NYĀYA-MAÑJARĪ

The Compendium of Indian Speculative Logic

JAYANTA BHAṬṬA'S

NYĀYA-MAÑJARĪ

[*The Compendium of Indian Speculative Logic*]

TRANSLATED INTO ENGLISH BY

JANAKI VALLABHA BHATTACHARYYA

VOL. I

MOTILAL BANARSIDASS
Delhi :: Varanasi :: Patna

First Edition : Delhi, 1978

ISBN: 978-81-2084-131-4

Also available at:

MOTILAL BANARSIDASS
41 U.A. Bungalow Road, Jawahar Nagar, Delhi 110 007
8 Mahalaxmi Chamber, Warden Road, Mumbai 400 026
120 Royapettah High Road, Mylapore, Chennai 600 004
Sanas Plaza, Subhash Nagar, Pune 411 002
16 St. Mark's Road, Bangalore 560 001
8 Camac Street, Calcutta 700 017
Ashok Rajpath, Patna 800 004
Chowk, Varanasi 221 0011

PRINTED IN INDIA
BY JAINENDRA PRAKASH JAIN AT SHRI JAINENDRA PRESS,
A-45 NARAINA, PHASE I, NEW DELHI 110 028
AND PUBLISHED BY NARENDRA PRAKASH JAIN FOR
MOTILAL BANARSIDASS PUBLISHERS PRIVATE LIMITED,
BUNGALOW ROAD, DELHI 110 007

To

My Parents

The late Pañcānana Tarkavāgīśa

and

The late mother Annapūrṇā Devī

न्यायाम्बुधौ कृतस्नानः शुद्धबोधः पिता मम ।
वितरतु कृपावृष्टिं पञ्चाननः शिवोऽपरः ॥
अन्नपूर्णा ममाम्बा च वरदा या स्वभावतः ।
ग्रन्थसमाप्तिकण्टकान् हरतु दिव्यधाम्ना सा ॥

PREFACE

Jayanta's Nyāyamañjarī became obscure in course of time in North East India because of the eminence of Vācaspati Miśra, Udayana, Gaṅgeśa Upādhyāya and Mīmāṁsakas. The rise of Navyanyāya in Bengal is another prominent factor since the Neo-logicians eclipsed the name and fame of their predecessors to a great extent. The decline of the glory of Kashmir as a seat of learning owing to political reasons is also a great factor which stood in the way of the attraction of the aspiring students from other states. Jayanta rose to prominence in his advanced age in Kashmir. Before the adequate publicity of Jayanta's master-piece 'Nyāya-mañjarī' the sun of the glory of Kashmir went down. Cultural vacuum in India was filled up by the rise of the Prābhākaras and the Naiyāyikas around Mithila and other seats of learning in the eastern zone in the later half of the middle ages. The rise of the Jaina logicians in the western zone is another factor which led to the isolation of Kashmirian culture round about the same period. Jayanta was known to Prabhācandra Sūri and Gaṅgeśa Upādhyāya. The latter knew him as jarannaiyāyika. Most probably he was not familiar with his great work. Vācaspati Miśra and Udayana Ācārya became the focus of attention of all students of the Nyāya-Vaiśeṣika systems. Moreover, Jayanta was not a systematic interpreter of the Nyāya-Sūtra. He selected all the important topics of Logic and defended the essential features of the Realistic views of the Nyāya system to the best of his abilities. He selected the right channel of defence and shattered all barriers of the Idealists and the Poet-philosophers. His contributions to Philosophy, Ethics, and Theology are of no mean order. His catholicity in Religion even in the present day wins the admiration of the religious reformers and thoughtful persons, devoted to social service. It is undoubtedly the good fortune of the twentieth century that the great work of Jayanta was unearthed in the Southern India and was published by the late Gaṅgādhara Śāstrī. The discovery of the text of Nyāyamañjarī proves its excellence. It led to acceptance in the remotest seat of national culture of independent India. The political turmoil is the predominant reason for its non-circulation in the states of India which were cut off from Kashmir by foreign invasion and internal feuds and constant political unrest in the intervening countries.

Through the grace of God I have been able to present the first volume of Nyāya-mañjarī which embodies the ways of true knowledge of the Indian Logic to the enlightened societies of the East and the West through the medium of English. This volume also comprises Epistemology and the fundamental elements of Theology and Religion. I completed my work long ago and got it published in the Calcutta Review. During the period of publication I could not read the proof-sheets owing to my protracted illness. I depended upon the office-staff for the correction of the published pages. I got them retyped and sent them for publication. Bad health stood in the way of revising the printed and retyped pages. Also I have not been able to go through the proof-sheets of the present volume myself owing to the want of prompt communication for unavoidable reasons. I am sorry to state that I have noticed a few errata and lacunas in the final stage since I had to depend solely upon a corrupt text. I have no opportunity of getting them corrected at present. I take the sole responsibility on my own shoulders and lay the blame on no other doors for these shortcomings. I have made up my mind to do justice to the published work and to annex all corrections to the second volume which will be published in the near future. I simply beg the apology of the present readers for the adverse circumstances which stand in the way of my prompt action to rectify the book to the best of my abilities. To err is human and as such I may crave the indulgence of the sagacions readers for the same.

I gratefully acknowledge my indebtedness to my beloved parents, teachers, friends and well-wishers whose constant encouragement has given me impetus to complete my work. My distinguished students and near ones have promised to help me by their suggestions and constructive criticism. In anticipation I express my thanks to them. I invite criticism and valuable suggestions from all sympathetic readers. I think that it is a work of national importance which will help in the future to raise the standard of research work both in India and abroad.

I acknowledge my indebtedness to my late father, Panchanana Tarkavagisa who had acted as pioneer to the translation of Nyāyamañjarī in Bengali. He paved the way which I have followed in English. He had to give up his work after making some progress since his weak eyes could not bear the strain of overexertion in his old age.

I express my thanks with gratitude to my publishers who have encouraged me all along with ungrudging co-operation and also to all my well-wishers.

Calcutta, J. V. Bhattacharyya
22.8.77

CONTENTS

		Pages
	PREFACE	vii
	INTRODUCTION	xxiii
	Āhnika—I	
1.	Benedictory Verses	1-2
2.	Heaven and summum bonum of life, learnt only from the Scriptures	2-3
3.	Fourteen Sources of Knowledge	3-4
4.	The place of Gautama's Logic as a source of Knowledge	5-6
5.	The usefulness of Logic. Preliminary discussion	6-8
6.	The Statement of Subject-matter—objection and rejoinder	8-11
7.	The main topics of "Gautama" Logic	11-14
8.	Interpretation of the compound word 'Tattva-jñāna'	14
9.	A brief discussion regarding the significance of all terms denoting subject matter	14-20
10.	The threefold procedure of the Nyāya Logic	20-22
11.	The definition of Pramāṇa	22-28
12.	An examination of the definition of Pramāṇa of the Buddhist school	28-33
13.	The definition of Pramāṇa of the Mīmāṁsā school	33-34
14.	The Refutation of the Mīmāṁsā view	34-46
15.	An examination of a few definitions of Pramāṇa other than the above two	46-52
16.	An examination of the definition of Pramāṇa of the Śāṅkhya school	52-53
17.	The definition of Pramāṇa and its division	53-57
18.	The Buddhist hypothesis of the two-fold division of Prāmaṇa	57-61
19.	The refutation of the Buddhist hypothesis	61-64
20.	The corroboration of the same truth by the different sources. Samplava (corroboration) of knowledge	64-69
21.	Enumeration of other sources of knowledge	69

22. Presumption of the Bhaṭṭa-School 69-79
23. Presumption included in Inference 79-81
24. The Refutation of the hypothesis of Śakti 81-85
25. Presumption based upon non-apprehension included in Inference 85-87
26. The contention of the Prābhākaras in defence of Presumption 87-88
27. The Refutation of Prābhākaras' defence 88-90
28. Presumption based upon the verbal testimony is not distinct from inference 90-92
29. Śrutārthāpatti refuted by the Prābhākaras 93-101
30. The refutation of the hypothesis of Dhvani 101-102
31. Abhāva (non-perception)—a distinct source of knowledge 102-107
32. The refutation of Non-perception as a distinct source of knowledge 107-115
33. Denial of reality to a negative fact 115-118
34. The Buddhist criticism—its examination 118-119
35. Eleven-fold division of non-perception 119-122
36. The reality of a negative fact 122-131
37. The contrary view of the Prābhākaras refuted 131-132
38. The clarification of Negation 132-133
39. The Refutation of the hypothesis of Probability and Rumour 133-135

Āhnika—II

40. The Definition of Perception 136-139
41. The view of Ācārya 139-141
42. The prima facie view—no place of Parāmarśa 141-146
43. Conclusive view—the perception of Capacity 146-148
44. Consciousness—not an instrumental cause of itself 148-153
45. The refutation of the charge of being too wide 153
46. The significance of the first constituent term 153-154
47. Sense-object contact 154-156
48. The refutation of the change of being too narrow 156-157

49. The significance of the term 'jñāna' 157-158
50. The refutation of the Buddhist hypothesis 158-162
51. The significance of the term 'avyabhicāri' 162-164
52. The various meanings of the term 'avyapadeśya' 164-165
(i) The traditional interpretation of the term 165-176
(ii) Some followers of the opposite school of interpretation 176-178
(iii) Some teachers of the Nyāya School 178-181
(iv) Some other Logicians 181-183
(v) The firm statement of the Nyāya view-point 183-184
(vi) The view of a small section of Logicians 184-185
53. The significance of the term 'non-erroneous' 185-189
54. The significance of the term 'Vyavasāya' (determinate) 189-193
55. The Definition of Perception as given by the Buddhists 193-198
56. The refutation of the definition of Perception of the Buddhists 198-209
57. The definition of sense-perception as given by Vārṣagaṇya refuted 209-210
58. The refutation of the definition of Perception of the Mīmāṁsakas 210-215
59. Proof of the truth of transcendental perception 215-219
60. Mental Perception 219-225
61. The refutation of the definition of Perception as proposed by the Sāṁkhya Kārikā 225-226
62. Inference—its definition 226-234
63. Induction based upon the law of identity and causality of the Buddhist hypothesis 234-235
64. The refutation of the Buddhist hypothesis 235-241
65. The Relation of concomitance—the basis of Induction 241-246
66. An Objection to the Validity of Inference 246-249
67. The Establishment of the Validity of Inference 249-261
68. The Sūtra containing the definition of inference explained 261-265

69. The function of the three constituent terms of the sūtra in question 265-267
70. The Meaning of the term 'Pūrvavat' 267-271
71. The Meaning of the term 'Śeṣavat' 271-273
72. The Meaning of the term 'Sāmānyatodṛṣṭa 273-275
73. Alternative three-fold division of Inference 275-279
74. Distinction between 'Śeṣavat' and 'Sāmānyatodṛṣṭa' 279-284
75. Past, Present and Future objects—an inference 284-285
76. An Objection to the existence of Time 285
77. Time—a Percept 285-287
78. Time—an inference 287-291
79. Division of Time 291-293
80. Space-Reality 293-295
81. Upamāna (Comparison) 295-297
82. Objection to its validity 297-298
83. Reply to it 298-303
84. The hypothesis of the Mīmāṁsakas 303-304
85. Its refutation 304-312

Āhnika—III 312

86. Śabda (verbal knowledge) 312-318
87. Distinction between Śabda and Inference 318-327
88. Objection to the Validity of verbal knowledge 327-328
89. A reply to the Objection 328-333
90. A general discussion : Intrinsic or extrinsic validity 333-334
91. The Mīmāṁsaka view : Intrinsic validity 334-345
92. The Mīmāṁsaka view of Intrinsic validity criticised 345-349
93. The Intrinsic validity of the Vedas 349-350
94. The refutation of the Mīmāṁsā hypothesis that the very conditions of a judgment produce its truth 351-366
95. The hypothesis of Non-discrimination 366
96. The hypothesis of misapprehension 366-371

97. The hypothesis in question involves the defect of overlapping 371-373
98. The refutation of the hypothesis of hallucination 374-375
99. The refutation of the hypothesis of the Subjective Idealists 375-376
100. The hypothesis of Non-discrimination is reaffirmed as a means to the intrinsic validity of true knowledge 376-391
101. The hypothesis of the Prābhākaras refuted 391-394
102. The Refutation of the hypothesis of a section of the Mīmāṁsakas 394-401
103. The Extrinsic validity of the verbal knowledge established 400-401
104. Objections to the existence of God 401-406
105. The existence of God established 406-420
106. The eternality of God's knowledge and other attributes 420-422
107. Incorporeal God 422-426
108. The hypothesis of the Mīmāṁsakas that sound is eternal affirmed 426-427
109. An objection to the hypothesis in question 427-430
110. Presumption employed as a proof of the hypothesis of the Mīmāṁsakas that words are eternal along with the criticism of it. 430-439
111. The hypothesis that a letter is only manifested but is not produced as well as its criticism 439-442
112. All the charges against the hypothesis of manifestation are answered 442-444
113. The hypothesis of manifestation is better since it obeys the law of parsimony 444-450
114. The summing up of the conclusion that sound is eternal 450
115. The commencement of the refutation of the thesis in question 450-451
116. The letters are many and are united by a universal 451-459
117. The proof of the universals belonging to letters 459-467

118. An objection to the hypothesis of the manifestation of sound leading up to its eternality 467-472
119. The refutation of the hypothesis of manifestation and the affirmation of the thesis of creation 472-477
120. The proof of the hypothesis that a sound is an attribute 477-483

Āhnika—IV

121. The authorship of the Vedas 484-485
122. The Vedas are eternal—refuted 485-496
123. The author of the Vedas—the creator of the universe 496-497
124. Single authorship of all the Vedas 497-499
125. The determination of the relation holding between a word and its meaning 499-505
126. The refutation of the eternality of the relation between a word and its meaning 505-513
127. The Vedas—a source of valid knowledge because of divine authorship 513-522
128. The Mīmāṁsaka method of ascertaining the veracity of the Vedas 522-525
129. The Validity of the Atharvaveda questioned 526-527
130. A reply to the said objection 527-533
131. Atharvaveda—a constituent of Trayī 533-538
132. Primacy of the Atharvaveda 538-543
133. The equality of the four Vedas (conclusion) 543-544
134. The validity of Tantra, Āgama, etc., discussed 544-550
135. The authenticity of the Āgamas of the Śaiva, Pañcarātra and such other Schools—established 550-551
136. The scriptures of the Buddhists are not authentic 551-554
137. The hypothesis that all Āgamas are authentic, being revealed by the trust-worthy persons 554-562
138. The proving of the hypothesis that a particular Āgama is authentic 562-563

139.	An objection to the Validity of the Vedas	563-566
140.	A reply to the charge of the falsehood of the Vedas	566-570
141.	A reply to another objection against the validity of the Vedas	570-572
142.	A reply to the above reply	573-576
143.	Nyāya—The meaning of Dharma	576
144.	The different meanings of Dharma refuted	576-578
145.	Do the Vedas involve contradiction ? No	578-585
146.	The Vedas have no veracity since they contain artha-Vādas—replied	585-592
147.	An objection to the validity of Mantras and its reply	592-602
148.	An answer to the objection that the Vedic sentences relating names of sacrifices are not true	602-605
149.	The Vedic words will be significant if they denote only the rites to be observed—Nyāya conclusion	605-617

Āhnika—V

150.	Introduction	618-619
151.	An objection against the acceptance of a universal different problems raised	619-626
152.	Concepts are possible in the absence of universals	626-630
153.	The Buddhist conceptualism—a negative general image	630-631
154.	The refutation of a negative general image (apoha)	631-639
155.	Universals negated and the hypothesis of apohas defended	639-647
156.	The proof of the reality of universals	647-650
157.	Objections against the reality of universals answered	650-661
158.	The refutation of the hypothesis of Apoha	661-664
159.	The conclusive proof of a universal	664-665
160.	The meaning of a common noun	665-666

161.	Words denote only an individual	666-677
162.	The hypothesis that a word denotes a universal refuted	677-683
163.	The hypothesis that a word denotes a concrete universal	683-684
164.	The complete meaning of a word includes invariably an individual	684-688
165.	The Meaning of a Sentence (Introductory)	688-689
166.	The Rival hypothesis of the Meaning of a Sentence	689-690
167.	The view that a Sentence Denotes an Idea	690-692
168.	The Refutation of the Hypothesis that an Idea is conveyed by a Sentence	692-694
169.	The object to be accomplished, being the most important, is the Meaning of a Sentence	694-697
170.	The proof of the Hypothesis—The Fruit of an Action being superior to the Action Itself	697-698
171.	Heaven renders no perceptible assistance to the Verb	698
172.	Heaven renders no invisible help to any action	699-702
173.	The refutation of the hypothesis that an action of a person is signified by a sentence	702-704
174.	The Determination of the Nature of an Activity	704-709
175.	Three factors of Bhāvanā	709-715
176.	The character of an injunction (vidhi)	715-717
177.	The definition of motif	717-719
178.	The two types of Bhāvanā	719-720
179.	A Śabda-Bhāvanā depends upon three constituent elements	720-721
180.	Relation between an Injunction and Bhāvanā	721-725
181.	The Śabda Bhāvanā constituting the meaning of a sentence examined	725-727
182.	A mandate is denoted by a sentence	727-731
183.	The causative and Optative suffixes differ in meaning	731-732

184.	Verbal proof being the only source of a command—How is a command communicated to us as the meaning of such and such word	732-734
185.	Niyoga inducing to an obligatory duty	734-735
186.	A Niyoga is a Spring of Action when its sense is grasped	735
187.	Injunction—a categorical Imperative	735-740
188.	A Prohibitory Injunction is deterring	740
189.	The Scope of Prohibition	740-746
190.	The four-fold division of a Mandate	746-747
191.	The different forms of Injunction	747-748
192.	Conclusion—an Injunction is the meaning of a Sentence	748-749
193.	The counter Hypothesis that the knowledge of an end is the motive of one's action	749-762
194.	The conclusion of the Topic	762-763
195.	The meaning of a Sentence	763-767
196.	The conclusive view—An End is the meaning of a sentence	767-768
197.	The Hypothesis—inner activity of the Soul is the meaning of Sentence	768-769
198.	The refutation of the hypothesis that a sentence conveys knowledge	769-771

Āhnika—VI

199.	An introductory discussion to ascertain the real nature of a word	771-772
200.	The Refutation of the hypothesis that letters convey a sense of Sphoṭa by an inference	772-778
201.	The manifestation of a sphoṭa by letters	778
202.	Inarticulate sounds manifest a sphoṭa	778-779
203.	The Perceptibility of a Shoṭa	779-781
204.	The proof of a vākya-sphoṭa	781-782
205.	The unreality of parts of a Sentence	782-784
206.	Sphoṭa enjoys the status of the Absolute	784-786
207.	An Introduction to the Refutation of Sphoṭa	786-786
208.	The Hypothesis that Letters convey a Meaning Established	786-790

209. The Hypothesis that Sphoṭa is an inference—refuted 790-801
210. The Perceptibility of a Sphoṭa refuted 801-810
211. The Hypothesis that a Word or a Sentence is partless refuted and the conclusive view on Sphoṭa 810-823
212. The Meanings of words communicate the meaning of a sentence refuted 823-828
213. That a Sentence conveys its own Meaning is the conclusion 828-830
214. The Hypothesis that words and Sentences are constituted by Letters Refuted 830-835
215. The Hypothesis that a Sentence conveys its own Meaning Established 835-836
216. The Alternative Hypothesis criticised 836-838
217. Jayanta's own theory of the communication of meaning of a sentence—Established 838-842
218. An Introduction to the hypothesis of mutual relation 842
219. Rival Hypothesis of this Topic 842
220. The Doctrine of Abhihita-anvaya 842-846
221. The Refutation of the Doctrine 846-848
222. An answer to the charges against the Hypothesis of Anvita-Abhidhāna 848-851
223. The concluding portion of the same hypothesis 851-854
224. The refutation of the hypothesis of Anvita-abhidhāna 854-857
225. Another Hypothesis and its refutation 857-858
226. The Knowledge of meanings as mutually related by Tātparyaśakti 858-862
227. An objection to the ascertainment of the meaning of the Vedas 862-867
228. The hypothesis that one learns the Vedas with the help of Grammar is not tenable 867-875
229. Inefficacy of the study of Grammar 875-880
230. The untenability of the hypothesis that Grammar makes an improvement upon words 880-883

231. Notion of a chaste word is puzzling 883-887
232. The definition of a chaste word is puzzling 887-895
233. The establishment of the hypothesis that chaste words are denotative 895-898
234. The hypothesis that corrupt words are eternal is not tenable 898-902
235. The chastity of a word is fit to be perceived with the aid of the authoritative words 902-912
236. The study of Grammar is compulsory 913-914
237. The concluding portion 914
INDEX 915

INTRODUCTION

Jayanta Bhaṭṭa is an obscure great scholar whom India may be proud of. He is like the moon in the misty night of December. He has written the monumental work 'Nyāya-mañjarī'. Though it should have been widely studied and discussed yet unfortunately it has not attracted the attention of Indian scholars as much as it deserves to do. We shall not try to find out the circumstances which were unfavourable to its study. We thank our stars that such a precious book was discovered and published by M. M. Gaṅgādhara Śāstrī towards the end of the 19th century A. D. In this introduction we shall not discuss so much about the merits of Nyāyamañjarī as about its author.

Abhinanda, son of Jayanta Bhaṭṭa, gave his pedigree in his family in his introduction to Kādambarī-kathā-sāra. We learn from it that Jayanta Bhaṭṭa's remote ancestor Śakti migrated to Kashmir from Bengal in the seventh century. He belonged to the Bharadvāja family of the Gauḍa section of Brahmins. The long journey undertaken by Śakti as described by Abhinanda, suggests that Śakti most probably migrated from Bengal to Kashmir. As he was a Gauḍa Brāhmaṇa the home of his ancestors was Bengal. But it is difficult to say with absolute certainty that Śakti migrated from Bengal. His grandson was Śakti Svāmin. He was a minister of Muktāpīḍa, also known as Lalitāditya. The great grand-son of Śakti Svāmin was Jayanta. We also learn from Abhinanda that Jayanta was a poet of no mean order and was also endowed with the gift of the gab. He was well-versed in the Vedic lore and the different branches of studies subordinate to the Vedas. Nay, he was well-acquainted with all the branches of the Śāstras. Nyāya-mañjarī was composed by him, for its author acquired the title of Vṛttikāra (the writer of a commentary). This glorious title, conferred upon him by a circle of scholars, points to the unqualified merit of the work.

The date of Jayanta is not clearly stated in the Nyāya-mañjarī. Prof. A. B. Keith holds that Abhinanda composed the synopsis of Kādambarī in the ninth century A .D. He takes pride in his father's title 'Vṛtti-kāra'. This title suggests that Nyāya-mañjarī had been appreciated by the learned scholars of his time. In other words, Nyāya-mañjarī precedes Kādambarī-kathā-sāra. If we accept the view of Dr. Keith, Nyāya-mañjarī was composed in the ninth century A.D. But Dr. Keith has not elaborately discussed the problem of the date of Abhinanda. So there is room for a doubt about its certainty. Let us discuss the problem of Jayanta's date *de novo*.

There are some incidental personal references, in the Nyāya-mañjarī of Jayanta, which throw some light on the age of its author. Jayanta mentions the name of Śaṁkaravarman, the king of Kashmir.

Yadapūrvamiti viditvā nivārayāmāsa dharmatattvajñaḥ /
Rājā Śaṁkaravarmā na punar Jainādi-matamevam //
(p. 248 N. M. Benares edition)

The king Śaṁkaravarmā stopped some religious custom as it had been unprecedented. Jayanta uses the verb in the past perfect tense (*liṭ*). Does the verb 'nivārayāmāsa' suggest that Śaṁkara varman had reigned long before Jayanta was born ? If it be so how is it that Jayanta's great grandfather was contemporaneous with the king Lalitāditya ? The reign of Muktāpīḍa extended over the period of thirty six years (from 733 A.D. to 769 A.D.) From this datum alone we are in a position to infer the date of Jayanta. Jayanta must have been born in the middle of the ninth century A.D.

Let us cite another verse from Nyāya-mañjarī, which will help us to understand the meaning of the verb in the past perfect tense mentioned above.

Rājñā tu gahvare 'sminnaśabdake bandhane vinihito 'ham /
Grantha-racanā-vinodādiha hi mayā vatsarā gamitāḥ //
(p.363 N. M. Banares edition)

Jayanta was imprisoned in a cave at the mandate of the king of Kashmir. He utilised his dreary days. He took to the writing of Nyāya-mañjarī. Thus, he got a relief from the pain of confinement. During the period of confinement the King Śaṁkaravarman most probably put a ban on the Nīlāmbara custom. Jayanta defends the action of the king as the said custom is immoral and not religious. The use of the verb in the past perfect tense suggests the skill of Jayanta in introducing bitter incidents without provoking the wrath of the then ruler.

Now the question 'Why was Jayanta imprisoned by the king Śaṁkaravarman?' arises in our mind. Jayanta remains silent on this point. Kalhaṇa in his Rājataraṅgiṇī furnishes us with a clue. If we rightly grasp it then the reason behind Jayanta's imprisonment becomes clear.

Dvijastayor nāyakākhyo Gaurīśa-sura-sadmanoḥ /
Caturvidyaḥ kṛtaṁ tena Vāgdevīkula-mandiram //
(Rāja-taraṅgiṇī 5/159)

Who is this Nāyaka? Stein thinks that the rhetorician Bhaṭṭa Nāyaka has been referred to in this verse. There is no sound reason at the back of this conjecture excepting the surname 'Nāyaka' itself.

A rhetorician is not necessarily a Vedic scholar, Nāyaka was not the name of the scholar. The title 'nāyaka' was most probably converted into a name. Jayanta deserved the title 'Nāyaka' in the fitness of things. In his versatile scholarship erudition in the Vedic lore, oratory and skill in composing poems he was second to none. He was honoured by the king who appointed him a teacher of the royal institute of learning attached to the newly built temples of Śiva. My revered father the late Pandit Pañcānana Tarka-vāgīśa in his introduction to Nyāya-mañjarī rightly identified Nāyaka with Jayanta. Thus, Jayanta became the most exalted teacher in Kashmir during the reign of Śaṁkaravarman.

Now, let us see why Jayanta was imprisoned by the king Śaṁkaravarman, his very patron. Śaṁkaravarman waged wars of aggression abroad. He dissipated the resources of the kingdom in these wars. But he achieved marked success nowhere. It became a problem to him to meet the expenses of his vast army. He resorted to the oppressive system of taxation. Moreover, he was very extravagant and was particular about his personal comforts. He misappropriated the temple-treasures, being a slave of greed and vices. Being always encircled by some base and evil self-seekers his mind was so obsessed by their ill advice that he reduced the royal patronage till then enjoyed by the men of learning. Jayanta was a man of independent spirit. He was greatly devoted to the god Śiva. He was moral to the back-bone. Jayanta might have lodged his protest against the looting of the riches of temples. The arrogant king Śaṁkaravarman could tolerate no just opposition. Jayanta was a great stalwart. The opposition, led by him, had considerable weight. In order to put down this opposition Jayanta was imprisoned by the king. As the king was a terror to his subjects so Jayanta did not dare record the account of his imprisonment. We refer to a few lines of Rājataraṅgiṇī in order to make our readers familiar with the extortions of the king Saṁkaravarman (Prajā-pīḍana-paṇḍitaḥ) (5/165) Devādīnāṁ sa sarvasvaṁ jahāra yosad-yuktibhiḥ (5/166) Catuḥ ṣaṣṭiṁ suragṛhān mumoṣetaradañjasā (5/169) Nimittam maṇḍale' muṣmin sa-vidyānām anādare ... Rājñām pratāpahānau ca nānyaḥ Śaṁkaravarmanaḥ (5/179)... Anyaiśca vividhairyatnair vyadhād grāmān sa nirdhanān (5/175). No king in Kashmir excelled the king Śamkara-varman in dishonouring men of letters in various ways. Kalhaṇa gives the story of oppression of the subjects and that of dishonour shown to the learned men at the hands of the said king in a nutshell. Does not the imprisonment of the greatest scholar for defending a just cause illustrate the worst type of dishonour accorded to the learned society by the king? From the various suggestions scattered here and there we infer that Jayanta was imprisoned in a cave during the reign of Śaṁkaravarman (883-902 A. D.)

Jayanta's Nyāya-mañjarī is full of copious references. A careful study of them may throw some light on his age. In this context the mention of the references to very early works is useless. Jayanta refers to Kuṭṭanimatam, a work of the eighth century A. D. The view of the Cārvāka system as adumbrated in the Tattva-upaplava-siṁha has been criticised by him. The name of the work is not known to Jayanta. The book was most probably written in the first half of the ninth century A. D. Jayanta criticizes the view of Yukti-dīpikā, a work of the 8th century. He also quotes a verse from the first canto of Śiśupāla-vadha. Māgha belonged to the eighth century A. D. Abhinanda, in his Kādambarī-kathā-sāra, mentions Jayanta Bhaṭṭa, his father as the illustrious vṛttikāra. This book was most probably written in the second half of the ninth century A. D. We may roughly calculate the age of Abhinanda on the basis of the genealogical tree, mentioned by him.

We shall now discuss another important problem, viz. the relation between Jayanta and Vācaspati Miśra. The pandit Surya Narayana Sukla, in his introduction to Bheda-siddhi, holds that Vācaspati Miśra was a pupil of Jayanta Bhaṭṭa. He quotes a verse from Nyāya-kaṇikā which is a commentary on Vidhi-Viveka of Maṇḍana Miśra. It runs thus :—

Ajñāna-timira-śamanīm
para-damanim̐ Nyāya-mañjarīm̐ rucirām /
Prasavitre prabhavitre
Vidyā-tarave namo gurave //

The very name 'Nyāya-mañjarī' has tempted the pandit to make a hasty conjecture. He has forgotten to take the date of Nyāya-sūci-nibandha into consideration. The working of the date in this work is very ambiguous. We shall discuss the date of Vācaspati afterwards. The same pandit, in the Nyāya-mañjarī edited by him holds that Vācaspati Miśra is earlier than Jayanta. He equates 898 vatsara with 841 A. D. He also holds that Jayanta refers to the view of Vācaspati Miśra. Jayanta refers to the view of ācārya. Who is this ācārya? Is he Vācaspati Miśra?

If we carefully analyse the view of Acārya then we fail to identify Vācaspati Miśra with Ācārya. Vācaspati, in his commentary on Nyāya-vārttika, has shown much originality. None of his original views finds a place in Jayanta's Nyāya-mañjarī. Moreover, Jayanta is not a student of Vācaspati. Why should he mention the name of Vācaspati ? There is no proof that Vācaspati was Jayanta's teacher. The epithet 'ācārya' does not apply to him. Nyāya-mañjarī, mentioned in the Nyāya-kaṇikā, is a treatise on Mīmāṁsā. The term 'Nyāya' is very popular in the Mīmāṁsā literature. Nyāya-mañjarī signifies that it explains all the Nyāyas given in the Mīmāṁsā-sūtra. Therefore we strongly assert that Vācaspati was not a pupil of Jayanta. Vācaspati himself mentions the name of Trilocana as his teacher in the Nyāya-system. Trilocana has his original views on perception. Jayanta is absolutely innocent of these views. Moreover in no work of Vācaspati is his acquaintance with the land of Kashmir to be found. Vācaspati had no knowledge about religious toleration, the peculiar cult of Kashmir in the eighth and the ninth centuries A. D. He was strictly conservative in his out-look.

The date of Nyāya-sūci-nibandha, is Saṁvatsara, Prajñānānanda Sarasvati holds the above view. According to this view Vācaspati was a contemporary of Devapāla who probably reigned from 815 A. D. to 854. Vācaspati makes mention of a great ruler 'Nṛga'. Who is this Nṛga? Indian history throws no light on such a ruler. How is it that an emperor has escaped the notice of historians? Nṛga is an epithet but is not the name of a king. The Mahābhārata informs us of the great king Nṛga. Though the king performed many pious deeds yet he committed many sinful acts. From the above account we make out that Vācaspati used it figuratively. He did not openly condemn his royal patron. As he was very orthodox he could not justify some acts of his patron. Devapāla was a Buddhist king. He bestowed liberal grains on Buddhist monasteries. An inscription, belonging to his reign, refers to a grant to a Buddhist monastery built by a king of Java and Sumatra. The king's attachment to Buddhism displeased Vācaspati who neither suppressed his feeling nor clearly expressed it. He gave vent to his inner feeling in a subtle manner. Thus we see that Vācaspati was a senior contemporary of Jayanta. If we carefully examine the reference, contained in the Nyāya-mañjarī of Jayanta, we learn that Jayanta did not know much of his senior contemporary philosophers of distant lands: Jayanta was thoroughly conversant with the earlier views. At his time the communication of current thoughts was not easy. Avantivarman restored peace at home and became a great patron of learning. At this period Jayanta was a learner. He had to read the old classical works of the different branches of Sanskrit learning. He became a sound scholar when a civil war broke out in Kashmir. Kashmir which was previously a place of attraction for the men of letters belonging to the different parts of India, being a renowned seat of culture suddenly turned out to be a field of military action—a beloved place for warriors. The atmosphere of Kashmir became too hot for the advancement of learning. The import of new ideas into this land was suddenly stopped. Thus, Jayanta had no opportunity of being acquainted with the current thoughts of other parts of India. After this civil war Śaṁkaravarman ascended the throne of Kashmir. Jayanta rose to prominence. But fortune did not favour him for a long time. A sudden reversal of fate took place. He was imprisoned in a cell. He was cut off from the surrounding world. He became confined in the circle of his ideas. He found out some tragic relief in composing a work on the Nyāya-system of thought. The period of his imprisonment was indefinite. He found ample leisure to bestow his best thoughts on his composition. He repeatedly pondered over the problems he discussed. He dived deep into the matter and tried to reach the very bottom of every item. The wealth of knowledge and mental alertness which he possessed won for him a place in the forefront of Indian philosophy.

Some scholars hold that Jayanta flourished during the reign of Pārtha or that of Paṅgu. The verse" .... nivārayāmāsa .... Rājā Śaṁkaravarmā" is the hinge upon which all their arguments hang. The use of the verb in the past perfect tense (nivārayāmāsa) leads them to think that Jayanta must be posterior to Śaṁkaravarman with whom he had no personal acquaintance. The events of the said king could not come within the circle of Jayanta's experience. These scholars have missed the sense of the past perfect tense. A person may use a verb in the past perfect tense to denote such events as happened in a distant country or at a period of time which is beyond the range of his sense-organs. The use of past perfect does not necessarily imply that it refers only to such an event as falls outside the life history of the person who uses the verb. Moreover, there is no reliable record in the history of Kashmir that the reign of the said king was notorious for the persecution of men of letters. Again, we know the genealogical table of Jayanta. If we calculate the age of Jayanta on the basis of the said table then we arrive at the conclusion that Jayanta was born during the reign of Avantivarman. Hence we can confidently say that Jayanta was contemporaneous with Śaṁkaravarman.

Prof. Macdonell and some Indian Pandits place Vācaspati

Miśra in the twelfth century A. D. Their calculation of the age of Miśra has been wrong because they have wrongly identified the senior Vācaspati Miśra with the junior Vācaspati Miśra. The junior Vācaspati Miśra is better known as abhinava Vācaspati Miśra. He is the author of Khaṇḍanoddhāra a work containing the refutation of Khaṇḍana-Khaṇḍa-khādya of Śrīharṣa from the Nyāya standpoint. But they do not see how it is possible that Udayana writes a commentary upon Vācaspati's work.

The late Pandit Vindhyesvari Prasada Dvivedi holds that Vācaspati Miśra flourished during the reign of the king Nṛga in the tenth century A.D. He equates the Vatsara, mentioned by Vācaspati Miśra with the Śaka era. In that case he becomes a contemporary of Udayana. He has little opportunity of writing a commentary on the Nyāya-Vārttika-tātparya of Vācaspati Miśra. When an earlier commentary is roughly handled by the critics, the posterior generation of the same school finds the necessity of defending the views of their teacher. An able disciple of the school writes a commentary upon the previous commentary. It is a general rule that there is a long interval of time between a commentary and its sub-commentary if the second commentary is not written by the direct disciple of the author of the former one. We can strongly assert that Udayana was not a disciple of Vācaspati. In the Bhāmatī commentary of Vācaspati there is a reference to a sovereign ruler. His resources and prestige lie beyond the reach of imagination of the other kings. If Nṛga is the king how is it that there is no trace of him in the history of India. Nobody knows the existence of the king Nṛga in the tenth century A.D. We appreciate the creation of the pure imagination of Vindhyesvari Prasada but cannot rely upon its contribution. We have already pointed out that the king Nṛga is Devapāla. Thus we cannot accept the hypothesis of Vindhyesvari Prasada. According to our hypothesis Vācaspati Miśra is a senior contemporary of Jayanta Bhaṭṭa; the Nyāya-vārttika-tātparya of Vācaspati has not been referred to in the Nyāya-mañjarī and Jayanta is absolutely innocent of Vācaspati. Gaṅgeśa in his Tattva-cintāmaṇi (upamāna-khaṇḍa) has mentioned the name of Jayanta as qualified by the epithet 'jaran Naiyāyika' (an old logician). We cannot infer the age of Jayanta from this epithet as Gaṅgeśa's knowledge of the chronological order is not dependable.

The main task, undertaken by Jayanta, is to defend the views of Vātsyāyana expressed in the Nyāya-bhāṣya against the criticisms offered by the rival schools. He is a sincere and devoted student of the Bhāṣya school. Though the Buddhists are the worst enemies of Vātsyāyana yet Bhartṛhari, Kumārila, Prabhākara Rāja and others are no less formidable opponents. Jayanta wields his pen to give an answer to the charges brought forward by the critics of Vātsyāyana. He also subjects the rival hypothesis to severe criticism. At the time of explaining the views of his master he also introduces new matter into his work. His style of writing is inimitable. His language is forceful. His selection of words is very happy. Even when the discussion of a topic is very long, the presentation of the subject does not appear to be insipid to the readers. He does not at the same time sacrifice accuracy at the altar of his artistic expression. His analysis is very minute. He does not engage himself in logic-chopping He focusses his attention upon the subject-matter. His mind is broad and fair. He appreciates the merit of the arguments of his opponent if they are sound. He does not condemn anything and everything which comes from the pen of his opponents. He is also very bold in his statement. He spares nobody however great he may be. He does not hesitate to be out-spoken He fearlessly declares that Prabhākara has borrowed such and such part of his thesis from the Buddhists without acknowledgment. Therefore, Prabhākara is a plagiarist. Sometimes the caustic remarks, flung upon his masterly opponents, go beyond the bounds of decorum. Sometimes he overdoes and loses the balance of judgment. Though Jayanta is very cautious in the choice of words yet he being influenced upon by the style of writing of the earlier writers, unwittingly heaps contumely upon the great opponents of the Nyāya school. His self-restraint in the tempting places might have been much more appreciated. The use of harsh words or that of abusive language does not display the greatness of one's mind. Modesty in every sphere of life is praiseworthy. The language of the Buddhist critics is very bitter and pungent. These critics have no respect for the great teachers of the Nyāya school. Though the sarcastic remarks might have provoked the pious wrath of Jayanta yet he should have restrained himself and dressed his arguments and remarks in polite language.

Jayanta is a sound scholar. He has studied several branches of learning. He has had no scruples to go through the text-books on Buddhist Logic. Though he holds a very poor opinion about the narrow outlook of the Cārvākas yet he pays close attention to the proper understanding of their system. His knowledge of the Mīmāṁsā school is very comprehensive. He is thoroughly acquained with the two broad divisions of the Mīmāṁsā school, viz. the Bhāṭṭa and Prābhākara schools. He is also aware of the nice shades of difference in views among the followers of these two schools. He mentions the views of Bhartṛmitra and those of the modern logicians of the Prabhākara school. He has studied all the recondite works on Pāṇini's grammar, viz. the Mahābhāṣya of Patañjali, the Vākyapadīya of Bhartṛhari, etc. The Naiyāyikas do not generally read the Vedic scriptures specially the Atharva Veda. Jayanta is a sound Vedic scholar. His study of Vedic literature is very extensive. That is why Jayanta is in a position to review the hypothesis of the Mīmāṁsakas with apt reference to the Vedic texts. It is also superfluous to add that he intimately knows all the details of the Nyāya school. In other words, he is like a moving library. It is for this reason that he was able to complete his voluminous Nyāya-mañjarī when he had been cut off from the external world, being imprisoned in a cell. He received no help from outside. He had no books to consult. He had to depend absolutely upon his memory and scholarship. It is a wonderful feat which has seldom any parallel in history. The authors of the modern age receive all facilities i.e. they are supplied with the books they require while they write books behind the prison bar. We shall do injustice to Nyāya-mañjarī if we simply take it to be a commentary. It is an encyclopedia of logic, metaphysics, ethics and theology. It represents the history of Indian philosophy of a few centuries. If an author of the history of Indian Philosophy is not acquainted with Nyāya-mañjarī then his work will remain incomplete for ever. His data will not be sufficiently collected.

Besides the resourcefulness of Nyāyamañjarī it contributes much towards the infusion of catholic spirit into Indian culture. Jayanta has grasped the essence of true religion and expressed it in clear and convincing terms.

Jayanta mentions the six schools of logic, viz., the Nyāya school, the Sāṁkhya school, the Buddhist school, the Jaina school, the Cārvāka school and the Vaiśeṣika school (asyāṁ janatāsu prasiddhāyāmapi ṣaṭtarkyam). This remark will throw some light on those who will write the history of Indian Logic. It is interesting to note the ancient scholars did not recognise that the logic of memory always refers to such a content as is contradicted by our sound experience. Therefore, memory *per se* is incorrect. The hypothesis of memory, suggested by Jayanta, has not been accepted universally.

Jayanta has also criticised the pragmatic test of true knowledge. The knowledge of an object which successfully leads the knower up to the object or helps him to avoid it is true. The Buddhists say that the determinate perception, being constructed by imagination, is not true. But it cannot lead one up to the object in question because it is short-lived. The fundamental doctrine of the universal flux itself contradicts the definition of true knowlelge as offered by the Buddhists. From the standpoint of the Buddhists there is only a logical distinction between Pramā and Pramāṇa as they are the two aspects of one and the same phenomenon of consciousness. Jayanta has refuted this hypothesis.

Jayanta subjects the hypothesis of Pramāṇa as suggested by the Sāṁkhyists to severe criticism. According, to them the mode of intellect (Buddhi) which assumes the form of an object is Pramāṇa. Jayanta boldly asserts that this hypothesis is closely akin to that of the Buddhists. He does not pay much importance to this hypothesis since the hypothesis of the Buddhists has been repudiated by him. In this context he has also proved that novelty is not the criterion of true knowledge.

He has elaborately discussed the division and the definition of Pramāṇa. He refers to the different views regarding the division of Pramāṇa. His criticism is mainly directed against the Buddhists. He subjects the twofold division of true knowledge as offered by the Buddhists to severe criticism. The Buddhists hold that there are only two kinds of objects, viz. (1) exclusively particular reals and (2) concepts manufactured and objectivized by our imagination. They also hold that this division of objects is based upon experience. We learn from our perception that this is a blue object, that this is not a non-blue object and that there is no other kind of object. Jayanta challenges the very evidence of perception and points out that perception can only reveal a present object but can do nothing more.

In this way Jayanta proceeds to do justice to the hypothesis of the Naiyāyikas. Having established the fourfold division of Pramāṇa, he does not spare the hypotheses of the Bhāṭṭas and the Prābhākaras. He tries his level best to prove that presumption is not a distinct source of knowledge. He holds that presumption cannot be distinguished from inference. He also holds that a distinct source of knowledge is not to be postulated to know negation. Negation is perceived. It may also be inferred in some cases.

In this connection he has tried his best to establish the hypothesis that negation is objectively real. He mentions the twofold division of negation, viz. pre-negation and post-negation. The negation of an object which will come into being is called pre-negation. The negation of an object which has ceased to exist is called post-negation. The classical fourfold division as suggested by the Vaiśeṣikas has been ignored by him. He tries to explain all kinds of negation in terms of the two types of negation. He follows the foot-step of the Nyāya-Bhāṣya-kāra. But his explanation is not satisfactory since he misses the fundamental difference holding between the negation of identity and that of relation. Moreover, the eternal negation of an object in its relational character cannot be translated in terms of pre-negation.

Jayanta exhibits all his scholarship to solve the problem of perception. He makes mention of a good number of views of the long forgotten logicians. He fairly discusses these views. In spite of his wide scholarship he fails to touch the centre of the problem of perception. Does our knowledge begin with a judgment? Is the indeterminate perception of the Nyāya School a judgment? Is it a feeling or a form of consciousness? Does the criterion of truth apply to it? Wherein lies the difference between the normal and the super-normal perception? Does super-normal perception come under the province of perception? Jayanta's idea of super-normal perception is not very clear. Moreover, Jayanta avoids some problems which he should have tackled with a firm hand. How are we aware of the awareness of an object? The causal theory of perception implies that the object which conditions its own perception should be present at the time of its perception. The phenomenon of consciousness is very short-lived. It lasts only for two kṣaṇas. Again, the determinate perception of an object is preceded by its indeterminate perception. If these two conditions of perception are taken to be essential then the intuition of an awareness becomes a problem.

Jayanta discusses the problem of inference from the standpoint of the old logicians. His contribution to the solution of the problem of inference is mainly the destructive criticism of the Buddhist hypothesis. The Buddhists hold that in order to arrive at a generalization one is to depend upon the relation of identity or that of causality. Jayanta strongly refutes this view. He also establishes the truth of inferential knowledge. One of the (purposes) of inference is to prove that the transcendental objects are rightly inferred. Jayanta plays his part well in order to bring home the point in question. But the problem of induction involves a few basic problems which are for empiricism hardnuts to crack. Jayanta does not raise them. Is induction at all possible from the empirical point of view? Jayanta anyhow solves this problem. He does not dive deep into the matter. He has also failed to work out the suggestions of the Nyāya-Vārttika-kāra. He thinks that his task will be completed if he defends the Nyāya-Bhāṣya-kāra against the attacks raised by the hostile camps.

Jayanta's treatment of Upamāna is fairly long. Gaṅgeśa refers to his view. The hypothesis of comparison as offered by the Mīmāṁsakas has been admirably refuted by Jayanta. He has proved that Upamāna is a distinct source of knowledge but not an inference. Upamāna is not a piece of indirect knowledge based upon analogy. But it is the ascertainment of the meaning of an unknown word based upon analogy.

Jayanta with right earnestness tries to establish the hypothesis of the Naiyāyikas that Śabda is a distinct source of knowledge. The knowledge, derived from the sentence of a trustworthy person, is true. Though it is indirect yet it is not inferential. He refutes the view that verbal knowledge is an inference. He meets the objection of the Buddhists who hold that verbal knowledge *per se* is not true. In order to prove the thesis of the Naiyāyikas that the truth of the Vedas is not self-evident he raises the fundamental problem, viz. whether or not the truth of knowledge is self-evident. He also discusses the other aspects of the problem, viz. whether or not the factors to which a piece of knowledge owes its origin are responsible for its truth. After having discussed all the rival views he arrives at the conclusion that the truth of a piece of knowledge is not self-evident. A factor in addition to the recognised factors of a piece of knowledge is required to bring about a piece of true knowledge. The Vedas are not also immune from this general rule. In this context Jayanta has also discussed some of the well-known theories of illusion. He has established the Nyāya view of illusion, viz. a mistake consists in misinterpreting a thing. When one cannot read an object in the right context he wrongly places it and commits a mistake. Therefore a true or false knowledge implies that it is necessarily a judgment. Even if a judgment is false it contains a reference to a real object. The Naiyāyikas assume that there is no contradiction in Nature. Truth or falsehood applies only to a judgment. Jayanta shares the same view with them. He incidentally refers to the hypothesis of illusion of a section of the Mīmāṁsakas whose thesis bears a close resemblance to that of the Advaitins. If we can ascertain the exact date of these Mīmāṁsakas then a flood of new light will be shed on the history of Indian Philosophy.

Jayanta enters into controversy with the Mīmāṁsakas, regarding the character of sound. He closely examines the hypothesis of the Mīmāṁsakas that sound is eternal and arrives at the conclusion that sound is non-eternal. He also holds that it is an attribute of the sky. The other topics of Nyāya-mañjarī will be discussed later on in proper places. We simply reiterate our honest opinion about Jayanta that he is a devoted student of the Nyāya-Bhāṣya-school, having abilities of no mean order.

—ooo—

ĀHNIKA I

1. Salutation be to Śambhu (the highest source of good), who is the seat of eternal bliss, consciousness and mysterious powers and who by His mere desire creates everything from the tuft of grass to the personal creator of the universe.

2. I bow down to the wife of Bhava (Śiva) whose locks of hair on the fore-head are decorated by the crescent of the moon and who is verily the river of nectar—the extinguisher of the fire of all worldly sufferings.

3. I tender my salutation to the lord of Gaṇas (a class of divine beings) who is the sun removing the darkness of obstacles and whose feet are illumined by the rays of the crest jewels of gods and demons.

4. The great work of Akṣapāda, the mine of precious gems of arguments—is superior to all such works since it has been highly spoken of by Śiva Himself (the demolisher of the cities of demons).

5. Let the discerning wise people take their bath in this great flowing river of Sarasvatī which ardently flows into the ocean of Akṣapāda's logic.

6. We make an appeal to the great scholars to the effect that they may look kindly upon this work by a mere peep at it though their mind is fatigued, being in constant touch with the great works displaying wonderful skill in depicting matters of wide interest and arousing strong emotion.

7. I have culled this essential herb from the wild garden of herbs of logic and have churned this lump of butter from the milk of Logic of Akṣapāda.

8. We claim no originality of thinking to discover new truth but have fascinating style to express the old ones in an attractive form. Let the critics examine it for themselves.

9. The very flowers by which garlands have been repeatedly prepared arouse curiosity even in the mind of those wearers of garlands when they constitute a new garland, being arranged in a new order.

10. The good men appreciate even a work of little worth presented to them since they are unaware of turning down the request of a supplicant.

11. Let the great savants of learning who are about to enjoy sportive walk in the garden of words adorn their ears with this (Nyāyamañjarī) new blossom of logic.

12. The tree of logic, planted by the great sage—Akṣapāda, has grown in its bulk and is bent down under the burden of its fruits of thick juice tasting like nectar.

13. I cannot climb up this tree because my powers are limited and hence it is further beyond my powers to test its merits in toto.

14. I take pains only to discuss some selected topics of that great work. I make an appeal to the great thinkers who are noted for their friendly appreciation to show me a great favour by a kind perusal of this work.

15. The conduct of the great ones is very strange. They do not feel happy even if their merits are innumerable. But they are elated with joy if they find little merit in others.

16. Blessed are the authors who are fortunate enough to behold the face of the great scholars beaming with joy when the latter go through the works of the former and dive deep into the topics of great interest, being personally approached for the favour of criticism.

Merit and Demerit, Heaven and Hell are only knowable from the Scriptures.

The intelligent persons know for certain that no earnest man can reach the desired goal if he does not know the right means to the end. Hence the people, desirous of attaining the goal of life, are in search of the adequate means. The human end is twofold, viz. tangible and intangible and hence the means will be also of two kinds. Those who like to attain the worldly end have been initiated into the proper means by the practice of the senior experts and have learnt themselves its efficacy by actual experiments, adopting the joint method of agreement and difference. Whenever a person feels hungry he does not make a search for the injunction of the sacred lore but moves straight to eat something. The injunctions of the scriptures such as a dirty man should bathe, a hungry person should eat, etc., are not essential. But all persons are ignorant of the invisible human ends such as Heaven and Final Emancipation from all sorrows since their mind is enveloped by the innate darkness of ignorance. In this case, the scripture alone throws light to illuminate them. It serves the purpose of divine eyes to find out the proper means. Like sages, we have no mystic intuition which will reveal the intangible goal since such a vision arises from the constant practice of deep meditation. Hence if we are serious about the invisible human destination, we should have to depend upon the scriptures alone.

The fourteen sources of knowledge.

The scriptures are divided into fourteen branches. The learned scholars hold that there are fourteen sources of knowledge. Among them the four Vedas are enlisted. The first of them is the Atharva-Veda, the second is the Ṛgveda, the third is the Yajurveda and the fourth is the Sāma-veda. These four Vedas are essentially embodiments of the instructions of the means to the summum bonum of human life, e.g. 'A man who covets Heaven should perform Agnihotra sacrifice', 'The self should be realised', etc.

The Smṛti texts, composed by Manu and others, throw light on the means to the invisible human ends, e.g., the aṣṭakā śrāddha ceremony, the tonsure-ceremony, the establishment of a room for the free supply of drinking water, etc. The fruits of the religious acts which have not been mentioned in the scriptures will be discussed in the chapter on injunction. All the acts enjoined by the scriptures ultimately lead up to the human ends and should not be taken as they seem to be barren. History and the Purāṇas generally elaborate the Vedic matters by means of the narration of various legends, etc.

It has been stated:—

One should elaborate the sense of the Vedas by means of History and Purāṇa Literature since the Vedas dread a man of little learning who is apt to mar the sense of them. The Vedas, the Purāṇas and the Law-books are the sources of knowledge since they are direct embodiments of the prescriptions of the means to human ends. The auxiliary Vedic works such as, Grammar, Astronomy, Phonetics, Ritualistic treatises, Prosody and Etymology, are also sources of knowledge since they throw light on the meanings of the Vedic words, etc. (In other words, they help to understand the meaning of the Vedic texts.) The very designation 'subsidiary Vedic texts' shows that these works directly help the understanding of the Vedic works. The Mīmāṁsā Literature is also a source of knowledge since it solves all the seeming contradictions involved in the Vedic sentences and clarify their meaning and supply us with all the details that are required for the implementation of the Vedic injunctions.

Bhaṭṭa says :—

When a person ascertains the religious rites in and through the Vedic texts the subsidiary acts which complete them are supplied by the Mīmāṁsā treatisc.

Hence, it is not the seventh subsidiary work annexed to the Vedic text since it is part and parcel of the Vedic texts, being intimately connected with them. Some apparently disconnected words of Vedic sentences yield us a consistent meaning when the logical rules of interpretation contained in the Mīmāṁsā, text are applied to them.

Confirmation of the Introduction of the Study of Nyāya (Logic).

The extensive Nyāya Literature is the main pillar upon which all branches of learning rest since it establishes the validity of the Vedic rites confidence in which may be shaken if the validity of the Vedas is gainsaid by the unfair criticism of the bad logicians. In that case, the people will hesitate to perform the Vedic rites which mean a lot of expenditure of hard-earned money and stupendous labour. If the Vedas themselves (the lord) are at a discredit then their off-shoots (the attendants) have no solid ground to stand upon in order to improve the position of the Vedas. That is why Akṣapāda has composed his great logical treatise which teaches us canons of logic by means of which all the bad logicians will be easily silenced and the validity of the Vedas will be re-affirmed. This glorious achievement is due to the greatest branch of learning which is called the source of knowledge since it throws light on the means to the highest human end. Though the term 'Vidyā' denotes knowledge yet it does not mean the awareness of an ordinary object such as a jar and so on but the knowledge of the means to the highest end. The compound word 'Vidyā-sthāna' conveys the source of such knowledge. In some of them this character is directly grasped and in others it is indirectly grasped. These branches of study are fourteen in number. It is stated thus :—

'The sources of knowledge and dharma are fourteen in number, viz., the Purāṇa, Tarka (logic) Mīmāṁsā, Dharma-śāstras and the four Vedas together with the six auxiliary sciences.'

It is also stated in some other work.

'These fourteen branches of study are the six ancillary sciences, the four Vedas, Mīmāṁsā, the extensive literature of logic, the Purāṇa and the Dharma-śāstra.

Among the Fourteen sources of knowledge the Logic of Gautama only has been enumerated.

The term 'Tarka' in the first verse is synonymous with the term 'Nyāyavistara' in the second verse. They denote the same science of logic. 'Nyāya' and 'Tarka' denote inference. Inference has been elaborately discussed in this science of logic. The Sāṅkhyists, the Ārhats (the Jainas) and the Kṣapaṇakas (the Buddhists) superficially initiate a very small section of their disciples into the deep science of inference. The validity of the Vedas cannot be established if we make use of their logic to do so. Thus the logic of these schools does not deserve the title of logic.

The Buddhists are very proud of the superiority of their power of argumentation. But as the drift of their logic is to cotradict the truth of the Vedas so their logic cannot be included in the branches of learning headed by the Vedas etc. We shall also demonstrate the hollowness of the arguments, advanced by the Buddhists at every step. The wretched Cārvākas, on the other hand, should only be neglected since their unworthy logic has no scope for being enumerated as one of the branches of learning.

But the Vaiśeṣikas closely follow the Naiyāyikas. 'Tarka' or 'Nyāyavistara' which figures in the six systems of logic widely known among people denotes the science of Logic of the Vaiśeṣikas as well.

Moreover, the logic of Gautama which bears the designation ānvīkṣikī' is counted as one of the four branches of learning.

Ānvīkṣikī, the three Vedas, Vārttā (Commerce) and the eternal Political Science constitute the four branches of study. The term 'anvīkṣā' signifies inference since it corroborates the evidence of perception and verbal testimony. The science which aims at the elaboration of such inference is called 'Ānvīkṣikī'.

Now, a question arises if the four-fold branches of study exhaust the entire curriculum then how is it that the fourteen different kinds of learning have been already mentioned. There is no real contradiction between these two divisions of learning. Commerce and Political Science are only of secular interest and consequently cannot find a place in such branches of learning as have spiritual significance as well. The three Vedas and Ānvīkṣikī being also included in the former list of study, the branches of learning are truly fourteen.

The justification of the study of the Logic of Gautama—Preliminary statement about its usefulness.

Now, if the function of logic is only to establish the validity of the Vedas then there is no need of it since Mīmāṁsā can easily replace it. In the Mīmāṁsā literature the vedic rituals as well as the validity of the Vedas have been discussed. This contention is true on its surface. But we should bear in mind that the principal subject-matter of Mīmāṁsā is the interpretation of the Vedas and the discussion of validity is a side-issue. Every branch of study has its own province. Mīmāṁsā is the science of interpretation but is not a work on Logic and Epistemology. The Mīmāṁsakas are not adept in defending the validity of the Vedas. We shall show later on that they have exhausted all their energy, traversing the blind alleys of logic, beset with thorns. The evidence of no single source of knowledge, even including perception, is conclusive unless and until it is strongly corroborated by other independent proofs. The unaided verbal testimony which depends upon perception for its existence is certainly unreliable. A sentence can only independently convey its meaning on the strength of the established convention but for the determination of the truth of its meaning the knowledge about its author is indispensable.

The meaning of a sentence is true if the author of it is trustworthy but not otherwise. This point will be elaborately discussed later on. Before the advent of Akṣapāda who was there to establish the validity of the Vedas ? (The purport of the objection is that if the Vedas do not carry their own validity then all attempts will fall through to prove their extrinsic validity). But it is indeed a feeble objection.

Who has interpreted the Vedas before Jaimini ?

Who has given the analysis of words before Pāṇini ? Who has made a study of metres before Piṅgala ? From the dawn of creation these sciences are in vogue on earth like the Vedas. The so-called authors do not invent logic, grammar etc. but they discuss the existent subject-matters either in an elaborate manner or in an abridged form. Now another question crops up in our mind : if the great minds admit that the validity of the Vedas is intrinsic then does not our effort go in vain to prove a settled matter ? We say 'No' since we make an attempt at removing a possible doubt or illusion of a layman. The science of logic will prove to be a fruitful study to them who are under the spell of doubt or illusion. That is why the study of logic is introduced. The study of Mīmāṁsā is not meant for them who are conversant with the sense of the Vedas. It has been stated that 'the Mīmāṁsā Sūtra and its short commentary are not intended for the Vedic scholars.'

There are four different types of people. The first type represents the ignorant. The second one stands for the doubtful. The third one embraces such persons as always misjudge. The fourth one includes only the men of correct ideas. The author of the Nyāya Sūtra is a sage whose mind does never err. He enlightens the ignorant by his logical treatise (the vehicle of instruction). He hereby removes the doubt of an oscillating mind and corrects the mistake of an illusory mind. It is proper that the study of logic should be introduced for the benefit of these three types. How does one know that the sage in question sees objects in their true perspectives ? An answer to the question runs thus:—The acquisition of the true view of the world may be due either to the practice of penance or to the worship of deity or to the close study of some other books. Let it be so, still the answer is not satisfactory. If the third alternative answer is accepted then we shall also be able to gather the correct view of the world from that work and in that case the work of Akṣapāda is useless. This point has already been met. We have already stated that no author repeats the same old story. A new author puts the old matters either elaborately or briefly. This conduct of an author justifies his new enterprise. Moreover, the mentality of the readers is diverse. This is what has been stated. The study of Akṣapāda's logic is at least fruitful to those who get their ignorance dispelled, doubts solved and mistakes corrected by it. That is why the great teacher has composed it.

A General Statement of the Subject-Matter in the first Aphorism of Gautama's Logic (Objection and rejoinder).

The first aphorism of Gautama's Nyāya-Sūtra runs thus :—The final emancipation from all sorrows is attained through the true knowledge of Pramāṇa, Prameya, Saṃśaya, Prayojana, Dṛṣṭānta, Siddhānta, Avayava, Tarka, Nirṃaya, Vāda, Jalpa, Vitaṇḍā, Hetvābhāsa, Chala, Jāti and Nigrahasthānas (these terms will be explained by Jayanta himself. English equivalents are not given here because Jayanta shows much independence in their interpretation).

Why does the first sentence thus commence ? What is the drift of this question ? If a teacher delivers a series of lectures which result in a book then he cannot but commence his work without beginning with a sentence since the whole of his lecture cannot be delivered all at once. Without speaking out the first sentence the second one cannot be given out. Now if you find fault with the first sentence only because it is the first one then the book which consists of a large number of such sentences cannot be composed.

Now the objector replies:—'Do not think that I do not know all these'. He holds that he has been misunderstood. The purport of his question is this : "Why does the author give the broad division of his subject-matter and the ultimate end of his book, leaving aside the main topic at the outset. Now if the objection amounts to this then a reply may be given to this effect that the subject-matter of a book together with the broad division of its contents and the end towards which it drives should be given in the beginning in order to encourage the listeners. The learned scholars decline to lend their ears even to the contents of a small treatise if the broad outline of the subject-matter and its end were not known to them at the initial stage.

No learned man undertakes such an action the details and the utility of which are not known to him. Bhaṭṭa says to this effect, "Neither a person undertakes an action nor he cares to read a book unless he realises the usefulness of either of them."

Very well. How does a listener become acquainted with the said utility at the out-set? It is a hard nut to crack. It requires much reflection to tackle it. The question gives rise to other difficult questions. Do we suddenly realise the utility of a book as soon as we read the mere statement of its utility? Or, does it flash in our mind whenever we follow the logic of it? How do we make the correct estimates of its utility unless we know the truth of the statement? If it is held that even a man, who entertains a doubt as to the utility of a book proceeds to read it then a man may also proceed to perform a Vedic rite without being sure of its efficacy. If it is held that when a man understands the utility of a book following its logic he reads the whole of it but not otherwise. Now, if he proceeds to listen to a book, having thoroughly grasped its utility then the fallacy of mutual dependence invalidates such a solution. The fallacy of mutual dependence runs thus :— If we listen to the recitation of a book then we know its utility and if we know its utility then we care to listen to the recitation of a book. The final answer is this that a listener knows the utility of a book from the very first sentence but cares to listen to it even if he hesitates to accept the truth of all the statements of the book.

The purport of the solution is the statement of the psychological condition of a reader which is favourable for a reader to read a new book. The mere knowledge of the utility of the book is necessary only for his movement. The reader may doubt the validity of the statement of utility and the truth of the subject-matter of the book. In spite of this irresolute condition of his mind he proceeds to read the book.

If a man is not convinced of the validity of the Vedas then it is not proper for him to undertake to perform very difficult Vedic rites in a hesitant mood. An undertaking which demands little, is easy to perform and does not entail tremendous labour and heavy expense upon a performer but has a very bright prospect is taken up. The intelligent persons, during the course of their lecture, know for themselves within a few days whether the study of the subject is conducive to a big result or a small one.

If a person goes on to scrutinize the result of his undertaking from the very start of an action then he will never make progress but will surely court failure in life.

A diseased person generally sends for a physician, gets himself examined by him and follows his prescription. But if he doubts the efficacy of his prescription and hesitates to follow it then his disease will simply wax strong.

Hence a man, knowing the utility and the broad outline of the subject-matter from the first sentence, should listen to the book in a reverential mood with the expectation that its study may prove useful.

Some learned scholars have discussed the usefulness of the first sentence of a book in a different manner. A sentence in which the constituent words are not mutually connected is to be rejected as it conveys no sense resembling in this respect an expression like 'ten pomegranates' etc., of which words are not syntactically connected. Even a sentence which conveys sense, having its constituent words mutually connected, should be rejected as worthless if it answers no purpose like the following interrogatory one, "Are the teeth of a crow good or bad ?" A sentence which points to a useful object is accepted. A sentence which serves no purpose is rejected. The first sentence of a book, indicating the utility of the book, removes all our doubts as to its acceptability. If the first sentence had not described the goal of the book then the objector would have rejected the book on that very ground. The first sentence attracts the readers and silences the hostile critics, fulfilling all initial requirements. The drift of the contention of these scholars is that the first sentence should convey the aim and object of a book.

The very statement of the aim and object of a book does away with all our misgivings with regard to it since the condition which prepares ground for rejection has been excluded. Others hold that the first sentence calls up either a doubt as to the realization of the end expressed in it or a feeling of probability of its realization. But any one of these two feelings is roused up only by the expression of the end in question by the first sentence. Either doubt or the possibility concerning the realization of the end gives impetus to us to read or listen to the book.

But the first sentence makes us aware only of the end in question since it expresses only its meaning but nothing else. But a doubt arises in the mind of a listener in due course when he thinks that a sentence of a man turns out to be sometimes true and sometimes false. When he notices that the author is pure, good and honest he thinks that the above statement may be true. There, it has been stated well that the only object of the first sentence is to express the usefulness of the book.

At the outset it is proper to speak out what attracts a listener to lend his ears to it. There is no other motive than to convey the end in question.

The contents of a book should be narrated in order to prove its utility which follows from their knowledge to invite the attention of a listener.

The relation between a book and its contents and that between the contents and the result of its study are not clearly stated by its author. These two relations are easily grasped, since they are implied though they are not explicitly stated by suitable terms. The relation of the signifier and the signified holds between the science of logic and its contents. So the knowledge of the latter leads up to the final emancipation from all sorrows (mokṣa) and the relation of the means and the end holds between the contents and mokṣa, the goal. The specified relations are grasped by us to the exclusion of other possible relations because the relations themselves as stated clearly indicate their appropriateness.

The narration of the main topics of the science of logic.

The main topics of the science of logic are sixteen in number. They begin with Pramāṇa (the source of valid knowledge) and end in Nigraha-sthāna (the source of defeat in a debate). An adequate treatment of them will take place later on. Let us now give a rough sketch of them. The source of the true knowledge of an object such as perception etc., is called Pramāṇa. The object of such true knowledge is called Prameya such as Ātman etc. The form of consciousness which reveals its substantive as simultaneously qualified by the two or more incompatible predicates is called saṃśaya (a doubt). [In other words, a doubt is a discursive judgment in which the subject is predicated by two or more incompatible predicates. It is really the semblance of a judgment since it ends in indecision.] The realization of the good and the avoidance of the evil and the means to such realization or avoidance is called Prayojana (the spring of action). A positive instance by means of which the invariable relation of concomitance holding between the probans and the probandum is ascertained is called Dṛṣṭānta. An object possesses two characters, viz. common and exclusively particular. If it is known as such by means of proofs and accepted as such then it is called Siddhānta. Whenever our inferential knowledge is demonstrated we do so by means of a syllogism consisting of a number of propositions designated as Pratijñā etc. Each of these propositions is called Avayava. When two rival hypotheses are offered to explain a fact one is preferred to the other for its having stronger reasons. The more reasonable one seems to us to be the probable explanation. The knowledge of such probability is called Tarka. Nirṇaya is the arrival at a truth by means of the establishment of the hypothesis of one's own school and the refutation of that of his rival school. A dispassionate discussion which results in the finding out of the truth is Vāda. Jalpa is such a debate in which the contesting parties care only to win anyhow and in which there is only a free play of intellectual powers. A species of Jalpa is Vitaṇḍā. What is not a true mark but appears to be so is called a Hetvābhāsa. The adverse criticism of a sentence by means of the distortion of its meaning is called Chala, Jāti means an opposition by a counter-argument simply based upon resemblance or difference, but not upon sound grounds. Nigrahasthāna is such as never gives a true picture of a fact but always a false one.

The first sūtra consists of compound words. The list of main terms of logic has been given by a compound. These items have been subsequently defined by appropriate sūtras. In the light of those sūtras we know that some of the component words of the compound word have only singular number. In the expounding sentence which explains the above compound word the component words which have singular number should have such inflexion as indicates the singular number. The words such as Pramāṇa, Avayava and Hetvābhāsa should have inflexion indicative of the plural number in the expounding sentence. The remaining words of the above compound word should have only such inflexion as is indicative of the singular number. Thus, the thorough agreement between the general statement and the specified ones has been perfectly maintained. The compound in this particular instance is dvandva which conveys the sense of mutual conjunction.

The above explanation is not satisfactory. The word 'tattva' is a dependent one since it refers to Pramāṇa etc. for the complete expression of its meaning. Such a dependent word should not be compounded with another word. The principal word in a compound is allowed to be compounded though it is related to an uncompounded word. In the sentence 'Rājapuruṣaḥ śobhanaḥ' the word 'śobhanaḥ' relates to puruṣaḥ. The word 'rājapuruṣaḥ' is a compound one. The word 'puruṣaḥ' plays the main part since emphasis is laid on its meaning. But in the compound word 'tattvajñāna' the word 'jñāna' is the principal one and the word 'tattva' has the subordinate one. In that case, the word 'tattva' which enjoys a subordinate status in the Sūtra of Gautama cannot be compounded. A similar case may be cited viz. in the sentence 'ṛddhasya rājñaḥ puruṣaḥ' the word 'rājñaḥ' is not allowed to enter into a compound word as its component. The drift of the argument is that the compounding of the word 'tattva' is inadmissible.

Some commentators meet this objection in a different way. They hold that the term 'jñāna' is also related to the words 'Pramāṇa and others' since they are also objects of knowledge. If the word 'tattva' is related to the words 'pramāṇa etc.,' the above objection arises. But if the word 'jñāna' is related to the words 'pramāṇa etc.' then no such difficulty arises. The solution of the above problem is simply this, the word 'tattva' which has no other 'correlative term' is compounded with 'jñāna', a principal word in spite of its reference to other terms. The proposed compound is 'karmadhāraya'. The above linguistic solution is not satisfactory since it goes against the conclusion of the Nyāya Logic. No knowledge is in itself true or untrue. If a piece of knowledge correctly reveals an object, it is true. If not, it is untrue. Truth or untruth is an extrinsic property of knowledge but not intrinsic. The word 'tat' has a definite meaning. It conveys the sense that the meaning in question is either a positive or negative real well-determined by a source of true knowledge. The essence of such a real is 'tattva'. The piece of true knowledge which reveals such an essence is called tattva-jñāna. The essence of true knowledge i.e. truth is cognized by another piece of knowledge. The sources of true knowledge etc. are determined by a piece of knowledge other than the objects of it. The use of tattva as an object of knowledge is very significant since it throws light on the essential teaching of Nyāya-Logic, commentators should not be perplexed by the linguistic objections. The admissibility of such condemned terms in a compound word is noticed in many instances. A well-accepted example is 'Devadattasya gurukulam'. The place of a word in a compound word is an important factor. The mutual relation of words should be maintained. If the sense is clearly expressed by a compound word of which any constituent term, principal or subordinate, has relation to other uncompounded words, there is no bar to their forming a compound word. The celebrated grammarians follow this diction.

Pāṇini commences his work with the title
'The science of word'. The commentator asks
"of which words?"

An examination of the compound in the compound word Tattvajñāna.

The compound word has the sixth case-ending attached to it. It has syntactical relation with the word 'tattva'. The sixth case-ending indicates the non-specified relation holding between Pramāṇa etc. word and tattva. Then he explains the two other compound terms, viz., tattvajñāna and niḥśreyasādhigama. Tattva is the object of the verb to know since it is being known and niḥśreyasa is being attained it is the object of the verb to attain. The answer is 'of classical and Vedic Sanskrit words'. Now, the complex sentence turns out to be the science of classical and Vedic words. The Sanskrit sentence is like the 'laukikānāṁ vaidikānāṁ ca śabdānuśāsanam'. Patañjali, the great commentator of Pāṇini approves of the compounding of śabda and anuśāsana in spite of the double relation of the word śabda which has a subordinate place in the compound word 'śabdānuśāsana'.

Therefore the sixth case-endings in the three words, viz., Tattvaniḥśreyasa and śabda are quite correct, being in accordance with the decision of the great commentator on Pāṇini.

An examination of the hypothesis that Tattvajñāna is a means to the attainment of Niḥśreyasa.

Now it should be proved how the true knowledge of the sixteen topics of Gautama's logic leads up to the attainment of the highest good (niḥśreyasa). The declared purpose of it is to prove the validity of the Vedas. Go on with your business. Why do you take up the tedious task of discussing the sixteen topics? Our answer to such a question is that the true knowledge of the twelve objects beginning with the soul and ending in apavarga (the absolute cessation of all sorrows) is the direct means to the realisation of the final state of freedom from all sufferings and that the true knowledge of other objects is not conducive to the goal of life. We shall discuss all these points later on. When our erroneous knowledge is dispelled by the true knowledge of the soul etc., our cycle of worldly existence, based on errors, comes to a stop. That is why the objects of the true knowledge must be instructed. We learn only from the Vedas that the true knowledge of objects such as the soul etc. leads to the absolute cessation from all sorrows.

The validity of the Vedas is established by an inference. The unfailing mark in that inference is the utterance of a trustworthy person. We shall discuss the details of the mark later on. Perception alone helps us to detect the relation of invariable concomitance holding between the probans and the probandum. No other forms of knowledge help us in this matter since all other forms of knowledge land in *regressus ad infinitum* which baffles all attempts. If one has the direct experience of the good results of the medical science then he will understand without the least doubt that the utterances of an āpta (a seer—a trustworthy person) are true. (Jayanta means to say that the medical science is a branch of the Vedas. If the statements of it tally with the facts, i.e., if the diagnosis, prognosis and treatment as suggested by it prove to be true then its validity is established. The Vedas, being the work of the same author, will also be valid). Upamāna (comparison) also gives us assistance in some sphere of activity (viz., the detection of the relation holding between a word and its meaning). Therefore, the four proofs should also find a place in logic like the real objects such as the soul etc. Though doubt and other contents of the sūtra are included by their very nature either in the proofs or in the objects of the true knowledge, yet they have been separately treated because they induce a person to the syllogistic reasoning. Syllogism which establishes the validity of the Vedas helps us to realise human ends.

No body uses syllogistic arguments to prove an unknown or a well-established object but a doubtful one. Hence doubt is an accessory of syllogism. No one uses syllogism if it serves no purpose. A positive instance again helps us to detect the relation of invariable concomitance holding between the probans and the probandum. Thus, it is intimately connected with induction and thereby with syllogism.

Siddhānta (the establishment of the subject) also is a necessary condition of the demonstration of a syllogistic argument since it fulfils one of the conditions of an inference. It correctly asserts that the object to be inferred definitely belongs to the subject of inference. Thereby it counteracts the fallacy that the object to be inferred does not belong to the subject of inference. Now, a question arises in our mind, "Why do we pay special attention to Siddhānta ?' The purport of this objection is that if we entertain a doubt as to the belonging of an object to be inferred to the subject of inference then the fallacy stated above is surely negated by it (by the very doubt). There is much sense in this objection. But we should bear in mind that we do not always use syllogistic arguments to prove doubtful cases but also prove established facts by means of syllogism. There is no such rule that the syllogistic argument should only be used to prove doubtful cases. Hence, Siddhānta should be distinctly treated.

If we employ a syllogistic argument to convince others then all the premises should be used since they are helpful to them for their better understanding. A syllogistic argument, consisting of 5 premises, is called parārtha-anumāna (an inference meant for convincing others).

Now, another question arises in our mind. 'Why should Dṛṣṭānta (a positive instance) and Siddhānta (an object established) be separately treated ?' The drift of this objection is that as they constitute the meanings of the first and the third propositions (Pratijñā and Udāharaṇa) so it is superfluous to reconsider them afresh. A tentative reply is that if you argue like this then Inference, a distinct source of valid knowledge, should not be enlisted in the list of the sources of valid knowledge since the second proposition which is called Hetu signifies it (i.e. Inference). The objector may say, that it matters little whether Inference finds a place in the list or not. The further rejoinder to this objection is this :—Every item has its proper place in the system of logic. All of the five constituent propositions together signify syllogism. They should only be discussed when the turn of syllogism will come up. Siddhānta, Dṛṣṭānta etc., precede syllogism. Hence, they should be separately treated. If the order of this system is not obeyed then the system of logic has no other topic to discuss than the five constituent propositions of a syllogism.

Tarka is separately discussed because it has a special function to pave the way for one of the two rival hypotheses. When two rival hypotheses are known to us to explain a fact our mind naturally hesitates to cling to one of them under the supposition that each of them is almost equally strong. Tarka steps in to remove the state of indecision. It strengthens the arguments in favour of one of these two rival hypotheses by removing all doubts. At the same time, by exposing defects in the other rival hypothesis, it relaxes the force of all arguments put forward in favour of the alternative predicate. In a dispassionate debate Tarka is used inorder to eliminate the bias from the mind of one of the two debators. The function of Tarka does not cease until the truth of one of the two rival hypotheses is established. The final ascertainment of truth (nirṇaya) employs a tarka in order to work out its result, viz., the termination of a syllogistic argument. If an unending chain of syllogism goes on for ever without reaching a final conclusion then no body would have been eager to seek the services of such a fruitless chain of syllogism.

Now an objection is raised as to the importance of nirṇaya as a distinct topic. The purport of it is that it is superfluous to take up nirṇaya separately since nirṇaya itself is tattvajñāna (the true knowledge of the real nature of the specified objects of logic). The rejoinder to this objection is as follows :—There is really much force in the above objection. Still, the nirṇaya in question has a special feature of its own. The true knowledge of the sixteen topics is acquired through the instrumentality of a distinct valid source of knowledge, viz., an inference. As it requires the operation of a syllogism for its very establishment so it is a mover of a syllogism. But the nirṇaya in question arises when the debate has been concluded. (In other words, when the dual fight of a thesis and its antithesis is over and the antiparty is utterly crushed, nirṇaya emerges). The syllogistic process reaches its destination and comes to a standstill. Nirṇaya is the very goal. It stops the movement of a syllogistic process. Hence, tattva-jñāna, the mover of a syllogism, cannot be identified with this nirṇaya. We cannot know the true character of this nirṇaya unless it is separately treated.

Another objection is raised against the separate treatment of anumāna. The Nirṇaya in question is no better than an inference. But such an objection is untenable. Nirṇaya is the result of inference but in itself is not an inference. If it had been an inference then it, like an inference, would only remain a process and would have yielded no result and as a consequence an inferential process would have continued interminably.

Now a further objection is raised. The objector holds that inference coupled with tattvajñāna is nirṇaya. He gets over the above difficulty since an inference has a goal to reach, viz., tattvajñāna. A reply to this objection is as follows:—If nirṇaya is not special then who will say that all inferences lead to tattvajñāna. Some inferences are right and the rest are wrong. Inference does not imply that it is right. A fallacious reasoning leads to a wrong conclusion. Thus instead of the true knowledge of tattva we may get the erroneous knowledge of tattva. Therefore the objection is not tenable.

Now, a further objection is raised. The purport of it is as follows : Doubt precedes inference and inference, being a mental process, reaches a definite conclusion by its very nature. Now the act of inference which is preceded by a doubt and succeeded by tattvajñāna is nirṇaya. Such an objection does not hold good. All inferences are not correct. There may be a wrong argument which though preceded by a doubt will yield only a wrong conclusion (nirṇayābhāsa). There is no such rule that a doubt invariably precedes inference. In fine, in order to establish that a definite conclusion which is drawn from a syllogism, has a distinct character of its own, nirṇaya deserves a distinct mention......

Enough of it.

Suppose two contesting parties put forward the two distinct trains of syllogism in order to prove their opposite views on a certain topic. Both of them cannot be correct. If one of them refutes the other and arrives at a final conclusion, then this final conclusion is Nirṇaya. We arrive at Nirṇaya through a different process of thought. Hence it demands a special treatment.

In cases of dispassionate discussion a teacher employs a syllogism in order to prove the soundness of his thesis, brings home his point to the mind of the other debators by removing all doubts and wins their approval. A teacher should hold such a debate with his pupils and class-mates who are not prompted by love and hatred. When the guileless honest people become dejected and depressed by the unsound arguments fabricated by the wild imagination of bad logicians, Jalpa (wrangling) and Vitaṇḍā (cavil) are permitted to be employed even by the honest logicians in order to restore conviction to the above persons so that they will cling to their original hypothesis and fortify it. On special occasions even to the persons desirous of final emancipation such an unfair debate becomes serviceable. We shall discuss it later on.

The study of defective marks renders some service to a syllogistic argument since it helps us to discriminate between the sound and the defective minor premises which constitute a syllogism. If we know the defective marks then the marks which are not so are easily recognised to be true. Now, an objection arises in our mind viz. "Why do not we reverse the order of treatment?" If we know at first the true mark then the wrong mark can be easily detected. Though there is much truth in it yet when a proposition containing a middle term is to be used two things are to be noticed, viz., the employment of the true mark and the avoidance of the false one. In order to avoid the false mark we should know it to be such. Truly speaking hetvābhāsas belong to a species of Nigrahasthāna. But they are mainly pointed out in a dispassionate debate to invalidate the counter syllogism. That is why they have been separately treated. In cases of debate like Jalpa or Vitaṇḍā type, Chala, Jāti and Nigrahasthāna are freely employed. One should know them thoroughly at first so that he will be able to play better the game of defence by not allowing his opponent to hurl them at the propositions employed by him.

On special occasions one under painful necessity uses them though it is not possible to use them always. Again, if his opponent uses them, he will be able to remedy them. One should know them as they invariably accompany Jalpa and Vitaṇḍā and are their part and parcel. For this very reason, they have been separately treated.

The Buddhists who have received wrong training in the art of logic are very vociferous. Little bits of wrong premises sound much. These logicians are skilled in the employment of vitaṇḍā i.e. destructive criticism, having no positive stand of their own. If one is not well equipped with the knowledge of Jalpa, Vitaṇḍā etc. he cannot meet them and be able to win victory in such debates over them.

A common man is generally uncritical in his acceptance of views. He follows the beaten track of his fellowmen. Such a person is generally led astray by the bad logicians. The compassionate sage Gautama comes to their rescue and teaches them all specimens of bad logic so that the simple minded people may not be misled by these designing logicians.

Similarly, the other topics of logic, viz., a doubt etc. should also be taught so that the knowledge of the validity of the Vedic lore may be deeply rooted in their mind.

The science of Logic of Gautama rightly deserves a place among the sources of knowledge since it restores the validity of the Vedic scriptures.

The celebrated commentator says to this effect : The Logic of Gautama which like a lamp illuminates all other sources of knowledge, i.e., branches of learning, shows means to all actions and acts as a support of all dharmas, has been rightly ennumerated in the list of the sources of knowledge.

The sage has shown the path which leads to the destination of the absolute cessation of all sorrows. There are other objects of knowledge in this world. They have no bearing upon the final goal of life mentioned above. Hence he did not discuss them.

The Three-fold procedure of the Nyāya-Logic

The procedure, adopted by the Nyāyasūtra to discuss its topics, is three-fold, viz., the nomenclature of its topics, their definitions and an examination of them. The introduction of a topic by its name is called uddeśa (denomination). The definition (lakṣaṇa) of a topic is the statement of such property as reveals its essence. An enquiry into the appropriateness of a definition is called an examination (parīkṣā). Now, a question arises in our mind :—The fourth kind of procedure is noticed, viz., division. The sūtra mentions the broad divisions of Pramāṇa, Siddhānta, Chala, etc., which admit of division. So the statement about the procedure is not exhaustive. The objection appears to be true but does not stand a thorough criticism. The reply to the above objection is as follows:

It is admitted that the initial *sūtra* of a topic sometimes contains division but it is also to be noted that the very *sūtra* denominates all the species. Hence it is nomenclative. As the *sūtra* pointing to division discharges the function of denomination, it should be considered as to be nomenclative. When a *sūtra* mentions the common name it is called *Uddeśa*. But when a *sūtra* mentions the designations of all the species it is called a *sūtra* of division (*vibhāga*). But in the *Uddeśa* and *vibhāga sūtras* the common element is nomenclature. The celebrated *Nyāya bhāṣya-kāra* adopts this line of defence. An objection has been raised as to the propriety of the *sūtra* which deals with *pramāṇa* since division of the *pramāṇas* has been mentioned only. The *Bhāṣya-kāra* gives a final reply with the remark that the *sūtra* in question is in order since it is nomenclative. The *sūtra-kāra* mentions the names of all the species subsumed under *pramāṇa*. Hence the disputed *sūtra* is nomenclative (*Uddeśa*). Therefore we arrive at the conclusion that the procedure of discussing a topic in the *Sūtra* form is three-fold only.

Nomenclature comes first. If a matter for discussion is not designated it can neither be defined nor examined. There is an order of succession between a general definition and that of its species. If a generic property is not defined, specific properties cannot be defined, since the property of a species cannot be defined if the common property of the genus is not defined. Hence the definition of a species always follows that of a genus.

The very nature of an examination clearly shows that it follows a definition if the property of an object is not exactly stated by means of a definition, how can it be examined? No order of succession obtains between the definition of a genus and its division. The general definition may precede or succeed the division of its species. There is no ruling with regard to an order of place. There may be first general definition and then division or there may be first division and then general definition. Thus the topic on nomenclature is exhaustively discussed.

Then the *sūtras* which relate to definition will be explained. The task of thorough discussion will be done to the best of our intellectual powers alongwith the *sutras* which deal with definitions in a relevant manner. We shall not take an extra trouble of explaining and dicussing the *sūtras* which concentrate upon the examination of a topic.

After the explanation of the first *Sūtra* of Gotama's Logic the second one will not be explained, since it neither embodies a definition nor contains such materials as are conducive to a definition. It will be discussed in its appropriate place alongwith *apavarga* (the absolute cessation of all sorrows) since the content of this *sūtra* is secondary to the treatment of *apavarga*.

The definition of Pramāṇa

The deflnition of Pramāṇa will be discussed in the *sūtra* on the division of *Pramāṇa* since it finds an appropriate place therein.

Pramāṇa admits of four-fold division, viz. Perception, Inference, Comparison and Verbal Testimony.

Now, the following matter is going to be discussed. What is a pramāṇa ? What is the nature ? What is its definition? The matter of enquiry being discussed the bearing of the sūtra upon Pramāṇa will be taken up. The theme in question is being discussed. Pramāṇa is the collocation of the two types of objects viz., consciousness and unconscious ones which co-operate to produce such an apprehension of objects as is other than an illusion and a doubt. Pramāṇa consists of two opposite elements viz. consciousness and unconscious objects. The definition of Pramāṇa is what produces such an apprehension as is other than an illusion and a doubt. The etymological meaning of a pramāṇa is what is an instrument of the true knowledge. The suffix which is atttached to the root 'ma' denotes an instrument. An instrument (Karaṇa) is defined to be the causa sui of an act (sādhaka-tama). The nominal suffix 'tamap' added to the stem 'sādhaka' indicates a sense of comparison. It presupposes the other objects with which it is compared. There must be other conditions of an act amongst which it is the most efficacious. That is why it is called sādhaka-tama. Now, if the collocation of all conditions is the instrument then how can a comparison among them take place since the collocation is one and there are no other conditions outside the collocation? If the collocation of all conditions is the instrument of the true knowledge of an object, then how can it make room for comparison? The object which is being truly known is also one of the conditions of such knowledge. In that case, it becomes merged in the collocation of all condition and loses its individuality. Thus, the object of knowledge itself, being one of the members of the collocation, turns out to be the instrument of the knowing process. Thus, all acts of true knowledge become objectless from this stand-point since the object of knowledge is included in the collocation like the sense-organ, viz., eyes, etc. Who will be the subject of an act of knowledge? The subject who knows an object by means of an instrument in the shape of collocation is also one of the conditions of an act of knowledge. As a condition it is engulfed by the collocation of all conditions. Thus, the subject ceases to be the subject and becomes an instrument.

If this absurd conclusion is accepted by the contender then the fundamental position of Nyāya-Epistemology is at stake (jeopardised). Nyāya epistemology embodies a pragmatic appeal. If the subject of true knowledge, its object, its instrument and the act itself maintain their individual distinction then and then only the essence of Nyāya Epistemology finds its perfect expression. The people at large do not approve of this hypothesis, since in the conversion we find no indication of a collocation as being used in the shape of an instrumental case. No body says that he sees an object by means of the collocation of all conditions but he asserts that by means of his eyes he visualizes an object. Therefore, no collocation of all conditions is an instrument. Hence, the collocation of conditions is not pramāṇa.

A reply to these objections is as follows :—

An instrument is such as gives the most efficient service to produce an act. The word 'pramāṇa' denotes the instrument of true knowledge. Hence it is reasonable to hold that the collocation of all conditions of true knowledge is pramāṇa. No other case excepting the aggregate of all of them can be the most efficacious one to produce it. When all the conditions assemble, the effect takes place. When one of them is absent the effect does not come into being. Therefore, the assemblage of all conditions is superior to all. None of them singly does get the credit for making a special contribution towards its effectuation. None of them alone wins the distinction of doing a special service since all of them combine to do the effect in question and share in common the credit for production.

Now, the objector may contend that a condition which is directly connected with an effect has only a distinctive feature. This contention does not hold good since what is indirectly connected with an effect is also a condition. Moreover, all the conditions of an act of knowledge are directly related to the act in question. Let us take the example of an act of perception. All the conditions, viz., the senseorgan, the inner organ, the object, etc., combine together to produce the act of perception. Now, the objector may contend that a condition, the immediate presence of which brings about the effect, possesses a distinction. In other words, such a condition should be the instrument. Such a solution is not tenable since sometimes the immediate presence of an object is responsible for its perception. In a dark night when the sky is enveloped by clouds heaped upon clouds and pitchy darkness prevails a lady is suddenly revealed by a flash of lightning. It is generally believed that in this case the flash of lightning has a distinctive mark which no other condition possesses. Therefore, the flash of lightning to the exclusion of all other conditions is the instrument. But here is a point worth noting that if all other conditions excepting the lady assemble then the perception of the lady will not take place. As soon as she appears on the scene the perception in question takes place. The lady is the object of the act of perception. If we had struck to the above proposition then in this case the object itself would have been an instrument. The distinctive feature of an instrument lies in this that its presence is invariably and immediately followed by the appearance of an effect. No condition, included in the collocation of all conditions, individually possesses the exceptional mark of distinction. Now, the collocation of all conditions alone possesses that mark of distinction. Therefore, it is logical to call it an instrument i.e. causation. When the collocation of all conditions takes place the effect invariably comes into existence in close succession. Therefore, the collocation of all conditions is alone capable of being the most effective producer of an act. An act of knowledge is not an exception to the general rule.

Now, the objector may indulge in a further contention that since the subject and the object of an act of true knowledge are invariably connected with true knowledge, they should also possess the distinctive mark recognized by all. A true knower is the locus of the act of true knowledge. A true object is what is grasped by the act of true knowledge. In other words, the subject or the object of every piece of true knowledge are invariably related to it as its subject or object. The contention is true. But the objector does not dive deep into the nature of the subject and the object. The subject and the object mentioned above acquire their real relational character only through the medium of assemblage of all conditions which produces true knowledge in order to render the relation of the subject and the object with true knowledge possible. In the absence of this assemblage true knowledge does not come into being and the subject and the object of true knowledge lose their primary significance. They are so only in the secondary sense. None but the collocation of all conditions deserves the distinctive mark of effectuating true knowledge. Hence the assemblage of all its conditions is the instrument of pramā (true knowledge) i.e. causa sui.

Now, a further objection is being raised. A collocation in itself has no process by means of which it can produce an act. How can it be an instrument, having no process? The answer to it is that it works not by an independent process of its own but by means of the processes of all the conditions included in it. The assemblage is a common property of all conditions. Hence it cannot do away with their individual traits. When these conditions assemble together each one of them retains its own characteristic feature. The individual property of each one is recognized.

Is collocation different from the individual conditions? If it is so then why is it not observed to be so? If it is identical with the conditions then all conditions turn out to be the instrumental case. In that case, the usage such as a subject, an object, etc., should be abolished. Such an objection does not invalidate the hypothesis in question. When all the conditions assemble at a point of time the property of assemblage is directly perceived. If the objects such as the cooking pot, water, fire, rice, etc., stand apart then the knowledge of assemblage does not arise. But when they stand together they are known to possess a common property, viz., assemblage. When many conditions assemble they possess a common property of assemblage. But in case of threads a bundle of threads being united a distinct type of assemblage comes into being. It is called a piece of cloth. The piece of cloth is distinct from its constituent threads assembled. In spite of a distinction between the first and second type of assemblage an assemblage irrespective of its types exists as a matter of fact. An assemblage as compared to each of the individual members that assemble is an instrumental case. The objection, mentioned above, does not hold good. An object may assemble in a collection. But the assemblage itself is the instrument. Therefore the charge that a piece of true knowledge becomes objectless i.e. deprived of its object to reveal turns out to be pointless. Similarly, the subject of an act of knowing unaffectingly stands as a subject in the much debated assemblage of the conditions. Thus the fourfold division involved in an act of true knowledge is shown to be honoured.

Another objection has been raised from the linguistic point of view that an assemblage does never take the third case ending which is indicative of the instrumental case. An answer to it is this that the term 'assemblage' is never used independently of an assembling member. Hence in Sanskrit Literature no such usage, viz. 'I all with an assemblage' comes to our notice. But a lamp or a sense- organ or anyother appropriate object takes the third case-ending to convey the idea that the object denoted by the stem to which the third case-ending has been added is the instrument. The underlying secret is not known to all. Such a usage is permissible only when the nature of producing an effect, belonging to the assemblage of all conditions is attributed to any member included in the assemblage. Not only in the field of Epistemology but also in the common practice the above-mentioned condition holds good. Let us cite an illustration viz. 'one cooks with a pot.' Such usages on the strength of attribution come to our notice. When an assemblage acquires the character of an instrument depending upon the conditions included in it such an assemblage is the cause par excellence of true knowledge.

The other critics come forward and take an exception to the above hypothesis. They argue in the following manner:—An assemblage is nothing but all the conditions assembled together. The double character of the members is incomprehensible. One of such conditions lying outside the assemblage may be an object or a subject or something else. But when they assemble together to produce an effect they become an instrumental case. What is the underlying reason behind the formulation of such a hypothesis. In the absence of a clear rational ground the subject and the object should be never an instrument. The other conditions which generate true knowledge which is other than an error or a doubt is an instrumental cause i.e. the cause par excellence. In the Sanskrit grammar the third case-ending signifies this character of the condition in question I see with a lamp; I see with eyes; I know by means of a mark, I ascertain with the help of a word, I determine with my inner organ and so on. These are the classical examples in support of the second hypothesis of the critics.

Now a question arises in our mind viz. 'should there be only three kinds of conditions ? The reply is that in Epistemology these three types of conditions are enough and that this hypothesis agrees with that of yours. In the actual world there may be other types of conditions, having different contributions to the effectuation of an act : Let us take concrete case viz. the act of cooking. A container of the articles to be cooked is necessary. The act of cooking is not possible without the remote help received from the container and so on. Similarly, the other types of conditions are to be assumed in consideration of their necessary contributions towards the actualisation of an act. In the production of the effect viz. a piece of true knowledge no difference in the nature of contributive function is noticed among the instrumental causes mentioned above, viz. a lamp, eyes, an inner organ and so on. All such conditions are to be included in the instrumental cause. The most contributive condition is defined to be an instrumental cause. The meaning of 'tamap', is 'the most' in English. The superlative should have significance. What is the significance of the suffix 'tamap' in the effectuation of knowledge ? The answer is that there is some significance. This significance is grasped by every body. Nobody uses the subject or the object as an instrumental cause. But he rightly uses 'eyes', 'an inner organ', 'a lamp', 'a word' and 'a mark' as an instrumental cause as he notices the differences of a subject and of an object from an instrumental cause. Thus we conclude that the four-fold division of true knowledge generally called a proof or a source of valid knowledge, the subject of true knowledge, its object and the act of knowing truly, is completely covered by the second hypothesis. Therefore we arrive at the final complete definition of a proof of true knowledge that is the collocation of all conditions other than a subject and an object partaking of the nature of consciousness and unconsciousness and productive of the knowledge of an object other than an error or a doubt, is the instrumental cause of true knowledge.

An examination of the Definition of Pramāṇa of the Buddhist School

These who hold that some forms of consciousness are pramāṇas lack deep insight into the Science of logic. Some kind of consciousness is the result of pramāṇa but cannot be itself a direct pramāṇa. The term 'pramāṇa' etymologically signifies an instrument. A pramāṇa is that by which something is correctly known. What is the meaning of the predicate 'is correctly known' ? The answer is that true knowledge is generated. The people at large also hold that they know it by means of a pramāṇa. They also lend their support to the view that an instrument is really a pramāṇa. In Sanskrit literature we find that the word 'pramā' is also synonymous with the word 'pramāṇa'. This 'pramāṇa' is truly the result of pramāṇa, the instrument. Thus a piece of knowledge which is other than a doubt and an illusion is the result of a pramāṇa. Such a piece of knowledge generates an inference of the soul or that of the internal organ of such true knowledge as gives information about its object whether it is acceptable or avoidable. Under some circumstances it acts as an instrument and becomes a pramāṇa. But if a piece of knowledge which is neither an illusion nor a doubt does not produce another piece of true knowledge then it should not be called a pramāṇa, though some thinkers wrongly call it a pramāṇa. It is widely known all over the country that the unconscious objects such as a lamp, a sense-organ, etc. are instruments of knowledge. If we accept the view of some thinkers that knowledge is only pramāṇa then we shall have to discard the popular view. Therefore, it should be noted that if a piece of knowledge is included in the collocation of conditions which determines a resulting consciousness then it is called a pramāṇa. A number of illustrations may be cited to substantiate our point. If a perceptual judgment is taken into consideration then the antecedent simple perception acts as an instrument which produces the subsequent judgment of perception. In case of an inference the knowledge of the mark is instrumental to the knowledge of the object marked. In case of analogy the knowledge of similarity is an instrument of the analogical knowledge. The auditory perception of a word leads to the knowledge of the object denoted by it as an instrument. These pieces of knowledge are pramāṇas. Therefore, it is rightly stated that the collocation of conditions including both consciousness and unconscious objects is a pramāṇa.

Some other logicians hold that a phenomenon of consciousness which reveals an object is pramāṇa provided that the revealer and the revealed owe their existence to the same set of conditions. Every object in this universe is momentary. The Universe does not become empty and worldly transactions go on undisturbed since phenomena belonging to one series generate phenomena of other series through the agency of a cause and its accompanying conditions. When a phenomenon of consciousness is generated its antecedent phenomenon of consciousness is the material cause and the object which determines it is the co-operative efficient condition. But when an objective phenomenon is generated the antecedent object-phenomenon is the material cause and the antecedent phenomenon of consciousness belonging to the parallel series is the co-operative efficient condition. A phenomenon of consciousness is produced by a phenomenon of consciousness and an object, but an object, on the other hand, is also produced by an object and a phenomenon of consciousness. Thus, a phenomenon of consciousness never fails to reveal an object which owes its existence to a set of conditions similar to that of conditions determining the phenomenon of consciousness, the revealer. Such a phenomenon of consciousness is a pramāṇa.

This view does not stand to reasons. If it is admitted then an absurd conclusion is forced on us, viz., what does not produce a piece of consciousness as an effect would become a pramāṇa. [The causal relation does not hold between pramāṇa and pramiti but the relation of the determinant and the determined holds between them from the Buddhist standpoint.] Therefore, the so-called pramāṇa is never the generator of pramiti. Thus, the Buddhists fail to explain pramāṇa. Again, these logicians defend themselves that a phenomenon of consciousness which appears to be possessed of a process in the shape of its object is held to be a pramāṇa. It has been stated to this effect that the very object of consciousness puts on the garb of a process and the pramāṇa appears to be possessed of a process. (The Naiyāyikas subject this view to a severe criticism. The points of their criticism are as follows). A phenomenon of consciousness, the illuminator and the object, the illumined simultaneously come into being. The object in question is an effect of another antecedent momentary phenomenon of consciousness and another antecedent transient object but cannot be an object of its simultaneous phenomenon of consciousness. The object in question may be an object of its immediately antecedent phenomenon of consciousness. (The drift of this argument is that a momentary phenomenon of consciousness cannot appear as possessed of an effect, having produced no effect during its existence. The pramāṇa of the Nyāya school is either actually present or remains so through its process when its effect comes into being. But a momentary phenomenon of consciousness can be in no way present when its effect comes into being. Hence, a short-lived phenomenon of consciousness cannot be a pramāṇa.)

These logicians defend their hypothesis in a different manner. Their further contention is like this. A phenomenon of consciousness is invariably determined by an object if they are effects of the similar sets of conditions and are compresent. A phenomenon of consciousness is aware of an object by its very nature of being conscious and the object, being unconscious by its nature, becomes an object of awareness. If their invariable relationship is explained in this way then wherein lies the difference between the phenomenon of consciousness and its object since they are the effects of the similar sets of conditions.

The sense of this argument is this that dependence upon the similar sets of conditions for coming into being and simultaneity control the invariable relation of the determinant and the determined. This relation governs its character of being pramāṇa. The causal relation does not play a part for the determination of a pramāṇa. The critics join issue with them and point out that they are requested to explain the question, viz., why does a phenomenon of consciousness illumine an object if they are effectuated by the similar sets of conditions and are compresent ? They may answer like this that a phenomenon of consciousness reveals because it is luminous by its very nature and an object is illumined because it is dead matter by its very nature. If this is their reply then a further question arises:—How can their difference in nature be explained since they are the effects of similar sets of conditions ? They may offer an answer to this effect that the difference in material and efficient causes in this pair explains the diversity of their character. But this reply does not hold good. This point will be elaborately discussed in connection with the refutation of the doctrine of the universal flux.

They hold that according to the hypothesis of presentative consciousness, consciousness remains always the same in spite of the fact that the different objects such as yellow or blue objects are presented to it. If they had held the hypothesis of presentative consciousness then the definition of pramāṇa, viz., what generates true knowledge is pramāṇa, would have been too wide since it is applicable to all conditions of consciousness alike and even to sense-organs such as eyes, etc. But they subscribe to the view that consciousness is representative. The special merit of this view lies in this that the relation between an idea and its object is exact and well-defined. An idea which seizes the form of an object as its booty reveals it and it alone. According to this view, representative consciousness itself is pramāṇa.

Jayanta subjects this view to a severe criticism. He points out that this view has been offered with the motive of proving subjective Idealism. This view will be thoroughly criticized when the refutation of Subjective Idealism will be discussed. The main point of criticism is that the same idea cannot be both the subject and object at the same time. Moreover, the reality of external objects cannot be proved if one subscribes to the view that consciousness is representative. Is an external object an inference or an object of perception ? It cannot be an inference since no inferential knowledge is possible, the relation of invariable concomitance being absent. What follows from the representative view of consciousness is that an idea remains devoid of form when an object is not presented to it and assumes the form of an object when an object is presented to it. But have those who subscribe to the view that an external object is merely an inference ever witnessed such formless consciousness (an empty idea) ?

The other alternative suggestion that an external object is the object of perception is not tenable since nobody is aware of the two forms, viz., the form of an object and that of an idea. Even if for the sake of an argument it is admitted that the two forms are cognised, such a view will face the difficulty of being involved in a regressus ad infinitum. As the form of an idea is not cognised by a formless idea so the idea which cognises it should have a form. The form of an idea will also be grasped by another idea having a form and so on ad infinitum.

Again, an object is not grasped by a formless idea. In order to transfer the form of an object to an idea the object should surrender itself to the idea. Thus the object disappears and the representative idea alone exists. The reality of a formless object and the existence of an objectless idea being unthinkable, another object, its substitute, should be postulated. This object is also grasped. Therefore, there must be an idea to grasp it. This object, too, will surely be merged in the idea in order to transfer its form to it and so on ad infinitum. Thus, a representative idea remains alone, having no corresponding object. Hence, another object is to be postulated. Thus we see that these assumptions will go on ad infinitum without a stop. If the representative view of consciousness is accepted then the subject-object-relation holding between an event of consciousness and its object is determined by the relation of causality.

An object which generates an event of consciousness is revealed by its effect consciousness. Such a solution being in thorough agreement with the nature of things, stands above criticism. The Naiyāyikas mean to say that among the conditions of consciousness an object is only grasped by it owing to the peculiar nature of the real objects. But this law holds good only in cases of true perception but does not hold good in cases of indirect knowledge such as inference, etc. The representative view of consciousness is also open to these charges. These points will be elaborately discussed later on. Even if we, for argument's sake, assume the representative view of consciousness then pramāṇa cannot be distinct from pramiti (the result). Therefore, the hypothesis in question is absolutely untenable.

The view of the Mīmāṁsakas

Śabara holds that it is proper that those who hold that consciousness itself is pramāṇa but has no distinct result should be surely refuted. But though he admits that consciousness itself is pramāṇa yet he shows that the result, achieved by pramāṇa, is distinct from pramāṇa, viz., cognizedness belonging to the object of consciousness. This cognizedness is the mark by means of which we infer consciousness. Consciousness is an act—a process. All acts are inferred from their results. (Now, how do we know that consciousness is an act?) The answer is that a knower cannot achieve a result if he does not perform an act. The causes get themselves united in order to generate an imperceptible act. If it is not postulated then why do they unite without a purpose ? If they do not unite then a result cannot be produced. A cause bears a significant name only when it is related to an act. A thing, supposed to be a cause, does not acquire the title 'cause' but only passes by its old designation unless and until it is related to an act. A man who runs after an effect should not search for such a thing as is not a cause. Thus, if the importance of an act be minimised then all the worldly transactions would collapse. In fine, he adds that as the already existent facts such as rice, water, fire, the cooking pot, etc., become united with a view to performing the act of cooking which was not yet existent so the soul, the sense-organ, the inner organ and the independent object being united the act of perception (knowing directly an object) comes into being. The act of consciousness is not directly known since an external object outside the body of the knower is grasped by the sense-organ. He implies that the act of awareness is not intuited since the two forms (the form of an object and that of consciousness) are not grasped. Though consciousness itself is not intuited yet it acts as a means to the awareness of an object like the invisible sense-organ, viz., the eye, etc. Though consciousness itself is not directly known yet it may be indirectly known by means of its result, viz., cognizedness belonging to its object.

The actual words of the commentary of Śabara are as follows : When an object remains unknown no body cares to know whether a preceding act of consciousness exists. But when an object is known the preceding act of consciousness is inferred. Thus the view of Śabara has been faithfully represented.

It has also been stated by the author of Śloka-vārttika:- No object is cognized if the act of consciousness does not precede it. Cognizedness belonging to an object cannot be explained if the preceding act of consciousness is not presumed. Afterwards, to solve the apparent contradiction the proof is presumed. (In other words Kumārila holds that presumption establishes the existence of the act of consciousness. Both Śabara and Kumārila hold that no body is directly aware of his consciuosness). Jayanta puts the view of Śabara in a nut-shell. The act of consciousness, denoted by the term 'consciousness,' is the proof. It is an inference. The mark by means of which it is inferred is cognizedness belonging to an object. The word 'consciousness' may imply a sense-organ since a sense-organ produces some forms of consciousness. The primary meaning of the word 'proof' is never a sense-organ. The purport of this view is that consciousness alone is a proof which is always an inference, being supersensuous. The proof in question brings about a result, viz., cognizedness belonging to an object. Though Śabara and the Buddhists agree to the point that consciousness is the proof yet they differ in certain respects. According to the Buddhists, Pramāṇa and pramiti, are one and the same thing where as according to Śabara pramiti, the result, is distinct from pramāṇa.

The refutation of Mīmāṁsaka view

Jayanta joins issue with Śabara. He points out that it is a matter of great regret that the learned Vedic scholars are at their wit's end under the threat of hostile criticism from some quarters. They arrive at a strange conclusion since all acts of knowing are not mediate. The judgment 'an object is known' is an example cited by them. The perceptual judgment 'a cloth is white' presupposes the direct awareness of the colour whiteness as its antecedent condition. Similarly, the perceptual judgment 'an object is known' should also presuppose the direct awareness of the awareness of the object as its antecedent condition. Why do you get nervous to speak out the verdict of your experience ? If you hold that the perception of an external object reveals only the object and that perception is not self-conscious, then the Buddhists who deny existence to the external objects may only be defeated.

The view of the Mīmāṁsakas that consciousness is not directly introspected because it is an act is not tenable. They assume a wrong hypothesis that knowing is an act whereas it is an effect partaking of the nature of a result. Moreover, an act belonging to a perceptible substance is directly perceived. According to the Bhaṭṭas, the soul is directly intuited. But the act, belonging to the soul, they say, is not directly introspected. Has it committed an offence ? What is the offence of an act of knowledge that it transcends introspection ? Now, they may contend that a supersensuous act belongs to the perceptible causes, over and above physical motion admitting of such divisions as upward motion etc. But this view is not tenable. Is this act eternal like a universal or non-eternal property of a substance like colour ? If it is eternal then its result should be ever present since an act always inheres in the substance. If the second alternative is accepted then an act is to be accomplished by a cause. Another act should also inhere in the cause when the cause brings about the act in question and so on ad infinitum. If it is held that an act is produced by a cause, devoid of an act then it is more logical to suppose that the causes in which no act inheres, bring about the so-called result of an act. An act has nothing to do.

Now it is contended that the word 'kāraka' directly points to an act and that a substance does not acquire causal efficiency if an act does not inhere in it. It is true that etymological meaning of the word 'kāraka' is that what does something. But it may be argued that it does not bring about an act but only a result. This argument is met thus. The verb 'to do' included in the body of the word 'Kāraka', directly points to an act. In the sentence 'Caitra weaves (Karoti) a mat' every word denotes a distinct object. The nouns 'Caitra' and 'mat' denote two distinct things. Similarly, the distinct meaning of the verb 'weaves (Karoti) cannot be ignored. It is nothing but an act. Caitra and a mat become cases because of their direct relation with this act. A reply to the counter-argument is as follows. A thing does become a case because of its connection with a supersensuous act since the act being transcendental no body can see a thing as a case. The detection of the case-character of an object implies the direct awareness of the connection of the act with itself. If we cannot recognize a case to be such then all our transactions with cases should be impossible. How can a man, desirous of a result, make an attempt at procuring a suitable cause (a case in grammar) to serve his purpose since the case-character of a thing bound up with the connection with an act remaining ever unknown ?

Jayanta holds that according to him the character of a Kāraka (a case) is not supersensuous. The case-character of a thing means the assemblage of all essential conditions. (When a thing enters into a specific relation with an act it is called a Kāraka (a case—the producer of an act). In order to generate an act it requires the assistance of some other conditions. When all the conditions assemble in order to make the thing fit for generating the act in question it acquires the character of a case. The persons, desirous of a result ascertaining all these points get hold of the favourable conditions and derive the intended result.

The Mīmāṁsakas contend that if a thing does not possess an act then no conditions can help it. (In other words, if consciousness is not an act but a mere result then the co-operation of conditions is useless). The Naiyāyikas meet this argument thus:—If a thing possesses an act then the co-operation of conditions is not needed to produce the act and thereby the result. Now, the Mīmāṁsakas further contend that the thing, combined with the conditions, produces the act in question. The Naiyāyikas give a reply to them. They hold 'Has the result offended against you ? Why do you not accept that the result is directly produced by the joint effort of the thing in question and its co-operating conditions ?'

The Mīmāṁsakas have already raised the point that the meaning of a verb cannot be ignored. A reply to this point is as follows: The meaning of the verb 'to do' is the act of a material object. It is virtually motion. We do not deny existence to motion which is visible to all. In every case we perceive various acts like the burning of fire, etc. But we deny existence to an imperceptible act. The Mīmāṁsakas further contend that the verb 'to cook' has a meaning which should be taken as something different from the act of burning, etc., since without its assumption the final result, viz., boiling can never be obtained. If existence is denied to it then what for will these cases combine ? Such a contention does not carry much weight. The purport of the contention is that the cases produce the act in question. Now two questions arise viz. (1) Do the cases jointly generate it ? or (2) Does a case singly produce it ?

If the Mīmāṁsakas answer the first question in the affirmative then it should be admitted that each does not singly generate it. Now, if each individual case by itself is not capable of producing the act in question then how will the cases do it when they combine ? If they answer the second question in the affirmative then any one of the cases may generate it without receiving co-operation from other cases. In that case, the act, the meaning of the verb 'to cook', does not constitute the end for the realisation of which the cases combine.

When do the cases combine ? Does the act come first and does the combination of cases follow it ? Or does such a combination come first and does the act follow it ?; If the act precedes the combination in question then what is the good of admitting it ? If it is admitted that there is no need of combination then the result would also be brought about by them even when they stand disunited. If they hold that the cases jointly produce the act in question then they will have to admit that none of them singly possesses an act. If it is admitted then an absurd conclusion will be forced on them that the fuel will not burn unless and until it is combined with the cooking pot. (a case stands for a condition).

Faggots burn but do not cook. (The Mīmāṁsakas mean to say that when the cases combine they produce an act which is other than motion). This contention is not tenable. The said faggots burn alike when they are either combined with the cooking pot or remain alone. The cases assemble together not with a view to bringing about a distinct act but a result. Now, what is the nature of this result ? Is it Independent of our will ? Or, is it a creature of our will? (What we can either make or unmake or transform according to our sweet will is called sādhya. Any object the nature of which we can neither make nor unmake nor transform according to our sweet will is called siddha.) If the result is independent of our will then what will be the nature of the combination of all independent objects ? The free combination of cases cannot take place if the result is determined. The Naiyāyikas should say that the result is not independent of our will but a creature of our will (sādhya). Now, if they accept this interpretation of the result then the result is nothing but an act. In the above example, the act in question is that of cooking which is other than motion.

(The Naiyāyikas join issue with them and point out then the above conclusion is not tenable.) Do not say so. A result cannot be an act. In the above case, the result is boiled rice. It is certainly not an act. If you say that the word 'pāka' is synonymous with the word 'Odana' then we have no quarrel with you. The Mīmāṁsakas further put a question to the Naiyāyikas. What is the meaning of the verb 'to cook' ? If an act is not its meaning, then the verb will have nothing to denote. (In an indirect manner they suggest that the act of cooking is distinct from motion).

A reply to this contention is being given thus :—

The combined motions of all cases assembled together such as the nominative case Devadatta and others directed towards a common result constitute the act of cooking. This is the meaning of the verb 'to cook'. In the above example each case has its distinct act, e.g., the fuel burns, the pot sustains the content, etc. We also experience each of these acts as distinct. But when these acts combine to bring about the common result, we overlook their individual character and consider the collection of verbs as a single verb. This single verb is the verb 'to cook'. Several sages also confirm our conclusion. The people say 'Devadatta cooks' 'fuels cook', 'the pot cooks' and so on. The

Mīmāṁsakas point out a defect in the above conclusion. If this is so then why do not the people say that the soul cooks? They mean to say what actually happens when Devadatta cooks. He moves the ladle. The movement of his body and limbs is due to the activity of the soul since the body is static by its very nature. The final source of activity being the soul, the sentence 'the soul cooks' should have been noticed if movement is the only act. (Jayanta meets this objection). The sentence 'he cooks' cannot be framed since the soul is the unmoved mover. The soul has no activity. It has the qualities of desire and aversion. They are the springs of volition which is also a quality. Volition causes motion in the material object.

III

In fine, we beg to state that the motion of the cases (i.e. conditions) brings about the result. No activity other than motion is witnessed. Motion is noticed in Devadatta, the nominative case and also in other cases. After a series of motions the result, viz., boiled rice, comes into being. This much is noticed. No other act is experienced. The Mīmāṁsakas hold that the soul has a distinct activity which is called bhāvanā. The verb 'to do' denotes it. (The literal meaning of bhāvanā is making something). Every sentence reveals it as its primary meaning. Such a view is also refuted by an argument mentioned in the above paragraph. No activity of the soul is noticed. The soul is no doubt, an agent. Its agency does not depend upon its activity. A soul becomes an agent when the quality of Kṛti (volition) inheres in it. Consciousness and other similar inner states of the soul are attributes but not acts since they are not creatures of our will. The Mīmāṁsakas put forward a counter-thesis. They argue like this 'To know' is a verb. Therefore, to know denotes an action. This action, as a matter of fact, belongs to the soul. This counter-thesis does not stand to reasons. There is no hard and fast rule that all verbs denote actions. The verb 'gadi' which is included in the classical list of verbs denotes a portion of a face. Let us analyse the sentence 'I know a jar' and see what is revealed by it. A jar denotes the object of knowledge. 'I' stands for the the soul, what does the verb 'know' convey? Does it denote an act since it is supersensuous ex-hypothesis. If it is held that the result of the action is presented to consciousness then the result itself should be denoted by the verb 'to know.' Therefore, consciousness is not an act. If consciousness were an act then the commentator on the Mīmāṁsā sūtras should not have separately mentioned consciousness and an act. He states that as consciousness and an act are also recognized so they should be eternal.

The drift of the above statement is that consciousness does not belong to the class of acts. The view that consciousness is transcendental, being an action, is not sound. Moreover, if it is held that consciousness is an act then it cannot be inferred since the major premise is impossible to frame. A positive example being absent, an induction is impossible. An act being imperceptible, the example, viz., an object of knowledge in the shape of an external object as qualified by an act, is an absurdity. The Mīmāṁsakas put a question to the Naiyāyikas, viz., 'How do you account for your inference of the soul?' (The purport of this question is that if you infer the existence of the soul without citing a positive example then why should not we be allowed to infer consciousness in a similar manner?) Such a plea is not tenable. When an induction is based upon similarity a positive example is indispensable but if it is based upon other grounds such as a universal then a positive example is not necessary. The syllogistic argument of the soul will be discussed in a subsequent section. The external objects do not contain the character of cognisedness when they are known. We have already stated that no body has witnessed cognisedness belonging to an external object. Presumption also cannot prove the existence of consciousness which partakes of the nature of an act. An object is immediately known whenever it comes into contact with the sense-organ. The awareness of an awareness follows the perception of an object in quick succession. Hence, the means of the proof of self-consciousness belonging to an object. Or, is it an objective illumination? The first suggestion is not tenable. The act of perception is transcendental. When an object is perceived how can a person grasp it as an object of the act of perception? We cannot frame a judgment if we do not know the predicate before. Similarly, we cannot frame the judgment that this is the object of perception if we are not beforehand aware of the perception in question. The second suggestion of objective illumination is not also tenable. If an object is known because of its own property then all beings would be omniscient with the least effort on their part since an object reveals itself without any reference to the self. The Mīmāṁsakas contend that an object does not reveal itself because of its own property but its illumination is conditioned by its relation to a subject. This suggestion of condition is not tenable. A lamp by its own nature reveals an object but does not depend upon the subject. Similarly, an object by its own property becomes revealed and the subject has nothing to do. Therefore the view that the illumination of an object is conditioned by its relation to a subject does not hold good. (The self contributes nothing towards the illumination of an object.)

(Now, the Mīmāṁsakas may further contend that as the number two is the property of an object but is not perceived by all so the objective illumination is not grasped by all.) The so-called illumination belonging to an object as its property does not bear a resemblance to the number 'two' etc. Since the number 'two' is perceived only by him whose copulative judgment referring to the two units of number produces it. But the above law of perception does not apply to the case of the illumination which belongs to an object as its property.

The number 'two' is only perceived by him whose copulative judgment referring to the units of number produces it. Now, which is held by the learned logicians to be the locus of illumination ?

If illumination is a process of the subject then it requires another activity of the subject in order to be perceived since an inactive cause can produce no result.

The Nyāya view on this point has been already stated that illumination (saṁvedana) is a quality of the soul. You may hold that it is mental activity in accordance with your system. But we hold that Jñāna and saṁvedanā are two synonyms.

We do not subscribe to the view that saṁvedana (illumination) is the result of the knowing process since if it belongs to an object then every body should be omniscient.

(In order to explain a fact, viz., illumination of an object, we presume the existence of knowing process.) If the object is the seat of saṁvedana there would be no difference of opinion between Śabara and Kumārila. A knowing process would be no more an inference but a presumption. If both the subject and the object are held to be the seats of saṁvedana then the two defects vitiate the view, viz., the obliteration of the difference in view between Śabara and Kumārila and the omniscience of all.

If saṁvedana is a mental process which belongs to the subject then it will also be transcendental like consciousness. In that case, saṁvedana itself should be an inference. It cannot be the mark of inference of a knowing process. If another act of saṁvedana is required to reveal it then a regressus ad infinitum will be forced on them since each act of saṁvedana is transcendental.

The alternative possible suggestion that saṁvedana is self-luminous will be refuted later on. A judgment of perceptual illusion that this is silver is due to the combination of apprehension and mutilated memory. 'This' is apprehended and the universal of silver is remembered. The possibility of the judgment lies in this that apprehension and memory are not distinguished from each other. If saṁvedana, the result of knowing process, is self-luminous then the result of an apprehension will be grasped as it is in itself and that of memory will also be grasped as it is in itself. In that case, the difference between apprehension and memory will be clearly grasped. Thus the ground which makes the appearance of an illusory judgment possible will be cut off.

How can you explain that the result of the knowing process is self-luminous since it does neither reveal itself as a form of apprehension nor as a form of memory ?

As there is no possibility of the third alternative so how can the result of knowing process be revealed ? No body has ever experienced a case of illumination which lacks its distinctive feature.

An awareness reveals itself as an act of awareness and an object is grasped as an object. An awareness is never misidentified with its object. They are presented to our consciousness as distinct from each other. Now, if you hold that consciousness is self-luminous and when it reveals itself it assumes the form of its object then you really conceal the nature of objects like the Buddhists.

If you hold that consciousness is self-luminous then the view that saṁvedana (the illumination of an object belonging to it) is the result of knowing process is untenable.

In fine, we beg to state that the knowing process which is inferred by means of its result as a mark is not a means of proof.

Some other logicians hold that a means of proof is such as is a special cause of true knowledge and does not reveal an apprehended object. This view is not tenable. There is no difference in the nature of the means of proof either if it produces such true knowledge as reveals a novel object or if it produces such true knowledge as reveals an apprehended object. When a means of proof is directed towards an object already apprehended which effect is produced by it ? The answer is that it produces true knowledge. Does it repeat the same true knowledge as has been produced by it ? In that case, the answer is absurd since what has been produced cannot be reproduced. No, it produces a fresh piece of true knowledge (though it reveals one and the same object). Does it serve any purpose, producing a fresh piece of similar true knowledge ? Yes, it discharges its casual efficiency by producing another piece of true knowledge. The question of purpose does not affect a tangible result. A means of proof does not take into consideration the question of utility. Whom are you going to take to task ? A means of proof is an inanimate object. Can it be an object of rebuke ? When an object perceived before comes within the range of vision of a man and becomes connected with his sense-organ (eyes) the perception of it, the above object, takes place. Do you make a formal complaint against him to this effect ? Why do you not shut up your eyes ? Why do you look at things already perceived by you ? As the means of proof does not produce in this case such true knowledge as is subsequently contradicted so it cannot cease to be a means of proof. Do not think that means of proof absolutely renders useless services when it produces true knowledge of an apprehended object ?

When a person repeatedly beholds objects of hatred like a person with a snake round his throat, a wolf, a shirk, a poisonous snake, etc., he apprehends danger from it and makes up his mind to take to his heels. On the other hand, when a person beholds an object of his liking such as sandal, camphor, a necklace, a lady, etc. his heart leaps with rapturous joy which he alone experiences.

The objector says something to the contrary. He points that when the same means of proof successively produces another piece of true knowledge referring to the same object the predicate is presented to the subject with much more specification in the second judgment. (i.e. there is always novelty in the product of a means of proof).

This contention does not convince us. The subsequent judgments, produced by the same means of proof, do not necessarily supplement the first one by adding new features to the predicate. When an uninterrupted series of perceptions, focussed upon a single object takes place, is not the same object perceived ? Does each of the perceptual judgements reveal a new object ? If a person catches hold of an object, places it on his palm and beholds it a hundred times then the object with its same predicates will be perceived by him. No new predicates will be presented to his consciousness. A fresh objection has been raised by the objector. If a means of proof does not cease to produce its result after the appearance of its first result, viz., the true knowledge of an object, then it will unceasingly go on with the production of its results and stop nowhere since it has transgressed the bounds of the law of production, viz., a single piece of true knowledge by a single means of proof.

A rejoinder to this objection is as follows : The perception of an object does not flow in a continual series when the sense-organ, the instrument of the above perception, comes into contact with another object, or when the observer becomes inattentive to the object of his perception, or when one of the conditions of his perception is missing. If a series of perceptions, pointing to the same object, goes on without a stop then a regressus ad infinitum will be forced on the upholder of the view. Jayanta's solution to this objection is as follows : A regressus ad infinitum of this type does not strike at the root of our hypothesis. It would have struck at the root if we had admitted that the first perception would not come into being unless the series of subsequent perceptions had not arisen.

A regressus ad infinitum is to be avoided when it comes into collision with the law of causality or when it undermines the basic tenets of one's own school. But if it does not interfere with the conclusions of one's own system then it may be admitted against our will.

Again, if it is held that a means of proof produces such true knowledge as reveals only a new object then recognition, which is a source of true knowledge, should be discarded.

Now, if the objector argues that recognition produces such true knowledge as throws light upon some new predicate of the subject, e.g., the present existence of the object then he simply deceives us.

The judgment which immediately precedes recognition clearly suggests that an object endures as long as the conditions of its destruction do not assemble. Recognition simply corroborates the evidence of its predecessor judgment. The unambiguous verdict of recognition is that it grasps an endurable object.

In fine, we beg to submit that one should not obstinately stick to the conclusion that a means of proof produces such true knowledge which reveals only a novel object. The object urges that if you do not subscribe to our view then memory should be regarded as a piece of true knowledge.

This objection is not tenable since recollection is not a piece of true knowledge since it knows an object which has already been apprehended but because of the fact that its object is not one of its causal factors.

How is it that memory is not generated by its object ? When memory comes into being its object ceases to exist. If this is your argument then how is the inference of the past rainfall generated by an existent object ? The answer is that the subject of inference is also inferred and that it produces the inference in question. The subject of inference is a river. The river at a particular place has swollen because it contains a large quantity of extra water which has been supplied by a contiguous up-country over which it flows. The past rainfall is, now, non-existent but the river which is also inferred as the subject of inference exists at the time of inference. Therefore, an inferential knowledge is conditioned by its real and existent object. How do you account for the origin of the mental perception in the form that one's brother will turn up to-morrow due to the causality of its existent object ? The answer is that the object of the perception in question is his brother who lives in a distant country. He is qualified by the future act of coming which will take place tomorrow. He also knows this predicate, produces the perception in question. Therefore the pure mental perception (pratibhā) is not an exception to the above rule. But, in case of memory, its object is not thought of as one of its conditions. Take the example of the memory of a son of his dead father. The father is dead and gone and his body has been consumed by fire. There is no trace of his existence. Still, he is easily recalled. Though the object is non-existent yet memory takes place. Therefore, memory is not conditioned by its object. Even when the object of memory exists in a distant country the existence of the object is not considered as an invariable condition of memory. Hence, an object of memory does not condition it.

If memory is excluded from true knowledge because of its being not conditioned by its object then the definition of a means of proof should not be qualified by the phrase 'not productive of such true knowledge as grasps a known object.' Moreover, Jaimini himself has stated that verbal testimony is a valid source of knowledge only when it produces such a knowledge which reveals new matter, not known before. But why do you overdo by an extension of the application of this test to all cases of means of proof ?

An Examination of other definitions of Pramāṇa

Some other Buddhists hold that Pramāṇa is broadly defined to be such as does not baffle movement. A means of proof is that which does not frustrate the movement of a knower. The negative predicate has a positive meaning. It signifies what leads to the attainment of the object revealed by apprehension. How does a pramāṇa help us to get hold of an object ? It reveals an object. This revelation sets up movement in the knower either to get hold of an object which is conducive to pleasure or to refrain from an object which is a source of pain. A man attains an object when he moves for it, being prompted by its illumination. The connecting link between a means of proof and the attainment of its object is a process of the former, viz., the revelation of the object.

The knower attains the object but the people think that the means of proof causes him to attain it because it shows the object to him. A parallel case may be cited. The people say that the king robs a man of his property though his soldiers actually do the act of his instance. Here the pronouncement of an order amounts to the actual commitment of an act. The character of a means of proof is its capacity for leading to the attainment of an object, shown by itself, is called a means of proof. Both perception and inference partake of the character of leading to successful attainment. Hence the broad definition of a means of proof is sound. The object of pure sense-perception is real and exclusively particular. It is very shortlived and endures a moment only. Though it is impossible to attain it yet a phenomenon of its series is attained. Hence the meaning of 'leading to successful attainment' is the production of determinate perception which refers to a number of a series of objects similar to that of the basic pure sense perception.

Though the object of an inference is always a creature of imagination yet the imagination being based upon the solid rock of the unbroken succession of real objects, a man attains a real object under the guidance of an inferential knowledge. A familiar example will explain our contention. A man mistakes the rays of a gem for a gem. If he proceeds to have it even under the guidance of illusion, be attains a gem. Similarly, a man proceeding to get hold of an imaginary object under the direction of inference attains a real object. In fine, a means of proof is what leads to the attainment of an object of determinate knowledge. Though the object of determinate knowledge is unreal yet the source of imagination being real, a real object is attained. Hence, the hypothesis that a means of proof leads to the attainment of the object of determinate knowledge is proved.

Therefore, a judgment such as the conch-shell is yellow, etc. is not true though a man who proceeds to attain the object referred to by the above illusory judgment gets conch-shell since he does not attain the object as revealed by the judgment. The judgment reveals a yellow conch-shell but a white conch shell is attained. Therefore the non-frustration of a means of proof signifies that a means of proof successfully leads to the attainment of an object as revealed by the judgment, the spring of action.

This view is not sound. Jayanta asks the Buddhists to answer a question, viz., "Does a means of proof lead to the attainment of an object of pure sense-perception ? Or, 'Does it lead to the attainment of an object of a judgement ?' An inference is not directly based upon sense-perception. Hence, it is an idle talk to hold that inference leads to the attainment of an object of sense-perception. In case of perception—an object is surely revealed but is never attained since it endures only for a Kṣaṇa (the minutest unit of time). Again, the object of a judgment is hardly attained. The Buddhists themselves admit that the object of a judgment is not a real one and that an unreal object is hard to attain. They hold that when imagination imposes superstructure upon reality the object imagined is unreal and that the object upon which imagination does not prevail is real. A man may accidentally attain a real object. But it is never an object of perception and inference. Hence, a knower can never attain it, moving in accordance with the direction of any means of proof.

Now, the Buddhists may contend that the attainment of a member in the series of the real object is as good as the attainment of a real object. Such a contention is not tenable. The hypothesis of a series is not established since the dilemma whether the series is identical with the individuals included in it or not cannot be perfectly solved by them. This hypothesis will be elaborately refuted in the chapter on the refutation of the universal flux.

The followers of the Buddhist Idealism contend thus :— Well, it is admitted that a series has only an imaginary existence. The above definition of a means of proof does not suffer from a defect since it applies only to the world constructed by Nescience. Nescience alone solves all the difficulties which beset the definition. It has been actually stated by them that it is a definition of the means of proof which holds good only in the conventional world. From the metaphysical point of view the external world has no real existence. Reality behind it is consciousness. Everything in this universe is essentially consciousness. The distinction between the knower and the known is a creation of Nescience. If we look at the world from the point of view of reality then there are no such things as the means to attainment and the attained. This is the essence of the Buddhist doctrine. Such a view does not stand a severe scrutiny of reason. It exhibits only an attitude of escapism. What is this Nescience ? Is it real or unreal ? The causality of Nescience should not be invoked to explain anything unless and until its nature and character are not defined. The world of differences does not owe its existence to the impressions due to Nescience. But it will be established that the world of differences is absolutely real. If you accept the imaginary existence of a series then why do you not assume the imaginary objects such as universals, wholes, etc. If you urge that the latter objects should be assumed because such suppositions involve a number of insoluble problems such as the problem of relation, etc. then a reply to this argumentation is that the conjecture of a series is open to the same charges. They are simply hoping against hopes. Hence the definition of a means of proof in the form that what leads to the attainment of an object revealed by perception is a means of proof is absurd. It is no definition at all.

Moreover, this definition is too narrow to cover all cases of valid knowledge. It does not apply to such true knowledge the object of which arouses in our mind a feeling of indifference.

What is this negligible object ? It is such an object after which nobody strives since it is simply neglected. In that case, it should be included in the class of such objects as are to be avoided. Such a view is not reasonable. An object of neglect is experienced by us all with a peculiar trait of its own. It cannot be discarded.

The objects which should be avoided are sources of pain. The objects which are worth-having are conducive to pleasure. A man carefully avoids the former and receives the latter. Our attitudes towards avoidable and acceptable objects are well-established. In case of indifferent objects which are neither received nor avoided a distinct feeling is expeerience by us.

Our experience is the only source of its existence. When an object worth having is perceived by us we feel an attraction for it. On the other hand when we behold an avoidable object we feel hatred for it. But when we see a negligible object we neither like it nor hate it.

The Buddhists may urge that a negligible object is an avoidable object since it is not worth having. But there is no sanction of reason behind it. We cannot hold a thesis like this that a sexually undeveloped person is a male because he is not a female or that he is a female because he is not a male. A neuter person is one who is neither a male nor a female since he is known to us to be such. Similarly, a negligible object is neither attainable nor avoidable since it is experienced by us to be such.

When a man passes through a road a tuft of grass or a leaf is presented to his consciousness. He neither feels inclined to receive it like an umbrella nor wishes to avoid it like a snake. But he feels an attitude of indifference towards it. Therefore, the definition of a means of proof that what is conducive to the attainment of an object is a means of proof is not sound since the perception of a negligible object is also true though it is not conducive to its attainment. The Buddhists may urge that the perception of a negligible object is a means of proof though it is not conducive to the attainment of the object and that it is so since it has a function like a means of proof, being not itself conducive to the attainment of an object. It is stated that a king is known as a slayer though he simply issues an order of capital punishment. Similarly, a piece of true knowledge may be simply called as conducive to the attainment of an object when it simply reveals an object.

Such a conclusion is not tenable.

If the definition of true knowledge is only confined within the precincts of its power of revealing its object then it will be too wide since this definition also makes room for the illusory experience of water on the locus of the bright rays of the sun, i.e., a mirage as it reveals its object.

Now, the Buddhists contend that in the case of illusion the object of the basic sense-perception is the real ray of the sun but it produces a judgment which reveals an imaginary object, viz., water. Hence, it turns out to be false as it produces a contrary judgment. One and the same means of perception has three different functions as it produces three distinct results, viz., it reveals a true object and produces a judgment which stirs up activity to get hold of the object and also reveals what is invariably connected with the object e.g. transitoriness but does not become a means of proof of the perception of transitoriness as it does not produce a subsequent judgment. A piece of knowledge which does not reveal a particular aspect of an object is not a means of proof of it. Let us take an example. When we perceive a blue object the perception of a blue object is the means of proof of it since the above perception produces a judgment referring to the blue object.

Every real object of the universe is momentary and hence the blue object is momentary. The transitoriness of an object is its essence. It is not distinct from the object itself. It is also grasped when the object is perceived. But the perception of the blue object in question is not a means of proof of its momentariness, since the perception of it does not produce a judgment which points to its transitoriness. But the judgment reveals the blue object as an endurable one. But the continuity of the blue object is merely imaginary. Hence, the imaginary element contributes to the untruth of the judgment. Thus, the sense-perception of the blue object is not a means of proof of its persistence. This is the sum and substance of the revised thesis of a section of the Buddhists.

If you amend your definition in this manner then the definition of the means of proof involves much more defects. You have stated that a means of proof leads to the attainment of an object by means of a process, viz., a judgment. Hence, as the perception of an individual ray of the sun is not a means of proof because of its production of a judgment referring to a contrary object so the perception of an individual should not be a means of proof because of its production of a judgment pointing to a series which is contrarily opposed to that of the true object. If the judgment points to an imaginary series why does the knower move for the attainment of the object of perception knowing full well that the object cannot be attained, being momentary ? If it is further contended that the knower moves to attain the object because he has wrongly identified the individual object with the imaginary series when it should be acknowledged that an illusion leads to the attainment of an object. In that case, such a perception is not a means of proof. Therefore, a means of proof is not conducive to the attainment of an object. Moreover, the attainment or the non-attainment of an object entirely depends upon the desire of a person. The awareness of an object is the only product of a means of proof. Therefore, in order to frame the definition of a means of proof the character of knowledge, its product, should be accurately specified. In fine, it is reasonable to hold that the essence of a means of proof does not lie in its conduciveness to the attainment of an object.

An examination of the definition of Perception of the Sāṁkhya School

The Sāṁkhyists also hold that the mode of intellect is a means of proof. When an object comes within the range of our sense-organ a change takes place in it (sense-organ). It catches the form of the object in question. This image of the object, seized by the sense-organ, exerts influence upon the Intellect. The Intellect also transforms itself into a similar image of the Intellect. This mode of Intellect attributing itself to transcendental consciousness (Puruṣa) as its property is a means of proof. Transcendental consciousness, possessing attribution of Intellect, becomes the knower of a definite object fixed up by Intellect. The mode of Intellect which is called cognition or apprehension or determinate knowledge is unconscious since it is a property of unconscious Intellect. Its result is the revelation of an object. It does not belong to Intellect. Cognition or apprehension or determinate knowledge is not a property of him who reveals an object. Therefore there is no co-ordination between a cause and its result. A means of proof—the mode of Intellect does not belong to Transcendental consciousness since the means of proof is such as possesses cognition or apprehension or determinate knowledge as its property. The result of a means of proof is the revelation of an object. It does not belong to Intellect.

The Sāṁkhyists may contend that when Intellect evolves modes become very transparent. Puruṣa, stainless by its very nature is reflected into serene Intellect and as a result of this reflection, the revelation of an object which is a property of Intellect is ascribed to transcendental consciousness and intellect appears to be conscious. If you stick to this position then your very statement contradicts your own tenet. The property of Puruṣa does not really belong to intellect and viceversa.

Your hypothesis is not different from that of representative consciousness of the Buddhists. The refutation of the Buddhist hypothesis amounts to that of your hypothesis.

All the details of the system of Kapila will be elaborately refuted in the subsequent section. Here, we only point out that if one follows his system he will fail to find a means of proof in it.

We summarily remark that the other definitions of a means of proof framed by the other system-makers suffer from defects. For this very reason those who belong to our camp hold that the assemblage of conditions such as defectless eyes, etc., is a means of proof since it is the cause of true knowledge.

The definition and division of Pramāṇa

The means of proof, stated above, admits of four kinds. The author of Nyāya-sūtra says to this effect 'Perception, Inference, Comparison and Verbal testimony are the means of proof. In this sūtra, the name and division of the subject-matter have been given. In this context, the definition of the general subject-matter, its division, the definitions of its specified forms should be given. The next four sūtras which discuss the definitions at the four sub-classes of pramāṇa are as follows 'Indriyārtha-sannikarṣotpannam, etc. (arisen from the contact of the sense-organs with their objects etc.) In this sūtra the general definition of Pramāṇa and its division have been given. By the single sūtra the great sage has realised two ends viz. he has mentioned the four divisions of Pramāṇa and the general definition of Pramāṇa.

The term 'Pramāṇa' in close proximity of the terms 'Pratyakṣa (Perception), Anumâna (Inference), Upamāna (Comparison) and Śabda (Verbal Testimony) points to the fourfold division of Pramāṇa (means of proof). But no term denoting the number 'four' is given there. Moreover, there is no such term as 'only' is noticed to indicate the restriction imposed upon the number of the division of the means of proof. In that case, how do we know that the division is exhaustive and complete ? Our answer to this question is that the number is indicated by the very meaning of the terms themselves like the sentence 'Feed three persons of the Garga family'; the sentence 'Bring Yajñadatta and Devadatta' purports to convey that only two persons are to be brought though there are no terms to indicate the number and the exclusion of the other number. Similarly, if it is stated that Perception, Inference, Comparison and Verbal Testimony are the means of proof then these very names by the force of their meaning suggest the exact character of the intended division, i.e., they are only four neither more nor less. Thus from the very name of the species we understand the suggested division. The etymological meaning of the term 'pramāṇa' supplies us with the definition of Pramāṇa pointing to its general feature. The cause par excellence of true knowledge is called Pramāṇa. The suffix attached to the root of 'Pramāṇa' denotes the sense of an instrument. Thus the cause of Pramā (true knowledge) is Pramāṇa. It has been shown before. The sūtra which embodies the definition of Upamāna (comparison) containing the term 'sādhya-sādhana' in the middle suggests by a linguistic device that 'sādhya-sādhana' (sādhyapramā—true knowledge) (sādhana-karaṇa—a cause—the cause of true knowledge) is the common character of all sorts of means of proof. The net result is that a cause of true knowledge is a means of proof. If a cause of knowledge produces such a judgment as is partly true and partly false then it may be as well a means of proof. In order to meet the anticipated difficulty three terms such as arthotpannam (caused by the real object of knowledge), avyabhicāri (non-illusory) and vyavasāyātmakam (determinate) should be borrowed from the sūtra on perception and combined into the other sūtras defining the other types of means of proof so that the causes of memory, illusion and doubt are excluded from all classes of means of proof. Thus, the above three terms become the common factors of all the four sūtras which define the four different types of means of proof.

The term 'arthotpanna' (owing its origin to a real object)

prevents the cause of memory from being a means of proof. The terms 'avyabhicāri' excludes the source of illusion from being a means of proof. The term 'Vyavasāyātmakam' shuts out the cause of a doubt from the list of means of proof. This, the boiled down meaning of the whole thing amounts to this that a means of proof is the cause of such knowledge as is generated by a real object, is not doubtful and is not illusory. Thus we get the definition of a means of proof in its generic character and the division of it from a single sūtra.

If a single sūtra serves two independent purposes, viz., the division of pramāṇa and definition of pramāṇa in its generic character then a defect in the use of a sentence is noticed. A sentence should convey a single meaning. But if it communicates two meanings then it really splits itself up into two sentences. A sentence represents a unit of thought. It should not represent two. If it does so it violates the fundamental rule of the use of a sentence. The sūtra of Gautama suffers from this defect.

A reply to this is as follows : A sūtra is immune from this defect since it is an agreed assumption that a sūtra may point to more than one meaning either by its consistent terms themselves or by their meanings.

When a matter is known only by the means of verbal testimony to the exclusion of other means of proof the sentence which expresses it should have only one meaning. If it signifies two meanings then and then only the charge of the bifurcation of the single unit of thought into the two units of thought etc. invalidates the truth of the sentence. In such cases only a sentence should never convey two meanings.

Let us take an example. The Vedic injunction is: 'A person, desirous of kingdom in the Heaven, should perform the Vājapeya sacrifice'. This injunction is an illusion of Utpatti Vidhi which simply narrates the name of a sacrifice. If we try to extract two meanings from it then it will shape itself as a case of guṇa-vidhi as well. A guṇavidhi signifies merely a guṇa (a subsidiary element) of the main action already enjoined by a precious injunction. The second meaning of the injunction in question amounts to this that a sacrifice should be performed in order to attain Heaven and that wine should be the most important article to be used in this sacrifice. Thus the one sentence has two incongruous meanings. According to the first one the action enjoined by this sacrifice is completely a new one. But, on the other hand, according to the second one the action enjoined is merely a repetition and so on. It is impossible on the part of a sentence to yield such two incongruous meanings. But the precious sūtras ingeniously indicate a lot of meanings which have been already determined by the different sources of knowledge. But it is a glorious feat on the part of the sūtras that they yield manifold meanings. Such a feat should not be condemned as defective. It is called a sūtra because it indicates many a meaning. This is really an excellent device adopted by the authors of the sūtras that they give the readers to understand a good deal of things by means of a single sentence containing a minimum number of syllables. The device, adopted by them to indicate so many meanings, is as follows:—the filling up of the understood, the use of one to serve multiple purposes and repetition of a word. The sūtras follow a set of rules to convey so many meanings. There is nothing faulty about them.

There is no such rule as determines the priority of treatment with regard to the division of genus and its definition. But there is a rule that the definition of the species must follow the division of its genus and its definition. A single sūtra may simultaneously discharge both functions, viz., division and definition by means of tantra (serving many a purpose).

The definition of a species is not possible if the corresponding genus remains undefined. But we may divide a genus into species and define it as we like. We may at first divide it into species and then define it. Or, we may at the outset, define it and then divide it into species as in the case of Siddhānta (tenet) and chala (wrangling). Or, we may simultaneously define it and divide it into species. In order to do it if the device of tantra (serving many purposes be one and the same thing) or the device of āvṛtti (the repetition of something) is adopted then it suffers from no defect.

An objection to the division of Pramāṇas

Let us now postpone the consideration of devices, viz., tantratā (the use of the same sūtra to serve multiple purposes) and āvṛtti (the repetition of the same word) adopted in the sūtra in question to indicate the number of the means of proof since the logicians of the rival schools do not agree to the point that the number of the means of proof is four. It will be established that the number of the means of proof is exactly four when it will be proved to the hilt that their number is neither more nor less. But it is difficult to prove the above thesis. There are many hypotheses on the point at issue. The Cārvākas (materialists) hold that perception is the only source of knowledge. The Buddhists assert that there are only two sources of knowledge, viz., perception and inference. The Sāṁkhyists subscribe to the view that the three means of proof viz. perception, inference and verbal testimony should only be admitted. The Mīmāṁsakas and others arrive at a conclusion that the number of the means of proof is more than four. How do you come to the conclusion that the means of proof only admits of fourfold division? A reply to this question is as follows. We shall refute later on the view of the Cārvākas when the validity of an inference will be discussed. We shall point out the difference of the verbal testimony from inference when we shall subsequently define verbal testimony. Hence the Buddhists do not follow the right path.

The Buddhist hypothesis of two-fold Division of Pramāṇas

The Buddhists refuse to accept the Nyāya thesis. They hold that the means of proof admits only of two kinds since the knowable objects are only of two types and the difference in the type of knowable objects alone accounts for the variety of the means of proof.

The objects are two-fold, viz., perceptible and imperceptible or exclusively particular and universal. As those two objects mutually exclude each other so the existence of the third type of objects is impossible. (Each being the negation of the other they exhaust the whole universe and exclude the middle). How do you come to know the non-existence of the third type?

The reply to this question is that perception, the great, throws light on it. Perception which is directed towards a blue object grasps it as a blue object. This part of our hypothesis is agreed to by all. The perception of a blue object differentiates it from a non-blue object since it is not revealed by the awareness of a blue-object. What is revealed by the awareness of a blue-object is a blue-object and what is not revealed is a non-blue-object. Hence the possibility of the existence of a third type is ruled out. Is the third type an object of the awareness of a blue object or not ? If you say 'Yes' then it is nothing but a blue object. If you say 'No' then it is nothing but a non-blue object. There is no such object as is neither blue or non-blue.

How do we define a blue object ? An object which is revealed by the awareness of a blue object is blue. An object which is not revealed by such an awareness is non-blue. The same rule holds good in the case of perceptible and imperceptible object. An object of perception is perceptible. An object which is not an object of perception is imperceptible. The pssibility of the third type of objects is also excluded. We should also follow the same logical path in order to disprove the possibility of the existence of a third type of objects other than a particular and universal. Thus we see that perception fixes up its own object.

It has been stated that perception determines its own object, excludes its negation and suggests the absence of a third kind. All these three functions are discharged by a single means.

If this view is not accepted, an object cannot be completely known in all its aspects with the result that the practical utility of his knowledge will be nil. No body will proceed either to attain an object or to avoid it. (He means to say that an object is not known as attainable unless we know as well that it is other than avoidable and vice-versa).

It has been stated that a person who seeks fire does neither sit idle nor leaves the place when he beholds fire. It is a truism that sense-perception simply apprehends an exclusively particular point of reality which lies within its range but does not judge it. But it should be admitted that perceptual judgements which follow in its wake determine the object, exclude it from its negation and preclude the possibility of the third alternative;

otherwise, all practical transactions would collapse. If it be so, the relation of contradictory opposition existing between an object of perception and its non-object is known to us since perception reveals its object as absolutely excluded from its non-object. Inference contributes its quota to the understanding of the proposition that there is no middle term between an object of perception and its opposite (non-object).

Of the two opposites if one is known then its other is excluded from that piece of knowledge because of their nature involving mutual contradiction. The suggested third if any is also included in the contradictory opposite since it is not revealed by the awareness of an object.

Now a question arises in our mind. If you had ever grasped the third one like the second one then the third one would surely have an independent existence like the two objects (an object and its opposite). How do you come to know that the relation of contradiction or non-contradiction exists between the known and the unknown? The reply to this is as follows:—Oh sound logician, in order to know the relation of contradiction the knowledge of the opposite is not necessary since the object is known as opposed to those which are not revealed by its awareness. An object is said to be opposed to that which is not grasped when the object is presented to our consciousness. Hence, as non-awareness indicates the relation of contradiction so the distinct awareness of the opposite should not be sought after. There is no middle term between the two contradictory terms. Thus the two-fold division of all objects is absolutely established. Thus there is no middle term between the following pairs of terms opposed to each other, e.g., existent and non-existent, eternal and non-eternal, successive and simultaneous. Perception reveals only a perceptible object, viz., an exclusively particular point of reality. An inference reveals a universal which lies beyond the ken of perception.

There are two kinds of knowable objects which are well established by two kinds of the means of proof. Then say, why we should postulate another distinct type of the means of proof and what for?

It is not reasonable to hold that the verbal testimony also like an inference reveals a universal which is imperceptible.

One and the same object should not be revealed by more than one means of proof since they would oppose each other to secure the priority of appearance and either of them would be redundant. If the second means of proof knows an object in the same way as the first one has done, then the services of the second one are futile. The learned ones hold that if a means of proof reveals only what has been already known by its predecessor then it simply kills a dead man. The second cannot grasp the object in question in a different manner since it is to contradict the evidence of the first one. The persons conversant with the laws of thought hold that the co-operation of various means of proof is impossible. When many a means of proof reveals one and the same object it is technically called samplava (mutual co-operation). But it is hard to establish that there are common objects of many a means of proof. The idea of mutual co-operation on the part of the means of proof is discarded. Perception and inference cannot co-operate since inference cannot reveal an exclusively particular point of reality and perception fails to reveal a universal.

How can an inference which depends upon the relation of concomitance for its existence prove the existence of an exclusively particular point of reality which is neither similar nor dissimilar to any object of the universe.

Sense-perception is causally connected only with a real point of reality. How can it grasp a universal which is created by imagination ?

The so-called other means of proof such as inference, verbal testimony, etc. will have no distinct objects to reveal.

Then an exclusively particular point of reality is grasped by sense-perception and the objects other than the reals are within the range of inference based upon the relation of invariable concomitance.

There is really speaking, no object which is to be grasped by many means of proof. It is a good news for us that like the plurality of means of proof applicable to a case neither a whole nor a universal does exist.

If you admit that an inference and verbal testimony apply to the field of perception then you should also admit that they would also produce such knowledge as is produced by perception. But the resultant knowledge of these means of knowledge or cognition is not similar. The Buddhists say to this object : When the object of the different means of knowldge is one the knowledge arrived at by them should be the same. But perceptual knowledge is never similar either to the inferential knowledge or to the verbal knowledge. The light of the stars or the light of the moon is entirely different from that of the sun who illumines the whole universe.

They also hold that what is sensed is absolutely different from the object of verbal knowledge. A blind man does not see an object but gets an idea of it when he hears a word denoting it.

They also add that the experience of burn when a man is burnt by fire is totally different from the knowledge of burn produced by the word 'burn'. In fine, they submit that as only two types of objects have been established by them by means of the logical procedure stated above so the third means of proof does not exist over and above perception and inference. It should also be admitted that the plurality of the means of proof does not apply to the same case.

The Refutation of the Buddhist hypothesis

A rejoinder to the Buddhist view is as follows : It has been stated that perception is competent enough to exclude the possibility of a third type of objects and thereby to deny existence to the means of proof other than perception and inference. But such a stand is not logical.

An indeterminate perception which cannot connect the antecedent event with the consequent one cannot bear so heavy a burden on its shoulders. The determinate forms of knowledge are nourished and strengthened only by imagination. How can you hold that such knowledge establishes and arranges the real objects of the universe ?

Or, let us assume for the sake of argument that the blue and the non-blue exclude the middle. But the same method fails when we try to know an object as being perceived or as being inferred. When a perception of an object takes place it reveals the object as it is in itself but does not reveal it as a perceptum. An object is cognized in the form that this is blue but never in the form that I perceive a blue object. What is meant by its perceptibility ? Does it exist in a sense-organ ? Or, is it the fact of being an object of self-conscious sensuous cognition ? Of these two alternatives the first one is known only through the joint method of agreement and difference but not directly perceived. Kumārila Bhaṭṭa says to the effect—

That a sound is an object of auditory perception is never directly grasped. When I hear a sound, if my cognition assumes the form that it is a sound but not that it is an object of hearing. But that it is heard is indirectly known through the joint method of agreement and difference. A deaf man cannot hear a sound. A man having normal power of hearing hears a sound. Hence, a sound is heard by the ears of a man. It is a case of inference.

Now, you may suggest the second alternative that when an object is sensed by a person he knows that he perceives it. But it is not a fact that the knower is aware of his perception of an object. When an object is perceived by a person, he is not aware of his perception since no perception is introspected at that time. If the perception of the object is not introspected then it is impossible to know that the said object is an object of perception. How do you know that when an object is perceived an introspection of perception does not take place ? Are not two forms simultaneously present in our consciousness ? No, we never experience in cases of perception a difference like this, that this is perception and this is an object of perception. Only one form is cognized. In the fitness of things there should be only the form of the object perceived but not that of perception. This point will be discussed later on.

The Buddhists contend that if a direct awareness is not self-conscious it cannot reveal an object. Jayanta quotes the line of the Buddhist text to prove his honesty of representation 'Na pratyakṣo . . . . prasidhyati' (But this view is not tenable). If we are at first aware of our awareness then object-consciousness cannot follow it. Hence how can the perception of an object take place ? Now, the Buddhists may contend that an awareness being self-conscious, reveals its content. In that case they are to face the two horns of a dilemma. Is an awareness an object of another piece of awareness or self-luminous ? If they hold that it is an object of another piece of awareness then a regressus ad infinitum becomes inevitable. But such a regressus ad infinitum in this case defeats the very purpose of the hypothesis in question (the initial awareness will never be revealed since an unending series of awarenesses will go on in vain). Therefore, if they stick to the decision that perception, being introspected, reveals its object then the whole universe would be blind and dumb. The Buddhists cannot, also, hold that an awareness is self-luminous since if an awareness be an object of its own self then it will be no better than ordinary objects, e.g., blue, yellow, etc. We shall subject the hypothesis of the self-luminous character of an awareness to an elaborate and severe criticism when the thesis of subjective Idealism will be refuted.

The Buddhists may argue that an absurd conclusion will be reached if their hypothesis is not accepted. If nobody is aware of his awareness then it makes no difference whether an awareness appears or not. In that case everybody would be either absolutely ignorant or omniscient. Such an indirect proof is not tenable. As soon as an awareness comes into being the person having awareness becomes a knower. The essence of an awareness is to illumine an object. Whenever it arises it reveals an object. How is it that there is no difference between an absent and present awareness ? When the awareness of a blue object, etc. arises in the mind of a man he becomes a knower. But when an introspection of happiness, etc. takes place in his mind he becomes an enjoyer. This definition of a knower or that of an enjoyer is not too wide to be applicable to a non-knower or to a non-enjoyer. When a perception takes place we are not aware of it. Hence, the perception in question does not assume the form that I perceive an object. As a perception is not introspected so it can neither be differentiated from mediate knowledge nor can suggest that there is no third form of knowledge other than immediate and mediate awareness. How can perception prove the existence of only two types of objects ?

We have shown before that the inference which has been adduced by the Buddhists to prove the existence of only two kinds of objects is based upon the evidence of perception that a perceptible object is incompatible with an inferred object.

We have already pointed out that perception is not capable of enlightening such an incompatibility of its object with that of an inference. If such an incompatibility is not perceived, an inference based upon it is an impossibility. If it is not proved that the objects admit only of two types then the desire for establishing only two kinds of the means of proof should be given up.

Or even if we admit for the sake of an argument that there are only two kinds of objects then how can the further distinction of the means of proof due to their difference in the assemblage of conditions and results be gained ? The sets of conditions which determine perception and inference are distinctly different from those of conditions which determine verbal knowlege and comparison. Moreover, the results which the former pair yields are also different from those of the latter pair. These differences account for the corresponding change in the nature of the means of proof. Hence, the hypothesis that the means of proof admits of only two kinds is not tenable. This argument also refutes the hypothesis of the Sāṁkhya school that there are only three kinds of the means of proof. We shall establish that the fourth means of proof is determined by a different set of conditions and the resultant knowledge is a class by itself.

Re-affirmation of the co-operation of the different Sources of knowledge (Samplava)

Moreover, the Buddhists under the sway of delusion have argued against the application of the plurality of the means of proof to a single object. Nobody can establish the existence of an inference if such an application does not take place.

If one does not grasp that the relation of invariable concomitance holds between the probans and the probandum then the probans in question does not point to the probandum. The knowledge of the relation of invariable concomitance in question implies that of the two concomitants. The probandum, one of them is a concept, the knowledge which is ex-hypothesis inferential. If the Buddhists stick to this hypothesis then an inference is an instance of circular reasoning. (If we do not know the probandum then we cannot grasp the relation of invariable concomitance. Again, if we do not know the relation of invariable concomitance then we cannot grasp the probandum in question).

Now the Buddhists may suggest that the probandum is known by a fresh inference. In that case a vicious regressus ad infinitum is inevitable since the fresh inference requires another inference to reveal it and so on.

In order to avoid a vicious regressus ad infinitum the perception of the probans and the probandum should be admitted. In that case an application of the plurality of the means of proof to a single object takes place.

The Buddhists contend that this criticism is based upon a misunderstanding of the conclusion of the Buddhist Logic. They add that inference and verbal knowledge reveal imaginary objects. Imagination supplies a person with the knowledge of invariable concomitance. Hence, neither a regressus ad infinitum vitiates, invalidates the hypothesis in question nor an application of the plurality of the means of proof is required for the justification of the hypothesis.

The sum and substance of the Buddhist point of view is that conceptual knowledge which follows a true sense-perception in close succession is stamped by the perceptual image and consequently assumes the form of perception. The content of conceptual knowledge, the conceptual image is purely imaginary but still it excludes itself from such other conceptual images by its very nature. All syllogisms refer only to conceptual images. As any one who mistakes the rays of a gem for a gem and proceeds to attain the object obtains it, so in the case of an inference though a conceptual image is mistaken for an image of real object yet a real object is attained when a man works under the illusion since reality is at the root of the conceptual image in question. Hence, inference and perception can never have a common object. How can the hypothesis of the application of many means of proof to a common object be possible? How can the Buddhist theory of inference be open to the charge of a regressus ad infinitum ?

This statement is merely a hoax. The relation of invariable concomitance has been specified by the Buddhists as the relation of identity or that of causality. Does it belong to reality ? Or does it belong to an imaginary image ? It cannot belong to an imaginary object. A real object is always produced by a real object. A real object is only identical with a real object. Hence, the relation of invariable concomitance belongs only to a real object. The conceptual image does not represent a real object but the relation belonging to a real object is determined in and through the medium of an imaginary image. Really, a strange solution is this : The relation of invariable concomitance belongs to real objects. But two general images which are imaginary beings play the part of a probans and a probandum. Thus the relation in question exists on one locus but something else is the source of its knowledge. The object inferred is one thing but a man who infers moves for another and attains an object other than the inferred one. All this is mere deception and nothing else.

Moreover, a concept is in no way related to a real object. Hence, it cannot bear a close resemblance to a perceptual image. Hence, thinness and vividness which are asserted of concepts do not impart validity to them since they are far away from the domain of reality.

The induction from the Buddhist point of view is not based upon sound proof. It is a mere conjecture. Hence, the conclusion which is deduced from such induction carries no material validity. If the Buddhists believe that the universality of the relation of invariable concomitance is really conceptual then why do they run the risk of proving its material validity?

If the perception of a universal is not assumed then the relation of invariable concomitance cannot be discovered. Hence, the cause of inference is very much weakened. Moreover, one who discovers the relation of invariable concomitance cannot perceive the probans (a mark) for the second time. Hence, those who are against the admission of application of the plurality of proofs to a single fact really fail to establish the validity of an inference.

An exclusively particular cannot serve as a mark. If a concept is a mark its knowledge cannot but be indirect, i.e., inferential. If an inference is based upon another inference then either a regressus ad infinitum or a vicious circle will invalidate all cases of inference. Such defects take away much from judgments. Hence the possibility of the plurality of proofs cannot be rejected. How can you reject the plurality of proofs without rejecting an inference which is generated by the knowledge of invariable concomitance with that of the mark.

Moreover, even if the existence of only two kinds of objects is admitted then there is no bar to hold that both perception and inference apply to one and the same object. An object which is to be perceived at one time at a place goes beyond the range of perception if it changes its place and time. But it is inferred. An object which is now inferred from this place is perceived from that place or will be perceived at a subsequent period of time. The doctrine of the universal flux will be refuted later on. The Buddhists have postulated the hypothesis of a series in order to justify the hypothesis that what is perceived is attained. They may subscribe to our hypothesis that various proofs apply to one and the same object without any prejudice to their own hypothesis since a series is not in the least affected by it.

The Buddhists have a motive behind the rejection of the application of the plurality of proofs to a single object. They intend to deny existence to a universal, etc. A fit reply will be given to them by re-establishing the hypothesis of a universal, etc.

The fire of your criticism consumes the impurities which cling to our hypothesis. It is a good news to the logicians that like the application of the plurality of proofs the distinct existence of a whole and that of a universal will be re-established.

The Buddhists argue against the application of the plurality of proofs on the ground that an assumption like this contradicts other assumptions and is redundant. The charge that it is superfluous has been met by us when we have proved that a proof should not be unnecessarily qualified by an adjective of revealing a novel object. We do not even find contradictory nature in it. When a proof comes into being it does not cancel any antecedent judgment like the negative judgement that this is not silver. A concrete object is possessed of many properties. A particular means of proof discovers sometimes one particular property in it. In this situation let us see what is meant by its contradictory nature. The Buddhists may explain the contradictory nature in this way that if perception, inference and verbal knowledge have a common object then the knowledge of it should have been similar (i e. when a man perceived fire his mediate knowledge of fire should have been similar). Some logicians meet this objection thus—In the case of an object common to various forms of consciousness the conditions which determine each form of consciousness being different; the resulting consciousness in each case is different like the perception of an object, lying at a close quarter, differing from that of it lying at a distance. Other logicians point out that the diversity in the character of consciousness is explained not by the difference in the conditions but by the difference in the nature of the objects. In the above example the near object is not the same as the distant one. When an object is looked at from a distance it is seen as qualified by its general feature. But when it comes nearer, it is seen along with its special features. Perception, inference and verbal knowledge differ from one another because of the difference in their objects.

Our visual perception grasps an object as qualified by its specific property. The inferential knowledge grasps the subject of inference (the minor term) as qualified only by the object inferred (the major term) on the strength of an induction. A piece of knowledge which arises from a word reveals an object, its meaning, as associated with the word itself. The knowledge of a word meaning is always verbalised. How do the Naiyāyikas now hold that the different proofs apply to the same object since they have admitted that no piece of knowledge has the same object ? Oh yes, the Naiyāyikas admit that no two such pieces of knowledge have the same object. Still, they stick to their decision that many proofs apply to one and the same object. They mean to say that the substratum underlying the diverse properties is one and the same. When the application of many proofs to a single object is spoken of, a reference to the identical substratum is made. These two rival hypotheses, viz., application and non-application of many proofs to a single object will be more elaborately discussed later on. However, it has been already established that many proofs apply to one and the same object. The great commentator on the Nyāya-sūtra has given an appropriate example. From the words of a trustworthy person we learn that fire exists at a distant place. A person proceeds in that direction relying upon his words. When he comes near he sees smoke and infers its existence. When he advances further and approaches fire he sees it with his own eyes, etc., etc. In some cases restriction is imposed upon the function of proofs. As for an example the Vedic Injunction alone that one who intends to attain heaven should perform Agnihotra-sacrifice throws light upon the attainment of heaven by means of a Vedic sacrifice but perception and inference do not enlighten us. When one hears the roaring of thunder he infers its cause which he neither perceives nor learns from the scripture. One directly knows that his hands are two but he does neither infer the number nor does learn it from the lips of another person. In the majority of cases all proofs apply to all objects but there are few cases in which a particular proof has an exclusive object of its own.

Thus all the charges levelled against the Nyāya hypothesis of the application of all the different proofs to a case have been adequately met. The fear of negative criticism has been removed. The above hypothesis is now proved. All the long cherished intentions of the Buddhists to establish the two hypotheses that there are only two means of proof and that there are only two kinds of objects have been nipped in the bud. Thus, all the hypotheses that the number of the proofs is less than four have been examined.

Enumeration of other extra sources of knowledge

Now the hypotheses that the number of the proofs is more than four is being examined. Prabhākara holds that the number of the means of knowledge is five. They are perception, inference, verbal testimony, comparison and presumption. The Bhāṭṭas include non-apprehension in the list of the means of knowledge and hold that their number is six. Some add tradition or rumour and probability to the above list and hold that they are eight in number. The Cārvākas who are well-trained in the logical discipline hold that the fixation of the number of the means of knowledge is an impossible task.

Presumption of the Bhāṭṭa school

The Bhāṭṭas explain presumption in the following manner.

Whenever a fact known to us or learnt from a verbal source seems to be apparently absurd and requires the assumption of some other facts to explain it, it is called presumption. The phrase 'known to us' requires further explanation. It means the fact which is known by means of any of the five means of proof. The phrase 'learnt from a verbal source' signifies that it has been learnt from the nonscriptural source or from the scriptural source. The meaning of the sentence thus learnt seems to us to be apparently inconsistent. We postulate some other facts in order to explain it. It is called presumption. The source of our knowledge of the primary fact being six, presumption correspondingly admits of six-fold division. The word 'dṛṣṭa' signifies 'awareness' in the widest sense. Thus 'Śruta' presumption gets itself merged in the Dṛṣṭa presumption. Why has the first one been treated separately? Its separate treatment suggests that presumption in this case solves apparent contradictions which is noticed in the matter brought in only by the verbal testimony. Hence its object is different from those of other five forms of power presumption.

Let us cite an example of presumption based upon perception. We perceive fire and see its effect, i.e., the burning of an object which comes in contact with it. But we fail to explain why it does burn. This apparent riddle leads us to postulate its power of burning which is not visible.

An example of presumption based upon inference is as follows: We infer the motion of the sun from the mark, i.e., the occupation of different spaces. The motion of the sun appears to us to be a riddle. It is solved only if it has the power of moving. An example of presumption based upon comparison is cited as follows. We see a gavaya (a blue deer). We remember a cow. The individual cow which is remembered is cognised as qualified by its close resemblance to a blue deer. It is not within the range of our vision. The awareness of the resemblance of a gavaya belonging to a cow is the resulting consciousness of comparison. How is an individual cow thus qualified presented to our consciousness? It cannot be perceived since there is no sense-object-contact. It cannot be inferred since no invariable mark is present. We do not understand through the medium of a word since there is no such word as denotes it. But it appears to be mysterious that it is presented to our consciousness. Hence, we assume that the object in question has the power to be cognised in this way. Presumption itself is a distinct means of proof since all these cases of presumption have for their objects 'transcendental power'. Power inherent in an object can never be perceived and cannot also be inferred since an inference is invariably based upon the knowledge of the relation of invariable concomitance which is dependent upon perception for the discovery.

The relation of concomitance admits of two kinds, based uponeither the method of agreement or that of difference. These two kinds of invariable concomitance help us only to understand the essence of a substance and its essential properties. But its power being still subtler, is beyond the reach of them. It is not enlightened by them. There is little chance for verbal testimony and comparison to throw light upon it. Hence it is only presumption which has such power as its exclusive object. Let us give an example of presumption based upon presumption. The knowledge of an object through the instrumentality of a word seems to us to be apparently inconsistent. To remove this inconsistency we assume that a word has the power of expression. In spite of its power of expression a word fails to convey its meaning if it is not assumed to be eternal. This topic will be discussed in the chapter on verbal testimony. Presumption, based upon non-apprehension, has been illustrated by Śabara himself, the commentator on the Mīmāṁsā-sūtra It is as follows. One cognizing the absence of the living Caitra at home finds that this experience is inconsistent. In order to solve this consistency he assumes his presence somewhere outside his house.

Why is it not a case of inference since the known probandum is established on the strength of the perception of its mark? No, it is not a case of inference since the assemblage of conditions which determine inferential knowledge is absent. According to the rules laid down in the logic of the Naiyāyikas the conditions such as the presence of the invariable mark in the subject of inference, etc., only determine a specific form of knowledge which is called an inference. The assemblage of the above conditions is conspicuous by its absence when one is aware of Caitra's presence outside his home. Shall we infer the presence of Caitra outside who is absent from home ? Or shall we infer the presence of Caitra on the outside which is other than a house ? But a mark which is suitable for the purpose is not available.

None of the following marks such as Caitra absent from a house, containing the negation of Caitra; the negation of Caitra in his house; or non-perception of Caitra in his house belongs to the subject of inference. Neither Caitra's house nor Caitra nor the negation of Caitra nor non-perception of Caitra belongs to either Caitra or to his existence outside his house. Hence, none of them is a genuine mark. Moreover, in the case of an inference, the means of proof should be logically prior to the conclusion but on the contrary in the case of a presumption the matter to be proved comes first and the means of proof is found out later on. In this case we get the result of our enquiry first. Hence, it is not a case of inference. The argument, put forward by the Mīmāṁsakas, is as follows. From the astrological calculation we learn that Caitra is still alive. The absence of such a person from his house appears to us to be a riddle. It leads us to assume that he is somewhere outside his house so that the problem is fairly solved. His mere absence from his house is not an invariable mark of his existence outside his house since it is connected with his conditional existence as well as his non-existence due to death. The awareness of the negation of Caitra in his house is necessary for the inference of his existence outside his house, since no probans, if it is not cognized, leads to the knowledge of the connected probandum, the awareness of the negation of an object arises when all the means of proof fail to cognize the object negated. But in the case of the point at issue there is the means of proof which cognizes his life. His life means his existence somewhere. The negation of Caitra cannot be known since the means of proof of his existence is available. The means of proof of his existence being at work, solves the contradiction between his simultaneous existence and non-existence. It restricts his non-existence to his house and his existence to the space outside his house.

When we know for certain that Caitra who is alive exists somewhere outside his house we come to know his absence from his house. Thus we at first know what we should have known later on. On the contrary, in the case of an inference when we know probans, viz., smoke, we have not the slightest knowledge of the probandum, i.e., fire. In other words, the order of knowlege is strictly followed. Does not this reversal of the order of knowledge in the case of a presumption amount to a defect in the procedure? 'Certainly not' is the reply given by the Mīmāṁsakas.

The Mīmāṁsakas further add in support of their view that presumption corroborates the findings of the two independent means of proof, viz., verbal knowledge and non-perception which grasp the existence and the non-existence of the same object, viz., Caitra. It simultaneously reveals the existence and the non-existence of the above object, i.e., Caitra. The verbal testimony indefinitely speaks of his existence. We know that he exists somewhere. But when we know for certain that he is absent from his house, we also definitely know that he lives somewhere outside his house. A presumption is not an inference because of this distinctive feature. Moreover, a presumption not being conditioned by the knowledge of invariable concomitance is different from an inference.

In the case of inference the relation of invariable concomitance holding between fire and smoke is grasped by a single means of proof. But in the case of presumption the relation of invariable concomitance holding between presence outside a house and absence from a house cannot be grasped by a single means of proof. If it is admitted by the Naiyāyikas that the relation of invariable concomitance is indirectly grasped by means of a hypothetical judgment that this is not possible if such and such condition is not available then we (the Mīmāṁsakas) take no exception to it. The major premise is obtained by means of presumption. The conclusion may be deduced from it by means of syllogistic process. If the subsequent part of the cognitive process is called an inference then the Naiyāyikas may do so as they like.

The relation of invariable concomitance holding between two objects just outside his house may be dicovered. But in this way the relation of invariable concomitance holding between an object negated and its negation can never be discovered.

When we see that Caitra is present in his house we conjecture that we cannot account for his stay at home if he is not absent from other places. Thus, we presume his absence from all the places other than his house. We cannot see all the places other than his house and come to know that he is absent from each of them. In this case, generalization, based upon observation, is impossible since the places are innumerable. How do the Mīmāṁsakas arrive at the general (universal) proposition "Where there is no fire there is no smoke?" The reply of the Mīmāṁsakas to this question is that the method of agreement contributes much to arrive at the required induction that smoke is the invariable concomitant of fire but exclusive use of the method of difference to arrive at the said induction is not worth trying. If we arrive at the correct generalization repeatedly observing the positive instances then why should we run after negative instances to arrive at the same truth in a roundabout manner ? In the present case, whenever we try to establish the relation of concomitance holding between Caitra and his absence in a general way we realise the real difficulty which besets it. The absence of Caitra cannot be abstricted from its locus. The locii of such absence are innumerable. Hence an induction is impossible but a summation of a few cases is merely possible. Hence Caitra's absence cannot be inferred.

Now, a question may arise that Caitra's absence may be definitely known by means of non-perception. 'No' is our reply. The reason is as follows : When we know negation by means of non-perception we know it as located upon a particular well-defined locus. But the negation of Caitra belongs to all places excepting his house. Hence it cannot be known by non-perception. The objector may urge that he will roam about from one place to another in order to know the negation of Caitra by means of non-perception. Such a contention is ṅot tenable. Though he may pay a visit to all the different places yet he cannot definitely know the exact locus of the negation of Caitra. He leaves Kauśāmbī for some other places. But a doubt may chase him that as soon as Caitra departs from Kauśāmbī he may return to it. To an ordinary man with a limited power of knowing things the negation of Caitra in all places outside his house cannot be known by means of non-perception but by means of presumption. He may still contend that the object in question may be easily inferred. The argument is as follows : All the other places contain the negation of Caitra because they are other than the place occupied by Caitra like the place in the vicinity of his house. Such an argument is set at naught by a counter-argument. The other places are not distinct from such places as contain his negation because they are distinct from the place which is very close to his house like his own house. The small body of a man is seen only at a particular place. If its negation had not existed in all other places then its small size would have been a puzzle which could not be solved. That is why it should be presumed that his negation exists in all places not occupied by him. Hence, the negation of Caitra under discussion is only ascertained by means of presumption.

Śrutārthāpatti

'Fat Devadatta does not take his meal during the day' is an incomplete sentence but has a reference to some understood part of it. The knowledge of such understood portion is called presumption based upon verbal knowledge. Whenever we hear an incomplete sentence but gather its sense with the aid of some portion not given, the knowledge of such portion is a distinct type of knowledge since it is due to none of the accepted means of knowledge such as perception, etc. The above knowledge is not direct since the taking of meal at night (supper) is beyond the range of our vision. It is not an inference since the above knowledge comes into the mind of one who is innocent of the relation of invariable concomitance. We cannot even entertain a supposition that it is due to comparison and so on. The knowledge of the taking of supper is surely verbal. The words which are heard are not competent enough to convey the above sense since the sentence which is heard conveys negative but cannot express a positive meaning as well. Moreover, in the above case, as long as the words such as 'At night he takes, etc.' are not heard the meaning, conveyed by the understood words, cannot constitute the meaning of the given sentence. Moreover, the meaning of the understood words, viz., 'the taking of supper' is neither a necessary element of the meaning of the given sentence nor inseparably related to it so that it invariably flashes in our mind even if it is not conveyed by the given words.

Therefore the knowledge that he takes his supper at night is based upon an authoritative sentence which is assumed by us. Let us now make an inquiry into the nature of the means of proof which leads us to do so. Our ears fail to hear such words as are not manifest since they have not been uttered. We cannot even infer the existence of the understood words since the words are also known even when the knowledge of invariable concomitance, one of the essential conditions of inference, is absent. Moreover, it is almost impossible to find out a mark which will be an invariable concomitant of those words which are eternal but transcendental. Therefore, we should presume a sentence which will solve all inconsistencies, involved in the given sentence, considering the context and other relevant matters.

The assumption of such a supplementary sentence with reference to the context, etc., has been admitted by the Mīmāṁsakas who are supposed to be experts in syntax. It has been stated in the Tantra-vārttika that the assumption of a supplementary sentence has been accepted by all. It is hard to find out a mark which is an invariable concomitant of the understood clause since it is transcendental ex-hypothesi. We cannot infer the words such as night etc. If the sentence 'he eats at night' be the probandum and Devadatta who is flabby but does not take his meal during the day be the probans then the probans in question does not belong to the subject of inference (the speaker of the sentence) but belongs to such a locus as contains the negation of the probandum and hence is not an invariable mark. Moreover, we find here no such property as can be proved by means of the probans in question just as we prove that a hill is fiery because it is smoky. Neither the sentence 'he does not take his meal during the day' nor its meaning can constitute the mark which will help us to infer the sentence 'he takes his meal at night.'

If the sentence containing the phrase 'at night' (i. e., the sentence that he takes his meal at night) is not heard then how can it be grasped as belonging to the subject of inference ? But if it is heard then there is no need of inferring it.

It is highly impossible to hold that the meaning of the sentence that Devadatta who is bulky does not take his meal during the day serves the purpose of a probans in connection with the inference in question. Nay, we cannot even assert that the inconsistency inherent in the sentence stirs our imagination to supplement it by the assumption of the sentence that he takes his meal at night in order to make it a consistent one.

Words denote universals. It will be an absurdity if they belong to no particulars. But there will be no inconsistency. We admit it. But in no case one can hold that a supplementary sentence is necessary to complete the sense of the above sentence. (Therefore the meaning of the sentence has no part to play in this matter). For this reason the sentence which is being heard implies a syntactical relation to some part of it not given here but as it stands in itself it falls to convey a consistent meaning. Hence, the given sentence implies it as a grammatical necessity. It illustrates presumption based upon testimony. It is to be noted here that if the portion of sentence is not presumed, the above incomplete sentence will not be able to communicate its meaning. Thus, the Mīmāṁsakas make out a case for Śrutārthāpatti.

Now, an objector raises a question as to the soundness of the above hypothesis. Why should not the meaning of the above complementary sentence be enough to communicate the meaning of the incomplete sentence ? The bulky size is the effect of the taking of nocturnal food. The effect in question being experienced should lead to the inference of its cause, viz., the taking of food just as smoke, being perceived, is a means to the inferential knowledge of fire. The taking of meal has been forbidden at a particular period of time but it must take place in some other part of the day. Why should a sentence be presumed ? Moreover, the sentence which is presumed is only for the understanding of the proper meaning of the sentence in question but not for acquiring merit. No body should find fault with the hypothesis that the meaning is directly presumed but not through the medium of the sentence which conveys it. Why should a partition in the shape of a sentence be allowed to intervene between the two meanings directly and indirectly acquired ?

The Mīmāṁsakas give a reply to the above objection. Oh, child, you are still inexperienced in the Philosophy of Grammar. A sentence which conveys a complete meaning is only a source of valid knowledge since an incomplete sentence conveys no meaning, being not self-sufficient.

A sentence is a complete whole in which each of its constituents (i.e., parts of speech) fulfills its duty and tends to convey the meaning of the sentence. These parts do never stop half-way but invariably complete its task, viz., the expression of the complete meaning of a sentence.

A sentence which expresses a complete meaning is a source of valid knowledge. Such a sentence bears a significant name. Therefore whenever we hear a portion of a sentence we should fill up the gap supplying the understood portion by our imagination. How can we get at the complete and consistent meaning if the understood portion is not supplied ?

In many cases, the Vedic injunctions are incomplete. By means of presumption, based upon testimony, they are made complete. But, in these cases if we do not complete the Vedic injunctions which enjoin rites then the sense of the clause to be inserted, being merely implied, will not be strictly Vedic.

The Vedic mantra (a prayer) which speaks of a kind of ceremony in honour of the departed ancestors (aṣṭakā by name) leads us to assume an injunction which enjoins aṣṭakā. Similarly, we assume Vedic injuctions on the basis of the direct wording of the Vedic mantras, e.g. the marks of gods given in the mantras etc.

Sometimes, we also assume a complete Vedic injunction on the basis of an incomplete injunction. The Vedic injunction one should perform 'Viśvajit sacrifice' is an instance of an incomplete Vedic injunction. The injunction does not contain a word which denotes the enjoyer of the fruit of the action. In this case, it does not carry the sense which it intends to convey. The object of an injunction is to induce a man to perform the rite prescribed by it. But a man who is aware of the fruit of the rite and intends to have it is persuaded to do it.

Hence, the above injunction should be supplemented by the word 'svargakāmaḥ' (desirous of heaven). The complete injunction amounts to this that one who is desirous of heaven should perform Viśvajit sacrifice. The injunction 'one who is desirous of the lustre arising from the holy study should offer Caru (rice boiled in milk) in honour of the sungod' is also incomplete since the meaning of the word 'caru' is ambiguous. It may mean either the pot containing rice to be boiled in milk or simply rice boiled in milk. Hence, another injunction which throws light on the deity to be worshipped and the article to be offered should be assumed to supplement it.

In cases of subsidiary rites such as Aindrāgnya etc., a general hint has only been given by the basic injunction as to their observance. In order to know the details of the rites which make them up we are to assume some injunctions which assert that the subsidiary rites bear a close resemblance to the principal rites which they belong to.

The Mīmāṁsakas conclude thus :—As in these cases, the knowledge of invariable concomitance is impossible so presumption based upon testimony cannot be replaced by inference. By means of this proof, the words which are not heard but form part and parcel of the incomplete sentence heard by us, are supplied. But if it is held that the objects, denoted by these words, are to be assumed but not the words then these objects cannot enjoy the sanctity which is shared by the meanings of the actual Vedic words. The net result of this discussion is that presumption, based upon six sources of valid knowledge, should be accepted as a source of valid knowledge. But on the contrary, presumption, if carefully examined, is not distinct from inference.

Presumption identical with Inference

If two things are not inseparably connected by a tie of relation then one of them cannot illumine the other. No person can know another object on the basis of the knowledge of an object. Moreover, the relation of invariable concomitance may exist between the two objects but if one does not know it to be such then he cannot infer the other, simply knowing one of the two. It should also be noted that a new born baby does not possess such a complicated process of knowledge. (It is not an elementary form of knowledge). In all cases of presumption it is not possible to know the specific relation existing between the two objects. But it is also a fact that they are known to be related in a general manner.

Moreover, the Mīmāṁsakas hold that in a case of presumption the proof that it (the given) cannot be established without this (the assumed solvent) is an instance of negative concomitance. The negative concomitance, being known, does also lead to the positive one that if it is assumed then it will be explained. These two kinds of concomitance (positive and negative) are the property of the probans. Hence, presumption is not other than inference. We shall prove that what is based upon the observation of negative instances becomes the probans when it is also grounded upon the observation of positive instances. Moreover, the so-called instances of presumption which are based upon perception and other forms of valid knowledge and are put forward to prove the existence of the supersensuous power of an object are really pointless since the supersensuous object in question does not exist.

Refutation of the Power of Cause

An effect which is produced only by its cause assisted by its conditions does not presuppose the supersensuous power of the cause for its coming into being.

The Mīmāṁsakas contend that the so-called cause is not a real cause if it is devoid of power to produce an activity. (In other words, what is capable of producing an activity is a cause. But what lacks it is not a cause). When a person intends to cut down a tree he lifts up an axe. But likewise he might have raised a shoe to do it. If its capacity for doing an action is not admitted then any cause would have produced any effect without any restriction since the essence of all substances is one and the same. The Mīmāṁsakas cite two examples to bring home the point at issue. If a man takes poison he meets his death. If a house is set on fire then it is burnt. If we enquire into the cases of these two effects then we find that the power, belonging to the so-called causes, constitutes the real cause. But in these two cases if their power is obstructed by the recital of incantations, though the causes are recognised to remain numerically identical yet their effect does not take place. How does one account for it without subscribing to the hypothesis of power ? Because the essence of the cause and the assemblage of conditions are not obstructed by the recitation of incantations. The essence of the cause remains unaffected and the assemblage of all conditions is now as it was before. The power of a cause to produce an effect is only obstructed. That is why the effect does not come into being in spite of the fact that the cause remains unchanged and all the conditions assemble. Moreover, it is also observed by us that even when two persons have service of the same status and draw the same pay they have differences in their enjoyments of life. This fact has led the Naiyāyikas to assume transcendental objects like virtue etc. as conditions of all effects. If you follow the same line of thinking then you will have to subscribe to hypothesis of transcendental power. This is the sum and substance of the Mīmāṁsā-contention.

The refutation of the hypothesis of Śakti

The view of the Mīmāṁsakas is not sound. The Mīmāṁsakas have contended that the selection of a particular cause for a particular effect points to the hypothesis of the supersensuous power of a cause. Let us now subject this hypothesis to a thorough scrutiny. We are not competent enough to frame a novel hypothesis of causality concerning the positive objects but follow the traditional view in our theory and practice. By our mere wish neither water does warm us during chill nor fire does quench our thirst. How do we come to know that these two are causally connected e.g. an axe and the act of hewing ? Either we discover the relation in question or we learn it from the experienced persons. When we discover it we have recourse to the joint method of agreement and difference. That is why when we intend to cut down a tree we take up an axe but not a shoe etc.

It should also be noted that whenever a cause-in-itself is present the effect does not come into being because like the cause itself the presence of conditions is also required for the appearance of an effect. As the conditions do not always accompany a cause so the effect does not come into being even in the presence of a cause. Virtue and such other subjects are also included in the list of essential conditions. If the assemblage of such conditions is absolutely necessary for the appearance of an effect then how we can contend that an effect must always appear because the mere cause is present. The hypothesis of merit and demerit should be admitted, otherwise, we fail to explain the variety of effects. It is not a fact that they are transcendental because they represent cosmic force. But they are so because of their innate nature just like an internal organ and an atom.

The Mīmāṁsakas have held that when some particular incantations are uttered the effects do not appear in spite of the assemblage of all conditions and the cause, e.g., poison and fire do not produce their effect. According to them the only possible explanation is that the power of the cause is obstructed under such circumstances. The Naiyāyikas point out that an effect does not appear not because the power of the cause is counteracted but because the assemblage of condition is disturbed by the introduction of a new factor. (They mean to say that the presence of a negative condition is also essential for the appearance of an effect but with the utterance of the incantation, mentioned above, the negative condition disappears from the scene). What does the person do, uttering the incantation if he does not counteract the power in question? No, he has not obstructed the power but has simply introduced a change into the very collocation of conditions, nay, he has replaced the old collocation by a new one. We should also bear in mind that a particular collocation of conditions is responsible for a particular effect and hence the effect in question does not appear. The Mīmāṁsakas take an exception to this explanation and point out that as no perceptible change is noticed in the nature of a cause so how is it that an effect does not come into being? If this is their contention then how will they explain why poison does not kill a person when it is not devoured?

Now the Mīmāṁsakas may give an answer that contact of poison with blood is also one of the conditions of death. If this is their answer then the Naiyāyikas will also argue that the absence of an incantation is also a negative condition of an effect such as burning, death etc. When a just person swears virtue prevents the appearance of an effect Similarly, an incantation finds a place in the assemblage of conditions and obstructs the appearance of an effect. Let us, for the sake of an argument, assume the existence of power. How does an incantation act upon power ? Does it destroy power or does it counteract its influence ? Certainly, it does not destroy power since with the disappearance of the influence of the incantation in question the effect of the cause is seen. If it is held that power is counteracted then the Naiyāyikas will also argue that the cause itself is likewise prevented from producing its effect.

The cause remains unaffected. "How is it that it does not produce its effect ?" says the objector. "The very question is also applicable to power" is the reply of the Naiyāyikas. The objector may urge that the unchanged nature of the cause is directly grasped. The rejoinder is that power also remains unaffected and its unchanged nature is inferred from its effect. The Naiyāyikas put a question to the Mīmāṁsakas whether power which is postulated by them is coexistent with the cause itself or it is an effect. If they hold that it is coexistent with the cause then its effect should always follow from it. Now, they may hold that power alone does not produce an effect but it requires the aid of concomitant conditions. If they subscribe to this view then the assumption of power becomes superfluous since the hypothesis that the cause itself accompanied by the conditions produces an effect better obeys the law of parsimony. What purpose will serve the hypothesis of Power ? If they hold that the power of a cause is an effect of the cause itself then is it an effect of the cause alone or of the cause combined with the conditions? If they answer the first question in the affirmative then an effect should always come into being since power continuously follows from its cause. Again, if they hold that power is an effect of the assemblage of conditions then the very collocation of conditions will only be sufficient enough to explain an effect. In that case what is the good of postulating 'power' which intervenes between the cause and its effect (i.e., a redundant tertium quid) ? Again they may urge that a cause which is devoid of power cannot produce an effect. If this is their contention then they surely invite a regressus ad infinitum since power, the effect, is produced by a cause which possesses another power which in its turn requires another power for its very existence and so on ad infinitum.

The Mīmāṁsakas go on defending their case thus :—An invisible object is postulated only to explain a perceptible object in a perfect manner but not to spoil one's own case. If a series of powers is assumed then the potentiality of a cause will be simply exhausted by the production of such a series and no effect will be produced. Hence, they postulate the hypothesis of only one power and hold that the logical problem of a regressus ad infinitum does not arise.

A critical review of this hypothesis is as follows :—If a perceptible object is not explained without the postulation of an invisible object then and then only they are at liberty to assume an invisible object. If a visible object is otherwise explained then there is no necessity of assuming an invisible object. And the Naiyāyikas have also proved to the hilt that a visible fact is explained without assuming an invisible object. They also hold that if the opponents are bent upon assuming an invisible object in order to explain a fact then they may do so provided that it does not involve a regressus ad infinitum like merit and demerit. Moreover, the latter should bear in mind that they also assume an imperceptible process of the causal factor like power in order to explain an effect. Now, the Naiyāyikas point out that if one of these two hypotheses of invisible objects explains facts i.e., an effect to the satisfaction of all, then why should the Mīmāṁsakas assume two invisible objects, violating the law of parsimony ? The Mīmāṁsakas contend that if a so-called cause which is possessed of power does not produce its effect in and through its intermediate process then it is not a real cause. The Naiyāyikas put a question to them. "How do they know that the cause possesses power ?" They may say in reply that they infer it from its effect. The Naiyāyikas take an exception to it that an effect owes its existence only to an intermediate process but not to power. The Mīmāṁsakas contend that a tree is not cut down even when a shoe is busy with its intermediate process. If this is the contention of the Mīmāṁsakas then they should admit that the intermediate process is perceptible but not transcendental since they do not infer the intermediate process of a cause from its effect but directly know the operation of the cause in and through the intermediate process before the appearance of its effect.

An intermediate process is always an inference. It is inferred only from its effect. An effect is a mark only of one of the two viz., power or an intermediate process. Hence, we cannot infer both of them on the strength of one and the same mark. Let us now pay our heed to the point at issue. Hence, the above illustrations of presumption which are put forward to establish the existence of transcendental power are really pointless. Even if we assume the existence of transcendental power for the sake of an argument then it is only an inference since the invariable relation which holds between two concomitants is an instance of causal relation. If the cause-in-itself is not sufficient enough to bring about its effect then and then only we should infer something else in addition to the presupposed cause in order to explain an effect and this may be called 'power'.

The instances of presumption which have been advanced to prove the eternality of sound will be refuted later on in the chapter on verbal authority.

Presumption based upon non-apprehension included in Inference

The examples of presumption, based upon non-perception, do really illustrate inference. The absence of a living person from his house constitutes a mark which indicates his existence outside his house. The absence of living Caitra from his house is the subject of inference. His existence outside his house is the probandum. The state of his being absent from the house is the probans. On previous occasions we have found that whenever a living person has been absent from his house he has been present outside the place of his residence. A similar instance may be cited. Smoke coexists with fire because it possesses smoke. Therefore, it has been a vain feat of wordy warfare to find fault with the reason and to refute the view that the proposition that living Caitra is present outside his house follows as a conclusion.

The Mīmāṁsakas have contended that if presumption is an instance of inference then presumption should not be a distinct source of the knowledge of a novel object. But such a contention is not tenable. Which object is grasped by presumption according to you ? Is it unqualified existence of Caitra ? Or is it his staying outside his house ? His existence pure and simple has been known from the astrological science. Hence, it is not a new object. The object to be known is his presence somewhere outside the house. How is this object included in the already cognised object ? The proof which generates knowledge of his absence from his house opposes the appearance of such knowledge as reveals his presence at home. But it throws light neither on his presence nor on his absence outside.

When the absence of a man from his house is perceived by us we cannot definitely know whether he is far away from his house or he is staying in the courtyard of his house. But if we know that a living person is absent from his house then we unerringly infer that he is, staying outside his house. Moreover, the knowledge of the absence of a living person from his house cannot be equated with the knowledge of his presence outside his house. The fact that a man is living is one thing but, on the other hand, the fact that he is staying outside his house is another thing. Moreover, it cannot be also held that the knowledge of the absence of a living person from his house is the same as the knowledge of that person staying outside his house. From the knowledge of the first object we pass on to the knowledge of the second object but these two pieces of knowledge are not identical. Our knowledge of smoke on the locus of fire is not the same as is the knowledge of fire. Smoke is different from fire. In this case, too, the absence of a living person from his house is distinct from his presence outside his house. The hill and fire are two known objects. We infer only their relation which is a novel object. Similarly, here too, the connection of the living person with the place outside his house is only inferred since it is such an object as was not known before.

If the Mīmāṁsakas do not approve of this decision that a novel object, i.e., the connection of the living person with the place outside his house, is known by us, then presumption, having no other new object to reveal, becomes simply superfluous. His absence from his house and his life during his absence from home are known by means of two distinct sources of knowledge. But if we infer his contact with some place outside his house then we see that inference has some scope for revealing an unknown object. But presumption has no such scope. It simply grasps an object which is already known. In case of presumption an object is postulated in order to solve an apparent contradiction involved in a given fact. An unknown object is not revealed by presumption which reveals only the postulated object. Hence, presumption reveals no new object. It has been stated in their authoritative work that as an object, which is known either through any source of knowledge other than the verbal testimony or through the verbal testimony, seems to involve contradictions so someother object is assumed to solve it. The object which is postulated is never denoted by a word. But whenever an object is supposed to solve a contradiction it is known. Presumption reveals only the postulated object known already. Hence, the object to be postulated is no new one. As in the case of an inference based upon the relation of self-identity the known object is an inference so in presumption the known object is only revealed. Hence, presumption is not a distinct source of knowledge. This is the sum and substance of our argument.

The contention of the Prābhākaras in the defence of Presumption

The followers of the Prabhākara school of Mīmāṁsā follow a different line of argument to distinguish between Inference and Presumption. In case of inference the so-called probans is not dependable if the probandum does not exist on the locus of the probans in question. The adjective phrase 'otherwise, not logically valid' qualifies a probans in case of inference. For example, smoke cannot logically exist on the subject of inference if fire does not exist there. But in case of presumption reverse is the order subsisting between the implier and the implied. Let us take a familiar example. It cannot be proved that a living person is staying outside if he is not absent from his house. When a living person goes out of his house he stays outside. They also explain the extract of Śabara's commentary to fit it in with this new hypothesis. The object which is known to us either through the verbal testimony or through the other means of knowledge causes us to postulate other objects. As such an object is the only source of postulation, so in the absence of it such a postulation becomes impossible. Again, if we have no opportunity of postulating an object then the object which is postulated cannot appear on the scene. Presumption reveals only an object which is assumed. Hence, presumption is not Inference. This is the sum and substance of Prābhākaras' defence.

The refutation of Prābhākaras' defence

This difference is merely verbal but is not based upon the observation of new facts. If the object to be known is not known before then how can one know that it will appear to us to be a puzzle without having such and such condition ? If one possesses the previous knowledge of the object then what is the good of exposing the puzzling character ? Because we have definitely known the object which we are now trying to know in this context. The Prābhākaras may contend that we have already known not merely the object but also the puzzling character without assuming such and such indicator. Oh so great is its difference from inference. Does not this statement amount to this that the knowledge of invariable concomitance precedes presumption ? If they say that the presence of a living person outside is impossible without his absence from house then they should also admit that if he is absent from his house then he is surely present outside his house. What is the nature of this impossibility ? If it is logical impossibility then the so-called presumption is no better than inference since the latter thought-process moves in a similar manner. If the probans is known before then and then only the probandum is known afterwards and if the probans is not previously known then the probandum cannot be known.

It is a wrong statement that the absence of living person from his house objectively determines his presence outside. If the absence from house is an established fact then its effect is subsequently produced by it since a cause is invariably antecedent to its effect. Such a cause alone is productive of its effect. Now it is to be noted here that if one tries to establish causal connection between the absence of a person from his house and his staying outside at the next moment then an absurd situation arises viz. at the very moment of his absence he neither stays in nor outside his house ? Hence, the causal relation does not hold between one's absence from house and his presence outside. But this discussion is fruitless since it has no bearing upon the point in question. In other words, such a discussion does not improve upon the Prābhākara thesis that presumption is a distinct source of knowledge.

Some logicians of the Prabhākara school hold that presumption is distinct from inference since in presumption the implier points to the implied and conditions the implied. In case of inference smoke is only the mark of fire but in case of presumption the absence from house indicates and produces presence outside. Such a thesis is likewise refuted. Moreover, the Mīmāṁsakas have already pointed out that the relation of invariable concomitance holding between the implier and the implied can in no way be discovered since a relation is discovered when the objects thus related are within the range of vision. Such an argument does not make an appeal to us.

The Mīmāṁsakas themselves are not sure of the truth of their argument. A doubt whether or not the invariable relation holds between the implier and the implied has arisen in their mind but they have not been able to arrive at the difinite conclusion that the above relation does not subsist between them. Hence, they have put forward another example to prove their thesis. The example in question is an follows:—When a living person is at home he is not out. But if they think that it is a better one then they should have given it at the outset. But it does not illustrate presumption based upon non-perception. The initial proposition of the Mīmāṁsakas is that there are six kinds of presumption. But they, cowed down with fear at the angry look of the Naiyāyikas, have taken to heels, deserting presumption based upon non-perception like a doe in a forest. Such an act, on their part, is extremely mean and unworthy of a noble man.

If you desert this young lady (in the shape of the former illustration of presumption) who absolutely depends upon you for her protection then how will the other ladies (the other illustrations of presumption) count upon your protection with confidence ?

If a negative fact is presumed on the basis of positive fact then it is an illustration of presumption based upon perception. But in that case it is not difficult to discover the relation of invariable concomitance holding between the above two facts. The simple reason is that an object of limited extension occupies only a portion of space and hence in the other spaces its negation can be easily known. If it is determined that smoke does not exist in a place where fire does not exist then does such smoke, according to you, play the part of a probans which establishes the existence of fire on its locus ? As you decide with regard to this example so we decide with regard to your example of presumption. (If you agree to the point that the above example illustrates inference based upon negative concomitance then the instance of presumption is in no way different from that of inference).

Now, the Mīmāṁsakas may contend that inference is based only upon the positive concomitance discovered in and through repeated observations. Such a contention is not tenable. If the Mīmāṁsakas hold that a negative fact is implied by presumption then they surely arrive at a wrong conclusion. But the Naiyāyikas hold that a mark which is either positively or negatively related to the probandum is conducive to latter's inference provided that the probandum in question is not already known. We shall prove later on that there are cases of inference in which the knowledge of the negative concomitance is essential. If we do not ascertain the positive and negative relations of the probans belonging to the subject of inference before the actual act of infering then we are not sure of the truth of an induction which leads to a deduction. The very propositions which the Mīmāṁsakas have put forward to prove the absence of living person from all places outside his house are the same as are required for the inferential knowledge of his absence. All the counter-arguments, advanced by the Mīmāṁsakas, are really semblances of reasoning since they are contradicted by the sources of valid knowledge such as perception etc.

Presumption based upon the verbal testimony is not distinct from an inference

The example of the so-called presumption, based upon the

verbal testimony, is a weak one, and is not different from that of an inference. It is really absurd to presume the part of sentence since the meaning of the absent part can be inferred from its effect which serves the purpose of a true mark. As you infer fire, the cause of smoke, on a hill seeing smoke, the effect of fire, in its cave, so you may infer the taking of meal, the essential condition of corpulence, noticing the great bulk of a person. We notice no difference in these two instances. From our repeated observations we have learnt that corpulence is the effect of the taking of meal. In some cases the mark is perceived but in other case it may be known by means of the verbal knowledge. There is no great gulf of difference fixed between these two marks, acquired by the two different sources of knowledge.

The Mīmāṁsakas contend that an incomplete sentence cannot convey its meaning. They do not mean to say that the sentence that corpulent Devadatta does not take his meal during the day fails to convey that he is corpulent but simply intends to suggest that the knowledge of his corpulence is conditional and that it involves a reference to its condition which is not given there. This hypothetical knowledge, being incomplete, is not a true one. Hence the source of this knowledge, i. e., the sentence, is not a means of true knowledge. Hence, the sentence in question should be made complete. This is the sum and substance of the Mīmāṁsā contention. Such a contention is not tenable. Now let us see which one of the following involves reference to something else. Is it a word or its meaning or its knowledge ? If it is held that a word involves a reference then it may be answered that as no inarticulate sound involves a reference so a word which does not refer to a meaning involves no reference to some other word. If it is further held that a word which refers to its meaning also involves a reference to some other word then the hypothesis requires further clarification. The upholders of the hypothesis should agree to the point that the meaning of a word also involves a reference to some other object. If it is admitted that the meaning of a word involves a reference to some other object then the hypothesis that the presumption of a clause is necessary becomes superfluous. Now, the Mīmāṁsakas may uphold the third alternative and assert that consciousness involves a reference. If this is their stand then the critics (the Naiyāyikas) point out that all forms of consciousness do not involve a reference to other objects. The critics admit that the knowledge of the meaning of a word involves a reference to other objects over and above its own object because its object involves a reference to them. But they also subscribe to the view that the auditory perception of a sound does not involve such a reference since sound itself, its object, does not involve a reference to other objects. Hence, in order to establish the referential character of meaning one should admit the referential character of an object.

Moreover, the Mīmāṁsakas presume a clause in order to establish the knowledge of some additional objects. Hence, it will be a simpler course to be adopted by us if we directly assume the additional objects themselves. What benefit do we derive, having recourse to the additional step ?

Now, the Mīmāṁsakas raise an objection that what is assumed does not follow from the Vedas. But the objection may be met thus :—

Even if we assume for the sake of an argument that a clause or a sentence is presumed then the meaning of the clause or of the sentence is not conveyed by the same since either of them is non-Vedic. The Mīmāṁsakas may contend that the Vedic text is of two-fold character. viz., the first type is heard, i. e., given and the second one is inferred and that what is presumed also pertains to the Vedic text. The counter argument of the Naiyāyikas is as follows :—

The subject-matter of the Vedic text admits of two kinds, viz., the first one is directly given by the Vedic texts and the second one is suggested by the first one. Thus, the suggested matter is also Vedic. In that case, why should we subscribe to a gratuitous assumption in the shape of a clause or of a sentence ? Hence, the new matter, i. e., the subject matter, which is derived from the direct Vedic text will be treated also as Vedic. Therefore, we can confidently assert that the hypothesis of presumption based upon the verbal testimony is in no way more satisfactory than that of the Naiyāyikas.

The refutation of Śrutārthāpatti by the Prābhākaras

Now, the followers of the Prabhākara school of Pūrvamīmāṁsā, a third party, appear on the scene. They refute the above two hypotheses and put forward a new hypothesis. The above subject matter, i. e., supper at night, is supersensuous and the relation of concomitance holding between supper and fatness cannot be discovered. Again, the hypothesis that a clause or a sentence which completes a Vedic sentence otherwise incomplete is to be presumed, has already been refuted. But if the subject-matter which is imagined is very general then it will be easy, on our part to discover the relation of concomitance. Let us see a few concrete cases. There are a few examples of Vedic injunctions in which the verb 'to sacrifice' has been used but the agent i.e., the nominative has not been mentioned. But in these cases the nature of the agent can be easily guessed. The verb 'to sacrifice' is transitive. Being such it produces some result. One who enjoys the fruit of the action is the agent since the relation of invariable concomitance holds between the enjoyer of the fruit of an action and the transitive verb like the verb 'to sacrifice'.

The drift of this line of thinking is that it is easy to arrive at a more general induction. The Prābhākaras quote a line from the commentary of Śabara in order to solve the apparent conflict between their view and that of Śabara. Śabara clearly writes that Presumption is dṛṣṭa (based upon sources of valid knowledge other than the verbal one) and Śruta (based upon verbal knowledge). Prabhākara interprets it in a different manner. He holds that the apparent meaning is not real one. It is only a popular saying. But the real meaning of it is that the complete Vedic sentence gives rise to such knowledge of objects as removes the apparent inconsistency involved in it (the Vedic sentence). Thus Prabhākara and his followers refuse to accept Śruta-arthāpatti (presumption based upon the verbal testimony) as one of the distinct varieties of Presumption and propound the thesis that the additional meaning which the words of the Vedic sentence do not cover is also conveyed by this sentence and the above knowledge is thus derived from the source of verbal testimony. As an arrow has a short or long process, i.e., it hits a near or a remote object or it pierces and passes through a thin or thick object quickly or slowly, so a sentence quickly or slowly conveys its meaning since the knowledge of the complete meaning depends upon a group of factors viz. the knowledge of the meanings of words denoting qualities, substances, action, etc. As long as the function of words conveying their meanings continues so long the knowledge of the meaning arises in our mind. But when its function ceases to work it produces no knowledge since the factors which determine knowledge do not exist.

A student, who is worthy of being initiated into the art of the proper use of words employed by the experienced persons, attentively notes the usage of the old teachers and comes to learn that such and such sentences are capable of conveying such and such meanings. The words which constitute these sentences determine the meanings of them which obey a number of specific conditions. If we reflect on the nature of conditions which regulate the conditioned meanings of sentences then we come to know that there are some cases which show that even silent words determine such meanings. There are a few Vedic injunctions which are elliptical in their character. An illustration of this type is 'Viśvajitā yajeta' a person who intends to enjoy heavenly bliss should perform the sacrifice called Viśvajit which is a means to this end. In this injunction the compound word 'svargakāma' (one who intends to enjoy heavenly bliss) is not given. Still, the silent compound word contributes its quota of meaning towards the conveying of the complete meaning of the above injunction. There are also some other injunctions in which the given words which are heard are given up since they do not help to convey the complete meanings of them (injunctions). An illustration of this type is as follows :—

Yasya ubhayaṁ havir ārttim ārcchet (the word 'ubhayam' (both) has been abandoned since it is not capable of expressing the complete meaning of a great Vedic injunction). (In connection with the directions of the new moon and the full moon sacrifices it has been stated that if both the articles which are to be offered are spoiled then Indra should be offered five plates of rice. Now, the prima facie view is that an emphasis should be laid upon the adjective 'both'. The conclusive view is that even if one of these two articles to be offered is spoiled then the compensatory rite should be observed. Hence, the word 'both' loses its significance since its absence opens up a wider scope. The actual traditional practice is that the word 'ubhaya' (both) should be given up. Thus, it has got no part to play when the meaning of the above two conjoined injunctions is conveyed). In some cases no importance is attached to a subordinate clause which does not shape the meaning of the main injunction, e.g., one sprinkles the articles with such clarified butter as remains after the conclusion of the Prayāja sacrifice. (There is direction for sprinkling the articles to be offered with clarified butter which remains after the conclusion of Prayāja sacrifice in the above Vedic sentence. Such a provision invites other considerations. There should be also some ruling with regard to the preservations of such clarified butter and the provision of a pot which will contain it. In the absence of such a ruling will the sprinkling of the articles with clarified butter be abandoned? A doubt arises in our mind. The Mīmāṁsakas hold that no qualitative change from the religious point of view is introduced into the nature of these articles by such sprinkling. In connection with that sacrifice it has also been stated that omentum should be given to Prajāpati. But it should not be sprinkled with clarified butter. The object of the sprinkling of the articles with clarified butter is not spiritual but merely secular. To smoothen the surface of the rough and coarse articles is the tangible aim. Omentum requires no such sprinkling. Therefore, in that case if any quantity of clarified butter exceeds the need of Prayāja sacrifice then it should be left aside. Hence, the sprinkling of articles with clarified butter is not an essential condition of the sacrifice in question. Thus, the Vedic sentence which describes such sprinkling is not an integral part of the Vedic injunction which throws light upon the performance of some Vedic rites. In other words, this Vedic sentence is not taken into consideration when the meaning of the main injunction is discussed).

Now, the boiled-down sense of the early discussion is this that when the meaning of a proposition corresponding to a relational judgment is ascertained it must be admitted that the words which are actually given do not determine the above meaning. If the truth of the above judgment is accepted then it also stands to reason that a sentence, a portion of which is not given may also directly convey a meaning. In that case what is the good of assuming the type of presumption based upon the verbal testimony? As in the so-called instances of presumption based upon the verbal testimony the meaning is directly conveyed by the incomplete Vedic sentences so the intermediate process of supplying the silent portion in order to render the sentence complete is superfluous. Now, a problem arises in our mind. It runs thus:—Should all the constituents of a sentence be ascertained? Moreover, if the meaning of a sentence is not completely grasped then how can the factors that determine the meaning be ascertained?

The solution of the above problem is as follows. Even when we hear a sentence in toto the words which compose it do not determine its meaning by their mere presence in the body of the sentence. But, on the contrary, if the meaning of a sentence is ascertained then we are in a position to understand which words really determine the meaning of the sentence. This is our view which has been already stated. Thus, if the meaning of a sentence of which some words are not heard is ascertained then in the light of that meaning we know that even the unheard words, too, determine the above meaning. Let us cite a few examples to vindicate the truth of our view that the unheard words determine the meaning of a sentence. The Vedic sentence 'svargakāmo yajeta' amounts to the complete sentence 'svargakāmo yāgena svargaṁ bhāvayet'. It means that one who aspires after heavenly bliss should make provision for heavenly bliss by means of a sacrifice. In the original form of the sentence the words 'yāgena' and 'svargam' are not given. But its meaning being transparent it is easy to follow that the unheard words determine the above meaning. We follow the meaning of the word 'agnicit'. The word stands for a sentence 'Yaḥ agniṁ cinoti'. The formation of the word is this (agni+ci the suffix 'kvip' denoting the agent). When we get the word thus formed, there is no trace of the kvip suffix which is dropped in the resultant form. But the meaning of the unheard suffix is definitely grasped. The word 'adhunā' also contains an element which is not heard. The combination of the pronoun 'idam' with the nominal suffix adhunā results in the word 'adhunā' (at present). The base of it is dropped though it conveys the meaning. Similarly, in the compound words and the words formed by the nominal suffixes the proper case-endings which are significant remain unheard. But we grasp their meanings. (The compound word 'rāja-puruṣaḥ' amounts to the sentence rājñaḥ puruṣaḥ (the servant of the king). The sixth case-ending corresponds to 'of'. It denotes the relation of the master to his servant. We follow its meaning though we do not hear it. The word 'Dāśarathiḥ' amounts to the sentence 'Daśarathasya apatyam pumān (the male child of Daśaratha). (The sixth case-ending is dropped in the resultant form though its meaning is clearly grasped). Similarly, we follow the meaning of the incomplete sentence 'Viśvajitā yajeta'. In the light of its meaning we come to learn that it contains the word 'svarga-kāmaḥ' which remains unheard. A viniyoga injunction is such as points to the relation between the end and the means of a sacrificial rite. (Some Mīmāṁsakas hold that the above injunction discharges its function with the help of six special proofs which are called Śruti, Liṅga. Vākya, Prakaraṇa, Sthāna and Samākhyā. They have been explained also in the manuals of the Mīmāṁsā works of the Bhāṭṭa School). The Mīmāṁsakas of the Prabhākara school contend that a viniyoga injunction discharges its function of pointing to the relation between the end and the means with the help of five proofs with Liṅga at the top and Samākhyā at the bottom. They also contend that Śruti, the first of the so-called viniyoga proofs, has got no part to play. Thus, no Śruti should be presumed in the absence of a direct Śruti. In fine, there is no scope for Śruta-arthāpatti in connection with the function of viniyoga injunction.

The Mīmāṁsakas of the Bhāṭṭa school contend that if the Prābhākaras mean to say that the meaning of a sentence is conditioned alike by the given and the silent then they should admit that all words which determine the meaning of a sentence, uniformly discharge their function of expressing their meanings. In that case there should exist no distinction between a word used in a primary sense and that used in a secondary sense from the Prābhākara standpoint. Moreover, the Bhāṭṭas have cited a fair number of examples, the proper interpretation of which depends upon the solution of the conflict among the six proofs of ascertaining the relation between the principal and the secondary elements of a Vedic rite. The solution presupposes Śruti, the first of the above six proofs, as the only solvent of all conflicts since the earlier one is held to be stronger than the latter. The Prābhākaras refuse to accept Śruti as a proof. Now how can they do justice to such example if they do not subscribe to the view of the Bhāṭṭas ?

The Prābhākaras face this objection thus:—The words which constitute a sentence and determine its meaning have got a part to play. But each of them does neither play the same part nor in the same manner. Words have different ways of expressing their meanings. Some directly express their primary meaning but others convey only secondary meanings. But the meaning of a sentence cannot suddenly appear if its essential elements denote no meaning. Again, if it is admitted that the constituent words have their contribution towards the meaning of a sentence then it goes without saying that the words will be admitted to denote the different types of meaning (primary, secondary, etc.).

The word 'lion' has a primary meaning in some sentences. But the very word, used in the sentences like the present one 'Devadatta is a lion' denotes a secondary meaning.

The word 'Ganges' has a primary meaning in the sentence 'He takes his ablution in the Ganges' (Gaṅgāyāṁ Majjati). But in the sentence 'A cowherd lives in the Ganges' (on the banks of the Ganges) (Gaṅgāyāṁ ghoṣaḥ prativasati) the word 'Ganges' denotes a secondary meaning. Thus, the Prābhākaras meet the first part of the objection raised by the Bhāṭṭas.

The Prābhākaras also meet the second part of the objection raised by the Bhāṭṭas. They point out that the Bhāṭṭas have lost sight of the real point. The real strength of a proof lies in its power of conveying the relation between the means and the end. If one proof conveys it much more quickly than another then the first one is stronger than the second one. The proofs have been arranged in order of their power of conveying the relation in order of time. The first proof gets the first preference since it conveys the above relation without the least delay. If we follow the sense of a Vedic text then we can understand which of these proofs renders us speedy service to grasp the relation between the end and the means. Thus, there is no necessity of presuming Śruti.

The Prābhākaras now argue against the hypothesis of the Bhāṭṭas. The Bhāṭṭas assume that such of the six proofs, viz. śruti, liṅga, etc. impart the power of conveying the relation holding between the end and the means to the viniyoga injunction. The very power of conveying such relation, being the same, how can one proof prevail upon another, preventing the due function of the so-called dependant proof in question? To meet this objection, they will have to revise their assumption and hold that the proofs do not uniformly impart the above power to the injunction in question. They should hold that the one is quick at imparting the power but another is slow to do so. If they admit it then they will find no difficulty in following the position of the Prābhākaras. They hold that all words do not uniformly convey their meaning. Similarly, all the proofs have not the same speed to convey the above relation promptly. What the Prābhākaras mean to say is that to have a proper solution an approach should be made from the side of the meaning of a sentence but not from the side of the words themselves. Therefore, the assumption of the power of words or that of a sentence is of no use.

The rites such as are observed in honour of Indra accompanied by Agni and others are called Vikṛta since the details of their performance are not directly mentioned. In case of Vikṛta rites no injunction which throws light on the observance of their subsidiary rites is found. But still none should infer an injunction which provides us with the required details. The very injunction which enjoins a Vikṛta rite furnishes us with all the details to be observed in connection with it. In some cases, the very injunction is correlative of the subsidiary actions. If the view is taken to be absolute then a question arises that there would be no distinction between a direct mandate and an indirect one the application of which is extended since both of them inform us alike of the details of subsidiary actions to be observed. An answer to this objection is as follows—There is no difference in the nature of the understanding of these two mandates. But there is a difference in the matter of the performance of the two sets of rites according to the direct and the indirect mandates. In case of a direct mandate one should observe rites as he is ordered by an injunction to do. But in case of an indirect mandate one should follow it so far as it has bearing upon the rite undertaken by him. (In other words, in the first instance all the details of a principal rite are furnished directly by the injunction. Thus, the performer has no choice to make. He is required only to obey the command. But in case of the performance of a subsidiary rite the details are not directly supplied by an injunction. They follow from the injunction which governs the basic principal rite. All the details of the main rite are not to be necessarily performed in connection with the observance of a secondary rite. Only the suitable ones are to be selected. Moreover, in connection with the performance of a principal rite some such details are observed as are not directly mentioned by injunctions. They are not to be counted upon as essential for Vikṛta karman. Thus Vikṛta karman is the pivot round which the selection of details revolves. Still a Vikṛta karman bears a close resemblance to the main karman since one is to observe a majority of the details of a main rite in connection with the performance of its corresponding Vikṛta karman.

Very well, if this is the solution offered by the Prābhākaras then they should admit that the husking of the cooked article should not be observed in case of milk-boiled rice which is prepared in a gold vessel, since such husking is incompatible with the vikṛta karman in which such milk-boiled rice is required. But why is husking mentioned here and abandoned after mature consideration ? The answer to this objection is very simple. Among the details of the main rite husking is included. It is a truism that the husking of milk-boiled rice is absurd on the face of it. Still, one should not argue like this that its incompatibility should not be exposed since it is absurd to think of it as an element of vikṛta karman. One should bear in mind that it has been stated that a vikṛta karman is similar to its corresponding main rite so far as the details of the latter are concerned. It is naturally expected that all the details will be observed in connection with the performance of a vikṛta karman. Husking is included in the list of the details of a main rite. Thus, husking has a possibility of being performed. To rule out this possibility the prohibition of husking has been mentioned. The main reason for this prohibition is this that the direct details are observed but the parts of the details are neglected in case of the extension of the application of an injunction.

Jayanta says in fine that the detailed discussion of the subject matter, of the other systems, which has been incidentally introduced into the work on Nyāya philosophy should no more be encouraged.

Some aspects of the thesis of the Mīmāṁsakas of the Bhāṭṭa school have been incidentally discussed. On a critical examination of their thesis we find that the hypothesis of presumption based upon the verbal testimony is only open to serious objections. Any one of the two hypotheses, viz. (i) both given and silent words determine the meaning of a sentence and (ii) the words of a sentence by means of their different intrinsic power of quickly or slowly conveying their objects express the meaning of a sentence without assuming other sentences or clauses, is a better substitute.

The refutation of the hypothesis of Dhvani

The second hypothesis that the words of a sentence by means of their intrinsic power completely express the meaning of a sentence is refuted by the hypothesis of the proud rhetoricians that a word, apart from its primary or secondary meaning, conveys a distinct meaning by means of the power of suggestion and that the meaning of a word in some cases suggests another distinct meaning. They say that a positive sentence suggests a negative meaning and that a negative sentence suggests a positive meaning.

The examples are as follows. The positive sentence "Oh pious one ! move here freely etc." suggest a negative meaning. The negative sentence "Oh traveller ! do not enter this house etc." suggests a positive meaning. (The words convey, at the outset, a primary meaning and afterwards with reference to the context and other factors the suggested meaning is presented to our mind.) Jayanta joins issue with the rhetoricians and holds that the words only by means of their power of expressing either primary or secondary meaning convey the final meaning of a sentence. In the examples cited above the objects meant are to be grasped by other sources of knowledge or are knowable by such proofs.

Or, one should not engage one self in dissertation with the students of pure literature since the learned scholars in the different branches of study become perplexed to ascertain the much complicated meaning of a sentence.

We shall not spend much time in discussions about the import of a sentence which befits the circle of the learned critics of literature since the ascertainment of such a meaning is not within the province of the logicians. Hence, we shall now return to our old topic. Our confirmed opinion on this topic is this that presumption does not differ in the slightest degree from inference.

Abhāva (Non-perception) is distinct source of knowledge

The Bhāṭṭas hold that the proof which reveals negation is a distinct one.

The proof which does not reveal a positive object reveals a negative object and is called the privation of proof (pramāṇābhāva). If we analyse the judgment that there is no jar here then we find that a proof which grasps only a positive object reveals a jar and that a negative judgement that there is no jar owes its existence to the privation of all proofs. If we dive deep into the matter then we see that the non-appearance of the knowing process of the knower directed to a jar is the proof which is called the non-perception of a perceptible object and the resulting consciousness assumes the form that a jar does not exist. (This hypothesis is not sound since the proof in question is not a form of consciousness). The alternative hypothesis is this. The knowing process of a knower which reveals a negative fact such as the negation of a jar is due to the absence of a proof positive. The judgment that there is no jar is the proof. The result of such a proof is that the negation of a jar is to be avoided or obtained etc. Kumārila has explicitly stated in his Śloka-vārttika to this effect:—

The first hypothesis of Kumārila is that the proof which is called the privation of a proof is really the negative mode of a soul—the negative mode which is the absence of all positive states such as perceptual consciousness etc. These positive states of the soul reveal only positive objects. The negative state, on the other hand, is the source of a negative judgement such as there is no jar. The second hypothesis is that the judgement which refers to an object other than a positive one (i.e., the negative judgement that there is no jar) is the proof in question and that the result of the judgement is that the negation of a jar is to be avoided.

An object other than a positive one signifies here the negation of a jar. The judgement that there is no jar here is not perceptual since it does not owe its existence to the sense-object contact. Sense-object-contact admits of two kinds, viz. conjunction and inherence. These two are fundamental types. There are other varieties of sense-object-contact. They arise from the combination of these two contacts such as conjunction-cum-inherence etc. Such a contact is not possible here. The state of being an adjective to an object, conjoined to a sense-organ, does not constitute the sense-object-contact in this particular case. The negation of a jar does not qualify the spot. What qualifies another object must be either in conjunction with it or inhere in it. A stick which is conjoined to a person qualifies him (a person possessed of a stick). The colour 'white' which inheres in an object qualifies it. This is the nature of an adjective which we learn from experience. The negation of an object is not conjoined to an object, its container, since it is neither a quality nor an action nor a universal.

Even it is taken for granted that the negation of a jar is visualised because of the sense-object-contact in the shape of conjunction cum the relation of the qualifying to the qualified then it would also be admitted that one visualises taste etc., belonging to an object to which his eyes are conjoined. The Naiyāyikas may meet this objection with the remark that taste is not visualised since it is not capable of being visualised. But this very answer goes against the perception of negation since it is imperceptible. Moreover, if the perceptibility of an object or its imperceptibility determines its perception or non-perception then why should the sense-object-contact with its six-fold division be assumed as one of the conditions of perception ? The capability of being perceived should alone determine perception. Therefore, the awareness of the negation of a jar is not visual. The Naiyāyikas put forward a cogent argument in support of their thesis. The say "When we attentively direct our eyes to a spot we perceive both the spot and the negation of a jar. But when we shut up our eyes we behold none of them. If both these pieces of awareness are alike dependent upon our eyes then how can we say that we perceive the spot but not the negation of a jar ? How can the proposed difference in the knowledge of negation be accounted for ? The Mīmāṁsakas boldly meet this objection and emphatically say, "Oh, yes there exists a difference between the perception of a spot and the awareness of negation. The negation of an object is not perceived because no sense-organ has contact with it."

If the eyes do not come in contact with the perceptible object then the perception of the object does not arise. Though the eyes make contribution towards the growth of the awareness of negation yet this contribution being indirect the awareness of negation is due to some other factors. As we have knowledge of heat at the sight of the brilliant colour of blazing fire encircled by the voluminous flames at a distance so we are aware of negation seeing the spot. In the above instance we infer heat on the strength of the perception of colour. Our eyes are not the unconditional antecedent to the knowledge of heat. Similarly, eyes are not the indispensable condition of the awareness of the negation of a jar which is not invariably connected with the visual perception of the spot. Hence, the awareness of the negation of a jar is not perceptual.

It has been stated thus : (in Kumārila's Ślokavārttika) The knower at the outset perceives the locus of negation. Then he recollects the object negated. Afterwards his inner organ in co-operation with the non-perception of the perceptible object produces the knowledge of negation without receiving direct help from the outer sense-organs. (Thus, the awareness of negation is never perceptual since it does not directly owe its existence to the sense-stimulus).

For the reason stated above, we have, sometimes, the knowledge of the negation of an object—the negation which lies outside the range of our sense-organs. Let us cite an example. A man who has thoroughly seen all the objects of Gauramūlaka, a village, has gone out of the village to a distant place. There he has been asked by a person whether Garga lives at Gauramūlaka or not. Now he who thoroughly knows Gauramūlaka recollects for sometime and knowledge dawns in his mind that Garga is not present at Gauramūlaka which lies outside the range of his sense-organs. Sense-organs play no part to produce this negative judgment. Hence, the awareness of negation is not perceptual. The negation of Garga, just cited above, is not an inference. Neither the locus of negation, i.e., the particular space in Gauramūlaka nor the non-perception of the object negated is the required mark necessary for an inference. The spot in question cannot be the mark since a man who is innocent of the invariable relation obtaining between the spot and the negation of an object is aware of such negation on the spot. Moreover, the spot in question contains both an object and its negation and it cannot be an invariable concomitant of the negation of an object alone. Moreover, a reliable mark rests upon the subject of inference without an exception. The subject of inference is, here, the spot. The spot is also the mark. The spot cannot rest upon itself. Hence, if the spot is the mark, then it does not belong to the subject of inference. Negations of objects belonging to the spot in question are innumerable. Moreover, the negation of an object does not belong to a particular spot. The number of its locii is countless. Hence it is absurd to discover that the relation of invariable concomitance holds between the spot in question and the negation of a particular object.

The non-perception of an object negated cannot play the part of a mark which leads to the inferential knowledge of the negation of the object since it does not belong to the object of inference. (The text-book does not refer to the old example. But it cites another commonplace example. We shall follow the text). The non-perception of a jar may somehow belong to a jar but does not belong to the spot which contains the negation of a jar. It may be urged that as non-perception of a jar contributes its quota towards the appearance of the awareness of the negation of a jar so it belongs to the spot. Such an argument involves the fallacy of mutual dependence. The fallacy may be thus illustrated. If the non-perception of a jar belongs to the spot, the subject of inference, the mark, i,e., the non-perception in question, becomes strong enough to produce the required inferential knowledge of the probandum in question. Again, if the inferential knowledge of the probandum correctly arises from the premises then the mark is known to belong truly to the subject of inference. Thus, these two propositions pre-suppose each other. Hence, it is impossible to establish that non-perception belongs to the locus of negation. The upholder of the view that the non-perception of an object is the mark may argue that if the probandum is inferred even by means of the defective mark then it is of no use to know it as belonging to the subject of inference. Moreover, if the mark in the shape of the non-perception is not discovered as an invariable concomitant of the probandum in question then how can it help to infer the negation of the object in question? The discovery of invariable concomitance depends upon the previous knowledge of both the mark and the probandum as it has been found in the case of smoke and fire. Now, if you stick to the above argument then it will be open to a serious charge since you do not show what sort of knowledge you have of the probandum in the shape of the negation of an object when the relation of concomitance obtaining between the probandum and the probans is discovered. If you hold that the probandum is inferred even at that time then it is a clear instance of mutual dependence. On the other hand, if it is held that the knowledge of the negation of an object is due to another distinct act of inference then this line of argument will be vitiated by the fallacy of a regressus ad infinitum. The mark, viz., non-perception is itself a negative fact. We must have recourse to the same process of thought in order to know it. (To infer a negative fact we require a mark which is also a negative fact. The mark, being a negative fact, is to be inferred. Another negative mark is thus necessary. It also cannot but be inferred by means of some other negative fact which is a mark, and so on ad infinitum. Thus, the fallacy of a regressus ad infinitum cannot be avoided.) Hence, we cannot count upon an inference as revealing negation. After taking a few baffled steps we will admit that a competent distinct proof produces the knowledge of negation and that negation is not an inference. It is not proper for us even to entertain a hypothesis that the negative judgment that there is no jar on this spot is due to either verbal testimony or comparison or presumption. Therefore, it stands to reason that the knowledge of a negative fact is due to a proof which is itself negative in its character since all the positive proofs exclusively throw light on the positive objects.

A proof and an object which is known by it should be alike in their character (similiasimilibus etc.). A proof which is negative in its character cannot reveal a positive object. Similarly, a negative fact cannot be established by a proof which is positive in its character. A proof which throws light only on a negative fact cannot be gainsaid. Therefore, a proof which is negative in its character should be admitted in order to enlighten a negative fact.

The refutation of Non-perception as a distinct source of knowledge

A refutation of the Bhāṭṭa Mīmāṁsā view stated above is as follows. It is a truism that a negative fact is admitted by the Mīmāṁsakas of the Bhāṭṭa school to be objectively real and distinct. One should not search for a distinct proof for its illumination since it is revealed by perception and similar other proofs already admitted by us. When a negative fact rests upon a spot which is within the field of our vision it is seen with our own eyes. But when it lies beyond the range of our sense-organ it is grasped by any other competent proof. The judgment that there is curd in the pot is a simple one. Similarly, the judgment that there is no jar here is a simple one. In the first case, both the objects, viz., curd and the pot stimulate eyes which produce the first judgment. Similarly, in the second case, the negation of a jar and the spot stimulate eyes which without being passive and functionless produce the second judgment. Now, how can the Mīmāṁsakas hold that the negative judgement is a complicated one ? They hold that the one element of it i. e., the spot is visualised whereas the other element of it is grasped by some-other proof. How can a distinction in the nature of the so-called awareness of the two objects be logically drawn? The judgment that the hill is fiery is a simple one but still it is a judgment by complication. It is a truism that the predicate of this judgment, viz., fire is not perceived and that its knowledge is mediate. If we take the growth of knowledge of fire into consideration then we find that the remembrance of the invariable concomitance obtaining between smoke and fire and such other thought processes intervene between the perception of smoke and the appearance of the knowledge of fire. But in case of the above negative judgment there is no such delay. No thought process goes between the perception of the spot and the awareness of the negation of a jar. Like the perception of the spot the awareness of the negation of a jar immediately and invariably follows the sense-object-contact, i.e., the functioning of the sense-organ, viz., the eyes.

The fire on the hill, as stated above, is beyond the range of our vision. But the negation of a perceptible object located upon a near locus is not so. The awareness of negation is causally connected with the senses. Its causal connection is based upon the joint method of agreement and difference. No man can see the above-mentioned fire in a hill in spite of the best activities of his eyes. The negative awareness is visual since it is produced when the eyes do not cease to function. Such an awareness closely follows the sense stimulus. The Mīmāṁsakas have pointed out that the colour of a distant fire is seen but its heat is inferred and that the knowledge of heat is not causally connected with the sense-stimulus. They urge that the awareness of negation is not likewise causally connected with the sense-organ. But this analogical argument does not hold good. The conclusion that no eyes are capable of feeling heat has been repeatedly arrived at. Every body knows that the sense of touch grasps only tactile objects. The eyes are capable of revealing colour and the sense of touch can only feel the touch of an object. Thus, in the above case, heat is only inferred since eyes are absolutely incapable of feeling heat.

The conclusion, reached by the Mīmāṁsakas, is one-sided. It is not applicable to the perception of negation.

If the awareness of an object which follows the visual perception of its container is not of sensuous origin then it does not follow that every such awareness as follows perception is non-perceptual. If this law had been universal then colour would not have been visualized. A fresh objection arises in our mind, viz, "How can negation which is colourless and has no connection with the eyes be perceived with eyes ?" An object is known as visualized when it is an actual object of perception produced by eyes. It is not so because it has colour. No coloured atoms are visualized. Whatever is connected with eyes is not visualized. The sky though connected with eyes is not visualized. Now, if the Naiyāyikas go to the other extreme and hold that an object which is not connected with eyes is also visualized then the very distant and the past objects such as Vibhīṣaṇa and others should have been visualized. The Naiyāyikas now make their position clear. They hold that the law that an object which is not connected with eyes is not visualized is applicable only to the positive objects. A negative fact though unconnected with eyes may be visualized. The narration of the six-fold division of sense-object-contacts touches only upon the positive objects. Whenever a positive object which is connected with the sense-organ is perceived, the sense-object contact is one of the six types mentioned in the Nyāya text book. The hypothesis that a sense-organ reveals only an object with which it comes in contact relates only to the positive objects. But a negative fact, being other than a positive one, is visualized though it does not come in contact with eyes. Such an admission does not interfere with the law of perception mentioned above. Now, if we stick to this conclusion then we smell a scent of possible anomaly that if a negative fact which does not come in contact with the sense-organ is perceived then all negative facts belonging to distant lands should also be perceived since they are also in no way connected with the sense-organ. Such an anomaly does not arise since the awareness of a negative fact is determined by the perception of its locus. The locus of a negative fact which is within the range of a sense-organ is only perceived. (Jayanta, himself, finds fault with this suggestion. He subscribes to another suggestion which is widely known among the circle of the logicians of the Nyāya and Vaiśeṣika schools. Or, a negative fact which comes in contact with eyes by means of conjunction-cum-the relation of the qualifying to the qualified is visualized. He cites an example to strengthen his case. Those who hold that the relation of inherence is perceived admit that the sense-object-contact is conjunction-cum-the relation of the qualifying to the qualified. Oh ! This unproved hypothesis is based upon an example which is not admitted by both the contending parties ! What a wonder ! The Naiyāyikas give the following answer. "No, do not say like this. Even from your stand-point the relation obtaining between a substance and its attribute cannot but be admitted. The awareness of a substance is not the same as that of an attribute. Therefore, a substance is not identical with its attribute. But neither a substance nor an attribute is perceived if any one of them does not come in contact with the sense-organ. Therefore, some sort of sense-object-contact must be admitted in order to explain the perception of an attribute. There is no time at our disposal to indulge in trifle matters.

The counter-thesis of the opponents that negation cannot qualify the so-called locus, i.e., the ground, in case of the negation of a jar since it has neither contact with the locus nor inheres in it, is not tenable. We shall prove on the score of experience that there exists a third type of relation which is other than the relation of conjunction and that of inherence and is called the relation of the qualifying to the qualified. The opponents have raised another objection that if the relation of the qualifying to the qualified added to the relation of conjunction were admitted then the perception of taste would have also taken place at the time of the perception of negation by means of this relation. Our answer to this objection is this that our opponents will also have to face the same difficulty since they admit the existence of the complex relation in the shape of conjunction cum inherence in order to perceive the colour of certain-objects. The purport of this reply is this that taste and colour co-inhere in an object. If colour comes in contact with our eyes by means of the relation of conjunction cum inherence then taste will also come in contact with the same organ by means of the same relation. Now, the opponents may contend that if such a relation suffers from defects then it should not be admitted and that its non-admission does not affect our position. Now, the Naiyāyikas subject the contention of their opponents to a severe scrutiny. They urge that if this is the position of the opponents then how do they explain that the eyes perceive colour with which they, the eyes, do not come in contact since colour comes in contact with the eyes only by means of the relation of conjunction cum inherence ? The very function of eyes by means of which an object is perceived is called a contact. Or, it may be asserted that the sense-organs are fit to perceive an object and an object is fit to be perceived. Either the function of a sense-organ or the reciprocal fitness explains the perception of an object such as colour, etc. The relation of conjunction cum inherence has no part to play. Now, if this is all what the opponents have got to say then negation should also be perceived since the sense-organ functions or there exists mutual fitness, the prerequisite conditions of perception. If a sense-organ is admitted as an instrument of the perception of an object then it must have contact with the object. But if they refuse to accept the hypothesis that the sense-object-contact is a necessary condition of perception then they blow hot and cold with the same breath.

For the reason stated above, it should be admitted that there are six kinds of fitness and that they correspond to the six-fold sense-object-contact. The mere statement of non specified fitness will not do. A fit object which is invariably perceived comes in contact with the sense-organ but, on the contrary, an object which comes in contact with the sense-organ is not necessarily fit for being perceived. If the above hypothesis is accepted then the possibility of visualizing taste or such other qualities is ruled out. Thus taste is never introspected though it comes in contact with the inner organ (manas) since the inner-organ is neither capable of introspecting it nor taste is capable of being introspected.

Even if it is admitted that fitness is the sole condition of perception then it cannot be proved that negation lacks fitness. Now, if the Mīmāṁsakas argue that negation should not have a positive property then the Naiyāyikas meet this argument with the following counter-argument, viz., the opponents also admit that many a positive property belongs to negation. There are only two alternatives open to the Mīmāṁsakas. Either they should hold that negation is absolutely unreal because it defies all characterization or they should accept the Nyāya hypothesis that negation is perceived.

The following verse has been stated by Kumārila in support of his thesis. The content of it is this :—

A question whether or not such-and-such object existed in the village is put to a person who visited every part of that village. He falls to remember the object which he did not witness. On the strength of this non-remembrance he comes to know that such-and-such object did not exist there at the time of his visit. (The inner meaning of this verse is that negation is not a present object and its locus is a remote object. Both of them are beyond the range of perception. Negation is still cognized. Therefore, the awareness of negation is non-perceptual).

But this thesis does not stand the test of reason. When a person visits the village of Gauramūlaka which does not contain some objects he thoroughly perceives it and has also direct knowledge of the negation of those objects not to be found there in a general manner just as a person perceives the absence of light. (When a person perceives the absence of light his perception is expressed in a universal negative judgment that there is no light. There is no specification of the absence of all particular lights. When he is asked whether he has seen the absence of such-and-such light he remembers the absence of the particular light. Similarly, the visitor has perceived the negation of Garga.) Now, the person remembers the absence of Garga. The negation of Garga cannot be perceived since it is a past object. When he is asked whether Garga was there (during his visit) he, being truthful, says that Garga was not there after having remembered what he saw before. Now, a doubt whether Garga is now there or not lingers in his mind since Garga may go back to that village from some other place and stay there. Now, an objection is raised that the person did not know that he perceived the negation of all objects. (The purport of this objection is that the memory of the object of an act of perception which is not introspected is impossible.) The answer to the objection is that the remembrance of the object of perception which is not introspected is to be admitted here as the relaxation of this law is accepted by all in case of the remembrance of induction in connection with the inference of a familiar object. Thus when he is asked he remembers and gives the reply to all.

Now, an objection is raised that if one perceives all individual negative facts without knowing that he does so then he should simultaneously remember all of them but not a particular one. This objection is not sound. He remembers only that particular negation about which a question is asked. In other words, if there is an exciting factor to revive the memory of a particular negation such as a question, etc., then that particular negation is only remembered to the exclusion of the rest since the factors which are required to excite the memory of all particular negations are absent. We shall prove our point by an appeal to facts. All the letters that constitute a word may be simultaneously apprehended. But when the last latter is apprehended all the letters are simultaneously remembered. Therefore, in some cases, all the objects that we simultaneously apprehended are simultaneously remembered. But there are also some other cases which illustrate that the objects which are simultaneously apprehended are successively remembered. Thus, if the objects are perceived without being known that they are so perceived, they are not necessarily recollected simultaneously. Thus, if a person simultaneously perceives a number of objects having not known that he does so then there is no hard and fast rule that they should be simultaneously remembered.

Moreover, the statement of Kumārila himself that the locus —the village—has been only perceived amounts to this that the negations of all other objects are also perceived along with the locus but this perception is not introspected since the term 'only' signifies the negations of objects other than the locus. Kumārila himself subscribes to this view in the following verse.

When we determine a positive object and express our determination in the form that this is so and nothing else such determination necessarily involves a reference to the negation of other objects.

Thus when the village of Gauramūlaka with all its positive contents is perceived the negation of absent Garga is also directly cognized. Hence, the hypothesis that the awareness of negation is indirect should be given up. It should also be admitted that the negation of an object is perceived. The Mīmāṁsakas have rightly said that the negation of a jar belonging to the field of vision is not inferred. The Naiyāyikas approve of this point. The negation of an object which lies outside the field of vision is also inferred. An instance of the inference of negation is as follows. When in pitch dark night there is continuous and heavy shower of rain and the roots of corns are wet, the absence of the contact of the storm with the raining cloud is inferred. Another example is being cited to bring home on the above point. This example is the familiar example cited by the Mīmāṁsakas to illustrate presumption. It is as follows. We infer that Caitra is not out because he is in.

The negation of an object is also known on the strength of verbal testimony. The travellers, having heard the words of trustworthy persons, ascertained that there was no thief, etc. on the way.

The Mīmāṁsakas have also stated that there should be thorough similarity between the means of proof and the knowable object. They cite an analogous case in support of their hypothesis. They show that a positive object is grasped only by means of a positive means of proof. Such an argument is not convincing.

The absence of eye-disease is one of the conditions of perception. The absence of the probans on the locus of the negation of the probandum is one of the concomitant conditions which accompanies the probans to generate inferential knowledge. The absence of defects of a speaker such as absence of negligence, untruthfulness, etc. is the concomitant condition of verbal knowledge to be produced by the testimony of a trustworthy person. Thus, the negative conditions are also included in the totality of conditions that produces positive knowledge. Sometimes, a negative fact constitutes a probans which leads to the inferential knowledge of a positive probandum. The absence of rainfall leads to the inference of the blowing away of the cloud by the storm (the contact of the cloud with the storm). Thus, it is unreasonable to hold that a negative fact is known only by means of a negative means of proof. When a semi-divine being, viz., a Yakṣa is worshipped the articles of worship do not change in conformity to the object of worship.

The Refutation of the hypothesis that a negative fact is real

Now, the Buddhists, clad in red clothes, appear on the scene and make a remark that that discussion regarding the nature of a means of proof of a negative fact is tenable if a negative fact is real but the very foundation of this discussion is unsubstantial since a negative fact itself is conspicuous by its absence in the universe.

Negation is cognized but is never known as an independent object. (It involves a reference to some other objects). It is grasped as the negation of a jar (i.e., as qualified by space, time and jar, the object negated.) A negative judgment is expressed in the form that this is not here now. Though negation is cognized as indicated above yet it should be actually related to the three relata, viz., time, space and the object negated. If it actually comes in contact with them then nobody should find fault with the hypothesis that negation is objectively real. But, as a matter of fact, it remains always unrelated to its unavoidable relata. No relation exists beween it and time, space and the object negated since no relation such as the relation of conjunction, inherence, etc. unites them. No term which does not relate itself to another term qualifies it (an unrelated term). Now, it may be contended that the relation of the qualifying to the qualified connects them with one another. There is no need of assuming other relations. But such a contention is not tenable since the relation of the qualifying to the qualified presupposes some other basic relation obtaining between them (the qualifier and the qualified). A term which qualifies another term as an adjective is either conjoined to or inheres in that term. Two examples will illustrate this point. They are as follows: Devadatta is possessed of a stick. This lotus is blue. (In the first instance a stick which becomes a predicate of Devadatta is at first conjoined to him. In the second instance the colour 'blue' at the outset inheres in the lotus and then becomes a predicate.) Hence, the relation of the qualifying to the qualified is really not an independent relation. By the sweet will of a person the conversion of the terms of the relation of the qualifying to the qualified is noticed. Sometimes, an adjective becomes a noun and a noun becomes an adjective. Therefore, this relation is not objectively real but imaginary. No relation can specially exist between negation and the object negated since there is neither co-existence nor coordination between negation and the object negated. Let us take an example to illustrate this point. Suppose, a jar is present in a particular spot at a particular point of time. It cannot be absent from that spot at that point of time. Again, if the negation of a jar exists in a particular spot at a particular point of time then a jar cannot exist then and there.

The Naiyāyikas may contend that the relation of opposition holds between negation and the object negated. Now, let us see what is meant by opposition. If the negation of a jar is a pre-established real fact, comes to the locus of a jar and opposes it then it will be opposed to it like a mace opposing a jar. Such a relation of opposition does not exist between them. If it is assumed that a similar relation obtains between a jar and its negation then their co-ordination should be grasped as it is noticed in case of the destroyer and the object destroyed. The negation of a jar should produce some effect in order to negate a jar. But what is that effect ? If it does nothing in order to negate a jar then any object would have been opposed to any other object. If it is assumed that it produces another negative fact to oppose a jar then this hypothesis cannot escape the charge of regressus ad infinitum. The so-called sources of the destruction of a jar do not bring about its destruction since a positive object, being destructible by its own nature, does not require a destroyer for its destruction.

If a positive object is destructible by its own nature then there is no need of postulating a condition of its destruction. If it is indestructible by its own nature then the so-called conditions of its destruction have got no part to play.

For this reason, due to the operation of conditions like a mace, etc., a series of heterogeneous effects such as pot-sherds, etc., comes into being out of a jar, etc. Again if these phenomena are brought under some other series then a new series of effects will appear. But under no circumstances the negation of a jar (the destruction of a jar—a negative fact) will be caused by a jar. But it may be contended that the above negative fact (the post-negation of a jar) is something real and happens to be other than a jar. Such a contention will yield no result. Now, it may be further contended that the negation of a jar in general is a real fact since it is not cognized on its locus when a jar is brought there but it has been cognized on it when the jar has not been brought there because of the relation of opposition obtaining between a jar and its negation. This contention is not also tenable because the relation of opposition has been refuted. Again, if the negation of a jar is not different from a jar then a jar should have been an effect of a mace. Now, the Buddhists may argue that the pot-sherds which are produced by a mace constitute the very negation of a jar. Such a hypothesis, it is a pity, will lead to an absurd conclusion. If these potsherds are crushed then the negation of a jar is virtually destroyed. In that case, the destroyed jar will re-appear. Now, the Buddhists may revise their hypothesis and hold that the potsherds which produce no effects are called the negation of a jar. In that case, the potsherds may be the negation of a cloth as well because an unreal object cannot be distinguished from another such unreal object. This argument is based upon the assumption of the Buddhists that the negation of an object is unreal. It may be further shown, following the above line of argument, that a mace, etc., cannot effectuate potsherds, etc. (If a potsherd owes its existence to itself then it does not require conditions like a mace etc. for its appearance. But if it does not appear at all then the so-called conditions have no bearing upon it). Now, a question is put to the Buddhists regarding the nature of negation as supposed by them. Does it come into being or not ? If it does then it should be called a positive object like a jar. If it does not come into being but enjoys existence then it should be eternal. If it is eternal then is it related only to a particular object or to all ? Of these two alternatives we find no reason in favour of the first one. If the second alternative is accepted then the particular negation, being eternal and all pervasive, should oppose each and every positive object by its very nature. The net result of this opposition is that all positive objects, eternal or non-eternal, would have surely ceased to exist.

Now, if the Hypothesis of negation is discarded then the line of distinction which absolutely separates one positive object from another will break down and the one monotonous identity will engulf all the distinct types of objects. Thus, the human convention, of distinction based upon the classification of objects of the universe, will disappear from the surface of earth.

If negation does not enjoy objective reality, milk will be identical with sour milk and sour milk will be so with milk. Similarly, a jar will be a piece of cloth. A hare will have horns. The unconscious objects such as earth etc. will be possessed of consciousness, the very essence of the soul.

If we assume the hypothesis that negation is objectively real then the positive objects maintain their mutual distinction by means of their objective difference, which is a type of negation. But if we do not subscribe to this view and do not try to avoid the danger of the merging of objects into one another then a greater peril will surely await us.

The Buddhist criticism

As a positive object is admitted to be different from another positive one so it should be taken to be other than a negative fact with which it is associated. Now, let us see how its distinction can be maintained. If the mutual difference of the so-called negative facts is intrinsic, i.e., self-evident, then why will not the positive objects be so ? Have the positive objects committed any difference ? If difference, in all cases, is uniformly extrinsic then how is such an assumption tenable ?

If it is held that negation is different from a positive object because of its association with a positive object and a positive object is different from negation because of its association with negation then such an assumption involves the fallacy of mutual dependence. If it is assumed that every object, both positive and negative, is different from another object because of its association with another external negation then the fallacy of regressus ad infinitum will surely vitiate such an assumption since an unending series of differences is to be assumed in order to establish a single case of difference. Negation has its own innate character, viz., negativity. But it is common to all negative facts. Hence, it cannot constitute the differentia which distinguishes an individual negation from another. The distinction of one individual negation from another is due to the positive object negated by each individual negation. The objects which are negated by negation are positive. As they differ from one another so their corresponding negations mutually differ. From the above finding of facts it is reasonable to hold that the positive objects constitute the mark of distinction of the negative individuals but not the reverse.

Hence, it will be unwise to assume the hypothesis of a negative real since the apprehension of colossal chaos arising from it haunts us.

If negation has no objective existence then what is the meaning of the negative particle 'mā' ? There is no truth behind the hypothesis that every word has a real meaning.

We are the Buddhists who have earned name and fame in every circle of thinkers. We are expert in establishing the thesis that words have also imaginary meaning.

In some cases, a negative term, framed by attaching a negative particle to a term, presents to our consciousness an idea of a contrary object. When a negative particle is connected with a verb these two being together suggest to our mind an idea of the mere cessation of the action denoted by the verb.

Very well, let us accept the above Buddhist hypothesis. Now, a question is put to the Buddhists that if the Buddhists discard the hypothesis of negation then what purpose will be served by the elevenfold division of non-perception the only source of the awareness of negation ?

Eleven-fold division of Non-perception

1. Non-perception of the thing-in-itself :—There is no jar on this spot because no jar is perceived.

2. Non-perception of the cause of the object negated :—Here is no smoke because no fire is perceived here.

3. Non-perception of the pervader of the object negated :—Here is no touch of the cold because no water is perceived here.

4. Non-perception of the effect of the object negated :—Here is no fire the causal efficiency of which is not counteracted because smoke, the effect of fire, is not perceived.

5. Perception of the contrary of the object negated :—Here is no cold touch because fire which excludes cold touch is perceived here.

6. Perception of the effect of the contrary of the object negated :—Here is no cold touch because smoke which is the effect of fire that excludes cold touch is perceived here.

7. Perception of the pervaded of the contradictory of the object negated :—The destruction of a positive effect is not uncertain because it does not depend upon a factor other than the condition of its being for its destruction. Such non-dependence on the invariable mark of certainty is contradictorily opposed to uncertainty. Seeing the mark of certainty we frame the negative judgment of a positive object—an event that it is not uncertain.

8. Perception of the contradictory of the effect of the object negated :—Here is no source of cold touch because fire is perceived here.

9. Perception of the contradictory of the pervader of the object negated :—Here is no touch of snow because fire is perceived here.

10. Perception of the contradictory of the cause of the object negated :—Here is no horripilation, no grinding of teeth, because fire is perceived here.

11. Perception of the effect of the contradictory of the cause of the object negated :—There is no such person, on this place, as has the grinding of teeth, etc., because smoke is perceived here.

It is a truism that there are eleven types of non-perception. Non-perception is the source of a negative proposition but not that of objectively real negation. Now, the following question arises in our mind. Non-perception is that type of probans which is not different from the probandum. Such a non-difference of the probans from the probandum is admitted by the Buddhists themselves. The negative judgment or the negative proposition that there is no such-and-such object, being the probandum, non-perception, the probans, should be different from it. How can non-perception be the probans in this case? The Buddhists say in reply that there is much truth in this question, but the contender misses the inner significance of the Buddhist theory. Non-perception does not actually lead on to the actual negative proposition but to the potentiality of doing so. This potentiality is not different from non-perception. Hence non-perception is such a probans as is non-different from the probandum to be established.

Now, a fresh question arises in our mind. Potentiality, mentioned above, is a positive state but non-perception is a negative fact. How is it that they are identical ? The Buddhists give a reply to this question in the following manner. Those who know the real character of non-perception explain it thus. Non-perception is not a negative fact. It is not contradictorily opposed to perception. It is contrary to perception. It signifies the awareness of an object which is other than what is expected to be perceived. Such an awareness is denoted by non-perception. Thus the hypothesis that non-perception is the source of a negative judgment is also not open to the possible charge that if a negative fact presupposes non-perception as its source of knowledge then non-perception, being itself negative, should also presuppose another non-perception and so on ad infinitum. But non-perception of the Buddhist school, being an awareness of a positive object, presupposes no other awareness as it is self-luminous. Now, another question arises in our mind. If non-perception is the source of a negative proposition then can we frame, on the strength of non-perception, a negative proposition like this that a supersensuous object does not exist ? The Buddhists meet this objection in the following manner. They hold that the subject of a negative proposition is always a perceptible object. If a perceptible object which is expected to be perceived somewhere is not perceived but some other object is perceived then non-perception leads on to a negative proposition. We should also bear in mind that the subject of this negative proposition cannot but be a perceptible object. Hence we cannot, at our sweet will, frame a negative proposition which refers to any and every object without restriction.

In the Buddhist system the objects such as a jar, etc., that have been seen before are definitely known to be visible. If they are not perceived somewhere then they are referred to be negative judgments. The objects which lie always beyond the ken of our knowledge such as the sky-flower are never referred to by a negative judgment since they being not ascertained as visible objects non-perception does not precede it (the negative judgment in question) as its condition. But there is an exception to this rule. The negative judgment that Caitra is not a demon does not presuppose non-perception of a visible object as its condition. The reason behind the above statement is that Caitra is immediately known to be other than a demon. It is a fact that Caitra is perceived. Hence, he is not a supersensuous object by the logical necessity of the law of contradiction. Thus, the above negative judgment does not presuppose non-perception of the visible object as its antecedent condition. In other words, it is immaterial to enquire whether the demon in question is visible. In fine, the Buddhists arrive at this conclusion that the hypothesis that negation is objectively real is not tenable since a negative judgment or proposition is explained by non-perception as its condition.

The Establishment of the hypothesis that Negation is real

A refutation of the Buddhist thesis is as follows. There are two types of judgment, viz., positive and negative. Every body's experience bears evidence to their existence. They are illustrated by two examples, viz. there is a jar on this spot and there is no jar on this spot. The Buddhists are divided in their opinion as to the content of a negative judgment. Some of them hold that a negative judgment does not point to a peculiar object but is a mere construction of imagination. Others hold that it refers to an individual phenomenon of consciousness. (In other words, it is an empty form which is not determined by a real object but is constructed only by imagination. Or, it is a projection of consciousness which appears as an external negative fact.) These two statements about a negative judgment make no difference between a negative judgment and a positive one. Thus both of them should be either equally valid or invalid. By an arbitrary exercise of will they hold that a positive judgment is true but a negative one is false. Now, if both of them stand on the same platform then the peculiar object of a negative judgment should be thought out. The Buddhists hold that the non-perception of a jar is nothing but the awareness of a spot devoid of a jar. Such a statement is absolutely unreasonable. Let us examine the nature of the state of being devoid of a jar. Is it identical with the surface of the spot or not ? If it is identical then the spot, containing a jar, should also be referred to by the negative judgment that there is no jar on this spot since the surface of the spot remains the same whether it contains a jar or not. If the above state is different from the spot then it is really a negative fact but expressed only in a different language. Thus the contest is merely nominal but not real.

The Buddhists will not surely make a profit if they try to understand the state of being devoid in terms of a jar. Is it identical with a jar or different from it ? If the first one is accepted then it is a jar. If the second one is accepted then it is the negation of a jar.

The Naiyāyikas now quote the very example for the negative judgment which has been cited by the Buddhists. The judgment in question is that a jar does not exist here. The Buddhists hold that it refers to a spot devoid of a jar. The Naiyāyikas point out that the term 'here' which is one of constituents of the above judgment refers to a spot. They agree with the Buddhists in the point. The term 'here' of the positive judgment that a jar exists here similarly refers to a spot. Such a reference is admitted by all. The remaining portion of the here spot is not a vacuum since a necessary reference to some additional object makes it significant. The additional object may be called the state of being devoid of a jar or the negation of a jar. But the difference in name does not make distinction in the nature of the object referred to. But the Buddhists may contend that the portion of a negative judgment that a jar does not exist is only a construction of imagination. Such a contention is not tenable. The Buddhists hold that a negative judgment follows an indeterminate perception in quick succession like a determinate perception and they should admit that the negative judgment must share the same fate with the positive one.

All positive judgments which are constructed by imagination are based upon sense-perception. But a negative judgment should not be based upon sense-perception. The Naiyāyikas contend that no judgments which are constructed by imagination are true. Thus, the positive judgments do also turn out to be untrue. Now, the Buddhist may solve this difficulty thus :— the determinate perception of positive object is true since it closely follows a sense-perception (i.e. the indeterminate perception of the Nyāya school). But such a solution is not convincing since negative judgments, being also based upon the true positive judgments, cannot be true.

Now, the Buddhists may contend that the positive judgments are called as true because they are conducive to the attainment of a real object. If this is the purport of their contention then it may be pointed out that the negative ones are also true since they likewise lead to a real object. A question may be asked by them. What is the real object to be attained by means of a negative judgment ? A counter-question is put to them. What is the real object to be acquired by a positive judgment ? They may answer that it is 'blue'. We also give them the same reply that a similar object is also got at by means of a negative judgment. Whenever we come to by the object 'blue' it is obtained other than yellow, etc., which is subsumed under non-blue. As 'blue' with this characterization is obtained so it is not unreasonable to hold that the negation of yellow, etc., is also obtained. If it is not admitted then the attainment of blue cannot also be explained since it is impossible to think of 'blue' without the above characterization. You have already assumed in the chapter on definition that an object contains an exclusion from its other. You cannot retract now.

Happiness or sorrow arises in the absence of a foe or of a friend. A man places his feet on the way seeing the absence of thorn on it. A man is earnest to search for the material of a jar if he finds that no jar has come into being. A man refrains from taking medicine when he realises that he is free from disease. No thoughtful man can deny objective existence to negation having noticed that it actually exists and many worldly transactions are based upon it.

The Buddhists raise the following objection to the solution already enumerated. The object of an awareness is one of its conditions. Negation is absolutely devoid of all characteristic features. Hence it is not competent to produce awareness. How can it be an object of awareness ? This objection is not tenable. From the Buddhist position no real object which produces awareness is revealed by it since if it endures two or three points of time the doctrine of the universal flux falls down. The reason of the negative criticism is as follows. The so-called condition of awareness at first comes into being, then produces awareness and afterwards is revealed by its effect-awareness. These three events cannot simultaneously take place. Hence, the Buddhists should arrive at the conclusion that even a positive real which is revealed by apprehension does not produce it, not to speak of a negative fact. Later on, the Buddhist thesis that a real object imparts its form to consciousness will be refuted. In order to be consistent, the Buddhists should hold that positive and negative facts do not alike produce their awareness. But the Naiyāyikas point out that the Buddhist should admit that both the positive and negative facts should be defined as devoid of all characteristic features but it is pity that the Buddhists hold that the object of negative awareness is devoid of characteristic feature. A positive object is that which is the object of positive awareness but a negative one is that which is the object of negative awareness. Hence it has been stated in the Nyāya-bhāṣya that there are two kinds of Reality, viz., positive and negative. The Buddhists raise an objection to the above thesis of the Naiyāyikas that if a negative real produces awareness like a positive one then the line of distinction which separates a positive real from a negative one is sure to break down. What a deep insight of the fools ! Every body will admit that the positive awareness is different from the negative one. But how is it that objects, viz., positive and negative reals, revealed by these two types of awareness, do not differ in their mutual character ?

Moreover, oh fool ! you are to explain why does 'colour' differ from 'taste' though they alike produce the same effect viz., consciousness ? If you hold that difference in the character of awareness accounts for diversity in the nature of their objects then the character of the positive and negative reals should also be essentially different though they are endowed with the same causal efficiency since they generate dissimilar awareness. The Buddhists also admit that no difference in the nature of experience without assuming diversity in the character of its objects is explained.

According to the Buddhists true knowledge reveals a real object. It admits of two types. They point to the two distinct kinds of objects since they are mutually different and one and the same object cannot be revealed by each of them.

From the above conclusion it follows that the difference in the character of knowledge accounts for the distinction in the character of its object. A positive real is the object of a positive awareness and a negative one is that of a negative judgment. The existence of positive and negative awareness can in no way be gainsaid. Hence, they point to the existence of positive and negative reals. This is the corollary of the above finding. It should also be admitted by the Buddhists. But the Buddhists hold that negation is a mental construction. In that case, they should be thorough and consistent subjective Idealists. It is not proper for them to embrace half-hearted Idealism. It has been already proved that a negative real has practical efficiency, i.e., it is productive of some effect. A negative real produces at least its awareness. Hence, its power of production cannot be denied. But it is also a truism that a negative real cannot yield such result as a positive real does. In this connection, it should be noted that a positive real fails to do what another such real does. Hence the distinction in the nature of result does not take away the reality from a negative fact. The Buddhists cannot sacrifice a negative real at the altar of practical efficiency. Our direct knowledge contradicts such an attempt. The vain cry of the Buddhists merely dries up their throat.

The Buddhists have denied existence to negation on the ground that there is no possibility of any relation between negation and its locus. The possible relation of the qualifying to the qualified presupposes another relation as its basis. As the basic relation is impossible so the relation of the qualifying to the qualified cannot unite negation with its locus. The presupposition of a basic relation holds good only in case of a positive real. This rule does not apply to the case of a negative real.

Hence, the Buddhist criticism has no force behind it. The above law does not also apply to positive reals as well. We do not find that whenever an object is related to another object the former inevitably qualifies the latter. When a man presses a stick under his feet or carries it on his hand he is not cognized as possessed of a stick (daṇḍin). There is also no such law as shows that whatever qualifies an object is related to it by another relation. The relation of inherence qualifies its relata but is not related to them by an ab-extra relation. The relation of the qualifying to the qualified like the relation of universal concomitance or like that of a word to its meaning is a relation sui generis, i.e., a class by itself. It presupposes no other relation to unite its relata. The very source of this distinct relation is our experience. The adjective and the noun may change their mutual functions. Hence a noun may be sometimes cognized as an adjective and vice-versa. This syntactic relation may be reshaped by the will of a person. If a corresponding change by awareness takes place, awareness is not to blame. Hence, negation is connected with its locus such as the spot, etc, by means of the relation of the qualifying to the qualified. The sáme relation holds between time and the positive objects which are events in time. A verb, e.g., 'to go' in the active voice or a verb. e.g., 'to break' in the passive voice, used in the present tense is related to time by means of the same relation. (In other words, the sentence, "Rāma goes", purports to convey that the specific action, located upon Rāma, the subject, belongs to the present time and qualifies it. The sentences "The bread is divided into two pieces" imports that the resulting act of division, located upon the object, the bread, belongs to the present time and qualifies it. A relation other than that of the qualifying to the qualified does not hold between time and action as noted above. An action does not require the help of any other relation to relate itself with time). Similarly, the relation of the qualifying to the qualified holds between negation and its locus.

But the only relation which subsists between negation and the object negated is that of opposition or incompatibility. The relation of opposition or incompatibility signifies that the two relata are incoordinate, i.e., they cannot simultaneously occupy the same locus. The specific relation being fixed between negation and the object negated, the possible objection that on the destruction of a particular jar the universal destruction of all jars would emerge does not affect the Nyāya position. The destruction of a particular jar is only opposed to that particular jar but not to all jars. The Buddhists have goaded the Naiyāyikas with the two horns of a dilemma whether negation emerges or not, (i.e. is eternal). The Naiyāyikas meet it with the following reply: "Negation does not emerge" is the assumption of the Nyāya school. Moreover, even if it is admitted that negation emerges then it is not to be admitted that it is non different from a positive real since the positive facts themselves, viz., colour, taste, etc., which come into being are mutually different. Our experience bears convincing evidence to their mutual difference. The causal relation which holds between the condition of negation and negation is established by the joint method of agreement and difference. The emergence and the destruction of a jar depend upon their respective conditions. A jar depends upon a lump of earth, a stick etc. for its appearance. Similarly, it depends upon a mace and such other objects for its destruction. If somebody holds that a mace and such other instruments do not destroy a jar but produce a series of dissimilar objects then he must admit that the power of producing a series of similar objects has been negated. Otherwise, when the conditions like a mace, etc., assemble, a series of similar objects should have come into being along with the series of dissimilar objects. It may be further contended that a jar has the capacity for producing both the series of similar and dissimilar objects. Such a contention is not tenable. If a jar itself is sufficiently strong to bring about such effects then it should produce pot-sherds (broken pieces of a jar) in the absence of its contact with a mace, etc., and should also produce a series of jars in spite of such contact with a mace, etc. There should be no reign of law in the matter of production of its effects. Moreover, if the dissimilar objects owe their existence only to the intrinsic power of a jar then the conditions such as a mace, etc., will have no contribution towards the production of effects by a jar. The assumption of such conditions will be simply gratuitous. If the dissimilar effects are generated by the instrinsic power of a jar then the conditions such as a mace, etc., have no part to play. If it is beyond the power of a jar to produce such effects then the condition can offer no assistance to a jar to produce such effects.

If the stroke of a mace terminates the series of similar transitory jars and a series of another kind of momentary effects comes into being then what has happened to a jar so that it is not presented to our consciousness as before.

The contender may hold that a jar does not exist. The rejoinder is that this admission amounts to the acceptance of the thesis that negation is objectively real. In that case, the Buddhists indulge in verbal jugglery for nothing. They use the word abhavana whereas the Naiyāyikas use the word 'abhāva'. The word 'abhāva' is formed by the suffix 'ghañ' attached to the root 'bhū' prefixed by the indeclinable 'nañ'. But the word 'abhavana', is formed by the suffix 'lyuṭ' attached to the root, 'bhū' prefixed by the same indeclinable. Has the suffix 'ghañ' committed any offence against you ? Has the suffix 'lyuṭ' rendered some service to you ? The Buddhists admit that there is 'abhavana' of a jar but there is no 'abhāva' of a jar.

The Buddhists may contend that when the conditions such as a mace, etc., assemble, the jar in question does not acquire some new positive character but it simply ceases to exist in the next moment.

Such a contention is not tenable. The statement that the transitory jar does not exist in the next moment signifies that the negation of a jar exists. The Buddhists may further contend that they have stated that it is not. But they have not stated that the negation of a jar is. Such a contention does not hold good. The pronoun saḥ (ii) and the indeclinable 'na' (not) have two distinct meanings and produce two pieces of awareness of the two different objects. The awareness which corresponds to the pronoun 'saḥ' has for its object 'the jar', recalled in memory. The awareness which corresponds to the indeclinable 'na' has for its object 'negation'. We shall not waste our time in criticising the roundabout statement of a vain scholar.

Thus, the conclusion which follows from the previous discussions is that negation is a distinct type of knowable reality. The Buddhist thesis that negation is not objectively real but non-perception alone accounts for a negative proposition.

Moreover, non-perception cannot be comprised within svabhāva-inference, i.e., (it cannot illustrate that form of syllogism in which the middle term is non-distinct from the major term). The Mīmāṁsakas hold that negation is objectively real and non-perception is a distinct proof.

The non-perception of a cause, etc., may serve the purpose of a mark which leads to the inferential knowledge of negation. But the non-perception of a perceptible thing-in-itself is one of the conditions of the perception of negation.

There are eleven ladies in the shape of all kinds of non-perception in the harem of a section of the Buddhist Logic. One of them is negative proposition of an object which is generated by the perception of another object that is pervaded by the contradictory negation of the object itself in question. The destruction of a positive object which is an effect is not uncertain because it does not depend upon a factor other than its condition for its destruction. The destruction of an object which is dependent upon such a factor is uncertain. The state of being is more extensive than its mark, viz., non-dependence upon some other factors. Hence the knowledge of the non-dependence of an object upon some other factors leads to the negative proposition that it is not uncertain. This illustration of non-perception has been subjected to partial criticism. Its detailed criticism will be given in connection with the refutation of the doctrine of universal flux.

The sound logicians of the Mīmāṁsā school (the Prabhākaras) have denied objective reality to negation. Of this act of foolishness on their part we feel ashamed.

They hold that a jar is not perceived but its negation is cognized. The implication of such statement is that perception and non-perception respectively constitute the criterion of the objective reality or that of the unreality of an object. Such a view is not tenable. The positive or the negative character of an object is respectively determined by its perception or non-perception. But its perception or non-perception does not respectively amount to its reality or unreality.

We cannot perceive water hidden beneath earth. The non-perception of water, in this case, does not lead to the negative proposition that water does not exist.

Similarly, mere non-perception does not lead to all sorts of negative propositions. We think that the non-perception of hidden water is in no way different from that of the sky-flower and a demon.

The Refutation of the hostile views of the Prabhākaras

The Prabhākaras may contend that there exists a sharp distinction between universal and conditional non-perception. The non-perception of hidden water is conditional. The absolute non-perception leads to a negative proposition.

The sky-flower is never perceived. The demon is also never perceived. Still, the sky-flower and the demon do not stand on the same level of metaphysical existence. A demon may exist. The possibility of its existence is assured by the scriptures and inference.

The Prabhākaras hold that there is a temporary non-perception but its real non-perception consists of repeated non-perception. Such a thesis is merely an idle talk. By means of the specified non-perception, i.e., the non-perception of a visible object the negation of an object is determined. But it is not a fact that its non-perception is only determined.

If the Prabhākaras deny objective existence to negation then all the positive objects which are negated by their corresponding negations would be eternal since they do not subscribe to the hypothesis that they are transitory.

Now a question may be put to the Prabhākaras. What is the effect of a mace, etc., which acts upon a jar ? If they give a reply to it that the effect in question is a series of pot-sherds then the jar should exist and discharge its function since it is not destroyed.

The Prabhākaras may contend that it does not do so because it is not perceived.

Why is not this endurable and perceptible object perceived though all the conditions of its perception, viz., the sense-organ etc. assemble ? The real answer will be that it is not perceived because it does not exist.

The Prabhākaras should also hold that a negative judgment is self-luminous and cannot exist without having an objective reference since it is a judgment like all other positive judgments. (The implication of it is that negation is objectively real).

The Buddhists hold that the meanings of words are conceptual but are not real. But the Prabhākaras do not subscribe to this view. According to them the meaning of a word is real. What is the meaning of the indeclinable 'nañ' (not)? (Hence the reality of negation cannot but be admitted).

The Prabhākaras have discarded the time-honoured hypothesis that negation is objectively real. But some concession has been given to it since they cannot do without admitting it in some form. They have neglected the import of the commentary of Śabara. Wonderful is their skill in the art of interpretation! They interpret Śabara but they are indifferent to his spirit.

Enough of criticism. Further wordy battle does not behove us. Small men like us should pardon the mistakes of the great ones.

In fine, negation is referred to by a negative judgment which is expressed by the negative proposition containing the particle 'not'. This hypothesis has been established.

The Classification of the Negation

Negation admits of two types, viz., (1) Prāgabhāva (the negation of an object prior to its appearance—pre-negation), and Pradhvaṁsa abhāva (the destruction of the created object—post-negation). Some other logicians hold that the division of negation is fourfold, viz., prāgabhāva (pre-negation), Pradhvaṁsābhāva (post-negation), itaretarābhāva (mutual negation) and atyantābhāva (absolute negation). Another sect of logicians holds that it is divided into six classes, viz., the above four kinds with the addition of the two more types, viz. sāmarthyābhāva (the negation of capacity) and apekṣābhāva (the negation of an object confined to a limited space).

A detailed discussion about the definition and the character of the different types of negation is as follows:

The non-existence of an object before its coming into being is called prāgabhāva. The cessation of the essence of an object which has come into being is designated as pradhvaṁsa.

The other types of negation are not essentially different from prāgabhāva. Prāgabhāva in the shape of the non-appearance of an object belonging to the other objects which delimit the sphere of its appearance is called anyonyābhāva. When it transcends all limitations imposed upon, it becomes atyantābhāva. When it is restricted to a limited sphere, it acquires the designation of apekṣābhāva. If an object loses its capacity already belonging to it then sāmarthyābhāva is no better than pradhvaṁsa. If it denotes the negation of non-existent capacity, i.e., future capacity then it is not different from prāgabhāva.

The destruction of an object which has come into being and the non-appearance of such an object constitute the two natural divisions of negation. The other divisions of negation are merely artificial. The negative fact is a distinct kind of object of knowledge—a class by itself. It has been also established that it is perceived by our sense-organs. The hypothesis of the sage Akṣapāda that there are four kinds of proof is also sound.

The Refutation of the Hypothesis of Probability and Rumour

The thesis of the Naiyāyikas that there are only four kinds of proof has not as yet been proved since there are two more distinct types of proof. One of them is sambhava (probability). It means the knowledge of a part included in a whole by means of the knowledge of the whole itself. If the weight of an object is a Khārī then it is highly probable that its weight is a droṇa (Khārī included several droṇas in itself). If there are a thousand persons in the crowd then it is highly probable that there are a hundred persons in it (the number 'thousand' includes the number 'hundred' in itself). A series of rumours, the author of which has not been traced out, is called aitihya. The popular saying that there lives a Yakṣa (a semidivine being on this banian tree illustrates it. Such a saying is not an example of verbal testimony since the source of the above saying has not been found out and verified to be a trustworthy person. Such a contention is not sound.

The above mentioned 'sambhava' (probability) is not different from inferential knowledge. The probable knowledge of 'droṇa' on the basis of the knowledge of khārī is really a deduction which follows from an induction. (Where there is khārī there is a droṇa; Here is khārī. Therefore here is droṇa). But a rumour is not reliable, i.e. untrue. Who knows whether a Yakṣa lives on a banian tree or not? Has any person ever seen the exact features of the body of a Yakṣa? If the rumour is true then it is not different from verbal testimony since it is as good as a sound advice (upadeśa). We shall show in the subsequent section that the term 'āpta' is an adjective of upadeśa having the same inflexion if we expound the compound word in the sūtra Sāptopadeśaḥ.

The clever dialectician of the Cārvāka school (most probably Jayarāśi Bhaṭṭa—vide Tattvopaplava Siṁha p. 1) has proposed to expound the truth with the words "After Bṛihaspati we shall explain the truth in order to vindicate our views". But what he has actually done is this that neither proof nor reality (the object of true knowledge) can be defined and that their number cannot be fixed up. This is his exposition of the truth. In order to establish his point that the number of proof cannot be fixed up he has shown that there are some other forms of valid knowledge which are not based upon perception, etc. (Jayarāśi simply banks upon negative criticism but has no solid ground to stand upon. So Jayanta ironically remarks that he has other forms of knowledge which do not owe their existence to the known and accepted sources of knowledge).

The character of the other forms of true knowledge has been humorously described by means of a simile.

In nocturnal darkness a man with his eyes shut up knows whether the hand has its fingers contracted or extended. In order to establish his point he holds that this piece of knowledge is not produced by the touch-organ since his touch-organ is not pervasive and does not belong to his hand. But on the other hand, he illustrates cases which establish that perception and inference are the sources of true knowledge. At night the flame of a lamp is known to us from a distance by means of its rays diffused on all sides.

A person infers the existence of a cluster of lotuses, shaken by the breeze, by means of its fragrance carried to a great distance if he stands on a spot towards which the breeze laden with fragrance blows from the bed of lotuses.

The poor materialist logician does not know the character of perception and of inference but is adept in imagining almost such wild form of knowledge as has been shown above. We perceive the fingers as contracted by means of touch since the touch-organ is not incompetent to grasp, being itself pervasive. When persons drink iced water which reaches the farthest end of the alimentary canal (i.e. navel) they feel the cold touch of iced water all along inside the canal.

As we perceive conjunction by means of the touch-organ so we perceive the negation of it by means of the same organ. If we perceive a particular motion of fingers, i.e., contraction by means of a particular sense-organ (tactile organ) then we can also perceive the negation of contraction by means of the same organ.

The knowledge of a lotus by means of the smelling of its fragrance and the knowledge of the distant flame by means of the perception of its rays are instances of inference which presupposes the previous knowledge of the invariable mark as its antecedent condition. Is there any kind of knowledge which does not depend upon the four types of knowledge mentioned before? The Cārvākas have tried in vain to establish that the number of the sources of valid knowledge cannot be fixed up since they have failed to realise the nice shades of distinction existing among the four kinds of proof and their efficacy.

We confidently assert that the number of the kinds of true knowledge is strictly definite but not indefinite. Similarly, the definition, number etc. of the different kinds of objects of true knowledge are also definite and rigidly obey the logical discipline. The goal of the Cārvāka logic is that nothing can be conclusively said either of the objects or of their proofs. Their declaration of such a logical goal before the sound critics will simply bear evidence to the paucity of their intellect.

ĀHNIKA II

The Definition of Perception

The definition and the division of a means of proof have been thoroughly discussed. Now, the occasion of defining the species turns up. The author of Nyāya-sūtra selects at the out-set, perception for definition since it constitutes the foundation of all other sources of valid knowledge, being mentioned first.

Nyāya-sūtra on Perception

His definition of perception is as follows :—Perception is such consciousness as arises from the contact of a sense-organ with an object, has not the name of an object as its object (i.e. is not verbalised experience), is not an error (accords with its object) and is determinate. The term 'perception' (pratyakṣa) signifies the object to be defined. The remaining terms of the sūtra constitute the definition of perception. The aim of a definition is to distinguish it from similar forms of consciousness and dissimilar knowable objects. The similar forms of consciousness are inference and other sources of valid knowledge since they come under the same genus. The knowable objects are dissimilar since they are not subsumed under the same genus. Such an exact definition has been proposed by the above sūtra (aphorism).

A preliminary objection has been raised by some critics. They put this question to the Naiyāyikas whether the adjectival clauses such as 'as arises from the contact of a sense-organ with an object' etc. apply to the means of knowledge itself or to the assemblage of conditions of perception or to the resultant consciousness attained by the source of knowledge viz., perception. If the means of perceptual awareness is predicated by these clauses then the above sūtra signifies that consciousness, thus qualified by these adjectives, is perception, the means of knowledge. Now, if perception, the means of knowledge, is only specified that the adjectives mentioned above do not qualify the resultant-consciousness then the above definition of perception should be both too wide and too narrow. Let us see how it turns out to be too narrow. The cases of direct awareness which are really free from blemishes but are not qualified by the above adjectives cannot be recognized as perception. The sense-organ and other such inanimate conditions which produce true perceptual knowledge and rightly deserve the title of perception cannot be the means of knowledge since the above adjectives are not applicable to them. Let us also see how the above definition is too wide. If the perceptual awareness which is qualified by the above mentioned adjectives, does not generate a further resultant-awareness then the former instance of awareness will be called a means of knowledge. Moreover, if an instance of direct awareness, qualified by the above adjectives, produces either an impression or recollection or a doubt or an illusion will be entitled to the designation of a means of knowledge since the result to be produced by it has not been specified. Now, if the defender of Gautama contends that the adjectives which qualify the means of knowledge also qualify the result of it then he should postulate a new sūtra since such a sūtra does not find a place among the sūtras of Gautama. The above sūtra still remains open to the charge of being too narrow in spite of the proposed improvement. Therefore, the hypothesis that the above adjectives qualify perception, the means of knowledge is not tenable.

The second alternative hypothesis that the above adjectives qualify the collocation of all conditions of perceptual awareness—the result, is not tenable. If one subscribes to the second hypothesis then he should change the sense of compound word 'indriya-artha-sannikarṣa-utpannam' (arising from the sense object-contact) into that of the compound word indriya-artha-sannikarṣa-upapannam (the list of conditions being made complete by the inclusion of sense-organs, objects and their contacts in it). The compound words such as avyapadeśyam, avyabhicāri and vyavasāyātmakam and the term 'jñānam' should not be used in the primary sense of the words but should be used in the secondary sense. They should secondarily point to their conditions which bring about such consciousness as is signified by them (the above words). The upholder of the hypothesis will have to twist these terms in order to obtain such meaning as will suit their purpose. Such an attempt represents for nothing a laborious process. The third alternative hypothesis that the above adjectives qualify the resultant perceptual consciousness does not hold good. If the above sūtra represents both the means of perception and the result produced by it then the very construction of the constituent words of the sūtra indicates that there should be perfect co-ordination between the means of knowledge and its result. From the context it is evident that the sūtra intends to define the means of direct awareness. Such a means has also been described as an instrument. Consciousness which is produced by such an instrument is its result. How can there be co-ordination between an instrument and its result ? (Co-ordination implies the numerical identity between an instrument and its result). For the reasons noted above the above three alternative hypotheses are not sound. Moreover, it is also impossible to conjecture a new alternative suggestion which may satisfactorily interpret the sūtra. In fine, the drift of the objection is that the sūtra which defines perception is not tenable.

A reply to the above objection is as follows. It is a truism that the first two alternative hypotheses are open to the charges mentioned above. But we approve of the last one. It has also been pointed out that this one is not immune from the charge of the incoordination between the instrument and its result. This charge will be avoided by the insertion of the word 'yataḥ' (whence). The boiled down meaning of the above sūtra amounts to this that perception, the means of direct awareness, is that which is the source of such consciousness as has been specified by the above mentioned adjectives. Thus, the definition of perception is neither too wide nor too narrow. Moreover, we are not to twist the words of the sūtra to make out the real sense of it. By the mere insertion of the word 'yataḥ' every word of the sūtra becomes significant and all the words which constitute the sūtra convert it into an ideal definition of perception. Now, a question arises in our mind that in the original form of the sūtra the terms 'pratyakṣa (perception) and jñāna signify the same object but in the new form of it why are they (the two terms) not allowed to co-ordinate ? What is the purport of inserting 'yataḥ' into the sūtra ? An answer to this question is as follows. An instrument plays the part of the means of knowledge and consciousness resulting from the operation of that instrument is the result and that the instrument and its result are neither identical (i.e. they are distinct), nor refer to the same object. The net result of our discussion is this :—If the collocation of the conditions of perceptual consciousness is the instrument i.e. the means of awareness then consciousness described by the sūtra is the result. If, again, consciousness, thus specified, is the means of awareness then the subsequent judgment that the object of perception is either acceptable or avoidable or indifferent to us is the result.

How does the sense-perception which owes its existence to sense-object-contact bring about the resultant judgment that the object perceived is avoidable etc. by means of its operation since many discrete mental phenomena such as judgment of memory etc. intervene between the sense-perception, the means of awareness and the resultant judgment ? Let us substantiate our point. A man perceives an object, viz., a wood apple. Then he remembers that it is conducive to pleasure in the form that a similar object (an object belonging to its class) gave him pleasure in the past. Then he recollects his previous generalisation that all wood-apples are conducive to pleasure and applies it to the new object. The particular form of the application of generalisation is that this object belongs to the class of wood-apples which are conducive to pleasure. Having applied the above generalisation to the particular case he arrives at the definite conclusion that it (the object of perception) is conducive to pleasure. Then the resultant judgment that it is worth-having (acceptable) comes into being. The form of the judgment is that as this particular object which belongs to the class of wood-apples is conducive to pleasure so it is worthy of being accepted. In the meantime the initial perceptual judgment which arises from the sense-object-contact is long past but even its faint trace does not survive. How can we accept the hypothesis that a sense-perception plays the part of an instrumental cause to bring about the remote final judgment that the object of such sense-perception is worth having.

The view of Ācārya (Uddyotakara)

A great teacher of the Nyāya school holds a different view

on this point. He remarks, "Oh critics ! your criticism of the above view is sensible. The successive order of different judgments which follow in the wake of perception is really such as you have pointed out. We do not also hold that the initial perceptual judgment is the instrumental cause of the final judgment that the object of perception worth-having or otherwise etc". He now expresses his own view along with the negative criticism of the earlier one. The initial perception of an object owes its existence to the sense-object-contact. In this case, the collocation of its object, the particular sense-organ, their contact etc. is the means of the direct awareness of the object. This awareness is a mere result but not a means to a further valid knowledge. As it only begets memory so it is not a source of valid knowledge since memory is not a piece of valid knowledge. The initial perception revives the recollection of the induction that all such objects are conducive to pleasure. Though this memory-judgment which follows in the wake of the initial perception is not produced by a means of perceptual knowledge yet it may play the part of a means of perceptual knowledge. The above memory-judgment is followed by another judgment that the object which is being perceived belongs to the class of wood-apples which are conducive to pleasure like the wood-apple perceived before. This judgment owes its origin to the operation of the sense-organ assisted by the preceding memory-judgment This judgment is itself perceptual. But it is a source of inferential knowledge like the perception of smoke. As we infer fire which remains beyond the reach of our sense-organ so we infer that the particular object is conducive to pleasure on the basis of the above judgment. It is a truism that we do not subscribe to the hypothesis that an object possesses super-sensuous poser. But still we hold that the assemblage of conditions visible and invisible renders itself supersensuous. The so-called power is nothing but the assemblage of conditions. In this particular case, the collocation of conditions is beyond the reach of our sense-organs. Hence, the judgment that this object which belongs to the class of wood-apples is conducive to pleasure is inferential like the judgment that the hill is fiery since this judgment is brought about by the knowledge of its unfailing mark. Though the judgment that the wood apple is conducive to pleasure is deduced from the premises yet it in co-operation with the object in question, the sense-organ, the contact etc. produces the perceptual judgment that this is acceptable. The preceding judgment in itself is mediate, is a source of an immediate awareness by virtue of its association. The Author of Nyāya-bhāṣya, holding all these complicated processes before his mind, has remarked that if a judgment plays the part of an intermediate process then the judgment that an object is either worth-accepting or worth-rejecting or indifferent is the result of the means of perceptual knowledge.

Objection to the place of Parāmarśa Judgment in the Definition of Perception

Some interpreters of Nyāya-bhāṣya subscribe to a different view. They hold that judgments which arise in our mind one after another do not obey the above order. It is a fact that the initial perceptual judgment revives the memory of the induction that all wood-apples are conducive to pleasure. The phenomenon of memory is the cause of destruction of its condition, i.e., the initial perception. The very môment when the initial perception passes away it is followed by the judgment that the wood-apple just now sensed, is conducive to pleasure. This judgment is equivalent to the judgment that the wood-apple is worth-having. These two judgments are not mutually different from each other. The judgment which applies induction to a particular object, i.e., the minor term does not intervene between the judgment of memory and the final judgment. What is the good of assuming a judgment which is not introspected ? But it is contended that the judgment involving the application of induction to a particular case is introspected but is not a mere article of conjecture. In case of an inference the minor premise that the hill is smoky is immediately followed by the major premise 'what is smoky is fiery'. It is a memory judgment which owes its revival to the minor premise. Then a synthetic judgment appears in the mind of the person who infers. It assumes the form 'thus this is', the minor term contains the middle term which is an invariable concomitant of the major term. If this intermediate judgment had not appeared then the minor premise could not have effectuated deduction since it operates only to revive the memory of the major premise. What revives memory only cannot be admitted to be a source of valid knowledge. The memory judgment may be followed by the awareness of the major term but this awareness cannot assume the form that the hill is fiery, i.e. (the minor term accompanies the major term) since this judgment refers to a new element, viz., the relation of the minor term with the major term—not experienced before and this new element cannot be supplied by the memory judgment which simply repeats the old story. Moreover, those who deny existence to the judgment involving the application of induction to a particular case cannot explain the premise called upanaya, e.g., thus, sound is a created object—the premise which has been included in the Nyāya syllogism. It will be shown later on that as the premises are required for one's own understanding so they are required for the understanding of others. Hence, the hypothesis of a judgment involving the application of induction should not be discarded.

The critics oppose it thus :—

No judgment involving the application of induction intervenes between the memory of induction and the final deduction. Therefore, when a person perceives an object he makes neither much delay to accept it nor to reject it nor to be indifferent to it.

Though the knowledge of the invariable concomitant passes away yet it through its intermediate process becomes the source of true knowledge, i.e. deduction. The knowledge of the major term again is brought about by means of the minor premise. Deduction is not a piece of new information. We now know the major term as we have learnt it in time of induction. The perception of a wood-apple, etc. without generating the intermediate process in the shape of a judgment involving the application of induction produces the resultant judgment that the object of perception is worth-having etc. Moreover, in case of inference the resultant judgment that the object inferred such as fire etc. is worth-having etc. is not due to the causality of the recollection of the judgment that fire is conducive to pleasure. You should admit an intermediate judgment that fire which is inferred is also endowed with the characteristic feature of fire in general that it is conducive to pleasure. Which cause brings it about ? A sense-organ fails to produce it since fire, the subject of the judgment in question is not sensed. It is absurd to enter in the supposition that it is known by means of either verbal testimony or comparison. Smoke, the invariable mark of fire, cannot produce it since it produces another judgment involving the application of induction to a particular case—the judgment which is essentially required for the inference of fire. Smoke which is the content of the first judgment of application cannot produce the second judgment of application as a content of the first one since the first one does not exist when the second one comes into being. Let the point be clearly stated. The succession of judgments is as follows : At the outset there is the judgment involving the invariable mark (i.e., the minor premise occurs), then induction follows it (i.e. the major premise comes into being), then the judgment which links up the middle term, e.g., smoke with the major term by means of the tie of invariable concomitance takes place (i.e. the synthesis of the minor and major premises) and then the inference of an object such as fire is drawn (i.e. the conclusion is deduced from the above premises). The conclusion opposes the persistence of the third premise. Then the judgment of memory on the form that fire is conducive to pleasure arises. At this moment the third premise definitely passes away for good. When the judgment in the shape of the third premise ceases to exist smoke which is no more its content cannot by itself produce the judgment that fire is endowed with the characteristic feature of fire in general that it is conducive to pleasure. It may be contended that just after the remembrance of the judgment that fire is conducive to pleasure a fresh perceptual judgment having smoke as one of its objects is produced by the sense-organ. (The drift of this contention is that this fresh judgment will bring about the required intermediate judgment that fire is such and such), Such a contention is not tenable. Our experience bears no evidence to such an assumption.

On the other hand, even if it is admitted that the perception of smoke as described takes place then it should also be again followed by the remembrance if the above induction, i.e., the major premise and then the judgment involving the application of such induction to a particular concrete case should also come into being, In the mean time, the memory of the judgment that fire is conducive to pleasure has faded away. Hence, it would be impossible for this judgment accompanied by the judgment involving the applied induction to produce the judgment that the inferred fire is conducive to pleasure. But the perceived object is determined as conducive to pleasure because such knowledge appears at the time when the universal judgment that all such objects are conducive to pleasure passes away. Now, the upholder of the hypothesis may think in a different line and hold that the perception of smoke will not be followed again by the remembrance of inductive judgment and by the judgment involving the applied induction but the previous judgment referring to the applied induction will be revived in one's mind just after the remembrance of the judgment that fire is conducive to pleasure. When this judgment remains fresh in one's memory the judgment that the inferred fire is conducive to pleasure like the previously known fire will come into being. Such a line of defence is not tenable since when fire will be inferred (deduced) the judgment should be simultaneously remembered. Let us illustrate our point of criticism. At the same point of time the judgment that fire is conducive to pleasure will be remembered and the memory of the judgment that the hill contains smoke which is an invariable concomitant of fire will be revived. There is no assignable reason which will determine them to appear one after another. The simultaneous appearance of the two events of consciousness has been ruled out by this system of thought. However, let the two judgments appear successively. Still the above difficulty will not be solved. The two judgments, viz., 'fire is conducive to pleasure' and 'the hill contains smoke which is an invariable concomitant of fire' are remembered by us in close succession. Then the judgment that fire which is inferred is like fire that is conducive to pleasure comes into being. But this judgment does not refer to such an object as is referred to by its antecedent one. Moreover, the hypothesis of the succession of judgments does not help anybody to get rid of the real difficulty. Let us examine the order of the appearance of the judgments which are required in this context. The inference of fire comes first. The judgment that fire is conducive to pleasure is remmebered next. The memory of the judgment that the hill contains smoke which is an invariable concomitant of fire will be revived at the next moment. The second judgment is on the point of destruction at this moment. Then the fourth judgment that fire, an inference, is like the known fire which is conducive to pleasure comes into being. But at this moment the memory of the second judgment has already faded away. It is axiomatic that the memory of the judgment which has ceased to exist will not function to produce the judgment that fire is worth having. When fire is inferred on the strength of the premise that there is smoke, its unfailing mark, it is unreasonable to conjecture that the memory of the premise that there is smoke which is the constant concomitant of fire unnecessarily reappears. It is quite natural that if a person knows fire by means of inference then he remembers that fire is conducive to pleasure but not the premise that there is smoke which is a reliable concomitant of fire.

In fine, we come to the conclusion that the resultant judgment that an object of inference is worth having etc. is not due to the causality of such an intermediate judgment as involves the application of induction, since it is impossible to establish causal relation between them. Similarly the resultant judgment regarding the object of perception does not owe its existence to similar judgment. What is the good of assuming such a worthless intermediate judgments ?

The objection that if the hypothesis of the penultimate premise of the Nyāya syllogism (i.e., the judgment involving the application of induction to a particular case) is not assumed then the term 'upanaya' becomes meaningless will be discussed in the proper context when the premises of a syllogism will be taken into consideration. Hence in the absence of an intermediate judgment involving the applied induction perception will lead to the resultant judgment that such and such object is worth having or worth avoiding in and through such process as has been already described. It only awaits discussion what is, from this stand-point, the exact result of perception. The judgment that an object is conducive to pleasure is an inference since it is derived from the knowledge of the sure mark, viz., its belonging to the same class. Hence, it cannot be the result of perception. It is true that there is much sense in this criticism. But it is also a fact that the judgment that an object is conducive to pleasure follows sometimes from perception. When we discover the relation of invariable concomitance holding between the major term and the middle term both the terms are perceived by us. Let us illustrate our point by means of a familiar example. When we discover the universal relation of concomitance holding between fire and smoke in a kitchen we perceive both fire and smoke. The author of Nyāya-bhāṣya (a commentary upon Nyāya-sūtra) thinks of such character of the judgment that an object is conducive to pleasure as it is in time of discovery of the universal relation of invariable concomitance and has described that it (the above judgment) is the result of perception.

The Establishment of the Hypothesis that Conduciveness to Pleasure is perceptible

When we discover the relation of invariable concomitance how can we know that an object is conducive to pleasure since such a character is supersensuous ? If it is held that its capacity for giving pleasure is also inferred from the mark, viz., its belonging to the same class then a *regressus ad infinitum* is forced on us since the very discovery of the relation of invariable concomitance being an inference, an endless series of inferences should be postulated. Now it may be answered that pleasure, the effect of the object is felt and from the effect we infer its cause, viz., its power of giving pleasure. Such an answer is not tenable since if we do not know the relation of invariable concomitance holding between the terms, we cannot infer one from another. The relation of invariable concomitance is not to be perceived in this particular case since its power, one of the concomitants, is imperceptible. If it is inferred then a *regressus ad infinitum* will be forced on us as stated before.

Let us meet this objection. We do not subscribe to the view that power is supersensuous. Hence, it is not impossible for us to discover the relation of invariable concomitance holding between power and its effect.

The cause viz. force or power is, in our view, nothing but the assemblage of the cause and the conditions. This assemblage is easily perceived. But among the conditions the invisible residue of a previous unmerited action is also included. It is supersensuous. Hence, the assemblage under consideration is also beyond the range of perception since it contains an invisible element in it. Such an objection is not tenable. Merit, demerit and such other objects in some sense are not transcendental to our perception because they are in this context no better than an aspect of a material thing. They are so because nature has made them to be so. We shall discuss later on how merit and demerit are inferred from the diversity of this world. Thus the power of bringing about a result amounts to the assemblage of all conditions excepting the invisible principle, viz., merit or demerit. It is possible to perceive this power. Hence, it is justifiable to hold that the relation of invariable concomitance obtaining between the object such as a wood-apple and its belonging to the same class is discovered by the sense-organ since a wood-apple is grasped by our eyes. But pleasure which is derived from it is its effect. It is not perceived by our eyes. Now, how can you explain that the causal relations holding between a wood-apple and pleasure is grasped by our eyes, one of the two terms remaining outside the range of our eyes ? The answer to this question is that the relation is not visualised but is grasped by our inner perception.

We are immediately conscious of the feeling of pleasure, etc. by means of our internal organ but we see a wood-apple, etc. with our eyes. But we grasp the causal relation holding between a wood-apple and pleasure by means of our inner organ.

Now, a question arises in our mind that if we hold that we directly know a wood-apple to be conducive to pleasure then we should also admit that our inner organ, having no restriction, grasps external objects as well at its sweet will. In that case, has the hypothesis of external organ some solid ground to stand upon ? It also follows that there should exist neither a blind person nor a deaf man. Such an objection does not affect us. At the outset an external organ, coming in contact with the internal organ, does its work (i.e, produces perception). The external object which is grasped by our determinate perception, produced by the external sense-organ is also grasped by our internal organ. This is all what we admit. Such an external object imposes limitation upon the free movement of our internal organ and causes it to concentrate upon itself. Hence, our internal organ cannot grasp any and every object at its sweet will (i.e., in an unrestricted manner).

A further question troubles our mind that if at the time of the discovery of the relation of invariable concomitance an object is determined as conducive to pleasure by means of inner perception then why should we not have recourse to the same means of proof in order to demonstrate it as such ? Why should we depend upon the invariable mark, viz., its belonging to the same class ? Is it not superfluous ? We cannot entertain such a suggestion. In order to explain some cases of consciousness we assume the internal organ as their instrumental cause since either verbal testimony or the knowledge of the invariable mark or the external sense-organ fails to explain them and the facts of consciousness which are being experienced by us cannot be ignored. If we can prove that superseding the claim of a particular means of proof such as the knowledge of an invariable mark the internal organ has been arbitrarily asserted as the only cause of a particular phenomenon of consciousness then the charge that there is the only one means of proof, viz., the internal organ, applied to our decision but in the instance under consideration there is no scope for the four means of proof. We think that there is no further necessity of pushing the matter to a greater length.

Thus the commentator of the Nyāya-sūtra has thought only of the immediate judgment that a wood-apple is conducive to pleasure as the result of the visual perception of a wood-apple since he remembers the possibility of such immediate judgment at the time of discovery of invariable concomitance. It has been already stated that the judgment that it is worth-having is the same as the judgment that it is conducive to pleasure.

The Refutation of the hypothesis that Consciousness is the Instrumental cause of Itself

Why do you take so much trouble as to establish your point? Let a means of proof be identical with its result. The very perception of a wood-apple which is produced by our eyes may be called the instrumental cause since it appears to function in and through an intermediate process in the shape of the illumination of an object. This very perception may also be called the result since its nature is to reveal an object. Thus, the means of proof and its result will not be inco-ordinate as they are supposed to be. The means of awareness and its result do never co-exist in the same locus. It has been stated (in Diṅnāga's Pramāṇasamuccaya) that perception seems to us to be possessed of an intermediate process and thus turns out to be the means of awareness but is really a result. This hypothesis of Diṅnāga is not sound since it is open to the charge of depriving a means of awareness of its very essence.

If we analyse the word 'pramāṇa' into its elements, we get the root and the suffix. The primary meaning of the word is derived from them. The word signifies that by means of which something is truly known. Hence, it denotes the instrumental cause of true knowledge. An act itself is never an instrumental cause. But something else becomes the instrumental cause of an act which is to be accomplished. When we say that Caitra mows the sheaves of Śāli corn with a scythe, the subject, the object and the instrument are presented to our consciousness as distinct from the act itself. Similarly, when we say that a man sees a jar with his eyes, the subject, the object and the instrument should be held as different from the act of seeing. Hence, the act of seeing is not an instrument. Sometimes, the word 'pramā' and pramāṇa' are used as synonyms. The use of the word 'pramāṇa' in the sense of the resultant consciousness is not a faulty one since the use of a word in an unusual sense is sometimes noticed. The word 'karaṇa' which usually denotes an instrument is also sanctioned by the current idiom to denote simply an act (kṛti). Diṅnāga has suggested that if pramāṇa, the means of proof, and pramā, the resultant true consciousness, be not one and the same thing then they should not exist in the two separate locii. Such a suggestion is a sample of unprecedented eloquence. What does he purport to convey by the term 'adhikaraṇa'? If any real object is merely meant by it then they two point to the same object. The object which is grasped by the act of seeing is also the target of the instrumental cause of seeing, viz., the eyes etc. If the word 'Adhikaraṇa' denotes locus then it will not be found in the Buddhist literature. Every object having merely momentary existence, requires no locus to stand upon. But, on the other hand, we hold that the instrumental cause and its effect have been observed by us to stand upon the two distinct locii. Similarly, the eyes and the visual perception will be held to be causally connected though they do not stand upon the same locus.

On the other hand, in the same case two pieces of knowledge which are causally connected exist on the same locus like the knowledge of an invariable mark and that of the object marked and like the knowledge of a predicate and the relational knowledge, i.e., a judgment. There is no hard and fast rule that they must co-exist since the eyes do never exist on the locus of consciousness which is effectuated by them.

In some cases though the two distinct phenomena of consciousness are related to each other in the same way as an instrumental cause is to its result yet they co-exist in the same locus, viz., the soul. We may cite two examples to substantiate our stand-point. The knowledge of the probans and that of the probandum co-exist in the experiencing mind. The non-relational intuition of the predicate is, also, co-ordinate with the perceptual judgment which follows it in immediate succession. Such co-existence serves no purpose since eyes, etc., the instrumental cause, do not require such co-existence to bring about its result. It may be contended that if the cause and the result are of the same kind then they are co-ordinate elements belonging to the same locus. This co-ordination suggests that the antecedent condition determines the consequent one by means of an intermediate process and really becomes the cause of it, i.e. the instrumental cause. This suggestion applies to conditions other than a phenomenon of consciousness since consciousness, being itself a result does not require the help of an intermediate process to bring about a homogeneous result but requires it to produce a heterogeneous effect. As a matter of fact, the result which follows its conditions is consciousness. The awareness of an object which causes another phenomenon of awareness does not demand the aid of an intermediate process to do so. Now, the opponent may contend that the awareness of an object presupposes self-consciousness in order to generate another piece of consciousness. (When a person apprehends an object he becomes aware of the fact that he apprehends it. Later on, the awareness of an object leads to another act of awareness. Self-consciousness intervenes between these two acts of awareness. The suggestion is that self-consciousness is the intermediate process. Thus an act of awareness may be as well an instrumental cause.) A rejoinder to the opponent is as follows :—May we request you to explain self-consciousness ? Is it identical with or different from the awareness of an object ? If you hold that self-consciousness is not a separate act then it is absurd to assert that self-consciousness follows from the awareness of an object. If you subscribe to the view that the awareness of an object is distinct from self-consciousness then you really side with us. Moreover, let us dive into this problem and discuss whether consciousness which is absolutely contentless at the initial stage produces Self-consciousness that this object is known by us in and through an intermediate process engaging itself in generating the awareness of an object or consciousness which is the awareness of an object directly generates self-consciousness. After a thorough scrutiny of the above hypotheses we arrive at the conclusion that consciousness is by its nature object-awareness since the process of consciousness which is distinct from object-awareness and leads to object-awareness is not found out. The awareness of an object directly produces self-consciousness. Thus, consciousness is always a result at first but is never an instrumental cause in the initial stage. The people also approve of the hypothesis that consciousness is a mere effect but not a cause abinitio. They say in this manner. "We see with our eyes and we know by means of a mark". But we find no body to say "I know by means of consciousness".

The Buddhists review the above criticism and point out that the people designate eyes, etc. as an instrumental cause only when they produce the awareness of an object. But they do not call them as such if they do not generate the awareness of an object. It should also be borne in mind that they are so-called by the people because they are the cause of a cause but are not the direct cause of the awareness of an object. This review is not sound. The eyes and their like are the only cause but the cause of object consciousness is not produced by them. If they produce at all a cause then what is this effect cause ? If the Buddhists answer that consciousness which is a cause is generated by them then it is to be examined of which particular form of consciousness is the instrumental cause. It is a truism that no cause is held to be a cause if it produces itself. In other words, it is untenable to hold that consciousness is an instrumental cause if it applies itself to itself as a cause. The view current among the people that eyes, etc. which do not produce consciousness do not deserve the designation of an instrumental cause, is quite reasonable. If a condition does not operate to bring about an action then it does not become an instrumental cause. Hence eyes etc. which produce the act of cognition attain the status of an instrumental cause and the cognition which is thus produced is nothing but a result. Therefore, the designation of result given to consciousness is quite appropriate.

In fine, if we admit that the term 'pramāṇa' the instrumental cause of pramā, (a piece of true knowledge) is significant then it should also be admitted that the cause and its result are different. Hence, one and the same act of cognition cannot be both a pramāṇa and pramā its effect.

More illogical is he who holds that a single act of cognition may be designated as an instrumental cause of true knowledge, an object of true knowledge and its effect.

(The view of such a thinker is as follows. A concrete act of cognition is divided into three elements by a process of abstraction, a faculty of imagination. Every act of consciousness if self luminous). What is truly cognised is called prameya (an object of true knowledge). What illuminates correctly is called pramāṇa (an instrumental cause) and the awareness of a particular form is called a result. These three awarenesses are imagined to be different but are really identical. (This is the view of Diṅnāga vide Pramāṇa-samuccaya, chapter I, verse 11). We shall take this bad logician to task in the section on apavarga (the absolute cessation of all sorrows) in connection with the refutation of Subjective Idealism. Now, we refrain from an elaborate discussion of this view. Hence, it has been well stated that if the determinate perception is a pramāṇa then the judgment that the object perceived is conducive to pleasure, etc. is the result.

The refutation of the charge of being too wide

It follows from the previous discussion that in the Sūtra on perception all the adjectives given in it qualify the resultant form of perception since the sūtra with the word 'yataḥ' inserted into it points to this conclusion. That from which the resultant consciousness, arising from the sense-object-contact and having other characterizations, springs up is perception. The compound word 'indriya-artha-sannikarṣa-utpanna' (arising from the sense-object-contact) is given in the sūtra in order to distinguish this resultant consciousness from remembrance which is not produced by the object remembered and from the inferential knowledge which refers to an object lying beyond the range of sense-organs though it owes its existence to an object. Thus the definition of perception is not too wide since it does neither apply to the source of memory nor to that of inference. The inferential knowledge of the movement of sense-organ owes its existence to the sense-object-contact. An invariable mark which determines inference is, in this case, the sense-object-contact. Likewise we infer the motion of the sun by means of sun's contract with the different parts of the horizon. How does the adjective-clause 'arising from the sense-object-contact distinguish perception from inference ?" We solve this problem thus. The above-mentioned clause suggests that the sense-organ coming in contact with the object produces perceptual knowledge. The inferential knowledge of the movement of a sense-organ is not thus produced by the sense-organ. How do you mark off the origin of one knowledge from that of another ? An answer to this question is that the word 'utpanna' (generated by) clearly indicates their difference. It suggests that the sense-object-contact produces perceptual knowledge which refers only to such object as comes in contact with the sense-organ. The sense-object-contact does not produce the inferential knowledge of the movement of a sense-organ but simply indicates it. Therefore, the knowledge of the sense-object-contact is essential in case of an inference but, on the other hand, in case of perceptual knowledge, e. g., the direct awareness of colour the very presence of sense-object-contact is required. Its knowledge has nothing to do with perceptual knowledge.

The Necessity of the Assumption of Sense-Object-Contact

The sense-organs of smell, taste, sight, touch and hearing which are constituted by five elements such as the earth etc., will be described later on. The objects which are sensed are as follows : odour, flavour, colour, touch, and sound together with their respective species, some of the substances having these qualities, some other qualities such as number etc., belonging to the above substances and their movements such as going up, going down, lifting up and other such movements etc., and the genus and the species inhering in all of them, i.e., the universals. The followers of the Vaiśeṣika system hold that the sensed objects are those which are grasped by both the organs of sight and touch. Negation which has been proved as objectively real is also included in the list of objects. The contact of the sense-organs with their objects is six-fold. A substance is grasped either by the sense-organs of sight or by that of touch by means of the relation of conjunction. The quality such as colour etc., belonging to a substance by means of a complex relation viz., conjunction cum inherence. The species belonging to colour etc., such as colourness is grasped by means of a complex relation of the second degree such as conjunction cum inherence cum inherence.

Our eyes are in direct contact with a substance, i.e., they are directly conjoined to a substance, colour inheres in it and colourness, i.e., the universal belonging to the colour, inheres in it. Sound is grasped by the relation of inherence. The sky constitutes the ears and sound inheres in the sky. The universal belonging to sound, i.e., soundness is related to our ears by means of a complex relation, viz., inherence cum inherence and is grasped. Sound inheres in the sky which assumes the form of the ears under certain conditions and the universal of sound inheres in sound. It has been already explained that negation is related to our sense-organ by means of a complex relation, viz., conjunction cum the relation of the qualifying to the qualified and is directly perceived. The perceptual negation judgment is that there is no jar on this spot. A particular surface of the spot is conjoined to our eyes and negation qualifies the spot in question.

How can we prove the existence of sense-object-contact ? We say in reply because we cannot perceive a veiled object. If our sense-organs were competent enough to perceive an object with which they are not in contact then they would have grasped even the veiled objects. But it is a fact that they do not sense the veiled ones. Therefore, the hypothesis that the sense-object-contact exists is proved. Those who are opposed to this hypothesis may contend that the absence of a veil is one of the conditions of perception and that there is no necessity of assuming the sense-object-contact as a condition of perception. Such a contention is not tenable. As the sense-organs are the instrumental cause of the act of perception so they must be united with the other conditions of perception. The maxim based upon observation points to the totality of conditions that they yield results when they are mutually combined. Therefore the sense-object-contact should be admitted. We shall not elaborately discuss it now since it will be elaborately discussed in the chapter on the examination of sense-organs. The sense-organs of taste and touch, with the least shade of doubt, come in contact with such objects as they taste and touch respectively. As the rest sense-organs share some common character with the above two so it is assumed that they also come in contact with the objects of which they produce perception. If this is the drift of your reasoning then the sense-object-contact being clearly suggested to our mind why has it been directly mentioned ? It has been mentioned to indicate the six-fold division of sense-object-contact. The word 'utpanna' (generated by) suggests that both the sense-organ and the object condition the perception of an object. The object is what is perceived. As an objective case it determines the act of perception. How is it known that the object is causally connected with the act of perception ? The answer is that the objection question is only organised, the representative character of consciousness has been refuted and the definite relation obtaining between an act of perception and a particular object is hard to establish. You simply state the necessity of your assumption. But you have been asked to give the proof. How do you prove its necessity ? Our reply is that this is our proof. We cite other instances which clearly show that an accusative is the goal of a verb. In the sentence 'Sa vīraṇaṁ kaṭaṁ karoti (he makes a mat of a kind of straw) there are two accusatives 'vīraṇam' and 'kaṭam' of the verb 'karoti'. By the methods of agreement and difference based upon perception, and perception assisted by non-perception the causal relation subsisting between vīraṇa (straw) and kaṭa (mat) is detected. Similarly, the same relation holding between an object and its perception is detected. Let us take an example. A person in search of Devadatta visits his house but does not see him there since he is absent at that time. After a while, when he comes back he is seen by the person. Thus we see that when Devadatta is present he is perceived but when he is absent he is not perceived. Hence, by the joint method of agreement and difference, we learn that the perception of Devadatta and his non-perception follow respectively his presence and absence. Straws and a mat are distinctly perceived by all. It is, therefore, reasonable to admit that the causal relation subsisting between them is detected by means of the joint method of agreement and difference. But an object is never cognized as distinct from its awareness. Hence, the application of the joint method of agreement and difference, in the above case, to ascertain the causal relation subsisting between an object and its perception, is inadmissible. The distinct awareness of an object consists in this that the true perception of an object does not take place when an object lies beyond the field of perception. The opponent seems to take his stand upon the doctrine of Subjective Idealism and intends to refute our hypothesis in the light of it. We shall meet the argument of our opponent in the proper place. The word 'utpanna' of the adjective clause suggests that as the joint method of agreement and difference proves that the sense organs are the necessary conditions of perception so it proves that the object which is perceived is also a condition of its perception.

The Refutation of the charge against the Definition of Perception that it is too narrow to apply to Inner Perception of pleasure etc.

Do not think that the adjective clause which arises from the sense-object-contact excludes the inner perception of pleasure etc. from the province of perception but, on the contrary, includes it. The internal organ is also one of the organs of consciousness. It causes the inner perception of pleasure etc. The internal organ has not been included in the list of sense-organs because it is not elemental like the external sense-organs, e.g., the organ of smelling. The perception of an object may be produced by four or three or two contacts. When we perceive the colour of an external object four contacts are required to produce its perception. The individual soul is conjoined to the internal organ, which is in contact with the external sense-organ which is united with the coloured substance in which colour, the object in question, inheres. The inner perception of internal phenomena such as pleasure etc. requires two contacts to be produced since the external organs such as eyes etc. have no part to play. The transcendental perception of the soul by a sage is produced only by a single-contact since in that stage a third object does not exist besides the soul and the internal organ. The adjective clause 'arising from the sense-object-contact' has been rightly used since the inner perception of pleasure etc. is included in the class of perception. The sūtra on perception does not include the contact of the soul with the internal organ in the list of the causal factors of perception though it is one of its conditions because the above contact is the common factor of all forms of consciousness but not a special condition of perception.

The Service of the term jñāna

The word 'jñāna' (consciousness) mentioned in the sūtra stands for the substantive. There are several adjectives and adjective clauses in the sūtra, e.g., 'indriyārtha' etc. They require at least a noun to qualify. If their function is gone then their very existence will be threatened. Another alternative suggestion may be offered. The word 'jñāna' (consciousness) has been given to exclude (pleasure) etc. Pleasure also arises from the sense-object-contact. The assemblage of conditions which is the source of pleasure should not be mistaken for a proof. But the source of true knowledge should only be called a proof. In order to indicate the instrument of true knowledge the word 'jñāna' finds an important place in the sūtra.

The Buddhists hold that Consciousness itself is pleasure

The Buddhists join issue with this solution. It is not proper to exclude pleasure, etc. by the use of the word 'Jñāna'. It is also beyond our power to exclude 'pleasure' etc. by the use of the word Jñāna. Pleasure, pain, desire, hatred, and volition are nothing but the forms of consciousness. The difference in causes explains the difference in the nature of effects. If one notices that the different effects follow from one and the same cause then he arrives at the conclusion that the character of an effect is not determined by its cause but it is accidental.

The Buddhist argument has been expressed by the following verse. An effect of one kind and that of another owe their existence to the two different sets of causes. Is pleasure really different from consciousness? No, 'certainly not' is the answer since pleasure owes its existence to such a cause as produces consciousness. In a nutshell, the Buddhist argument is that pleasure is a form of consciousness because it is produced by the same cause as produces consciousness.

The Refutation of the Buddhist hypotheses from the Nyāya-stand point

This syllogism is not sound. The material validity of this conclusion is questionable. Pleasure is a feeling which is an object of consciousness. It is intuited as a joyful state. On the other hand, the essence of consciousness lies in illuminating an object. The evidence of our direct experience on this point is incontrovertible. Inference cannot make head against a fact, the object of sound experience. In other words, inference is not strong enough to establish the identity of pleasure with consciousness. The Buddhists cannot even hold that pleasure, pain etc. are essentially consciousness and the transformation of them are mirth, dejection etc. Different names may be given to these derivatives according to the sweet will of a person. The Buddhist position will not be affected by this act of naming. But the Buddhists forget the main point. We are always aware of our awareness as illuminating an object but no feelings of pleasure and pain are intuited as revealing an object. Thus an awareness involves a reference to its object. Our direct experience teaches that it is the essence of awareness. But pleasure or pain is never experienced as involving a reference to an object.

The awareness of pleasure and that of pain are two distinct forms of consciousness. They are not different by their own nature, as a doubt and an illusion differ from each other by their essential character. A doubt and an illusion partake of the essential character of consciousness, viz., the illumination of an object. A doubt is experienced as revealing an object. The object of a doubt is indefinite. An illusion also reveals an object. It either mistakes one thing for another or reveals an absence of object. But neither pleasure nor pain is experienced as an awareness revealing an object. Pleasure and pain are merely inner phenomena. They are only objects. They are other than consciousness. The awareness of pleasure and pain are distinct from each other on the basis of their references to the objects like the awareness of a jar but unlike a doubt which is essentially different. (In other words, the awareness of pleasure distinguishes itself from that of pain because pleasure and pain which are referred to by them are mutually different. The awareness of a jar is also distinct from that of other objects because a jar which is referred to is distinct from the other objects. But a doubt is distinct from the other forms of consciousness because the specific character of this type of consciousness is essentially different from that of the other forms of consciousness. But the awareness of pleasure is not essentially different from that of pain but the objects of these two awarenesses are only different.

Now the Buddhists may contend that pleasure, pain, etc. are not merely objects of knowledge since they are self-luminous; they are also self-conscious. Hence, they are identical with consciousness. This contention is not tenable. The hypothesis that consciousness is self-luminous has been refuted and will be more elaborately refuted. If consciousness is not self-luminous then how is it that pleasure, pain etc. are to be admitted as self-luminous ? The reason behind our criticism is obvious since no body experiences pleasure, etc. as self-conscious consciousness. Very well, in the face of criticism, the Buddhists may press their point with great force. They may argue that if pleasure is not self-luminous then as there will be no distinction between pleasure that has arisen and what has not yet arisen along with the result viz., either people should always enjoy pleasure or they should never enjoy it. Such an argument does not hold good since pleasure is intuited only when it comes into being. Hence, we do not follow the argument of the Buddhists why there should be no distinction between pleasure that has come into being and what has not as yet come into being. But a serious charge rebounds upon the Buddhists since a self-luminous object like a lamp is a public property the benefit of which is shared by all alike. If the Buddhists stick to the hypothesis that pleasure is self-luminous then though it may arise in a particular series yet it should render happy the members of the other series as well.

Moreover, does a single individual phenomenon of consciousness possess the complex character of partly pleasure and partly pain ? Or does an individual phenomenon of consciousness partake of the character of pain ? If the Buddhists subscribe to the first alternative then one should simultaneously experience both pleasure and pain contrary to each other with the appearance of his consciousness which is partly pleasure and partly pain. If the Buddhists accept the second alternative then as some forms of consciousness are to be held as pleasure and some other forms of consciousness are to be held as pain so they should also admit the verdict of experience that some other forms of consciousness are neutral and that they are neither pleasure nor pain but they reveal their objects only. The last type of consciousness is not absolutely blank, i.e. objectless. It involves a reference to an object such as a jar. It is known to us by means of the joint method of agreement and difference. This type of consciousness even involves a reference to an object which has ceased to exist. This assertion is made on the strength of our experience. In the light of this type of consciousness if we try to understand the real character of the consciousness of pleasure then we arrive at the conclusion that consciousness itself is not pleasure but it involves a reference to pleasure which is its object as it does with regard to a jar, its object. Moreover, we can strengthen our position on the basis of our experience that consciousness which is not pleasure illuminates it since it is sometimes experienced by us. (The sum and substance of this argument is this that we can explain the awareness of pleasure in terms of neutral consciousness but fail to explain neutral consciousness in terms of the awareness of pleasure). Hence pleasure or pain is not consciousness.

The Buddhists infer that pleasure is consciousness because the conditions of pleasure and those of consciousness are the same. The reason is materially invalid. The inherent cause being the soul, is the same. Similarly, the non-inherent cause which is the contact of the internal organ with the soul is also the same. But the efficient causes are different. The efficient cause of pleasure is the universal of pleasure whereas the efficient cause of consciousness is the universal of consciousness. These causes should assemble together to produce the effect. The universal of pleasure cannot exist alone but requires a locus, viz., an individual in the shape of a phenomenon of pleasure to stand upon. Hence, before the appearance of pleasure, how can the universal of pleasure be present there ? How can the universal of pleasure be united with the other causes of pleasure ? Which will be the specific relation that binds them together ? If the universal of pleasure stands unrelated then how can it be a cause ? A reply to these objections is this:— It will be proved later on that all the universals are omnipresent. Hence, the universal of pleasure is present there. It co-operates with the other causes of pleasure in order to bring about the effect, viz., pleasure. Co-operation is the specific relation. Moreover, the universal in question behaves like merit and demerit. The invisible principle of merit and demerit is the cause of the śāli corn which is the source of pleasure or pain of all beings. They co-operate with the other causes of śāli corn, viz., seeds, the earth, water, etc. Similarly the universal of pleasure co-operates with the other factors of pleasure. Hence consciousness and pleasure are not identical since their efficient causes are different.

The difference in the efficient causes accounts for the diversity in the nature of effects. The natural colour of a jar is destroyed when it is burnt by fire. A new colour emerges. The emergence of this new colour is due to the causality of a distinct efficient cause.

All logicians do not agree on the point that consciousness is always preceded by another antecedent consciousness. But pleasure, pain and other feelings are invariably preceded by the knowledge of an object which one seeks either to obtain or to avoid.

Pleasure, pain, etc. are not always preceded by the direct awareness of an object. When they are not preceded by the direct awareness of an object they are invariably preceded by the remembrance of an object.

In some cases, the self-consciousness of a resolution leads to pleasure. Therefore, the proposition that pleasure and other feelings are preceded by consciousness is universal. It may be contended that consciousness is also preceded by consciousness and that there is no distinction between pleasure, etc., and consciousness. The hypothesis that consciousness precedes consciousness will be refuted later on. The dawn of consciousness of a foetal baby is not preceded by antecedent consciousness. The appearance of consciousness after a period of unconscious state due to an attack of swoon is not due to the said antecedent consciousness. Some points of criticism in a nut-shell have been indicated here. The above hypothesis will be elaborately discussed and criticised later on. Thus, we see that there is a distinction between pleasure, etc., and consciousness. The 'Jñāna' (awareness) has been given in the sūtra on perception in order to preclude pleasure, etc., from perceptual awareness.

The Refutation of a probable doubt that the adjective avyabhicāri is enough to suggest the noun jñāna and that the use of the term jñāna is redundant

It is a fact that truth and falsehood are the specific properties of knowledge. Among many adjectives, the adjective 'true' finds a place in the sūtra. It being applicable only to knowledge, the term denoting the noun, viz., awareness, is unmistakably guessed since the property of 'truth' belongs to none else. In that case, is the term 'jñāna' not superfluous? The whole objection is based upon a wrong assumption that truth and falsehood are the specific properties of awareness since unreal pleasure is also experienced by all. Which pleasure is experienced as unreal? The pleasure which is derived from doing forbidden deeds such as the enjoyment of another's wife, etc. is a false one. What makes pleasure false ? What makes a piece of knowledge false ? False knowledge is such as asserts a predicate of a thing which has not in reality the property corresponding to the predicate. Similarly, false pleasure is also a case of wrong reference. Does not the pleasure derived from the enjoyment of another's wife produce pleasant sensation ? Does not a false knowledge, e.g., the mistaking of conch-shell for silver reveal an object ? Yes, it is a piece of knowledge but a false one. Similarly, the instance of pleasure mentioned above is undoubtedly a pleasant feeling but at the same time a false one. It is not false since it is nothing but a pleasant feeling. If you argue like this then the mistaking of conchshell for silver is not false since its essence lies in the illumination of an object.

You may answer that though an illusion reveals an object yet it contains a wrong reference. We may also answer in the same strain that though false pleasure is a pleasant feeling yet it is not produced by a real cause. Now a question may be put to them. Is it produced by a cause which does not produce pleasure ? We may also raise a similar question. Is an illusion produced by a cause which does not produce consciousness ? Your answer to the question will be that it is produced by a real cause but its reference is wrong since it is contradicted by perception. Pleasure is produced by a condition which is conducive to pleasure but such a condition has been prohibited by the Śāstras such as the enjoyment of another's wife. Is not another's wife a real condition of pleasure ? In case of an illusion also the object which is wrongly referred to is also real. But we call it as unreal since it is contradicted by perception. Similarly, though another's wife is a real source of pleasure yet it should be called unreal since it is condemned by the scriptures. How does the scripture contradict it ? How does perception contradict an illusion ? "The object which is referred to by an illusion is not true" is the verdict of perception. It is also declared by the scriptures that the cause which produces pleasure is now a source of true pleasure. Is not that object conducive to pleasure ?

As the object referred to by an illusion is the condition of untrue knowledge so the condemned source of pleasure produces such pleasure as turns out to be misery in the end. Such bitter pleasure is called unreal. Enough of this verbal jugglery. For the same reasons pleasure should also be admitted to be unreal. Hence the adjective phrase 'not untrue' does not invariably qualify apprehension.

Some other logicians hold that this foolish disputation is of no use. The word 'avyabhicāri' may not be suggestive of the term 'jñāna' but the word 'vyavasāyātmaka' (determinate) suggests it. The adjective 'determinate' is not applicable to pleasure, pain etc., but is applicable only to consciousness. It is a truism that the word 'determinate' finds a place in the sūtra in order to exclude a doubt from perception. It is not only competent enough to exclude a doubt from perception but also it is competent enough to distinguish perception from pleasure, pain etc. since it is impossible to use an expression like this that pleasure or pain is determinate. Thus, without mentioning the word 'jñāna' perception is easily distinguished from pleasure, pain etc. In spite of this fact the word 'jñāna' should find a place in the sūtra since the noun should be mentioned by the denotative term. All the adjectives are given in the sūtra. But if the noun is conspicuous by its absence then the adjectives, having no noun to qualify, will surely lose their significance (they will float in the air having no solid ground to stand upon). Moreover, the attention of the listener will be diverted, having no concrete object to concentrate upon. Hence, though the word 'a jñāna' is suggested by the power of suggestion belonging to the adjectives yet the noun i.e. jñāna should be specifically mentioned in the sūtra. If we do not mention what is intelligently guessed by an adequate expression then the word of the sūtra would be "pratyakṣam pratyakṣam' since everything else, given in the present sūtra, can be easily guessed. Therefore, the sūtra has done the right thing viz. the use of the word 'jñāna' in order to state clearly the substantive.

Various meanings of the word Avyapadeśya

(i) The negative thesis that words do not interpenetrate real objects will be established when we shall refute the hypothesis of the Buddhists on this point. When words interpenetrate our knowledge it is called vyapadeśya i.e. it becomes inter-woven with words. In order to exclude such knowledge from perception the word avyapadeśyam (not inter-mixed with words) has been given. The old logicians interpret this term in their own way. What finds expression in words is called 'vyapadeśyam'. Thus, an expressible knowledge is designated as vyapadeśyam. The awareness which arises from the sense-object-contact and is named after its object such as the awareness of colour, the awareness of taste etc. is called as 'vyapadeśyam' The term 'avyapadeśyam' finds a place in the sūtra to suggest that no such expressible awareness is the resulting form of perception. Such an interpretation is untenable. The mere association of an apprehension with a word cannot discredit it as untrue. If the awareness of colour or that of taste is represented by language but it rightly refers to its object and does not oscillate between two objects then how can it be called as a false one ? If it contains a wrong reference then the term 'avyabhicāri' given in the sūtra is competent enough to exclude it from the domain of true perception. In that case, is not the term in question superfluous ? In due course it will be shown that the awareness interpenetrated by a word owes its existence to the source of valid knowledge. What will be its fate ? Will it be excluded from the state of being the resulting perception by the mere term 'avyapadeśyam' contained in the sūtra in spite of the fact that it is generated by the source of valid knowledge ? It is not also produced by the source of an inferential knowledge. There is also no provision in Gautama's logic of the fifth source of valid knowledge. Thus, the four-fold division of valid knowledge would be too narrow to include it within itself. Hence, it is a riddle which defies the finding of our intelligence (or it represents a glaring instance of oversight on the part of our intelligence). Therefore, we arrive at the conclusion that the so-called interpretation is really a misinterpretation.

Some teachers of the Nyāya School have shown, that the term 'avyapadeśya' excludes some other form of knowledge from the domain of perception. A man who learns the meaning of a word from the usage of an experienced man solves his doubt about the identity of an object on hearing a sentence indicating the name of the intended object from the mouth of an expert. He listens to the sentence of an expert that this is a jack-fruit tree. He ascertains that the yonder object having branches etc. is signified by the word 'jack-fruit tree'. Though the apprehension of the tree is of sensuous origin yet it should not be solely sensuous since if the sentence which throws light on its name had not been present then his present apprehension would not have arisen. Hence words and his sense organ have jointly produced it. It is an effect of the joint effort of the two types of causes. As words play an important part in its production so it is called as Vyapadeśyam. Such an apprehension is excluded by the term 'avyapadeśyam'. This apprehension is not a class by itself. Therefore, the proposal of a fifth type of knowledge does not mature. But the people hold that it is a piece of verbal knowledge. If somebody asks him, "How do you know that this is a jack-fruit tree" then he says in reply, "I have been instructed by Devadatta that it is so and so". But again, he does never say even in a dream "I have seen it with my eyes that it is a jack-fruit tree". Though we know from the joint method of agreement and difference that the sense-organ is one of its conditions yet words play the part of an instrumental cause in its production. For this reason, the author of the Nyāya-sūtra has not framed the definition of verbal knowledge in such a way as to exclude the dependence of verbal knowledge upon a sense-organ as its condition. The definition of verbal knowledge as given by Gautama is this that the knowledge which is derived from the words of a trustworthy person is verbal. It shows that the room of verbal knowledge is spacious. Gautama also approves the entry of a sensuous element into the body of verbal knowledge. But he has narrowed down the scope of perception as he shuts his door against an element of verbal knowledge, having qualified perception by the term "avyapadeśya". Hence, experience interpenetrated by words cannot be the resulting form of perception. Therefore, the term 'avyapadeśya' has been used to exclude the above experience from the perception proper.

The subsequent interpreters do not assent to the above conclusion. If such apprehension as is produced by the joint causality of the two distinct factors is excluded from perception then it turns out to be a piece of false direct knowledge but the definition of false knowledge does not apply to it. Again, if it is true then it should be decided with which kind of true knowledge it is to be identified. Word-interpenetrated experience is verbal since it is causally connected with words as its causal relation is detected by the joint method of agreement and difference. It is also sensuous since it is causally connected with the sense-organs and its causal relation is also similarly detected.

It is also incompatible to hold that word-interpenetrated experience is verbal since it is produced by the two distinct sources of knowledge. Again, if it is held that it is a class by itself then such a hypothesis meets with the dilemma which has been shown before.

How is it that the previous teachers, having noticed the perilous journey on the path of logic, have accepted the popular view that such an experience is verbal on the strength of the evidence that it has been instructed by Deva Datta that this is a jack-fruit tree ? What a fine decision ! The author of Nyāya-Sūtra, being a man of super intellect, has little faith in popular saying like an ordinary fellow. The character of an object is not such as the people believe and express. The people say that this small reservoir of water is reserved for the use of Nandin though the bathing place is used by all the sages. But even in the face of this criticism if we try to make out the real intention of the author of the Nyāya-Sūtra then we arrive at the conclusion that this piece of knowledge is verbal. Gautama cautiously defines perception and adequately qualifies it with the purpose of excluding any element of verbal knowledge from it. But on the other hand, he does not qualify the definition of verbal knowledge so as to exclude it from the partly sensuous one. From this attitude of his mind, we come to the conclusion that piece of knowledge which is produced not by words alone but by words accompanied by some other factors required for the appearance of some other form is of knowledge surely verbal.

A critical review of the above hypothesis is as follows : The author of the Nyāya-Sūtra is not an instructor of moral duty like Manu so that we should hold that the piece of knowledge in question is verbal as he so commands.

On an adequate examination of the nature of this object we find that this piece of knowledge is perceptual since it is causally determined by the sense-organ and this causal connection is based upon the joint method of agreement and difference. When its sensuous origin will be negated it is wise to hold that it belongs to another kind of valid knowledge.

We shall follow a different line of interpretation since we are divided in our opinion. In other words, we mean to say that we may be right in our interpretation but our opponents are not satisfied with our interpretation. Therefore, we should try to convince them.

Another Interpretation to avoid the defect of being impossible

The adjective 'avyapadeśyam' given in the sūtra is to guard against the possible defect of the definition of perception in being impossible. A critical thinker discusses the point thus :— If an object to be defined is existent then its definition is given. But perception which arises from the sense-object-contact does not really exist if perception refers to the object as qualifed by a word which denotes it. The so called perception referring to a qualified object as indicated above is essentially verbal. The distinction-perceptions cannot be established if their reference to their corresponding different objects is not admitted. The function of consciousness is simply to reveal an object. The judgment that a man has a stick or the judgment that a man is white is distinct since each one refers to the relational object containing noun qualified by an adjective. Similarly, the judgment that this is a cow is distinct since it refers to an object which is qualified by its name. Such a judgment (i.e. a judgment similar to the last one) is verbal since a word is the only instrumental cause of it. No sense-organ can play the part of an instrumental cause to bring about the above judgment since the predicate lies beyond the range of eyes and the subject is beyond the reach of ears.

Nobody has ever experienced that a perceptual judgment is the joint effect of the two different sense-organs. An exception may be cited in this connection. As objector may urge that a word interpenetrated experience owes its existence to the inner organ just like the judgment that the Bandhūka flower is scented. But we should also remember in this context what has been stated about this type of judgment. When a word or a mark or a similar source of knowledge fails to discharge its function as an instrumental cause and an effect in the shape of a judgment arises in our mind we entertain a hypothesis that the inner organ plays the part of an instrumental cause to generate it. But if the possibility of a source of knowledge as an instrumental cause is not ruled out then the causality of the inner organ should not be relied upon. If we violate this rule then the inner organ should be the only source of valid knowledge. A word is the instrumental cause of the judgment in question. It reveals itself and the object meant by itself like thousand-rayed sun. Therefore, though the judgment that this is a cow refers to a cow which is a perceptible object yet it is not perceptual but mediate, i.e. it is derived from a word. A question arises in our mind with regard to this hypothesis. We have heard the word 'cow', etc. when we have been initiated into its signification. The word has ceased to exist. How is it that the judgment in question is due to the instrumentality of the past word ? Do not think that we entertain such an absurd hypothesis. Though the word is not heard at the time of the formation of the judgment yet it being recalled in our memory, generates it.

When the particular word consisting of many letters is heard do we really perceive all the letters at a time ? (When we actually hear the last letter the first has passed away. Thus, a complete word is never heard. The last letter is heard but other letters which are absent are recalled in our memory. The relevant portion of our point is this that when a word conveys its meaning all the letters are not perceived). Is there any distinction between the communication of sense by the two different words ? A word expresses its meaning when all its constituent letters are supplied by memory and another word carries its sense when its last letter is only audible and the rest are supplied by memory.

We arrive at the conclusion that the judgment in question is due to the instrumentality of words which are not directly given to us but are recalled in our memory. As a word reveals itself along with a supersensible object so it does with a perceptible object. Thus it should be admitted that judgment of this type refers to an object which is qualified by a word which denotes it.

An experienced teacher refers to an analogous case. He holds that the word 'saṁjñitva' is a classical example of an object having a word as its predicate. Let us see the derivation of the word 'saṁjñitva'. The noun 'saṁjñā' is the base. The nominal suffix in 'having the sense of 'matup' suffix has been attached to it. The resultant form is 'saṁjñin'. Again, the nominal suffix 'tva' denoting the sense of an abstract quality has been attached to the word 'saṁjñin'. But the nominal suffix 'tva' denotes a relation when it is attached to a word which is derived from a basic word with a nominal suffix implying the sense of the 'matup' suffix added to it. Thus the word 'saṁjñitva' denotes the relation obtaining between 'saṁjñā' and 'saṁjñin'. If we recall the ruling of the learned grammarians on this point in our mind then we see that the 'tva' suffix after a word derived from a root with a verbal suffix attached to it or that derived from a base a nominal suffix attached to it or a compound word signifies a relation. The term 'saṁjñā' stands for a word. Thus the import of the word 'saṁjñitva' is that an object which is denoted by a word is presented to our consciousness along with its denotative word as its predicate. We are aware of no awareness which is not associated with words. When definite words are not presented to our consciousness there is possibility of some general words being associated with our consciousness. If words are not associated with consciousness then consciousness lacks its power of illumination.

Bhartṛhari says to this effect

There is no such consciousness in this universe as is not associated with words. We are aware of all awarenesses as qualified by words. Thus the definition of perception turns out to be merely verbal having no real thing to define. Anticipating the possible charge of absurdity to be levelled against the definition of perception the author of the Nyāya-sūtra puts in the adjective 'avyapa-deśyam'. The consciousness of a person who is innocent of a word and of its denotation and of their relation is not associated with words. When the direct awareness of a person who is even conversant with words, their meanings and their mutual relation arises from the contact of the sense-organ with an object in immediate succession it is not associated with words. It helps to bring back the proper words to our minds. Such an awareness which is an antecedent condition of word-interpenetrated experience does not owe its existence to the words. No word contributes to the power of illumination of awareness. The power of illumination constitutes the essence of conciousness. No body's experience is interpenetrated with an adjective thus, denoting an object close at hand when he has the initial sense-perception known as indeterminate perception. Though the judgments such as this is a cow, etc. come under the species of verbal knowledge yet the initial sense-perception is a fit object which is to be defined. Therefore, the definition of perception is not futile. In order to meet the charge of absurdity which may be levelled against the definition of perception the adjective 'avyapadeśyam' has been given in the sūtra.

The Refutation of the above hypothesis

Some teachers of the Nyāya school disapprove of this solution. They believe that the judgment that this is a cow owes its existence to the sense-object-contact, and also hold that it cannot be a piece of verbal knowledge. Moreover, they point out that this judgment does not refer to an object which is qualified by a word since an instrumental cause of such a judgment is not possible. Words are the source of such judgment as has the subject supplied by them. But let us now find out the instrumental cause of a judgment in which the word plays the part of a mere predicate. Our auditory organ is not the instrumental cause in question since it cannot produce its result by fits. If we closely examine the process of associating the synthetic judgment that this is a cow with words then we at once abandon the idea of entertaining the hypothesis that the auditory organ is the instrumental cause of it. The first step towards the association of the judgment with words is our knowledge of the relation between a word and its meaning. Then the word which is recalled in our memory is associated with the objective consciousness. How does the auditory organ come in to produce the judgment in question ? The inner organ unaided by an external sense-organ, is not competent to produce a judgment which refers to an external object; otherwise, no body should be blind, etc. The objector may urge that the words alone play, here, the part of an instrumental cause and may suggest that one should not search for another instrumental cause. Such a contention does not hold good. The object of a verb cannot be its instrument. The objector cites an illustration in support of his view that sun light is both the object and the instrument of the verb to see. We see sun's light by means of itself. This is not an apt illustration. The illustration arises from the wrong identification of one act of seeing with that of another. There are two acts of seeing. When sun's light is an instrumental case it is not an objective case and vice versa. We see an object, e.g. a jar by means of sun's light; light is merely the instrumental cause but is not the objective case. When we see light it is merely an object but not an instrumental cause. What is the instrumental cause in this case ? We see light only with our eyes. Therefore, the eyes are the only instrumental cause. When we see light we require no instrumental cause like light. How is it that we see without light ? We are to accept facts but cannot challenge them. We see an object such as a jar with the aid of light. But when we see light we require no such aid. Who is to blame ? Sun's light is, at first, seen independently of any other light with our eyes. It endures long and serves the purpose of an instrumental cause when the other objects are beheld with the same organ. This conclusion seems to us to be reasonable.

Sound endures only two time-atoms. It is audible. If it plays the part of an instrument when the consciousness of an object which is grasped by a source of knowledge other than the auditory organ is produced then how can it be an object of such awareness ? A word is a means of knowledge like smoke but is never an object of such knowledge. In other words, a word itself is not referred to by a judgment which owes its existence to its instrumentality. When a word, being recalled in our mind, leads to the knowledge of an object, i.e. its meaning let us pay attention to the following steps. At the outset we remember a word. Then we know the object denoted by the word. Thus, when we know the object it is in no way possible for us to cognize the word itself. Thus, no judgment refers to an object which is qualified by its denotative word. Moreover, the judgment that this is a cow is causally connected with the sense-object-contact since its causal connection is determined by the joint method of agreement and difference. How can you per force, i.e, violating the law of logic, hold that the above judgment is a piece of verbal knowledge ? Though it is due to the function of a sense-organ in co-operation with the impressions of the knowledge of words yet it is asserted by you to be a piece of verbal knowledge. Then we see that you are a great logician indeed.

It has been pointed out by you that neither the visual organ nor the auditory organ is instrumental to the production of such a judgment as refers to an object as qualified by its denotative word. But, oh Sir, why do you not hold that such an object is perceived with our eyes alone ?

Very well, you may contend that our eyes do not apprehend an object which is not visible. Hence, the judgment which refers to an object which is qualified by its denotative word is not visual.

This contention does not hold good. How do you hold that your illusion is optical when you mistake the rays of the sun for water ? The eyes are not in contact with water. Therefore, your statement is baseless.

We beg to mention in this connection that water which is at first recalled in our mind is perceived with our eyes. Similarly here too, why is not the word which is at first remembered perceived with our eyes.

Now, you may contend that a word which is essentially a sound ever remains beyond the reach of our eyes. We also put this question to you, viz., "Is water which is not in touch with our eyes, ever seen with our eyes?"

You may still contend that if sound is at all visualized then only one kind of sense-organ, viz., the eyes, should be admitted. We also meet this contention with the following counter argument. If you admit that an object which is not in contact with our eyes is visualized then all the objects of the universe should be perceived with eyes. In other words, every body having normal eyes should have seen each and every object of the universe.

Why do you illustrate an illusion by which the rays of the sun are mistaken for water ? What is it that makes an illusion? Is it so since the sense-organ does not produce it ? Or, is it so because it does not correspond to the object referred to by it ? Now, if it is held that it is illusion because of its non-sensuous origin then the phrase 'not produced by the sense-object-contact' being sufficient to exclude an illusion from perception the phrase 'not corresponding' should be abandoned as superfluous. As the latter phrase finds a place in the sūtra which defines perception so it is admitted that the essential character of an illusion lies in its non-correspondence. Thus it should be surely assumed that the illusory judgment which refers to water not united with the sense-organ is produced by the sense-organ.

As the optical illusion of water refers to water lying beyond the reach of our eyes so why do you not subscribe to the hypothesis that the perceptual judgment refers to an object which is qualified by its denotative term ?

As you hold that the colourless objects such as time, etc. are visualized, why do you not maintain that an object which is characterized by its name is also visualised ? Moreover, the causal relation obtaining between the perceptual judgment which refers to an object as qualified by its name and the sense-organ will not be contradicted.

An objector to the view may contend that he cannot support the above view that sound is visualized as long as he is alive. He advises his rival thinkers to give us his tenacious attempt at bringing home the point that an object qualified by its name is visualised.

(If this contention is thoroughly scrutinized then its hollowness will be transparent). Moreover, if the above judgment is said to be a piece of verbal knowledge as it has been suggested by objector then he should explain how he does acquire the knowledge of signification. A word cannot communicate its meaning if the signification of a word remains unknown. The signification of a word is not grasped if one has only the indeterminate perception of the object denoted by it. The objector stands committed to the view that all determinate perception is a piece of verbal knowledge. Therefore he cannot hold that the knowledge of the signification of a word is due to the determinate perception. The knowledge of the signification of a word is not acquired if it does not come through a distinct source of valid knowledge other than a verbal one. If it is held that the signification of a word is learnt from the verbal testimony then it is an instance of circular reasoning. No body understands that the object which is signified by a word is qualified by the word itself. If it had been so then the meaning of the word 'cow' would have been grasped as the word 'cow' itself.

The last sentence of the above paragraph requires a bit explanation. If we take a concrete case then our point will be clear. If the word 'cow' denotes a cow as qualified by the word 'cow' then it will also be an element of its meaning (the word 'cow' will signify itself).

If a term signifies its denotation as qualified by itself then the knowledge of a mark should also lead to the knowledge of the object marked as qualified by the mark itself.

But fire is never inferred as qualified by smoke. Similarly, a cow and such other objects are never known as qualified by their denotative terms. The state of being signified is never a property of an object. If it had been so then it would have been grasped by the indeterminate perception (i.e. the initial sense-perception) just as colour is sensed.

The Buddhists, the bad logicians, hold that the words cannot signify the real objects. They should be vanquished by an appeal to the evidence of determinate perception. If you (the objector) hold that the so-called determinate perception is a piece of verbal knowledge then how can you win victory over them (the Buddhists)?

How do you hold that a word relates itself with an object which is perceived ? A word should be at first related to its object. At this stage it should be known independently of the word itself. If it is held that a word at all stages associates itself with its meaning then the knowledge of an object would be piece of verbal knowledge. It that case, the Buddhists will surely get the upperhand of you.

You also work under an assumption that the diversity of objects alone accounts for the difference in the character of an awareness. Owing to the obstinate inclination to cling to this wrong assumption you have had to imagine that the object of a determinate perception, being qualified by a word, is distinct from that of an indeterminate perception. Proceeding in this path do not you realise that you mistake perception for verbal knowledge ? What a perversion of intellect ! Doing so you have become an object of the following censure viz. "Oh fool ! you only see honey but do you not see the pit under your feet—the pit where you will drop".

Thus, the judgment that this is a cow is perceptual since it is produced by the eyes in co-operation with the recollection of a word.

It is reasonable to hold that it has not been the creation of the internal organ alone. It is due to the function of the external organ since it is causally connected with it and the causal relation is determined by the joint method of agreement and difference.

Some stalwart followers of the line of the objector come forward with a new objection and hold that it has been proved to the hilt that the judgment that this is a cow and such other judgments do not refer to objects, qualified by their denotative terms. Now, how shall we distinguish a determinate perception from an indeterminate one ? Because an apprehension is not distinct from another if the latter does not refer to a distinct object. When we hear the term—'a club-man', a man who carries a club is present to our consciousness. If this consciousness were not a distinct one then it would have been simply an awareness of a man. Again, a man and a club are not present to our consciousness as unrelated since the club qualifies the man i.e. the relation of the qualifying to the qualified governs this consciousness which arises from the knowledge of the term 'a club-man' (The drift of the whole argument is that the difference in the nature of an object explains only the difference in the corresponding awareness). The acts of consciousness corresponding to the words 'remote, near, slow, quick, successive, simultaneous etc.' refer to an object which is either qualified by space or by Time. Otherwise, the distinction in their meanings would not have been grasped.

If you put a question to me whether Time or Space is directly known then I simply ask you to put this question to your experience but not to me. It is a fact that an object qualified by Time or Space is presented to our direct awareness but on the contrary, it is also strange that they themselves (Time and Space) are never perceived.

This admission also points to the acceptance of the hypothesis that the relation of inherence is perceived under certain circumstances. The judgment that the cloth rests upon this (the collection of interlaced threads) reveals that the cloth inherent in the threads, is perceived. (Thus, the relation of inherence which unites the cloth with the threads is perceived).

The judgment that this is a piece of cloth is distinct from the judgment that this piece of cloth inheres in the threads. If the relation of inherence which subsists between this piece of cloth and the threads is not perceived then the distinction between the above two judgments will not arise since the apprehension of the cloth alone cannot account for the distinction. Now, a second alternative suggestion on this point is as follows: The difference in the two awarenesses focused upon the same object is explained by the distinction in the nature of conditions. The following illustrations will bring home our point. The same post is differently presented to our consciousness when it stands close at hand or is far away from us. The same thing is differently perceived when it is seen with normal eyes or with diseased eyes. The alternative hypothesis does not stand to reasons. The difference in the nature of awareness due to the diversity of conditions is hard to establish. The condition brings about some special feature in the effect viz., an act of awareness reveals but cannot alter an object in the least. But the Naiyāyikas hold that when one is aware of an object he is not aware of the awareness of an object. The act of awareness which is marked by some distinction is not intuited. The object which is presented to our consciousness has no distinction. But it is a fact that a distinction is presented to our consciousness. Thus, the line of the hypothesis is dangerous. The awareness of a near object does not differ from that of the same object, being distant though their conditions are distinct but they differ since the objects are not the same.

When we look at an object from a distance we perceive it as outlined by its general features only. But when we see it from a close quarter we behold it as qualified by its vivid distinctive features.

Māgha has given a description that lends support to our view. He (Vāsudeva) knew at first the object as a collection of rays when it just entered the field of his vision. When it came closer to his sight he saw his form and knew it to be a corporeal being. When it approached nearer still the limbs being distinctly seen he knew that being as belonging to the male sex. When that person gradually came very close to him he recognized him to be Nārada.

We do not mind whatever else may account for the diversity of acts other than that of awareness but the difference in the act of awareness is absolutely due to the diversity of objects.

Some teachers of the Nyāya school join issue with the above thinkers. They hold that the distinction of awareness is not only due to the diversity of objects but also is due to the difference of means. The objector has pointed out that when an object is presented to our consciousness we are not aware of the awareness of an object and if it is held that an act of awareness acquires a distinction without a reference to its object then the hypothesis is beset with enormous difficulty. But such a criticism comes from the lips of a person who is innocent of the Nyāya system of thought. The appearance of apprehension amounts to the perception of an object accordingly to our system. But we are not self-conscious of this act of perception. When we have the indeterminate perception of a person, the object of such perception is only presented to our consciousness but the awareness of this perception remains absent. Though the awareness of an awareness does not take place yet the object is cognized. When the determinate perception of the same object takes place it acquires distinction as it is conditioned by the awareness of its predicate. The above perception is expressed in the judgment that a person is possessed of a stick or clad in a white cloth. This judgment is not self-consciousness but reveals the same object. Thus, the hypothesis in question does not meet with disaster though it acquires a distinction without referring to a distinct object. We also beg to mention in this connection that the judgment that this is a club-man refers only to a person. If you ask, "Who is a club-man" then the answer is "A club-man". Thus we see that the term 'club-man' denotes simply a man having no intimate connection with a club—since in the judgment that a man is a club-man, club-man being a case in apposition with the subject 'man'. Moreover, when we say "Feed a club-man —and give it to a club-man" then we ask some body to feed a man or to give him something. But in these cases the acts of feeding and giving have no bearing upon the stick. Now, a few cases may be pointed out to contradict the above solution. When we say that a club-man is climbing up a mountain the club belonging to him also ascends the mountain. In the Vedic literature, too, the sentence that an assistant priest (Maitrāvaruṇa) having a stick in his hand gives direction to his subordinate priests purports to convey that the said assistant priest should have a stick in his hand since the function of giving directions follows from the previous text. The objector cites, also, another analogous sentence to confirm his view. The Vedic sentence that the priests with red turbans on their head should roam about, does not purport to convey that they should roam about but should have red turbans on their heads since in a śyena sacrifice (a sacrifice which is performed with the object of killing an enemy) the roaming about of the priests has been already enjoined by the basic injunction. (In other words, the objector means to emphasise the point that the distinction of an awareness is explained only by its special object. When we see a club-man we do not merely see a man but a man having a stick. The stick which qualifies the man is also perceived along with the man, qualified by it). A review of the above criticism is as follows: Though there is much truth in the statement of the objector yet a man having a stick in his hand mounts the hill but the stick itself does not ascend it. The above Vedic sentence directs that a priest having a stick in his hand should give directions to his subordinates but not the stick itself should do it. Similarly, the other text does not direct that only the red turbans should roam about. Its direction is that the priests who have red turbans on their heads should only move. In every case, the noun which is signified by a compound word becomes the sole object of knowledge. If both the noun and the adjective had been the objects of knowledge then the corresponding knowledge would have been expressed in the proposition that there are a man and a stick but not in the proposition that there is a man having a stick. Now, the objector may contend that the knowledge should not be expressed in the proposition that has been pointed out by the critic since the relation of the qualifying to the qualified determines the form of knowledge. The contention of the objector is not tenable since the net result of this determination is that the sole object of knowledge is only the noun. Let us find out the meaning of the word 'daṇḍin'. The word 'daṇḍa', occupies a subordinate place in the derivative word 'daṇḍin'. Its literal meaning is that one possesses a stick. Hence, it signifies only a person but does not signify both a person and a stick. Thus, our knowledge of 'before' and 'after' etc. that of 'slow' and 'quick' etc. and the judgment that a cloth inheres in threads etc. refer to such objects as are qualified by space, time and the relation of inherence respectively. These factors viz., space, time and the relation of inherence are included in the conditions of knowledge and determine its distinctive character. But they are never cognized as a cloth is cognized. Thus, the judgment that a slab of stone is heavy refers to a substantive the predicate of which refers to a supersensible quality. This imperceptible quality which is an inference is one of the conditions of the judgment. It is inferred from its effect viz., the going down of the slab of stone. It is needless to multiply the number of examples to establish our point the conditions which are not perceived contribute to the distinct character of a judgment framed by them. Hence, the judgment that this is a cow does not refer to an object as qualified by its name. Therefore, it is not a piece of verbal knowledge. But it is a clear case of perceptual judgment. The judgments of this type come within the province of perception, so the assertion of the futility of the definition of perception becomes baseless. Hence, the adjective 'avyapadeśyam' has not been given in the sūtra to meet the charge that it is impossible to define perception.

What is the function of this adjective ? We simply repeat

the answer, given by the celebrated teachers of the Nyāya school that it has been given to exclude such knowledge as arises from the two distinct sources of knowledge within the field of perception. The hypothesis that the experience of objects qualified by denotative words is perceptual has not as yet been conclusively proved. When we perceive an object before us we apprehend only the objective features belonging to it. But when we know that the object 'cow' is denoted by the word 'cow' we entirely depend upon a sentence which enjoins that such and such word signifies such and such object for our knowledge, though we may learn the relation of signification subsisting between an object and a word from other sources of knowledge yet the verbal testimony is the only source of knowledge in some cases. Suppose, when an experienced teacher imparts instructions in nomenclature to a common man with regard to objects in the following manner that this is a cow, this is a jack-fruit and so on, the denotation of a word is learnt only from the source of verbal testimony.

For this obvious reason, a man in the street takes this piece of knowledge as arising from the verbal testimony since he is satisfied with this instruction which contributes a new information to the stock of his existing knowledge.

Though his sense-organ plays some part in the acquisition of this knowledge of signification yet he would not have known that this object is denoted by this word if he had not listened to the above instruction. Hence, the verbal testimony plays the most important part in this context.

Hence, the author of the Nyāya-sūtra does not formulate a moral ordinance if he holds that the adjective 'avyapadeśya' excludes the knowledge of signification from the province of perception because he has realized the important role of verbal testimony in its production. Hence, we arrive at the conclusion that the term under discussion is indispensable for the exclusion of such knowledge as owes its existence to the two distinct types of sources of knowledge.

Some other logicians argue thus. The above teachers of the Nyāya school may represent their view that the term 'avyapadeśya' excludes only such knowledge as arises from the two distinct types of sources of knowledge and that this knowledge appears only when the signification of a word is learnt from a sentence employed for instructing the name of an object. If this is their view then the judgment that this is a cow, meant for communicating the acquired signification, should be necessarily generated by the two distinct types of sources of knowledge since the judgment is produced by the sense-organ together with the memory of a sentence learnt by us. We remember that we have correctly learnt that this word signifies the object in question since we have been taught by Devadatta, a reliable person, and so on. Now, the question is "Why do not you exclude such a judgment from the field of perception by the term in question?" Now, they may contend that words do not directly condition the above judgment but their memory. Such a contention is not tenable. The memory of words does also condition the knowledge of signification. The syllables—the constituents of a word, which come in succession are not simultaneously heard by us. When the last syllable is heard the preceding ones have disappeared. Does a word operate in a different manner to produce the knowledge of its signification by means of its last syllable which is either heard or recollected? They may further contend that when the knowledge of signification is communicated by a judgment the judgment is produced by the sense-organ together with the memory of the word denoting an object as an accessory condition. They may also point out that the sentence of an expert, expressing a significant word, directly condition the knowledge of the signification of a word. This contention is not also sound. When the signification of a word is communicated by a judgment the sentence of an expert, pointing out the significant word, is remembered. If it were not recalled in mind then we could not know that such an object is denoted by such a word. When it is recollected that Devadatta has instructed that the word 'cow' denotes this object a person expresses his judgment in the proposition that this is a cow. Therefore, the judgment in question is due to the revival of the memory of the above sentence.

Hence, the judgment in question is a piece of verbal knowledge since the sentence instructing the denotative word conditions it. If they (some teachers of the Nyāya school) subscribe to this view then the determinate perception of the poor logicians will be absolutely precluded from the field of perception.

Even, if the knowledge of the signification of a word is ascertained by some other means of knowledge (say, inference) then the statement that this knowledge of signification is a piece of verbal knowledge cannot be controverted (since a sentence, conveying the required signification, may be imagined as a condition of the subsequent judgment).

The Naiyāyikas firmly stick to the hypothesis that the validity of determinate perception is the life blood of their Epistemology. Hence, the knowledge which owes its existence to the two distinct types of sources of knowledge should not be designated as a piece of knowledge derived from the verbal testimony. The relation of signification subsisting between a word and the object signified is grasped by means of various proofs. Each of them plays its own independent part. Kumārila also holds that the source of the true knowledge of the relation of signification is three-fold. Hence, the verbal testimony alone should not be saddled with the burden of revealing the said relation. When we receive the instruction that this word signifies the object before us and assimilates it we perceive it all along. Similarly, when in order to communicate our acquired knowledge we frame the judgment that this is so and so, we perceive the object as before. Hence perception plays more important part in these two cases. In other words, the sense-organ constitutes the very canvas of this judgment whereas the verbal testimony supplies us with the mere embroidery. Hence, the tentative hypothesis that the term 'avyapadeśya' has been used to exclude such knowledge as is the joint product of the two distinct sources of knowledge is not without its defects (i.e., is not fair). The import of this argument is that the judgment in question is perceptual. Realising the limitation of the hypothesis in question as contrasted with the previous hypothesis, offered by a band of ancient logicians, the ancient thinkers seem to us to be more reasonable. They hold that the term 'avyapadeśya' excludes interpenetrated with word perception from the field of valid perception. Moreover, the term 'vyapadeśya' conveys more literal sense.

Very well, if we accept the hypothesis of the ancient logicians then the objection, raised before against it, dogs it. It is neither invalid nor a class of valid knowledge by itself, i.e., it is a fifth type of valid knowledge. In other words, it has neither head nor tail. But we may meet this objection thus: the ancient logicians intend to mean that word-interpenetrated perception may be analysed into two elements, viz., (1) its knowledge-element and (2) its word-element. The knowledge-element, represents perception. It is generated by the sense-organ. If it illuminates its object aright then it is a piece of valid perceptual knowledge. Again, if its word-element, i.e., the designation of the above perception such as the apprehension of colour or that of taste is stressed upon then it does not discharge the function of an apprehension (i.e., the words, e.g., the apprehension of colour etc., do not reveal colour but simply signify an object. Thus, the word 'apprehension' plays the role of an object. Hence, in the capacity of a word, it is not at all, a piece of knowledge. Thus, there is no possibility of its being called a fifth type of valid knowledge, i.e., a new species of valid knowledge.

Another logician holds that the term 'avyapadeśya' has been used by the author of the Nyāya-sūtra to remove a possible wrong impression that determinate perception is derived from the verbal testimony. The possibility of this wrong impression is due to the following factors that the object which is one of the conditions of this perception is associated with a name and that it also allows itself to be word-interpenetrated. This piece of knowledge is sense-perception since it is causally connected with the sense-organ and its causal connection is determined by the joint method of agreement and difference. Moreover it is not derived from the verbal testimony.

This piece of knowledge is sense-perception since it is vivid, that it is not word-interpenetrated at the time of its appearance, is causally connected with the sense-organ and gets the sanction of the popular view.

Though, in some cases, the recollection of the name of an object is one of the conditions of determinate perception yet it is not derived only from the knowledge of the word since the sense-organ plays the important role of a cause but the remembrance of the name plays the subordinate part of an accessory condition like a lamp to the eye.

Now, if the hypothesis that determinate perception is sense-perception is thus proved then a new difficulty is to be faced viz., indeterminate perception does not come within the province of perception.

On the other hand, some critics think that the so-called determinate perception is derived from the verbal testimony since it is a piece of verbalised knowledge. Now, a retort to this critical remark is as follows :

If even some word-interpenetrated knowledge is proved to be sense-perception then there is no doubt that apprehension which is absolutely free from the association with words is sense-perception.

Hence, the author of the Nyāya-sūtra includes both indeterminate and determinate perception within sense-perception by the term 'avyapadeśya'.

All the different views of the great teachers of the Nyāya school on this point have been faithfully represented here. Let the competent reader select for himself any one of them, that makes an appeal to his mind to be true.

The word Non-erroneous

The adjective 'non-erroneous' excludes erroneous perception from the field of true sense-perception. An illustration of perceptual error is as follows. In summer when the sun shines scorching the forehead with its heat its rays obliquely strike on the surface of the sandy soil and are thrown back. The reflected rays assume the form of waves. They appear as an ocean. The appearance of the rays as an ocean is false since what is presented to consciousness does not correspond to reality. One thing is mistaken for another. The erroneous sense-perception is excluded from the realm of true sense-perception by the adjective 'non-erroneous'. The indeterminate perception (sensation) is such apprehension as follows in immediate succession the initial contact of the eyes with the object. It produces the determinate perception of water. It itself reveals only water. In the stage of indetermination one does not judge but as soon as he opens his eyes for the first time water is presented to his consciousness as a shining object. The Buddhists hold that indeterminate perception has the rays of the sun as its object but as it generates such determinate perception as reveals water so it is erroneous. Two consecutive perceptions which are causally connected cannot but have the same object. Hence, the Buddhist hypothesis is not sound. We have also proved that determinate perception which also refers to (reveals) the name-marked object is sense-perception. The reference to the old topic suggests that determinate perception which refers to absent water is an error of sense-perception. Hence, indeterminate or determinate perception which makes a wrong reference is erroneous. Such an erroneous sense-perception is to be excluded from the province of perception in question. The mistake of the rays of the sun for water refers to an absent water. Hence, it is not produced by the sense-object-contact. Therefore, the phrase 'generated by the sense-object-contact' excludes all errors from sense-perception. Thus, the exclusion of errors from sense-perception being established, what is the use of the adjective 'non-erroneous' ? Such an objection does not hold good.

The illusion in question is produced by the sense-object-contact since it depends upon the sense-object-contact for its appearance. If a man shuts up his eyes he cannot cognize water in a desert. A real object is one of the conditions of this awareness since no unreal object is presented to our consciousness. There are the three different hypotheses, framed by the great teachers of the Nyāya school, with regard to the presented form of an illusory experience. Some of them hold that some of the rays of the sun, which conceal their specific character and assume the form of water correspond to the presented form in question. Let us now explain how some rays appear as water. The three necessary conditions of illusion are as follows. We perceive only those features which are commonly shared by the waves and the rays of the sun. But the rays of the sun do not give rise to the doubtful knowledge that they are either the rays or the waves like the well-known instance of doubt that it is either a post or a man. They produce only a judgment of memory that they are water which is known before to be contrarily opposed to them. If these conditions are fulfilled then the external object itself, being coloured by the subjective element contained in the judgment, fails to reveal itself in its objectively real specific character but appears as water.

Some other teachers hold that water, the memory of which is recalled by the knowledge of its resemblance to the yonder object, is presented to our consciousness. The form which is presented to our consciousness is its ālambana. But the object which is close at hand, is not its ālambana. No unreal object, e.g., a sky-flower, is presented to our consciousness. So, water which really exists in some other part of the country is recalled in our mind owing to the revival of the impression of similarity. Such water is presented to our mind.

The third batch of logicians hold that the condition of awareness is one and what is presented to our consciousness is something different. The rays of the sun constitute the objective condition of consciousness but what is revealed is water.

An ālambana is such a condition of apprehension as is other than the agent and the instrument. Therefore, a supersensible object like an atom is never an ālambana. These three hypotheses on illusion will be more elaborately discussed later on. The sense-illusions which are causally connected with the sense-organs and the external objects arise from the sense-object-contact. Hence, such illusions cannot be excluded from the province of true sense-perception if we simply qualify the true sense-perception by the adjective phrase 'generated by the sense-object-contact'. If it is a fact that subjective hallucinations arise independently of the external sense-organs, they are precluded from the true sense-perception by the above phrase 'generated by the sense-object-contact'. The adjective 'non-erroneous' will not be required to do so. It runs thus :

A lover with his eye-sight distorted by the excessive pressure of love, excited by separation, sees his beloved lady by him though she is actually far away from him.

Now a question arises in our mind, viz., "How does an object-less hallucination reveal a form ?" i.e., "How does it refer to an object ?" Our answer to this question is as follows :

The objects which are generally recalled in memory are presented to our illusory experience. In some occasions the revival of memory is determined by some known factors. In some other cases, the knowledge of resemblance excites memory. Love and grief, sometimes, revive the old impressions left by some object on our mind. An object is recalled in our mind if we are in the habit of perceiving it repeatedly. Some eye-disease which is at the root of optical illusions helps to revive remembrance. Sometimes sleep, sometimes repeated pondering over an object and sometimes the unbalanced condition of the three humours make us recollect the known object. If memory takes place and the known factors which revive memory are conspicuous by their absence then the principle of merit and demerit is asserted to be the exciting factor.

No body knows whether or not a child has the double vision of the moon. If it is answered in the affirmative then the principle of merit and demerit is alone responsible for the revival of the memory of the moon. If it is held that an object which conditions perception is only cognized then the subject-object relation holding between an act of perception and its object is fairly established. An absolutely unreal object which is incapable of conditioning awareness is never cognized. In case of hallucination the hallucinatory object such as a lady, etc., has no chance of being perceived since it does not stand close to the person but being recalled in our mind is presented to our consciousness. The initial adjective, i.e., 'generated by the sense-object-contact' excludes hallucination from the realm of true sense-perception since its origin is independent of the sense-object-contact. But there are cases of sense-illusions. The judgments, viz., "This conchshell is yellow", "This is water" etc. illustrate this type of illusion. They arise from the sense-object-contact. The term 'non-erroneous' has been given to exclude the sense-illusion from the range of the true sense-perception.

A person sees from a distance the bare common outline of an object which is shared by the two objects belonging to different classes, viz., height. He fails to see the specific features, e.g., the crooked holes or hands and legs, etc., of the two distinct species of objects which the above feature belongs to. The experience of the common character awakens the impressions of the two specific features by the law of association. He remembers the two features belonging to the two different kinds of objects. He, then, is aware of alternative predicates at the same time of one and the same subject before him. Such an indeterminate perception is called 'doubt'. Though doubt arises from the sense-object-contact yet it is not true sense-perception. The adjective (determinate) has been applied to true sense-perception in order to exclude doubt from the field of true sense-perception. An objection appears in our mind thus: The inner organ being the only cause of doubt, the adjective phrase 'generated by the sense-object-contact' is sufficient to exclude doubt from the true sense-perception. In that case, what is the use of adding another adjective, viz., 'determinate ?' The objector should not interpret the following passage of the Nyāyabhāṣya in the light of his hypothesis and suggest that the Bhāṣya-kāra also, hints at the truth of the same. The passage of the Nyāyabhāṣya that the invariable mark of the existence of an internal organ consists of the facts of remembrance, inference, the knowledge derived from the verbal testimony, doubt, instinctive intuition, dream, conjecture and the intuition of feelings of pleasure, pain, etc., and inner phenomena such as volition, etc., does not corroborate the view of the objector. A doubt expressed in the form that it is either a pole or a man is produced by the external sense-organ. But it is also a truism that there is a type of purely subjective doubt. An illustration of it is as follows : When an astrologer has made two false predictions if he makes a third one then he hesitates to believe whether or not it will turn out to be true. This doubt is purely subjective since the inner organ is its sole cause. But who shall call the doubt of a person who sees an object with his eyes open and asserts alternative predicates of it that it is either a pole or a man as purely subjective? An error consists of mistaking one thing for another. The object, in front of us, has one definite predicate. But when we doubt it, we assert alternative predicates of it (i.e. we assert many incompatible predicates of it). We say that it is either a pole or a man. Thus, we perceive it differently from what it actually is. Hence, a doubt is an error. Thus, the previous adjective 'non-erroneous' really excludes doubt from the true sense-perception. The term 'determinate' being superfluous, should not be used to preclude it.

Such an objection is not tenable. A doubt is essentially different from an error. Moreover, their causes are definitely distinct. An error is a piece of determinate knowledge which reveals an object wrongly. If we either mistake a pole for a man or we mistake a man for a pole then the predicate is the wrong one. But the nature of doubt is defined as a piece of uncertain knowledge revealing a subject as predicated of two or more irreconcilable predicates at the same time. In other words, when we doubt, our mind oscillates between the two contradictory or contrary predicates of one and the same subject and fails to arrive at a decision. But when we err, we have a definite knowledge. A definite predicate is asserted of the subject. Thus the certainty and the uncertainty of knowledge constitute their essential difference. Such a distinction in their character is experienced by all. The condition of error is also different from that of doubt. Error is conditioned by the remembrance of a property which does not belong to the object in front of us. In other words, an object comes in contact with our sense-organ. It awakens the impression of a property experienced in the past by us. This property which does not belong to the object is remembered by us. Our sense-organ which is in contact with the object and is accompanied by the recollection of the property produces a judgment of sense-error that the object has the property (which is really supplied by memory). The person who remembers silverness at the time of the contact of the mother-of-pearl with his eyes or recollects water-ness at the time of the contact of the rays of the sun with his eyes has illusory experience. But doubt is conditioned by the recollection of the two specific properties, the perception of general outline of an object etc. The disjunctive judgment that this is a pole or a man is preceded by the memory of poleness and man-ness disjoined, i.e., by the recollection of the two disjoined alternative predicates of the subsequent judgment. Thus, a doubt is a class by itself. A separate adjective is required to exclude doubt from the province of the true sense-perception.

If we subscribe to the view of the band of the great logicians viz., 'Pravaras' then the term 'avyapadeśya' is competent enough to exclude doubt and error from the range of true sense perception since it is impossible to hold that doubt and error are indeterminate. The sensation (i.e., the indeterminate perception of the object before us such as a pole etc.) owes its existence to the function of our sense-organ. But in the case of a doubt or an error it is immediately followed either by the remembrance of the one predicate or by that of the two such predicates. An error or a doubt arises from the one or from the other intermediate inner phenomenon. They also illustrate word-interpenetrated experience. The memory of the predicate which is the essential condition of the judgments of doubt and illusion supplies the doubting and the erring persons with the words, the designations of the predicates of judgments. The adjectives 'non-erroneous' and 'determinate' should not be given to exclude them (error and doubt) from the domain of true sense-perception. We have got something to say in this connection. We have already refuted the hypothesis of the Pravaras since we have established that the objects associated with their names are revealed by perception. The objector may contend still that though it is admitted that the hypothesis of the Pravaras has been thoroughly refuted yet it can never be established that doubt and error are produced by our sense-organs since the eyes cease to function when they detect similarity and the memory of the predicate is revived. After the cessation of the operation of the sense-organ an error or a doubt appears. The sense-object-contact is never the immediate antecedent of either of them. Therefore, the initial adjective phrase 'generated by the sense-object-contact' is competent enough to preclude error and doubt from the province of true sense-perception. Such a contention is not tenable. It has been stated that the sense-organ continues to function even after the intervention of memory. The unceasing operation of the sense-organ is known by means of the joint method of agreement and difference since such an error or a doubt as has been indicated above does not arise in the mind of a person who remains with his eyes shut up. When a doubt and an error arise in our mind they are not pieces of word-interpenetrated experience, made to be so by our voluntary effort. When they arise they are intuited as dissociated with words but awaken the recollection of the designation of the objects referred to by them. The recollection of the predicates refers only to them. How the memory of the terms denoting them revived ? The remembrance of the terms denoting the predicates presents them (the terms) before the mind. The recollection of the denotative terms as an essential factor of an error or a doubt has not been proved.

As a piece of determinate perception is not associated with the words denoting its objects, so error and doubt owe their existence to the function of our sense-organ but are not word-interpenetrated. Now; how is the initial adjective phrase competent to exclude such error and doubt from the realm of true sense-perception ? Hence, it is highly reasonable to qualify true sense-perception by the above two adjectives viz., 'non-erroneous' and 'determinate' so that doubt and error are excluded from the province of true sense-perception. Thus we have explained all the terms that constitute the exact definition. But the term 'Pratyakṣa' embodied in the definition stands for the object to be defined. It conveys a conventional sense and signifies also a particular species of knowledge. If it had expressed only the etymological meaning of the word, it would not have conveyed the above meaning. Let us explain why the etymological one falls short of the accepted conventional meaning of the term. The compound word 'pratyakṣa' is derived from the original words 'akṣam' and 'pratigataḥ'. The original meaning is that which depends upon the sense-organ, the generator. Such a meaning of the term may apply as well to pleasure etc. Hence, the conventional sense is more appropriate in this case. Another alternative suggestion is that it should stick to the etymological sense since the word 'jñāna' (consciousness) has been definitely mentioned in the sūtra. The original sense of a word if it is clear, should not be sacrificed. The scholars do not approve of such a meaning as is both etymological and (yoga-rūḍha) conventional (rūḍha). If it is admitted that a word has two kinds of meanings, etymological and conventional, then it will also be held that it does not simultaneously convey both the meanings but only helps the selection of its meaning. Now, one should rationally explain "How is some form of consciousness dependent upon the sense-organ?" If it is held that the term 'pratyakṣa' applies to those objects which are attached to the sense-organ then it should apply as well to 'stye' and such other objects. Again if it denotes such objects as inhere in the sense-organ then it should denote as well colour and such attributes that inhere in the sense-organ. Moreover, if it denotes the constituents of the sense-organ then it should denote as well atoms etc. that constitute the sense-organs. Hence, we should hold that it applies to such consciousness as is generated by the sense-organ. The term 'pratyakṣa' is not an example of the class of 'avyayībhāva' compound (the resultant form of this compound word becomes an indeclinable word) because the word 'pratyakṣa' takes the masculine form when it qualifies a noun in the masculine gender and it takes the feminine form when it qualifies a noun in the feminine gender. The corresponding forms are 'Pratyakṣaḥ puruṣaḥ' and 'Pratyakṣā strī'. These illustrations are enough to prove our point. Here, there is no need of multiplying the number of examples.

Hence, true sense-perception is such consciousness as is qualified by the given adjective phrase and adjectives e.g. 'generated by the sense-object-contact' etc.

Akṣapāda, the highly intelligent logician, has framed a defectless definition of sense-perception whereas the definitions of perception, given by the rival schools, do not satisfy the mind of the critical thinkers. Dharmakīrtti has defined perception (sensation) as such form of consciousness as is free from determination by imagination (i.e. as is not the product of synthetic imagination) and is not incorrect. This definition is not sound.

The Buddhists' definition of determinate perception

Imaginary knowledge (kalpanā) is that the objects of which are expressible in words. (The Buddhists suggest that such knowledge produces confusion in our mind. The objects are presented to our mind as identical with their names (words). Such presentation is the product of synthetic imagination). Jayanta puts the following question to the Buddhists. Why do they not subscribe to the hypothesis that the synthetic judgments of perception are true ?

(Jayanta, now, dives deep into the matter and raises the crux of the problem). Is determinate perception invalid according to you (the Buddhists) due to someother discrepancy besides the alleged defect that it reveals an object which is expressible in words ? (The clause 'which is expressible in words' has been used by them instead of the clause 'which is expressed in words' with a definite purpose. They have used the clause in order to bring all sorts of determinate perception under its scope. The determinate perception, as a matter of fact, of a dumb and of a child does not reveal such an object as is expressed in words. But that object is still expressible in words). The Buddhist rejoinder to the question is that the real nature of the determinate perception will not be discussed if it is not pointed out that its object which is expressible in words is unreal since all the objects signified by words are imaginary and therefore unreal. When a word expresses its meaning it does so if the listener grasps the relation of the word to the object signified by it. But an exclusively particular point of reality is never denoted by a word. Again, reality is only exhausted by a multitude of such particular points of reality. No other kinds of reality are apprehended. The synthetic judgment of determinate perception which is the product of imagination does not arise from the sense-object-contact. Their causal connection is not determined by the joint method of agreement and difference. Such a judgment takes place even if it is not preceded by the sense-object-contact. Even, if such a judgment, the product of imagination, is preceded by the sense-object-contact, it is only generated by the synthesis of the memory of the name of its object—the name that has been learnt before. If the sense-object-contact had generated it, it would have done so before the intervention of the memory of name. But it is a fact that it does not do so. The Buddhists also subscribe to the view that if the sense-object-contact fails to produce it at an early stage then it will not also generate it after the appearance of the memory of the scene.

It is stated in the following verse of a work on Buddhist Logic. If the sense-object-contact does not bring about the synthetic judgment of determinate perception before the appearance of the memory of the name etc. because of its inadequacy then it cannot do so after the appearance of memory because of the same limitation. Hence, a conclusion is drawn that such perception takes place even when the object has ceased to exist.

Moreover, though the sense-object-contact persists yet it is to be admitted that it depends upon the memory of name to produce the desired effect. In that case, the memory of name stands between the sense-object-contact and the determinate perception and separates the one from the other.

The Buddhists say :—

Even though it is admitted that an object has some part to play in the production of a determinate perception yet it should also be admitted that the said perception depends upon the synthetic imagination which links up the memory of name. In that case, the object should be separated from its determinate perception.

Now, the Naiyāyikas may contend that the sense-organ, accompanied by the memory of signification, produces such a perception. Such a contention is not tenable. The contention of the Naiyāyikas is based upon an assumption that the cause, accompanied by the accessory condition, produces its effect. Such an assumption is unwarranted. It is shattered by the horns of a dilemma that the benefit which the cause derives from the accessory condition is identical with the cause itself or not.

Moreover, the judgments of determinate perception such as 'This is a man with a club' etc. do not immediately follow from the sense-object-contact. But they presuppose many an intermediate process. The Buddhists state clearly:—If one knows the qualifier, the qualified, their mutual relation, their actual order and all such prerequisite conditions then and then only he has the determinate perception of an object. Some hold that the indeterminate perception or sensation which follows directly from the sense-object-contact cannot furnish the knower with so many details (i.e. cannot amount to such a complicated process of perception). It has also been stated in this context. How can we call the determinate perception which is manufactured by the recollection of signification, is a superimposition upon sense-perception due to an act of imagination and is not directly related to the real object as true optical perception? Now, an objection may arise in our mind with regard to the above critical remarks. There are two types of the judgments. The first type is illustrated by the judgments of pure imagination i.e. unrestricted imagination. Such judgments are purely imaginary. The second type of judgments contains the form of 'this' a yonder object. These judgments such as "This is blue" etc. illustrate the second type. Of them let the judgments, belonging to the first type be false. Who will care to prove them to be true as they are not based upon reality? But why should not the judgments that belong to the second type be true since they contain the form of the real objects and are causally connected with them. This is the sum and substance of the possible objection anticipated by the Buddhists. A rejoinder to this hypothetical objection is as follows. But all these judgments which are manufactured by imagination remain absolutely unrelated to the points of reality. A point of reality is completely grasped only by indeterminate perception. It has been stated by the Buddhists. No portion of an exclusively particular point of reality remains unapprehended by an indeterminate perception and no subsequent determinate perception should be assumed to apprehend it. It is a fact that some cases of determinate perception contain the forms of real objects and are very vivid like an indeterminate perception. They are so because they closely follow an indeterminate perception which is only causally connected with a point of reality. The form of an indeterminate perception is also imparted to determinate perception, its immediate successor. No determinate perception has direct relation to a point of reality since an indeterminate perception alone receives the form of a real object. In other words, a determinate perception merely repeats the story of its antecedent indeterminate perception and is invalid, having no new information to give.

The images produced by imagination reveal always unreal forms. They do never exactly copy the forms of real objects. There are five kinds of imaginative judgments viz. (1) judgment having a universal as its content, (2) a judgment having an attribute as its content, (3) a judgment having an action as its content, (4) a judgment having a word as its content and

(5) a judgment having a substance as its content. They are called imaginative judgments as they sometimes superimpose difference on a single unit or as they sometimes superimpose identity on the two different objects. There is no real difference between an individual and universal. A judgment involving a universal is imaginary because it abstracts a universal from an individual and imagines a difference between them. Nobody experiences like this that this individual has cowness. Nobody apprehends difference. But a difference is imagined as belonging to a single unit.

The imaginative judgment involving an attribute follows the step of its predecessor. There is no difference between a substance and an attribute. But a difference is imagined to exist between them. A substance which possesses an attribute and an attribute are never separately experienced. But it is strange that one intends to thrust difference upon them.

The judgment involving an action is also a case of thrusting difference on a single unit like the previous one. An action is never distinct from the substance. When we say that Devadatta does, we see neither more nor less than Devadatta.

The judgment involving a word i.e., a name is imaginative since it imagines oneness in the two different things. The judgment that this is 'Caitra' attributes identity to them i.e., it imagines that the name is identical with the object named.

The above judgment has two contents viz., 'Caitra' and 'this' 'Caitra' stands for the word and 'this' represents the real object. There is perfect co-ordination between them. The co-ordination implies their thorough identity. How is such co-ordination possible ? The illustration of the judgment involving a substance is that this is a club-man. The club, being a predicate of 'this', there is perfect co-ordination between 'this' and 'club'. They are two distinct substances. This co-ordination suggests the imaginative character of the judgment involving it. If imaginative judgments superimpose difference on an object which is really one and if they superipose midentity on an object which is really different then why do not the subsequent true judgments appear to cancel them like a true negative judgment negating the illusory judgment that this is silver (when we mistake an oyster for silver)? A reply to this question is as follows. If a real object appears to us to be another then a sublative judgment arises in our mind to negate it. We may illustrate our point by the following example. When we mistake the rays of the sun for water a sublative judgment has a scope to appear in our mind. But in the case of imaginative judgments universals and other such objects are not real. So we have no chance of mistaking one real object for another. But the imaginative judgments only revolve round co-ordination or in co-ordination and confine themselves to an individual. Hence, no sublative judgment has an occasion to arise in order to contradict an imaginary judgment which does not mistake one real object for another. Therefore, no imaginative judgments are the judgments of illusion. But they are not true because universals and such other objects which are revealed by them are unreal. Therefore, the Buddhists hold that these judgments are neither real nor unreal but are a class by themselves. There is no need of further discussion.

Thus these five types of judgments are creatures of imagination. They also reveal a world of unreal imaginary objects like difference etc. The Buddhist logician, having realised that the imaginative judgments are absolutely untrue, has added the phrase 'free from determination by imagination' to the body of the definition of true sense-perception.

Jayanta gives a reply to these objections from the Nyāya point of view

A retort to these objects is as follows. The Buddhists have made a mess of arguments. They have really rambled too much and talked a lot of nonsense. But they have failed to fix up a definite condition that clearly determines the invalidity of the imaginary judgments of perception. Let us suggest the possible alternative conditions of their invalidity and examine them one by one: (1) Is a determinate perception invalid because it reveals an object which is expressible in a word and thus points to an imaginary object? (2) Or, is it invalid because it does not arise from the sense-object-contact, being dependent upon the remembrance of signification for its coming into being? (3) Or, is it invalid because it depends upon many troublesome complicated processes for its appearance? (4) Or, is it invalid because it is dissimilar to the initial indeterminate perception which lacks representative character and because it judges ? (5) Or, is it invalid because it apprehends an object already apprehended ? We may clarify our point and say that a determinate perception grasps an object which has been sensed by its antecedent indeterminate perception. (6) Or, is it invalid because it mistakes one thing for another ? This reason has been expressed in a different language that it superimposes identity on the two different objects (i.e. it mistakes identity for difference). (7) Or, is it invalid because it refers to a universal and its like which are contradicted by the dilemma of relation etc. Hence, it is surely sublated. It is not fair to hold that a determinate perception is invalid because it grasps an imaginary object. How do we know that its object is imaginary ? Because it apprehends an object which is expressible in words. (The Buddhists mean to say that a real object is exclusively particular and as such it cannot be expressed in a word. A word denotes something universal. A universal is a mere concept. It is manufactured by our imagination. Hence, it is unreal). We shall establish the point that an object denoted by a word (i.e. the meaning of a word) is real. Which is this object that is denoted by a word ? It is the very same object as is revealed by an indeterminate perception. Are universals and such other objects apprehended by an indeterminate perception ? "Oh yes, they are apprehended" will be our answer. Moreover, the Buddhists should not hold that a determinate perception is invalid because its object is riddled with contradictions. These contradictions are proved by the persistent dilemma of relation. They will be got rid of as we shall refute the horned syllogism of the Buddhists. A perceptual judgment like a judgment of illusion that this is silver is not as a rule held by the Buddhists to be contradicted by a corresponding negative judgment that this is not so and so. The Buddhists should not hold that a determinate perception does not arise from the sense-object-contact because it depends upon the remembrance of a word which is presented to consciousness when the relation of a word to its denotation is grasped. The sense-organ continues to function even after the production of an indeterminate perception because it gets a new impetus when it is united with an accessory condition in the shape of the remembrance of a word. A sense organ which has hereto failed to produce a determinate perception, produces it when it receives the help of a favourable accessory condition after a lapse of time. How can it be prevented from producing a new effect ? We shall refute the dilemma of benefit afforded to the cause by its accessory conditions in the subsequent chapter on the refutation of the doctrine of universal flux. If the Buddhists admit that the eyes depend on the lamp for the sensation of colour and then they will surely be easy prey to the dilemma levelled against us and have no chance of escape. They also subscribe to the hypothesis that no single cause produces an effect. Thus, the dilemma set up against the hypothesis that a cause accompanied by an assemblage of conditions produces an effect will also place the Buddhists in an infinitely undesirable position. In these circumstances, if both the contesting parties are to blame then one of them should not be singled out as target of condemnation. As the assemblage of conditions such as a sense-organ (the eyes), light, the union of the internal organ with the external one, the object etc. produces a true sense-perception so the collocation of conditions which includes the remembrance of the name of an object in itself will also produce the true perception of colour since each condition has always its quota of contribution towards the production of an effect. A determinate perception of which the remembrance of the name of its object is a condition is not consequently imaginary in its character and is not invalid thereby. The Buddhists also hold that an indeterminate perception viz. the sensation of taste is preceded by the remembrance of colour which constitutes the antecedent condition. Now if the Buddhists urge that the above illustration of determinate perception, offered by the Naiyāyikas, is not a true one and is not true then this illustration of indeterminate perception of the Buddhists, laid on the table, should also be treated as non-perceptual and untrue. Another charge against the validity of determinate perception is that the object of preceding indeterminate perception is clouded by the revived memory of the name of the object of the following determinate perception. But we cannot follow the true implication of this charge viz. the eclipse of an object. It appears to us to be an enigma. The illumination of an object is never obstructed by a condition of consciousness such as a lamp or the internal organ. The remembrance of the name of an object is one of the conditions of perception like the internal organ. As such it plays its part to bring about its perception. How should it conceal an object from our sight ? The Buddhists may contend that a word (i.e. the name of an object) which is recalled in memory obstructs the illumination of the object in question. Such a contention is not tenable. A word like an act of consciousness or like a lamp reveals an object but does never throw an object into the shade. The Buddhists might have said it in a figurative sense. They mean to say that the revival of the memory of a name suspends the function of a sense-organ. Such an argument of the Buddhists is also untenable since a sense-organ still continues to operate.

As an indeterminate perception (the initial apprehension) is brought about by a sense-organ so a subsequent perception (i.e. a determinate perception) is generated by a sense-organ since in both cases their causal relation is determined by means of the joint method of agreement and difference. It is not a fact that when a person recalls a word in his memory he shuts up his eyes and imagines that this is a piece of cloth. Now, the Buddhists may contend that when we remember the name of an object the object of the antecedent indeterminate perception has passed away, since it enjoys momentary existence. The passing away of the object has been figuratively expressed by the sentence that it is obstructed from our vision. But such an attempt to save their skin is really hoping against hope since the doctrine of universal flux will be refuted later on. (The Buddhists advocate the pragmatic test of truth. The object of a perception is never reached. We perceive an individual hut we never get it if we move towards it since it is transient. They hold that the pragmatic test will be satisfied if an individual of the series which the object of perception belongs to is reached). Moreover, even if we assume the hypothesis of the universal flux then we can show that an object is perceived. We shall simply follow the practice of the Buddhists and hold that the object which is grasped by a determinate perception is the same as is sensed by the preceding indeterminate perception though these two objects are not numerically identical yet they are the same in the sense that they belong to one and the same series. The Buddhists have also done something when they hold that a person gets the same object as is rightly apprehended by him. Thus, the suggestion of obstruction is absolutely untenable. Thus, a determinate perception which depends upon the remembrance of signification for its appearance is surely generated by the sense-organ. How is it that it is not a case of sense-perception ?

It has been stated that a determinate perception is not true because it presupposes troublesome complicated processes such as the perception of the subject, the awareness of the predicate and so on. Such a statement of reasons is a very cheap way of criticism. It is not a fact that a judgment is wrong because one undergoes a lot of trouble to frame it.

It has been rightly remarked that the perception of a person is not wrong if he perceives, climbing up a mountain. If the sensation of colour is compared with that of taste then we see that the former requires a lot of troublesome conditions such as the procuring of a lamp etc. Should that sensation be untrue thereby?

It has been stated that a judgment of perception is invalid because it is qualitatively different from an indeterminate perception which contains no element of recognition and because it judges. But this argument is not sound. An awareness does never judge.

It is a knower who alone judges. We shall bring home the point that it is the subject who sees, remembers, recognizes, judges, longs for an object, hates it, strives for it, catches hold of it, gives it up and enjoys pleasure derived from it. Even if we admit that an awareness acquires the power of judging, having come in contact with an object then does it follow that an awareness which judges should be invalid ?

The Buddhists may contend that even if it is assumed that a determinate perception grasps such an object as has been apprehended by an indeterminate perception then as an indeterminate perception alone apprehends an object in its entirety, a determinate perception is invalid because it knows what is already known. The import of the Buddhist contention is that a determinate perception is insignificant as it repeats an old story (literally it presses what has been pressed). But this contention is not sound. We have already met the Buddhist argument. We have mentioned in this connection that novelty does not constitute the criterion of true knowledge. Even if a piece of knowledge apprehends a cognized object then it is not bereft of its property of truth.

The judgments, the products of imagination, superimpose identity on the different objects and difference on the identical objects and are therefore false as they mistake one thing for another. The falsehood of an awareness consists in mistaking one thing for another. A determinate perception is not a case of mistake because a mistake is detected when it is contradicted. But we find no such judgments as contradict the five kinds of imaginative judgments which have universals etc. as their contents and which have been described by the Buddhists. Hence they do not illustrate mistaking one thing for another.

An individual is different from a universal. A substance, the possessor of an attribute, is not identical with a host of attributes. An individual and a universal, a substance and an attribute etc. are so perceived as they are in reality. Hence a determinate perception is uncontradictably a synthetic judgment. We shall prove this point later on.

A real thing and its name are really distinct from each other. They are also presented to our consciousness as mutually distinct. Hence, it is not a case of superimposition of identity. The judgment that this is Devadatta does not import that 'this' is the same as the name 'Devadatta'. The Buddhists cannot hold that the name 'Devadatta' is wrongly thought of as the object Devadatta i.e. occupies the place of (Devadatta) and is presented to our consciousness. It is not a case of ascription of identity. They cannot also hold that the object Devadatta, is in reality nothing but the name 'Devadatta' and is presented to our mind as a word. What is the true import of this judgment?

It is a distinct judgment ! It has a special condition viz. the remembrance of a name. This condition possesses a distinct causal efficiency which contributes to the special character of its effects. In other words, this judgment inherits its distinction from its uncommon powerful condition. The distinct character of this judgment has been already established.

The judgment that this is a club-man i.e. a man with a club signifies that this is identical with a club. It has been illustrated as an example of superimposition of identity by the logicians of slow understanding. The judgment that this is a club does not point to Devadatta but the judgment that 'this is a club-man' does it. In the term 'daṇḍin' the basic word 'daṇḍa' and the nominal suffix 'in' are distinctly presented to our consciousness. The term 'daṇḍin' signifies one who has a 'daṇḍa' (stick). Our judgment corresponds to the real order of things. There is a man named Devadatta. There is a distinct object viz. a stick. It belongs to his hand. A man has a stick in his hand. The objects which stand related in reality are presented to our consciousness as such. Hence, there is no superimposition of identity in the above case. The act of imagination does not discharge the two-fold function viz. (i) it does neither ascribe identity to two different objects nor (ii) it does create imaginary difference in a single unit.

An action is really different from a substance in action. They are also presented to our consciousness as such. When we see an object move we know the true nature of an action.

Hence a determinate perception which apprehends an object as qualified by an action, an attribute, a substance, a designation and a universal is not untrue.

We, the Naiyāyikas, gladly subscribe to this part of the hypothesis that it is not illusory but on the contrary, we record our emphatic denial to the other part of the hypothesis that no determinate perception is true.

If the Buddhists hold that all determinate perception is false because a few cases of determinate perception are contradicted then the Naiyāyikas as well make a counter proposal that all indeterminate perception is false because the double vision of the moon, an example of indeterminate perception, is false.

Let the examples of determinate perception which refers to imaginary objects be false. We take no exception to this decision. But why should the concrete cases of determinate perception which refer to the real objects as they are in reality and are generated by the sense-organ be false ?

The Buddhists put forward a thesis that determinate perception inherits its form from its immediate antecedent indeterminate perception. The suggestion of this thesis is that a determinate perception has no touch with the real object and is not causally connected with the sense-organ. This thesis is untenable because an awareness is formless by its own nature but cannot acquire a form if it does not come in contact with an object. The Buddhists may contend that the fact of succession of an indeterminate perception will furnish it with the required form. A memory-image sometimes follows an indeterminate perception in immediate succession. But the memory-image does not bear a resemblance to that of an indeterminate perception. They hope against hope to establish their thesis.

The Buddhists have stated that the whole of an exclusively particular point of reality is apprehended by an indeterminate perception. This point has been confuted. It has been pointed out in this connection that even though it is assumed that a determinate perception cognizes what has been apprehended yet it remains equally valid. Not to speak much of an indeterminate perception we do not follow quite well what is at all apprehended by an indeterminate perception.

The Buddhists hold that the object of an indeterminate perception is an exclusively particular point of reality which is distinct from all homogeneous and heterogeneous objects.

Some other thinkers assert that the object of an indeterminate perception is the summum genus of all existent objects viz. the genus of existence i.e. being. But another band of thinkers advocates that an indeterminate perception apprehends a word which constitutes the knowable reality.

Some other thinkers hold that a real substance is variously qualified by an attribute, an action, a substance, a universal and the properties and accidens and it is apprehended by an indeterminate 'perception'.

It is a wonder of wonders that there are so many conflicting hypothesis with regard to the very object of perception. But this perception is the highest court of appeal to settle the dispute of the conflicting theories centering round a transcendental object. But how is it possible to settle the dispute over the contradictory evidences of perception viz. 'this is perceived' and 'this is not perceived'? In order to convince others of his hypothesis a person has recourse only to others.

We cannot find shelter in oath and refrain from all mental

activities. But, on the other hand, we try to find out the true object of perception by means of someother methods.

The object of a determinate perception is determined by its antecedent indeterminate perception. By the method of backward calculation we shall fix up such an object of an indeterminate perception as paves the way for the appearance of its succeeding determinate perception.

The Buddhist hypothesis that an indeterminate perception apprehends an exclusively particular point of reality which is distinct from all sorts of homogeneous and heterogeneous objects, is not tenable.

If an exclusively particular point of reality is the object of an indeterminate perception then how can a judgment of imagination, its immediate successor, having a universal as its content all of a sudden come into being ?

A determinate perception should imitate the form of an indeterminate perception.

Moreover, if the Buddhists admit that the exclusion from heterogeneous and homogeneous objects is apprehended by an indeterminate perception then the Naiyāyikas may as well point out that a universal which is not distinct from the above exclusion is the object of a determinate perception. (The Naiyāyikas suggest that there is no qualitative difference between a determinate and an indeterminate perception. If the suggestion is true, the Buddhists are to face an awkward situation).

The exclusion mentioned above is not really different from the object excluded (i.e., it is non-different from the exclusively particular point of reality). Hence the apprehension of the object excluded (i.e. a particular point of reality) implies that of exclusion.

Thus, the awareness of a universal being implied only by the apprehension of an exclusively particular point of reality, the hypothesis that an exclusively particular point of reality is the sole object of an indeterminate perception does not stand to reasons.

The monists who hold that existence is the only reality subscribe to the hypothesis that existence is the exclusive object of an indeterminate perception. This hypothesis is not sound.

Even if it is admitted that the summum genus viz. 'existence' is apprehended by an indeterminate perception then how will a monist account for the appearance of the direct awareness of its subordinate species? If the genus of existence is the sole object of an indeterminate perception then the doctrine of monism with all its implications is established.

The genus of existence cannot be apprehended if its subordinate species are not apprehended along with it. The antithesis that the subordinate species are not mere creatures of Nescience will be established later on.

The hypothesis that the sole object of an indeterminate perception is a word which is the only underlying reality is similarly confuted by us (the Naiyāyikas). How do we visualize a word?

How is a word (i.e. the name of an object) presented to our determinate optical perception if we are unaware of the relation of a word to its meaning (i.e., the object denoted by it) or if we are oblivious of it or if we fail to revive its impression before the actual perception?

If the hypothesis that a substratum is qualified by a variety of inherent properties such as a universal, etc., catches popular fancy then let us give our consent to it.

A substratum of various properties, etc., is not identical with its properties and accidens since they are not cognized being constantly present in it. Again, if we hold that substratum is not something distinct from its properties and accidens but is constituted by them, then the whole is surely distinct from its parts, i.e., constituents.

The upholders of the above view which has been criticized by us may point out that a substratum is not always cognized as identical with all its properties, etc. but with a particular property or accidens whenever or wherever it comes into being or becomes the object of enquiry. Such a revised thesis is also not tenable. Because we do not entertain the idea that there is perfect co-ordination between a substratum and its property. They too never co-exist on the same locus because a substratum is the very locus of its properties, etc. but is not identical with them.

The very real object which is apprehended by a determinate perception is experienced by an indeterminate perception. The only difference lies in an indeterminate perception that it does not reveal the object as qualified by its name.

What is the character of an object when it is apprehended by an indeterminate perception? A reply to this question is as follows: Put this question to an indeterminate perception but do not put it to the rival contesting parties.

We believe that our critics will thoroughly agree with us if they impartially scrutinize the content of an indeterminate perception. They are asked to solve this problem with an unbiased mind.

A substratum is sometimes apprehended together with a universal, a substance, an action or an attribute. Whatever is apprehended by a determinate perception is apprehended by an indeterminate perception.

The object of a determinate perception has only an additional object for the original object is only associated with its name which is supplied by memory. But there is not the slightest difference of a determinate perception from an indeterminate one so far as their real objects are concerned. Therefore all sorts of perception apprehend the same set of objects. Only this point of difference is to be carefully observed that one kind of perception (i.e., a determinate one) is preceded by the memory of the name of an object but the other one (i.e. an indeterminate perception) is not similarly produced.

Therefore, in the definition of perception, offered by the Buddhist logician the phrase 'free from creation of imagination' is superfluous because there is no such possible consciousness as will be excluded by it.

We find no utility of the adjective 'abhrānta' (nonerroneous) in the definition of perception as offered by the Buddhists since it does not prevent the possible overlapping of some undesirable form of consciousness. The Buddhists may now contend that the above adjective excludes some types of illusory perception from true sense-perception. Some illusions are produced by the defective senses. The defect in the eyes is brought about by the timira disease (detachment of retina), the quick motion of a stationary object during a boat journey. The indeterminate perception of the double moon, that of the circle of blazing fire and that of the moving trees illustrate non-imaginary perceptual illusions. They are excluded from the circle of true perception by the adjective 'abhrānta'.

The critics have truly pointed out that there is no justification for the term 'abhrānta' since the phrase 'free from creation of imagination (kalpanāpoḍham)' checks wrong entry of illusion into the sphere of true sense-perception.

But the Naiyāyikas hold that the single moon is the object of an indeterminate perception. The perceptual judgment which succeeds it misreads the object in question. We perceive the rays of the sun but judge them as water. They suggest that all cases of indeterminate perception are true but some cases of determinate perception are wrong.

The Buddhists point out that retina is divided into two parts by some disease and cannot but have the double vision of the moon. This double vision is immediate and, therefore, is an instance of illusory indeterminate perception.

If the Buddhists argue in this way then it may also be asserted that the rays of the sun, reflected in the sandy soil assume the form of water and are immediately perceived as water. But why do not the Buddhists call it as an instance of illusory indeterminate perception? Even if they admit it to be such then their hypothesis that an awareness which is generated by a real object is true and an awareness which is produced by an imaginary object is false should not hold good. Moreover, a piece of knowledge is not falsified unless and until it is contradicted by another piece of knowledge. But if it is held that everything in this universe has only momentary existence then a piece of knowledge cannot be contradicted by another piece of knowledge. There is no need of further criticism.

Dharmakīrti, a logician of sharp intellect, could not correctly put the two words together in order to define perception. If he makes a demonstration of his keen intellect, let him do so. But it is a fact that the logicians of his camp all over the country are silent at the defeat of Dharmakīrti.

Some other philosophers such as Varṣagaṇya have defined sense-perception as the mode of sense-organ, i.e., the unsynthesized impression of an object passively received by a sense-organ. This definition also suffered from the defects and is confuted, therefore, by similar reason. It has been also shown that the soul does not become the subject in and through the operation of the intellect. (If the mode of a sense-organ or of the intellect is the proof and if the awareness of an object is the result determined by the proof then there is no co-ordination between the proof and the result. The result belongs to the soul, the proof belongs either to a sense-organ or the intellect.)

The Mīmāṁsakas' definition of perception refuted

Perception is that form of consciousness which arises from the contact of the sense-organs with the existent real object in the mind of a person. As it throws light only on the existent perceptible objects it does not reveal 'Dharma'. For this reason the sūtra which deals with perception has been interpreted by the followers of Jaimini that it is not a direct definition of perception. They hold that the initial proposition of Jaimini is the definition of Dharma. Dharma has been defined as the end of human life which has been revealed only by the Vedic injunctions. Though the definition of perception has no direct bearing upon the initial proposition, i.e., upon Dharma yet it has been given to indicate that perception has nothing to do with the illumination of Dharma. If this is the real intention of Jaimini, the sūtra which deals with the definition of perception does not introduce a new subject-matter but speaks about something already known. If the interpreters insist on the point that the above sūtra embodies the definition of perception then they act unwisely since the so-called definition does not escape the defect of being too wide.

The boiled-down meaning of the sūtra amounts to this that when the sense-organs come in contact with the existent objects, an awareness which arises in the mind of a person is called perception. This definition of perception is as well applicable to the cases of doubt and illusion since they are also due to the sense-object-contact. Now, if the compound word 'sat-samprayoga' is interpreted as the contact of the sense-organ with the existent real object then hallucinations which are not conditioned by the real existent objects should only be excluded from the province of perception but doubt and illusion which are conditioned by the real objects should not be excluded. The compound word 'sat-samprayoga', they add, may be analysed into its components in a different manner. The second meaning is not also lost sight of. When the contact of the sensa-organ with the existent objects of references takes place true sense-perception issues forth. The indeclinable prefix 'sam' in the 'samprayoga' indicates such a sense-object contact as excludes doubt and illusion.

It has been stated in the following verse (of the Śloka-vārttika of Kumārila). The indeclinable word 'sam' signifies appropriateness or fitness. It excludes inexact sense-object-contact. When a judgment of illusory perception that this is silver arises from the contact of the sense-organ with the pearl-oyster such an inaccurate contact is excluded because it leads up to the perception of silver.

But the appropriateness of the sense-object-contact being supersensuous it cannot be perceived. But it may be stated that it is inferred from the effect. The effect of the sense-object-contact is an apprehension. But if it is not adequately qualified, it does not indicate the appropriateness of the sense-object-contact.

There is neither a single word nor a letter nor the slightest indication found in the sūtra to qualify the resulting consciousness. The object of the compound word signifying the contact of the sense-organ with the real object has been narrated as to exclude hallucination from the field of perception. Another interpretation of the same word representing the precedence of the sense-object-contact as the determining condition of perception amounts to the same thing and is, therefore, superfluous. Now, the Mīmāṁsakas may contend that it is unnecessary to insert in a word to qualify the resulting perception since the proper adjective of it is supplied by the people themselves not trained in any particular school of logic. If this be their contention then the critics may as well hold that there is no necessity of taking the pains of stretching the sūtra to such an extent as to show its competence to embody the definition of perception since the people, innocent of the definition of perception as given by the systems of logic, know perception as an accomplished fact.

Regarding this matter the renowned commentator on the Mīmāṁsā sūtra (the Vṛttikāra) has made his own observation. He states that perceptual consciousness which does not correspond to its object is illusory. He also adds that if our sense-organ does not come in contact with such an object as is referred to by the true perception then the true perception does not dawn. He simply makes a reciprocal change of place of the words 'sat' and 'tat' in the sūtra and transforms it into a defectless one, i.e., an ideal one. But such an attempt ends in wordy nothingness. This new definition of perception is applicable to a doubt as well. According to him the apprehension of an object is a true perception if it arises from the contact of a sense-organ with the object apprehended by it. Again, the apprehension of an object is surely an illusory perception if it does not arise from the contact of a sense-organ with the object apprehended by it. (In a case of doubt there are two alternative suggestions. One of them represents true perception. Therefore, the definition is too wide).

The Mīmāṁsakas contend that the definition is exact since a doubt throws light on the two distinct objects but one's sense-organ does not come in contact with both of them in order to generate it (a doubt). Such contention is not tenable. Unlike a copulative judgment which refers to the two independent objects standing side by side unrelated lika 'Dhava' and 'Khadira' (two trees belonging to different species) a doubt does not refer definitely to the two objects. A doubt is an indefinite state of knowledge which oscillates between the two alternatives. The well-known illustration of doubt is that this is post or a man. But it is, of course, a truism that the sense-organ must have come in contact with one of the two objects. But it is also a fact that the two objects have been alternatively referred to by it. The eyes come in contact with that object which has been referred to by it. Hence, the definition of true perception applies to it and this application cannot also be avoided by some tactful manipulation.

Now the Mīmāṁsakas may give a new turn to the contention and say that there is no need of taking so much trouble in criticizing them since they do not intend to define perception since the definition of perception has been assumed at first and it will be an idle job to repent it. Moreover, the Sūtra repeats the description of perception which has been learnt from the people at large but enjoins that perception is not a source knowledge of Dharma. Perception is not a source of knowledge of Dharma because it apprehends only an existent object. Dharma is not an existent fact because it is not an event in time, being conveyed by verbs such as 'should worship' 'should give' 'should offer libation' etc. Why does the text of the sūtra embody the description of perception ? The reason is that it embodies the minor premise. If a critic takes an exception to the conclusion that perception is only a source of knowledge of an existent object then a reply is given to him that perception reveals only an existent object since it arises from the contact of the sense-organ with an existent object. The sūtra represents perception with the definite object of embodying the above reason for its inability to apprehend Dharma. If one remarks that it is not true that perception owes its existence to the real sense-object-contact then his opinion is refuted by the sūtra. Perception arises from the real sense-object-contact because it partakes of the character of perception. It has been stated in the Śloka-vārttika that the very essence of perception consists in its being produced by the real sense-object-contact and that remaining conclusions follow from it. Or, it may be stated that the very definition of perception determines the essential character viz., the essence of perception. (Thus Kumārila establishes the utility of the sūtra on perception.)

Kumārila suggests an alternative interpretation and holds that the essence of perception should be utilized as an independent stop towards the negative conclusion so that perception is a source of knowledge of Dharma. As our normal perception does not apprehend Dharma so no perception apprehends it. The sūtra on perception does not suffer from the defect of being too wide since it purports to convey some other significance than the mere definition of perception. Such a conclusion does not make an appeal to the mind of a person adept in logic. The following question may be put to him : Does normal perception reveal Dharma ? Or, does transcendental perception of the stages reveal Dharma? But we all agree to the point that normal perception does not reveal Dharma. Why does he take so much pains to prove an agreed thesis ? But as he does not subscribe to the thesis that transcendental perception of the sages is a fact so why does he try to prove that transcendental perception does not reveal Dharma ? If transcendental perception is a fiction as Kumārila believes then there will be no minor term, i.e., the subject of inference will be absent. Hence no conclusion will be deduced in spite of the middle terms such as an illuminator only of the existent object, a perception etc.

The Mīmāṁsakas may contend that they assume the conclusion of the rival school and base their argument upon it. What is the nature of this conclusion ? Is it based upon sound logic or not ? If they accept the first alternative then they will also hold that transcendental perception is real since what is logical in one system is also the same in the other systems as logic knows no partiality. Again, if the proof of transcendental perception is not sound then it has got no solid ground to stand upon in all the systems.

If they assume the existence of transcendental perception with its predicate as given in the rival system and assert some negative predicate of it afterwards then they make a contradictory statement.

The rival thinkers hold that transcendental perception is an illuminator of Dharma. If the Mīmāṁsakas assume it *in toto* and subsequently state that transcendental perception which is an illuminator of Dharma is a non-illuminator of Dharma then they flatly contradict themselves.

In inference we should not depend upon the observation of the subject of inference made by others. This is what has been stated by Kumārila himself in connection with the refutation of Mādhyamika system. If we have no first-hand knowledge of a mark, we cannot infer on the basis of it. So, if we are not ourselves sure of the subject of inference, but are in possession of a second-hand knowledge from the rival school, we should not proceed to make an inference.

The Mīmāṁsakas may contend that it is an admitted method of destructive criticism, i.e., *reductio ad absurdum.* This method consists in assuming the conclusion of a rival party in examining it and in drawing an absurd conclusion from it. The rival party holds that an existent object is only apprehended by perception and perception arises from the real contact of our sense-organ with an object. On that very ground it is justly pointed out that perception is not a proof of Dharma. Is there any defect in this procedure ? No, this is not so.

The method which has been adopted by the Mīmāṁsakas is not really the method of *reductio ad absurdum.* Their attempt looks like drawing a picture on the void, i.e., without having a canvas or its like. (In other words, if existence is denied to transcendental perception it is silly to hold that the said perception is not a proof of Dharma.)

It is not sound to discuss whether the sky-flower is fragrant or not. It is needless to discuss whether their method is proper or not. Let it be the method of *reductio ad absurdum.*

We may also use the same method on our side as a defensive measure. We do not arrive at the generalization that no perception is a proof of Dharma. Who knows that nobody's perception reveals Dharma ?

You cannot know that I do not perceive Dharma. I cannot know that you do not perceive Dharma. Both you and I cannot know that he does not perceive Dharma like us.

If you introspect the contents of the perception of all beings then you have yourself become a sage. In that case why do you vainly hate a sage ?

Oh Vedic scholar ! I just remind you of the fact that your acquisition of the knowledge of the real supersensuous objects is second hand. (The Vedic literature presupposes that there is somebody who is directly aware of the supersensuous objects). Therefore, I entreat you not to find fault again with the narration of supersensuous objects made by others.

Nobody can contradict a well-established fact or theory. It is also futile to lend one's approval to something not based upon sound proof. Please hold in your passion for discarding transcendental perception but try to find out ways and means of establishing it.

Cognition of transcendental perception

Now, if the critic of transcendental perception states sound reasons for his disapproval then we are prepared to accept them. But if he fails to do so then we shall believe that he has none to his credit.

The critic may join issue with us and reply that the Naiyāyikas are well conversant with the logical art of establishing positive theories, but not merely adept in negative criticism. He accepts the challenge and enquires about the positive proof in favour of transcendental perception which apprehends Dharma. A reply to this question is as follows : The competence of this perception lies in its superior quality. We only perceive the near objects with our eyes when we receive assistance from light. The cats (the enemies of mice) perceive objects situated on a spot enveloped by pitchy darkness. It is learnt from the Rāmāyaṇa that the king of Vultures, Sampāti by name, saw the daughter-in-law of Daśaratha (Sītā) from a distance of a hundred yojanas (a yojana=4 miles roughly). The superior quality of perception varies in degrees like the superior quality of the colour 'white', etc. The truth also remains implicit in the above statement that when the quality or perception varies in degrees a section of the class attains the highest degree of perfection. Those whose perception reaches the highest degree of perfection are called 'sage'. The most excellent perfection of perception is constituted by the apprehension of subtle, separated from the field of vision by partition, remote, past and future objects. The Mīmāṁsakas argue against the above hypothesis thus : Though perception reaches the climax of perfection yet it cannot violate the law which governs the nature of its objects. Dharma is not at all a perceptible object.

Kumārila states that when one comes across the superior quality of perception he notices that a man, possessed of the superior power of vision, perceives only visible objects. The examples of the perception of subtle or remote objects point to this direction. We may have excellent ears but cannot perceive colour with our ears.

Kumārila further adds that the superior order of genius and memory is observed in men but nobody comes across such superior order of sense-perception as apprehends the transcendental objects.

Such criticisms are not fair. It is a truism that though Dharma is transcendental to normal sight yet it is sensed by the sages. The above examples, cited by us, show that a very distant object (an object lying at a distance of a hundred yojanas) and an object covered by darkness, are beyond the reach of our normal eyes but still are respectively sensed by Sampāti and a cat. A natural reaction to this sort of reply is that if a sage perceives a transcendental object then he should also perceive odour, taste, etc., with his eyes. Kumārila argues in this strain. If one imagines that an omniscient sage grasps every object of the universe by means of a single source of knowledge then he should admit that the sage perceives taste, etc., with his eyes.

The point towards which Kumārila drives is not based upon the solid rock of facts. The other sense-organs of the sages are endowed with super-excellent powers like the eyes. Hence, the fantastic hypothesis that a sage perceives taste, etc., with eyes is not to be conjectured. The Mīmāṁsakas may contend that the Naiyāyika should not imagine that a sage perceives Dharma with his eyes. The Naiyāyika gives a pertinent reply to this that Dharma is not invisible like taste, etc. The Mīmāṁsaka argument is based upon the misrepresentation of the above sentence that taste and similar qualities other than colour are always imperceptible. This sentence is reduced to the logical proposition that some objects are not perceptible. It is not a universal negative proposition that no objects excepting colour are perceptible. Moreover, how does the Mīmāṁsaka know that Dharma is not perceived with eyes? The Mīmāṁsaka replies that an object is known to be not fit for perception when it is not perceived with eyes though it is present before the eyes. Let us take the example of sound. It is not perceived with eyes though it enters the field of vision. (An answer to the above question is only suggested that Dharma is transcendental.)

The Naiyāyika reviews Kumārila's arguments and points out that the latter cannot say from his experience that a sage, though endowed with super-eyes, cannot perceive Dharma because Dharma and the excellent power of the eyes of a sage are imperceptible to him. Therefore, Kumārila should not hold that Dharma is not a fit object which is perceived with eyes. This is the concluding portion of the above topic.

Dharma is the eternal fulfilment of Duty. Past, present and future do not put a limit to it. Is it not a rash act to hold that

Dharma is perceived with eyes ? Surely, it will be rash on our part to hold that it is perceived with the mortal eyes of you and me. But it is not at all difficult for the omniscient sages to behold it.

The knowledge or eternal Dharma is only derived from the Vedic injunctions such as 'should sacrifice', etc. How can it be learnt from the sources of knowledge other than the Vedas ? But this argument is not based upon the observation of facts but only upon the technicality of the Mīmāṁsā system. We have got nothing to do with the eternality or non-eternality of Dharma. As we know that the act of going has an object in view, viz., the reaching of some other place so the sages will know that the religious acts such as the performance of Agnihotra (the recitation of praises in honour of Fire-god) will lead the performer to heaven. Is it an act of rashness to draw a conclusion like this ? If the Mīmāṁsakas find fault with the external sense-organs and cannot admit of the excellence of them then we (the Naiyāyikas) do not insist on the acceptance of the former hypothesis put forward by us, viz., the sages perceive Dharma with their supernormal eyes.

When a sage meditates on Dharma and practises constant contemplation upon it he intuits Dharma with his internal organ like a love-sick person who beholds his beloved lady by means of meditation alone.

The reason behind such intuition is that the internal organ is competent to comprehend all objects without an exception and there is no such object in the universe as defies its penetration. We have also got a lot of examples to show that men, practising meditation upon objects which are beyond the reach of sense-organs, have clear and vivid vision of them.

It is stated that men, oppressed by lust or excessive grief, disease, insanity, a dream of thieves etc., have clear, distinct vivid vision of imaginary objects as if they are before him.

The Mīmāṁsakas may contend that the above examples illustrate false knowledge and it is not fair to establish the true transcendental perception of the sages after their analogy. Such a contention will not hold good. The point of similarity towards which we drive is that the transcendental perception of the sages is as clear and vivid as the above examples of false knowledge are. When we say that a sound is like a jar we do not mean that they resemble each other on all points. The clear and vivid vision of imaginary objects springs up from the constant practice of contemplation upon them. Again this habit of contemplation is determined by lust, excessive grief, etc. The truth of such vision is contradicted by the corresponding opposite true judgment. But the transcendental perception of a sage is not untrue because it is not contradicted by another judgment. The quality of clearness and vividness is commonly shared by these two pieces of knowledge (true and false). Again, if we devote ourselves to the continuous practice of some activity such as the act of jumping then we do not acquire an unprecedented excellence in it thereby. He who practises the act of jumping (high or long) everyday with undivided attention, springs up or forward only a few steps more, i.e., makes a very little progress in his act but does neither jump over the mountain nor the ocean.

A rejoinder to this objection is as follows. The act of jumping is a property of our body. Phlegm is one of the constituents of our body. Inertness is an innate attribute of it. It offers perceptual resistance to the progress of jumping. The act of jumping does not reach the climax because it faces hindrance all along. But our knowledge reaches the highest summit because there is no obstacle to its upward journey. The state of excellence laboriously acquired by the body on the previous day, is not retained by it on the following day. But by mere practice phlegm and fat are considerably reduced. The body becomes light. The person is able to jump over so much distance as his body permits.

Statement of intuitive knowledge

But in case of knowledge when we repeatedly concentrate upon an object each act of concentration leaves an impression behind it. These impressions accumulate on our soul. They construct the stable background of our knowledge. When they are arranged in a perfect order they produce the highest form of knowledge.

Let us take an example which shows the acquisition of proficiency in learning. A young student undergoes a prescribed course of discipline such as the strict observation of the vow of celibacy, the regular revision of the old subject-matter learnt by him, etc., in order to learn the Vedas by heart. He acquires permanent impressions thereby. They, being stable as they are, help him to recall the matters read by him in memory with perfect facility and dexterity.

Or, as gold, being slowly purified in a closed vessel, acquires matchless beauty, so the inner organ of a sage is capable of perceiving all knowable objects by the constant practice of meditation.

On the other hand, the inner organ of worldly men like ourselves being enveloped by the veil of passions we do not acquire the highest stage of knowledge, i.e., omniscience. Is there any object which is not directly grasped by the pure inner organ of the sages ? The reason of this direct awareness lies in the fact that all the impurities of their mind are consumed by the daily practice of meditation. The method of cleansing the impurities of the inner organ such as worldly attachment, etc., will be elaborately discussed in the chapter on Apavarga (Final emancipation). Thus, when the sages consume all the inner drosses and acquire high proficiency in the art of concentration by the constant practice of meditation, they attain to faultless omniscience.

We foresee sometimes future events. An illustration of the true judgment of foresight is that my brother will come tomorrow. Such foresight is called as Pratibhā Pramāṇa. This piece of valid knowledge is not hallucinatory. It is not a doubt. It is not even negated by its contradictory judgment. Its source is not a defective sense-organ. Therefore, it should be treated as a piece of valid knowledge.

If it is negated sometimes by its true contradictory judgment, it will turn out to be a false one. But if the brother actually comes on the day predicted then will not it be a true one ? Do the critics call it a true judgment ?

If the critics point out that the correspondence of the judgment in question to facts is purely accidental then it is replied that the plea of accidental correspondence does not hold good since the real object has been truly revealed beforehand.

An argument against the validity of this piece of knowledge is this that it is not generated by an object since the brother who is the object referred to is absent at that time. Certainly, this argument would have held good if he had known his brother as present on that occasion. But he knows him as a possible event in future. This idea of possibility, too, is an event of the present time. The brother under consideration is present as a possible object which is perceived. Hence, how can the argument of the critic that it is not produced by an object be tenable ? The critics contend that it is unreasonable to hold that an object is grasped with a future characteristic feature. What is a future characteristic feature ? A feature does not exist now but will come into being at a later period. It is really the pre-negation of an object which is limited in time. How can a negative fact be related to a positive object ? Because, they are incompatible with each other by their very nature. This misdirected old criticism is untenable. It is not the pre-negation of the person (i.e., of the brother in question) but the pre-negation of the contact of the person with the house in question. This pre-negation is not incompatible with the person. The brother, the substratum, actually exists. He is recalled in our memory because he is anxiously expected at the time of dinner. The brother who is thus recollected is presented to our consciousness in the form that he will come here tomorrow. The brother in question is one of the conditions of prophetic vision (pratibhā-jñāna). Hence, this type of knowledge which is not hallucinatory but is conditioned by a real object is really valid.

This type of valid knowledge is direct but not indirect. Indirect knowledge admits of three species. It belongs to none of them since it does not depend upon a word, a mark and resemblance for its appearance. It may be objected that it cannot be direct since it is non-sensuous. Such an objection is not tenable since the inner organ determines it. Now, if the inner organ could independently apprehend external objects then there would have been no blind person in this universe. Such an objection has been met before. It has been answered that the external object which has been perceived with eyes is only intuited by the inner organ. Thus, the objection that there would be no blind person is fairly met. It has also been stated before that a piece of knowledge which is true but comes into being on the absence of the acknowledged conditions of knowledge such as a word etc. is an instance of valid inner perception. It bears a close resemblance to the judgments such as 'ketaka flower is sweet-scented'. 'Sugar is sweet' and so on. The critics are not in a position to take an exception to it with the remark that the direct awareness of a sage is not determined by a definite set of conditions like the normal perception. The implication of the previous line is that it is not perceptual. The answer to the above charge is that the transcendental knowledge of a sage is always perceptual. If it is not direct it is not the knowledge of a sage. Some hold that the knowledge of a sage is in toto derived from the scriptures. The implication of the conjecture is that it cannot be direct. All the sources of the knowledge of a sage have not been exhaustively given but have only been illustrated by means of a single instance. The Vedas are one of them. No such knowledge arises in the mind of a sage as does not spring up from a source.

Now, another objection arises in our mind that foresight is non-perceptual since perception refers only to a present object. Kumārila has stated that an object which is present and comes in contact with our sense-organ is only sensed. Moreover, it should also be noted that the differentia of perception is that it apprehends a present object. Such an objection is not tenable. The objectors themselves have been stated in another place that an object with its future property is apprehended. When silver is perceived it is also perceived that it will last long. In fine, it is also established that the perception that my brother will come to-morrow reveals a future object. As the perception of an ordinary man refers to a future object so the transcendental perception of the sage refers to future Dharma.

Thus, the argument against omniscience offered by Kumārila is refuted. Kumārila has stated that : As an ordinary person grasps a particular type of object by means of a particular kind of proof so a similar object was grasped by a similar proof in the past.

Now, the following objections appear in our mind. Is omniscience constituted by a single act of transcendental perception or by many acts of transcendental perception ? The first alternative is not possible since the incompatible objects like heat and cold are never present in a single act of consciousness. By many acts of consciousness all the objects of the world are not known. Do these acts of consciousness arise simultaneously or successively ? They cannot simultaneously arise since the internal organ, the instrument of consciousness is so small that it cannot simultaneously produce many acts of consciousness. If it produces them one after another, it will not be able to generate the direct awareness of all objects concealed in the womb of the three worlds by the ten millions of Manu periods. How are the sages omniscient? A rejoinder to the objection is as follows : The sages will simultaneously perceive all the objects all over the world by a single act of perception.

The argument against the co-presence of the incompatible objects in one act of perception has no binding force since the contrary qualities such as 'blue', 'yellow', are co-present in the awareness of a picture. We may also cite instances which show that we simultaneously feel heat and cold on some occasions. They are as follows : a person who has descended the icy cold water of a lake up to his navel with the upper part of his body exposed to the spark-like hot rays of the sun in a midday of the summer season simultaneously feels heat and cold. If the sages perceive all the perceptible and imperceptible objects past, present and future in the universe by a single act of perception, how can they be distinguished from God, the greatest teacher of the universe ? There is a clear-cut distinction between them and Him. His omniscience is eternal whereas that of the sages is acquired as it arises from the practice of meditation.

One cannot meditate upon an object which has not been known before. If the Vedas are the source of Dharma what is the use of meditation ?

If the sages are pioneers to know the true nature of Dharma from the Vedas then the well-ascertained proposition that the Vedas are the only source of Dharma is never contradicted. This is the final argument of the objector.

Our reply to the above objection is as follows : There is an element of truth in the above objection that the sages are initiated into Dharma by the Vedas. Afterwards when they reap the fruit of meditation the transcendental perception of Dharma flashes in their mind. The net result of it is that the ascertainment of the truth of the thesis that the Vedas are the only source of the Dharma becomes shaky. Moreover, the eternal perception of Dharma belonging to God is the source of Dharma. God is the author of the Vedas because of His perception. This point will be discussed later on. If God's eternal perception is proved then the above thesis that the Vedas are the only source of Dharma is not conclusively proved. Therefore, the argument offered by the Mīmāṁsakas, against the possibility of the transcendental perception of Dharma by the sages, is not convincing. The Mīmāṁsakas have argued that Dharma cannot be perceived by the sages because an existent object is only perceived and perception arises only from the contact of the sense-organ with an existent object.

Now, the view that the scriptures are the only source of Dharma, i.e., the merit arising from the performance of the acts enjoined by the Śāstras, has been confuted by the following argument: Every word informs us only of known facts. The Vedas are nothing but the sum-total of words. Hence, they possess the character of words. Each of the words cannot furnish us with a piece of knowledge of an object not known before. (In other words, words do not denote novel objects. The Vedas which are words do not signify novel Dharma. Dharma is grasped by some other means of proof. Thus the Vedas are not the only source of Dharma). A jar, being a knowable object, is to be perceived by somebody in the universe. All these counter-arguments are easily available (to silence the objectors). Why do you vainly present a picture of a series of defective arguments to negate the existence of transcendental perception, resulting from meditation and revealing all objects of universe-transcendental perception which is based upon uncontradictable reasons.

Therefore, the sūtra on perception, put forward by Jaimini thus interpreted, (i.e. meant for the refutation of transcendental perception) is really irrelevant. It has been already shown that the sūtra does not serve the purpose of the definition of perception.

Some logicians suggest a different definition of perception. They hold that the consciousness which arises from the contact of the soul, the internal organ, the sense-organ and the object and which is other than inferential knowledge and such other indirect knowledge is called perception. This definition suffers from the defect of being too narrow and also too wide. It does not apply to the introspection of pleasure of the soul and of consciousness itself, since it arises either from the contact of the two conditions of the above ones or from that of the three conditions of them. It also applies to the case of perceptual illusion and so on.

Sāṁkhya definition of Perception refuted

Īśvara Kṛṣṇa, on the other hand, has defined perception as a clear and distinct image of its corresponding object. This definition is not defectless. But it is very wide since it is applicable to an inference which is also a clear and distinct image of an object. Rājā, the author of Yuktidīpikā explains the above definition of perception given in the Sāṁkhya-Kārikā in the following manner : According to him the indeclinable 'prati' signifies 'in front of'. Hence, perception is the clear and distinct image of an object which is in front of the person concerned. This definition, taken in the light of this interpretation, does not overcome the defect of being too wide since it applies to an inference as well. Like the perceptual judgment that this is a jar, the inferential judgment that this hill contains fire refers to an object which is cognized to be in front of the person concerned. The object of every awareness is, of course, clear and vivid. The above interpreter, contends thus : In case of perception an image has only been mentioned whereas in case of inference and verbal testimony the images have been specified. In the latter two cases, processes of framing images have been specifically mentioned, viz., in case of an inference the image is framed by means of a mark but in case of verbal testimony the image is produced by means of a word. As a special rule restricts and narrows down the wide application of a general rule so the special images distinguish themselves from the particular image. Hence, an image which is other than the special ones is perception. If this line of defence is final, perception would not have been defined at the outset. When inference and verbal testimony will be described we shall be able to recognize perception as distinguished from them. Hence, if the definition of perception does not contain the adjectival clause 'which arises from the sense-object-contact', it is not logically maintained that perception is distinguished from inference, etc. Hence, the above definition is not sound.

It is needless to speak much about it. For the reason indicated above the definitions of perception offered by the other systems are without defects. So, the definition of perception, framed by Gautama, attracts the mind of high intellectual attainments.

Inference—its Definition

When perception which is the presupposition of all other sources of knowledge has been defined, Inference which occupies the next place in the hierarchy of ways of knowledge will be defined in the wake of the treatment of perception.

Inference which is dependent on perception admits of three kinds, viz., (1) Pūrvavat, (2) Śeṣavat and (3) Sāmānyatodṛṣṭa (Nyāya-sūtra I. 5).

The essential character of inference will be discussed at the outset and then the sūtra will be thoroughly explained.

We know for certain at first that the sign possesses five characteristic features and that the relation of invariable concomitance between the sign and the signified belongs to it. The passage from the definite knowledge of the sign thus characterized to the definite knowledge of the thing signified, which is not an object of perception is called inferential knowledge.

The determinate knowledge of the sign or the sign thus known together with the recollection of the relation of invariable concomitance between the sign and the signified belonging to it is called the means of inferential knowledge (inference as a process is the proximate cause of the valid inferential knowledge. The knowledge of the thing signified is its result. If the knowledge of the thing signified is called a means then the judgment that the thing signified is acceptable, or avoidable, etc. will be the resultant form of inference. It has been fairly decided that the proximate cause or an instrument of the true knowledge is called a means par excellence. The term 'liṅga' is full of significance since its primary meaning is that a liṅga is that by means of which an object, lying beyond the reach of perception, is grasped (liṅgyate—made known). A sign possesses five characteristic features which are as follows :

(1) The presence of the reason (sign) in the subject (minor term), (2) the presence of the reason (sign) in the positive example, (3) the absence of the reason from the negative example, (4) the reason being not contradicted by other sources of true knowledge, and (5) the reason being not counterbalanced by another reason. The knowledge of such reason, possessed of these five characteristic features, is the proximate cause of the inference of consequence.

Pakṣa is the subject (i.e., the locus of the object signified) regarding which there is a desire to establish the point by inference that the thing signified belongs to it as its adjective. The object signified is tentatively asserted of it as its adjective. The syllogistic proposition that the middle term (the sign) is the predicate of the minor term (pakṣa) leads to the conclusion that the minor term is predicated by the major term (the signified object). Another positive example confirms the truth of the concluding proposition. A negative example (vipakṣa) is such as contradicts the conclusion. The absence of the reason from such a case is essential. The reason is free from contradiction if the conclusion is contradicted neither by perception nor by verbal testimony. If a reason is not counterbalanced by another reason (i.e., the minor proposition is not challenged by another counter-minor proposition), another (conclusion) which creates doubt about the truth of the conclusion does not arise. A reason which is possessed of these five characteristic features leads to the inference of a conclusion. The faulty or apparent reasons are those which are devoid of any one of these five characteristic features. They will be elaborately discussed later on. A faulty reason is called the asiddha (unreal) when it does not belong to the subject. An example of it is as follows :—

Sound is eternal because it is visible. A faulty reason is styled the opposite when it is an invariable concomitant of the contradictory term of the major term. An example of it is as follows :—Sound is eternal because it is created like the sky. A faulty reason is designated as the indefinite when it does not universally belong to the positive instances (i.e. when the middle term is not distributed). An example of it is as follows:—Sound is eternal because it is knowable (the reason is not absent from the opposite examples i.e. non-eternal objects are also knowable). A faulty reason is called Kālātyayāpadiṣṭa (contradictory if the probandum is contradicted by our true experience or knowledge. An example of it is as follows:—

Light which is a constituted whole consisted of light particles is not hot because it is a created object like a jar. A faulty reason is called inconclusive when it is not immune from being counterbalanced by another reason. An example of it is as follows:—Sound is non-eternal because eternality is known to be absent from it (sound) as it is absent from a jar. This is counterbalanced by another proof. Sound is eternal because non-eternality is not found to be present as it is not found in the sky. If the five characteristic features characterize the reason, the reason becomes the invariable concomitant. A criticism of the Nyāya theory that the five characteristic features of a true reason are necessary for distinguishing it from a faulty one is as follows:—The Buddhists subject the Nyāya theory to severe criticism. Very well, you have stated your point of view. But we have got something to speak against you. A true probans is invariably concomitant with its probandum if it possesses only the three characteristics in lieu of the five ones mentioned by you. If the probans is thus characterized then its possibility of being associated with a probandum which is contradicted by a piece of valid knowledge is ruled out since invariable concomitance and contradiction are incompatible. The example of this type of faulty reason selected by you is absolutely unreasonable.

In the syllogism "Fire is not hot because it is a product; the reason, a product, has the three conditions; over and above them it has another feature, viz., it is concomitant of the major term, 'not hot' which is contradicted by touch-perception. But if this reason is carefully examined then it is clear that it does not possess the three conditions of a sound reason. A sound reason must be present in the subject of inference. But the above reason does not belong to it. In the subject of inference the presence of a major term is doubtful. It may or may not be present in the subject of inference. But its absence in the subject of inference should never be determined by another proof. If its absence is determined then the subject of inference ceases to be so. A reason which is present in such a defective subject of inference should not be taken as belonging to the subject of inference. Moreover, the positive relation of invariable concomitance holding between this middle term and this major term has not been discovered. Had it been so, its discrepancy would have been detected then and there. A generalisation based upon the observation of positive instances refers to all cases. Thus the major premise is "Whatever is a product is not hot". When we verify it we see that fire is a product but is hot. Thus how can the major premise be arrived at ?

It is contended that all the positive instances excepting fire (the subject of inference) have been observed and the above generalisation has been based upon them then our retort to it is this induction is not universal since the class of the subject of inference has been excluded but in case of true induction this class cannot but be included. This all-inclusive induction is called antar-vyāpti.

As this reason is not invariably concomitant of the major term in question, the conclusion drawn from the reason in question looks like approaching an impotent person with a prayer for love.

The negative instances should also be observed so that we may arrive at the true induction. But the foundation of induction is the method of agreement. The method of difference is merely a corrective process which clears the way to induction. As the verdict of the observation of the positive instances does not go in favour of the above induction so there is no possibility for the method of difference to work on it.

Moreover, what you intend to infer is that fire is not-hot. But it is perceived that fire is hot. Thus fire turns out to a contrary instance. But fire being a product the reason is present in the contrary instance. Therefore the above reason does not fulfil the conditions of a true reason. But, on the contrary, it becomes a faulty reason. Hence the alleged condition of a true reason that it should not be invariable concomitant of such a major term as is contradicted by another proof is logically untenable. How do we know that the alleged condition is an essential one ? The mere non-perception of contradiction does not lead to the conclusion that there is non-contradiction here since persons who are not omniscient cannot know truly non-contradiction. If the condition of a true reason be non-contradiction, all reasons cease to be true ones since according to the Buddhists a reason devoid of one of the three essential conditions ceases to be a sound one. In fine, non-contradiction should not be one of the conditions of a true reason. This is the sum and substance of the critical remarks made by the Buddhists.

A retort to the above objections is as follows:—It has been stated that when the relation of invariable concomitance holding between the two positive objects is known to be universal, we know for certain that the mark in question is not an invariable concomitant of the object marked since fire, the subject of inference, is perceived as characterized by such property as is contrary to the property intended to be established as belonging to it. But his statement is not convincing. It is a truism that an induction is universal but is not a case of perfect enumeration. Thus in order to arrive at a generalization we shall not consider all the individual cases one by one. If we do it, we shall have to face too insurmountable difficulties. First, we shall not be able to generalize because we cannot take into consideration all the particular cases since they are infinite in number. Secondly, if induction is a mere summation of perceptions then deduction is superfluous since the conclusion is a known fact. Let us take a concrete case to bring home the point in question. If all places which contain smoke and fire are perceived, it is generalized that where there is smoke there is fire. If it is inferred that the hill is fiery because it is smoky then this inference is truly superfluous since it simply repeats the story of the previous perception. The hill in question must have been perceived before as containing smoke and fire since the above generalization is impossible without such perception.

Thus, we arrive at an inductive truth referring to all particular cases in an abstract manner, e.g., where there is smoke etc. But we do never refer to all particular cases such as a hill, a forest, a house etc. in order to arrive at a generalization.

This being the method of discovering the universal relation of concomitance it is not an idle pursuit like the offering of a love proposal to an impotent person. We find no justification in leaving aside this method of difference in order to discover the universal relation of invariable concomitance.

When the relation of invariable concomitance is discovered in an abstract manner and its truth is reaffirmed by a reference to the subject of inference we call it as antar-vyāpti (really universal). When we infer that the hill is fiery we discover that the relation of concomitance holding between smoke and fire exists in all places such as a forest etc. outside the hill. In this stage though the relation in question is believed to be universal yet it is called as tentatively universal (bahir-vyāpti). At a subsequent period of time when it will be inferred that the forest is fiery it virtually becomes antar-vyāpti. Let us now discuss the point in question. We arrive at an induction that what is a product is not-hot in an abstract way but do not refer to fire, the subject of inference. Thus, the relation of concomitance holding between the above two terms is established. Now, in the syllogism, "The body of luminous substance (a whole) is not-hot because it is a product" the atoms which constitute the body of luminous substance illustrate the contrary example. No thinker can mention such an absurd reason. It may be pointed out that the moon, the stars etc. are constituted by luminous atoms but they are not hot. A thinker may frame a syllogism of which the product is the middle term and not-hot is the major term. The major premise is based upon the tentative induction which must be verified in order to accept as universal induction. At the time of framing the premise no contrary example has come to his notice. But no proposition having the subject of inference as a term should be cited as a contrary example.

Now, the Buddhists contend that nothing really possesses the two mutually contrary characteristic features. If the subject of inference possesses the major term as its attribute then it really becomes a similar example. If it does not possess it then how is it that it is not a contrary example. It cannot also be held either that the subject of inference alternately becomes a similar example and contrary one or that it is neither a similar example nor a contrary one. The import of this contention is that a neutral subject of inference is an absurdity. But such a contention is not tenable since it strikes at the very root of inference and does away with it. It is a truism that a thing is not endowed with the two contrary characters. But it is in the nature of inference that an object should be exclusively selected as the subject of inference. If we do not do so then it will not be possible to find out either a similar example or a contrary one since they are independent of the subject of inference for their very existence as possessing unquestionable authority to decide the fate of the subject of inference i.e., they act as the unquestionable standard of verification. If the character of a contrary example is attributed to the actual subject of inference and the syllogistic process is vitiated thereby then the sound process of deduction might also be invalidated by such a contrivance.

Now, the Buddhists may contend that in case of sound inference the subject of inference viz., a hill is not definitely known as containing the negation of the major term whereas in the above case the subject of inference viz., a body of luminous substance is definitely known as containing the negation of the major term viz., not-hotness (coldness). If this is their contention then is the hill in question definitely known as containing fire before the actual inference takes place? If they answer in the affirmative then why is fire inferred at all?

Now, the Buddhists contend that there is neither the positive judgment that the hill is fiery nor there is the negative judgment that the hill is not fiery but there is the disjunctive judgment that the hill is either fiery or not-fiery. Hence, the hill which is the subject of the above disjunctive judgment is a case of doubtful contrary example The Buddhists may hold that a reason which belongs to a doubtful contrary example should be a faulty one like one belonging to a contrary example. If a reason which belongs to a doubtful contrary example becomes a faulty one like a faulty reason belonging to a contrary example then the very possibility of inference is threatened. Hence, we should not invalidate a syllogistic process by making a reference to the subject of inference as a case of contrary example. But the reason is faulty because it is not invariably concomitant of the major term in question (i.e., the relation of invariable concomitance does not hold between the state of being product and the state of being not-hot (cold). But it is a truism what has been again pointed out by you that the reason does not belong to such a subject of inference as is not contradicted. But we also take a note of this criticism and hold that the predicate of the above subject of inference is contradicted by perception. We also point out in this connection that the reign of contradiction does not only extend over the subject of inference but also over a reason.

There is no such subject of inference as is absolutely independent of a reason since it is a reason by means of which some predicate is asserted of it (the subject of inference). (In other words, we establish the conclusion that a hill is fiery because it is smoky. We prove that a hill, the subject of inference, contains fire because it has smoke (the reason).

But when we try to establish something as belonging to the subject of inference as its attribute and directly perceive that another attribute which is contrarily or contradictorily opposed to the above attribute belongs to it, the reason which belongs to the subject of inference is contradicted, i.e., is connected with the negation of the attribute to be inferred (i.e., the major term) since perception contradicts the relation of invariable concomitance holding the major term and the minor term.

Thus, it should be admitted that one of the essential conditions of being a true reason is that it should be invariably concomitant with such a thing to be inferred (i.e., a major term) as is not contradicted in any locus of their compresence. But the reason belongs to the subject of inference viz., fire. Thus the condition of being a faulty reason, viz., its non-presence in the subject of inference, does not invalidate it.

If you hold that the non-contradictoriness of a reason is not possible to ascertain then, Oh great logician ! how do you ascertain the contradictory character of the subject of inference ?

If you make sincere attempts to find out contradiction but fail to do so then you should admit that there is no contradiction. But if you deny the truth of this maxim then all your practical transactions will be impeded by imaginary doubts.

The Buddhists hold that the sound reason has only three characteristic features. But a reason, thus characterized, may fall a victim to another defect of being contradicted, viz., it may be imagined to be concomitant of a major term, the presence of which in the locus of a reason is contradicted by some other proof. Therefore, non-contradictoriness should be distinctly included in the list of the conditions which are essential for a sound reason. The Buddhists hold that contradictoriness and invariable concomitance are mutually incompatible with regard to a reason which is marked by the three characteristic features mentioned by them (the Buddhists). This incompatibility is not universal. In some cases it holds good. In other cases, an exception to it is noticed. In other words, contradictoriness and invariable concomitance are compresent in some reasons, marked by the above three characteristic features. But invariable concomitance which belongs to a reason, marked by the five characteristic features, reaches the ideal state of perfection since such a reason excludes contradictoriness. In this case, the hypothesis of incompatibility between invariable concomitance and contradictoriness is truly sound. In case of a reason, marked only by the three characteristic features, the hypothesis of incompatibility is not logically tenable. Thus, it has been stated that the hypothesis is partially tenable and partially untenable. Enough of this discussion.

The relation of invariable concomitanee based upon the law of identity and causality as held by the Buddhists

The Buddhists have said that the recollection of niyama (a rule) is one of the conditions of inference. What is this niyama? It is the real relation of invariable concomitance holding between the middle term (the probans) and the major term (the probandum). It is also called an indissoluble connexion between objects or ideas. It is also designated as their constant compresence. The Buddhists hold that the laws of identity and causality constitute the ground of indissoluble connexion between ideas or objects. The Naiyāyikas demand a further explanation on this point. They say that the Buddhists should not stop with this sort of incomplete answer but as logicians should find out the real ground of invariable concomitance. The Buddhists (the

Bhikṣus) have discovered that the relation of invariable concomitance is based upon the laws of identity and causality. A positive object is identical with some object. How can it be different from that? A śiṁśapā (an individual belonging to a species of tree) is a tree. So a śiṁśapā constitutes the probans for the probandum that it is a tree. This probans is based upon identity. This is a tree because this is a śiṁśapā. (This judgment is analytic). Thus the indissoluble connexion between these two ideas is based upon the law of identity (this law is really appriori in character as it is not discovered after observing facts, but by the action of our thought a creation of our imaginative mind). What is an effect is absolutely dependent upon its cause for its very existence but is never independent of it. When an effect is cognized it leads to the inferential knowledge of its cause. It may be illustrated thus:—Here is fire because here is smoke. Smoke being an effect of fire smoke, the effect, is a reason. The indissoluble connexion subsisting between smoke and fire is based upon the law of causality. (The judgment based upon the law of causality is empiric). The Buddhists hold that the Naiyāyikas exhibit an attribute of escapism when they state the mere rule of invariable concomitance but not the ground of two-fold indissoluble connexion.

The Refutation of the Buddhist Hypothesis

A reply to the above objections is given thus :—We prefer the crude hypothesis of the rule of invariable concomitance offered by the persons of obtruse intellect—the hypothesis which has been stigmatized as the walking on foot to the laws of identity and causality—the grounds of the knowledge of invariable concomitance as devised by the men of sharp intellect. If the law of identity is the ground of invariable concomitance, the middle term becomes identical with the major term. In that case it is impossible to establish that the middle term is a mark of the major term since if the middle term is not cognized as a distinct term, the major term is not known to us. (If we do not see smoke in a hill, we cannot know that fire exists in that hill. The conclusion follows from the premises). (In an analytic judgment are the two terms simultaneously apprehended or not? If the mark i.e., the middle term, is apprehended then do we apprehend the thing marked (i.e., the major term) along with it or not ? If the thing marked and the mark are not simultaneously apprehended then how is it that the mark is identical with the thing marked ? If they are simultaneously present to our consciousness then the thing marked is perceived like the mark. In that case is it not useless to infer the thing marked ? No, the Buddhists may contend that inference has its justification since it is necessary for sublating a contrary character which may be ascribed to the thing marked. Such a defence is not tenable since when an object is truly determined there is no scope of ascribing an opposite character to it. Let us take a concrete case. If we see the head, hands etc.—the distinct limbs of an organic whole then we cannot conjecture that the yonder object is a post. In the above example the limbs, the head, hands, etc. being distinct from the man who has them, we may possibly attribute the essential character of a post to a man since the above limbs are not identical with the whole, the man. We may assume that as we do not see the whole but the different parts of it so we may ascribe some contrary attribute to it. But in the Buddhist example of svabhāva anumāna the śiṁśapā tree is identical with a tree. Hence, when we determine a śiṁśapā tree as a śiṁśapā tree we cannot attribute an attribute which is contrary to the essence of a tree to it. Moreover, in the above case, we determine a śiṁśapā tree as a tree. We have definite knowledge of its generic character. But we have not as yet identified its species. If we at all commit a mistake, we may take one particular species for another i.e., we may mistake a śiṁśapā species for a non-śiṁśapā species. But if we have definite knowledge of the specific character of an individual then we cannot commit a blunder as to its generic character i.e., if we definitely know an individual as belonging to the species to śiṁśapā then we cannot take it for a non-tree.

If the species of śiṁśapā is perceived by a percipient then is it not borne out by our common experience that the genus remains transcendental to his sense-organs ?

Moreover, if the reason is identical with the consequence then as it is inferred that it is a tree because it is a śiṁśapā so it should be inferred that it is a śiṁśapā because it is a tree since the judgment "a śiṁśapā is a tree" is analytical. Similarly, as the conclusion that it is non-eternal follows from the premise that it is an immediate successor of effort and that the premise that it is an immediate successor follows from the premise that it is non-eternal. If the identity of reason with the consequence is accepted, the difference holding between productivity and successiveness to an effort and that between such successiveness and non-eternality should die out. This difference is based upon sound logic. When we infer that this is non-eternal because this is a product, is a similar example which testifies to the truth of the induction concerned available ? But if we infer that this is a product because it is non-eternal, a contrary example which invalidates the underlying induction is available.

Now, the Buddhists may contend that there is a great gulf fixed between full-fledged relation and invariable concomitance. A relation belongs to both the terms, i.e., the relata. On the other hand, the relation of invariable concomitance implies the dependence of one term upon another. The essence of a śiṁśapā is an invariable concomitant of the essence of a tree but the latter is not an invariable concomitant of the former. Similarly, successiveness to an effort is an invariable concomitant of non-eternality but not the vice-versa. A similar case may be cited. Smoke is the invariable concomitant of fire but not the vice-versa. The Naiyāyikas point out in this connection that they completely endorse the view of the Buddhists but the latter should take note of the significance of their hypothesis. It amounts to mere concomitance based upon the empirical law but not to invariable concomitance based upon the law of identity. In case of identity a śiṁśapā is never perceived as a non-śiṁśapā. Now, if a tree is identical with a śiṁśapā then whenever a tree is seen it should be seen as a śiṁśapā. But when we see a catechu tree we see a tree but not a śiṁśapā. When we see lightning we know it to be short-lived, i.e. non-eternal but do not know that its non-eternality immediately succeeds an effort. How does the relation of identity hold between the above two pairs ?

Several examples may be cited to demonstrate that the reason is absent but the consequence is seen to be present. If the one exists without the other, but they are held to be identical then such a statement is deceitful.

Now, the Buddhists may contend that though a flash of lightning is non-eternal and a jar is non-eternal yet the non-eternality of the latter is different from that of the former since the non-eternality of the latter only follows an effect in an immediate succession. Such a contention leads to another conclusion that a property, belonging to an individual substratum, is exclusively private. Thus, there is no common property which is shared by all. Hence the relation of invariable concomitance which is asserted to be shared by many individuals cannot be possible. Therefore, the possibility of inferential knowledge which is based upon the knowledge of the relation of invariable concomitance should be ruled out. But fire, being the cause of smoke, it is reasonable to hold that smoke is the invariable concomitant of fire but not vice-versa, since smoke is different from fire. On the other hand, where the reason is identical with the consequence any one is the invariable concomitant of the other. The relation of mutual invariable concomitance does not hold between non-eternality and productivity. Hence in the above case, the identity of the reason with the consequence cannot be maintained.

Either the Buddhists should discard the relation of invariable concomitance based upon the law of identity or they should justify the following conclusions viz. it is a śiṁśapā because it is a tree and it is the immediate successor of an effort because it is non-eternal. Identity and non-identity exclude a middle term. A new point should be added to the above points of criticism. In order to illustrate an inference based upon identity the Buddhists cite the following example, viz., sound is non-eternal because it is a product. Is it really an analytical judgment? Let us analyse the concepts "non-eternality" and "the character of being a product" and see whether they are identical. The meaning of the term 'non-eternality' is 'meeting destruction'. The meaning of the term 'the character of being a product' is 'having a new beginning'. An object which comes into existence meets its destruction. The appearance of an object is not asserted to be its destruction. Therefore, how is it that the reason is identical with its consequence?

The Buddhists contend that if the term 'non-eternal' signifies 'destructible' then the conclusion should assume the form that sound is destructible but not non-eternal. Such a conclusion is surely false since it is difficult for us to comprehend the conclusion that sound is destructible as we do in case of the conclusion that the hill is fiery.

Destruction is negation. It cannot be a property belonging to a substratum since when we cognize destruction its substratum, i.e., the object destroyed, is never present to our consciousness.

Moreover, if the word 'anityatvam' (non-eternality) is grammatically analysed, we see that the nominal suffix 'tva' has been attached to the word 'anitya'. The suffix 'tva' signifies an abstract quality which is, of course, positive. Thus the boiled-down meaning of the word 'anityatva' is positive essence of the non-eternal. Now, if the word 'non-eternal' has a negative meaning then how is it that it has a positive essence, because a positive essence is incompatible with the negative real? Thus, the word 'anityatva' denotes real existence marked by the two terminations (ends). The word 'kṛtakatva' (the character of being a product) denotes existence which belongs to a real object, being brought about by its cause. Thus, the reason is existence and the consequence is existence. Hence, it is an instance of inference based upon the law of identity.

The refutation of an example of inference based upon the law of identity

The contention of the Buddhists is not tenable since the reason and the consequence are not presented to consciousness in the form as described by them. If the Buddhists stick to their contention then the syllogistic form should be like this : A sound is existent because it has existence. But this form is conspicuous by its absence. On the other hand, the current syllogistic form is that sound is non-eternal because it is a product. The object to be inferred is such existence which inheres in a real object which is brought about by its cause. But this thesis is not tenable. Destruction which is one of the two ends by means of which existence is marked is absent at that time and hence fails to describe existence accurately.

Now, the Buddhists may hold that destruction is one of the boundary lines of existence, though actually absent, is supplied by our imagination. If this is their answer then the Naiyāyikas will also hold that destruction, though actually absent, may qualify sound, being supplied by our imagination.

As a present predicate is asserted of a subject so a future predicate may be asserted of a subject in the same manner.

Thus, the judgment "sound is destructible" is possible since the problem of the relation of an absent predicate to its subject is solved. Hence, there is no point in subscribing to the conjecture that existence is to be inferred. The Buddhists have taken exception to the attachment of a suffix which denotes an abstract quality to a negative term. But they have done it quite unwisely. Those suffixes denote the essence of the meaning of the words which they are attached to (i.e. their essential property). They are attached to words which denote positive reals because these reals possess the uncommon property. Similarly, it is a fact that the suffix 'tva' is attached to the word 'abhāva' which denotes a negative real. In other words, a negative real has also some unique property. Hence, the word 'anityatva' denotes the abstract property of a destructible object which may be comprehended. The word 'kṛtakatva' denotes the abstract property of an effect which is produced but not existence (unconditional). But the Buddhists may contend that it should denote such existence as belongs to an object which has been brought about by its cause. In that case, the Naiyāyikas give a retort to them that it will be better if it simply denotes the abstract property of a product which characterises it. No better purpose will be served if a different track is followed.

(The Buddhists try to bring home their thesis that there is invariable concomitance based upon the law of identity). They argue that if the appearance and the destruction of an object are the two unique distinct properties of an object, the subject of inference and the example cannot have the same reason and a general proposition cannot be formulated. The peculiar property which belongs to a jar does not belong to sound and what belongs to sound does not belong to a jar (the same reason should belong to the subject of inference and to the example). If it is held that there is only one property which is commonly shared by all the positive objects, then they will have to face an absurd conclusion viz. when an object comes into being all the objects of the universe should come into being and when an object meets its destruction all the objects of this world should cease to be. The Buddhists arrive at the conclusion that existence is a better substitute for appearance and destruction and it should be resorted to as reason and consequence. The Buddhist thesis is not sound. Because though the different subjects have distinct properties yet they are presented to our consciousness as the same.

The reason behind our point of view is that the destruction of a jar is not the jar itself. If it were identical with the jar itself then an inference in the above case that sound is non-eternal because it is created like a jar would have been impossible, because the same reason does not belong to the subject of inference and to the example, the reason being different in each case as it is not other than its substratum.

Moreover, a single common property, viz., destruction, does not belong to all objects of the universe. Therefore, the Nyāya thesis is not open to the objection that when an object is destroyed all objects should meet destruction.

Thus, though the attributes of the different objects are distinct yet they are apprehended by us as the same attribute. The net result of this apprehension is that there is no hindrance to our inference since there is perfect harmony between the reason belonging to the subject and that belonging to the example.

Though the attributes are distinct yet they are presented to our consciousness to be the same. Hence, there is no difficulty in the formulation of a general proposition i.e., the major premise based upon induction. Thus the relation of concomitance obtains between the middle and major terms. One does not require the presence of a public property, shared in common by many but only similarity, in order to formulate a general proposition. That is why the author of the Nyāya-sūtra does not make mention of the common attribute but only of the similarity of attributes. The reason proves what is to be established through its similarity with the example. The proposition which contains the reason is called 'hetu'. The example has the characteristics of the subject because of its similarity with it. The proposition which refers to an example is called 'udāharaṇa'.

Therefore, the syllogism which contains origin and destruction as its middle and major terms does not illustrate an inference based upon the law of identity since the middle term is distinct from the major term. Thus the refutation of the Buddhist thesis is thoroughly established. Similarly, an effect cannot be the reason by means of which an inference is made. Does the relation of cause and effect take place between the two momentary objects or between the two series of momentary objects ? When the doctrine of the universal flux will be refuted we shall point out that the relation of cause and effect does not take place between the two instantaneous objects. If such a relation at all takes place between them, it is very difficult to comprehend because of the subtle character of them. The two series of smoke and fire have merely imaginary existence and hence the causal relation does not subsist between them. The Buddhists hold that the reality of an object consists in its practical efficiency. If inference is from smoke, the effect to fire, the cause, smoke, having the characteristic features such as bad odour, dark colour, ascending the sky, etc. should constitute the reason. Concrete smoke with all the attributes is the effect of fire. Some of its attributes cannot be taken away by means of abstraction. It cannot be held that smoke with these limited characteristic features is not the effect of fire. Smoke with all its attributes is the effect of fire as it is evident from the joint method of agreement and difference. Now, if it is established that smoke with all its attributes is the effect of fire then the Buddhists may revise their thesis and hold that smoke, which is not specified by its peculiar attributes but is marked only by its class-character and is concomitant with fire, leads to an inference of fire. If this be the case, the Buddhists vainly make mention of the reason as an effect but should only speak about its concomitance. The relation of concomitance is the means of inference.

Now, the Buddhists contend that the Naiyāyikas have also admitted the actuality of inference from an effect to its cause. The type of inference styled śeṣavat illustrates the above point of view. Kaṇāda has given a list of real relations as the basis of inference. He holds that inference is either from effect to cause, or from cause to effect, or from one term conjoined to the other correlative term, or from the one form inherent to the other correlative term, or from the negative term to its positive correlative term. The Buddhists establish their point that inference is from effect to cause as they get the support of Kaṇāda.

The Naiyāyikas meet the Buddhist argument and point out that it is not the intention of Kaṇāda to enumerate all the real relations which constitute a basis of inference but mentions them by way of illustration to prove his point that the invariable concomitance between the ground and the consequence constitutes the sound basis of inference. We infer fire from smoke and rain-fall from the swelling of the river-current not because of their causal connexion but because of their invariable concomitance. This is the final conclusion of the Nyāya school.

Now, a question arises, "How is it that the relation of concomitance subsists between the pair of the two opposite terms, viz., a positive term and its correlative negative term ?" A positive term and a negative one are related to each other as ground and consequence. If we find the presence of one of them, we infer the absence of the other. Thus the relation of invariable concomitance subsists between them, i.e., the pair of the two opposite terms. Kaṇāda does not exhaustively enumerate all the relations but he merely illustrates some of them in his Vaiśeṣika-sūtra.

There are in this world various other reasons which constitute the real ground of inference. Let us illustrate our point, citing a few examples. Noting the setting of the sun, the rise of stars is inferred.

Seeing the full-moon in the sky the swelling of the sea is inferred. Noting the rise of the star called Agastya some infer that the birds are resting upon the dry sea-shore, forming a long line.

When the ants proceed in a long line and carry off their eggs on their mouth the travellers anticipating imminent rainfall by inference make haste to repair their thatched cottages.

Thus we see that there are various reasons which constitute the sound basis for inference but invariable concomitance is not based upon the laws of identity and causality.

The popular view of invariable concomitance, based upon the laws of identity and causality, has been neglected by the philosophers of extensive knowledge. The Buddhists prompted by sheer puerile obstinacy, are eager to lend their support to it.

It is a logical blunder to hold that the reason is either an identical term or an effect. In the Buddhist logic, the middle term and the major term denote the two concepts. The concepts are negative in character as they embody exclusion. Thus, the ground and the consequence remain confined in the imaginary world of concepts, i.e., negation. But the invariable relation of concomitance subsists between the particulars which are objectively real. And it is held to be an object of conceptual knowledge in the Buddhist system. How does it conform to the Buddhist Logic ? We have elaborately discussed this point in the first chapter. There is no special occasion for dilating on this point. In fine, the major premise which conditions the conclusion refers to the relation of concomitance subsisting between the middle term and the major term. It does not point to the invariable connection based upon the laws of identity and causality as the disciples of Buddha have conjectured.

The Buddhists put this question to the Naiyāyikas : "On the dictation of which proof do they (the Naiyāyikas) hold the indissoluble connection of the Buddhist school amounts to the invariable concomitance of the Nyāya-school". The Naiyāyikas also put the same question to the Buddhists : "On the dictation of which proof do they (the Buddhists) know that the laws of identity and causality are the source of indissoluble connection ?" (Of course, the answer of both the schools will be the same, viz., observation). Nothing can be gained by this unfruitful ramble.

Thus we have explained invariable concomitance. Let us now see what is suggested by recollection, contained in the phrase 'the recollection of invariable concomitance'. Our contention is as follows :

Generalisation always precedes the deductive conclusion, i.e., inference. It is nothing but the discovery of the universal relation holding between the middle term and the major term. But a man living in an isle abounding in coco-nut trees (nārikela-dvīpa) cannot infer fire from smoke. When he infers fire he does not observe the relation of invariable concomitance. But when he observes the relation of invariable concomitance he does not infer.

Hence, he has observed before the relation of invariable concomitance holding between the middle term and the major term. When he tries to deduce the conclusion he presupposes the major premise as its antecedent condition. But it flashes in his mind as a judgment of memory. If the matter is carefully scrutinized by us then it is clear that the major premise which precedes a deduction is a judgment of memory.

Does not the true knowledge of the object to be established arise in our mind if we see the middle term as an invariable concomitant of the major term ? But we do not always recollect the major premise.

When we infer something which has been repeatedly inferred we do not remember that we recollect the major premise as the condition of inference. Though it does not belong to our conscious plane, we must assume that it subconsciously precedes our conclusion.

Some logicians hold that the recollection of the major premise, i.e., the invariable concomitance holding between the middle term and the major term which is recalled in our mind by the present condition, i.e., the perception of the reason is the cause of inference. In some cases, the perception of the reason as belonging to the subject of inference takes place. There are some other cases where this perception does not take place. We shall also discuss about the inference of supersensuous objects such as God, the principle of merit and demerit, sense-organs, etc. later on. Thus, when the invariable concomitance holding between the middle term and the major term is remembered in a manner described above, the knowledge of the object to be established by means of the true reason is called an inference. This is the final conclusion of the Nyāya-school.

An Objection to the Validity of Inference

If inferential knowledge is valid then there is scope for discussion about its definition. But its validity does not stand the fire of criticism.

The primary meaning of the word 'pramāṇa' (the source of valid knowledge) is only accepted—but not its secondary meaning. Hence it is very difficult to find out the meaning of the word 'anumāna'—the means of inferential knowledge. The primary meaning of the word 'liṅga' (mark or reason) is to be sacrificed. The secondary meaning of it is to be accepted. It denotes in a secondary sense such a mark or a reason as belongs to the subject of inference. Such a meaning of the term is not sound. Suppose, if we try to establish that fire belongs to some particular place, say, a hill, then the well-known reason does not belong to it (the subject of inference). Because specified smoke which plays the part of a reason does not belong to the minor term. (Smoke the origin of which is linked up with fire is the true reason). This sort of smoke belongs to fire but not to the hill. If the hill is to be inferred then the relation of invariable concomitance does not subsist between the hill and smoke thus specified. Because we cannot generalize that where there is smoke there is a hill. Again, if it is held that both the hill and fire are to be inferred then smoke, the reason, neither belongs to the minor term nor is the invariable concomitant of the major term. Because such smoke does not belong to both the hill and fire and moreover, we cannot generalize that where there is smoke there are both the hill and fire. Again, if the hill as containing fire is to be inferred then the above reason does neither belong to the subject of inference nor is, invariably, concomitant of the major term. No body perceives that smoke belongs to the hill which contains fire. No body generalizes that where there is smoke there is a hill which contains fire. The conventional meaning of the term 'pakṣa' according to which it denotes the subject of inference having the object to be established as its attribute is to be abandoned so that the reason possesses the characteristic of belonging to the subject of inference. The secondary meaning of it is to be accepted. It signifies, now, only the object to be established. Thus the secondary meaning represents only a portion of the primary one. Thus the relation of invariable concomitance is shown to subsist between pakṣa in the secondary sense and hetu (the reason). Thus, the definition of anumāna (inference) turns out to have a secondary meaning like the definition of perception according to which perception is what arises from the sense-object-contact. Therefore, inference is not a source of valid knowledge.

The other points of criticism are noted below. If a particular object is to be established then the relation of invariable concomitance between it and the reason cannot be established. (We may infer fire but cannot infer the particular fire which belongs to the hill in question. If we infer fire in general then we apprehend what has been already apprehended. It is like doing what has been done. Moreover, fire, having no peculiar trait of its own exists nowhere. Hence the talk of inference is an absurdity.

It is an act of foolishness to pin faith in concomitance as an invariable relation because though we experience a hundred instances of concomitance holding between the two terms yet we notice cases where such concomitance does not take place.

All objects change in character when their time, space and circumstances alter. Hence, it cannot be held with certainty that the so-called relation of invariable concomitance remains constant for good.

The capacity of all objects changes as their time, space and circumstances alter. Hence, it is very difficult to infer an object on the basis of our previous experience.

Even if we admit that the relation of invariable concomitance exists, it is very difficult to discover it without the shade of doubt unless and until we apprehend all the objects of the three worlds. We may entertain a doubt about the origin of smoke from a cause other than fire so long as we do not perceive all the particulars of smoke and fire as causally connected.

The persons who like you (the reputed Naiyāyikas) can directly perceive all the objects of the universe are to be assumed as endowed with the divine eye. Do they feel the slightest necessity of inferring an object ?

If the Naiyāyikas hold that the relation of invariable concomitance is not confined within the realm of particulars but obtains between the two universals, we, the Cārvākas, take a strong exception to this view since a universal has no objective existence in the real universe. (Thus, the possibility of discovering the relation of invariable concomitance by means of the transcendental contact in the shape of a universal is ruled out). If it is repeatedly observed that one thing goes along with another thing then it is not decidedly concluded that the relation of invariable concomitance obtains between them. Because in the face of the repeated observations of concomitance say, a thousand times, a tentatively accepted probans has every chance of not accompanying the expected probandum. A particular character of property or relation of an object has been repeatedly observed by you. But when the very same object is observed by you in a different time and place you see it to be entirely different.

We do not join issue with you if you definitely hold that smoke accompanies fire. But how do you arrive at the conclusion on the score of repeated observations that smoke does not exist in the locus where there is no fire ?

If we merely observe the concomitance of the two things in a particular place, we cannot infer the presence of one of them in another place from the perception of the presence of another. Because, a probans cannot be the invariable concomitant of a probandum unless and until it is definitely known that the probans absents itself from a place where the probandum does not exist.

If the relation of invariable concomitance is definitely grasped then we admit that the knowledge of that invariable concomitance is the invariable condition of inferential knowledge. But it is also a fact that the relation of invariable concomitance cannot be ascertained if we are not sure of the fact that a probans does not belong to a locus where its probandum does not exist.

If the Naiyāyikas hold that the knowledge of the presence of a probans in a similar instance and that of its absence in a contrary instance lend to the unmistakable discovery of the relation of invariable concomitance then we point out that they subscribe to an impracticable hypothesis. We, of course, approve of the thesis that a probans in order to be an invariable concomitant must not belong to a contrary instance. But the number of contrary instance is innumerable. Let us take a concrete case to illustrate the point in question. There are many places in the universe where fire does not exist. They constitute the contrary instances where smoke should not exist if it is an invariable concomitant of fire. It may be possible for a superman to behold all these places and thereby to discover the relation of invariable concomitance obtaining between smoke and fire. But it is impossible for an ordinary man like us to perceive all these contrary instances.

In fine, we come to the conclusion that either the relation of invariable concomitance does not exist or if it exists at all, its perfect discovery is next to impossible. Hence, the Naiyāyikas should give up all hopes of establishing the validity of inference.

If the Naiyāyikas are not satisfied, we adduce a further proof which is sure to invalidate an inference. Let us examine the syllogistic process itself. Examining it we find that every syllogism is fallacious. The truth of the third premise has not been established but has been simply assumed. The property of invariable concomitance does not belong to the probans.

Therefore, the thoughtful logicians, having failed to be convinced of the validity of inference, have sincerely advised all persons to relax their confidence in the efficiency of inference. If a blind man who gropingly proceeds through a hazardous way depends mainly upon inference then his fall is inevitable.

Moreover, some logicians who are adept in syllogistic reasoning deduce a particular conclusion with much care to explain a fact. Some other better logicians do not share in the view of the earlier ones but explain the same fact in a different manner. (Hence, inference is not a reliable instrument of knowledge since it is not the source of perfect knowledge).

The Establishment of the Validity of Inference

A reply to the above objections runs thus :

What is the exact import of the objections raised by the Cārvākas ? Do they intend to invalidate inference per se, or, do they find fault with the several definitions of inference offered by the different logicians of the Nyāya school ? They cannot confute the validity of inference per se since its validity has been universally accepted.

A woman, a child, a cow-herd, a cultivator and such other persons know another object (lying beyond the ken of their sense-organs) by means of its sure mark with absolute certainty.

If validity is denied to inference then all worldly transactions cannot be conducted with the mere help of perception. All the people of the world should remain motionless as if they are painted in a picture.

The man in the street accepts or rejects perceptible object when he infers that it is conducive to pleasure or pain from the mark that it is similar to the object experienced before as such.

If the objectors hold that the beauty of inference lies in its inexplicability because neither the validity of inference per se can be confuted nor it can be defined. This admission amounts to this that the sole target of objection is the definition of inference. Such an objection is unsound because of the following reasons. The perception of any object does not lead to the inferential knowledge of any other object. But the knowledge of some particular object leads to the inferential knowledge of some other particular object. This is the law which governs inference.

But if it is held that such knowledge takes place because of the inner essence of all objects then the real problem is only avoided but not solved. Our experience teaches that the knowledge of the relation of invariable concomitance makes inferential knowledge possible. Thus, on the basis of the knowledge of an object, the knowledge of some other object takes place. Hence, we conjecture that there is some relation between the objects if the knowledge of one of them leads to the knowledge of the other.

Those who are conversant with this relation have no faith in the hypothesis that the laws of identity and causality govern the relation in question. We, the Naiyāyikas, believe that it is the relation of invariable concomitance which counts. The relation of invariable concomitance implies that if the probans exists in a locus, the probandum exists there and that if the probandum does not exist in a locus, the probans does not exist there.

What is the ground of this relation ? If it is answered (by the Buddhists) that the relation of invariable concomitance is based upon the laws of identity and causality then we point out that the question is not squarely solved but it persists as it was before.

Let them (the Buddhists) solve the problem, viz., why does smoke arise from fire but not from water ? The only possible answer is that smoke and fire are so related because we learn their relation from experience. If this is the answer then the relation of invariable concomitance requires no laws besides experience as its basis. How do we know that the relation of invariable concomitance obtains between the two objects ? The answer is :—because experience teaches us that they are so related. The answer given by the Naiyāyikas is in no way different from that given by the Buddhists.

The field of reasoning is well-defined. It plays its part well only within its limited sphere. But we cannot explain why there are fundamental differences in the inner essence of objects by means of reasoning. We have got to accept the data of our knowledge but not to explain them. Reasoning is not competant enough to do it.

Again, a suggestion may come that an object points to another object because of its own inner essence but not because of the relation of invariable concomitance. We point out in this connection that such a suggestion is not amenable to reasons because the knowledge of one object does not lead to that of another if these two objects are not known to be connected by the tie of invariable concomitance. Hence inference presupposes the knowledge of the relation of invariable concomitance as its necessary condition.

Now, the opponents may raise a further question : viz., why does the relation of invariable concomitance hold between the two objects ? The enquiry regarding the basis of this relation will not be reasonable since the declared basis of this relation, viz., the law of identity and causality has been already discredited by sound logical arguments. Hence, the relation of invariable-concomitance will only be elaborately discussed. It is not fair to hold that inferential knowledge is merely a judgment of imagination. Because, it has been stated that if an object is an invariable concomitant of another object then and then only the knowledge of the former leads to the knowledge of the latter. If the mere presence of the relation of invariable concomitance without being cognized had led to the knowledge of its invariable concomitant then the inhabitants of the island which bears a significant name 'nārikela' (the island which abounds in coconut-trees) would have inferred fire merely seeing smoke but not knowing its invariable relation to fire. But it is a truism that in such cases inference is absolutely impossible. Therefore, the Naiyāyikas strongly assert that the knowledge of the relation of invariable concomitance definitely conditions inference. It has been stated by the Cārvākas to negate the thesis of Naiyāyikas that it is impossible to establish the relation of invariable concomitance holding between the two objects.

In order to counteract the objections raised by the Cārvākas some logicians hold that the relation of invariable concomitance (holding between the two objects) is grasped by the inner perception.

The elaboration of their view is as follows:—A man perceives that smoke and fire co-exist in the same locus. He comprehends by means of the method of difference that smoke is not present in the locus where fire does not exist. Then he synthesizes the results obtained by the joint method of agreement and difference and frames a judgment by means of the internal organ that smoke is the invariable concomitant of fire.

Is there any logician who will not subscribe to the thesis that all the objects of the universe are within the reach of the internal organ since it is powerful enough to grasp an object which lies beyond the range of the external sense-organs ? But it should also be noted that in order to comprehend the relation of invariable concomitance obtaining between smoke and fire it is not necessary that all the particulars belonging to the classes of smoke and fire should be perceived. We are to comprehend this relation as obtained between the two universals. In this case, we are to know that the relation of invariable concomitance obtains between all particulars of smoke and those of fire taking only note of their class-characters.

The Cārvākas and some other logicians have stated that a universal is not objectively real. This point of view will be refuted in the chapter on the meaning of words. Some other logicians hold that a sort of perception which is as good as the transcendental perception of the sages is to be postulated in order to grasp the relation of invariable concomitance. They state the reason behind the assumption of this distinct kind of hypothetical perception. The relation of concomitance obtaining between the middle term and the major term may be determined by means of the universals inhering in them (these two terms). The relation of concomitance holding between smoke and fire amounts to that of concomitance subsisting between the universals of smoke and fire. The positive aspect of the relation may be grasped by extra-ordinary perception acknowledged by the Naiyāyikas. But the negative aspect of the relation should also be grasped in order to grasp its invariable character. Therefore, we should also know that smoke does not exist in the locus where fire does not exist. The locii of the absence of fire are innumerable. No universal as non-fireness inheres in all such locii. Hence they (all locii of the negation of fire) are beyond the range of mental perception even. The relation of invariable concomitance holding between smoke and fire cannot be grasped if we do not perceive that every particular of smoke in this universe goes along with some particular of fire and no container of the absence of fire contains smoke. If this relation is not grasped in this manner, it cannot produce sound inferential knowledge. It has been proved that inference is a source of true knowledge. As effect must have its cause. Therefore, an act of perception which grasps the relation of invariable concomitance cannot but be admitted. This perception should also be admitted to grasp all the particulars concerned. Though we are not aware of its mode of operation, it is based upon sound logic. Hence, they hold that this type of perception has only logical existence.

Some logicians of the Mīmāṁsā school are not convinced of the justification of the logical existence of the hypothetical perception described in the preceding para. Thus, they hold that a universal judgment that the middle term is the invariable concomitant of the major term is framed on the basis of the repeated observations of the cases of the concomitance of the middle term and the major term. They further add that the knowledge of the absence of the middle term on the locus where the major term does not exist is not necessary for the framing of the above universal judgment. It has been stated that the concomitant probans leads to the knowledge of the probandum though it is not actually experienced that the absence of the probandum is the invariable concomitant of the absence of the probans.

The purport of the above text is as follows :—

The universal judgment that this object is an invariable concomitant of that object, arises from the repeated observations of the cases of their concomitance. The evidence of the universal experience is on our side.

The universality of the universal judgment, i.e., the major premise is like the truth of a general proposition. If the middle term is found to exist in the contrary example then the universality of the major premise is counteracted just as a negative example contradicts the truth of a general proposition. The universality of the major premise, viz., where there is smoke there is fire, is not so long counteracted as long as we are not aware of the fact that smoke exists in a locus which contains the absence of fire. They hold that if a judgment which counteracts the universality of a general proposition does not actually arise then it is irrational to apprehend the possibility of such a judgment. If a judgment which counteracts a general proposition does not actually arise in our mind from experience then one should not indulge in idle conjectures which may be expected to counteract the universality of it. (The Mīmāṁsakas hold that a proposition is true unless it is contradicted by a contrary proposition. Again, a contrary proposition does not arise if the conditions of a proposition are not defective. A jaundiced man perceives that a conchshell is yellow and generalises that all conchshells are yellow. The general proposition, framed by him, is contradicted. Similarly, if the major premise is based upon non-observation or mal-observation then it will be surely contradicted. But if it is based upon sound observation, i.e., repeated observations then there is no scope for the appearance of a counteracting preposition.

The Necessity of the Determination of the Negative Counterpart of Concomitance

The above hypothesis is not sound. Without the confirmation of the negative hypothetical judgment, viz., if the probandum does not exist there, the relation of concomitance holding between them is not established to be invariable. This point has been discussed in the chapter on presumption. The relation of invariable concomitance is indicative of an object. Hence, it does not reveal an object by its mere presence but a person must be aware of the relation in order to infer an object. The relation of invariable concomitance holding between the two objects is exactly this that if the concomitant middle term exists at a spot then the major term does not exist there then the concomitant middle term also does not exist there. The repeated observation is that which cognizes the relation in its entirety. If such observation grasps only the positive aspect of the relation then it is only partially comprehended since the other aspect of the relation, viz., the negative counterpart, remains unrealised.

Some other logicians hold that though it is a truism that all the locii of the absence of fire are not united by a universal and that the hypothesis of the transcendental perception is not worthy of being accepted yet the relation of invariable concomitance in its entirety, i.e., in the positive and negative aspects is comprehended by the internal organ.

As we perceive the co-existence of smoke and fire and frame a universal judgment "Where there is smoke there is fire", on the basis of our perception, so we perceive the co-existence of the absence of fire and that of smoke. We are in a position to frame a universal negative judgment, viz., where there is no fire there is no smoke because water and such other objects where fire does not exist are never perceived to contain smoke. Though it is a fact that the universals are omnipresent yet it does not mean that all the universals exist everywhere by means of the relation of inference. (Let us take a concrete case to illustrate the point in question. The perception of the relation of agreement that where there is smoke there is fire together with the perception the negation of smoke in a river where fire does not exist stimulates the imaginative perception to discover correctly the invariable relation of concomitance holding between smoke and fire. To discover this relation between them it is unnecessary to behold all locii of the negation of fire.

As we convey the positive aspect of the relation of universal concomitance by means of a general proposition because the relation holds between the two universals. But it is difficult for us to convey the negative counterpart of the relation of universal concomitance by means of a general proposition because the individual negations of the terms entering into the relation of concomitance rest upon the different loci which have no common property. But the difficulty is thus solved. The individual negations of the terms may be expressed in a universal negative proposition since a reference to the locus of negation is not an essential element in the above proposition. When we say that there is no fire we do not refer to all the individual cases of fire, existing in different places and negate them. But we simply hold that there is no such object as is characterized by the universal of fire-ness. If an object negated is characterized by a universal then the negation of it is expressed by means of a universal negative proposition. The determination of universal concomitance does not involve a necessary reference to all the individual cases as its condition.

As the relation of concomitance holds between the two positive objects so it obtains between the corresponding negative terms. The relation of concomitance obtaining between the two positive objects is called the positive aspect of the relation (anvaya). The relation of concomitance holding between the negative terms corresponding to these positive terms is called the negative counterpart (vyatireka) of the relation. If the middle term and the major term are negative then the relation of concomitance holding between them constitutes the positive aspect. But the relation of concomitance holding between the corresponding positive terms is called the negative counterpart.

As the positive aspect of the relation of invariable concomitance holding between the two negative terms is perceived so the negative counterpart of the relation of invariable concomitance holding between the two negative terms is surely perceived.

The concomitant (the reason) and the major term (the consequence) in the relation of concomitance follow a definite order. But the negations corresponding to the above two terms are also related to each other by the relation of invariable concomitance but their order becomes reverse in the negative counterpart. In other words, the negation of the concomitance of the positive aspect becomes the major term in the negative counterpart; and the negation of the major term of the positive aspect becomes the concomitant of the negative counterpart.

It should be noted that the same rule applies to the case of the relation of universal concomitance holding between the two negative terms. The negative term, corresponding to the positive term which plays the part of a concomitant in the positive aspect, becomes the major term. The negative term, corresponding to the positive term, which plays the part of a major term becomes the middle term in the negative universal proposition. The universal proposition is framed on the basis of the reference to the above two universals. The negation of smoke is not grasped if smoke is not characterized only by smoke-ness, similarly the negation of fire is known. But it is derived from perception. Similarly, a major premise which involves a reference to the negative terms is also universal because they represent the positions of the universals. As the transcendental perception of a sage is not required for the framing of the former proposition so it is not necessary for the production of the latter one. The relation of universal concomitance holding between the two positive objects and between the two negative objects is detected by the internal organ. No need of further discussion. Therefore, it has been proved that the relation of invariable concomitance is objectively real and that there is a source of comprehending it.

The establishment of the five conditions of a sound reason

We cannot infer an object existing in a place unless and until we perceive that its reason is there though we are definitely aware of the fact that the relation of universal concomitance holds between the reason and the consequence. Hence, the perception of the reason for the second time is required as one of the conditions of inference. (To find out the relation of universal concomitance the reason has been firstly perceived), the belonging of the reason to the subject of inference is called pakṣadharmatā (The minor premise of the western logic is the pakṣadharmatā of the Nyāya Logic). (But we must be sure of the fact that the reason belongs to the subject of inference. This condition of the reason is directly apprehended by perception). If it is definitely known that the reason belongs to the subject of inference and that the relation of invariable concomitance in both its aspects, positive and negative, obtain between the reason and the consequence even then the reason is invalidated, provided that the presence of the consequence in the subject of inference is disproved either by perception or by verbal testimony or by some counter-argument. Two more conditions should be fulfilled by the sound reason in addition to the three conditions, generally accepted by the logicians, viz., the presence of the reason in the subject of inference, its presence in the positive examples and its absence from the negative ones. The presence of the consequence which the reason accompanies in the subject of inference should neither be contradicted nor be disputed by a counter-argument, The existence of inference cannot be disputed because it is based upon universally sound experience. Similarly, the definition of the proof as framed by the Naiyāyikas is sound. The Cārvākas have levelled a charge against it that the definition is not expressive of the object to be defined. But if they carefully examine it then they themselves will ascertain that it is faultless. Even if they have a special hatred against the definition of inference, they cannot deny existence to inferential knowledge.

The refutation of the secondary charges against the validity of inference

We fail to understand the other charges levelled against inference. It is as follows:—The 'pramāṇa' (the source of valid knowledge) has not been primarily used in the present context. Hence, it is next to impossible to find out any meaning out of the word 'anumāna'. The line of defence is this that the defect in the use of words subtracts nothing from the nature of true knowledge, the goal of definition. Even if we admit for the sake of argument that the words such as pakṣadharma etc., have been secondarily used then does it suggest that the true knowledge itself defined by it has been partially expressed? If the definition is newly worded then the purity of knowledge will not be affected.

The last charge brought against the validity of inference is that if a particular is the consequence then no reason is its concomitant and that if a universal is the consequence then an old story is only repeated (a known object is established). This charge is also not very fair. A universal itself is not inferred. The presence of a universal in the subject of inference is inferred but not a bare universal. The suffix 'matup', conveying the sense of 'belonging to', clearly points to the Nyāya stand-point.

A retort to Objections

The objectors have described a good number of pitfalls of inference, viz., changes in circumstances, space and time which transform an object to a considerable extent. But they are not really fatal to inference. If the relation of universal concomitance is truly grasped then there is no chance of invalidation on the part of an inference. If an act of inference is contradicted then the person who infers is to blame (but the critic should not find fault with the process of reasoning).

The objectors have also stated that an inference is easily invalidated either by a counter-argument or by perception or by such a reason as is the invariable concomitant with what is contrarily opposed to the original consequence. This statement is nothing but the vain wasting of words since if a sound reason is employed then no such disaster ensues.

If the reason employed in the counter-argument is really sound then the reason, employed in the first argument does not prove the consequence. The so-called reason does not deserve the title 'reason' but is a child of fancy. For this very reason, it illustrates fallacy. We shall discuss this point later on. If a defectless reason is properly employed then it does not disappoint us by its failure to prove the conclusion. On the other hand it rightly proves the conclusion as it does no disservice to the cause of the validity of an inference.

If a man reaches his goal by means of sound reasoning then he can never be compared with a blind man who gropingly proceeds.

If sound logicians take cautious steps to arrive at a conclusion then the conclusion cannot be retroverted by mere accusation.

Non-acceptation of inference as a source of valid knowledge implies the stop of all worldly transactions

Those who are more adept in logic hold that inference admits of two types, viz., utpannapratīti (objects inferred are familiar) and utpādya-pratīti (objects inferred are unfamiliar). The inference of God, etc., illustrates the second type.

Whoever does not approve of the common process of reasoning e.g., the inference of fire by means of smoke, the reason, they freely exercise their power of reasoning and prove the consequence by means of the reason, without being tutored by the logical discipline of the Naiyāyikas.

Those who are in the know of the reality of all objects refuse to believe in the validity of such inference as proves the existence of the soul, God, the omniscient and the next world.

The unsophisticated persons cannot so long follow such conclusions as are drawn by the Tārkikas from their premises as long as their mind is not polluted by the crooked logicians.

These remarks simply speak of their atheistic turn of mind or of their ignorance but do not confute the validity of inference. The process of reasoning is not invalid because the method of knowing the relation of universal concomitance is complicated.

The said relation is discovered by means of some of the following sources viz., the verbal testimony, the act of inference, the indirect method of *reductio ad absurdum* and perception. The difference in the nature of the source itself does not introduce any change into the nature of the relation of universal concomitance.

When the problem of God will be discussed it will be elaborately proved that the evidence of inference bearing upon God etc., is very strong. No need of a long talk at present.

Subscribe to our thesis that inference is a source of valid knowledge. Its validity is not discredited by your faultfinding remarks.

We have already remarked that if the validity of inference is not acknowledged then all persons will be motionless like the statues of stone.

The Sūtra containing the definition of inference explained

Having established the validity of inference we shall now resume our duty of defending the terms of the sūtra which defines inference. The word 'anumānam' of the sūtra denotes the object to be defined. The portion 'tat-pūrvakam' constitutes the definition. 'Tat' is a pronoun. It signifies perception which follows from the context. The compound word 'tat-pūrvakam' conveys that which owes its existence to perception. If the apparent meaning of the word is accepted, the definition of inference becomes too wide as it comprises 'comparison', 'the final ascertainment of a thesis' etc., within itself. In order to make the definition exact by excluding them from the province of inference the expounding sentence should have the initial word in the dual number. Thus, the meaning of it will amount to this that inference is that of which the two acts of perception are the cause. Are any two perceptions the cause ? No, any two perceptions are not the cause of inference but the two such acts are to be specified. One of them is that which discovers the relation of universal concomitance. The second one is the perception of the presence of the reason in the subject of inference. The two constitute the cause of inference alone but not of comparison, etc. The perception of the universal concomitance is not the immediate cause of inference. It exerts its influence in and through its memory revived. The perception of reason in the subject of inference is the direct cause of inference.

An objection to this sort of interpretation arises in our mind. Perception which is supplied by the context is a non-specified one. The pronoun 'tat' refers to it. How does the interpreter give the twisted meaning of it, viz., the two specific perceptions ? A reply to this objection is as follows : The definition of the reason to be given later on is this that the reason is that which proves the object to be established through its similarity with the example. The reason is the instrument of inferential knowledge. Hence, it is the object of the present definition. The reason cannot prove the object to be established if its similarity with the positive example and its dissimilarity with the negative one are not cognized. Hence, one should depend upon the source of such knowledge. We are to move in a vicious circle if we have recourse to some source other than perception. We have very often drawn the attention of our critics to this point. Though the context supplies us with perception in general but not the particular perception which lies at the root of inference yet the pronoun 'tat' refers here to the particular perceptions, viz., the perception of the universal concomitance and the second perception of this reason.

Now, an exception is taken to this definition. It is pointed out that it still remains too wide as the previous definition has been since it applies to some other forms of fallacy such as 'Savyabhicāra', 'Viruddha' etc. This objection does not hold good since the reason has been qualified by the adjective clause 'which proves the object to be established'. In case of fallacy the reason does not prove the object to be established. The true nature of the relation of universal concomitance will be minutely discussed in its proper place. But the source of the knowledge of universal concomitance is only stated here. If perception rightly discovers the relation of universal concomitance then no fallacy of reasoning can ensure since the relation of invariable concomitance is not taken amiss. If we define the species of anumāna, having repeated all the generic features as its property then the definition of anumāna excludes all fallacies since it is a species of pramā (true knowledge). In order to make this definition exact it is to be shown that it sharply distinguishes the species of inference from the other species such as comparison, etc. which are subsumed under the same genus of pramā. The compound word 'tat-pūrvaka' which constitutes the definition does it nicely. All the species of valid knowledge share the following characteristics in common. They are as follows : 'Which arises from the real object', 'which accords to its object' and 'which is determinate'.

A word and the reason do not function together to produce inference. Hence, inferential knowledge should not be defined as avyapadeśya (non-verbalised) experience. A word and the reason do not produce knowledge by themselves but their knowledge produces the desired effect. Two pieces of knowledge do not arise simultaneously. Hence, the verbal and the inferential characters of a piece of knowledge cannot be simultaneously recognised.

Now, the defect of being too wide may be mended. But how do you meet the objection that the definition is too narrow since the definition does not apply to that inference the reason of which is known by means of the verbal testimony, etc. Some logicians meet this objection to this effect that perception is the basic foundation of this knowledge.

Kumārila has stated that when the reason itself, being inferred, proves the object to be established it is proved by another fundamental reason that is perceived.

Another alternative view may be suggested here. The hypothesis that inferential knowledge is dependent upon perceptual knowledge signifies that the latter is generally dependent upon the former and that there is no hard and fast rule that perception is the only cause of inference. Hence, the definition is not too narrow. In order to have the clear understanding of the compound word 'tat-pūrvaka' it should be explained by the expounding sentence that inferential knowledge is that of which the other forms of knowledge constitute the condition. How are the mediate forms of knowledge denoted by the pronoun 'tat'? It can only refer to perception since it only precedes the sūtra on inference. The preceding sūtra contains the definition of perception. In order to define it the other forms of knowledge are distinguished from it. Thus, all the forms of knowledge do not remain absolutely unknown. Hence, it will not be out of context if the pronoun 'tat' refers to them.

Some thinkers take an exception to this definition. They ask whether the pronoun 'tat' signifies the instrument of perception of the resulting consciousness. If it denotes the instrument of perceptual knowledge, the compound word 'tatpūrvaka' should denote perceptual knowledge arising from the sense-organ. Inference, being generated by such knowledge, the word 'pūrvaka' should be repeated. In other words, the significant compound word should be 'tat-pūrvaka-pūrvakam'. Though one of them is not heard (not given in the sūtra), yet it is to be assumed. Thus the sūtra is open to the charge of the assumption of an unheard word.

Let the other alternatives be examined. Let us assume that the pronoun 'tat' denotes perceptual knowledge. Thus, the definition signifies that anumāna is dependent upon the resulting consciousness of perception. But the word 'anumāna' denotes the instrument of inferential knowledge. If this is the case then the knowledge which is generated by perceptual knowledge should not be the instrument of inferential knowledge as the wording of the definition 'tat-pūrvakam anumānam', suggests. The perception of the reason leads on to the knowledge of the object that is beyond the reach of sense organs. This indirect knowledge is not the instrument of inferential knowledge but is itself the resulting consciousness. Hence, the definition is not expressive. A rejoinder to the above objection is as follows: Though the above two alternatives are accepted yet the definition remains faultless. If the pronoun 'tat' signifies a sense organ, i.e., the instrument of perceptual knowledge then the compound word 'tat-pūrvaka' denotes the perception of the reason, i.e., direct awareness generated by the sense organ. It is the instrument of the mediate knowledge of the consequence. Hence, it is anumāna. Thus, the repetition of the word 'pūrvaka' twice is not necessary. Again, if the pronoun 'tat' denotes the resulting consciousness then the meaning of the compound word 'tatpūrvaka' is quite clear. The pronoun 'tat' conveys the perception of the reason. The compound word 'tat-pūrvaka' signifies the remembrance of the relation of universal concomitance. This remembrance is anumāna since it is the instrument of the mediate knowledge of the consequence since the latter follows the former in immediate succession. It has been stated that the remembrance of universal concomitance generated by an actually existing cause is anumāna. Thus coordination between 'tat-pūrvaka' and 'anumāna' is very clear since the compound word 'tat-pūrvaka' denotes remembrance mentioned above. The word 'anumāna' may be interpreted in the sense of resulting consciousness, i.e., it is synonymous with anumiti. Or, we may interpret the definition in a different light. We shall simply insert the word 'yataḥ' into the definition. The meaning of the definition turns out to be that anumāna is that from which the knowledge of an object lying beyond the reach of the sense-organ arises through the causality of perception. The process of 'anumāna' may be mentioned here in the following order of succession. The first step is the perception of the reason, the remembrance of the universal concomitance, follows it in close succession, the next one is, according to some, the judgment that the subject of inference is the container of the reason which is invariably concomitant of the consequence, then ensues the indirect knowledge of the consequence and then comes up the judgment that the consequence is worthy of being accepted or rejected, etc. in conformity to the processes described in the section of the definition of perception. Each member of this long series of judgments is causally connected with some other member. The causal tie holding between the two will be decided by the rule of logic. In fine, our teacher holds that only the compound word 'tat-pūrvaka' constitutes the sound definition of 'anumāna'.

The Function of the Three Words given in the Sūtra

Some other logicians interpret the sūtra in a different manner. They hold that the three words 'pūrvavat', etc., have been given in the sūtra so that the definition of anumāna may not apply to upamāna (comparison) and other forms of true knowledge. If only the compound word 'tat-pūrvaka' constitutes the definition of anumāna then it applies alike to upamāna, etc. To mend the defect of the definition the three words have been given in the sūtra. The reason admits of three kinds. They will be stated as an effect and soon. Or, the reason is held to be three-fold since it fulfils three conditions such as the presence of the reason in the subject of inference and so on. If the reason is three-fold, its knowledge is also secondarily called to be of three types. The complete definition of anumāna is that it is dependent upon perception and is the knowledge of any of the three types of the reason. Now they should explain the question "How do the words like pūrvavat, etc., signify the three conditions of the reason, viz., the presence of the reason in the subject of inference, etc.?"

Some logicians hold that the word 'pūrva' denotes the subject of inference in a particular universe of discourse, viz., three kinds of controversy with discussion based upon the rules of logic at the head since it (the subject of inference) receives the first attention. The word 'pūrvavat' denotes the reason since the latter belongs to the subject of inference as has been clearly expressed. The word 'śeṣa' denotes a similar instance since this locus is definitely known to contain the object to be inferred. The word 'śeṣavat' denotes the reason which belongs to a similar instance. Thus, it has been suggested that the reason belongs to the similar instance. Thus the second condition of the reason has been indicated by the word 'śeṣavat'. The compound word 'sāmānyatodṛṣṭa' suggests that the reason does not belong to contrary example. How is this meaning derived from it? The compound word is *sāmānyato-adṛṣṭam* since the vowel '*a*' has been inserted into it without any change in its sound. There is no trace of the reason, not to speak of some form of presence. Now, the locus of its absence is to be specified. From which locus is it absent? It belongs to the subject of inference as well as to the similar example. Only the contrary example remains to be specified. No trace of the reason is to be found in the contrary example. Thus the above three words point to the three conditions of the reason. Anumāna is that knowledge which depends upon the three conditions of the reason.

Some logicians hold that all the words of the sūtra constitute the definition of anumāna. The sūtra, thus interpreted, does not display the skill of its author in framing a definition.

It has been assumed in this science of logic that five conditions are necessary for a sound reason. If a reason has only three conditions then the reason which has been adduced in the fallacy of *kālātyaya-apadiṣṭa* (the contradictory reason) or of prakaraṇa-sama (counter-argument) should also pass for a sound one. Hence, only the compound word 'tat-pūrvaka' serves the purpose of a defectless definition.

The word 'trividha' (three-fold) expresses the division of

anumāna. The words 'pūrvavat', etc., denote the three kinds of anumāna which has been defined by the compound word 'tat-pūrvaka' and bears also the epithet 'Nyāya'. The nomenclature of the divisions clearly points to the three-fold character of anumāna. But why does the author of the Nyāya-sūtra use the word 'three-fold ? Surely, he is not here particular about the economy of language as he is not elsewhere. He names the different types of Siddhānta, Śabda and Chala and mentions their number as well.

The Meaning of the word Pūrvavat

When an effect is inferred from its cause it illustrates the type of inference called 'pūrvavat'. We infer that rain will come when we behold the cloud gathering in the sky.

Some logicians take an exception to this thesis. They hold that the term 'pūrva' denotes a cause. The word 'pūrvavat' denotes an effect since an effect has a cause. Thus, the primary meaning of the word 'pūrvavat' is an effect. Thus, the type of inference which is called 'pūrvavat' is to be illustrated by the inference of a cause by means of an effect but not by the inference of an effect by means of a cause. It is impossible to infer an effect from a cause. First, it is unreasonable to think that an effect is a subject of inference. Is it existent or not ? If it is existent then what else is to be established ? If it is non-existent, it, being unreal like the sky-flower, cannot be the subject of inference. Now, the syllogistic argument may be put in the form that an effect exists because its cause is existent. In this case, the reason and the consequence are two inco-ordinate objects. It is as absurd as is the syllogism that sound is non-eternal because the crow is black. Now, in order to establish the existence of an effect, if we posit the existence of a positive condition as a reason then the reason does not belong to the subject of inference. It is an example of asiddha fallacy (the unreal reason). In order to prove the above consequence if the presence of its negative condition, i.e., the presence of the pre-negation of the effect is adduced then the contradictory negation of the consequence is proved by some other source of valid knowledge. Hence, it is a case of contradictory reason if the existence of both conditions, positive and negative, is put forward, then it simply illustrates the fallacy of the fallacious reason (anaikāntika). How can we establish the existence of an effect ?

The existence of the positive condition constitutes the unsound reason. The existence of conditions positive and negative constitutes the unsound reason. The existence of the negative condition constitutes the contradictory reason. How can the consequence in question be established ?

Again, to prove the existence of an effect a non-specified cause cannot serve the purpose of the reason since the relation of universal concomitance must hold between the reason and the consequence. A particular effect is generated by a specific cause. Hence, a non-specified cause is sure to illustrate the insufficient reason. If it is held that the specific cause will be put forward as the reason then it will be pointed out that even a wise person fails to find out a specific cause. The following illustration is sufficient to bring home our point. Sometimes we notice that massive clouds which are as dark as the leaf of a lotus-plant and look like moving mountain vanish into nothingness without shedding a drop of rain.

If it is held that the cause from which the effect follows in immediate succession constitutes the reason then the very effect will be perceived when the remembrance of the relation of universal concomitance takes place. In other words, the inference of an effect is simply superfluous.

The unholders of the original thesis may contend that the Buddhists also lend support to their view. They also hold that an effect is inferred from a cause. The Buddhist text runs to this effect. The appearance of an effect is inferred from the totality of all conditions. It has been described as identical with the conditions since it depends upon nothing else.

The fools have failed to understand the Buddhist text. They misinterpret the word 'utpāda'. It denotes the capacity for producing an effect. Its root-meaning is that by which an effect is brought into existence. This capacity which belongs to the conditions is here inferred. It is not different from the conditions themselves. Hence, it is an instance of analytical inference. The correctness of our interpretation has been borne out by the portion of the verse 'sa svabhāvo' anuvarṇitaḥ.

Some other logicians (some Mīmāṁsakas) join issue with the objectors and sharply condemn them. They hold that the objections have been raised by such persons as are not adept in the framing of syllogisms: An effect is not here the subject of inference. Its existence is not the consequence in question. An inco-ordinate reason is not applicable. But the clouds are the subject of inference. It is to be established that they contain rain which will drop in the immediate future. The gathering of the clouds in the sky and such other features of them constitute the reason. Hence, the objections mentioned above have no scope. We may cite an example to confirm our statement. This smoke is fiery because it has darkish white colour like the smoke in the kitchen. (The proposition that this smoke is fiery is in the sense that this smoke co-exists with fire in one and the same locus). What is established by an act of inference is that smoke has fire. In a similar manner, we hold that those clouds will shed rain in the near future because they have assembled in the sky etc. like the clouds experienced before. Hence, the clouds which contain the future rain are inferred. Kumārila Bhaṭṭa says to this effect. The subject of inference containing the consequence is an inference. The spot which contains fire is to be inferred in this manner. Some other logicians hold that the smoke, which is generally adduced as the reason, may also be the subject of inference.

The word 'pūrva' truly denotes a cause. The word 'pūrvavat' denotes the property of a cause. Let us take a concrete case. The cloud is the cause of rain. Its property, viz., the gathering of the cloud in the sky etc. is signified by the term 'pūrvavat'. This property constitutes the reason. Moreover, there is no linguistic defect in the statement of the proposition. A non-specified cause has not been stated as the cause of rain. Thus, there should be no chance of noticing the absence of rain in spite of the presence of the cloud. The cause has been specified. It is not at all difficult to find out the specific cause of an effect.

The cloud which rends the cave of a mountain by its thundering looks like a black bee, or a wild buffalo or a black cobra or a Tamāla tree and the massive body of which becomes frequently tawny brown being lit up by the constantly flickering light of the slender line of lightning never fails to associate itself with rain.

If you do not subscribe to this view then it may be pointed out by way of protest that fire should not be inferred from smoke, having some specific property. Thus, the vital force of inference will be destroyed. In other words, if the specific character of a cause or of an effect cannot be detected then the very possibility of inference is cut off.

If an effect is held to be inferred from the immediate antecedent cause then it is apprehended that it is sure to be perceived earlier. But such a fear is unreasonable. When we actually infer rain, drops of rain do not fall on our head from the cloud. At least our experience does not give evidence to such a situation. Such knowledge is inferential as points to the consequence which is beyond the range of our sense-organ at the time of inference. We shall cite such examples where rain does not actually fall but is imminent.

(Let us take another example, make a comparative time estimate between inference and perception of a future object which will shortly come into existence and see which of these two takes place earlier). The object in question is a piece of cloth which has not been as yet produced. The last thread is moving for conjunction with the other threads which have been already conjoined in order to produce the piece of cloth. There is no obstacle to its production as no movement that may destroy the last thread is noticed in the *fibres* of it—the very constituents of thread. No fear of its non-appearance is entertained. This is the situation when the above piece of cloth is inferred from the movement of the last thread for conjunction with the rest. Now, we see that the piece of cloth is known earlier by means of inference than by means of perception. Let us compare and contrast the two processes of knowledge side by side and see the possible length of time to be taken by each of them for the apprehension of the said object. That is to put it in one word, let us see the time-limit of inference. First let us perceive the mental movement and see the time-limit of inference. First, we perceive the movement of the last thread for conjunction, then remember the relation of universal concomitance, then apply this relation to the particular reason present in the subject of inference and lastly arrive at the conclusion that the consequence is present in the subject of inference. Thus, we see that three or four moments are required from the start to the finish. Secondly, perception cannot also take place if the object is not present. Let us at first count the different moments of the operations of the causal factors that precede the apearance of the piece of cloth to be perceived and calculate all of them from the same starting point. The first moment contains the movement of thread. It is followed by separation. It does away with its previous conjunction. The new combination of the thread takes place. Then, the piece of cloth emerges into existence and it does not possess its colour and other attributes. These attributes appear in the next moment. The piece of cloth is the material cause of its attributes. The cause must precede its effect since it is accepted by all that a cause and its effect cannot be simultaneous. From the above statement it is clear that when the above piece of cloth comes into existence it is devoid of colour. It cannot be perceived at the moment when it is produced. It becomes a coloured object when its colour appears in the next moment. When our sense-organ will come into contact with the coloured object our perception will take place. Thus, we see that a good number of moments intervenes between the starting point and the perception of the object in question. Therefore, it is unreasonable to hold that there are cases in which the perception of a future object takes place earlier than its inferential knowledge.

The non-appearance of the said effect owing to the absence of its condition or cause is not possible. The cause has been qualified by a clause which shows that there is no destructive movement in the parts of the cause. Hence, no apprehension arises in our mind that the cause is to meet its destruction before the production of its effect. Hence, the starting movement for conjunction is to be necessarily followed by the series of effects in the proper order. The above mentioned Buddhist text has been interpreted as an illustration of the inference in question, being analytical in its character, has been already refuted. The people infer an effect from the competent cause but not from capacity. No need of further discussion.

Śeṣavat

The Śeṣavat type of inference is that by which a cause is inferred from its effect. Let us take an example viz., we infer rain in the country over which the river has flown, seeing its peculiar current. In the above example in accordance with the strict syllogistic form the contact of the river with the ante-adjoining-country which has heavy shower of rain is to be inferred. The swelling of the river due to this contact is the reason. From the abnormal swelling of the river the contact of the river with such an ante-country is inferred. The river is in contact with an ante-country (a country over which it has flown) where a heavy shower of rain has fallen because it has its stream studded with foams, muddy and very rapid (strong) like a river seen before in a similar condition.

Or, a particular country may be the subject of inference instead of the river. This country is adjoined to another ante-country which has heavy shower of rain because it has a river with swollen stream. If we adopt any one of these two syllogisms then our reasoning will not be open to the charges of the inco-ordination between the reason and the consequence etc. It is merely a verbal statement that a cause is inferred from its effect. But, in reality, the subject of inference plays the part of the consequence as well as that of the reason as it has different aspects.

Kumārila Bhaṭṭa has clearly stated to this effect. He holds that the subject of inference is both the consequence and the reason. It becomes the consequence when it is qualified by something which has not been established. It also acts as the reason when it is qualified by something which has been experienced or determined before. (As a container of an unknown content it becomes the consequence whereas it is the reason when it contains the known content.) The swelling of a river is due to many a condition such as the collapse of embankment, snow-break etc. Hence, a particular cause cannot be inferred from an effect. (It is an objection on the ground of the plurality of causes). The objection is met in the following way.

Who can know that the peculiar swelling of the river—the swelling which is only due to the heavy rain-fall ? The river abounds in eddies, having its water risen very high. Its water is very dirty. The stream is studied with setting foams owing to the wild dance of waves. If man fails to see the peculiarity of an effect, he is to blame since there is nothing wrong with the syllogism, based on the relation of universal concomitance.

Let us take the objections one by one and discuss their merits. If the current of the river is embanked somewhere then the waters of the river swell somewhere else. Hence, the swelling of the river is not due only to the heavy shower of rain. Thus, the reason in question is insufficient.

When the ants come out of their nests and march in a line and carry off their eggs, we infer rain from the above movement of ants. But if the sticks are thrusted into the nests (holes) of ants then they come out and march for another shelter. Hence, we cannot safely infer rain from the movement of ants. The reason in question is uncertain. But if the sticks are thrusted into the nests (holes) of ants then they come out and march for another shelter. Hence, we cannot safely infer rain from the movement of ants. The reason in question is uncertain.

At the advent of the rainy season we infer rain on hearing the scream of peacocks. Sometimes such an inference is falsified. Suppose, somebody exactly imitates the scream of a peacock. If he infers rain, hearing human cry then his inference is surely falsified. The embankment of the flowing river, the molestation of ants' nests (holes) and human cry similar to the scream of a peacock do not contribute towards the insufficiency of the reason. On this flimsy ground it is improper to invalidate an act of inference. On a closer examination it is not difficult to find out a true reason and distinguish it from a false one.

Rain-fall is the remote cause of the swelling of a river. At the outset drops of rain fall on the ground from the cloud. Then they mingle together and flow into the river.

The Meaning of Sāmānyatodṛṣṭa

When we infer the consequence from the reason which is neither a cause nor an effect this inference is styled as sāmānyatodṛṣṭa. Let us take an example, viz. the taste of a wood-apple is inferred from its colour and so on. Colour and taste co-inhere in a wood-apple. They are not causally related to each other. Even from the Buddhist point of view these two distinct momentary events which are com-present are not mutually related by the causal nexus. If we infer the taste of the subject of inference from the colour inhering in it, the objections, mentioned before, such as the reason not belonging to the subject of inference etc. are really pointless with regard to the above inference. But the commentator of the Nyāya-sūtra has given a different example of this type of inference. It runs thus : The sun has motion because he comes into contact with the different objects at distant places. This example is not appropriate. The contact with the different parts of the horizon or the sky or the space is not perceptible, but that of the sun with a hill (a perceptible whole) is perceptible. We really infer a cause from its effect. Therefore, the example in question is an illustration of the śeṣavat type of inference.

Moreover, what is the meaning of such a contact ? The sun does not come into contact with hills etc., situated at distant places. Moreover, the reaching of a different place means the contact with a different place. He does never come in contact with a hill etc. If he does come into contact with anything then he is in contact either with the sky or with the space. But this contact is imperceptible because it inheres also in the sky or the space. The perception of conjunction of the perceptible objects is admitted only. The contact in question is imperceptible like that of the air with a huge tree, or, like that of a foetal child with its mother's womb.

Now, a logician may hold a brief for the commentator to revise the above syllogism and assert that the reason is the perception of the sun in a different country but not the contact of the sun with a different country. The perception in question may also be traced somehow to the motion of the sun as its remote cause. The motion of the sun is the direct cause of the contact of the sun with the country. The perception of the sun at a distant place is due to his motion. The revised syllogism runs thus: (The sun is perceived at a distant country i.e., above distant garden in the evening). The perception of the sun above the garden is generated by the motion of the sun because it is a perception at a different place or because it is denoted by the phrase 'the perception of the sun in a different country' just like the perception of Devadatta in a different country. Even if we accept this revised syllogism we cannot but hold that the said perception of the sun is the indirect effect of the motion of the sun.

Darśanatva is not a universal belonging to all cases of perception like the universal of gotva (cowness) which inheres in all cows. But the suffix 'tva' attached to the word 'darśana' denotes an abstract noun. It denotes the power to produce 'perception'. It is not supersensuous and eternal. It is nothing but the accessory condition of perception itself.

Hence, it is identical with the contact of the sun with another country. Such a contact is produced by his motion. In a similar manner, it may be pointed out that if the reason is denoted by the word 'darśana' then the type of the inference will remain the same. The contact with another country, is possible only through motion. The defenders have only used another term to denote the reason. But they fail to make any actual improvement. The perception of the sun at a distant place is possible if the sun has motion. What is the result of such a motion? He comes into contact with such a place. The perception of the distant sun is possible if he is in motion. The word is really perception. But it simplification is the contact with a distant place. The attempt at defence by a cover of a word cannot protect the weak point. The same old reason turns up in spite of the use of the new term 'darśana'. Hence, the revised syllogism is nothing but an instance of the śeṣavat type of inference.

In fine, the instance of the sāmānyatodṛṣṭa type of inference as cited by the commentator on the Nyāya-sūtra is not sound. The instance, shown by us, viz., the inference of taste from colour, is up to the mark. We have shown many instances of syllogistic arguments in which the reason and the consequence are not causally connected when we have disputed with the Buddhists.

Further Types of Inference

Having assigned the above meaning (the sense of having the suffix 'matup') the tripartite division of inference has been described. But this division has been discarded as a house of cards by the logicians. The reason establishes the consequence because the relation of universal concomitance holds between them, but not because the reason is either the cause or the effect of the consequence. Therefore, the above three-fold division has no solid ground to stand upon. The suffix 'matup' is to be replaced by the suffix 'vati'. The basis of division should be different. The division has been given in a different manner and sense. Let us see what is signified by the pūrvavat type of inference. Whenever we discover the universal relation of concomitance holding between the reason and the consequence, we perceive them thoroughly and distinctly. If we establish the homogeneous consequence on the perception of the homogeneous reason, they are similar to those reasons and consequences which have been perceived before. Hence, this type of inference is designated as pūrvavat. Let us take an example to bring home our point. In a kitchen we find that smoke and fire co-exist. In a hill we infer fire from smoke. Now a question arises in our mind. We definitely apprehend all the distinctive features of an object by means of perception. But we cannot know the details of an object by means of inference. How is an act of inference similar to that of perception ? Truly so. But the particular reason which is perceived along with all its details establishes fire which is similar to the fire as experienced before. As there is no difference with regard to their distinctive features so it will not be unreasonable to hold that the act of inference is similar to that of perception.

The śeṣavat type of inference throws light on residue. It is an indirect proof. In order to explain a fact there are many possible alternative suggestions. If all the possible rival suggestions are cancelled and other suggestions are considered to be irrelevant, then the remaining one is definitely known to us to be the cause.

The example of it is as follows : Suppose, we infer fire at a spot. We have simply a general knowledge of fire. Now we try to find out its fuel. What is its fuel ? Several hypotheses are suggested to our mind. We entertain a doubt about its fuel. We think that it may be produced either by the dried-up grass or by dry leaves or by faggots. When they are eliminated, no other hypotheses that fire is produced by an earthen lamp or by a piece of stone are worthy of being entertained. The conclusion that fire is produced by the dried clod of cow-dung is indirectly arrived at. The indirect proof of the hypothesis that sound is a quality will also illustrate that type of inference. There are six broad divisions of Reality in the Vaiśeṣika Bhāṣya. Let us settle the question that sound comes under which division. We have no proof positive to establish our hypothesis. Sound may be either a substance or a quality or an action. Let us leave aside the hypothesis that sound is a quality. And let us try the other two. Sound may be either a substance or an action. These two possible alternative suggestions are refuted. The other alternative suggestions that sound is either a universal or the relation of inference or exclusive particularity are not attended to as they are impossible. Hence, it is indirectly inferred that sound is a quality. This type of inference is called as śeṣavat because the remaining one is inferred. (In other words, we have a number of possible hypotheses with regard to an object before our mind. We leave one of them aside. We examine the rest and find them to be inadequate. At the same time we do not waste our time over the scrutiny of absurd hypotheses. Then we hold that the residual hypothesis is proved.

The Sāmānyatodṛṣṭa type of inference is as follows : The consequence is a super sensuous object. It is not perceived even when the relation of universal concomitance is discovered. Moreover, it is to be noted that the relation of universal concomitance does not obtain between the reason and the consequence but between the universal of the reason and a universal which belongs to the consequence. When an imperceptible object is inferred on the basis of the relation of universal concomitance between the two universals it is called the sāmānyatodṛṣṭa type of inference. Let us take an example, viz., we infer the existence of the organ of hearing from the auditory perception. The sense-organs are supersensuous objects. Hence, they are never perceived. But we have discovered that the act of hewing and such other acts depend upon an instrument such as an axe, etc., as their cause. Thus we infer the instrumental cause from the act of perception such as hearing, etc.

Some take an exception to this line of interpretation with the suffix 'vati' attached to the stem 'pūrva'. They point out that if we subscribe to this view then there should be only one type of inference but the three-fold division of inference should not hold good. The reason which has not been known to be an invariable concomitant does not prove the consequence. The individuals, belonging to the classes of the reason and the consequence, are innumerable. Hence, it is different to discover the positive and negative aspects of the relation of universal concomitance obtaining between the reason and the consequence. Therefore, we should hold that the said relation of universal concomitance is a generalisation. Such an abstract relation of universal concomitance is known alike in all the three types of inference. The so-called three types should merge into one type which bears the title of 'pūrvavat' since they are all similar to one another.

Such an objection is not tenable. Though they are similar from the broader point of view yet there are vivid minor differences among them. If you hold that all the said different types of inference are one because all inferences are grounded upon the relation of universal concomitance then we admit your contention to be true. But our point of view is this that though they are all similar because of the same common property yet they may be classed under the three different types because of their other differences. Let us illustrate our point. Smoke and fire have been perceived before. Now we infer the same fire from the same smoke. Hence, this type of inference has been designated as 'pūrvavat'. It signifies that this type of inference depends upon perception as its cause.

Now, a question arises in our mind that if we infer fire which has not been perceived from such particular smoke as has not been seen at the time of the discovery of the relation of universal concomitance then does this inference depend upon perception as its cause? Who says that it does not belong to the type of 'pūrvavat?' If it be so, how do you define 'pūrvavat' as an inference of the same fire from the same smoke? The answer is that we do not mean the particular but the universal.

As you take notice only of the universals but not of the particulars so the pūrvavat type of inference should be identified with the sāmānyatodṛṣṭa type of inference. This objection does not hold good since the consequence in the sāmānyatodṛṣṭa type is only an inference, being imperceptible. In the other type of inference which is grounded upon the method of residue the consequence is known only through the process of elimination of the possible ones. Our previous illustration that this fire is produced by the dried clod of cow dung or that sound is a quality points to this direction. In the sāmānyatodṛṣṭa type of inference the consequence which is imperceptible by its nature is inferred. The inference of the auditory organ has been mentioned as an example. Therefore, inference admits of threefold division because of the possibility of these differences. This division is also amenable to reasons.

We have no need of placing the different examples before our readers. The three different types of inference may be shown to apply to one and the same example. Desire, being an effect, has a locus to stand upon because it partakes of the character of an effect like a jar. If a locus is only to be established then it is an example of the pūrvavat type. If a distinct locus is to be established by a process of elimination of the possible ones such as the body, the sense-organs, etc., then it illustrates the śeṣavat type. As the locus which is to be established is a supersensuous object so it is also an example of the sāmānyatodṛṣṭa type.

The Distinction between the śeṣavat type and the sāmānyatodṛṣṭa type

In which aspect does Śeṣavat differ from Sāmānyatodṛṣṭa? The procedure of Śeṣavat is one and that of Sāmānyatodṛṣṭa is another. Desire, being an effect, stands upon a locus which is other than the body, etc., because it partakes of the character of an effect and because of the cancellation of the judgment that the body or any material object is the seat of desire. This is the mode of operation of Sāmānyatodṛṣṭa. Śeṣavat operates in this way. The body or the sense-organ or the inner organ is the possible locus of desire. The possibility of each of them of being a locus is cancelled. The possibility of being a locus of desire is not to be extended to time, space etc. Therefore, the residual substance, viz. the soul is the seat of desire. There is no hard and fast rule in the Śeṣavat type of inference that the consequence must be a supersensuous object. The fire, kindled by the dried clods of cowdung is proved by means of it. The consequence of Sāmānyatodṛṣṭa is always a transcendental object. Therefore, the threefold division of inference has been nicely stated.

Some other philosophers (the Mīmāṁsakas) on the other hand hold that Sāmānyatodṛṣṭa is that type of inference in which no particular similar to the consequence has been perceived even at the time of the discovery of the relation of universal concomitance. The illustration of it is the inference of power of action. An action which belongs to Devadatta remains imperceptible. The judgment that Devadatta moves refers only to Devadatta since his action is not perceived. The judgments that Devadatta stands still and that Devadatta moves refer alike to the same person.

The predicate of the judgment is a compact series of conjunctions and disjunctions. Hence, this judgment does not always arise. If an action is a transcendental object then can we infer it ? The answer to this question is as follows. An effect is an event in time. So, it depends upon its cause for its coming into being. If the substance-in-itself is its cause then effects will constantly issue of it since the paramount cause is always there. But the effect does not always come into being. Hence an action which is distinct from the cause is inferred, It should be noted that power is also thus inferred. An action and power are intrinsically transcendental. The syllogistic argument which proves them is a particular type of inference. The person who goes to infer the consequence has perceived no such particular before, i.e., its species. It is not an inference of the particular because it is impossible to discover the relation of universal concomitance holding between the particulars. The thesis that all actions are transcendental is not reasonable. All actions are motion of which upward movement and such other movements are the species. This movement is referred to by the judgment "It moves" and so on. This is a perceptual judgment. Hence, it is not tenable that all actions are an inference. If conjunction and disjunction would have been referred to by such a judgment then the form of the judgment should have been that it is united and disunited but not that it moves since the judgment accords with its object. We classify the objects of the universe, following the difference in the nature of reference of judgments. Otherwise, the awareness of a jar should have referred to something else. If the judgment that it moves refers to its conjunctions and disjunctions then an object which stands still should be referred to by the judgment that it moves since it has every possibility of containing both conjunction and disjunction.

A stable post on which a hawk sat and from which it flew away should be referred to by the judgment that the post moves. Now, the Mīmāṁsakas may contend that the judgment involving of movement refers to a continuous series of conjunctions and disjunctions but the above judgment does not hold good. The past and future conjunctions and disjunctions are included in the series. But they can never be perceived. Hence, we should take note only of present conjunctions and disjunctions. If Devadatta stands still after having walked some distance then conjunction and disjunction belong to him. As such why should not he be referred to by the judgment that Davadatta moves ?

The ground is also seen to contain an uninterrupted series of conjunctions and disjunctions. It should also be referred to by the judgment that the ground moves like the men moving on the ground.

Now, the Mīmāṁsakas may contend that the predicate 'moves' is asserted only of that person whose action brings about conjunction and disjunction and that the predicate in question does not apply to the ground since it does not produce them (conjunction and disjunction) not action in itself. If they go so far then it is proper to admit that the above predicate refers only to an action but not to conjunction and disjunction since such a reference is established by the joint method of agreement and difference. If conjunction and disjunction are referred to by the predicate 'moves' then they have to explain why they hold that the person moves but not the ground though both the person and the ground contain alike conjunction and disjunction. Now, the Mīmāṁsakas may further contend that the judgment that Devadatta moves is only to be framed but not the judgment that the ground moves because the action of Devadatta is only responsible for conjunction and disjunction.

Such a contention is not tenable. The action being supersensuous, we fail to know whether the action inheres in Devadatta or in the ground since it is only inferred from its effect, viz., conjunction and disjunction. But the effect is shared in common by both Devadatta and the ground. Now, our experience teaches that the following judgments under the specified conditions do not arise in our mind. When Devadatta walks on the ground we do never judge that the ground moves. When the breeze constantly blows over the banks of a river and has connection with and disjunction from the slabs of stone on them we do never judge that the slabs of stone move. Therefore we arrive at the conclusion that the verb 'to move' refers only to an action but not to conjunction and disjunction. When the bird mounts high towards the sky we perceive that it flies. In the unsupported sky no conjunction is perceived since such a contact with the sky belongs to the supersensuous sky as well. It remains ever imperceptible like the contact of the air with the tree. (If the two conjoining terms are not perceived then their contact is not perceived). It may be held that the contact of the bird with a particular portion of the sky which is marked out by a flood of light is perceived. But such a defence is not tenable. When the sky is enveloped by the Tamāla dark clouds we perceive in the dark night that the glow-worm is flying.

In that sky there is neither broad light nor darkness having parts. There no object with which the contact of the glow-worm and from which its separation will be perceived. When the earthquake takes place we experience that the earth is quaking but neither conjunction nor disjunction is seen. Again, if it takes place at mid-night of the dark fortnight, no object is seen but the shaking of the earth is experienced. Hence, the awareness of movement does not refer to conjunction, etc. but only to action. Again, if an action is absolutely transcendental, it cannot be inferred. You may hold that it may be indirectly inferred. Every effect has a cause. Conjunction and disconjunction are effects. Therefore, they have a cause. This cause is no other than an action. Such an inference is not tenable since the relation of universal concomitance cannot be established. For, you hold that a substance-in-itself is not the cause of conjunction, etc., but is the cause when it is qualified by an action. As an action, being absolutely transcendental, is hard to perceive so a substance as qualified by an action is imperceptible. Moreover, it is very difficult to perceive the essence of a cause. Hence, it is difficult to detect the relation of universal concomitance even in a similar example like a jar, etc. But when we infer a transcendental object like the soul we face no difficulty since the object to be inferred has the dependent character. We all perceive that a jar is dependent upon its cause, i.e., parts. Hence, in the similar example, the relation of universal concomitance is perceived. Therefore, we come to the conclusion that an action is not inferred from its effect. The action is not also inferred from conjunction. The last effect of an action is conjunction and the action perishes in the next moment. Hence, an action which is actually present cannot be inferred from conjunction, its effect. The predicate 'moves' refers to a present action. It cannot be inferred from conjuntion and disjunction so long as it is present. An action comes into being in the first moment. It produces in the second moment disjunction which destroys the earlier contact in the third moment. In the fourth moment it produces a fresh subsequent contact with some other object. In the fifth moment it passes away. The subsequent contact is not perceived when it comes into being since the perception of an object is causally determined by its object. If it (the subsequent conjunction) is the reason of the inference of an action, the perception of the reason is necessary. When such perception takes place the action has passed away. Hence, the action which is actually present cannot be inferred. The hypothesis that an action is an inference has been refuted in the general introduction. The hypothesis that supersensuous power is an inference is also refuted in the light of this criticism. The hypothesis that supersensuous power is objectively real has also been elaborately refuted in the earlier chapter (i.e., in the section on presumption).

Hence, the inference of transcendental action and power is not an instance of the Sāmānyatodṛṣṭa type of inference. The illustration of this type has already been given.

We have explained the terms 'pūrvavat' and 'Śeṣavat' either by attaching the 'matup' suffix or by attaching the 'vati' suffix.

Thus we have presented three-fold division of inference before our readers. Such a division stands to reasons.

As the moon-beams become lustreless in the presence of the rays of the sun so the definitions of inference as given by the learned scholars of the other schools become unconvincing when they are compared and contrasted with those of inference of this school.

The definition of inference as put forward by the Buddhist is to be criticised in the light of the criticism of universal concomitance as propounded by the Buddhists. Śabara Svāmin holds that the relation of universal concomitance is based upon the repeated observations of concomitance. He defines inference accordingly. He is to be pitied. (He does not take note of the positive and negative aspects of the relation of concomitance. Hence, the universality of such relation is open to criticism.) We fail to understand how do the followers of the Sāṁkhya school explain inference. The universals are not distinct from the individuals. An effect is identical with as well as different from its cause. When an effect is identical with its cause the universal belonging to the effect is also identical with the cause. If the universals have no distinct existence then the relation holding between the two universals cannot be accepted from this standpoint. Therefore, the relation only obtains between two particulars. Thus, it is difficult to establish the universality and the generality of the relation of concomitance.

Past, present and future objects are inferred

Now, a new matter is going to be discussed. Our normal perception which has been defined as arising from the contact of the sense-organ with the object, etc. generally refers to present objects only. Does inference also reveal only present objects? Or, can it reveal objects belonging to the other periods of time? The answer to these questions is that the past, present and future objects are revealed by inference. The past rainfall is inferred from the swollen river. The future one is inferred from the gathering of clouds. The present fire is inferred from smoke. The Mīmāṁsakas hold that the Vedas alone reveal past, present, future, subtle, enveloped and remote objects but no other proofs can do it. This view is not sound. Because, like the Vedas, other sources of valid knowledge reveal similar objects. We have already stated that the super-sensuous perception of the sages reveals objects belonging to the different periods of time. Sometimes, we also perceive distant objects.

An objection to the very existence of time

Some logicians take an exception to the above hypothesis. They point out that if time is established to be objectively real then the discussion about the knowledge of the objects belonging to the three different periods of time becomes relevant. But it is a pity that it is difficult to prove the existence of Time. If time does not exist, the division of time into past, present and future is absurd.

As we perceive a jar, etc., so we do not perceive Time. The ideas such as 'slow', 'quick', etc., do not refer to time but only refer to events. The above ideas do not constitute the reason from which time is to be inferred since as the relation of universal concomitance holds between smoke and fire so it does not obtain between the above ideas and time.

How will you explain the difference in the meanings of these ideas ? A reference to the different series of the moments of actions answers the above question.

It is not reasonable to assume that time is nothing but the vibrations of planets, stars etc. and that it is not distinct from ordinary actions.

The use of the different units of time such as a muhūrta (48 minutes), a yāma (3 hours), day and night, a month, a season, an ayana (a half-year) and a year may be explained as conventional. The convention is based on imagination.

If time is held to be a partless substance which is one eternal and all-pervasive then how can we divide it into parts and use them as past, present and future ?

Some say that time is a perceptible object

A reply to the above objection is as follows : Some logicians hold that Time is perceived. When an event is perceived it is perceived as qualified by time. In other words, time is a predicative predicate in a perceptual judgment. The judgments such as 'it has been gradually done', 'it has been simultaneously done', it has been quickly done, 'it has been slowly done', etc. do not refer only to events since the diversity of judgments presupposes the variety of objects. How is it that colourless time is perceived ? If you raise an objection like this then how do you yourself explain the perception of colourless colour ? Or, how do you explain that the coloured atoms are not perceived ? Our experience can only give an answer to these questions. Ask your experience and learn from it what is perceived and what is not. Simply discover the facts but you do not try to find out the 'why' of everything. Now, it may be argued against the perception of time that among the substances only coloured ones are perceived. The perception of all substances, is also not determined by it. If it had done so then atoms would have been perceived. The law should be re-stated in the following manner that all substances which are perceived are coloured. Praśasta Deva has also said that only three substances have perceptibility, colour and fluidity. It is not a divine mandate so that it should not be transgressed. A mere verbal statement cannot solve the problem, viz., which object is perceived and which is not since the perceptibility of an object lies in its being the object of an apprehension, produced by a sense-organ. If it is perceived, you should not argue against its perception on the ground that it is colourless. Let colour belong to the earth, water and light. We have nothing to object to it since they are experienced as such, i.e., coloured. A man who keeps his eyes shut up cannot have perceptual judgments like these that it is quickly done, etc., since they have a necessary reference to time. Therefore, time is perceptible.

If time is perceived at all, why is not it perceived as a subject in a perceptual judgment like a jar ? Our answer to this query is that the intrinsic property of time is responsible for it and time is not to blame on that account.

Time is always the predicate of a coloured object in a perceptual judgment but is never a subject like a stick. (Though a stick becomes a predicate in a perceptual judgment yet it becomes a subject in another judgment. But time becomes never a subject in a perceptual judgment.) But the sky is never perceived even as a predicate. The sky is imperceptible not because it has no colour.

If it is held that when the coloured objects such as a stick, etc., become a predicate they are perceived but the colourless objects such as time, etc., are never perceived as a predicate. Such a view is not tenable. The colourless predicates such as universals, etc., are perceived. The law that the coloured objects as a predicate are perceived may be restricted only to the sphere of substances. But we point out that such restriction is not possible as the reasons have already been stated. Whenever objects are perceived with eyes whatever comes within the range of eyes is perceived and it does not matter whether the object is coloured or not or whether it is a substance or not. Thus, we also perceive gold to be heavy and hence gravity belonging to such substances, is perceived. The hypothesis that gravity is only inferred from the falling down of the substances which it belongs to, is not tenable.

Hence, whatever is perceived with eyes either as a subject or as a predicate should be included in the list of perceptible objects.

Therefore, time is a visible object, Space is also a perceptible object because of the same reasons though the hypothesis in vogue holds that it is inferred from the concepts 'near', 'remote', etc.

Time is an Inference

Some other logicians hold that the judgments such as 'Devadatta has a stick'. 'The lotus in blue', etc., are different as their contents are diverse. They also hold that though time is not perceived yet it is an inference because there are judgments containing such peculiar contents as owe their existence to time.

None can argue against the existence of time because it is not perceived as he can neither deny existence to the bottom of the Earth nor to the other side of the moon since neither of them is perceived.

Though impressions are transcendental yet as accessory conditions they help the sense-organs to produce the recognitive perception. Similarly, transcendental time produces such perceptual judgments as refer to slowness, swiftness, etc. In connection with the discussion about the definition of perception it has been elaborately discussed whether the difference in the nature of perceptual judgments arises from the diversity of objects or from the variety of conditions. It is needless to reiterate the old matter.

We have arrived at the conclusion that determinate perception is not untrue. Hence the perceptual judgments which refer to slowness, swiftness, etc., are not imaginary.

If we minutely observe an effect such as a piece of cloth or a similar object and its coming into being then we come to know that we cannot perceive all the conditions of it. Though all the perceptible conditions such as threads, the beams set in a loom, the shuttle, the weaver, ete., are the same yet we perceive the effect in a different manner at different times. Sometimes, we perceive that an effect is swiftly produced. Sometimes, we also perceive that it is slowly produced. We are to find out some other cause to explain the difference existing in these two judgments.

Now, the objector presses his point that the above concepts are not objectively determined by time but by actions such as vibration, etc. Some vibrations are swift, some are slow. They determine judgments such as 'it is swiftly done', 'It is slowly done', etc. In other words, the objector explains time in terms of known objects.

This view is not tenable. How does he explain swiftness or slowness belonging to vibrations themselves ? What will be the objective ground of these concepts ? There are judgments, viz., 'This vibration is moving very slowly', 'That vibration is moving very swiftly', and so on.

Some hold that vibration is surely the *sine qua non* of these judgments but it is not the ordinary vibration of Devadatta, etc., which determines the ideas of succession, simultaneity, etc. The vibrations of planets, stars, etc., condition them. Thus, time is nothing but the vibrations of planets, stars, etc.

The vibrations of planets and other heavenly bodies constitute the basis of conventional time. The time which is measured by us for our use such as yama (three hours) ahorātra (day and night), prahara (one hour and a half), etc. There is innate difference in vibrations. Hence, it is not difficult to explain different times. But if we subscribe to the hypothesis that time is one, then in order to explain different times current in the conventional world, one should assume limiting adjuncts which impose limitation upon time. But if we do not subscribe to the above hypothesis, we are not to assume that different conventional times are due to the action of limiting adjuncts. The different vibrations are not seen. How will they be measured ? The different units such as a 'daṇḍa', 'prahara' etc., are the means by which it is indicated. When time is measured it is expressed by the sentences such as 'This much time makes up a daṇḍa''. This much time constitutes a muhūrta''. This much time is taken up by a prahara'', etc. When many acts are performed in a particular moment or within a prahara we know that they have been simultaneously done. When they are performed in different moments we know that they have been successively done. Hence, the objector comes to the conclusion that the vibrations of planets, etc., themselves are time and that they are inferred from the invariable mark, constituted by daṇḍa, prahara, etc. The astronomers, who know the secret of time, subscribe to this hypothesis. This hypothesis is not tenable. When we see the moon and other luminaries we see their motion and other activities.

The sun has slowly gone down. The cold-rayed moon has swiftly risen. Mars and Venus seem to have ascended simultaneously.

Now how are we to account for the term 'slowly' contained in the sentence. 'The sun has slowly gone down'? Are we to infer the vibration of some other planet in order to explain it ? If we do it then we are to face the charge of *regressus ad infinitum*. Hence, we arrive at the conclusion that the vibration of planets is not time and that time is a distinct substance. Succession, simultaneity and such other terms are used because they all contain a reference to time.

Does succession flow from the intrinsic nature of time which has been assumed by you ? If you answer the first question in the affirmative then you should have held that succession independently follows from the intrinsic nature of effects such as a cloth, etc., which are being perceived by us and the assumption of time is superfluous. If you answer the second question in the affirmative then the new hypothesis is open to the fallacy of *regressus ad infinitum* since each condition, being dependant, requires the aid of another.

It will be foolish to indulge in such futile argumentation. We can dispense with objects such as the white colour and so on if we follow the above procedure. If a quality is white by its intrinsic nature then let a substance to white be its intrinsic nature and the hypothesis that a quality is a distinct object is redundant. If it is held that a quality is white because of its possession of another quality then the hypothesis is open to the fallacy of *regressus ad infinitum*. You should not also hold that the argument against the distinct reality of time holds good since a similar argument against the distinct reality of quality is available. The use of temporal expressions such as succession, simultaneity, etc., with reference to events in time, viz., a cloth, etc., is due to a distinct cause which is other than the events themselves. Another cause should not be sought afterwards to attribute causal efficiency to the above cause. Hence, time is the cause of the use of temporal expression, viz., simultaneous, etc.

The ideas such as 'far' and 'near' based upon space, are distinct from those, viz., 'young' and 'old', based upon Time. If time is not assumed then this distinction cannot be upheld. Devadatta and other persons who occupy the distant spaces are known to us as remote objects. They who occupy the near space are apprehended as near objects. But if the former are junior in age then they are cognised as young. But on the other hand, if the latter are senior in age then they are cognized as old. Hence the temporal ideas such as 'prior' and 'posterior' cannot be explained if Time is not assumed. Hence Time is thus inferred. Time is one in number like the sky. It has no intrinsic diversity. Sound is the mark of the sky. As sound remains always the same and as there is no such mark as points to the diversity of the sky so the sky is one. Time is omnipresent in dimension since the use of temporal expressions is everywhere noticed. It is partless since no parts, the locus of the whole, are observed. As partless it is self-sufficient. It is a substance because. (it requires no locus to stand upon.). It is, also, eternal since the conditions of destruction viz. the separation of parts etc. do never arise.

Three divisions of Time

Time is an individual. It admits of no division. How is Time divided into three divisions, viz., the present, the past and the future ? As it admits of no division, so how do you hold that the present, the past and the future objects are inferred ? Our answer to this question is this that time does not really divide itself into three parts. But though the division of Time is absent, yet in order to establish the conventional division of Time some condition is assumed. What is this condition that imposes apparent division upon Time ? We answer that it is an action.

The three divisions of conventional Time, viz., the present, the past and the future do not represent the real divisions of an action of the abovementioned condition of Time. If they (i. e., the present, the past and the future) really had done so, then an action would be the only ground of all divisions of Time. What is the necessity of assuming Time ? An action is a series of operations which extend over a few consecutive moments in order to bring about a result and is determined by it i.e., the result. Let us cite an example to illustrate it. The act of cooking rice is a series of operations such as the placing of a pot, containing unboiled rice, on the burning oven, boiling of water, reducing the rigid conjunction of the parts of rice to a state of loose one and ultimately the softening of the parts of rice and ending in the operation of elminating the watery portion. The determinant of an act is its result. It has the three parts (present, past and future). The act which commences from the placing of a cooking pot on an oven and ends in taking it down from that is called the act of cooking. As it continues till the emergence of a result, i.e., boiled rice so it is called the present action, i.e., an action covering the present time. The sentence 'He cooks' illustrates it. The sky which is limited by a jar because of its association with the latter is called the sky enclosed by a jar. Similarly, Time which is associated with an action which extends over a few moments and is characterized by it is called the present one. A series of actions which are qualified yielded results still characterizes Time. Such Time is called the past time. The sentence "He cooked" illustrates it. Time which is associated with such an action is called the past one. An act which is qualified by such result as will emerge is called the future action. The sentence "He will cook" illustrates it. Time-which is conditioned by such an action is thus called the future one. Hence, the expressions the 'present', the 'past' and the 'future' apply to Time. Some hold that the present time does not exist. They argue in the following manner : When a leaf falls down from a tree the two spaces are only perceived, viz., the space which has been covered by it and the space which will be covered by it but the space which it covers at the present moment is not perceived. This argument is not relevant since conventional time is not indicated by space. But it is only indicated by an action. The manner of its indication has been already described. The use of temporal expressions owes its origin to the divisions of Time by means of acts. Some temporal expressions represent the divisions of conventional time, viz., Kṣaṇa (4 minutes), Lava (16 seconds), Kāṣṭhā (8 seconds), Kalā (4 minutes), Nālikā (24 minutes), Muhūrta (48 minutes), Yama (3 hours), Ahorātra (day and night), Māsa (a month), Ṛtu (a season), Ayana (the half-year measured by the sun's apparent course north to south of the equator) a period of 6 months measured by the sun's motion either on the north of the equator, or on the south of it, Saṁvatsara (a year), Yuga (quinquennium or a period of twelve years or a period of a few thousand years), Manvantara (Manu's period) and Kalpa (a day of Brahman). It is needless any more to argue to prove the existence of Time.

The ascertainment of various lunar days helps the performance of the Vedic rites. Let us cite examples. One should observe particular Vedic rites on the day of the full-moon and on the day of the new-moon. Particular Vedic rites are observed during different seasons. The knowledge of the advent of a season is gathered from the observation of distinctive phenomena.

Let us cite examples. A Brahmin should kindle sacrificial fire in spring, a Kṣatriya in summer, a Vaiśya in autumn and a carpenter in the rainy season. But we are in a position to know the different lunar days and seasons if we only calculate the lunar motion and that of the sun in conjunction with the different signs of the zodiac, following the method given in the science of astronomy. There are also well known popular signs by means of which the different seasons are detected.

When the cuckoos peck mango blossoms with the edge of their bills and sing sweet notes we know the advent of spring.

When the creepers on the roadside wither, being dried up in the scorching rays of the sun and we smell the sweet scent of the jasmine flowers during our journey on road we know the approach of summer.

When the hills put on a glossy appearance having clouds over their peaks and the peacocks indulge in wild dance on them, stretching out their spotted tail the setting in of the rainy season is indicated.

When the sky as blue as the water of Jamunā is decorated by the milky way, resembling a pearl necklace it indicates the advent of autumn.

The breasts of the youthful damsels remaining warm in spite of their prolonged enjoyment in the long nights welcome the presence of the dewy season.

The wind, being saturated with frost, blows roughly, opens the kunda-buds by its contact, speaks of the approach of winter. Therefore, though Time is one yet becomes many, being associated with the different actions.

Determination of Space

Space which has been established should also be considered in the light of arguments similar to those already stated.

The ideas of the East, the West, etc., being different from those of the objects, located in space, such as the idea of a tree, etc., lead to the inference of a distinct cause. Though Space is one because of the same mark yet it admits of tenfold division.

When the sun circumambulates, the contact of its rays with the different sides of the table land of the Mount Meru serves the purpose of a condition that ideally divides Space into the East, the West etc., and other directions. The different directions are the East, the South-East, the South, the South-west, the West, the North-West, the North, the North-East, the nether direction and the upper direction. As ten deities preside over these ten directions so Space which is one admits of ten divisions and these ten spaces acquire fresh designation after the gods such as Āindrī (presided over by Indra), Āgneyī (presided over by Agni (Fire), Yāmya (presided over by Yama (god of death), Nāirṛtī (presided over by Nirṛti, (the evil spirit), Vāruṇī (presided over by Varuṇa). Vāyavya (presided over by Vāyu), Kauberī (presided over by Kubera), Āiśānī (presided over by Īśāna), Nāgīya (presided over by Nāga), and Brāhmī (presided over by Brahman).

Another point draws our attention for the clarification of the ideas of Time and Space. We infer Time and Space either indirectly from a few judgments or directly from the existent marks which are perceived. But the very ground of their inference gives us to understand that they admit of division. How is it that each of them is one ? When we know Time and Space it is revealed to us that there are times and spaces. But we have already discussed the matter and pointed out that all the ideas of Time and Space, being similar in their nature, point to the hypothesis that each of them is merely one. We also realise that no times and spaces are absolutely real. What is the east from one point of view is the south from another point of view. The country which is to the east of Surāṣṭra is to the south of Mālava. The distinction between 'slow' and 'quick' is not absolutely fixed. The time which is known as the future will become the present and the past. Similarly, what is slow becomes quick and *vice versa*. Hence, all differences of space and times are only relative.

In other works of the allied systems of Nyāya and Vaiśeṣika Time and Space have been elaborately discussed. For this reason, the elaborate treatment of them has been given up. Moreover, it is well known that in this world the garrulous persons are despised by all.

The hypothesis that Time exists is proved. It is either perceived or inferred. It admits of manifold divisions. But at the same time its manifold divisions are only conditional, i.e., relative. Hence, Gautama, the author of the Nyāya-sūtra, has concluded that inference reveals the present, the past and the future objects. This conclusion is sound.

The end of the chapter on Inference.

Upamāna (*Comparison*)

In the Nyāya-sūtra which treats the classification of Pramāṇa Upamāna has been mentioned after Anumāna. Following the serial order of the Pramāṇas the definition of Upamāna is given here.

Upamāna is the knowledge of an object to be ascertained by means of its similarity to a known object (N.S.I.).

The earlier logicians have described the specific character of Upamāna thus : An assertion which enlightens the similarity of an unknown object to a known one and helps to ascertain the relation of denotation of a word and its meaning is Upamāna. A citizen who has never seen a gavaya (Boselaphus tragocomelu) but desires to know it, puts to an expert forester the question, "What is the form of a gavaya ?" He replies that it is like a cow. This instructive sentence informs of the similarity of an unknown object to a known one and thereby communicates that the term 'gavaya' denotes this unknown object.

This instruction, being itself composed by words, is no better than that of a trustworthy person. Hence, it belongs to the sphere of verbal knowledge and as such it should not be recognized as a distinct source of knowledge. As it brings about a distinct result, viz., the ascertainment of the relation holding between a term and the object denoted by it, so it should be held as a distinct source of knowledge. If we subscribe to such a hypothesis then the member of distinct sources of knowledge should be endless. Though the sentences of the ordinary persons and the Vedic sentences consisting of injunctions and prohibitions yield numerous distinct results yet they do not transcend the domain of verbal knowledge.

A reply to this objection from the above standpoint is as follows : When a person, according to his belief in the truth of a word or out of his reverence for the utterer of a word, comes to know independently of any other means of knowledge that the word correctly denoted the object which it stands for, the word is recognized as the verbal authority since it is the independent source of valid knowledge of an object. When a person advises a person to adopt some other means of knowledge in order to know the object it is not determined only by the instruction. Words, i.e., the instructions, given by a reliable person, play here only a secondarly part to enlighten the object in question. We also see that they (words) play no important part in a syllogism consisting of propositions, e.g., this hill is fiery since it is smoky like a kitchen. The person who follows the trend of the proposition knows that the hill is fiery. But he comes to the conclusion not because of his implicit faith in the veracity of the words, uttered by a reliable person without any reference to the middle term but because of his knowledge of the sound middle term and the sound premises. If the forester had not instructed the means of knowing the gavaya, viz., the similarity of a gavaya to a known cow to a citizen desirous of knowing a gavaya then his instruction would have been the verbal authority. But a gavaya is known by means of similarity referred to by the above instruction. It is surely a distinct proof though it consists of words. The citizen who sees the animal does not merely know that it is denoted by the term 'gavaya' from the instruction of the forester but experiences its similarity to a familiar cow. Does not the citizen identify the animal by the instruction of the forester? We do not deny that the instruction has helped him to identify it. But it is a truism that his instruction purports to suggest some other means, viz., similarity which points to its proper identification. The determination of the animal which does not immediately follow from the hearing of the instruction is not verbal knowledge but it is such knowledge as is obtained by comparison. Though the instruction, given by the forester, consists of words yet it is reasonable to hold that it is a distinct proof called comparison. It seems to us that the lines of the commentary on the Nyāyasūtra in this context bear evidence to this hypothesis. We do not quote these lines as they will unnecessarily increase the bulk of this work.

No more elaboration is required.

The contemporary logicians hold that the knower who has

heard the instruction, given by the forester, directly perceives that the unknown particular bears a close resemblance to the known particular. This sensuous perception of resemblance which is called upamāna generates the knowledge of the relation between the term and the object denoted by it. Like the perception of smoke it (the knowledge of resemblance) leads to the identification of an object which has not been sensed though it contains sensible property. Hence, it is a distinct proof. The citizen, who has learnt the instruction, rambles in the forest, sees an animal similar to a cow and then remembers the instruction of the forester that a gavaya is like a cow. Recollecting it he comes to know that the term 'gavaya' applies to it, that is, this is denoted by the term (gavaya). The knowledge of the relation between the term and the object, denoted by it, presupposes the knowledge of the term and the object denoted by it. The resultant knowledge that this is designed as a gavaya is called upamiti. The proximate cause of it is called upamāna.

Perception is not competent to reveal the relation between a term and the object denoted by it since the figure of a wild gavaya is only sensed by him for the first time.

We do not even ascertain the relation between a word and the object denoted by it hearing the instruction given by the forester since when the forester has given the instruction the animal 'gavaya' is not perceived. When we know for certain that this is the word and that this is the object denoted by it we distinctly know that a definite relation holds between the word and this object, otherwise, we fail to do it. For this reason, Kaṇāda has stated that a name cannot be given to an object unless the latter is perceived, as an effect cannot be produced unless the material cause is within the reach of our eyes.

A Refutation of the Hypothesis that Comparison is a Distinct Proof

An objector subjects this hypothesis to severe criticism. In answer to the question of a citizen the forester replies that a gavaya is like a cow.

The above sentence purports to convey that an animal which resembles a cow is a gavaya by name. It also throws light on the relation holding between the term and the object, denoted by it.

The above relation does not obtain between a word and an individual since the individuals are innumerable. But it has been decided that it obtains between a word and a class which includes all the individuals in itself.

It has been stated that the perception of an object precedes the assignment of its name and that of the material cause precedes the production of its effect. Is it a Vedic injunction ? Can nobody violate it ? But the main purport of this statement is that the knowledge of an object always precedes that of the signification of a word.

The knowledge of the object may be acquired through perception or through some other source of knowledge. There is no hard and fast rule that the perception of an object should always precede the knowledge of an object. The remembrance of an object also, leads to the knowledge of the signification of a word.

The animal which has been seen there is called a ruru (a species of deer). Sometimes, we introduce an imperceptible object by the mention of its marks and name it. Let us illustrate this point. You will know the person to be Caitra—the person whose teeth are long, body is covered with hair, complexion is dark, stature is short, eyes are large and jaws are flat. Similarly, it is not impossible to instruct a person that the name 'gavaya' applies to an animal which bears a close resemblance to a cow.

It may be argued against the thesis mentioned above that if the object is not perceived, the instruction that a gavaya is like a cow is not believed to be true. It may be answered that though the instruction is not accepted to be trustworthy yet the relation of denotation holding between the word 'gavaya' and the animal resembling a cow as suggested by the instruction is not discredited as incorrect. But as long as we do not perceive a gavaya, curiosity as to its form lingers in our mind and instantaneously dissolves with the perception of a gavaya.

In fine, the objector holds that the object which is established either by perception or by verbal authority requires the help of no other proof for its establishment.

The Establishment of the Thesis that Comparison is a Distinct Proof

The Naiyāyikas of established reputation meet that above

objection thus :-When we acquire the distinct knowledge of the relation of denotation from the instruction of the said forester (such knowledge is distinct from verbal knowledge) because the object is not perceived at the time of receiving the instruction. Though from the instruction we know a gavaya to be like a cow yet we cannot rely upon this knowledge. This piece of knowledge by description is not so convincing that all our inquiry about the known object gets a satisfactory answer.

The knowledge which arises from the instruction, being heard, does not solve all the rational doubts about its content. Verbal knowledge carries with it a sense of completion and depends upon no other proof for the complete expression of its object. But the knowledge, derived from the instruction is incomplete and depends upon perception for the right communication of its object.

In this case the words of the forester fail to produce such complete knowledge and hence it is highly probable that they fail in their task.

If it is held that the relation of denotation obtains between a word and a universal (a class) then it is also a fact that a universal is not definitely known unless an individual is perceived.

When the form of a gavaya is made known to us by the instruction of a forester we have no faith in the veracity of this statement. Hence, the relation of denotation which holds between a word and the object, denoted by it, as derived from the said instruction, is not accepted to be correct.

For this very reason it is held that the naming of an object and its communication are preceded by perception. Sometimes, perception is not the proximate cause of the knowledge of the relation of denotation. It produces such knowledge through the medium of memory. Let us illustrate our point. The relation of denotation holding between the word 'ruru' and an experienced deer (belonging to a species of deer) is known by means of memory. Similarly, the relation of denotation between Caitra and a particular person is known by means of known characteristics such as having long teeth, etc. But regarding the point at issue it is to be noted that though the bare resemblance to a cow has been imparted by the above instruction, yet the knowledge of a gavaya, arising from it, is not free from a doubt about its true communication, since the instruction in question does not exactly throw light on a gavaya but depends upon some other proof for the perfect illumination of its object. When a person will see the individual with his eyes and notice that it is like a cow, his doubt about the truth of the instruction will be removed. The contention of the objector is not tenable since the instrument of perceptual knowledge, being the sense-object-contact, etc., cannot produce the knowledge of the relation of denotation.

You hold that the perception of the animal produces the apprehension of likeness. We take no exception to it. But the very apprehension of resemblance is, according to us, a distinct source of knowledge, called comparison.

As the perception of smoke in a hill leads to the inferential knowledge of fire which is beyond the range of perception so the perception of a gavaya resembling a cow in a forest generates the knowledge of the supersensuous relation of signification holding between a word and the object denoted by it. This piece of knowledge is a distinct type of knowledge based upon comparison. As is case of inference the recollection of the previously known universal concomitance holding between fire and smoke is the accessory condition so in the case of knowledge, based upon comparison, the remembrance of the content of a previous instruction inparting resemblance plays the part of an accessory condition. In inference, when we discover the relation of universal concomitance we do not find that this relation obtains only between the particular consequence and the particular reason but between the consequence and the reason in general.

But when we draw a conclusion from a major premise by means of a minor premise that the middle term belongs to the minor term (e.g., there is smoke in the hill) we specify the character of the major term to some extent (e.g., we deduce such fire as belongs to the hill). Similarly, in case of comparison when we hear the said instruction we have simply a general idea of an object denoted by a word, e.g., a gavaya. But when we perceive a particular object, i.e., when we perceive an individual gavaya, having resemblance to a cow we truly come to know for certain that this is the same object as is denoted by the word 'gavaya'.

Do not think that this is a piece of inferential knowledge since knowledge based upon comparison depends upon neither positive nor negative concomitance.

In fine, we arrive at the conclusion that the judgment that this is denoted by the word 'gavaya' is derived only from comparison but not from any other source of knowledge.

Some logicians may raise various objections against this hypothesis, viz., "Such a judgment does not exist", "Its validity is doubtful", "It is contradicted", and "It is merely imaginary". Such objections are not fair. This is a piece of true knowledge since it satisfies all the tests of truth. The source of it is comparison. As there is nothing wrong about it so it is reasonable to hold that it is a species of true knowledge. Theauthor of the Nyāya-sūtra points to the same conclusion in his sūtra "Prasiddha sādharmyāt-sādhya-sādhanam".(the establishment of the object of inquiry through resemblance to a well-known object.

The compound word 'prasiddha-sādharmyāt" may be differently interpreted. Either it may be an example of Karmadhāraya compound or that of Tṛtīyā-tatpuruṣa compound or that of Bahuvrīhi compound. If we try to understand the import of the first one then it signifies the well-known resemblance of a gavaya. If we intend to understand the import of the second one then it conveys the resemblance of a gavaya to a very familiar object. If we are interested in the sense of the third one then it represents a gavaya whose resemblance to some other object is well-known. Upamāna (comparison) is sādhya-sādhana because of prasiddha-sādharmya (because of the perception of such resemblance or that of an object having resemblance to a familiar object). The compound word 'sādhya-sādhana' requires interpretation. The word 'sādhya' denotes the relation of a word to an object denoted by it. The word 'sādhana' stands for the act of knowing it. The compound word 'sādhya-sādhana' represents the knowing of the relation of a word to the object denoted by it. Or, the word 'sādhya' stands for the knowledge of the relation of denotation holding between a word and the object meant by it. The word 'sādhana' means generation. Thus, the compound word signifies the generation of the knowledge of the said relation of denotation. The knowledge of the resemblance of an unfamiliar object to a very familiar object plays the part of an instrument. It is called Upamāna (comparison). The result which it brings about is the knowledge of the relation of a word to the object denoted by it.

The author of the Nyāya-sūtra states that a piece of valid knowledge which acts as an instrument is called a proof and the compound word 'sādhya-sādhana' is clearly suggestive of this hypothesis. This convention has been adopted in every case of a proof. The compound word 'sādhya-sādhana' has been put in the middle of the sūtra with the idea that it will be syntactically connected with all the preceding and the succeeding definition of a proof.

The perception of resemblance is comparison (upamāna). But the nature of resemblance is a controversial matter. The problem whether or not the resemblance is complete or partial has not been solved. So a doubt as to the validity of the knowledge based upon comparison may occur in our mind. The author of the Nyāya-sūtra has removed this possible doubt. An object to which the knowledge of resemblance to another object is due is called 'similar to that'. Hence the discussion regarding the character of resemblance is superfluous. As an universal is the source of the idea of oneness so resemblance is at the root of the idea of similarity.

Is the definition of Upamāna (Comparison) in any way useful to this spiritual science which teaches the doctrine of final emancipation from all sorrows?

From the authoritative scriptures we learn that the knowledge of the self together with that of all the accessory details, leads to final emancipation. The veracity of the scriptures and speech is established by means of inference. Perception is the source of induction. Hence, as the three proofs, viz., perception, inference and verbal authority have a special service to this science so they should be exclusively discussed. (But Upamāna, having neither proximate nor remote usefulness, should find no place in the Nyāya-sūtra) The objection is really true to a great extent. But still comparison is serviceable to the performance of a Vedic rite which enjoins the killing of a gavaya since a gavaya cannot be killed if one is not acquainted with it. On the strength of the instruction that the plant of Mudgaparṇī is like the stem of kidney-beans, comparison has special service to identify the plant of Mudgaparṇī. In such matters the proof of comparison has a unique part to play.

The kind-hearted sage Gautama has defined the proof of comparison in order to render a useful service to all though the said proof has no bearing upon final emancipation.

If this is the motive of the sage then a lot of other things like the Vedic rite, the said plant, etc., should also be instructed. There is no scope for such an objection since the Nyāya-sūtra, being a science of sources of valid knowledge, teaches only such proofs as act as an instrument to bring about the knowledge of an object. The number of proofs is only four neither more nor less. This point has been established by an argument. The objects which are suitable to the realization of final emancipation are exclusively discussed in this work.

The Determination of the Nature of Comparison from the Standpoint of the Mīmāṁsakas

The followers of Jaimini do not subscribe to the above thesis. They hold that knowledge derived from comparison is different from that which has been asserted by the Naiyāyikas. After having heard the instruction of a forester that a gavaya is like a cow he goes to a forest on some errand and sees a gavaya. Then he remembers a cow, seen by him, in the city. Afterwards he knows that a cow is like a gavaya. He derives the resultant judgment from the perceptual one "A gavaya is like a cow" called Upamāna. It is called Upamiti. This judgment refers to the unperceived cow as endowed with resemblance to the gavaya which is being perceived. Or, it refers to the resemblance belonging to such a cow. Therefore, it (Upamiti) is generated by the perceptual judgment that a gavaya is like a cow since it refers to a cow which is beyond the range of perception. No instruction is heard to inform us of the content of this judgment and hence it is not a piece of verbal knowledge.

It is not also a judgment of memory, since it refers to such an object as has not been experienced before. We have not experienced before that a cow is like a gavaya. Though we admit that an object is similar to another if they possess in common many elements, yet an object is known to be similar to another when the other correlative term is presented to our consciousness.

The judgement is not arrived at by an act of inference, since it occurs in our mind independently of an induction or of a deduction. Moreover, the resemblance which belongs to a gavaya does not constitute the reason since it does not belong to the subject of inference. The resemblance which belongs to a cow does not constitute the reason since it does not belong to the subject of inference. Moreover, the resemblance which belongs to a cow does not constitute the reason in question since it is not an established fact but is an element in the initial proposition to be established. The limbs of a city-cow such as horse, etc., do not constitute reason since they remain beyond the range of vision of a person staying in the forest and the reason which is not perceived cannot serve the purpose. Any limb of the gavaya does not serve the purpose of a reason since it does not belong to a cow, the subject of inference, like the resemblance belonging to it. Thus the Mīmāṁsakas put their conclusion in a nut-shell. It is as follows:—

The judgment that a city-cow which is not perceived is similar to a gavaya occurring in the mind of a knower who resides, at the time of the judgment, in a forest, is Upamiti. It is a class by itself and is distinct from the other species of knowledge such as perception, etc.

The Refutation of the Mīmāṁsaka Hypothesis Concerning the Nature of Comparison.

The hypothesis of the Mīmāṁsakas is not sound since it is not based upon experience. The judgment that an unfamiliar gavaya is like a very familiar cow is experienced by us but not its simple conversion (i.e., a cow is like a gavaya).

A citizen who has not heard the instruction that a cow is like a gavaya rambling in a forest sees an unseen animal resembling a cow. Seeing it he judges and states that it is an indefinite animal which is similar to a cow. But he does neither judge nor state that a cow is like this. No body does so. Hence the judgment that a cow is like a gavaya is not true since such a judgment is an after-thought, carefully constructed but not natural.

It is useless to find out its exact instrument. Let us assume, for the sake of argument that the judgment that a cow is like a gavaya is possible. But it is a judgment of memory. So, it cannot be a class by itself. As such no distinct instrument is required to produce it. Thus, upamāna is not a distinct proof.

The Mīmāṁsakas join issue with the Naiyāyikas and hold that it is a truism that an individual cow is remembered by law of similarity when a gavaya is seen. But the cow is never remembered as similar to a gavaya since its similarity to a gavaya which is being perceived now has not been experienced before. Hence, the judgment that a cow is like a gavaya is not that of memory. The Naiyāyikas take an exception to this solution and point out that the defensible argument of the Mīmāṁsakas does not hold water since the similarity of a gavaya as belonging to a cow has been experienced before.

The Mīmāṁsakas retort that the critical remarks, offered by the Naiyāyikas, seem to them to be very strange since a person who has not seen a gavaya at an early date has experienced its similarity as belonging to a cow.

The Naiyāyikas reply that such a defence is untenable since the person has experienced its similarity as belonging to a cow without knowing distinctly gavaya.

The Mīmāṁsakas review the argument of the Naiyāyikas and hold that the suggestion of the Naiyāyikas that something has been experienced but all the properties have not been distinctly grasped appears to them to be more unintelligible. The Naiyāyikas hold that some particulars have been experienced but not distinctly. It is a truism that such an experience is an absurdity. A reply to this review has been given by the Naiyāyikas. They hold that their thesis is not that they are not able to account for it. The explanation given by the Naiyāyikas is as follows. When a citizen sees a gavaya in a forest, he does neither recollect an elephant nor a camel nor a horse but remembers an individual of a distinct class. The memory of a distinct object is not revived without having the sufficient reason. On the strength of this established law the Naiyāyikas hold that the individual which has been perceived as similar to this gavaya by a person, is recalled only in his memory whenever a gavaya is perceived but nobody else can remember it. Though nobody can definitely place the awareness of the judgment that a cow is like a gavaya in the history of his experiences yet the existence of such an experience is to be necessarily assumed since the relation of universal concomitance, holding between an individual cow which has been repeatedly seen and a gavaya as united by the relation of similarity, is remembered. It is absolutely impossible on the part of a villager to frame the judgment, based upon his experience, that a cow is like a gavaya if he has no previous experience of a gavaya. Hence it is reasonable to hold that similarity to a gavaya is experienced when a gavaya is not distinctly cognized. Therefore the thesis of the Naiyāyikas is not unintelligible. But it is a truism that at that stage of knowledge the judgment that a cow is like a gavaya is not framed on the basis of previous experience.

Very well, let the thesis of the Naiyāyikas be rational. But it should answer a question of the Mīmāṁsakas. How can a villager know that a cow is similar to a gavaya if he has no definite knowledge of a gavaya, the other correlative of the relation of similarity ? The reply, given by the Naiyāyikas to this question is as follows. If the Mīmāṁsakas raise this question, they simply contradict their previous statement.

They (the Mīmāṁsakas) hold that similarity, like a universal resides wholly in each of its many locii. Hence, if the other correlative of the relation of similarity is not cognized, similarity is perceived. Again, what is similarity according to them ? They say that the common possession of many limbs is called similarity. These limbs can be perceived even by a villager if he has never perceived a gavaya.

If the Mīmāṁsakas hold that the villager does not know that cow is like a gavaya even if he perceives those limbs which are shared in common by the two similar objects (a cow and a gavaya). They now discard the above definition of similarity that similarity is the common possession of many limbs. The revised definition of similarity as offered by them is that similarity is the unique source of the awareness of similarity. The former definition of similarity is too narrow to be applied to the picture of a cow, etc. This definition also suffers from the defect of being very wide since it applies also to an animal which is dissimilar to a gavaya. A dissimilar animal also possesses some of the same limbs such as hoofs, etc., as a cow possesses. Now, the Mīmāṁsakas may hold that they do not know the exact number that constitutes the number 'many' which is required for the idea of similarity. But they may hold that the number of common limbs should be such as produces the idea of similarity. But such a defence is not satisfactory. It really repeats the revised definition of similarity stated above that similarity is that which generates the idea of similarity. Hence, the implicit awareness of similarity is logically possible even when a gavaya has not been perceived at all. Therefore, the judgment that a cow is like a gavaya is that of memory.

The Mīmāṁsakas may justify their position in the following manner. The Naiyāyikas hold that when the instruction of a forester is received the relation of denotation holding between the term 'gavaya' and the object 'gavaya' is not grasped without the shade of a doubt. But with the perception of the similarity of a cow belonging to a gavaya (i.e. comparison) it is rightly and distinctly grasped. Similarly, the said similarity of a gavaya is vaguely experienced at the initial stage when a gavaya, the correlative, remains unknown. But it becomes clear and distinct when the similarity of a cow belonging to a gavaya is perceived (i.e., when comparison reveals the said similarity). This is the sum and substance of the contention.

The above contention is not tenable since the very perception of a gavaya contributes towards the vividness of the knowledge that a gavaya is like a cow whereas comparison does not do it. The Naiyāyikas will simply pay the Mīmāṁsakas back in their own coins—the coins which they have paid to the Naiyāyikas. The coin is in the shape of sentence which runs thus :—Comparison cannot exclusively claim as its own an object which has not been grasped by some other proof. The so-called exclusive object is supplied by perception.

The Mīmāṁsakas raise another question, "How does this perception of a knower, staying in a forest contribute towards the vividness of the knowledge that a cow in a village is like a gavaya ?" The Naiyāyikas reply "we are not to blame for our observation since it is a fact that the very perception of a gavaya is followed by the vivid memory that a cow is like a gavaya".

That Mīmāṁsakas advance a further argument in support of the view that comparison is a distinct source of valid knowledge. They argue that as perception lays hold only of a near object, so the judgment that a cow is like a gavaya is not perceptual since the cow resembling a gavaya, remains beyond the range of our vision.

The Naiyāyikas meet this argument in the following manner. They hold that the judgment that a cow is like a gavaya merely acts as a memento since it bears the stamp of likeness on the face of it. If this knowledge pertains to memory, it cannot be a piece of valid knowledge since the Mīmāṁsakas hold that novelty is the only criterion of valid knowledge. (If it is not a piece of valid knowledge, there is no ground for advocating in favour of comparison as a separate source of valid knowledge). Even if it is admitted that it does not pertain to memory, it may be inferential since it is deduced. Hence, no other distinct source of knowledge should be assumed. The syllogism which proves the point of the Naiyāyikas is as follows. The cow which is being remembered is like this (a gavaya in front of the knower) because the first one possesses many common limbs that is, many limbs belong equally to the individuals of the both species. (The cow which is being remembered is the subject of inference. The consequence to be established is 'is like this'. The reason is the possession of many common limbs. The example in this inference is the second individual of the gavaya class). If the second individual does not come near at hand, more general major premise is to be found out. This major premise requires reference to (no positive) examples. Where there is the possession of many common limbs there is resemblance like the above two. The reason is not doubtful since the limbs which belong equally to the individuals of the two species have been specified. Moreover the reason is not unproven like the consequence since it has been admitted that there is a sharp distinction between the possession of common limbs and resemblance. An inexperienced lad, a resident of the cocoanut island (an island where cows and gavayas are not found) does not have the judgment that the cow, seen in a village, is like this gavaya (which is being perceived now in the forest). On the strength of the absence of experience of the said boy it is to be admitted that the judgment that a cow is like a gavaya is only deduced from a major premise which is arrived at by induction and that such a judgment cannot take place independently of induction. Hence, the judgment in question is not produced by comparison because it is either inferential or recollective or impossible, on account of the reason stated above. Now the Naiyāyikas put a question to the Mīmāṁsakas, "Does comparison render any unique service ?" It amounts to this : "Does it stand the pragmatic test of a proof ?" Kumārila himself has admitted that when a definition has been given even with the slightest intention of examining it, an eye has been kept on its usefulness so that nothing has been superfluously stated.

Now the Mīmāṁsakas say that they have proved the efficacy of comparison. The detailed procedure of performing a Vedic rite in honour of the sun-god by offering an oblation of milk boiled rice is learnt from its resemblance to a sacrifice which is performed in honour of the god of fire. With regard to the Vedic rite in honour of the god of fire the injunction is self-sufficient and complete since there is ample provision for the details of unknown subsidiary actions such as the placing of rightly prepared cakes on eight earthern pot-sherds etc. But the injunction, "one who is desirous of acquiring the lustre of the holy study should offer an oblation of milk-boiled rice to the sun god", enjoins only the principal action and the article of offering but does not give information about the performance of the subsidiary actions. The main action cannot be performed if the minor ones, the means to an end, are not prescribed.

Now, questions arise in our mind "How shall we find out the subsidiary rites ? Which will be the rites ?" Now, we see that there is similarity between corn and barley, boiled in milk and puroḍāśa (a cake prepared from cereal) since both of them are prepared from cereals. Moreover, the respective deities of these two rites resemble each other as they have lustre. Owing to this similarity, comparison throws light on the nature of subsidiary rites so that these rites in honour of the god of fire can be applied to the rite in honour of the sungod. Moreover, there is another point which is worth-noting that if a substance which has been enjoined as a means is not available then its substitute will suffice to complete the action. Suppose, barely has been enjoined to prepare a particular food to be offered. If barley is not available we take wild rice as a substitute for barley on the strength of comparison.

The Vedic sentences which reveal the rites to be performed in honour of the sungod and the god of fire point to their similarity on the basis of comparison but not on the basis of perception and inference. Hence, they prove the efficacy of comparison. If comparison had no part to play then how can the injunction concerning the rite in honour of the sungod refer to the injunction regarding the rite in honour of the god of fire ? Therefore we, the Mīmāṁsakas, hold that comparison renders a special service in such cases.

Kumārila also points out another utility of comparison. If barley is somehow defective then wild rice acts in its place as its substitute in a Vedic rite. This is the desired goal of the definition of comparison. He also adds that when the points of resemblance are not too many, the resulting judgment is that one is partially like another and when the points of similarity are too many the resulting judgment is that one is closely alike another.

The statement of the Mīmāṃsakas Involves Inner contradiction

A defect in the above solution has been pointed out by the Naiyāyikas. The subsequent remarks of the Mīmāṁsakas do not tally with the true character of comparison as depicted by them. They have taught that comparison reveals that a familiar object is like an unfamiliar one. They have held that comparison reveals that a well-known cow is like a gavaya which is not seen before and hence it remains entirely new and unfamiliar. Having said all these they cite such examples as run counter to their thesis. (In other words, the examples go in favour of the Nyāya conclusion). Consequently, comparison produces the judgment that an unfamiliar rite in honour of the sungod is like a rite in honour of the god of fire. The second rite is familiar because the details of its subsidiary actions are given. The first rite may be compared to a gavaya. The second one may be compared to a cow. The above judgment corresponds to the judgment that a gavaya is like a cow. If the Mīmāṁsakas were not off their guard then they would have shown that the rite which is complete in its minor details is like the rite of which details are missing. But it is strange enough that they have proved the reverse.

Now, the Mīmāṁsakas may contend that the solar rite which is in need of minor details reminds one of the rite, observed in honour of the god of fire. Hence, the first one approaches the second one for the minor details.

The Naiyāyikas join issue with the Mīmāṁsakas and hold that even if the above explanation is taken for granted then the object which is required is settled by memory alone. In that case, is there any necessity of assuming comparison as a distinct proof? If the Mīmāṁsakas hold that as the rite, observed in honour of the god of fire, is remembered so its minor details are borrowed. They also add that the object which is remembered flashes in our mind along with such extra objects as memory cannot supply. Hence, a distinct type of knowledge based upon comparison has been admitted. The Naiyāyikas point out that they cannot argue in this strain. The reason of controverting it has been already mentioned. (Memory is not valid knowledge since it simply reveals known object. If comparison revives memory only, it is not an instrument of sound knowledge). Hence, there is no need of keeping the discussion up any more.

The Naiyāyikas advance an additional point that the object which is revealed by knowledge, based upon comparison, cannot play the role of the scriptures. It can neither induce a person to do something nor dissuade him from doing an action. Hence, a person who requires definite knowledge by means of comparison cannot apply the minor details of the rite in honour of the god of fire to the solar rite on the basis of the above knowledge since his knowledge has no force of injunction.

If the Mīmāṁsakas stick to their hypothesis then no substitute can be taken in. The Mīmāṁsakas, if they are sincere to their conclusion, cannot hold that wild rice is like barely but that barely is like wild rice. But the judgment that barley is like wild rice serves no useful purpose. (The net result of this discussion is that barely is the substitute for wild rice but not the converted proposition).

The killing of a gavaya is a means to some sacrifice. But comparison as defined by you does not help to know a gavaya and to select a substitute. Therefore all intelligent persons should accept the definition of comparison as offered by the greatest of all sages (i.e. Akṣapāda).

The end of the second Āhnika (Chapter).

ĀHNIKA III

Sabda (*Verbal Authority*)

The sūtra which deals with the classification of proof mentions verbal authority next to comparison. Hence, the author of the Nyāya-sūtra proposes to define verbal authority just after the definition of comparison.

The sūtra which embodies the definition of śabda runs thus "Āptopadeśaḥ śabdaḥ". (A reliable assertion is *śabda*). If the definition is merely "upadeśaḥ śabdaḥ" (an assertion is sabdaḥ) then only the two synonyms are put together to frame the definition with the result that it becomes too wide as it applies also to a word which does not produce true knowledge. In order to make definition complete, we are to borrow a few words from the sūtra which constitutes the definition of perception and to construe them with the word 'upadeśa' (all assertions) in the sūtra in question: the word 'jñāna' 'artha' 'vyavasāyātmaka' and 'avyabhicāri' are to be borrowed. The word 'jñāna' (consciousness) represents the result of an assertion. The word 'artha' reveals the nature of the resulting consciousness and the adjective 'vyavasāyātmaka' (determinate) expresses its form. A doubt is eliminated thereby. The adjective 'avyabhicāri (non-erroneous) excludes an error. The complete definition of śabda signifies that an assertion which is productive of such knowledge as is neither memory nor doubt nor an error is a means of verbal knowledge. Thus, an assertion, which is qualified by such adjectives as are taken from the sūtra on perception, constitutes the reliable source of verbal knowledge.

Some other logicians hold that the adjective 'āpta' (reliable) has been given to convey the exact character of the definition in question. In the sūtra "the sense-organs such as nose, tongue, skin, eyes and ears spring from elements" the word 'bhūta' has a definite purpose to serve and its utility will be shown later on. Similarly, the adjective 'āpta' 'has been used to refute the hypothesis that rumour is a distinct source of knowledge and has the object in view to establish that 'rumour' (aitihya) is distinct from śabda.

Some other logicians hold that the word 'upadeśa' (assertion) constitutes the exact definition of śabda pramāṇa (the means of verbal knowledge). The adjective 'āpta' has been used to indicate the correctness of the assertion. Some adjectives should not be unnecessarily borrowed from the definition of pratyakṣa (perception), and construed with the definition in question since there is scope for defining a species only when the genus has been defined. When the definition of pramāṇa i.e., the means of true knowledge, has excluded such instruments of knowledge as produce memory, etc., the definition of śabda should be such as exclusively contains the differentia from all other species subsumed under the same genus. The word 'upadeśa' (assertion), though it is a synonym of śabda, is competent enough to discharge the above function like the word 'buddhi' in another sūtra. Hence, there is no need of taking the trouble of borrowing adjectives from another sūtra.

Another logician holds that one should neither take the trouble of referring to the distinguishing features of pramāṇa, the genus of all proofs nor borrow adjectives from some other sūtra to fill up the gap in the definition of śabda and that the complete definition of śabda is the assertion of a reliable person. Such an assertion as is either insignificant or, calls up memory, or, leads to a doubt, or, carries no true information is to be excluded. If we take notice of the etymological meaning of the word 'upadeśa' (an assertion) then we make out the truth that the very word 'upadeśa' excludes such assertions as are either insignificant or produce a doubt, etc.

The deceptive sentences of a vagabond knave illustrate false assertions since they are a source of error. The definition is too wide as it is also applicable to them. In order to mend the defect in the above definition, the adjective 'āpta' (reliable) is to be given. If a rumour is a source of true knowledge, it is not distinct from a sound inference. In fine, it is to be noted that the wording of the sūtra which constitutes the definition of śabda pramāṇa should be rigidly adhered to and not a single word from a previous sūtra should be borrowed in order to frame the definition in question.

Let the definition be so framed. But, let us examine the etymological meaning of the word 'upadeśa'. An upadeśa is that by which something is communicated (upadiśyate). But the meaning is not clear. It is that by which the knowledge of something is conveyed (abhidhīyate). Still, the meaning is not very clear. The act of abhidhāna denotes the act of cognizing. The boiled down meaning of the verb, together with the suffix attached to it, amounts to this that the instrument which produces knowledge is an upadeśa. In that case, the term, 'upadeśa' should also denote eyes and other sense-organs which produce consciousness. Now, the upholder of the above view may contend that the word 'upadeśa' does not denote consciousness in general but some specific form of it. He suggests that specific consciousness is that which resembles its cause (the instrument). (Thus, he tries to tide over the difficulty since perception does not resemble the sense-organ which produces it.

If we accept this interpretation the reflection of a leg by means of which the leg is inferred should be upadeśa. A word which is sound in essence should be non-upadeśa since the consciousness which is produced by a word does not resemble its cause. Moreover, if consciousness signifies only the awareness of sound, the auditory sense-organ becomes the only source of such awareness. In that case, the word 'upadeśa' should denote only the auditory sense-organ. The awareness of sound should not be confused with the understanding of the meaning of a word. A sound by itself cannot produce such understanding Hence, a word, when it is taken as a mere sound, cannot be denoted by the term 'upadeśa'. Thus, we see that it is next to impossible to find out the specific character of the act of conveying the knowledge of something (abhidhāna kriyā). Therefore, we cannot define 'upadeśa' as an instrument of such an act.

An answer to these *prima facie* objections is as follows :—

The abhidhāna kriyā denotes the apprehension of the meaning of an audible object through its instrumentality. It is the conventional meaning of the act. An object the knowledge of which is produced by a word which consists of a number of alphabets (sounds) is held to be denotative. A number of audible alphabets (sounds) makes us apprehend a thing—a thing signified by it. Hence, a word is a collection of such sounds. But what is not audible is not a word such as a sphoṭa (a subtle entity which is assumed for the communication of the meaning of a word). What is audible is a word. As alphabets are audible so they constitute a word. But if it is held that a word is that which conveys the knowledge of someother object then a mark such as smoke, etc., should have been a word. A word, the relation of denotation of which remains unknown, is not really a word since such a word cannot convey the sense. An objection arises in our mind. Every event of consciousness represents the knowing of something. As there is no distinct form of consciousness which is signified by the verb "to denote" so every form of consciousness is meant by it. In that case, as a word is not the only source of such consciousness so the above definition suffers from the defect of being too wide.

A reply to this objection is as follows. It is a truism that to be aware of an object is to know it. An awareness which is produced by the sense-organ such as the eyes as its special cause is called perception. The knowledge of an object which is produced neither by a sense-organ nor by a word is the inferential judgment. The knowledge of an object, produced by an audible word, is verbal knowledge. To be perceived, to be inferred and to be denoted are not synonymous with one another. A word which produces this distinct form of consciousness is called an upadeśa. But if this very word indicates the intention of a speaker then it is treated as a mark but not as an upadeśa. No more ? Let us put a stop to this discussion.

Vātsyāyana, the commentator on the Nyāya-sūtras, has explained the term 'āpta'. The person who has the intuitive knowledge of merit and intends to communicate correctly the result of his experience and who is a competent teacher is called an āpta. There is no hard and fast rule that the subject-matter of his teaching is to be intuited since an inferred matter may also be taught. Such an indirect knowledge does not cancel his qualification as a teacher. If he intends to impart his experience to somebody then it does not mean that he is partially disposed towards him. The title 'teacher' applied to a man, indicates that he is efficient in the art of teaching. If a person who does neither take an interest in anything nor shrink from it, is deaf and dumb then what shall he do, being incapable of imparting his lessons. A person may be a capable preacher and seer of merit. But if he is partial to somebody, he holds his tongue and does not like to utter a single word. A seer-teacher should not be interested also in the subject-matter which he intends to teach. Such a person is rarely seen. The status of being an āpta should neither be monopolised by a sage nor by an Aryan. The definition of an āpta should be elastic that it may be either applied to a sage or to an Aryan or to a mleccha (a non-Aryan). If this be the case, there will be no paucity of an āpta in the society.

Some hold that the essence of an āpta lies in the freedom from such defects as are error, inadvertence, etc., and a man, having no such defects, is an āpta. It must be also admitted by them that a teacher should not have imperfect knowledge of the subject-matter which he undertakes to teach. If we do not subscribe to this view then the title of āpta which is in vogue would be denied to all.

Or, the aim of this system of logic is to establish the validity of the Vedas. God, the author of the Vedas, is only āpta. The definition of an āpta, taken in its literal sense, is applicable to Him alone since he has really intuited merit. (He has the direct awareness of merit.) It is fair to hold that the intention of disseminating valuable ideas has actuated him to compose the Vedas since it will be proved later on that he is compassionate. He is also a competent teacher since it will be proved that all the sources of knowledge with the Vedas at the top have been composed by him. Let us stop here with regard to the definition of an āpta. And let us now discuss why Śabda has been singled out to be defined as a distinct source of knowledge.

The Buddhists contend:— We discern no distinction between verbal knowledge and inferential judgment. Therefore the definition of inference is to be applied to śabda. Hence a distinct definition of śabda should be sought for. The following arguments strengthen our contention. Both inferential judgment and verbal knowledge have no immediate object to reveal. As both of them depend upon some relation to enlighten an object they indicate only the general feature of an object. If the relation is not discovered, both of them fail to bring about their intended result. As the particulars are innumerable so it is very difficult to discover their relation. As we infer fire, perceiving smoke so we make out the meaning of a word, hearing it. As there is positive and negative relation between a reason and a consequence so there is positive and negative relation between a word and the object meant by it. If a word is employed to convey the knowledge of an object then it denotes the object. As in the inference of fire smoke plays the part of the subject of inference so a word becomes the subject of inference since the the object, denoted by it, belongs to it. In the former example smokeness is the reason. In the latter case the universal, belonging to the word, will discharge the function of a reason. As the conditions and objects of verbal knowledge and inferential judgment are similar, so verbal knowledge is identical with the inferential judgment. Hence, we should not differentiate one from another in view of minor differences.

(Some of these differences are as follows). These impressions, left by the previous experience of alphabets, are the accessory condition of verbal knowledge. Moreover, the truth of the verbal knowledge is ascertained when we learn that the sentence, the source of the said knowledge, has been uttered by a trustworthy person. Again, we are also to read the intention of the speaker of the sentence in order to make out its exact sense. These are the distinctive processes which invariably precede a piece of verbal knowledge unlike an inferential judgment. On the score of these peculiar conditions we cannot hold that sabda is a distinct type of proof. As the knowledge of the definite relation between the reason and the consequence is the special feature of an inferential judgement so is not the verbal knowledge determined by the knowledge of the relation between a word and the object denoted? It may be argued that as a sentence has a directive force so inference being not distinct from śabda should enjoin us to take a course of action. Such an argument is not tenable since though the reason in the shape of the waving of the hand etc. is the cause of inferential knowledge yet it possesses a driving force.

In case of an inference when a very familiar object is to be established no reference to an example is required as no major premise is presented to conciousness in case of verbal knowledge when a very familiar object is communicated by a word. No reference to an example is necessary. But in both the cases a reference to an example is a necessity when unfamiliar subject is touched upon. As reference is an incentive to the unfolding of creative imagination so in some cases the coinage of new words such as 'aśva' etc. illustrates the work of creative imagination.

As a defective reason, being adduced does not help us to know an object correctly so when a word, having multiple senses, is applied, it does not convey a definite sense.

Moreover, when verbal knowledge is produced by a sentence, it does not carry along with itself the conviction that it is correct. But we do not know it to be true unless and until we ascertain that the sentence has been uttered by an āpta (a trustworthy person).

Therefore, the learned scholars hold that verbal knowledge is inferential because it is known to be valid if it is in agreement with the unquestionably true of a trustworthy person.

Moreover, a word can only help us to infer the intention of a speaker aright but not an external object because there is no absolute certainty of the faithful representation of an external object by it. We correctly infer that the speaker intends to communicate such and such object because he utters such and such words like me. A word serves the purpose of a true reason if the consequence is the intention of a speaker.

Distinction Between Śabda and Inference

A reply to the above objections is as follows :

Śabda admits of the two kinds viz., a word and a sentence. But a sentence reveals its meaning without depending upon the knowledge of the relation between a sentence and its meaning. We have learnt from experience that those who are conversant with words and their meaning make out the general sense of the entire verse, newly composed, whenever they listen to it. But an inference necessarily presupposes the knowledge of the relation between the reason and the consequence. How can we imagine that śabda bears a very close resemblance to an inference? But though a word depends upon the knowledge of significance in order to communicate its meaning yet it differs from inference since the conditions of these two types of knowledge and their contents are different. The object which is denoted by a word is different from that which is established by inference. The Word 'fiery' conveys only the locus of fire and this point will be proved later on. But the proposition that the hill is fiery signifies the conclusion of an inferential process. The very conclusion constitutes the subject-matter of an inference. The inferential process results in establishing the conclusion that the hill is fiery. We come to know that there is fire or that the hill is the locus of fire. It has been stated in the second chapter of this work that the consequence of an inference is the subject of inference (i.e. minor term) as predicated by the major term.

It is not possible to contend that there are words which express the sense of a sentence? The words such as 'gomān' (a man who is possessed of cows), aupagavaḥ (a man who is a son of upagu) and kumbhakāra (a man who makes pots) illustrate the above point. It may be admitted that there is much truth in this contention. Still, they do not produce such knowledge as is absolutely complete in itself. Take the word 'gomān'. It does not satisfy our inquisitive mind. We still hold enquiry viz. who is gomān ? (A sentence is complete in itself. It has syntactical relation with no word which is not included in it. But it expresses a complete idea. It is the unit of our thought. A word implies syntactical relation with some other words which are not its constituent in order to express a complete idea. Hence, under no circumstances, a word can rise to the status of a sentence.)

(An objector may contend that the knowledge of the meaning of a word may not be inferential but the knowledge of the meaning of a sentence is surely inferential. Jayanta proves the hollowness of such a contention).

Moreover, the conclusion which is drawn from the premises is a judǵment. As it is a judgment. So it has a subject and a predicate. The subject of the judgment is cognised at first and the awareness of the predicate succeeds it.

The resulting judgment of an inferential process is that the hill is fiery. The hill, the subject of this judgment, is known at first and the predicate, fire, is known afterwards. But the verbal knowledge which arises from a sentence is also a judgment. The predicate of it is known at first and the knowledge of the subject and that of the predicate in a verbal judgment take place on a reverse order. Thus, the contents of verbal and inferential judgments are different. Hence, śabda is not included in inference.

Now it may be contended that as the subject of inference, as qualified by the consquence, is established in an inference so let a word, as qualified by the object, denoted by it, be established in a verbal judgment. Such a contention is not tenable. A word is the cause par excellence of the verbal knowledge. If it is assumed that verbal knowledge is inferential then a word, being the cause par excellence of it, is the reason. In that case, the reason cannot be the subject of inference.

Now, the objector may defend himself against the review, citing example from the works of the critics. Kumārila establishes fire by means of a peculiar syllogistic argument. It is this that smoke is fiery because it has smokeness like smoke in a kitchen. Some logicians hold that the place which contains fire is the consequence. Some other logicians hold that smoke is the consquence. Similarly, the meaning of a word is inferred. The syllogistic process is as follows. The word 'cow' contains the object denoted by it because it has cowness, i. e. the universal, which belongs to the word 'cow'. This is the defence of the objector in a nut-shell.

Such a defence is hardly tenable, The objector intends to establish a consquence, assuming a word as the subject of inference. Let the character of this consequence be determined at the out-set. Do you establish that the word is qualified by the object denoted by it or that the word has the power of conveying its meaning or that the word is qualified by the knowledge of its meaning? It is possible to prove the first alternative. There is no bar to hold that the hill contains fire. But we cannot hold in a similar manner that a word contains the object signified by it. It may be argued "As an object is conveyed by a word, so a word, having denoted it, contains it by means of the relation of denotation." Such a defence is not tenable. An object is not denoted by a word as long as we do not know that it is presented to our consciousness by the word itself. If the object is not denoted then it cannot stand upon the word as its locus. When the knowledge of an object is produced by a word, the object only stands upon a word as denoted by it. In that case is there any necessity of assuming that the object is located upon a word? If it is held that an object finds its locus in a word because it is denoted by the latter. In this way the object which is located upon a word is made known as such. The object, the knowledge of which is produced by a word, is denoted only by it. Such an argument is an instance of circular reasoning. Therefore it cannot be established that a word is qualified by an object to be denoted by it. The second alternative that a word is qualified by a power of conveying a sense cannot be established. Nobody employs a word to this effect. A person does neither utter a word nor listen to it to determine its power of expression. Everybody either listens to a word to learn its meaning correctly or utters a word to communicate his knowledge of an object to others. A word-in-itself is not to be assured as the subject of inference. A word, as qualified by a predicate mentioned above, is not also to be assumed as the subject of inference. But the upholder of the view that śabda is not other than an inference may plead his case in a slightly different manner. He urges that even though it is admitted that the above two alternatives are not tenable yet there is no bar to hold that a word, as qualified by the knowledge of an object, is the subject of inference. Such a defence does not hold water. A word as qualified by the knowledge of an object, cannot be the subject of inference because there is a great controversy over the issue whether or not the knowledge of an object is an established fact when the word is merely heard and the conclusion of the said inference is not drawn.

When the word is only heard the knowledge of an object being conspicuous by its absence, how is it possible that a word is qualified by the knowledge of an object? It may be held that the knowledge of an object is possible even before the drawing of the conclusion of the said inference and that the word as qualified by the knowledge of an object may be taken for granted. Such a hypothesis does not stand to reason. If the knowledge of an object is available before the operation of the inferential process then is not the syllogistic process redundant ?

The opponent stands his ground and holds that such a criticism is applicable to all accepted types of inference e. g. the inference of fire. (He means to say that such a criticism does not affect our point of view). Such a defence is not tenable. Smoke does not produce fire but merely indicates it. But in the present case a word produces the knowledge of an object. Hence, there is scope for controversy over the matter whether or not the knowledge of an object is an accomplished fact when the word is only heard. But in the case of a regular inference, there is no room for the said controversy. Therefore the above three alternatives which have been suggested to prove that a word is the subject of inference do not hold good. In fine, a word cannot be the subject of inference.

Moreover, if the word 'cow' is the subject of inference, the reason in the shape of cowness (the universal) belonging to all words 'cow' is to be cognized to the subject of inference. Then, the relation of invariable concomitance holding between the reason and the consequence is to be remembered. Then, the reason must be cognized as qualified by the relation of concomitance. Then, the object which is denoted by the word is inferred. As it takes a long interval of time to complete the inferential process so the word 'cow' the essence of which is sound — the subject of inference passes away by this time. Sound is not a durable object like a hill but it lasts only for two time-atoms (the time-atom stands for the minutest unit of time). An unsophisticated person does not know that the word has the object (i. e. the word is intimately related to the object). But he realizes that there is no perceptible relation between the word and the object. Hence, by no means the word can constitute the subject of inference. As there is no possibility of establishing the subject of inference as qualified by an object upon it so there is a gulf of difference between verbal knowledge and inferential knowledge so far as the objects of knowledge revealed by them are concerned.

The conditions that determine inferential knowledge and those that determine verbal knowledge are not the same.

Inferential knowledge depends upon five conditions such as the belonging of the reason to the subject of inference etc. The conditions of it have been stated before. But the verbal knowledge does not require them for its coming into existence. If it be so then as the word cannot be the subject of inference so the universal of cowness that belongs to the word cannot constitute the reason. The object, denoted by the word 'cow' cannot be the subject of inference because whenever the word 'cow' is uttered the dilemma whether the object 'cow', denoted by the word 'cow', is presented to our consciousness or not goes to controvert the above assumption. We cannot also hold that the object 'cow' being qualified by the word 'cow' is to be established since the word 'cow' does not belong to the object 'cow' by means of the relation of denotation. An assumption of location in such cases is open to the charge of involving a circular reasoning. If we hold that the object, denoted by a word, is an inference then the knowledge of the object takes place only when the five antecedent conditions are fulfilled such as the presence of the reason in the subject of inference etc. But if the object is not known before then the five conditions which determine its knowledge are not available. Therefore, the hypothesis that the object which is said to be denoted by a word is an inference does not stand the test of reasoning. Moreover, if it is urged that as a word qualifies an object so the former belongs to the latter then the object should be treated as the subject of inference as qualified by the word, belonging to it. But a man in the street who is innocent of the relation of causality between smoke and fire sees with his own eyes that smoke belongs to the subject of inference. Similarly, a person who is ignorant of the relation of denotation should have known that a word belongs to the denoted object. But it is a truism that such an ignorant person does not do it. Therefore, a word cannot belong to an object. Again, it is not possible to demonstrate that wherever there is a word there is an object and wherever there is not object, there is no word since the application of the joint method of agreement and difference presupposes space and time but in no space and in no time they are related. An object does not exist in that part of space where a word belongs. The Mīmāṁsakas hold that a word which is heard is uttered by the mouth and resides there whereas the object is cognized on the ground. But the Naiyāyikas hold that a word is heard in the sky, confined within the ear-hole. Let this new point be ignored. When a word exists the object denoted by it does not necessarily exist. Now, it may be argued that though when the word 'Yudhiṣṭhira' is pronounced, the object, meant by it, does not exist yet the very word is inseparably connected with the meaning of it. Now, a question may be put to the opponents of the Nyāya-school. It is as follows:-"When does a word relate itself with the object denoted by it ? Does it do so before the knowledge of the object or afterwards ?" If they answer the first alternative in the affirmative then it may be pointed out that such a relation is not possible since the object, being not present before our mind, is as good as a non-entity. Again, if they answer the second alternative in the affirmative then it may be pointed out that if the knowledge of the object is acquired from the word without knowing the relation of denotation then there is no possibility of grasping the relation in every case. Therefore, such a relation of denotation is insignificant. Again, if, it is held that the knowledge of the object presupposes the knowledge of the relation of denotation and the knowledge of the latter presupposes that of the former then it is a case of circular reasoning. The absurdity of the application of the negative method to the relation is also evident from the trend of the above argument.

When an experienced person asks another experienced person to do something he utters two sentences. In one sentence a particular word finds a place. In the other sentence it is conspicuous by its absence. An inexperienced learner who listens to these two sentences notes the presence of a particular word in one of the two sentences and its absence from the other one. He watches the movement of the junior person. By the joint method of agreement and difference he makes out the meaning of the words contained in the sentences. Thus, we see that the joint method of agreement and difference helps us to determine the relation of denotation of a word. Hence, the above joint method, being applied, has a special service to ascertain the relation of denotation. Kumārila has stated that if a word is related to an object then that object is only denoted by that word. The contention of Kumārila is true. But it will also be pointed out in this connection that the knowledge of an object arises from a word because of the convention. The joint method of agreement and difference establishes the connection of a word with a particular object because of a convention. Moreover, in order to find out the relation between a word and an object as fixed by a convention by means of the joint method of agreement and difference, we shall proceed from the side of a word (i.e., we are to depend much more upon a word). By the joint method of agreement and difference we discover the relation of concomitance holding between smoke and fire. We infer fire from smoke. But we do not likewise know an object if we merely hear a word.

Moreover, when we infer fire from smoke we do not know definitely that they co-exist in the above locus. But when we know an object to be here from a word we know the object to be here even before the communication of this information by the word. Let us illustrate the point. When a boy who is ignorant of a word and of its meaning sees an object he understands that it is denoted by this word from the action of an experienced person who has carried out the explicit order of another experienced person.

When a convention is set forth to the effect that this particular object should be denoted by this particular word, the relation of denotation is undoubtedly different from that of concomitance. This relation is the invariable condition of the verbal knowledge of an object denoted by a word. In fine, it is to be noted that the relation of universal concomitance obtains only between the reason and the consequence but the relation of denotation is distinct from it and is merely one of the accessory conditions of verbal knowledge. Thus, the verbal knowledge is distinct from the inferential one like perception since the conditions which determine these two types of knowledge are separate and the objects referred to by them are not one and the same. Some logicians hold that śabda is a distinct source of valid knowledge because one is to remember the order of succession of the letter that constitutes a word in order to know the object denoted by it. The critics have subjected this hypothesis to a severe criticism and remarks that the distinctive character of śabda cannot rest upon this inadequate ground. We are not in the least inclined to hold brief for the same hypothesis since it is absolutely unsound. The critics have shown that śabda is included in inference because śabda and the utterance of a reliable person deserve the same treatment as they closely resemble each other. Such a critical remark is too fair since the results, arrived at by them, are different. A sentence which is uttered by a reliable person does not produce knowledge because it has been uttered by a reliable person. But the knowledge, produced by such a sentence, is asserted to be true because it has been spoken of by a trustworthy person.

Kumārila also endorses the above conclusion. The knowledge produced by a word, reveals an object. The reason that the sentence has been asserted by a trustworthy person points to the consequence that the knowledge, produced by such a sentence, is true. Thus, the consequence is different from the object of the verbal knowledge. An object, denoted by a word, is known prior to the ascertainment of the truth of such knowledge. The object of knowledge is surely distinct from the truth of its knowledge. Thus śabda is distinct from inference. We, at first, know the meaning of a sentence and then infer that it is true because it has been uttered by a trustworthy person. If this is the case then how will śabda be included in inference?

When we hear a sentence which is uttered either by a trustworthy person or by a non-trustworthy person it uniformly communicates its sense. A reason which fulfills the three specific conditions leads to the inferential knowledge but does not produce verbal knowledge.

It is unfair to hold that if the validity of verbal knowledge is not established then such knowledge merely refers to an imaginary object since it is universally experienced that words produce the knowledge of objects.

Thus we refute the hypothesis that words convey only the intention of a speaker. The intention of a speaker is not denoted by a word but an object is denoted only by it. A word serves the purpose of a reason from which the intention of the speaker is inferred or guessed. We infer the existence of the sky from a word which as a sound is its effect. But any and every word being denotative does not denote the sky. When a word is uttered it first communicates its meaning but it may afterwards point to the intention of its speaker. Under these circumstances it is to be admitted that when an intention arises in the mind of a person it has no connection with a word which denotes it since no word is uttered at that stage. If the object as denoted by a word remains unknown at the time of the appearance of an intention then it cannot be held that an intention is qualified by the meaning of a word. (The drift of this argument is that an intention is never denoted by a word at the initial stage of its appearance).

A Critical Review of the Hypothesis that sabda is a Source of Valid Knowledge.

If it is established that śabda is a sourse of valid knowledge then we should discuss either śabda is a distinct proof or it is included in one of the recognized proofs.

A proof is that which produces true knowledge. But words, being a product of imagination, do not produce the true knowledge of the real objects. The meaning of the word may be, somehow, made out but it can be identified neither with a universal, nor with a particular, nor with a concrete universal. There is no eternal relation of denotation holding between a word and an object. If it exists at all then how can such a relation as obtaining between a word and a transcendental object be comprehended? The meaning of a Vedic sentence in the subjunctive mood cannot be grasped. It is held that the mental activity which causes the action, denoted by the given verb to be done, and the command denoted by the injunction stand to each other, as a noun relates itself with its adjective, by means of the relation of identity or some other relation. We cannot follow that either words or their meanings or sentences which are held to communicate the interrelated meanings of words or the subtle power of a word which is supposed to reveal its meaning cannot produce the knowledge of a real object.

It is not reasonable to hold that when the knowledge of an object is produced by a sentence the validity of it is assured if the sentence is known as being uttered by a reliable person or as being eternal.

Even if it is admitted that the words are eternal then it is to be established that either the Vedic sentences are composed by an author or they are eternal. If it is held that they are composed by an author it is impossible to find out the author.

Even if it is assumed that they are composed by a single author then it is difficult to comprehend that he has no enemy and is one, omniscient and compassionate.

There are many āgamas (scriptures) which involve contradictions. Now it is difficult for us to ascertain that which books of them have been composed by God and which ones have not been composed by Him.

There are many defects which are noticed in the Vedas which are assumed to be the work of God. They are as follows viz. (1) contradiction, (2) repetition of the same idea, (3) non-obtainment of the result assured by the Vedas and (4) the arising of the contrary result.

If God were the author of the Vedas then the Artha-vāda section of the Vedas (the section which contains recommendation, praise, condemnation, a reference to history etc.) would not have involved material contradiction, mutual contradictions and references of ephemeral objects.

The Vedas inform us of the eternal objects and instruct us to do some actions by which some results are accomplished. Now, a doubt arises in our mind viz., either do the Vedas initiate us into eternal objects or do they teach us to do some actions or do they intend to do the both? In fine, the authority of the Vedas cannot be rationally established. You may admit the authority of the Vedas because either they furnish you with the means to your livelihood or they command your unconditional reverence.

The Justification of The Authority of Speech

The review of the above criticism is as follows. All the defects, pointed above, will be remedied in the proper order. Hence the objector should not live in the fool's paradise that his criticisms are unanswerable. Oh long lived one, you should know that the truth of the Vedas stands well-established.

Now, how can the objection that a word does not relate itself with a real object be answered? It has been asserted that words do not produce the Knowledge of the real external objects. The words are produced by such imagination as holds out false hopes that they are related to the real objects. They, by their own nature, produce such imaginative judgments as do not refer to the real external objects. Let us cite an example to illustrate our point, a sentence like a hundred elephants simultaneously stand on the finger-end' is a classical one. Here words, by their very nature, are somehow related to the objects.

It may be argued against the conclusion that the sources of perception such as eyes etc. also produce illusory experience. A bundle of hairs is mistaken for a peacock-tail. In every such case the sense-organs do not come in contact with the real objects in order to produce knowledge. Such an argument does not hold good since only the diseased sense-organs e. g., suffering from the detachment of retina, produce illusion. But they do never by their intrinsic nature produce illusion. Regarding the false verbal knowledge, it may be stated that such knowledge is only due to the defect in the speaker and that a word is not its source. Such an argument is not tenable. If a man who has defects, is dumb then he who cannot utter a word cannot produce illusion in others. If a defectless person utters the sentence that there stand a hundred elephants on the tip of a finger then the sentence is sure to produce illusion. Hence, the conclusion does not follow from the above observation that it is in the nature of words to produce illusion but the defect in the speaker does not produce illusion. Moreover, whenever a true judgment exerts its counter-acting influence the sense-organs such as eyes etc. desist from producing illusory judgments. If we know that the yonder object is not silver then the object cannot produce the illusory experience that it is silver (i. e. we see the object with our eyes and do not mistake it for silver). But if we truly know a hundred times the knowledge arising from the sentence that there stand a hundred elephants on the tip of a finger to be incorrect and to be cancelled by a true judgment even then the sentence that there stand a hundred elephants on the tip of a finger again produces a false imaginary judgment. As words are the creature of imagination so they produce illusion in the face of a real counteracting contradictory judgment. This is what is called the dissociation of words with the real objects. It has been stated in the Buddhist logic thus : "Imagination begets words and words beget imagination and they are inseparably connected with each other. So the discordance of words with the real objects constantly follows from the very nature of words. This is the sum and substance of the argument of the Buddhist logicians against the validity of verbal knowledge.

A reply to this objection is as follows. The contender might have subscribed to the hypothesis of the objector if no sentence had produced the true knowledge of a real object. So far as we understand the nature of a word we know for certain that there is a perfect agreement between a word and a real object denoted by it. If the sentence that there are fruits on the banks of a river is uttered by a trustworthy person then it produces a true judgment in the mind of a listener and there is no material contradiction of it. A person who hearing this sentence moves for the fruits gets them. Now, the objector may contend that a false judgment, in some cases, leads to a successful result. He cites an example to corroborate his statement. A man who mistakes the ray of a gem for a gem proceeds to obtain it and gets hold of it. Similarly, the false judgment, arising from the above sentence, is crowned with success. Thus, a false judgment does not stand on the way of obtaining a good result. Such a contention is not tenable. This matter will be thoroughly discussed later on.

Now, let us see whether or not the sentence that there stand a hundred elephants uttered by a trustworthy person, produces a true judgment. Such a conjecture is absurd since a good man, possessed of excellent merits, is not so fickle as to utter such a sentence.

A trust-worthy person advises people not to utter an incoherent sentence like the sentence that a hundred herds of elephants stand on the finger-tip. Even if it is admitted that such a person utters an incoherent sentence like the above one then he does so with the intention of denying something and uses it as a mere symbol of contradiction. The sentence consists of empty words and its literal meaning is not insisted upon. If the sentence in question would have been used by him to convey a meaning then he had not prohibited people to use it. Thus the sentence which is uttered by a reliable person does never produce a false judgment. Hence, the hypothesis that a sentence does never represent the real objects is not tenable. Whenever a sentence misrepresents a fact or an object the speaker, i.e., the author of the sentence, is to blame.

Now, a fresh doubt about the negative relation between a sentence and the knowledge of an object arises in our mind. It is stated thus :—Either an erroneous judgment does not take place if a sentence does not precede it, or, it does not arise if the speaker has no defect in him. No such doubt arises in our mind.

A knave who does not utter a word deceives others, having recourse to the other methods such as a gesture, etc.

It may be argued that in the above case words are inferred from such gestures and it is the inferred words which produce illusory knowledge But such an argument does not hold good since it does not bear out the evidence of experience. A man who listens to the sentence that there are fruits on the banks of a river goes there but becomes disappointed as his experience contradicts the truth of the above sentence. Then he heaps contumely on the person but not on the words with the remarks, "I have been deceived by the wicked fellow : Fie upon him". If he is crowned with success then he praises the speaker of the sentence with the remark "He is a great man as he is a sooth-sayer." Thus we see by the method of agreement and difference that the defect in the speaker is causally connected with the falsehood of the judgment conveyed by his sentence. If a reliable person keeps silence then there is no scope of finding him. In that case no false knowledge arises as there is no knowledge. If an unreliable person advises something, a person who listens to it has illusory experience. Hence any and every word is not the source of illusion.

How do the defects in a speaker condition an illusion ? Because a person who has either merits or defects does simply utter a word. When a word is uttered it does so to convey its sense without giving us an opportunity of knowing the defects or otherwise in the person. An illusion which is produced in a listener is only due to the word of a speaker. A word assumes no corrupt form to produce it. The Naiyāyikas are really glad at this suggestion. The implication of this suggestion is that if the speaker is a meritorious person then the sentence "There are fruits on the banks of a river," uttered by him, produces true knowledge and that his words are capable of producing it. It follows from the above hypothesis that a person plays only the part of a speaker, and that a word presupposes no relation with the object to be denoted by it. But it is not reasonable to hold that a word expresses its meaning, being independent of its relation with the object. On the contrary it is reasonable to hold that it is the essence of a word that it reveals an object like a lamp. It should also be noted that correct or incorrect representation of an object does not constitute the essence of a word. A lamp reveals an object but it does not imply that a lamp always correctly reveals an object since the illusory perception of an object is also produced by a lamp-light. Words are also different from a lamp in some respects. A lamp reveals an object independently of any conventional rule. But words depend upon the relation of denotation in order to reveal an object. The truth or otherwise of words which communicate the knowledge of an object respectively depends upon the perfection or defect of the speaker. When the sentences such as the sentence "There are a hundred elephants on the finger-tip" are repeatedly uttered, they produce illusory knowledge in the mind of a listener since words which misrepresent facts possess the common character of revealing an object. Words are not to blame for this.

If a speaker repeatedly utters a sentence without considering whether or not the meanings of the component words are well-connected then he is only to blame for his inadvertence but not his words.

Some earlier logicians have held that the truth of the previous perception of the speaker—the perception which is at the root of the above verbal statement—is negated but not the syntactical relation of the words in the sentence "There are a hundred elephants, etc." A person communicates his direct knowledge through the medium of words to the other persons. If his basic perceptual knowledge is illusory then the verbal knowledge which is communicated by him is wrong. But if the basic perception is correct then the verbal knowledge is also right. If a person without perceiving an object instructs others then his power of judgment is not surely up to the mark, i.e. defective. Thus the truth or untruth of verbal knowledge respectively depends upon the perfection or upon the imperfection of a person, i.e., the speaker. Sabara Śvāmin has also subscribed to this view. He holds that verbal knowledge is, in some cases, true and it also turns out to be false, in some other cases.

The invalidity of verbal knowledge is due to the shortcomings of the speaker. It is not true to hold that words, by themselves, are never related to the real objects. The Buddhists have tried to prove by means of destructive criticism that words remain always unrelated to the real objects because existence has been denied to universals and such other objects which are denoted by words. Their negative thesis will be refuted later on.

An Introduction to the Discussion about the Intrinsic or Extrinsic Validity of all forms of valid knowledge

When a question regarding the validity of verbal knowledge is raised the followers of Jaimini hold that verbal knowledge is valid.

Let us, at the outset, discuss whether all knowledge is valid or not. Let us also decide whether knowledge carries along with itself the stamp of validity on the face of it or not. If it does not carry along with itself the stamp of validity on the face of it then does it derive it from an external source and do we know it from some source ?

Why do you introduce a broader issue, viz., the problem of the validity of all knowledge, leaving aside the point at issue, viz. the validity of verbal knowledge. It is a truism that the problem of the validity of verbal knowledge has not been singled out to be treated separately. But we have taken up the broader issue in order to solve the problem under discussion because the key to the solution of both problems is one and the some.

As the validity of all other forms of knowledge is either intrinsic or extrinsic so that of verbal knowledge will also obey the same rule. It is not reasonable to hold that verbal knowledge, being a class by itself, its validity has a unique character. Thus the question of validity or invalidity of all forms of knowledge should be uniformly treated.

(1) Do we recognize a piece of knowledge to be either true or untrue when we are aware of it ? (2) Or, do we know it to be so after testing it by some external standard ? (3) Or, do we know a piece of knowledge to be untrue whenever we are aware of it? Or do we know it to be true only when it is tested by an external standard ? (4) Or, do we know a piece of knowledge to be true without testing it ? Or, do we know it to be untrue only after testing it by an external standard ?

(We shall also remember in this connection that the problem of validity or invalidity has another distinct aspect which invites our attention : (1) Do the conditions which produce a piece of knowledge contribute towards its validity ? (2) Or, does a piece of valid knowledge require an extra factor for its coming into being ? (3) Does a piece of erroneous knowledge require an extra factor for its coming into being ? (4) Or, do the conditions which produce a piece of such knowledge determine its invalidity ?)

The Mīmāṁsakas hold that the Validity of a Piece of knowledge is Intrinsic.

The hypothesis that the validity as well as the invalidity of a piece of knowledge is intrinsic is not reasonable since when a person may move to get hold of an object, seeing it to be such and such he may be unsuccessful. Thus the truth of his knowledge is contradicted. If a piece of knowledge carries with itself sense that it is either true or untrue then does the mistake of the mother-of-pearl for silver carry with itself the sense that it is true or untrue ?

If a piece of knowledge carries with itself the belief that it is instrinsically true then how is it that it is discordant with its object ? Again, if it carries with itself the belief that it is not true then how is it that a person moves to bring the object referred to ?

This criticism refutes the third alternative hypothesis according to which the invalidity of a piece of knowledge is intrinsic and owes its existence to no additional factor but on the contrary, the validity of a piece of knowledge is extrinsic but it owes its existence to an extraneous factor. If the invalidity of a piece of knowledge had been grasped along with the awareness of itself then there would have been no movement in response to it. Again, the invalidity of a piece of knowledge could not have come into being if it were not generated by a special condition. It presupposes a distinct factor for its appearance. It owes its existence to such deficiency as assembles together with the condition of knowledge. Again, we know a piece of knowledge to be false when we definitely know that it is contradicted by its contradictory judgment. Hence, a piece of false knowledge does not arise independently of special factor and a piece of knowledge is not known as false whenever we are aware of it. Some (Buddhists) hold that the invalidity of a piece of knowledge is the negation of validity. They also hold that it is unreal as it is negation and that it does not owe its existence to an additional condition such as deficiency or some other factor.

The hypothesis is not reasonable since untrue knowledge admits of two kinds, viz. (1) illusion and (2) doubt and hence it is not unreal. Thus, the untruth or invalidity of a piece of untrue knowledge, being its abstract property, cannot be unreal. Moreover, the validity of a piece of knowledge does not owe its existence to a distinct factor. And the view that a piece of knowledge is known to be true afterwards when it is verified (i.e. when it is submitted to a real test and that validity owes its existence to a distinct factor will be elaborately discussed in the following paragraphs of this section. Thus, second part of the hypothesis that (a) the invalidity of a piece of knowledge is extrinsic and that (b) the validity of a piece of knowledge is extrinsic will also be refuted.

It has been stated that a piece of knowledge is true if it reveals an object in its true character. The truth of a piece of knowledge is its non-discrepancy with the object referred to by it. Now, if the said truth depends upon a distinct factor for its appearance and if it is cognized to be such only in relation to something other than itself then it is called as extraneously determined and known. But with regard to these two aspects it is absolutely independent of any outside influence. Now, if it is held that the validity of a piece of knowledge is extrinsic then three questions arise in our mind, viz. "What is the extraneous factor that brings it about?" "What is the extra object by the aid of which the true knowledge requires to discharge its normal function?" And "What is the standard by which the truth of a piece of knowledge is tested?" If it is admitted that the validity of a piece of knowledge owes its existence to an extraneous factor then what is this extraneous factor? Is it nothing but the essence of the conditions that produce it? Or is it simply a qualitative improvement of the same conditions responsible for a piece of valid knowledge? If the assemblage of the conditions of a piece of knowledge and that of valid knowledge are basically the same, then the Naiyāyikas simply try to establish the established hypothesis. If the conditions are absent then a piece of knowledge which is an effect cannot come into being. In that case, there is no piece of knowledge which as an effect cannot come into being. In that case, there is no piece of knowledge the validity or the invalidity of which will be discussed. It is also very difficult to establish the hypothesis that the validity of a piece of knowledge depends upon a special factor which is distinct from the conditions, though all the conditions of a piece of knowledge and those of the so-called qualitative improvement of the same conditions is unreal like the sky-lotus, since its existence has not been proved. Hence, such an improvement, being a mere conjecture, cannot be the reliable condition of validity.

Let us take an example of true perception. The truth of perception does not depend upon the special quality of a sense-organ. It is hard to establish that such a special quality of the sense-organ is grasped by perception. The truth of perception is determined by a special quality that qualifies a sense-organ. All sense-organs, as the eyes, etc., are imperceptible. Hence, how can the quality be perceived since it belongs to a sense-organ, a transcendental object? It is not an inference since the relation of concomitance holding between it and its mark cannot be detected. Hence we arrive at the conclusion that a piece of valid knowledge is produced only by the defectless conditions.

If there had been a third type of judgment which is neither true nor false then the three different sets of conditions would have been necessarily assumed to explain the three different types of effects : In that case we are to hold that a true judgment is produced by a cause, possessed of a good quality, that an illusory judgement is produced by a defective cause and that a neutral judgment is produced by a cause as it is, i.e. by a cause which has neither a good quality nor a defect. But a third type of judgment is conspicuous by its absence. It is a truism that there are only two types of judgments, viz., true and false. Of these two types the false one is known to be produced only by the defective cause. It has been experienced that a jar which is produced by defective conditions has a distorted form. Similarly, the moon which has been perceived with normal eyes is one but when she perceived with diseased eyes she is known to be two.

It has been established that an illusory judgment is produced by the defective cause and that the third type of judgment which is neither true nor false is conspicuous by its absence. Hence, we arrive at the conclusion that the true judgment is produced by its normal cause, having no other qualification. There is no need of assuming the hypothesis that an additional good quality of the cause besides its normal property is necessary for the appearance of a true judgment. The assemblage of conditions (viz. the presence of the reason in the subject of inference, the knowledge of the relation of invariable concomitance holding between the reason and the consequence, etc.) which determines an inference is also known to contribute towards its truth when the conditions of an effect which have neither defects nor new good qualities (i.e. when they remain normal), assemble, they do not surely remain indifferent to produce their effects. Why should we assume that the conditions of consciousness require the assistance of a new good quality to produce a true judgment? For this reason, the hypothesis that the conditions have an extra excellence is to be discarded. The absence of any disease of the eyes such as glaucoma, jaundice, etc. has been expressed in a manner so that an impression is produced in our mind that the eyes have acquired a new virtue, viz., transparency. But it should be noted that the transparent eyes are nothing but normal ones, having no new excellence. When we apply ointments or collyrium lines to our eyes we do it with the intention of curing our eyes of their disease but not under the impression that a new good quality will emerge. In other words this device restores the eyes to their normal conditions.

Hence, the true knowledge is produced by the normal conditions. The false knowledge is produced by an excess of defects which interfere with their normal function. Therefore, the falsehood of knowledge depends upon an additional condition for its coming into being. Again, the falsity of knowledge, is determined, by an additional condition since the conditions of a true judgment cannot produce its opposite judgment.

The truth of a piece of knowledge does not depend upon a new good quality of its conditions for its coming into being. A piece of knowledge does not depend upon an extra-condition, viz., a new good quality to do its normal function. The illumination of an object by a sense-organ is due to its normal function for which it is indebted only to its conditions. The true knowledge simply reveals its object. The movement of the knower for the object revealed is due to his desire for the same. It intervenes between the knowledge of an object and the movement of the knower for it.

When a true judgment comes into existence it does not depend upon a new quality as its source. It does also independently play its part. It derives its nature of illuminating an object only from its own cause. The function of a true judgment is only to reveal an object. The movement on the part of a a knower for the revealed object is due to his choice and final resolution in favour of the same object.

When an apprehension comes into being it is not endowed with the character of illuminating an object. But it, being produced, reveals an object. Still, it does not depend upon something *ab extra* in order to reveal its object.

Some logicians have expressed the same idea in other words. A jar derives its existence from a lump of earth, a stick, a wheel a piece of thread, etc. but it depends upon none when it discharges its function of carrying water, i. e. it independently carries water.

Or (the mīmāṁsakas clarify their position)

A jar cannot independently carry water. It requires the services of a carrier to do so. But a true judgment requires the aid of nothing outside itself in order to reveal an object (It may be argued against the hypothesis that an act of awareness, being self-conscious, reveals its own object. The drift of this argument is that an awareness depends upon its own nature for the illumination of an object. The Mīmāṁsakas anticipate this argument and try to render it pointless in the following manner). An act of awareness being self-conscious, does not reveal its object. As the sense-organs such as the eyes, etc. without being conscious of their own existence reveal objects. But why an awareness should be self-conscious in order to its own object?

Śabara, in his commentary on the Mīmāṁsā-sūtras, has said to this effect. 'No body is aware of his awareness if the object is not cognized. When an object is cognized the knower infers that he has the awareness of an object because the object has been cognized'. Hence, a true judgment does not require the aid of its own awareness in order to discharge its own function, viz., in order to illuminate an object. Again a true judgment does not require the aid of an extra factor in order to apprehend its own essential attribute, viz., validity, since there is nothing else to be depended upon. Let us examine the rival hypotheses which explain the determination of the validity of a judgment. Does the determination of validity presuppose the knowledge of a new quality which occasionally springs up and qualifies the cause of the judgment to which the validity in question is supposed to belong? Or, does it presuppose the knowledge of the absence of a contradictory (preventive) judgment? Or, does it presuppose the consilience of the judgment with another true judgment? The first hypothesis that the determination of the validity of a true judgment presupposes the knowledge of a new quality of the cause of the judgment and that the validity in question is supposed to belong to the cause is not tenable since the presence of such a quality in the cause of the judgment will be immediately refuted in the following paragraph.

The new quality which is asserted to belong to the cause of a true judgment cannot be sensed since the quality which belongs to the super-sensuous cause is itself imperceptible.

The upholders of the first hypothesis may contend that the said quality of the cause may be inferred from the successful action which signifies the actual attaitnment of the object referred to by the Judgment. But such a success cannot be achived if a person does not move. The movement of a person cannot take place if he does not determine the validity of this judgment, the main spring of his movement. If a person moves in response to a judgment without determining its validity then the determination of the validity of the judgment at a subsquent period is fruitless. Again, if it is held that the determination of the validity of the said judgment precedes his movement then such a statement is a glaring instance of circular reasoning. When a person moves he knows that his action is successful. When he knows that his action has turned out to be successful he comes to know that the cause of his judgment has the specified quality. When he knows that the cause has such and such quality he determines that the judgment is true. And when he arrives at such a determination he moves for the object.

Moreover, if we know for certain that a contradictory judgment which prevents the appearance of its opposite is absent then it does not follow that the opposite judgment is true.

Is such knowledge of the absence of a contradictory judgment confined only to the present time? Or does it cover all times? If it is limited only to the present time then it is not capable of leading to the determination of the validity of the judgment in question. The knowledge of spurious cowries may not be contradicted for some time. But it is a fact that such knowledge is contradicted after some time. A person who is less than an omniscient being cannot comprehend that a judgment is absolutely free from all contradictions in all times.

Now, let us examine the second hypothesis regarding the test of the truth of a judgment. If it is held that consilience constitutes the standard by which the truth of a judgment is determined then what does consilience signify ? Does it mean that a judgment is consilient with another if they both refer to one and the same object ? Or, does it mean that a judgment is consilient with another judgment which refers to a distinct ? Or does it mean that a judgment is consilient with another judgment which refers to the utility of the object of the first one as its object? We draw the attention of those logicians who are in favour of the first meaning of the term 'consilience' and put this question to them "wherein lies the distinction between the prior and the posterior judgments so that the prior one is recognized as true if it thoroughly agrees with the posterior one". Moreover, if they hold that the truth will be asserted of the prior judgment on their consilience with a posterior judgment then they will not be able even after hundreds of years, to find out the final posterier judgment. If they go on examining a lot of judgment without accepting them as true but arbitrarily select one to be intrinsically true then why do they cherish hatred against the first one? (In other words, they cannot determine the truth of a judgment if they do not hold that judgment which constitutes the truth of a judgment if they do not hold that judgment which constitutes the standard of truth is intrinsicilly true. If they are compelled to hold that one judgment is, at least, intrinsicallly true then why should not they hold that the other judgments are also intrinsically true?)

It has been stated by Kumārila :

"If a judgment is to be at all accepted as intrinsically valid then why do you murmur at the acceptance of the intrinsic validity of the initial judgment ?

It may be held that a judgment is true if it is consilient with another judgment. Such a view is not tenable since our experience does not bear it out. The knowledge of a post is never in agreement with that of a jar. It may be said that the validity of the initial impellent judgment is ascertained when there is consilience between the knowledge of the object referred to by the judgment and that of the effect of the said object. Such a view is not tenable. If the validity of the second knowledge is not determined then how can the validity of the initial judgment be ascertained ? Moreover, wherein lies the distinction between the knowledge of an object and that of its effect ? For which reason should the first knowledge depend upon the second one for the determination of its validity ? It may be said in its favour that the practical efficiency constitutes the differentia of the second one. Let this point of view be substatiated. When water is absent we mistake at the outset the rays of the sun for water. How can one place his reliance upon the validity of a judgment of the first type ? But when one actually plunges in water, drinks it and bathes in it he experiences the practical utility of water. Such an experience is never contradicted. Hence, it guarantees the truth of the knowledge of water. This hypothesis is not sound. The sight of water and the experience of drinking and bathing falsify the above hypothesis. Moreover, when one sees a youthful damsel in a dream and embraces her he ejaculates semen without the actual contact with a real lady. Thus the above hypothesis is open to serious inconsistency.

The upholder of the above hypothesis may contend that the above emission of semen is not due to the embrace of a lady. But it owes its existence to the excessive sexual excitement or to the derangement of bile. Hence, there is no contradiction in the above hypothesis. Such a defence is not reasonable. Such an emission is causally connected with the dalliance with a damsel. This causal connection is determined by the joint method of agreement and difference.

Hence the hypothesis of consilience between the knowledge of an object and that of its result does not guarantee the truth of the knowledge of the object, since, the true knowledge of the practical utility of an object takes place even when the object is absent.

If a person does not move in response to his initial judgment then it is impossible on his part to acquire the knowledge of the utility of the object. Now, it should be admitted that he moves when the validity of the initial judgment is ascertained. In order to determine the validity of the judgment in question it should be recognized before that some special good quality of the instrumental cause of the judgment is responsible for it (the judgment in question). Thus, the tree of this hypothesis will ultimately have to face the havoc done by a see-saw in the shape of reasoning in a vicious circle as it has been indicated before. In other words, the movement of a person helps one to acquire the definite knowledge of the truth of the impelling judgment, its truth leads up to the determination of the special good quality of its cause, the recognition of such good quality helps the ascertainment of the truth of the judgment and such determination of truth impels one to move. Therefore it is a clear instance of reasoning in a vicious circle. If a person moves without knowing for certain that the knowledge of object towards which he moves is true then the subsequent determination of the truth of the impellent judgment though possible, is futile. According to the Hindu custom one should shave when the star is auspicious. But if he shaves and then enquires whether the star is auspicious then such investigation is surely profitless. Similarly, post movement enquiry about the truth of a judgment is absolutely fruitless.

An answer to the above objection is as follows. There are two types of movement, viz. (1) original movement and (2) imitative movement. An illustration of the first type is as follows. In order to test the condition of seeds some seeds of *śāli* paddy, etc., are sown in a flat cup containing very soft mud which has been properly watered. The cultivators observe the clever art of properly germinating the seeds. Then they unhesitatingly sow the same seeds in the paddy field. Their activities illustrate the second type. Now, let us come to our original point. When a wise man examines a judgment and makes it out to be true he moves for the object referred to by the judgment. This is an example of the first type of movement. When his movement is fruitful the wise knower accepts the knowledge of the practical utility of the object to be true. If a judgment referring to the same object arises in his mind at a later period, he will move with perfect ease for the object, having no shade of doubt. Therefore, the examination of the truth of a judgment after movement is not absolutely fruitless. This is what we have got to say.

A review of the above argument is as follows. The example, cited above, is not convincing. We shall firstly be sure of the fact that the seeds that are before us and those which have germinated are homogeneous. On the definite understanding of the homogeneity of these seeds the peasants unhesitatingly proceed to sow them. As all acts of consciousness have the same character but no individualistic distinction so the distinction of an act is to be indirectly known in and through either its effect and cause.

Can we infer that this act of knowledge is true because it is produced by such and such cause ? No, we cannot do it because the cause is beyond the reach of sense-organ at that time. We cannot also infer the truth of a judgment from the effect since it has been stated that in order to do so we are required to move at first. If our voluntary movement does not presuppose the determination of the truth of the impellent judgment then is not the quest after truth later on superfluous ? Thus, the above argument against the charge of futility is not adequate. Hence, the truth of a judgment cannot be inferred by means of the pragmatic method. One may hold that the truth of a judgment is determined if its cause is known to be defectless endowed with good quality. Then he surely imitates a person who, after having concluded the nuptial ceremony, enquires whether the time of the said ceremony is auspicious.

Those who hold that the truth of a judgment is extrinsic argue this. They describe a well-known incident. In a certain season abounding in full-blown flowers the bees suck the honey of flowers and hum very sweetly. A person conceals his body there behind the thick bower of creepers and plays on the lute. He who hears the music but does not see the player of the lute doubts whether the musical notes are the humming of bees. This very doubt prompts him to proceed towards the sound. When the player on the lute is seen the cause of the sound is definitely known. The doubt of the listener is solved. Then the listener is able to know which of the two alternatives of the above doubt is true. This is the finding out of the truth of a judgment by means of the determination of the exact cause.

If a man does not move for the object, he cannot realise the competency of the cause. Moreover, if he moves without ascertaining the truth of the impellent judgment then it is superfluous on his part to determine the truth of the said judgment. Again, if the upholders of the extrinsic validity of a judgment hold that movement presupposes the determination of the truth of the impellent judgment then they will surely face the fallacy of mutual dependence. The determination of the truth of the judgment is the prerequisite condition of movement and such movement leads up to the determination of the truth of the said judgment.

Thus we arrive at the conclusion that the hypothesis of the extrinsic validity of a judgment cannot avoid the following charges, viz., reasoning in a vicious circle, mutual dependence, *regressus ad infinitum*, superfluity, etc. Therefore, the determination of the truth of a judgment is self-evident. Therefore, we (the Mīmāṁsakas) arrive at the three conclusions, viz. (1) 'The truth of a judgment does not depend upon an additional factor for its coming into being' : (2) 'A true judgment discharges its function independently of an additional factor'. and (3) 'The determination of the truth of a judgment presupposes no act of knowledge other than itself'. The final great conclusions which these three conclusions point to the conclusion that the truth of a judgment is self-evident since it is absolutely free from the three conditions that determine the extrinsic character of the truth of a judgment.

Kumārila says :

"The truths of all true judgments are innate in them since if the truth of a judgment is not its inherent property then it cannot be imparted to it by an influence *ab extra*".

The Refutation of the Hypothesis that the Falsehood of a Judgment is Intrinsic

The falsehood of a judgment owes its existence to a defect belonging to a cause. A judgment is known to be untrue only with reference to a contradictory judgment. Hence the untruth of a judgment is an extrinsic property. Hence the first three hypotheses being not amenable to reason the fourth hypothesis is the best of all. The hypothesis amounts to this that the truth of a judgment is intrinsic and its falsehood is extrinsic.

When a judgment arises in our mind we are not in a position to determine whether it is true or it is untrue. Hence, this oscillating state of the mind gives rise to a doubt.

The nature of a true judgment is the revelation of an object. This is the common property of the true and the false judgments It is well-known that the awareness of the common character of these two kinds of judgment is a source of doubt.

We cannot know that a judgment is either true or otherwise unless and until it is consilient with or contradicted by another judgment. Hence, both truth and falsehood are extrinsic properties.

This hypothesis is not faultless. It is a truism that the revelation of an object follows from a true judgment. When a judgment comes into existence it is not coloured by the state of indecision. But as a general rule it should be *prima facie* provisionally accepted that the truth of a judgment is intrinsic and self-evident. When a person, knowing an object, moves for it he does so because he takes his knowledge to be true but does not doubt its varacity. This is the concluding part of the hypothesis that the truth of a judgment is selfevident. There is an exception to the above general rule. When a judgment is contradicted it is known to be untrue, i.e., it misrepresents its object. The untruth of a judgment is not self-evident. A judgment is known to be false when we are aware of another judgment which negates it. There are two factors which help to determine a judgment to be false. They are as follows, viz., the determination of the contradictory judgment and the awareness of a defect in the cause of judgment. Śabara states that a judgment is false when the cause of it is defective or when the judgment is known to misrepresent its object. Kumārila, the author of Śloka-vārttika has stated that the truth of a judgment is innate in it but if a judgment reveals an object at a place where it is absent or if it is known that its cause is defective then its claim to truth is lost. But as a contradictory judgment contradicts its antecedent opposite judgment so the former has a reference to the contents of the latter. Of the pair of the two opposite judgments the antecedent one is contradicted by the subsequent one because both of them refer to the same object. (Let us take an example : The judgment "This is red" is contradicted by the judgment "This is not red". The first one asserts that this is red. The second one denies that this is red. Hence, one establishes a claim but the other one disowns its claim. Thus these two judgments refer to the same object, viz., 'this' the subject of these judgments being one and the same, the 'act' associated with the copula 'is' denies the predicate. A judgment is false if its cause is known to be defective. The awareness of a defect as belonging to a cause, is not mentioned in a judgment though such awareness contradicts its truth. It does so because the defect as belonging to the cause of a judgment, cuts off the root of the truth of a judgment. (Let us take an example : We have jaundiced eyes. But we do not know them to be such. We see a conch-shell. We judge that this is yellow. But when we learn that our eyes are jaundiced we come to know that the predicate 'yellow' is wrong. The awareness of the defect in the eyes, i.e. jaundice, falsifies the judgment that this is yellow. The predicate 'yellow' owes its existence to jaundice, but not to the cause. It is in the nature of defect to produce such false knowledge. The two contrary predicates are predicated of the same subject. The cause produces the real one. The defect is responsible for its contrary one. Thus, the possibility of the opposite predicate is due to the defect in the cause.) The Mīmāṁsakas put forward such an example as is found in the Vedic literature. It has been enjoined in the Vedas that water should be sprinkled from a Camasa (a spoon used for sprinkling water) in a Darśa-Paurṇamāsa sacrifices (Vedic rites observed in new moon and full moon). A Camasa is a means to the performance of Darśa and Paurṇamāsa sacrifices because it is one of its necessary implements. But it has also been enjoined that a person who is desirous of gaining cattle should give water to a cow, carrying it with a pot used in connection with milking. In the second injunction an emphasis has been laid on an animal which is the desideration of the performer. The above-mentioned pot is an essential implement in the second rite. It serves well the purpose of giving water to a cow. But in connection with the performance of this rite a Camasa has no utility. (A Camasa and a milk-pot may be used alike in the second rite. The purpose of giving water to a cow may be served by both of them. The use of milk-pot has been prescribed by the Vedas. Hence, though there is no opposition between a Camasa and a milk-pot yet the use of a Camasa has been cancelled by the Vedic injunction.) Similarly, though the knowledge, produced by a defective sense-organ, is due to the defect yet the truth of the knowledge in the second example is cancelled because it has been generated by the unauthorised or unvedic cause.

Kumārila, the author of Śloka-vārttika, has endorsed the same view and clarified the Mīmāṁsā point of view. He holds that though the judgment, produced by a defective cause, and a true judgment, produced by the same cause, only devoid of the defect, do not refer to one and the same subject, yet the subjects, referred to by them, suggest that these two judgments seem to refer to one and the same subject, i.e., they have the same subject 'This'. Hence, there is the possibility of opposition between them. As in the Vedic example a Camasa is enjoined instead of a milk-pot so a judgment, produced by a defective cause, is contradicted by a judgment, generated by the defectless cause.

If these two kinds of opposite judgments do not arise to contradict or oppose the truth of their corresponding rival judgments then the innate truth of the judgments remains uncontradicted. In that case, there is no justification for starting a suspicion as to its truth. Kumārila has also stated that if the cause of a judgment is not found out to be defective then the judgment is not baselessly suspected to be untrue.

Let me state some wise sayings on this point. Kindly note them :

A doubt exists in this universe. It assumes the form of that this is either a post or a man. Every body's personal experience bears witness to its actuality.

But without sufficient reason if we doubt the veracity of a piece of knowledge then we cannot transact worldly business. If one entertains non-interesting doubts at his sweet will, he while embracing his wife, may stop and imagine her to be his mother. The son of Parāśara has said that a man who is distrustful of every act of knowledge meets with disaster. Oh Arjuna ! a suspicious person finds happiness neither in this world nor in the next one.

Let us now take a hypothetical case. A judgment arises in our mind. A corresponding contradictory judgment also arises in our mind. In that case, the truth of the first judgment is doubtful. Then a third judgment referring to the same object is required for the final verification. As a limited number of cases decides the truth or the otherwise of a judgment so the fallacy of *regressus ad infinitum* is got rid of. But though there is a reference to a third judgment for the determination of the truth or the otherwise of the first judgment yet the hypothesis of the intrinsic validity of a judgment is not sacrificed. If the first judgment is consilient with the third one then the intrinsic validity of the first judgment maintains its *status quo*. The second judgment wrongly ascribes untruth to the first one. The duty of the third judgment is to cancel the attributed untruth of the first one but not to establish the truth of it by means of its consilience. If the second judgment is consilient with the third one then the first one is held to be untrue. The hypothesis that the untruth of a judgment is extrinsically determined is agreed upon. The third judgment does not impart the truth to the first one by means of the consilience of the first one with the third one but functions to remove the imaginary suspicion of untruth.

Kumārila has also said in his concluding remark that three or four judgments are only required for the final solution of the truth of a judgment in the manner described above. No more judgments are necessary for this purpose. This admission lends support to the view that the truth of a judgment is intrinsic and self-evident. This is the sum and substance of the Mīmāṁsā view of Svataḥ-prāmāṇyam.

The truth of the Vedas is also intrinsic as they have no other source of truth

The truth of every type of valid knowledge is self-evident. Hence, on account of the same reason, the truth of verbal knowledge is also self-evident. It is not fair to hold that the relation holding between a word and its meaning is naturally accidental. This point has been discussed before. The truth of verbal testimony is innate in it because words are the source of our knowledge. Some exceptions are noticed because the speaker of the untruthful words has defective knowledge. Kumārila has said that the speaker is responsible for the untrue words. In case of a sentence, made by a human being, if the author has the required qualification, i. e., he has complete knowledge of the thing stated then his words have unquestionable intrinsic truth because his qualification removes all possible defects. But his qualification does not contribute towards the truth of his words since the qualification is not a logical condition of its truth. It has been already stated before that the truth of words is discussed because they produce knowledge. The Vedas enjoy the intrinsic truth without the shade of a doubt because as they have no author so no defect is even suspected to cling to them. We should also take note of the fact in this connection that defects find a passage to words only through the agency of their speaker. As nobody has ever experienced the contradiction of the truth of the contents of the Vedas so the truth of the Vedas remains uncontradicted.

Kumārila, in his Śloka-vārttika, has said:—

"As there is no author of the Vedic sentence so it is more quickly grasped that the Vedas are free from all defects. For this very reason nobody suspects the untruth of the Vedas".

Jaimini has also stated in his Mīmāṁsā-sūtra that the Vedas are intrinsically valid because they do in no way depend upon Bādarāyaṇa, the compiler of the Vedas, for their appearance. (This sūtra, apart from this literal meaning, is impregnated with the wealth of hidden meaning. He suggests that all words consisting of letters are eternal and their relation with the objects meant is also eternal, but their relation is not due to a convention set up by human beings. The words, being eternal, are not made by a person. Hence, they are intrinsically true. Though Bādarāyaṇa is a great repository of the Vedic lore yet the authorship of the Vedic mantras should not be ascribed to him.

The untruth of a sentence is due only to a defect (imperfect knowledge). As this defect belongs to every human being so it has been truly remarked that a sentence which has no human author is necessarily true.

Again, if the truth of a sentence is due only to the qualification (perfect knowledge) of its author then as the qualification belongs only to human beings so it is not consistent to hold that a sentence which has no human author is true.

On the other hand, the qualification of a person does not bring about the truth of a sentence. The truth of a sentence is innate in it by its inherent character. The critical thinkers hold that the qualification of an author does not contribute to the truth of his sentence but simply removes the defect which is the source of the untruth of a sentence.

The refutation of the hypothesis that the truth of a piece of valid knowledge is intrinsic.

The refutation of the above thesis is as follows. Even if we do not ascertain the truth of the judgments which have reference only to worldly objects, but we proceed to our ordinary works on their basis then it is useless to discuss the problem whether it is intrinsic or not (i. e., extrinsic). We should rather prefer indecision. But intelligent persons should not undertake Vedic rites, a means of the attainment of transcendental objects without being sure of their truthfulness since they entail upon them a heavy expenditure of wealth and a lot of troubles. Therefore, the question of the truth of the Vedas should be settled. We shall also prove later on that the truth of the Vedas is extrinsically determined.

The Mīmāṁsakas have tried their best to prove the hypothesis of intrinsic validity. Let us (Jayanta) now examine their hypothesis. What is the exact meaning, of the compound word "Svataḥprāmāṇyam" (a judgment itself is self-evidently true) ? Does the truth of a judgment emanate from the judgment itself? Or, does a judgment reveal its own truth to itself. The thesis that a judgment itself is aware of its own truth is not tenable since it is not amenable to the rule of logic. Let us clarify the point of criticism with reference to a concrete case of perception. When the perception of a blue object correctly reveals a blue object as blue, the perceptual judgment is true so far as the blue object is concerned. The judgment is true in such a limited sense because it is learnt that it owes its existence to the sense-object-contact. Is there anything to discuss this point ? But we should discuss the question, viz., "By which proof do we ascertain the truth of the above true judgment ?" Do we determine it by perception or by inference ? Because the other proofs are of no service in this matter. Let us scrutinize the merit of perception at first with regard to the point at issue.

A true perceptual judgment itself can neither reveal its own truth nor reveal that of its resulting form. In other words, a perceptual judgment can neither grasp the truth of its own self nor that of the illumination of the object. Of these two the perceptual judgment is the knowing process of the knower.

It remains ever transcendental, according to the Mīmāṁsakas. Therefore, it cannot grasp the truth of its own self since the process itself remains beyond the grasp of its own self. The resulting form of perception is the illumination of an object. It is in no way connected with the external sense-organ. Therefore, the truth of the illumination of an object is never perceived. The inner perception cannot be competent enough to perceive it. It is impotent to ascertain the truth of the resulting form of the perceptual process since the inner perception is absent when the illumination of an object takes place. The judgment that this is blue is not experienced to be immediately followed by another judgment that the antecedent judgment is true. But if it is admitted that the said second judgment is experienced by us then this second one assures us of the truth of the first one. Hence, the hypothesis that the truth of a judgment is self-evident should not be tenable. The net result of the above discussion is that perception fails to grasp the truth of a judgment.

Now, it may be held that the truth of a judgment is inferred. Either the truth of the process of perception or that of its resulting form is to be inferred. The truth of the resulting form cannot be determined by means of inference since no mark, an invariable means to inference, is known to us. But the result, i. e., the illumination of an object, is the effect of the knowing process of a knower. So, it is the mark of the said process. This mark or the middle term is universally accompanied only by such a major term as is an activity. Hence, by means of this mark we infer the mere existence of an activity, i. e., a process in itself but nothing else. Hence, the truth of a knowing process cannot be inferred from the above mark. Now, if it is urged that the above result leads to the inferential knowledge of the truth of the knowing process then these two questions are put to the Mīmāṁsakas, viz., "Does the mark remain unqualified ?" "Or is it qualified by the adjective 'true' ?" If the first question is answered in the affirmative then any and every result true or untrue will lead to the inference of the truth of a judgment. In that case no judgment should be false. With regard to the second question no definite answer can be given since there is no tangible way of finding out the truth of the mark. This point has been already discussed.

If the Mīmāṁsakas contend that the very experience is the source of the illumination of an object, because the blue thing reveals itself as the object of awareness of blue this awareness itself is a piece of true knowledge but nothing else. The same logic applies to the cases of illusion when we mistake mother-of-pearl for silver because there is only the experience of silver but not that of its truth.

Now, the Mīmāṁsakas may contend that when we mistake mother-of-pearl for silver a corresponding contradictory judgment arises, contradicts it and invalidates it. Let us consider the different cases of illusion. The illusory judgment that this is silver is contradicted by a contradictory judgment that this is not silver later on. The illusory judgment that this is a genuine cowry is contradicted by a contradictory judgment that this is not a genuine one at a subsequent point of time. The illusory judgment that there are two moons in the sky is experienced by a person who is suffering from the detachment of retina. It is contradicted by a contradictory judgment which arises in the mind of another person, having normal sight. The illusory judgment that this conch-shell is yellow is experienced by a person, having jaundiced eyes. It is contradicted by a contradictory judgment when he is cured of his disease. Thus all the illusory judgments have to face afterwards contradictory judgments. If this is the fate of almost every illusory judgment then it is reasonable to assume its truth. This point has been discussed before.

The Naiyāyikas argue against this contention. They say that there is much truth in your assertion. But if you contend in this manner then you say in another way that the truth of a judgment depends upon the knowledge of the absence of its contradictory judgment. Now, does the knowledge of the absence of the said contradictory judgment synchronise with the judgment ? Or, does it arise at a later point of time ? The Mīmāṁsakas cannot fairly answer these two questions. It has been already shown that the line of defence does not stand to reason. Again, if we were perfectly aware of the truth of a judgment at the time of its appearance then we acting up to this judgment would have never been baffled. But it is a fact that we are deceived. Hence, we think that we transact our normal business even when the truth of the impelling judgment is believed to be highly probable but is not definitely ascertained.

Now, the Mīmāṁsakas contend that though the impellent judgment amounts to be a doubt yet it is not experienced to be such. No body experiences an object and expresses his judgment in the form indicative of a doubt. When we perceive silver do we say "This is silver or not ?" But we communicate our perceptual judgment by means of the proposition that this is silver. An ordinary person who is under the sway of a doubt does not proceed to have the object which is doubted. But when he is sure of the object he moves for it. Why do you ascribe the character of a doubt to a judgment which is not experienced to be so ?

The Naiyāyikas join issue with the Mīmāṁsakas and establish their point by the following argument. It is a fact that the judgment in question refers to a single object and that there is no oscillation between two alternatives. But still it does not furnish the knower with a means to determine the true nature of the object. Hence, it, by force of logic, represents to it as a doubt. A doubt, also, assumes the form of a judgment. For example, when the ascetics, having no fixed abode, see a well from a distance they think that there is water in the well. Though the prior judgment that this is silver refers to a single object yet it is virtually nothing but a doubt. Again if its truth is ascertained then how can it be contradicted sometimes after ? On the other hand, if it is known to be untrue then how can it impel a person to move ?

As we can know it neither as true nor as untrue so it should be a doubt. Why are you (the Mīmāṁsakas) angry upon us (the Naiyāyikas) ?

It is a truism that though this event of consciousness is not experienced as a doubt yet it is logically established that it is a doubt. Even if we move for our accustomed objects, a true judgment does not guide us. We infer that this is a doubt from a major premise obtained by an induction.

(All movements are preceded by a doubt)

This is a movement.

Therefore, this movement is also preceded by a doubt. The conditions of a judgment are absent whereas the conditions of a doubt are present. Let us illustrate our point. The object which is sensed is the common property of true and false judgments like height, etc. (common to a man and a post). We are not at that time aware of any specific property of the said object which invariably produces a true judgment. In the absence of such a specific property the awareness of the common property revives our acquired impressions and brings about the remembrance of both the predicates of a judgment, viz., true and untrue, as these two features have been alternately experienced by us. So, we hold that there is an assemblage of the conditions of a doubt. Why should not a doubt be produced by them ?

The Mīmāṁsakas may meet this argument in the following manner. The act of consciousness in question is a true judgment because whenever it appears in the mind of a knower the invariable mark of its truth is revealed to him but on the appearance of a false judgment no such mark is noticed.

The Naiyāyikas examine this contention in the following manner. Oh Sir ! kindly define the distinct feature of the said mark since we ourselves cannot make it out, being shallow minds. If the vividness of an awareness constitutes the distinction then a false judgment that this is silver, having a reference to the mother-of-pearl, has the same vividness since such a judgment does not contain the impurity of indefiniteness. Again if you hold that the absence of the misapprehension of untruth constitutes its distinction then we also point out that such a distinction also belongs to a false judgment that this is silver, referring to the mother-of-pearl. When such a judgment (this is silver) arises in our mind we do not suspect it to be untrue as we do on hearing the sentence that there are a hundred elephants on the tip of a finger. Moreover, if you hold that an apprehension is vivid because it is other than a doubt then we shall also mention that the misapprehension of silver is also vivid since there is no oscillation between two incompatible predicates in it. Now you may hold that a judgment has a distinctive mark of truth in the shape of having no contradictory judgment to cancel its truth. But we are obliged to put a question to you for our information. Can you name a situation when contradiction does not arise at all ? The non-appearance of contradiction is an absurdity. We are sure of the fact that contradiction arises to invalidate a judgment at all stages. If we reflect long on this special feature, we cannot define it. Last of all, you may hold that the distinctive mark of truth is constituted by the accordance of a judgment with its object. Then we simply reiterate our old criticism that such a distinctive feature is not grasped by us when the judgment makes its appearance. Another point in the above criticism is that even if such a distinctive feature is admitted to be grasped then how does a person move for an object on the basis of a judgment which lacks such a distinction ? The last point in the criticism is that even if a person grasps the above distinctive mark of his impellent judgment, why is he deceived on moving for the object ? The impellent judgment may be in the form that this is a post but not a man. Even such a judgment is proved to be untrue when it is verified by an actual movement.

The common people transact all their ordinary business on the basis of their doubtful knowledge. No other alternative is left to them as they carry on their daily business on the basis of their problematical knowledge. (Jayanta suggests here the foundation of the logic of chance. Knowledge is experimental in its character. Its guidance is not infalliable. More or less we always take a leap in the dark).

(The concluding paragraph of Jayanta's critical remarks is as follows). We are not bent upon proving the thesis that a judgment, on its appearance, partakes of the character of a doubt. But what we mean to say is that when a judgment comes into being it is not known to be true. We shall call a judgment as one of doubt if it remains indefinite as to the nature of its truth. (In other words, the thesis that the truth of a judgment is self-evident does not stand to reason. If it does not carry the assurance of its own truth along with itself then it is not certainly true. Thus, it involves an element of uncertainty. As it is doubtful to some extent so it comes within the province of a doubt in the wide sense). It has been proved that the truth of a judgment on its coming into being cannot be grasped. The truth of a judgment can neither be directly apprehended nor be indirectly known by inference. Hence, the thesis that a judgment cognizes its own truth is hard to establish.

The Refutation of the thesis that the conditions of a Judgment produce Its own Truth.

The Mīmāṁsakas put forward another thesis that the truth of a judgment owes its existence to no extra factor. Such a thesis is not tenable. Every effect has a cause responsible for its existence. But the truth of a judgment is also an effect. The said truth is a real entity but not an abstraction, manufactured by imagination. But it is not eternal but an event in time. Hence, it is an effect. As it is an effect, it does not owe its existence to itself. (The primary meaning of the Sanskrit sentence "Prāmāṇyasya svata utpattiḥ" is that the truth of a judgment originates from itself.) Hence, the above thesis in question is absurd so far as it is taken in its primary sense.

Now, the Mīmāṁsakas may revise their thesis and hold that the truth of a judgment does not depend upon an extra special quality of its cause apart from the conditions of its existence. They also hold that they do not subscribe to the view that the said truth being not an effect an extra quality of the cause is not responsible for its existence. Such a thesis is not also sound. A good effect cannot come into being if its cause does not possess an excellent property. As effect is either good or bad. Of these two the good one is produced by a qualified cause but the bad one is generated by a defective cause.

A cause which is neither qualified nor defective does not exist. Therefore a neutral effect i.e., an effect, which is neither good nor bad is impossible.

A cause, productive of a true judgment, produces its own effect, being assisted by an extra good quality belonging to it because it has causal property. In this syllogism, the cause of a true judgment, is the subject of inference. The production of its effect with the assistance of an extra good quality is the consequence. The causal property of the cause constitutes the reason. The cause of a false judgment is cited as its positive example. Or, another syllogistic argument may be put forward to prove the Nyāya thesis. A true judgment is produced by a cause which receives the assistance of an extra good quality over and above its natural property in order to produce it because it partakes of the character of an effect like a false judgment. Jayanta means to say that a true judgment is not generated by the bare cause of consciousness. As a false judgment is produced by the cause of consciousness in co-operation with some defect belonging to it so a true judgment should be the joint product of the same cause and some good quality belonging to it. As a defect is not a natural property of the cause so the good quality.

We learn from the medical science the excellent qualities of the sense-organs. The physicians prescribe medicine for the normal persons not to repair their diseased organ but to impart fresh vigour to them, i.e., to introduce a qualitative change into them. On the application of these medicines the sense-organs acquire a state of health much superior to that of their normal life. The people call this excellent state of health as free from defect. It is not a state of health, negatively determined, e.g., free from disease but positively qualified. No more disputation. Hence, the thesis of the Mīmāṁsakas that a true judgment does not depend upon as extra good quality of its cause for its coming into being, is not amenable to reason.

The third point in the thesis, put forward by the Mīmāṁsakas, is that the instrument of a true judgment depends upon nothing else to discharge its own function. Let us analyse this statement in order to make out the correct meaning of the term 'pramāṇa' which has been predicated above. Does it denote the assemblage of all conditions that are responsible for a true judgment ? Or, does it denote only the cause which is included in the totality of conditions ? Or, does it denote the resulting consciousness, i.e., a true judgment ? It is a truism that the collection of conditions independently produces its effect. This admission does not mean that the collocation is conscious of its own power. It depends on some other factor not included in itself for the knowledge of its causal efficiency. But the cause which is included in the collocation of conditions absolutely depends on the other co-operators in order to bring about its effect. A true judgment, being itself an effect cannot condition itself. True knowledge, being only an effect, has nothing to do. Hence, the question of dependence or of independence does not attract our reflective mind. But when the true knowledge implies a person to move it is definitely dependent upon his will. This is merely a brief criticism of the above thesis.

The Mīmāṁsakas have also held that the truth of a judgment is self-evident. A judgment independently determines its own truth. It depends upon no factor to do so. There are only two alternate courses open to us. Either the truth of a judgment is not at all determined or the truth of a judgment is determined only through the agency of some factor. No body can hold that the truth of a judgment is determined and such determination automatically takes place. With regard to this point we have already said that when the initial impellent judgment arises in our mind we do not definitely know that it is true. A true apprehension of blue is not so aware of its own truth as it is aware of the blue object. After a lapse of time the truth of it is rightly determined. Hence there is no chance of the automatic determination of the truth. It is ascertained to be true because it leads to a successful movement.

A judgment has a very short span of life. (It lasts only two kṣaṇas, i.e., minutest units of time). If we fail to determine its validity during its existence, how will it be possible for us to do the same later on ? It ceases to exist at that time. Hence, the truth of it cannot be determined. (This is, of course, the possible objection from the Mīmāṁsaka point of view), Jayanta meets this objection thus. He holds that this is a childish objection. The Mīmāṁsakas hold that the false judgment is transitory like the true one but its falsehood is extrinsically determined. A judgment is determined to be false only when the truth of its contradictory one is known as true at a later period. At that time the false judgment does not exist. How can the falsehood of a judgment be determined ? The Mīmāṁsakas may contend that though the judgment is dead and gone yet it may be recalled in memory and thus be judge. Or, they may hold that a judgment may be releventiy passed upon the several conditions that produce the judgement in question in the following manner that they are the source of a false judgment. This road is uniformly open to the Naiyāyikas to defend the thesis of extrinsic validity.

Jayanta meets other objections raised by the Mīmāṁsakas.

They take an exception to the thesis of extrinsic validity on the ground that if the truth of a judgment is determined later on then such determination is either open to the fallacy of mutual dependence of it is futile like the quest for a particular star after the shaving of head (like the placing of the cart before the horse). With regard to these objections the Naiyāyikas have got something to say. They classify the objects to be known under two broad classes, viz., transcendental and secular. Regarding the transcendental objects they are of opinion that when they are definitely known to be true the people move for their attainment. The fallacies of mutual dependence, vicious circle, etc., do not affect their thesis. But with regard to the ordinary objects of every day experience a person moves for their attainment when he does not determine the truth of the impellent judgment but thinks that the truth of it is highly probable. Again, he turns away from an object when he thinks that the falsehood of the impellent judgment is highly probable. The popular experience establishes the judiciousness of the Nyāya thesis. We have said this before. But the movement for an ordinary object does not presuppose the determination of the truth of the impellent judgment. Hence the Nyāya thesis is not open to the fallacy of mutual dependence. But the Naiyāyikas admit that the ascertainment of the truth of an impellent judgment after the successful movement is futile. But still such an ascertainment is purposeful to some extent. When a trustworthy person gives us an advice about an ordinary object we act up to his advice and move for it. We getting hold of the object, learn that the utterance of a reliable person is invariably true. Such a knowledge helps us in an indirect manner to determine the truth of the Vedas, the source of verbal knowledge, viz., other scriptures, etc. the source which deals with the transcendental objects. Though the determination of the truth of a judgment referring to an ordinary object is futile so far as its own object is concerned yet it has some worth, having an important part to play. Therefore, the Nyāya thesis is immune from all blemishes. Now, another question is raised. What is the meaning of the compound word 'pravṛtti-sāmarthya'? Because the Naiyāyikas hold that the determination of the truth of a judgment depends upon it (pravṛtti-sāmarthya). The old teachers of the Nyāya school explain it in the following two ways :—(1) Pravṛtti-sāmarthya is the confirmation of the knowledge of an object in its experienced order after its pragmatic test. (2) Or, the discovery of the unique property of an object is pravṛtti-sāmarthya. These two meanings do not come to us to be highly satisfactory. But the commentator on the Nyāya-sūtras explains it thus : The term 'pravṛtti' generally denotes movement. But the deeper meaning of it is the putting of the knowledge to a practical test. Sāmarthya means the experience of the actual result, i.e., the experience of the practical efficiency of the said object. In other words, if a judgment is put to the pragmatic test and satisfies the knower then it is true. The truth of a judgment is determined by the adoption of the pragmatic method.

Wherein lies the distinction of the knowledge of the practical efficiency of an object from a judgment referring to the object ? If there is no distinction between them as instances of knowledge then the truth of the former, being extrinsic, requires the services of another knowledge for its determination. The third one requires the services of a fourth one and so on ad infinitum. Hence, the Nyāya thesis is open to the fallacy of regressus ad infinitum. This point has been discussed before. Such a charge has not been appropriately brought against the Naiyāyikas since the human behaviour feels no urge to submit the truth of the knowledge of the practical efficiency of an object to a scrutiny. The truth of an impellent judgment is not to be tested in order to set him to doing. We move for an object and obtain it. Now, if it satisfies all our practical needs that are expected of it then there is no point in examining the truth of the experience of the effects of an object. Why does the fallacy of regressus ad infinitum vitiate the Nyāya thesis ? We do not raise the problem whether the knowledge of the effects of an object is valid or not because we never entertain a doubt about its validity. Let us take an example to clarify our point. We see water and judge that this is water. This judgment prompts us to move. But we also know that a similar judgment takes place even when we mistake the rays of the sun for water. Hence when a judgment that this is water arises in our mind a doubt about its validity naturally dawns in our mind. But a man is aware of the effects and uses of water only when he gets down into it. Hence such knowledge is always true. Therefore the truth of it is never questioned. As there is no doubt about its validity so no argumentation is required to establish its truth since a doubt is the mother of argumentation. Or, as we experience the specific forms of the practical efficiency of water so we determine the truth of the knowledge of them.

What is the exact nature of the specific form ? The acts of cleansing the impurities of a body, sipping, bathing, offering libations to gods and departed ancestors, washing the clothes, removing fatigue and heat and indulging in sports like swimming etc. and various other practical uses of water constitute the said specific nature which points to the truth of the experience of the practical efficiency of water. If a man has an illusory experience of water and proceeds to have it then he cannot perform all these acts by means of the water referred to by the false judgment. Now, it may be argued that all these acts are also performed by imaginary water in a dream. A fitting reply to this argument is that everybody is directly aware of the vivid distinction between waking consciousness and dream consciousness. Therefore, the argument of the opponent is not sound. When we are not under the sway of slumber, we all know that we remain awake and do not sleep. Thus, we all experience the distinction between waking and sleeping states. In our waking state no object other than real water is noticed to accomplish all those effects i.e. objects. Therefore, the very experience of the specific acts of water assures us of the truth of such an experience. Or, examining the nature of the cause of our experience we shall be in a position to determine the truth of the knowledge of the effects of an object, i.e. its practical efficiency. Śabara has also stated that if the conditions of an apprehension are thoroughly and carefully examined and no defect is found out then they are taken to be defectless since there is no proof to substantiate their defect. We, the Naiyāyikas, also subscribe to this view. An object to be apprehended has no defects such as unsteadiness, the similarity of an object to another object, the source of mistake etc., light has no defect such as dimness etc., the knower has no defect such as disturbance from hunger, thirst etc., and the eyes have no defect such as the detachment of the retina, etc, the weakness of lens etc. The Mīmāṁsakas themselves also admit that the knowledge of an object which is derived from that of its effect and from the instruction of a reliable person is true. Therefore, we have the definite knowledge that the awareness of the practical efficiency of an object is true because it is produced by the defectless conditions.

The Mīmāṁsakas come forward and review the hypothesis of the Naiyāyikas. They put to the Naiyāyikas the following question : (if this is your final view) why do not you scrutinize the conditions of the initial judgment which sets up motion ? Why do you examine only the conditions of the knowledge of practical efficiency. The Naiyāyikas give a fitting reply to them. They say, "Oh dear friends ! you do not think that the conditions of the initial impellent judgment have not been examined through an inadvertence. If they are examined then is the hypothesis of intrinsic validity established ? Does such an examination refute the hypothesis of extrinsic validity, proposed by us ? But when an impellent judgment arises in the mind of a person he becomes very much anxious to get at the fruit of his knowledge but exhibits no such eagerness for scrutinizing the conditions of his judgment. That is why the conditions of the knowledge of practical efficiency are thus examined. Thus, the truth of the initial judgment is established by means of the knowledge of the effect of its object. Is there any man who, leaving aside the proximate means, has recourse to the remote one ?"

No body doubts the truth of the knowledge of the practical efficiency of an object but on the contrary, every body knows it to be true because a doubt obeys a universal law in order to come into being. A doubt does never arise in the mind of a person if he has no previous knowledge of the two predicates of a disjunctive judgment. Let us take an example of a doubt "This is either a man or a post". A man who is ignorant of the fact that height is the common property shared by both the man and the post does not doubt the yonder object to be either a man or a post. Similarly, a person should know that the consciousness of height is the common property of the true and false judgments. Otherwise, he cannot doubt that it is either true or false. Whenever we have the knowledge of practical efficiency during our waking state we see that there is a perfect accordance of this piece of knowledge with its object. As there is no previous experience of discordance between the above piece of knowledge and its object so it is known only to be true. The present means of the determination of its truth will do the same function in future. Hence, the truth of the knowledge of practical efficiency will always be uniformly determined. Even when the truth of the knowledge of practical efficiency is not determined, the truth of the impellent judgment is determined on the basis of the former knowledge. But the truth of judgment is never self-evident. When a judgment comes into being nobody can recognize it to be either true or false because it bears no distinctive mark. And in the knowledge of practical efficiency no distinctive mark is noticed. Therefore, it should also be treated as an ordinary judgment.

Now, the Mīmāṁsakas may raise further objections to the thesis of the Naiyāyikas. Should the knowledge itself of the distinctive mark of an object be proved to be valid ? Or, does the truth of such knowledge remain unascertained ? If we answer the first question in the affirmative, the fallacy of regressus ad infinitum invalidates our assumption. If we answer the second question in the affirmative then we simply contradict our own statement and come to our wit's end. But all these arguments are merely samples of irrelevant talk because they are directly contradicted by our experience. We do not like to enjoy the devilish delight arising from the refutation of all these arguments. Thus we reiterate our conclusion that the knowledge of the practical efficiency of an object assures us of the truth of the impellent judgment. It has been stated in the Nyāya-bhāṣya that a man moves for an object when he rightly cognizes it and if his movement is crowned with success then his knowledge is proved to be true because of its accordance with its object. (At the outset the judgment, being not clouded by a doubt, is assumed as true and later on it is proved to be true). Similarly, the falsehood of a judgment is extrinsically determined. Hence, both the truth and the falsehood of judgments are extrinsically determined. We think that this hypothesis is better than the previous one.

A philosopher who is proud of his learning (Akalaṅka Bhaṭṭa, the Jaina Philosopher, has been referred to) holds that the truth of the knowledge of an object that has been frequently obtained when the knower has moved for it is self-evident and the truth of the knowledge of an object which has not been frequently obtained by the knower moving for it is extrinsically determined. But he holds that when an object has been frequently moved for and obtained the knowledge of such an object it is intrinsically true. He really does not follow what he preaches though his attention has been invited to his statement. Repetition literally means the doing of an act again and again. When it applies to the obtaining of an object it has a secondary sense. It signifies the frequent movement towards an object. When we very often perceive our body or the walls of our house or a post erected in our house, we have an opportunity of verifying our perception a thousand times by an actual movement. Thus, the truth of such perceptions has been established by the successful movement. The truth of such perceptions is not self-evident. The repetition which applies to the obtaining of an object can have no other sense. Hence, the statement of the above philosopher is an absurdity. Therefore, the validity of knowledge is extrinsically determined.

Some philosophers hold that the examination of the truth of knowledge cannot be logically held. Is its truth determined by a valid proof or by an invalid one? If it is done by a valid proof will the proof itself be examined or not? It is next to impossible to examine a proof. Hence a proof escapes an examination, and you hold that the truth of the resulting knowledge is to be tested by the untested proof. But it will be still better to hold that there is no need of verifying the resulting consciousness but our movement for all practical purposes will directly ensure from the proof because the former alternative suggestion is open to the fallacy of regressus ad infinitum. The hypothesis that the truth of a judgment is self-evident has been already discarded. A man moves for a secular object without examining the truth of the impellent judgment. But when he runs after a transcendental object he critically examines the truth of his impellent judgment beforehand. In other words, he must be sure of the truth of impellent judgment in the later case at the outset.

In fine, the truth of the Śāstras which deal with the means to the transcendental ends should be critically examined. We have arrived at the conclusion that the truth of such Śāstras is extrinsically but not intrinsically determined. There is no need of discussing the bad hypotheses which rest upon logic chopping and afflict our mind.

In order to refute the Doctrine of the extrinsic truth of a judgement the Hypothesis or non-Discrimination is substituted for the hypothesis of Misapprehension

The very learned section of the Mīmāṁsakas (i.e. the Prābhākaras) hold that it has been nicely done that the ill-trained Mīmāṁsakas have been defeated by the wicked logicians like the kāśa flowers, blown away by the gust of the wind at a great distance during the autumnal season. They do not know how to defend themselves as they subscribe to the hypothesis of misapprehension, i.e. in a judgment of illusion an absent predicate is asserted of the subject but at the same time they maintain that the truth of a judgment is self-evident.

How can we appreciate their skill in a logical approach? If the hypothesis of misapprehension is admitted then it is easy to come across such judgments as are contradicted. In that case it becomes truly unavoidable to call in question even the truth of such a judgment as has not been contradicted since all the judgments both contradictory and contradicted are alike because of their common property. If the truth of a judgment is doubtful then its verification by means of consilience etc., necessarily follows in the wake. Therefore, the conclusion that the truth of a judgment is extrinsically determined becomes inevitable.

The hypothesis of misapprehension is refuted because no judgment is contradicted

If no judgment is contradicted in the world then no knower should rationally doubt the truth of a judgment since it has no similarity to something which produces illusion. If no doubt as to the truth of a judgment arises in his mind then why should he look forward to some other judgment for its verification? The truth of a judgment becomes automatically self-evident.

Why is it that there is no such judgment as is contradicted? We all experience that there is a large number of instances of illusory judgments which are contradicted, for example, we mistake the mother-of-pearl for silver. The Mīmāṁsakas say "You are inexperienced in the science of logic since the judgments, cited by you, are incapable of being contradicted. Do you really understand the very meaning of your statement when you hold that, viz., a preceding judgment, is contradicted by a succeeding one? But we do not follow the meaning of the term 'contradiction'. If contradiction signifies destruction then it does not hold between the so-called pair of opposite judgments since every judgment is subject to destruction. In that case each judgment which is destroyed by its immediate successor should be contradictorily opposed to the latter since the relation of the destroyer and the destroyed holds between them according to the universal rule, applied to all judgments. If contradiction denotes the non-coexistence of the two judgments in the same locus at the same time then such an absurd conclusion will inevitably follow. It is a fact that the judgments which are never contradicted do not co-exist in the same locus at the same time.

Now, the Naiyāyikas may revise that hypothesis and hold that contradiction is the wiping out of the impression produced by the contradicted judgment. Such a hypothesis is also untenable. Because we know that even an impression, produced by a true judgment, is wiped away. Sometimes, an impression, produced by a contradicted judgment of illusion survives the counteracting force of a contradictory judgment, but does not fade away since the object referred to by a contradicted judgment, happens to be remembered after a lapse of time.

Now, the Naiyāyikas may hold that contradiction is such as takes away the object referred to by a judgment. In other words, contradiction takes place when it suggests that the contradicted judgment has not revealed an object which should have been revealed. It is impossible to apply such a meaning to contradiction. When an object has been revealed, it is beyond the power of a contradictory judgment to declare it as unrevealed. A contradictory judgment does not appear in our mind in a manner so that the object which has been known may become unknown at the very moment.

Now, the Naiyāyikas may hold that a contradictory judgment is one which points to the negation of such an object as is referred to by a preceding judgment. Does the contradictory judgment refer to the negation of an object as co-existent with the object negated or as subsequent to it ? It may be held that the contradictory judgment refers to the subsquent negation of an object and contradicts a preceding judgment which refers to the object negated. In that case, contradiction would take place between two such judgments as are free from contradiction. A jar existed at a spot. It has been destroyed at present by the stroke of mace. The judgment which refers to the negation of the jar, thus destroyed, would contradict the judgment which refers to the jar, as occupying a spot before its destruction. In that case the so-called contradictory and contradicted judgments will simultaneously arise in our mind. The implication of the negative one is that this is not a jar. The implication of both is that this is a jar and this is not a jar. Thus, this should be both positive and negative at the same time. In that case, which one would contradict and which one would be contradicted.

Now, contradiction may mean the annulment of the resulting form of a judgment. Such an annulment is not possible. As the resulting form of a judgment has come into being so it cannot be bodily removed from the field of consciousness. A contradictory judgment does never imply that the result which has come into being has not come into being.

Now, contradiction may be defined as the suspension of some particular remote consequence of a judgment of perception or some other form of knowledge viz. the resolution of avoiding or accepting the object referred to by the judgment. Such a definition is of no service since the above resolution is not a consequence of a judgment which is accepted to be true.

The volitional reaction which results in the actual rejection or acceptance of an object depends only upon the will of a person. If the volitional turn of mind is set at naught then the judgment which is at the root of it should not be contradicted.

The sum and substance of the above discussion is that there is no such thing as contradiction. There are also other reasons which point to the same conclusion. Does contradiction hold between two judgments having the same content or having the different contents ? The relation of contradiction does not hold between two such judgments as have the same content since we have no experience of contradiction in a series of judgments pointing to the same object. The relation of contradiction does not hold between two such acts of knowledge as refer to the different objects since the knowledge of a post is never contradicted by the knowledge of a jar. If a subsequent act of knowledge points to an object which is other than that which is referred to by its antecedent judgment then does it mean that the latter is contradicted by the former ?

Moreover, when the truth is assured of the preceding judgment it stands on a firm footing. But when a new judgment arises in our mind at a subsequent period it remains weak since its truth has not been established. If some experience is at all contradicted then the weak one should be reasonably contradicted by the strong one. In other words, the latter judgment should be contradicted by the former one. The Mīmāṁsakas mean to say that the former positive one should have contradicted the weak one i. e. the negative one since it has no firm footing in our mind. In other words, the truth of the former has been accepted as true and for this very reason it is stronger than the latter one. The former judgment should never be contradicted. But we have no such experience of contradiction. Hence, there is no such piece of knowledge as is contradicted. Hence, we are not entitled to entertain a doubt as to the truth of any judgment on the ground of its similarity to a contradicted judgment. As we cannot doubt the truth of a judgment so there is no need of applying the pragmatic test to a judgment for the determination of its truth. Hence, the hypothesis that the truth of a judgment is extrinsic does not hold good.

The hypothesis that illusion consists in misapprehension is refuted because it is baseless

Now, existence has been denied to contradiction. Should the illusory judgments such as 'This is silver' (the mother-of-pearl is mistaken for silver etc.) pass on as uncontradicted judgments ? (This question has been put by the Naiyāyikas to the Mīmāṁsakas of the Prabhākara school). A reply to this question is as follows : Oh dullards ! those judgments are not illusory because no cause whatsoever it may be, can be found out to explain their origination. A sense-organ cannot produce such judgments. If it had produced them then they would have constantly emanated from it. Even a defective cause cannot produce them. Such a cause exhausts all its potentialities to give birth to its own effects, fixed up by Nature. Hence, a heterogeneous effect will not be produced by it since it acquires no special efficiency by dint of its possession of defect to do so. The defective paddy of the *śāli species* would never have the efficiency of producing the Barley plant. Therefore, the so-called judgments of illusion are not really cases of misapprehension since no cause which will impart to them the character of mis-reading has been discovered.

The Naiyāyikas put a question to the Mīmāṁsakas. Is the knowledge of the mother-of-pearl as silver true ? The Prabhākaras give a reply to this question. They say "Oh fool ! 'This is silver' is not a single act of knowledge viz., an act of perception or an act of memory. This represents the perception of the shining object before us. The predicate silver represents the memory of silver experienced before. The knower has the impression of the experience of silver. When the shining object, the substantive of the above judgment is perceived, the impression of silver is excited by the law of similarity and the memory of silver is revived. A man who has never experienced silver cannot have the knowledge of silver in the form : 'This is silver'. If a man who has seen silver cannot recollect it at night or in the day if he misses to see the object as similar to silver".

Again, when we recollect an object but fail to locate it as a past event in time and space we hold that it is a case of mutilated memory. When memory is not recognised in its true character the distinction between memory and apprehension is not detected. The non-detection of difference is called non-apprehension (akhyāti).

As objects are revealed by the illusory experience so there are four rival hypotheses current among the contesting logicians. They are as follows : (1) misapprehension, (2) the presentation of the unreal, (3) projection of consciousness and (4) non-apprehension i. e. non-detection of distinction. Of these four hypotheses, the hypothesis of misapprehension has been discarded as there is no sufficient reason behind it.

The Hypothesis of Misapprehension is the Mongrel Offspring of the other Hypotheses

The hypothesis of misapprehension presupposes one of the three alternative hypotheses : (1) Silver which occupies some other time and space stimulates the sense organ to produce the consciousness of silver at this spot and at this time. (2) Or, the mother-of-pearl which conceals its own distinctive form and assumes the form of silver, produces the consciousness of silver. (3) Or, the stimulating object is one and its appearance is something different. The mother-of-pearl stimulates the eyes to produce consciousness but what appears is silver. Now, if the Naiyāyikas subscribe to the first alternative, viz., silver stimulates the eyes then the awareness of silver refers only to the unreal object. But it is not a case of misreading since the unreal silver is presented to such consciousness.

Now, the Naiyāyikas may contend that silver is real since it occupies some other time and space. But this contention is not tenable since silver, being at a remote time and space beyond the range of sense-organs, is as good as nothing.

Moreover, are existent time and space presented to our consciousness? Or, are the non-existent ones presented to our consciousness ? If with regard to the first alternative they answer in the affirmative then silver which is here and now has been presented. Hence, it should not be a case of illusion. If time and space are not present, i.e., be non-existent then they, like silver (absent), cannot stimulate the sense-organ to produce consciousness.

Now, the Naiyāyikas may plead their case in a different manner. They interpret the judgment "This is silver" in the following way : They hold that the memory supplies the knower with the predicate, i.e. silver. The predicate is wrongly referred to the mother-of-pearl as 'this', i.e., the subject of the said judgment. In other words, the judgment of memory that this is silver wrongly refers to the mother-of-pearl. It is a case of misreference. Let this view be examined. The Naiyāyikas hold that silver which is remembered is such an object as existed in the past. But how can a past object be referred to? Remembrance is nothing but consciousness. How does it refer to an unreal object? The Naiyāyikas may contend that as an act of recollection is not causally connected with an object so no object determines its character. Let this contention be examined. Let it be granted that memory is not produced by an object. Still, the other terms of consiousness bear resemblance to memory as all divisions of consciousness including memory are subsumed under the genus of consciousness. If this is true then it is difficult for the Mīmāṁsakas to agree with the Naiyāyikas in the point that in the judgment of memory "This is silver" such a predication takes place. The reason at the back of this note of dissent is this : How can the judgment of memory, which is not produced by an object, present an unreal object to consciousness? The reason is plain, viz., the act of memory is in no way connected with the object which is supposed to be presented by it. Now let us examine the second hypothesis. It amounts to this that the mother-of-pearl conceals its own form, assumes the form of silver and presents itself to consciousness. The Naiyāyikas strongly deny that it is not an illustration of the presentation of the unreal. Then it is indeed a novel drama in which the mother-of-pearl plays the part of Sītā. (The critic means to say that as an actor who is not Sītā creates the illusion in the mind of the audience that he is Sītā, so the mother-of-pearl which is not silver passes as silver.) Let us assume the suggestion of the Naiyāyikas and put this question to them.

Does this apprehension refer to the mother-of-pearl or silver? How do we truly know that the presentation of silver really points to the mother-of-pearl? They may reply that the awareness of silver, being contradicted, reveals the real object. Such a reply does not satisfy the critics. A contradictory judgment should not settle the object of the contradicted judgment in order to do justice to the problem in question. This much may be fairly admitted that a contradictory judgment negates the reality of the object referred to by the contradicted judgment. But the former cannot reveal the exact object of the latter. Moreover, if the knower be not in need of the object revealed by the illusory judgment then he will not run after it. In that case, there will be no occasion for the appearance of the corresponding contradictory judgment to contradict it. Now, which judgment will determine the real object of the above judgment? Hence, it is reasonable to hold that what is revealed by a judgment is its object. As silver is revealed by the above judgment so it is its object. The hypothesis that the mother-of-pearl conceals its own form etc. represents the opinion of a novice logician.

The third alternative hypothesis that the source of judgment is different from the object revealed by it is thus refuted. Those who explain the illusory judgment "This is silver" in the following way are in the wrong. They hold that the mother-of-pearl excites the sense organ to produce the judgment and what is presented to consciousness is silver. In this case, the mother-of-pearl cannot exert its influence upon the sense-organ because of its mere close proximity. The ground on which the mother-of-pearl stands is also similarly connected with the sense-organ because of its closeness.

What is presented to our consciousness should also objectively determine the judgment. It is strange to hold that the object which produces the judgment is different from that which is revealed by it. Therefore, silver which is revealed by the judgment is the object which produces the judgment that this is silver. If this is the conclusion which follows from the above discussion then the so-called misapprehension of silver does not differ from the presentation of unreal silver.

The refutation of the hypothesis that an unreal object is presented to consciousness

Is the hypothesis of the presentation of the unreal a better one ? Shall we accept it ? No, it is also untenable since it does not stand the test of reasoning. What does the phrase the presentation of the unreal signify ? Does it mean the awareness of an absolutely unreal object, i. e., the awareness of an object which exists nowhere ? Or, does it mean the consciousness of an object which exists somewhere but is absent from the present locus ? If the second alternative is accepted then the presentation of the unreal object amounts to the misapprehension of the real object since the logicians who uphold the hypothesis of misapprehension admit that silver does not exist in the present context but exists somewhere in the real universe. But nobody experiences an object which is absolutely unreal. The leaf of the sky-lotus-plant has never been experienced. Now, it may be contended that an unreal object is also presented to our consciousness since the impressions are regularly revived. Such a contention is not tenable since it is unreasonable to conjecture that the impressions of an unreal object remain stored up in our mind. The term *vāsanā* requires explanation. The impression which arises from the experience of a real object is called *vāsanā*. How does such a vāsanā revive the awareness of an unreal object ? (How does such a vāsanā owe its existence to the awareness of an unreal object ?) The upholders of the hypothesis of the presentation of an unreal object may subscribe to the view that this vāsanā is a class by itself and is also distinct from an impression. But they should explain why a particular vāsanā produces the awareness of silver but not of another unreal object since the unreal objects are not mutually distinct. Why does not the vāsanā which produces the knowledge of silver present the sky-lotus instead of it ? How is it possible that the law of presentation is obeyed by vāsanā ? We should not discuss the problem regarding the nature of vāsanā. An unreal object is absolutely impotent. Hence it cannot bear the burden of a true practical use. In other words, an absolutely unreal object has a place neither in the world of theory nor in the world of practice. Therefore, the hypothesis of the presentation of the unreal object is to be absolutely discarded.

The Refutation of the hypothesis that an Illusory Object is the projection of Consciousness

What does not exist is presented to our consciousness as a real one. Hence the hypothesis of the presentation of the unreal object is in no way superior to that of the misapprehension of an object. Therefore, the hypothesis that an illusory object is merely the projection of consciousness is better than that of an illusory one as framed by the other rival schools which propose that an external object is experienced. But the so-called external object cannot be proved to be an object of such experience. Therefore, consciousness itself plays the role of both the knower and the known.

The event of consciousness which apprehends as subject, projects itself as an external object and allows itself to be apprehended as an object. It is absolutely unrelated to the external objects but performs all the worldly transactions involving external objects. This is the essence of the hypothesis that the illusory object is nothing but the projection of consciousness. The refutation of the hypothesis under discussion is as follows : This hypothesis is also unsound. If consciousness plays the double role of the knower and the known then both the subject and the object are nothing but consciousness. In that case the consciousness should not express itself in the form "This is silver" but in the form "I am silver". Moreover, what is really an internal object is assumed to be appearing as an external object. Hence, the hypothesis of the projection of consciousness should turn to that of misapprehension. It also represents the presentation of the unreal object since the actual externalisation of consciousness is not possible. The upholders of this hypothesis may contend that the above criticism is pointless since consciousness is real. Such a contention does not hold good. The externality itself should be submitted to scrutiny. Let us see whether the alleged externality is real or not. The externality of conscious is not at all real since consciousness can never be external to itself. If the externality of consciousness is proved to be unreal then the hypothesis in question is virtually the view that the unreal object is presented to our consciousness.

The Hypothesis that an illusion consists in the Non-Discrimination of the two separate Acts of Knowledge is proved to be True in order to establish the hypothesis that Knowledge is Intrinsically True.

The above three hypotheses, viz., the projection of consciousness, the presentation of an unreal object and the misapprehension of an object interpenetrate one another. They also involve a logical contradiction. The hypothesis of non-discrimination is the best of all. The hypothesis which cannot be refuted by the upholders of the above three hypotheses is that of non-discrimination. In the hypothesis of the projection of consciousness it does not reveal itself as consciousness since it divides itself and reveals itself as an object i.e., something other than consciousness. The hypothesis of the unreality of an object is also based upon a wrong assumption since no object is presented to our consciousness as unreal. If our experience had recorded its evidence in favour of the above hypothesis then there would have been no incentive to our movement for practical purposes, i.e., for the attainment of the object of knowledge etc. The hypothesis of misapprehension is tenable if the object which is misapprehended is within the field of vision. But it overdoes when it holds that the object which lies outside the field of perception and does not produce consciousness is presented to consciousness. No critical thinker can indeed agree to the proposal. Thus the upholders of the hypothesis of misapprehension have accepted the suggestion that the object which is recalled in memory produces consciousness. Thus the remembrance of silver becomes unavoidable in order to explain the illusory judgment that this is silver. The memory of silver does not express itself in its true colour in the above judgment since the judgment does not assume the form of self-consciousness "I remember silver".

As the memory of silver and such other acts of memory assume an obscure form, so the logicians describe such indistinguishable memory as fading or indistinct or having lost its mark of distinction. The suggestion that memory assumes an indistinct form has been also accepted by the logicians of the rival schools. When an object which has been frequently inferred is inferred by means of a very familiar mark we implicitly remember the invariable relation of concomitance, belonging to the mark. The above implicit remembrance of the universal relation lacks the distinguishing feature of its specific kind.

The non-recognition of indistinct memory is called *akhyāti* (the term has been explained as non-discrimination). This form *akhyāti* has been used here in a privative sense. It means a failure to quote apprehension of an object.

Thus we see that all the contesting parties will not take an exception to the sense of akhyāti as described above. But the school of the Prabhākaras has eclipsed the fame of all other logicians having been able to give such meaning of the term as is accepted by all.

Now, a possible question arises in our mind with regard to the hypothesis of non-discrimination. How does the judgment "This is silver" illustrate non-discrimination ? The reason behind the question is this that 'this' refers to the substratum in front of us and reveals it in true character and though the predicate 'silver' is supplied by the unidentified, indistinct memory yet it is not possible to identify 'this' with 'silver' due to non-discrimination. An answer to this question is as follows : The yonder object, i.e., the substratum in question, is not clearly apprehended as the mother-of-pearl. If it had been clearly apprehended then there would have been no illusion in our mind.

The yonder object, i.e., the substratum in question, is presented to our consciousness only as a shining one. Silver is recalled in our memory owing to the operation of the law of similarity since the shining object, now cognised, is similar to silver. There are two distinct acts of consciousness, viz., the perception of the substratum in question and the remembrance of silver. But though they really differ from each other yet they are not mutually distinguished as such. Hence non-discrimination in the shape of a failure to detect their mutual distinction takes place. Therefore the term *akhyāti* does not denote the absolute negation of consciousness. The act of perception should always maintain its distinction from the act of remembrance since the object perceived is different from the object recalled in memory. The implication of this argument is that the judgment "This is silver" as interpreted by the Prabhākaras is inadmissible. The reply, given by the Prabhākaras is that if the distinction of the two separate acts of consciousness is not detected then can the non-detection of difference point to anything but to the identity of the indiscernible.

The hypothesis of non-discrimination does not justify itself if it takes its stand upon the above experience. The above judgment implies the identity between the subject and the predicate. In other words, what is this is silver. Does not this wrong detection of identity suggest the hypothesis of misapprehension? The objectors mean to say that the mother-of-pearl is wrongly interpreted as silver. The Prabhākaras meet this objection thus: The knower moves for silver because he fails to distinguish the perception of the mother-of-pearl from the remembrance of silver. As the two acts of consciousness are not distinguished so the knower identifies them, having subsumed them under the common genus of consciousness. This conclusion is arrived at when the problem is solved by the method of back calculation. This is the explicit statement of Prabhākara logic on this point.

(Some logicians apprehend that the two substrata of the two acts of consciousness are not known to be identical at the outset since such an admission is sure to lead to the hypothesis of misapprehension.) Thus they intend to modify the Prabhākara hypothesis to some extent. They hold that the two distinct acts of consciousness are not cognized to be different in the beginning. In the next moment they are cognized as identical. But we do not appreciate the merit of thus modified hypothesis.

If the identity between the two acts of consciousness is cognized then the hypothesis of non-discrimination will surely lose its ground and the hypothesis of misapprehension will be stated in an indirect manner.

Now, another question arises in our mind if we subscribe to the hypothesis of misapprehension. It runs thus: The contradictory judgment that this is not silver contradicts the antecedent judgment that this is silver. Such contradiction is experienced as a matter of fact. How is it to be explained by the Prabhākaras who uphold the hypothesis of non-discrimination.

The rejoinder to this question from the Prabhākara standpoint is as follows: Oh fools! You are not conversant with the true character of consciousness. We do not hold that the character of silver is at first attributed to this and that the contradictory judgment negates the attribution. But we hold that the contradictory judgment does not reveal such distinction as has not been detected before. 'This' does never signify silver. What is denoted by 'this' is not silver. This is always this and silver is always silver. There is no exception to this rule. It has been stated by the contradictory judgment that this is something else and silver is something other than silver. The difference between the two acts of consciousness is recognized by means of this contradictory judgment.

Now, another question with regard to the above hypothesis arises in our mind. The judgment "This is silver" may perfectly illustrate the non-detection of difference between the act of perception and that of remembrance. But how can the Prabhākara explain an illusory experience in a dream from the standpoint of non-discrimination ? (The objector means to say that the dream-experience does not arise from the failure to distinguish the act of perception from that of remembrance but only represents a single act of consciousness) The Prabhākaras meet this objection thus : Oh timid fellows ! critically judge the nature of your dream-experience.

Sometimes, the distinction of the act of remembrance from that of perception is not cognized. But the dream-experience is entirely constituted by remembrance the specific character of which is not recognized.

How will the Prabhākaras explain the above experience in terms of remembrance since it is not conditioned by the awareness of a similar object ? Such an objection does not hold good because the fact of remembrance is not determined by a single condition but by a plurality of such conditions. The inner organ which is over-powered by the contaminating influence of slumber is of course one of the conditions of remembrance. Even if we accept this answer then will the Prabhākaras solve the problem, viz., "How are the vision of the two moons and the experience of bitterness in sugar explained in terms of indistinct memory ? Oh fool of consumed brain ! Why do you not follow the Prabhākara argument though it is repeated to you again and again ?

The Prabhākaras hold that all cases of the so-called illusion are not explained in terms of the indistinct memory. But they admit that every case of such illusion is due to the non-detection of difference. In some cases, the so-called illusion consists in the indistinct memory-image. In some other cases, the act of remembrance is not distinguished from that of apprehension. But there are a few cases when the objects which are actually recalled in memory are not so cognized. In some other cases, the faculty of vision is divided into twain, being affected by certain diseases such as diplopia, etc. The organ of sight, being thus divided, cannot behold the single moon as such. There are other cases where the organ of taste, i.e., the tongue, coming in touch with the flow of bile experiences the bitter taste. Though the tongue is in contact with sugar yet it fails to experience sweetness belonging to sugar.

In this way the judgment that conch-shell is yellow is else explained.

In fine, the so-called illusory judgment is nothing but a failure to detect the difference between the two acts of knowledge. An illusory judgment is not such as does not accord with facts. An illusory judgment which does not so accord raises doubt as to the truth of a judgment.

One who does not doubt the truth of a judgment does not depend upon the accordance of a judgment for the ascertainment of its truth. So we do not subscribe to the hypothesis that the truth of a judgment is extrinsic.

As the truth of a judgment is intrinsic so the truth of the Vedas is self-evident. Thus the truth of the Vedas is not determined by means of the two negative conditions, viz., (1) the non-contradiction of the subject matter of the Vedas and (2) the absence of defects in the author.

The establishment of the hypothesis of Misapprehension in order to probe the hypothesis that the Truth of a judgment is Extrinsic

The hypothesis of non-discrimination is being refuted by the following arguments : It has been stated that in case of the so-called illusion there are two distinct types of consciousness, viz., (1) apprehension and (2) remembrance and they are not mutually distinguished but cognized as a single act of knowledge. Such a statement is not based upon sound logic since the judgment of illusion is intuited by us as a unit of knowledge like an act of recognition. What is a shining substratum in front of us is silver. This is the distinct manner in which it is perceived. What remains in front of us is silver. This perception resembles the true perception of silver. Silver is not presented to our consciousness as an object experienced before but as an object which is being experienced at present Remembrance is such consciousness as reveals an object which has been experienced before. But it does not reveal an object which is being experienced now. The Prabhākaras hold that consciousness itself is self-illuminating, i.e., self-conscious. It should be carefully examined in which form the awareness of silver presents itself to our consciousness. If it presents itself as an act of memory then their assumption that the act of remembrance assumes the non-recognizable defective form goes in vain. Again, if it presents itself in the garb of an apprehension then it is a clear case of misapprehension since remembrance appears as an apprehension. Now, the Prabhākaras may contend that the consciousness of silver reveals itself as a non-specific act of consciousness. Such a contention is not sound. As the act of consciousness refers to silver as its object so it is either apprehension or remembrance since an object-consciousness cannot but belong to either of these two classes. It should not also be held that it is a piece of vague consciousness which fails to reveal an object since it is introspected by self-consciousness and suggests, this consciousness cannot be identified with that of a person in a dreaming state. Moreover, the object-consciousness which reveals silver is in no way different from the self-consciousness illuminating 'this'.

The subject and the predicate of the judgment that this is silver are revealed by the same consciousness. Now, how do you distinguish the consciousness of the subject as an act of perception from that of the predicate as an act of remembrance ? 'This' which is revealed should be properly interpreted. If the piece of the mother-of-pearl with all its characteristic feature is presented to our consciousness then there is no chance of the remembrance of silver with the dawning of the above perception. If the perception of the said object provokes the memory of another similar object in obedience to the law of similarity then the remembrance of the object does not remain indistinguishable from the act of perception which excites it. If we perceive Devadatta and remember another person, his similar, then we have no confusion between these two distinct acts.

The awareness of this reveals only the non-specified substratum but not the piece of the mother-of-pearl. If the Prabhākaras subscribe to the above hypothesis, we feel the least hesitation to accept it. Let us now trace the growth of the judgment "This is silver". In the beginning we perceive the piece of the mother-of-pearl as characterized by the property which is common to it and silver. This perception excites such a common impression as is not incompatible with it. The impression, being excited, revives the memory of such specific property as is not incompatible with the above general property. As this specific property is recalled in memory in the said manner so the judgment, "This is silver" becomes possible. The above general property is at the root of the presentation of the specific property. The judgment implies that what is this silver. Thus, it suggests identity between this and silver. A person who is in need of silver moves for it when he thinks that he perceives silver. (Jayanta does not mention all the intermediate steps that lead to the judgment of illusory perception. It is not a case of normal perception. It is really knowledge by complication.)

Very well, the Prabhākaras have held that a knower moves for an object when he fails to draw a distinction between apprehension and remembrance. It has reached our ears that this idea has been borrowed from the school of Dharmakīrti. Dharmakīrti holds that a person moves for an object which is a combination of sensed and imaginary matters. The Prabhākaras are hard hit with this plagiarism. A man does not move for an object as long as he is not convinced of the fact that the perceptible object has been sensed by him. How can a person who is in need of silver go for it unless he strongly believes that he has perceived silver ? Therefore, it must be admitted that such a movement presupposes the perception of silver but not the indistinct memory of silver.

Now, the Prabhākaras have remarked that the upholders of

the hypothesis of misapprehension admit the conditionality of the recollection of a silver in the production of the Judgment that this is silver. This remark is partially true. The Naiyāyikas admit that the specific property of silver is recollected. Let us illustrate our point of view. When a substratum in front of us comes within the range of our vision we perceive it only along with its such general properties, e. g., its height, etc. as are shared in common by the two objects. Then the distinguished feature of the above two objects is recalled in our memory. A doubt follows in the wake of the above remembrance. Similarly, when we behold the substratum before us we simply perceive its non-distinguishing general character such as its brightness but not its distinguishing feature. Then, we remember the characteristic feature of silver with the result that we misread the yonder object as silver. Thus, the illusory judgment that this is silver flashes in our mind. The difference between a doubt and an illusion lies in this that a doubt is preceded by the recollection of the characteristic feature of the two objects whereas an illusion is preceded by the recollection of the distinguishing feature of a single object. Therefore, one who has no previous experience of silver cannot have the illusory judgment that this is silver. Again, if he does not behold a similar object such as a piece of the mother-of-pearl at dead of night then he cannot mistake any other object for silver. Though memory plays some part in the production of the above judgment of illusion yet this does not mean that memory alone constitutes the whole of it. One should not keep silence on this point only with the mention of memory since an illusion based upon memory is also experienced by us. Therefore, we, Naiyāyikas rather appreciate the truthfulness of the neo-Prabhākaras who hold that the illusory judgment follows in the wake of memory since they do not conceal the evidence of their experience.

The bad argumentation of the Prabhākaras regarding the cause of illusion has been refuted by the sound logicians.

If an effect is cognized as being produced by a particular cause then it is useless to discuss whether the particular cause is competent enough to bring about the particular effect.

An effect cannot come into being without being caused. When an effect takes place a cause is to be postulated. The cause of an illusory judgment has been already assumed. It is the defective sense-organ. Likewise the sense-organ accompanied by the existing impression is the cause of recognition.

We admit that the barley plants do not grow out of the defective śāli seeds. But still bad cakes are prepared from them.

In fine, we hold that the sense-organ, i. e., the eyes, being defective, is not able to grasp the peculiar shape of the mother-of-pearl, viz., its triangular shape. It visualises merely the common property, i. e., its brightness. Its awareness revives the memory of the characteristic feature of silver. The sense-organ in question in co-operation with the said memory produces the illusory judgment that this is silver. The sense-organ is relatively defective. When the sense-organ which produces illusion is judged from the point of view of a true knowledge it is called defective. If it is judged from the side of its own effect then it is a proper cause but not a defective one. Hence, the illusory judgment that this is silver is an instance of perceptual apprehension but not an instance of half-lost memory.

Now, let us see what is implied by the contradictory judgment that this is not silver. It negates such silver as has been apprehended before. In other words, it clearly signifies that what has been perceived by me is not silver. What is attributed is negated. What has not been experienced before is not attributed. If an object which is not attributed is negated, why is gold like silver not negated?

The Prabhākaras have given a different meaning to the said contradictory judgment. They hold that it clearly distinguishes apprehension from memory unrecognized before. It is really no explanation of the contradictory judgment. It is merely a play on words since it does not get the sanction of experience. The contradictory judgment does not suggest that the undifferentiated consciousness is differentiated. This point is too insignificant to deserve a long discussion. Hence, the memory of silver does not take place in connection with the illusory judgment that this is silver. The Prabhākaras may contend that silver is remembered because it was experienced some time in the past. In that case silver is recalled in memory in accordance with the normal laws which govern the occurrence of memory. But nobody is aware of its existence. Such memory cannot also be held to be supernormal for obvious reasons. When a person sees in a dream that his head has been cut off he should be ashamed of the statement that this experience involves the memory of such a fact as has not been experienced before. It may be contended that he experienced the cutting off of his own head in the previous birth. Such a contention has no worth at all. Why does he remember a particular incident of his past life? Is this memory governed by a law? How is it that a particular incident among the experienced ones is recalled in memory only at a particular period of time to the exclusion of the other ones? How is it that all experienced incidents are not remembered at all times?

The Prabhākaras put some questions to the Naiyāyikas. They run thus : If you discard the hypothesis that an unreal object is presented to consciousness, how do you explain the above dream-experience Which object does it refer to? The reply to the above questions is as follows : You will listen to the answer which will be given by us. But in a nut-shell we say now that the unreal object is never presented to consciousness. But we do never hold that an object which has never been experienced cannot be cognised.

Now, the Prabhākaras may put a question to the Naiyāyikas "if the object is not experienced by you how do you know that it is real." The answer to this question is this that though an object may not be experienced by a person yet it may be experienced by somebody else and thus may be called as real. An object which has been experienced by a person is not remembered by another person. Hence the Prabhākaras cannot explain a dream-experience in the same manner as the Naiyāyikas do. In other words, the explanation of the dream-experience as suggested by the Prabhākaras does not have the same merit as that of the Naiyāyikas.

The thesis of the Prabhākaras that the dream experience is representative by its nature but its representative character is not grasped by us should be thoroughly examined. Let us see the form which it acquires. If it attires itself in the garb of some other form of consciousness then it will be a clear case of misapprehension. If the Prabhākaras hold that the dream-experience is not at all cognied then dream would be the same as deep slumber is. It is a fact that we have some experience when we dream. But one cannot hold that the whole of dream-experience consists only of memory which remains ever obscure. Thus the Prabhākaras hope against hope to establish the thesis that memory assumes a mutilated form so that it is not recognised. How does the thesis of non-discrimination gain ground as the single moon is some times presented to our consciousness as the two moons.

The Prabhākaras may contend that when the eye-rays are divided into twain the single moon is not seen as such.

The Naiyāyikas take an exception to this defence. They hold that the eye-rays, being diseased, may not visualise the moon as one. But Oh Vedic scholar, how shall we conceal the fact that the double vision of moon is illusory? Now, the Prabhākaras may contend that the eye-rays, being divided, have the number 'two' and the perceiver fails to grasp the said number as belonging to its proper locus. Thus, they explain the said illusion in terms of non-discrimination. This explanation does not hold good since the eyes and their rays are always supersensuous.

When we behold the single moon do we perceive that the rays of the eye are one? But it is a fact that nobody will perceive that the ray of the eye is one since the eye-ray itself remaining supersensuous, reveals the object.

Now, if the Prabhākaras subscribe to this view then they should admit that the above case of valid perception is an instance of non-discrimination.

Moreover, they have explained the illusory judgment "Sugar is bitter" in terms of non-discrimination. They hold that bitterness is tasted but a person fails to taste it as belonging to bile. Such an explanation is as futile as the attempt of a drowning man who catches at a straw in order to save him.

The critics will not mind if the Prabhākaras hold that a person senses bitterness, assign a place to it, viz., sugar? The critics fail to understand it.

The excess of bile which remains deposited in a senseorgan is supersensuous like the eye-disease called diplopia. But it produces illusion, though undetected, as undetected fever causes headache. There is no need of pushing forward this topic any further.

Thus, we see that every case of illusion cannot be explained in terms of nondiscrimination. It should also be noted that the hypothesis of non-discrimination does not strike at the root of the hypothesis that the truth of a judgment is extrinsic.

In the judgment "This is silver" the predicate 'silver' may be supplied either by apprehension or by the mutilated memory. Thus, the truth of the judgment is called in question.

In order to ascertain the truth or otherwise of a doubt the standard of accordance is to be applied. When the truth of a judgment is determined by a reference to accordance with facts it is extrinsic.

Otherwise, the truth or otherwise of a doubt cannot be ascertained. The Prabhākaras cannot gainsay it. In fine, as the truth of a judgment refers to accordance for its determination so it is extrinsic.

The upholders of the hypothesis of non-discrimination believe that it is an antidote to the theory that the world has no reality. Such a belief is baseless. Memory plays on important part in the former hypothesis. Memory is not true as it is not produced by a real object. When our parents are dead and gone and their bodies are consumed, we have their memory. The implication of the theory of non-discrimination is that every judgment is true. Therefore, the world is real. But the upholders of the unreality of the world prove their thesis, illustrating the above memory which is based upon the unreal objects. The mere denial of an illusion cannot refute the thesis of the Śūnyavādins (the upholders of the unreality of the phenomenal world).

If it is held that there is a sound argument which counteracts the hypothesis that the truth of a judgment is not self-evident. The Śūnyavādins also approve of this trend of thought. Such a statement is not fair. If the critics were sincere then they should have straightly put forward the argument and discussed the matter. Why do they bring in the hypothesis of non-discrimination and discuss it ?

The main defect from which the hypothesis of non-discrimination suffers is this : As the true object which a judgment refers to has been ignored so the hypothesis of non-discrimination has been based upon a weak foundation. Thus, what has been stated goes contrary to experience. Therefore, their carelessness is strongly condemned.

It has been nicely stated : The spear has been only broken. But the god of love—against whom it was directed has not been killed. You have simply disgraced yourself but the object has not been accomplished. In other words, the Prabhākaras have not been able to prove the hypothesis of non-discrimination—the task undertaken by them. But in order to do it they have simply contradicted experience.

The upholders of the hypothesis of misapprehension may put forward three alternative suggestions in order to justify their hypothesis. These suggestions have been refuted one after another. But they have not been fairly refuted. Silver is the object which is revealed by the judgment "This is silver". Let us take it to be the first of the three alternative suggestions. Now, the critics subject this suggestion to severe criticism. They hold that silver is not present there but if it is the object of the said judgment and is revealed by it then the judgment in question involves the presentation of an unreal object. These critical remarks are not very sound since though silver is absent here yet it is present somewhere else. But those who hold that an absolutely unreal object is presented to consciousness assert that the object of an illusory judgment exists in no space and in no time. It does not exist in past, present and future times. It is absolutely unreal. Therefore, we do not feel the necessity of thinking that such an unreal object exists in some other country.

Now, the following question is put to the upholders of misapprehension. How is an absent object which is misread presented to our consciousness ? Jayanta says in reply to this question. "What shall we do if such an object is presented to our consciousness ?".

But an object which belongs to no time and occupies no space has never been experienced as yet like the sky-lotus.

The difference between an absolutely unreal object and an object which is absent from a particular space lies in this that the former has been never experienced nor will be, but the latter is experienced.

If an object is absent from a spot, how does it produce its perception at the spot ? Again, if it does not produce perception, how is it revealed by perception? Our answer to these questions is as follows: Even if we have mal-observation of an object, it provokes the memory of another object similar to it. The object thus recollected is somehow presented to the illusory judgment of perception. As an animal which is required at a spot is brought there with a noose tied round its neck so an object which is absent from a spot but is presented to our consciousness is not acquired to be physically present there. When an object is revealed within it makes us aware of the fact that it belongs to the outer world. Such presentation does not mean that we project our consciousness or we perceive an unreal object. The reason behind this statement is this that the object is perceived as distinct from the act of perception and that the presentation of an absolutely unreal object does never take place. Therefore, the mother-of-pearl, either concealing its form or attiring itself in the garb of another, is presented to our consciousness. This is the second alternative suggestion which may cling to in defence of our hypothesis of misapprehension.

But an objection to this suggestion has been raised before. The player who plays the part of Sītā in a drama makes necessary changes in dress. Does the mother make such a necessary change in its dress ? If it does not do then how is it referred to by the judgment "This is silver ?" We should not be laughed at if we say that we have witnessed the drama in which the mother-of-pearl plays the above part. We hold that what appears to be silver is really the mother-of-pearl. The substratum which stands in front of us reminds us of a particular piece of silver by virtue of its shining character bearing a close resemblance to that of silver. The substratum, without being characterized by its specific property is presented to consciousness. Something which is in front of us is apprehended to be silver. As a matter of fact, the specific property of the mother-of-pearl, viz., its triangularity, etc. is not detected. So, the mother-of-pearl is described as an object which conceals its own form. Again, as the remembrance of silver follows in the wake of its perception so it is called that it attires itself in the garb of silver. A large number of judgments of illusory perception is due to a defect in the object or a defect in the sense-organ. The following examples such as the mother-of-pearl appearing as silver, the rays of the sun being mistaken for water, the cloud being taken for the city of the Gandharvas, a piece of rope being taken as a snake, the vision of double moons, the conch shell being perceived as yellow, sugar being tasted to be bitter, the perception of a loose tuft of hair floating in the air, etc. illustrate the above class of illusion. This type of illusion takes place when an object which produces perception is misread as another. There is another type of illusion which is objectless. It owes its existence to a defect in the internal organ. There is no case of misreading. What is presented to consciousness is entirely supplied by memory.

The third alternative suggestion is this :-

The ālambana of a judgment is one thing but what is presented to consciousness is something else. This view is held by some logicians of the Nyāya School. What is an ālambana? Does it signify the object that is very adjacent to the perceiving mind? In that case the ground upon which the object is located should also be apprehended as an ālambana. If an ālambana is defined as an object which produces an awareness then the sense-organ such as the eyes should also be called an ālambana. But if it is defined as that which couses an awareness, becomes at the same time the object of such awareness and is referred to by the demonstrativa pronoun 'this', then the definition is free from all defects.

Now, a problem arises in our mind, viz., "What is an ālambana either of the illusory judgment that there are two moons in the sky or of the judgment that there is a tuft of loose hairs before the eyes?" A certain disease which is called 'timira' resides in the eye-ball and looks like a collection of loose hairs. The same disease divides the eye-rays into twain. The eye-rays, being detached from each other, separately behold the moon. Thus, one and the same moon is visualised as two. There is another form of timira disease which manifests another symptom. 'Timira' like smoke or fog takes shelter in pores of retina and stands in the way of the continuous flow of the eye-rays. The eye-rays come out in a scattered manner. When they come in contact with the rays of the sun, they appear as a collection of loose hairs. They become the source and object of the illusory perception since when the sun is not up or is down, such an illusory perception does not take place.

The white clouds constitute the source and object of the illusory perception of the city of the Gandharvas since they appear sometimes as a house, sometimes as a palace and sometimes as a rampart. Hence, the above three suggestions are the defectless supports of the hypothesis of misapprehension.

Another objection has been raised against the hypothesis of misapprehension that the hypothesis of the projection of consciousness and that of the presentation of an unreal object encroach upon the hypothesis in question. In other words, these three hypotheses interpenetrate one another and hence lack the mark of individual distinction. Of these three hypotheses the two hypotheses, put forward by the Buddhists, viz., the hypothesis of the projection of consciousness and that of the presentation of an unreal object will be refuted in the chapter on Apavarga where the thesis of Subjective Idealism will be rejected. Hence, there is no need of discussing the character of these two hypotheses. Thus, the charge of interpretation has been answered.

The prabhākaras have stated that they alone can claim the distinction of original thinking since the hypothesis of mutilated memory which has been contributed by them has been accepted by all of the contesting parties. With regard to this claim let the other parties give their own verdict. But we can say this much that the remembrance of silver precedes the illusory perception of silver. The memory of silver produces the illusory judgment that 'this is silver' due to knowledge by complication. In this judgment silver is the predicate. This is the process of the illusory perception of silver in a nutshell. In order to describe it we have, of course, admitted the efficacy of the hypothesis of the incomplete expression of memory, i.e., the hypothesis of mutilated memory. But our intellect does not stop here. We also admit that we are aware of the experience of silver. The hypothesis of mutilated memory is not the only peg upon which the theory of illusion is suspended. Therefore, we arrive at the conclusion that the hypothesis of misapprehension is immune from all defects.

The Prabhākaras have discussed various definitions of contradiction. Somebody defines it to be non-coexistence. Others define it as the wiping out of the impressions. Similar other definitions have been discussed. As the Naiyāyikas accept none of them, so let them be rejected by the Prabhākaras. Hence, the critics cry in the wilderness as their criticism is really pointless. They vainly dry up their throat. Now, let the term 'viṣaya-apahāra' (meaning literally, the taking away of the object) signify contradiction. It does not mean that the object which has been cognized has not been experienced. But it conveys the meaning that the object which has been cognized before has not existed at the time of its experience. It does not suggest at the same time that the object which has been experienced before is now non-existent, being destroyed. If it had conveyed such a meaning then in every case of its contradicted experience the knowledge of the non-existence of its object would have been true like the knowledge of the non-existence of a jar which had been cognized before but was destroyed afterwards by the stroke of a mace. Now, another apprehension arises in our mind. When an object exists at a spot but we commit a mistake that it does not exist, does the object possess the two imcompatible predicates, viz., existence and non-existence ? In other words, should we suppose that the object exists and does not exist at the same time since contradiction does not deduct anything from the predicative character of an object ? Such an apprehension should not be entertained since when we have definite knowledge of contradiction, the predicate of the substantive known before, is cancelled. We knew an object as silver at that time. But we now know that it is not silver but something else. This is what contradiction does.

Now, another question arises in our mind. Every phenomenon of awareness reveals only an object which is compresent with it. If this is the case then how can a subsequent judgment which contradicts an antecedent one imply that the object referred to by the latter was then absent ? What shall we do ? Because a judgment is born with such an innate function. When a jar is broken we know that it does not exist. Unlike it when a contradictory judgment arises in our mind we know that the object referred to by the opposite judgment did not exist at the time of its occurrence. We shall prove later on in the section on the refutation of the doctrine of universal flux that an object which is confined only within the bounds of present time is cognised.

Let us now consider the next definition of contradiction. Contradiction is such as sets at naught the resultant form of a knowing process. The judgment that the object which is being known is avoidable or acceptable is the resultant form of a knowing process. This point has been discussed in the section on the difinition of perception. The knowing process is surely contradicted because its resultant form is discredited. Now, a question may be put to us, viz., "How does a contradictory judgment dispense with the resultant form ?"

An answer to this question is this :—

If it completes its task while it sings or dances or repeats some sacred incantations or offers libation to fire then it requires no other intermediate process to realize its object. If it is held that an end is not directly attained and a chain of intermediate means awaits in the path which leads to the destination then how can we fix up the limit to such means ? How do we pass on from one means to another ? Another intervening means is required and so on *ad infinitum* In other words, if we admit that under no circumstances a goal is directly reached then the fallacy of *regressus ad infinitum* will surely discredit the very assumption itself. In fine, we should not doubt the efficacy of the above hypothesis raising unimportant questions. When a contradictory judgment arises it sets aside the resultant form of the opposite experience. Hence the latter experience is said to be contradicted.

Some object to the above conclusion on the ground that contradiction takes place when the object is one and the same and that it does not take place when the objects are different. But such an objection is not fair. They have taken a wrong view of contradiction. Contradiction is not applicable to Reality, i.e., to the objects known by us. Contradiction is confined within the sphere of judgments. A judgment is contradictorily opposed to another when the subjects of these two judgments are one and the same but their predicates are incompatible with one another. These predicates are asserted to be incompatible because they refer to such objects as are incompatible with one another. Now a question arises in our mind, viz., if an object is known to be possessed of variegated colour then why does not this judgment involve a contradiction? The answer to the question is this:—There is contadiction in the judgment because the subsequent judgment does not appear, cancelling the antecedent one. Many different attributes may belong to one and the same substratum. They are also known to co-exist harmoniously. There are judgments in which many different predicates are asserted to the same subject but none of them is incompatible with the other. There is no contradiction in the above judgment referring to the variegated colour because the subsequent judgment comes into being without negating the prior judgment in question.

It has been stated that the antecedent judgment being well established, the negating subsequent judgment which is a new comer on the field should be counteracted. But it is reasonable to hold that the subsequent judgment contradicts the antecedent one since cancelling the former, the latter appears. Moreover, the subsequent judgment alone contradicts the antecedent one since it correctly refers to the object of knowledge and is strengthened by some other proofs. Thus, the relation of contradiction holds between the two judgments. Again, if we subscribe to the hypothesis of misapprehension then the usage of contradiction becomes unmistakably proper. Therefore, this hypothesis is better.

The Refutation of the Hypothesis of a Section of the Mīmāṁsakas

Some Mīmāṁsakas who are not adept in the science of logic hold that the up-holders of the hypothesis of misapprehension define it as the mistaking of one thing for another, viz., the mother-of-pearl is mistaken for silver. But such a mistake does not take place since there is some sort of silver which is presented to our consciousness like the true silver. The silver which is an object of true knowiedge is accepted by all persons to be existent. It is called as common. The silver which is referred to by an illusory judgment is taken to be existent under abnormal circumstances. It is called as uncommon.

Thus they differ from each other. In modern language the former has existence but the latter has merely subsistence. The object which is referred to by the judgment "This is silver" is silver. The object will be silver even if the judgment in question is false. In some cases, silver is conducive to our business-transactions. In other cases, it is not so. What is conducive to our business transactions is laukika. What is not so is alaukika. The Naiyāyikas hold that the illusory judgment, "This is silver" refers to a piece of the mother-of-pearl. But it is really a piece of alaukika (uncommon) silver. As it is presented to our consciousness as silver so it is silver. But as it cannot be used as common silver so it is uncommon (alaukika).

The above thesis is put forward by him who is a creator of a new object but does not know the implication of judgments. The implication of the contradictory judgment is that there is no silver. The negative judgment that this is not silver negates the identity of silver. But it does not point to the uncommonness of silver.

It may be contended that the negative judgment that this is not silver signifies that this is not common silver. He suggests that the above negative judgment is incomplete but should be made complete by the insertion of an appropriate predicate, viz., 'laukika'. In the Mīmāṁsā literature the filling up of an incomplete sentence is noticed. The sentence 'saṁyajatraira-ṅgāni' is incomplete. It is completed by the addition of the appropriate verb 'saṁyujyantām'. Likewise, the negative proposition that this is not silver should be made complete by the addition of the predicate 'laukika'. This learned Vedic scholar has not as yet given up his method of explaining the Vedic texts but there is no scope of its application here. He holds that the negative proposition that this is not silver purports to convey that this is uncommon silver (the reading in the printed text is incorrect. It should be 'kathaṁ taddharmatvena alaukikatvaṁ gṛhyate'. This interpretation is absurd. Because if silver is not perceived then its property 'uncommonness' cannot be cognised. But if the above negative proposition conveys that this contains the negation of silver then no such trouble arises. The negation of silver does not presuppose the perception of silver since the negation of silver is not a property of silver. The negation of silver is surely cognised if the remembrance of silver precedes such cognition. There is no silver at the spot. Therefore, the proposition that uncommon silver exists should be no more spoken of. We cannot define silver as that which is revealed by the knowledge of silver but the correct definition of silver is this : "What is apprehended by the uncontradicted experience of silver is silver".

Does the difference in the nature of judgments referring to silver constitute the basis of the division of silver into two classes, viz., common and uncommon ? Or, does the difference in the nature of propositions, viz., positive and negative, constitute such a basis ? Judgments do not supply us with the basis of the above division. Sometimes, we, also, come across the judgment that this is not silver. The first one points to the existence of silver. But the second one refers to the negation of silver. But they do not respectively refer to common and uncommon silver.

Now, these Mīmāṁsakas may contend that the positive proposition refers to common silver and the negative one points to uncommon silver. Or, they may suggest that when we move for silver, seeing it, it is common silver and when we refrain from doing so, knowing it, it is uncommon silver. The Naiyāyikas take an exception to this contention or suggestion. What is a proposition ? A proposition is nothing but the verbal statement of a judgment. The above division of silver does not find a basis in the negative proposition. As a judgment does not establish the division so the negative proposition does not point to uncommon silver. Now, the Mīmāṁsakas may revise their hypothesis and hold that the pragmatic test works out the division. Silver which has practical utility is common. Silver having no such utility is uncommon. In that case women who are being embraced in a dream should be common. But a jar which is destroyed just after its appearance, i. e., which serves no purpose should be uncommon.

Moreover, a person who does not call the mother-of-pearl as silver knows for certain that it is not silver. But he does not know that this is uncommon silver. The Mīmāṁsakas may still urge that he knows it to be uncommon silver. If he knows it to be so then why does he move at all for it in order to achieve his practical end ? Now if the Mīmāṁsakas give a reply to this effect that one mistakes uncommon silver for common silver then the hypothesis of misapprehension which has been much decried appears on the scene to rescue them.

In fine, the Naiyāyikas remind these Mīmāṁsakas of the real situation that the latter should not cherish hatred towards the hypothesis of misapprenension and that they should frame a hypothesis in obedience to the evidence given by the universal experience.

The Mimāṁsakas are so much anxious to establish the hypothesis that the truth of a judgment is self-evident that they do not desire to take their wives out of their home (If they go out then others will get an opportunity of noticing their conduct and infer the purity of their character from their conduct. In that case, their chastity, i. e., the truth, will not be self-evident).

Even if the Mīmāṁsakas make all sorts of frantic efforts to prove their hypothesis, the self-evident character of the truth of a judgment will not be established because it has been established that there is a broad division of knowledge into two classes, viz., true and false knowledge. Moreover, we should also note that when a doubt arises in our mind in order to solve it we should have recourse to agreement between knowledge and the successful movement for the attainment of the object known.

The Mīmāṁsakas take a lot of trouble to prove the hypothesis that the truth of knowledge is self-evident. But there is no need of taking so much trouble since they cannot establish the pet hypothesis that there is no illusion and that the so-called illusion is explained in terms of non-discrimination between two distinct acts of consciousness. Why do they move about in a serpentine lane to reach the goal ? Let them travel by the main thoroughfare.

The hypothesis that consciousness projects itself does not hold good because an object is always cognized as an external one. In other words, as consciousness cannot externalise itself so the above theory is untenable. The hypothesis explaining illusion that an unreal object is presented to consciousness is untenable because an unreal object can never be known. The hypothesis of non-discrimination is equally wrong because it has been already subjected to severe criticism. Therefore, the men of light and learning should subscribe to the hypothesis of misapprehension.

As the misapprehension of an object is possible and a false judgment bears a close resemblance to a true one so the truth even of a true judgment is called in question. In that case, we are to depend upon accordance with facts for the determination of the truth of a judgment. Hence, the truth of the Vedas is extrinsic but not intrinsic.

The establishment of the hypothesis that the truth of verbal testimony is extrinsic

Though we, even, leave aside the hypothesis that the truth of perception and other sources of knowledge is intrinsic as an open questiton yet there is no room for doubt about the hypothesis that the truth of verbal testimony is externally determined.

When a person perceives an ordinary object or indirectly knows it but does not make himself sure of the truth of this knowledge he moves towards the object provided such an action does not demand much exertion from him. He does not feel much interest in ascertaining the truth of perception or some other form of knowledge because the task is a very easy one. But the Vedas, the best source of the verbal testimony, reveal transcendental ends of human life such as Heaven and Final emancipation from all kinds of sorrows. A judicious performer of sacrifice should not prepare himself for performing sacrifice such as Jyotiṣṭoma and such other sacrifices which entail great efforts upon the performer without ascertaining the truth of the Vedic injunctions enjoining them. Therefore, the truth of them should be surely determined. We also assert that their truth is only extrinsically known to us. A word produces the knowledge of an object. But how does it do it? When we carefully listen to the words of an experienced person and minutely watch the corresponding movement of another experienced person employed by the former, we know the meaning of a word, i. e., the relation of a particular word to a particular object. A word produces the knowledge of an object in a person who has known its meaning. We shall discuss later on whether the meaning of a word is natural or conventional. The character of a word is like that of a lamp, viz., it is the illuminator of an object. When a lamp shines it illuminates a near object which is either pure or impure. Similarly, when a word is employed by a person and reaches the ears of a listener it produces the knowledge of an object which is either true or false, either consistent or inconsistent, either fruitful or fruitless and either an action or an accomplished fact. This is what constitutes its nature. But the distinction of a lamp from a word lies in this that a word in order to communicate the knowledge of an object depends upon its meaning whereas a lamp produces the knowledge of an object without depending upon any relation with it. The truth or falsehood of verbal knowledge entirely depends upon a person who makes the statement. If a person correctly sees an object and is honest then the knowledge, communicated by him, is true. If he is otherwise then the knowledge, communicated by his statement, is false. It has been proved that a word has no natural relation to an object. Similarly, the knowledge, communicated by a word, is not naturally true. If the words had intrinsic truth in them then the statements of a deceitful person would not have been contradicted. The accordance or discordance of verbal knowledge with facts respectively depends upon the qualification or the defect of a speaker. It is not difficult to describe the qualifications which lie at the root of a truthful statement like the qualifications of a sense-organ. The qualifications and defects of a person are well known. Love, hatred etc. constitute his defect whereas his compassion and such other virtues constitute his qualification. The qualification of a person means that of his statement. The qualification of a person does not mean the good qualities belonging to his body as it does when we speak about the qualification of our eyes etc. If it is held that the good quality of a person does not contribute towards the truth of his statement then it may be as well pointed out that his defects should not be held responsible for the falsehood of his statement.

The good qualities of a person simply remove the defects

in a person but do not contribute towards the truth of his statement. This is the hypothesis of the Mīmāṁsakas, the Vedic scholars. They are only to take oath in order to establish it. The knowledge derived from a Vedic passage is true simply because no contradiction arises to counteract it. If this is the contention of a sect of thinkers then the passage, "One should enjoy a lac of beautiful damsels in order to obtain the dignified status of a Vidyādhara," should also be true. Somebody has made a remark to this effect :—

As object which is seen in a dream vision as belonging to some other islands can inspire the belief of no body in its existence though its reality is neither proved nor disproved by our experience. Similarly, a Vedic passage which informs us about a transcendental object the reality of which is neither proved nor refuted by a distinct proof is considered to be trustworthy by no body.

The Mīmāṁsakas may contend that the vision in a dream is not true because it is known to be produced by a defective condition. The defect which belongs to the inner organ is the sleep itself.

Now, the Naiyāyikas put the following question to the Mīmāṁsakas, "What have you got to say regarding the invalidity of the knowledge, derived from a sentence. 'One should enjoy a lac of beautiful damsels etc. ?" They may answer that the source of it, i. e., the author of it, is not known to us. If this is your reply then the source of the Vedas, according to you, is far less known to all. Now, how do you distinguish the Vedas from such sentences ? If you hold that the above sentence is not accepted by the great men then the source of the truth of the Vedas is to be traced out. The hypothesis, that the truth of the Vedas is to be accepted as a general rule as due to the fact that they produce knowledge, is not tenable.

If it is not definitely known that the author of a sentence has the direct knowledge of the object, signified by the sentence then its truth is not determined. But a sentence is not true if its meaning does not involve merely inner contradiction.

In order to prove the infallibility of the Vedas Kumārila holds that there is no author of the Vedas. Hence, the defects which, belonging to the conditions, invalidate the

Vedas float in the air, i. e., are not applicable to the conditions of the Vedas since the Vedas to not owe their origin to any such conditions. The hypothesis is not sound. If the Vedas are not composed by an author then they cannot be held to be true since the good qualities which are responsible for the validity of the Vedas will also be conspicuous by their absence. It is also not very reasonable to hold that the Vedas have got no author. We shall now discuss the point whether the Vedas have been composed by an author or not.

How can a person who has direct knowledge of all transcendental objects compose the Vedas and teach us ? Because the Vedas contain such injunctions as prescribe actions which are conducive to various transcendental results, lying beyond the range of all other proofs.

The Naiyāyikas give a reply to the above objection. Any and every man cannot compose the Vedas. The lord of all gods who is thoroughly competent to create the three worlds is the author of the Vedas. God surpasses all in his excellence, has omniscience, eternal bliss and compassion. He is immune from five evils such as transcendental illusion etc. He has neither worldly existence nor organic life nor sufferings.

Objections to the acceptance of God

What do you say with regard to god ? The possible answer to it is that He is deft in the creation of the world (three regions of the universe). The rejoinder to this statement is that you are too simple to follow the niceties of logic. God is not perceived like colour etc. Moreover, he is not also an object of inner perception like pleasure etc. He is nor also an object of transcendental perception of the sages since they have not been established as existent. God is not an inference since an inference in this case is not based upon perception. God lies beyond the range of perception. Every case of inference is based upon universal concomitance. There is no mark which may be universally and invariably connected with God. Inference based upon general ground is not applicable to God. Such a general mark is conspicuous by its absence. The earth and other such objects cannot be proved to be effects. At least no intelligent thinker will endorse this hypothesis. The unity of the parts of a mountain does not have the way for postulating a creator. The union of the parts of a mountain is distinct from a pot which is created by its maker. The parts of a mountain have assembled and been united together in a distinct way which excludes the idea that it is an effect. If for the sake of argument it is admitted that it has a beginning in time and is an effect, still it is not an invariable mark of the existence of God just like grass etc. The purport of the statement is that mountains etc. have a natural growth like that of grass etc. The vegetables and plants which grow wildly do not depend upon cultivators. Moreover, at the time of growth they are never perceived as such. As no creator is known to us as perceived, His non-perception is enough to establish his non-existence. But in the case of Earth and vast sheets of water the creator may be postulated as distinct from the visible creators. But such a postulation is not tenable since the mark will be too wide to arrive at a definite conclusion. If the case of the union of parts of a mountain is possible without a creator, the creation of Earth and water may be possible by a natural process. Therefore, the inference is fallacious. It is as fallacious as the inference that he is a Brahmin since he is a man. An inference must be based upon experience. This much may be admitted that the so-called creator is no better than a potter. Such an inference is contradicted since other specific characters as expected do not follow from the above conclusion.

A creator who has movement in the shape of intervening process has a body like a potter. If He has a body, He is not omniscient. He has imperfection and other limitations of his mental powers. If we infer the existence of God, He is no better than a potter. The creator of Earth is no better than a potter. But His other specific attributes cannot be established. How are they inferred ? Such a probandum has no similar instance to confirm its establishment. If the creator is merely established, then how will His specific attributes be established or known ? Now, will corporeal or incorporeal God create the earth etc? In this connection our observation is that incorporeal creator is never seen. If He is corporeal, His body is an effect like that of Caitra (a man). Is the body of God, being an effect, created by Himself or is it created by another God? It is unwisely rash statement that He creates His own body. If another creator is assumed then an infinite series of creators will be the logical conclusion.

Let us hold such a conclusion. What is the defect in such a conclusion? The defect is this that it is based upon no source of knowledge. You are perplexed to establish a single God. What will happen to you if you try to prove the existence of an infinite number of Gods. Will He create the universe by physical operation like potter? Or, will He create it by His mere will? These hypotheses are hard to establish. By physical operation nobody can create by hundreds of cycle of the worlds i.e. by hundreds of mythical years. Moreover, the unconscious atoms do not obey the will of Him.

Moreover, the hypothesis is open to other charges. Has he any purpose to serve by creating the universe? or, does He create the universe, having no purpose to serve? The second hypothesis is absurd since if He has no purpose to serve by creating the universe, then He is open to the charge of doing imprudent act. The first hypothesis requires no scrutiny since the contenders do not subscribe to it.

God has no desire to fulfil. As He is perfect He enjoys eternal bliss. He has neither love nor hatred. He is free from passions. He has no end to realize by engaging Himself in the task of creating the universe. We do not make out what is His object to serve. Does He undertake it out of compassions. Before the creation in the universe the individual souls are free from all passions, sufferings etc i.e. impurities like the liberated souls. Therefore they did not deserve compassion.

The very compassionate persons feel compassion only when their heart melts with pity observing the repeated sufferings of the creatures. But no body feels for the souls having no sorrow and other sources of sufferings like the soul at state of liberty. He also does not know to create such a world which provides us with enjoyments of pleasures alone. Even if He makes such a provision, such enjoyment is only short-lived. Such a weak defence does not carry any weight. Nothing is impossible for the great Lord since He enjoys limitless independence, and all the objects, in that case, submit to His inviolable command. If the contenders hold that the Lord of the creatures takes into consideration all the acts, good and evil, performed by the creatures and creates the world as the creatures deserve, such an explanation is not satisfactory. Let the unmerited acts alone create the world and the Lord of creatures has no business at all. The theorist may contend that the matter or elements require the guidance of the conscious being and that God is the fittest soul to create the world out of the unconscious materials. Such an assumption is not tenable. The souls are conscious beings who are competent to discharge the function of supervisors since all such materials are for them. There is no need of assuming another supervisor. Moreover, His absolute majesty is curtailed, being dependence upon the acts of all souls. Such limited majesty has no use at all. No king likes to enjoy a kingdom if he is to depend absolutely upon his minister and has no power to make choice of things and is to accept the choice of his minister as his own. If He is Lord, He should have absolute independence. If He cannot exert his own independence, such a Lord has no need. No body enquires the motives of the Lord if He does something.

The creator moves to create this universe from the sportive spirit. If you hold that the creator enjoys the feat of sport by creating this world having good and evil elements then we take an exception to this view that the world being devoid of pleasure as a result of his sport the God parts with His nature in the shape of blissfulness which He possessed before the creation of the world since He had all His desires fulfilled but no wants.

The great souls should not indulge in such sports as require much exertion and create panic in the hearts of all without an exception. Hence the Protector of the world is neither a creator nor a destroyer of it.

If God preserves the acts of all creatures of the three divisions of the universe then the possibility of the fruition of all acts at a time will be ruled out. In other words, the goal of universal liberation will be never reached. If the work ceases then the recreation of the world will not be possible since the varieties of the world will not be possible having no different kinds of acts as their efficient causes.

Now another hypothesis states that God goes on functioning for a period of a hundred years of which a day is much longer than the age of an earth and that after this period He feels a desire to destroy the created world. As a result the dissolution of the universe takes place. This period is mythological night of Brahman. When this night is over he feels an inclination again to create the world. By His desire the efficacy of the latent acts revives and the acts, being active construct this world. This hypothesis is not tenable.

If the creation and the destruction of the world depend upon the desire of the God, let it be alone the cause of the appearance and the disappearance of the world.

Let it be so. There is no need of the hypothesis of acts. If we examine the hypothesis as revised closely, we find that it is riddled with the three unanswerable objections. These are as follows, viz., (1) His Majesty turns out to be merciless; (2) He becomes merciless without any rhyme and reason since His act of creation of the world is cruel; and as (3) the desire of God is competent enough to bestow good and bad consequences, the injunctions and prohibitions of the Vedas become gratuitous assumptions. Another fresh problem appears to discredit the Nyāya hypothesis. It is this that the non-realization of the state of perfection is the inevitable logical conclusion since the desire of God overrules everything and if the God so desires, the liberated souls may be again bound down by the state of bondage. In other words they may be reborn as ordinary creatures. Therefore, we conclude that God is not responsible for the creation and the destruction of the world. The chain of logical arguments shows clearly that inference has no capacity for demonstrating the existence of God. Comparison has no scope at all. The eternal Vedas cannot rightly point to the existence of God. If the god is the author of the Vedas then the infidels like us can place no confidence in the statement of the Vedas. If it is stated that the Vedas are true because the God is their author and that God exists since the Vedas are the source of His existence then the argument is riddled with the unanswerable vicious circle. The existence of God cannot be established. If it is argued that the hypothesis of God is only a fair presumption to explain the existence of the world then we can boldly assert that such a presumption is not necessary as the world may be explained otherwise since all the sources of valid knowledge acceptable to us fail to establish the existence of God, God is conspicuous by His absence.

It is not fair to believe in the existence of God on the strength of a rumour current in the popular mind that God exists. It is no better than the baseless heresy that a Yakṣa (a kind of spirit) lives on the banian tree. The result of the close examination reveals that the elaborate statement in the mythological story of the creation and the destruction of the universe goes in vain since the moral philosophers cannot lend their support to such a whimsical world without plan and purpose.

The establishment of the existence of God

We, the theorists, say in reply to the above objections that it is a truism that our perception does not reveal a person who is skilled in constructing a mountain and other such objects. Similarly, the inference based upon the perception of similar objects is not capable of establishing the existence of God. Therefore, such an inference is ruled out.

But the inference which is based upon general observation has competence to prove the existence of God. We state our inference in the following logical proposition thus :—The earth and other such created objects are an effect. Such an effect is dependent upon a maker i. e. a creator who knows how to create and the purpose of creation. This is the probandum and the probans is the characteristic feature of an effect and the similar example is a jar.

In a short logical form :

All effects are dependent upon a creator.
The earth is an effect.
Therefore the earth is dependent upon a creator.

The formal validity is stated in the last syllogism. The material validity has been stated in the first one.

The rejoinder to the above distinct criticism

It has been stated that the earth is not an effect. Who says so ? Is he a Cārvāka or a Buddhist or a Mīmāṁsaka ?

How should a Cārvāka give a lie to the hypothesis that the earth is an effect because he holds that the Vedas have been composed by somebody though they are essentially different from other literary products.

It does not behove the Mīmāṁsakas to deny the earth the character of an effect. Śabara has clearly stated that the true character of an object is revealed to us though we do not know its origin. This piece of cloth has been produced by the combination of threads. But we can safely infer that it will be destroyed when the combination of threads will be served or when the threads themselves will be destroyed. Similarly, the knowledge of the destruction of hill and such other things which consist of parts may also take place. Sometimes, we witness the partial destruction of a hill. When some portion of a hill is damaged by the torrential rain falling from the cloud of the rainy season the mass of a projecting hill i. e. a rock slides down. Kumārila, the author of Śloka-vārttika has said that the relation of universal concomitance holds between the two terms the character of being an effect and that of being destructible and that they are co-extensive. The actual verse of the Śloka-vārttika says that if the middle term and the major term are co-extensive and each of them pervades the other then we can only infer the major term from the middle but no *vice versa*.

From the above statement, we may safely infer that the hill is an effect because it is destructible. Hence, it emboldens us to hold that it is not true that the character of an effect does not belong to a hill even from the Mīmāṁsaka point of view.

The Buddhists who do not tolerate the suggestion that some objects are eternal even at the time of universal destruction cannot disprove the hypothesis that the above-mentioned objects are effects. Hence, the conclusion that the earth and such other objects are effects stands irrefutable. In order to prove the conclusion that these objects are effects by means of a syllogistic argument we put forward the minor premise that they (these objects) possess the combination of parts. We directly perceive them as having the combination of parts.

The counter attack of the Buddhists runs thus :—We do not make out the cogency of the word 'such' in such combination,

When smoke in a kitchen is produced by mild fire, being kindled by the gentle fanning of housewife, it is very slender. But when smoke in a mountain is produced by the great trunks of big trees, being consumed by blazing fire which is fanned by the strong storm, it rises straight up to the sky and increases in volume. Shall not we infer fire from such smoke? Now, the objectors may contend that smoke in general is known to be universally connected with fire in general. Hence, one infers fire from smoke. We also point out that the combination of parts of a whole is universally connected with an agent who combines them. Hence, let us infer an agent from the combination.

(Now, the Buddhists take an exception to the Nyāya hypothesis from another point of view). They urge that the word 'combination' instead of denoting a real universal stands for a mere nominal identity. The Naiyāyikas say in reply "Oh Buddhists! do you admit the existence of real smokeness (the universal of smoke) in your system of Logic and Metaphysics?" The Buddhists may contend that there is an imaginary negative object on which the popular convention is based but there is no real universal. The imaginary negative universal of smoke is non-non-smoke. It distinguishes smoke from the sky, time, etc. Now the Naiyāyikas say in reply "Very well let us also follow the path, chalked out by you, and hold that there is a negative imaginary universal, viz., non-non-combination. It serves the purpose of a conventional universal and distinguishes the combination of the earth, etc., from the sky, time, etc.

Whenever, we have an experience of smoke we have a common idea. This common idea leads to the assumption of a common element which is negative in its character and is a construction of our imagination. If the Buddhists hold this view then they may find out such a negative common element in this case since we experience a common idea in every judgment referring to a combination of parts. But they may contend that the combination of parts which is known to be due to the operation of a creator does not agree in all fours with those which are not known to be such. The Naiyāyikas do not see much force in this argument. The different combinations of parts such as the combination of parts of a jar, that of a cloth, that of a house, etc., are not similar. The common element in a combination surely belongs even to the combination of parts of a hill. Hence, the word 'such' which qualifies combination as stated before has no significance whatsoever.

The wild plants and immovable objects have been cited as negative examples in order to invalidate the above generalisation. But we point out in this connection that the above cases are the subjects of inference and should not be cited as negative examples. If the objector cites the subjects of inference as negative examples then the very possibility of an inference will be cut off. As the time of the origin of this earth and such other objects lies beyond the range of our sense-organ so their creator is not seen by us. The truth of the judgment that a creator does not exist because he is not seen may be doubtful. But the creator of the big trees which have very recently grown is not seen by us. If we make a thorough search but do not find out the creator then we know for certain that the creator does not exist because he is not seen. Moreover, if the cases which we cite as negative examples are included by our opponents in the list of the subjects of inference then they strike at the very root of the fundamental law of inference since the generalizations which are materially invalid will surely pass as valid ones under the present device.

A reply to the above objection is as follows. Though the origin of some of the immovable objects is visible to us yet we do not see the creator because he has no body. An objection to the above solution may be put thus :—How can the so-called creator combine the parts of an object since he cannot put forth his energy in the outer world, having no body. We shall meet this objection later on that an incorporeal creator is active. If the creator is invisible then it cannot be held that he does not exist because he is not seen. Hence, the hypothesis that the widly grown trees have no creator does not fairly serve the purpose of negative examples.

The objectors have also suggested that the hypothesis of an invisible creator is superflous since the immovable objects are effects of visible causes such as earth, water, etc. Such a suggestion is not logically sound. Those who believe in the existence of the next world assume that the invisible principle of merits and demerits is also one of the conditions which are responsible for an effect. The followers of Bṛhaspati, i.e., the materialists, should also subscribe to this assumption in order to explain logically the world of manifold objects.

Now, it may be contended that the assumption of the invisible principle of merits and demerits as a condition is a necessary one because the variety of worldly objects is not explained without resuming it. If you argue in the following manner then we also point out that the assumption of an intelligent creator is a necessary one, since the unconscious conditions cannot produce their effects without being guided by an intelligent creator. Hence, the immovable effects are not produced without the imparted activity of a creator. They are not to be cited as negative examples. Therefore, they cannot contradict the truth of the major premise that all effects having parts are produced by a creator.

It has been objected that if the negative examples are taken as the subjects of inference then which will be the rule that decides the validity of inferential knowledge ? Such an objection is not fair. If the objector can prove without the shade of a doubt that a particular case is surely a negative example then who can hold that it is to be taken as a subject of inference ? If one argues that this fellow is a Brahmin because he is a man or that an object is eternal because it is knowable then even the creator of the universe will not be able to include a negative example in the group of the subjects of inference. An object cannot be designated as this or as that according to the sweet will of anyone of the contending parties. Regarding the immovable objects we have only stated that it has not been proved that they have not been created by a creator. Now, another fresh question arises in our mind. Even if we admit that the immovable objects are subjects of inference then the above generalization is not immune from an exception. The so-called subject of inference cannot but be either a positive or a negative example since an object cannot simultaneously have such two properties as are contradictory to each other. If the big trees are, in reality, created by a creator then they are positive examples. If they are not so created then they are negative examples. They are either positive or negative examples. There is no other possibility left to them.

An answer to this objection is as follows. If there is no such thing as the subject of inference then the positive and negative examples, implying a necessary reference to the subject of inference, become merely insignificant verbal expressions. A positive example is such as helps to prove that the predicate in question belongs to the subject of inference. A negative example is such as helps to prove that the predicate in question does not belong to the subject of inference. If the Naiyāyikas argue like this then they should define a subject of inference.

A positive example is that which illustrates the belonging i.e. the existence of the major term to it whereas the negative example illustrates the non-existence of the major term without the least shade of a doubt.

If the rival parties have a dispute over the matter whether the predicate in question belongs to a particular subject or not then the latter is called as the subject of inference. The Naiyāyikas also approve of the hypothesis that the two contradictory predicates do not simultaneously belong to a subject.

The subject of inference (pakṣa) has been so defined by a biased mind since it has been so framed by the propounder of a thesis to serve his interest. The mover of the thesis has introduced the new termin the above sense into the above designation of their logical literature.

Whenever a doubt, viz; whether a consequence belongs to the subject of inference or not, arises in our mind, a syllogistic argument is put forward to solve it. But if the consequence is unknowable or unknown then we do not put forward a syllogistic argument. This point has been already discussed. The subject about which it is doubted whether the consequence belongs to it or not is called a pakṣa. It remains a pakṣa until it is decided that the consequence belongs to it or it does not belong to it. When the decision is reached the above pakṣa becomes either a positive or a negative example. It is not fair to cite a particular case as a negative example so long as it remains a pakṣa.

Now, a fresh objection may be raised by our opponent. A reason is not sound if it belongs to a negative example. Similarly, it is not reliable if it belongs to a doubtful negative example. It is doubtful whether a creeper has been created by a creator. Thus the combination of parts is not a true reason. Such an objection is baseless. Let us take a familiar example. We argue that the hill is fiery because it is smoky. We do not definitely know that there is fire on the hill. Therefore, the hill is a doubtful negative example. Smoke belongs to the hill. Hence smoke should not be a reliable reason. If every subject where the presence of the consequence is doubted becomes a negative example then the very possibility of inferential knowledge is ruled out.

Now, the objector may contend that though the above subject, i. e., the hill has been converted into a pakṣa and has become a source of doubt whether the consequence in question, i. e., fire belongs to it or not yet smoke which belongs to it leads to the inferential knowledge of fire because the relation of universal concomitance holding between smoke and fire has been established with reference to the other cases. If this solution is accepted by you then we shall also prove our point in this manner. The earth and the big trees are doubtful cases. We do not definitely hold that they have been created by a creator. But they are effects. It has been ascertained with regard to the other instances that an effect is invariably produced by a creator. As they partake of the character of an effect so it is, also, to be accepted that the reason unfailingly points to the consequence with which it is universally connected. If you differ then you are to point out the negative examples which contradict the truth of his generalization.

Some other critics hold that the trees which grow wildly should not be referred to as negative examples. The above induction will be contradicted when the earth and such other objects will be cited as negative examples. These examples obstruct the very process of generalization. When we arrive at a generalization all the examples positive and negative are taken into consideration. Let us examine the process of generalization. Whenever we generalize we think that whatever has a combination of parts has been created by an intelligent creator. Again, when the process of generalization works in our mind, an idea that, there is no God etc., gets itself imprinted upon our mind. When it is inferred that fire is cold because it is the conclusion of the major premise that whatever is an effect is cold such a major premise does not arise. This major premise is arrived at by a process of induction. But whenever the process of induction is at work to realize the determinate final form, the contrary idea that though fire is an effect yet it is hot appears in our mind. As an impotent person cannot beget a son so the conclusion that such and such objects have been created by a creator does not follow from the suggested but intermediate major premise. This is the sum and substance of the objection.

Such an objection does not hold water. In connection with the definition of inference it has been proved that a broad generalization which is universally accepted is framed without any reference to a particular case. It is not a fact that when we infer that fire is cold, the inference is invalidated because induction is obstructed. But it is to be noted that the above inference is wrong because it is contradicted by our perception.

Moreover, your method of invalidating the inference that the earth and such other things have a creator will also strike at the root of the inference, put forward by you, that the apprehension of sound etc. being an act, is produced by an instrument like the act of hewing. Because when we arrive at the induction that all acts are produced by instruments, we are not aware of the fact that the apprehension of sound etc. is produced by an instrument, and hence this act of apprehension will falsify the induction. We should also note that the earth and such other objects are subjects of inference, i.e., they constitute the minor term in the syllogism in question. It is extra-ordinarily strange to contradict the truth of a syllogism by an appeal to its minor term.

Now, the objector may still press his point with the remark that the earth and such other things are contrary examples but are not really subjects of inference. The Naiyāyikas have described them as subjects of inference only to suit their purpose.

The Naiyāyikas meet this argument: Oh Mīmāṁsaka ! if you hold this view then the apprehension of sound etc. should not also be the subject of inference. It should be treated as a negative example. It should not be described as the subject of inference.

Now, the Mīmāṁsakas may contend thus : The judgment that the acts such as the apprehension of sound etc. are not produced by instruments is an absurdity. Therefore, the above apprehension and the like should not be treated as negative examples. The Naiyāyikas may also say in reply that as the judgment that the earth and such other things have no creator is an impossibility so they should not be described as negative examples.

Now, the Mimāṁsakas may point out that the creator of those objects is not perceived by any body. The Naiyāyikas also meet this objection thus. The instrument of the apprehension of sound etc. is not also perceived. Now, the Mīmāṁsakas may contend that the said instrument is not perceived because it is a transcendental object but not an unreal one. The Naiyāyikas also hold that such a contention is not convincing since the creator of the earth etc. is not perceived because He is transcendental but not unreal. Now, the Mīmāṁsakas may further contend that the existence of the instrument in question is inferred since an effect cannot be produced without the operation of an instrument. Such a contention does not satisfy the Naiyāyikas. They will also plead their case in the same strain that the existence of the creator of earth etc. is inferred since an effect cannot be produceed if there is no creator to produce it.

As the existence of the said creator is inferred so the judgment that the creator does not exist does never appear in our mind. In the absence of such a judgment it is glaring mistake to assert that the earth and such other objects are contrary examples.

When we notice probans but do not infer the probandum we entertain a doubt regarding the presence of the probandum in the subject of inference. Even in case of a very familiar probandum such as fire such a doubt is not to be avoided. If a doubt implies that the subject of inference when the presence of a probandum is questioned is to be taken as a contrary example then we cannot even infer fire from smoke.

In case of the syllogistic argument that the earth has a creator because it is an effect, if the reason, put forward, is held to be a fallacious one then smoke which is held to be a mark of fire may also be asserted as a fallacious one since fire is not seen on the hill at the time of inference.

Now, it may be contended that fire may be seen if we actually go to the place and move about in search of it. We simply say in reply to this contention, "Oh good sir ! ramble a hundred years with this idea deeply rooted in your brain". But it does not improve the condition of the above probans if the probandum is seen afterwards. It still remains to be fallacious at the time of inference. Again, if the person who infers fire does not go about to find out fire because he is not in need of it then what will you do ? In other words, how will you establish your case that smoke is not a fallacious reason when we infer fire on the hill and have no intention of seeing it ?

In fine, the probans, viz., being an effect or being a combination of parts, is not a fallacious one.

It has been objected that the particular which is inferred does not belong to the example which illustrates induction. This objection reveals only their superficial observation since such absence of the probandum does not negate the truth of the inferential knowledge, In other words, an inference of this type is not a fallacious one. Again, if a fallacy of this type is admitted then inference *per se* will be discredited. This very argument can be set against the inference of the auditory sense-organ, put forward by the objector. When we cut a tree with a big knife, it has been perceived by us to be a hard substance. Should our auditory sense-organ, the instrument of an action, be like it ?" "Certainly not" is the answer. It is different from the big knife. A dissimilar object being inferred, the probandum in question does not belong to the example. Let us clearly state our point. The sense-organ in question is supersensuous. But the instrument of the act of hewing is not supersensuous. Does anybody hold that the inference of such a sense-organ is thereby fallacious ?

Now, in order to safeguard his own position, the objector may hold that the general proposition is this: "All acts are produced by an instrument" Hence, we deduce only an instrument which one has no right to specify on the basis of the above generalization. Similarly, the general proposition, framed by the Naiyāyikas, is put forward thus : "All combinations of parts of a particular type are effectuated by a creator". The deductive conclusion which follows from it is that this particular combination of parts is effectuated by a creator. The Naiyāyikas may be allowed to state this much only but nothing more. In other words, they should not specify the creator as such and such. But it should also be noted that there is no such reason as contradicts the specific properties of the creator. Let us take a few concrete cases which illustrate the cancellation of some specifications. Sound is non-eternal because it is an effect. The reason in question contradicts some specifications of sound such as non-audibility, etc. The hill is fiery because it is smoky. We know on the strength of this inference that the hill contains such fire as sets at naught some qualifications, viz., "belonging to a kitchen" etc. Thus a reason is said to be contradictory when it establishes the contradictory negation of the probandum instead of proving the probandum. But it should not be called as a contradictory one when it proves a particular type of probandum which is dissimilar to that of the probandum illustrated in the example. The reason, employed in the above syllogism, does not prove that the earth and such other objects have not been created by a creator. The reason in question is absolutely different from the reason employed in the syllogism "This is a horse because it has horns." Therefore it is not a contradictory one.

Moreover, the reason in question does not illustrate the type of Kālātyaya Apadiṣṭa fallacy. This type of fallacy suggests that the reason which is employed to prove the presence of a probandum in a subject of inference must belong to it (the subject of inference). But it is learnt from the other sources of knowledge, viz., perception or verbal testimony that the probandum in question does not belong to the subject of inference. It has not been proved by perception or verbal testimony that the earth and such other objects have no creator. On the contrary, we shall cite passages from the Vedas which lend their support to the conclusion arrived at by the above syllogistic argument.

The reason in question does not illustrate the type of Satpratipakṣa fallacy. If a reason is employed in such a syllogism it is counter-balanced by another syllogism which proves the just opposite of the conclusion of the first one. The reason behind the appearance of the two opposite syllogisms is this: The exclusive possibility of one of these two syllogisms has not been determined. The two reasons which point to the two opposite conclusions are present in the subject of inference. The presence of such reasons constitutes the source of doubt. Besides this, there are other conditions of doubt. But in the present case, there is no such factor as leads to a doubt. Moreover, the probans in question is not such as does not stand in the relation of universal concomitance to the probandum. In some syllogisms the reason which is employed has no power to enlighten the intended probandum. Let us illustrate our point. The atoms are non-eternal because they have small size. The small size of an object cannot assure one of its non-eternality. But in the syllogism that the earth and such other objects are produced by a creator because they are effects, the relation, subsisting between 'being produced by a creator' and 'being an effect', is that of universal concomitance. The reason necessarily implies the consequence. The above relation has been discovered by us from sound experience. Hence, there is no room for the contradiction of the syllogism in question and there is no chance of the appearance of an obstacle which will stand in the way of arriving at the conclusion. If we employ an adequate reason in order to prove the existence of God then nobody finds an opportunity of throwing mud on it in order to discredit it.

In fine, we hold that the reason, viz., being an effect, put forward by us (as pointing to the existence of God), is not open to the charges which have been brought against it by our critics. Therefore, the existence of God is surely established on the strength of the sound reason indicated above. The truth of inference is admitted by all. We have also discussed a good deal to prove the validity of inferential knowledge. Hence, there is no obstacle to the path of proving the hypothesis that God exists.

Philosophers of the other schools of thought have put forward some other argument in order to prove the existence of God. Let us illustrate some of them. The gross elements produce pleasure and pain under the guidance of an intelligent being because they have sensible properties such as sound etc. like the musical instruments e.g., a drum etc. The gross elements perform certain acts such as the act of carrying a load etc., being presided over by a conscious principle like a horse. The fallacies which may be ascribed to these syllogistic arguments will be got rid of in the light of the defence adopted in the previous example. It has been also objected that the hypothesis "The earth has a creator" may be taken as proved. But it does not mean that the said creator has some exceptional atributes such as 'eternality' 'omniscience' etc. It simply means that there is a creator and nothing more can be asserted of him. From which source do the theists learn His specific attributes? Some logicians step forward and say in reply to this question that the Vedas supply us with the above attributes.

It has been stated in the Nārāyaṇa-Upaniṣad that He has eyes, faces, hands and legs on all sides and He unites Himself with merits and demerits and with the five elements in order to create heaven and earth (i. e., the whole universe).

Moreover, in the Śvetāśvatra Upaniṣad a verse runs thus: "He has no legs yet He moves. He has no hands yet He catches hold of objects. He has no eyes yet He sees. He has no ears yet He hears. He knows everything (He is omniscient). Nobody can know him. Everybody says that he is the most excellent soul". The above passage suggests that God is the creator of all and knows everything. Some Mīmāṁsakas hold that the Vedic texts which contain injunctions, laudations, condemnations, anecdotes and records of glorious exploits, purport to signify only rites to be performed but they do not lay emphasis on the promised objects. Such a view is absolutely wrong. It will be shown that the above texts signify in the same strain both the rites to be performed and the promised objects. As the Vedas are not the only source of God so the fallacy of mutual dependence is avoided. (If the Vedas had been the only source of God then the very existence of God would have been open to the said fallacy. If the Vedas are the source of true knowledge then the existence of God is established. Again, if the existence of God is proved then the Vedas are the source of true knowledge. Thus the whole argument moves in a vicious circle. But if the existence of God is proved by some other source of true knowledge then there is no scope for the above fallacy to vitiate the authority of the Vedas). Some Vaiśeṣikas hold that in the syllogistic argument "Earth has a creator because it is an effect" the relation of universal concomitance holding between the middle term and the major terms has its both aspects, positive and negative, satisfied. This middle term is based upon another middle term which is connected with its major term only by means of the relation of universal concomitance having only the negative aspect satisfied. As a distinct effect in the shape of pleasure, pain, etc., points to the existence of the soil which is other than the body so earth and such objects, being distinct effects, imply the existence of an omniscient creator having no parallel. It is a truism that the human being like us cannot create earth, etc. Earth and such other objects must be created by some creator as they are effects. So their creator is distinct from us, having very limited knowledge and power.

Some other logicians hold that the distinctive features of God are not established by means of an inference but only through the process of elimination of the other makers. This universe which is being perceived by us admits of diversity. It is the place where innumerable living beings enjoy various degrees of pleasure and pain. It is impracticable for a person other than one possessed of super excellent attributes.

Jayanta now records his own view. When a person sees smoke, smells its fragrance, recognises it to be issuing from the burning sandal-wood and distinguishes it from others, he infers fire as consuming the sandal wood from it. Similarly, we infer a distinct creator from a distinct effect. Likewise, we infer that the weaver who has made the cloth is very expert when we see a very fine cloth. A potter who has acquired proficiency in preparing various earthen objects such as a pitcher, etc., handles the materials in order to produce them on proper occasions. Similarly, God who is in the know of the processes of creating and destroying the universe where all creatures enjoy pleasure and pain can be the creator of the universe as he feels the necessity of creating and destroying it. For this reason the Supreme Lord is omniscient.

As the individual soul is relatively omniscient since it is the mover of all the sense-organs which sense only that respective objects, so God who is the mover of all individual souls is omniscient when He is compared and contrasted with them.

Vedavyāsa says in his Gītā, "There are two kinds of Puruṣas in this universe. The changing puruṣas belong to the first type. The unchanging ones are included in the second type. All composite bodies constitute the changing ones. The individual souls constitute the unchanging ones. The best Puruṣa is other than these two types. He is called the Supreme Soul. He is changeless. He is immanent in the three worlds. He controls and preserves them all."

The same idea has been repeated in the Māṇḍūkya-Upaniṣad. Two birds of the same kind very close to each other rest on the same tree. One of them tastes the delicious fruit. The other simply witnesses it without tasting it.

For this reason He is omniscient.

The ignorance of all creatures is due to passions in the shape of love, hatred, etc. But God is immune from all these feelings etc. and hence He is omniscient. The above defects accrue to the creatures since they enjoy pleasant and unpleasant objects. How can these defects cling to God who blesses all and has eternal bliss and consciousness? How are these shortcomings in the shape of love, hatred, etc. possible in God who has eternal, pure and serene consciousness? The reason behind the absence of these defects in God is this that they (defects) owe their origin to the wrong way of Thinking.

The eternality of God's consciousness and all other attributes

Is God's consciousness eternal? If he had remained sans consciousness even for a time-atom then various activities and enjoyments of pleasure and pain on the part of all living beings in this universe should have been absolutely suspended, since they presuppose the operation of merit and demerit for their coming into being and merit and demerit operate only under the guidance of His desire. Why do you assume that His consciousness persists during the period of dissolution? The answer to this question is this that His consciousness lasts till the commencement of the universal dissolution. But during the period of dissolution there exists no such condition which can destroy His consciousness. Hence it is assumed that His consciousness is eternal. His consciousness which grasps all sorts of objects, past, future, subtle, enveloped, etc., admits of no diversity, since if He had several acts of awareness then they would have been neither simultaneous nor successive. If His different acts of consciousness were successive then He would have no consciousness at least for sometime. In that case, all worldly transactions should have suddenly collapsed. If we assume that all acts of His consciousness are simultaneous then we should assume that each act of consciousness grasps everything in the universe, since He is omniscient. In that case, how can we distinguish one individual act of consciousness from another? His consciousness is said to be immediate because it bears a close resemblance to perceptual awareness. Though it resembles perception yet it is not produced by the sense-object-contact. It is like sunlight which reveals such objects as do not produce it. The other attributes of the Supreme Soul are also eternal like His consciousness, since they are not conditioned by the contact of the internal organ with the soul.

He has, indeed, neither sorrow nor hatred. He is not in need of impressions which, being revived, develop into memory. He requires no memory because He has always, the direct knowledge of all objects. For this very reason He requires no inferential knowledge. As a will to mitigate the sufferings of all creatures follows His nature so merit which constantly grows in Him is not excluded from Him. It has a great task to accomplish, viz., the creation of the universe. He has eternal bliss since it is learnt from the Vedas that He is ever blissful. A person who enjoys no bliss has no capacity for undertaking such a huge task.

Now a question arises in our mind. If His will is eternal like his consciousness and so is His bliss then the word will also be infinite. If He always wills to create the universe then it will never meet with destruction. Again, if it is admitted that He constantly wishes to destroy the universe then the destruction of the universe will go on day and night and know no stop. Such an objection does not affect our position. His will *per se* is eternal because it is not produced by the contact of the internal organ with the soul. But it is qualified sometimes by an object, viz., the creation of the universe and at other times by another object, viz., the destruction of the universe. During the interval between the creation of the universe and its destruction when the universe persists, the creator of the universe wills that this particular effect should follow from this particular action. A particular resolution of His mind is His mental activity. It has been stated in the Vedas that His Kāma and Saṁkalpa are 'always true, i.e. they are never baffled. The word 'Kāma' stands for will. The term 'Prayatna' signifies mental activity. Five attributes out of the nine ones of the soul belong to Him. They are as follows :—Consciousness, bliss, will, conation or mental activity and merit. The remaining four attributes, viz., sorrow, hatred, demerit and impressions do not inhere in Him. God is a distinct member of the class of souls. He is not a class by Himself. Patañjali in his Yoga-sūtra says that God is a distinct soul who has neither illusion, nor egoism, nor love, nor hatred nor fear of death, who has no undertaking, who has neither birth nor life nor worldly enjoyment and who has neither merit and demerit. The details of God are supplied either by the Vedas or by an act of inference or by the process of elimination.

Incorporeal God

Somebody puts a knotty question to the Naiyāyikas. It runs thus :—"Does corporeal or incorporeal God create the universe ?" The answer to the question from the standpoint of the Naiyāyikas is that incorporeal God creates this Universe. Now, a further question arises in our mind. Those who are associated with an action are real agents but those who are not so associated are not agents. The term 'agent' has no conventional meaning. As an incorporeal being has no action so it cannot be an agent. Is agency found anywhere in an incorporeal being ? One who has consciousness, will to do something and mental activity is called an agent. It has been stated that such agency surely belongs to God. The agency of our incorporeal soul is noticed when it moves its own body. As the soul moves the body merely by its will-force so the possible charge against the agency of the soul that it should undergo a lot of troubles in connection with its various operations has been replied.

If God does not behave like a potter, i.e., if He does not impart His mental activity to the constituent elements of the universe through the medium of His body like a potter then how does unconscious dead matter obey His will ?

The reply to this objection from the Nyāya point of view is this :—"As the unconscious body obeys the will of the soul so the unconscious atoms will submit to His will.

What is the motive of God behind the creation of this world? A question like this may be raised in order to negate the existence of God. But such a question is not at all fair. God's nature prompts Him to fashion this universe at one period of time. But the same nature prompts Him again to destroy it at another period of time. Why does His nature manifest itself at regular intervals ? If a person puts a question like this to us then we submit the following by way of reply. The person who raises the above question is a big fool. Let him behold the sun. He rises and declines regularly. Now if it is held that the nature of the sun-god is moulded by the merits and demerits of all creatures then our reply to it is this that the same rule applies to the hypothesis of God as well.

We may also hold that the creation of the universe is like a sport to Him. This does not show that this is an aimless task. If He engages Himself in this sport, He does not feel tired. Those who indulge in sports do not feel sorry for the hard labour. Or we stick to the view that out of sheer compassion for creatures He undertakes to create and destroy the universe. The objectors have taken an exception to this view. They hold that it is unreasonable to entertain such a view. But we review the argument of the objectors and reassert our original view. The reason behind our reassertion is as follows. The cycle of creation is beginningless. Hence, the souls are saturated with good and bad potential habits as they are tied down to the chain of merits and demerits. As they cannot enter into the main gate of final emancipation in such a plight so are not they objects of pity ? The actions, the fruits of which have not been enjoyed are not uprooted. But an action cannot bear its fruit if there is no world. Hence, the compassionate God is bent upon creating hell etc. in order to make possible the fruition of an action.

When the creatures incessantly enjoy the fruits of their actions they get tired. In order to give them recreation at some intervals He also brings about the destruction of the universe. Hence, the whole process of creation and destruction owes its origin to His compassion.

Now, another objection arises in our mind that the simultaneous destruction of all objects of the universe cannot be reasonably maintained. The residues of actions which have not borne fruits cannot be so obstructed that they remain impotent. Such a statement is also dogmatic. The potency of the persisting actions is suspended by the irresistible will-force of God. Thus, their power of bearing fruits is impeded. But when they are energized by the will-force of God they produce results. They remain fruitless when their power of bearing fruits is overpowered by the will-force of God. Why do they obey the law, imposed upon them by God ? The answer is that the unconscious objects without being guided or moved by a conscious being are never seen to produce their effects.

Now, a rival hypothesis may be pressed that the conscious souls should guide all merits and demerits of all creatures. Kumārila also lends his support to it. He holds that as all embodied souls can only perform actions so the conclusion is self-evident that they are the masters of their own merits and demerits, i.e., they control them. Again, if the same conclusion is proved by a distinct syllogistic argument then an old story is simply repeated (more literally, a proved conclusion is only re-established). Such a conclusion is not amenable to reasons. The individual souls are not controllers of their actions since they are many and are at cross purposes. Suppose, an immovable object which is the source of pleasure and pain of crores of creatures is to be constructed. Or, a king who affords happiness or suffering to crores of creatures is to be created. Can so many different individuals who are at cross purposes be united in inaugurating either of them ? Because they agree to differ. The members of an institution, educational or religious, sometimes arrive at an agreement to effectuate a work of common weal but not always. But when big palaces are under construction the artisans such as carpenters etc. who are employed there, follow the direction of the supervising engineer—the man entrusted with the sole responsibility. Even the small insects such as ants obey the same rule in collecting earth, i.e., in constructing a mould of earth. They do it in view of a public good. Or, they carry out the direction of their leader as the artisans follow the command of their head. How will many individuals agree to be united in order to construct a common immovable object which is a source of pleasure to some and at the same time that of pain to others ? Moreover, the hypothesis that the unconscious materials combine themselves to produce such an object has been already refuted. Hence, a single intelligent superintendent, who can guide unconscious merits and demerits is necessarily assumed. His control is as follows : When He desires, merits and demerits bear their fruits.

Hence, the existence of only one God is accepted by us. But the hypothesis of two or more Gods is to be discarded since the work for public welfare will remain suspended in case of a diversity of opinions or difference in plans among Gods. Suppose Gods are many and are at cross purposes. If the resolution of one of them is frustrated then he will cease to be a paramount ruler. Hence, the hypothesis of one God is better. The stored-up actions of all creatures commence to produce various effects in accordance with His will. Thus, the creation of the universe is fairly explained. Such actions remain inactive and no effects are produced if He so desires. Thus, the hypothesis of dissolution is nicely proved.

Kumārila has also taken an exception to the hypothesis of creation and dissolution and said thus :—The creation of the universe signifies that all objects in this universe are produced at once. The dissolution of the universe stands for the simultaneous destruction of all objects in this world. Such an assumption of creation and dissolution is not based upon sound logical basis.

Such an adverse criticism is not sound. Let us, now, set aside the hypothesis of universal creation and dissolution. No merit and demerit of a creature can by themselves bear fruits. They do so when they are guided by the will of God. Thus, the assumption of God is a necessary one, otherwise, all our religious practices will break up.

The Mahābhārata says to this effect :—

Every creature is ignorant. He has no control over his happiness and sorrow. According to the divine ordinance a creature goes either to heaven or to hell (i.e. as God sends him).

Now, a question arises in our mind. Let the will of God alone create and destroy the universe. If this is so, why are merits and demerits of all creatures assumed as conditioning the creation and the destruction of the universe ? As answer cannot be offered without assuming merit and demerit as factors of the universe. If God is absolutely independent of merits and demerits in the matter of producing the various objects then He is open to three charges, viz., (1) God's cruelty, (2) Vedic injunctions and prohibitions becoming a dead letter and (3) the unreality of final emancipation. Hence, God enjoys complete independence in controlling merits and demerits. But He is not absolutely independent of them. If He depends upon them, how is He a paramount ruler of the universe ? Such an objection does not hold good since a proof is not subservient to our needs. Or, if He is held to be dependent upon merit and demerit, His paramount lordship is not at stake. There is no need of continuing wordy battle with a contesting atheist who has focussed his attention upon an iota of sophistry.

As the bad logicians have set up fallacious counter-arguments against the sound arguments put forward by us and these arguments have been refuted so the existence of God who is able to create the three worlds has been established.

It is our conviction that we commit a sin if we talk with those who do not believe in the existence of God, established by sound logic. For this reason, it is highly reasonable not to enter into disputation with these fellows.

By His will the three worlds come into being, persist for a definite period of time and meet with destruction at the end of the cycle of existence. I bow down before the supreme lord, who is an embodiment of goodness, distributes the fruits of actions of all creatures among them and has eternal consciousness and bliss.

The favourite Hypothesis of the Mīmāṁsakas that sound is eternal is being asserted

It cannot be proved that the Vedas are composed by God even if the existence of God, the supreme being, as proficient in the creation of the three worlds, is established.

It may be suggested to our mind that God has created the Vedic words, fixed up the relation holding between a Vedic word and its denotation and composed the Vedas. This suggestion is not applicable to all words—not to speak of the Vedic words.

A word is a series of letters which manifest themselves in a close succession. But these letters are indestructible. How can they be created by God ? The relation of significance is not created by God since it represents the intrinsic power of words. As heat inseparably belongs to fire so the power of significance intrinsically belongs to words. Such power is an eternal property of words. The Vedas have not been composed by a person because they are intrinsically different from the ordinary poems composed by the poets. As the Vedas bear a stamp of distinction so no element of them has been composed by God.

We, the Mīmāṁsakas will take no exception to the hypothesis that God has created and destroyed mountains. But we stick to the view that the truth of the Vedas is intrinsic, i.e., self-evident because they are independent of an author. It is also a truism that though we deny authorship of the Vedas to God yet we are not sworn enemies of the hypothesis of God, the personal creator. The absolute independence of the Vedas explains the intrinsic truth of the Vedas. God may be a remarkable author or a competent creator but in no way helps the composition of the Vedas.

How are these letters eternal ? Do they not pass away as soon as they are heard ? How do you cherish the hope of establishing the hypothesis that the Vedas enjoy the absolute independence ? (The Mīmāṁsakas hold that sounds are eternal. The Vedas consisting of eternal sounds are also eternal. What is the basis of this assumption ? The Naiyāyikas raise the most fundamental question).

Let us discuss the pros and cons of the problem.

An objection to the hypothesis that sound is eternal

No argument which establishes the eternality of sounds flashes in our mind. But perception and presumption point to the hypothesis that sounds are eternal. The arguments which prove the non-eternality of sounds run thus :—

These reasons which point to the non-eternality of sounds are now being stated. Sound is an effect because it is experienced only when some effort precedes to produce it. The proposition that all effects are non-eternal admits of simple conversion as the character of being an effect and non-eternality are two co-extensive terms and pervade each other. If one of them is established as belonging to a subject of inference then the other term, also, necessarily belongs to it. In other words, these two terms are so related that each of them alternately becomes the reason of the other, i.e., when one becomes the reason, the other is the consequence and *vice versa*.

A sound is an effect to be produced by our effort because it is experienced by us only when we make an effort so that the air within our body comes in contact with a particular part of our body and becomes separated from it. A sound is also destructible because it is not experienced after its pronunciation. We know that a sound has perished because we do not experience it as lasting even for a moment soon after it has been pronounced. A sound is an effect because we use it as an object of the verb 'to make'.

Persons who make these expressions 'Make a sound', Do not make a sound', etc. know for certain that a sound is an effect. As the same sounds are simultaneously experienced in many places so they are effects. As they are produced in so many different places so they are localized in them. Again, a sound is non-eternal because a sound evolves from another sound. Let us take an example, viz., 'dadhyatra'. The semi-vowel 'y' evolves from the vowel 'i' because the semi-vowel 'y' bears a close resemblance to the vowel 'i' and because whenever we hear the former letter we are reminded of the latter. The semi-vowel 'y' is also subject to destruction because it is an evolute like the juice of grapes or that of sugar-cane. We also know that a sound is an effect because if there is an increase in the quantity of its cause then the effect, viz. a sound, increases in volume. When many persons with greater effort utter the word 'cow' the sound becomes very loud. But when a few persons with less effort utter the word 'cow' the sound becomes very small. As greater is the number of threads so bigger is the size of a piece of cloth and as lesser is the number of threads so smaller is the size of a piece of cloth. From the above relation holding between threads and a piece of cloth we know that a piece of cloth is the effect of threads. Similarly, we know that a sound is the effect of our effort.

(The Mīmāṁsakas, now, make their position clear and try to meet the argument put forward by the Naiyāyikas). They contend that the eternality of a sound is an established truth. A sound is experienced only when some effort precedes it. It is not produced by such an effort. Its manifestation is only due to it. As there is the possibility of the perception of a sound only when it is manifested by our effort so there is no hard and fast rule that a sound is an effect of effort since the latter precedes the former. The contact and the separation of the air with and from the certain inner parts help the manifestation of letters. But as they are very short-lived so when the letters are manifested by the aid of palate, etc. They do not last long after their utterance to be perceived by us. The use of the verb 'to make' is not decisive. It is sometimes loosely used. When we ask somebody to prepare fuels from a heap of cow-dung we use the root kṛ (to make) in Sanskrit. Or when we ask somebody to cut a log of wood into long pieces of wood, we use the root kṛ (to make)in Sanskrit. We do not ask the person to produce something. But we ask him to impart certain forms to some pre-existing matter. So, the use of the verb 'to make' does not invariably show that the causal relation subsists between an effort and a sound. The simultaneous perception of a sound in different directions is possible like that of the Sun even if the sound is one but not many. The hypothesis that the relation of causality holds between the two letters as one of them changes into another does not hold good since one is substituted by another. The word 'dadhi, ends in the vowel 'i' and retains its distinct form as long as there is no euphonic change. The vowel 'i' is replaced by 'y' when euphonic change takes place but the semi-vowel 'y' is a distinct letter. But the vowel 'i' does not change into 'y' as milk evolves sour milk. It is not advisable to hold that the semivowel 'y' is the effect of the vowel 'i' because these letters are uttered by the aid of the same inner limb i. e., palate. The consonants of the 'c' group, the semi-vowel 'y' and 's' are all palatal. If the two objects are similar, it does not mean that they are causally related to each other since the relation of similarity holds between two such objects as are not causally connected, e. g., the eyes and the petals of a lotus-flower are similar but are not causally connected. The rule of Paṇini's grammar regarding the euphonic change is that the vowels 'i' 'u', etc. respectively change into 'y', 'v', etc. when a vowel follows in immediate succession the former ones. It does not purport to convey that the vowel 'i' undergoes a change in form and becomes 'y' as milk changes its form and becomes sour milk. But it indicates that the above-mentioned vowel 'i' yields its place to the semi-vowel 'y' when there is possibility of euphonic change. The words, the objects denoted by them and the relation of significance holding between them are eternal. The instructive work simply informs of the presence of these words, meanings, etc. but does not create them. Moreover, milk changes into sour milk but *vice versa*. But the semivowel 'y' sometimes becomes the vowel 'i'. When the semi-vowel 'y' changes into 'i' we get the form 'vidhyati' from the root 'vyadh'. Hence, the hypothesis that the causal relation exists among letters cannot be established. If a word which consists of letters is uttered either by a strong man having loud voice or by many then the constituent letters do not increase in number. But they remain as they are. But an inarticulate noise increases in volume under the above-mentioned circumstances. Experience teaches us that the volume of an inarticulate sound increases but the letters do never increase.

Presumption has been put forward as a proof of the hypothesis that the words are eternal

The non-eternality of sounds cannot be proved by those resemblances of proof. But we now put forward presumption as a proof of the hypothesis that the words are eternal.

A word is uttered with the purpose of communicating its meaning. If it is held that a word perishes as soon as it is uttered then it cannot convey its meaning.

If a person employs a word the relation of significance of which is not known at all then it does never convey its sense. All persons who use words are unanimous in this point (that a word conveys its meaning).

We are aware of the relation of significance when we observe the activities of an experienced person who is employed by another such person. The relation of significance is cognised only when a long period of time has passed away after the utterance of words by an experienced employer.

The proof behind the above statement is as follows : An experienced person orders another experienced person with the following words 'Fetch a white cow'. In response to this mandate the latter brings there a white cow. There stands a boy who does not know the language of the order. But he watches the movement and activities of the man who has carried out the above mandate. Thus, he himself makes out the meaning of the whole sentence as he understands that the whole movement of this person ordered is based upon the thorough understanding of the words of the order. The person who has been ordered sets to work because the words, spoken by the person who gives the order, constitute the spring of his action and because there has been no other condition which impels him to work. The boy conjectures that he has understood something from the order, given to him. After sometime when he sees that an object is being brought by the person he understands that the person has followed the meaning from the above order. But the object, denoted by the above sentence, is not a simple but a complex one. It consists of many elements, viz., an attribute, an action, a universal and a particular. The sentence which embodies the order consists of many words. He does not understand the meaning of each word all at once. He hears these words in various combinations (positive and negative). He gradually learns the meaning of the word 'cow' after having repeatedly heard it in various combinations. He comes to learn that the word 'cow' denoted the universal of cowness or a concrete particular, i. e., an individual cow as a member of the cow-class or as qualified by the universal of cowness, as the Naiyāyikas suppose. Hence, it requires a long time to make out the relation of significance holding between a word and its meaning. Therefore, it is to be admitted that a word endures a long period of time but is not short-lived.

Now let us assume that the relation of significance holding between a word and the object denoted by it is grasped by us though the word itself is transient. But still the above-hypothesis does not convince us. If the word, the relation of significance of which has been grasped, passes away then how can we make out the meaning of another new word whose relation of significance has not been known to us ?

If the relation of significance of one word is known to us and another word can convey its meaning then all words should have communicated their meanings when the relation of significance of only one word has been detected.

Now, the upholders of the above hypothesis may also assume that when the speaker uses a word, he utters the word, fixes up its meaning, communicates its meaning to others and teaches others to use the word correctly. Such an assumption is not at all tenable. So many different activities cannot take place with simultaneous occurrence. Now, they may argue that when the meaning of a word has been grasped and the word has passed away, a new word appears and conveys the meaning of the nonexistent word since the new word is exactly the same as the old one. Such a hypothesis is not tenable. It is not reasonable to hold that one word is similar to another word since they do not possess many parts in common, being themselves partless. As the speaker himself does not know the meaning of the new word so he should not utter a word in order to communicate his idea, labouring under the apprehension that the listener cannot understand its meaning. Now, the upholder of the above hypothesis may contend that the speaker utters only such a word as is similar to another significant word. The so-called significant word also conveys its sense because it is similar to a third word which is supposed to be significant. If he adopts this line of procedure then the first significant word which was uttered at the dawn of creation should be referred to since the right use of all words which are similar to the initial word presupposes it (the initial word) as its basis. But as a matter of fact such a procedure cannot be adopted since the long series of similarities with the initial word at the start is never taken into consideration. In such a long series of similarities, the basis of similarity is lost sight of since the words being transient, the chain of similarity cannot be traced to a great length.

The words uttered in the long past cannot bear a resemblance to the words pronounced at present since the speakers being different, the conditions and the cause of these two sets of words belonging to the different periods of time, are different, viz., the mouths, the places of utterance, the efforts of the air within the body and the actual contacts of the air with the places of utterance and the actual separations of the air from them are different. If it is held that the communication of the meaning of a word is possible under the supposition that the word in question is similar to another word which has been known to be significant then such a communication of meaning will be surely false like the inferential knowledge of fire from the sight of mist resembling smoke. Therefore, as a word does not carry a sense because it is similar to another word so the hypothesis that a word (viz. a cow) endures long (i. e. eternal) is to be accepted.

Now, the Naiyāyikas may adopt a different line of argument and hold thus:—In case of inference we discover the universal relation of concomitance holding between smoke and fire because we focus our attention upon the common property of smoke, i. e., the universal of smoke but not upon the different particulars of the smoke-class. Similarly, we shall only take the persistent universal belonging to the letter 'g', but not the individual 'g' s into consideration with the net result that a word will have no difficulty in communicating its meaning.

Such a hypothesis is not tenable. The universal of smoke certainly exists. But the universal of all words is a wide common property. It belongs to letters which convey meaning and also to such letters as do not convey meaning. The universal which belongs to the word 'cow' cannot be proved. (Therefore it is difficult to hold that the word 'cow' conveys its meanings through the medium of a universal belonging to the word 'cow', by means of successive letters which are not related to one another as its constituents ? If the whole, i.e., the word 'cow' is not constituted then which locus does the universal of the word 'cow' belong to ? It is a truism that the universal which belongs to the pieces of cloth does never belong to the threads, i. e., the constituents of a piece of cloth.

Now, the Naiyāyikas may contend thus : Let the universal which belongs to the word 'cow' be not accepted as existing. But it is reasonable to hold that the universals which belong to the different letters 'g' etc. the constituents of the word 'cow', will do the above function. This alternative hypothesis is not also sound. The universals which are asserted to belong to the letters cannot be proved to be so. A particular is distinguished from a universal, if the relation of identity-in-difference holds between them. If a letter is repeatedly uttered then the different appearances of the same letter are experienced as identical. They are experienced to be so because the letter is one but not because they possess one universal. If the elements which manifest a universal in a particular are clearly distinct from those in another particular then the existence of a universal is clearly proved since the particulars possess very vivid marks of difference. The individual cows having different names 'Śāvaleya' and 'Bāhuleya' are vividly perceived to be mutually different. Though the particulars, i.e., cows are clearly different from one another yet they have a common name, i. e., a cow. The experience of identity in them is due to the fact that they all possess one and the same object, i. e., a universal. Hence the existence of the universal of cow-ness is accepted.

In the light of this experience let us examine the above hypothesis.

Have you ever experienced that the different utterances of the same letter, viz., 'g' look like the individuals of the class of a cow designated as Śāvaleya, etc. Why do you purport to hold that a universal belongs to so many different manifestations of the same letter ? When a child, an old man, a female and a parrot read a line the persons who listen to it recognize the difference in the speakers but do not recognize the difference in the letters uttered.

When Garga reads out a letter and Māthura does the same thing the speakers are only cognized to be different. We all experience that they are reading the same letter. Hence, there is no difference in the letter which is being uttered by the two different persons. When a person reads a line again and again the same thing is repeatedly uttered. If the same words, e.g., Gaṅgā, Gagana, Garga, etc. are repeatedly uttered then we notice no difference in these words themsleves. When a letter is pronounced with slow, moderate and fast speed there is difference in sound but not in the letter. The different utterances of the same letter are not like so many particulars of a class, viz., the individual cow 'śavala', etc.

Even if we admit that a universal, viz., gatva, belongs to the letter 'g' and that it expresses itself in and through various sounds slow, fast, etc. then it does not prove that the consonant 'g' is many. The recognition of difference in the universal 'gatva' is due to its accidents Similarly, why do you not hold that the consonant 'g' is identical in the midst of changing sounds and that a change in the sounds of the same consonant is accidental ? As the consonant 'g' essentially remains the same so the experience of identity is true and that of difference is untrue. The experience of difference is due to the defect in the organs of speech that are responsible for its manifestation. This hypothesis is also favoured by the economy of assumptions. In fine, there is no such universal of 'gatva' belonging to the particulars 'g', 'g', 'g', etc. We add a word more to the above conclusion in order to give an exposition to our point of view that the consonant 'g' occurring in the words 'go', 'guru' and 'geha' appear to be different owing to its association with the different vowels. Hence, it is our impression that the appearance of difference in a consonant is due to its accidental elements. We also believe that a vowel may also be associated with the accidental properties. As the accidental elements are uniformly associated with all letters so the same vowel appears to be different like a consonant due to its association with the said nonessential element. The universal, viz., 'atva' does not belong to the vowel as 'a' as the universal 'gatva' does not really exist. The eighteen-fold division of the vowel 'a' is based upon its accidental elements. The experience in the divisions of a vowel, viz., 'a' such as short, long and prolated follows from the difference in the nature of the sound itself. As the semi-vowel 'v' is different from the consonant 'g' so the vowel 'a' which is mute is not different from the vowel 'a' which is sonant. But the vowel 'a' is experienced to be the same in the midst of all the changing associations.

The objector may argue thus :— if the constituent letters of the two words are the same, how do the two words convey different meanings ? The objector illustrates his point citing the words 'āraṇyam' and 'araṇyam.' The word 'araṇya' denotes a forest but the word 'āraṇya' means 'forest-born'. There is no difference between 'a' in āraṇya and 'a' in araṇya since 'a' is short whereas 'a' is long. The Mīmāṁsakas meet this objection with the remark that the above difference in the sense lies in the sound itself. The length of the sound being not the property of the word itself how does it help to convey the meaning? The answer in this question is that it is like the speed of a horse.

As the speed of a horse serves the purpose of a man who rides it so the property of sound which is not a letter helps the letter to convey its meaning.

We cannot subscribe to the hypothesis that universal belongs to the vowel 'a'. The reason is as follows. The long 'a' and the prolated 'a' do not share the universal of atva in common. The short vowel 'a' and the long vowel 'a' do not share the universal of atva in common. Hence, the vowels like a, i. u, etc. do not admit of diffierence so they do not possess universals. All the letters do not possess a common universal of word-ness. If they had possessed such a universal then a word would not denote a distinct sense. Hence the analogy of smoke, i. e., the universal of smoke does not hold good in this case. In other words, it is not possible to hold that a word conveys its meaning by means of a universal belonging to it.

If we do not assume that a word is eternal then we cannot explain the communication of meaning by a word. Thus, the proof of presumption is the source of the true knowledge of the eternality of a word.

Some hold that presumption is not distinct inference. But it is not true that we cannot put forward a syllogistic argument in support of our hypothesis.

The syllogism runs thus:— A word is eternal because it communicates its meaning only when the relation of significance holding between it and its meaning is grasped. The positive example is smoke. The Mīmāṁsakas mean to say that when smoke is seen we are in a position to infer fire because we know that the universal relation of concomitance holds between smoke and fire. Similarly, when we hear a word which is sound we know another object provided that we are aware of the relation of significance holding between the word and the object. This knowledge is inferential because we are aware of the object denoted by a word on the strength of a particular relation holding between the word and the object. The next point, viz., the eternality of a word, has been explained by Jaimini in his Mīmāṁsā Sūtra (I. I. 18). He holds that a word is eternal because a word is uttered by a person in order to communicate its meaning to another person. The word lasts till the meaning is communicated. A word is uttered by a person. Another person hears it. He remembers the relation of significance holding between it and the object denoted by it. Then he understands that the word conveys this meaning. The word persists until and unless the meaning is not communicated. If the word does not endure, its meaning cannot be communicated. It is a permanent object like the soul because there is no source of its destruction. It does not perish on the destruction of its parts because it has no parts. How is it that it has no parts? Let us explain why it has no parts.

If we put forth very little effort to pronounce a letter then it may be inaudible but never becomes partly inaudible. The parts which make up wholes admit of two kinds. Some of them have made up wholes but the others have not as yet constituted wholes. Have the parts which are supposed to produce a letter effectuated whole or not? we perceive threads which are parts of a piece of cloth. But we see no such parts of a letter. We are not in a position to infer parts of a letter because there is no middle term. A letter does not persist like some other substance if its parts on which it rests are destroyed because it is a partless whole like the soul and requires nothing to stand upon. It cannot be held that a letter is neither permanent nor impermanent since a third alternative is not possible. Moreover, permanent and impermanent objects exhaust the whole of universe.

Hence, if a letter disappears for some time and does not meet its destruction then on its reappearance nobody can destroy it.

A letter is eternal because it is not numerable. Common people say that the word 'cow' has been eight times pronounced. But they do not hold that eight different words have been pronounced. Hence each letter maintains its constant identity among its different manifestations. When the repetition of an act is counted we use the suffix 'kṛtvasuc,' It is attached to a word when that on which the act of utterance rests is one and the same. Hence, only the act of utterance repeatedtly takes place.

It has been stated by Kumārila to this effect. If the locus of an act is one and the same then and then only the repetition of the act is possible. This repetition of an act is denoted by the suffix 'Kṛtvasuc'. As this suflix is used so the act of utterance which rests upon a single letter is repeated. It is attached to numbers. They hold that the suffix 'kṛtvasuc' applies to the words denoting numbers. From the use of kṛtvasuc we learn that an object is recognized to persist as identical in the midst of its various appearances. The representative auditory perception that this is that word 'cow' is a proof of its eternality (i. e. of the word 'cow'). The auditory perception is known to all listeners. It is not illusory since neither the sense-organ—the instrument of this perception, is suspected to be defective nor its object is suspected to involve contradiction.

The above act of recognition in question is an auditory perception since it is causally connected with the contact with ears. This causal relation is ascertained by means of positive and negative concomitance. The instrument which produces it is not known to be defective. Again, this piece of consciousness is not such as oscilates between two opposite predicates, i. e., it is not indeterminate. Moreover, we anticipate no such contradictory judgment as 'This is not such' which contradicts it. This judgment may be shown to refer to an object which is novel since it refers to an object which is qualified by the present existence. Moreover, though the recognitive judgment refers to an object which is known before yet it is accepted to be a piece of valid knowledge. The Naiyāyikas cannot discredit it like the Buddhists with the remark that it is a piece of invalid knowledge since they do not subscribe to the hypothesis of universal flux.

Some logicians hold that the recognition of a letter as same is due to similarity. Such a view does not hold good. Other logicians hold that such a recognition takes place because it refers only to the universal which the individual letters partake of. These two hypotheses have been already refuted.

(The points in criticism are as follows : Similarity consists in the possession of many parts in common with another object. As letters are partless so they are similar to none. No universal inheres in letters since each letter is merely an individual. No universal belongs to a word since a word cannot be shown to be a whole consisting of parts, viz. letters).

Some hold that the piece of consciousness which refers to a letter is not valid since it refers even to an absent letter, i. e. a letter which has disappeared. Such hypothesis is not tenable since when a word or a letter is cognized it has not disappeared. The very cognition of a word or a letter refutes the suggestion of disapperance.

The Naiyāyikas including Jayanta admit that a sound persists three or four atoms of time. Though it endures for this short span of time yet this short stay does not preclude the possibility of a sound of being recognized. But we do not perceive an object if it lasts only for an atom of time. The reason behind it is this that if an object passes away at the time of its perception then it cannot be perceived. (In other words, the object which is perceived is one of the conditions of its perception. The condition is always antecedent to its effect. The object, being the condition of its perception, precedes it. Again, an object which is perceived is required to last when its perception takes place. If an object lasts only for an atom of time then it cannot be perceived.) We shall discuss this point when we shall refute the doctrine of the universal flux.

We may also add in this connection. At midnight when the sky is enveloped by the dense cloud, as dark as black-bees, some object is recognized even by means of the short-lived flashes of lightning. Similarly, a letter is recognized to be one and the same by means of short-lived air-waves which give birth to an uninterrupted series of conjunctions and disjunctions of the air with and from the different parts of the mouth such as guttural, palatal etc. This is a case of auditory representative perception.

The Hypothesis that a Letter is only manifested but is not produced is untenable.

The Naiyāyikas come forward and refute the hypothesis of the Mīmāṁsakas. They hold that the very word "Mārutaiḥ" in the last verse of the preceding section reminds us of the line of criticism. Let us leave the argument on the strength of recognition at the outset. If we subscribe to the hypothesis of manifestation then we cannot explain the auditory perception of the distinct letters at the different periods of time.

All the letters are eternal and all-pervasive so each of them is present everywhere. In that case why do we hear a particular letter at a time to the exclusion of the others? What is the determining factor in this case?

Now, the Mīmāṁsakas may contend that the different 'dhvanis' manifest different letters. They define a dhvani as the air which blows within the body, comes in contact with a particular portion of the mouth and becomes separated from another such portion. Or, they define a dhvani as the conjunction and the disjunction of the inner air with some part and from some other part. Do these dhvanis make an improvement either upon the object of such perception or upon both of them? They may select any of these hypotheses. But each of them is defective. If it is held that some change is introduced into the instrument of hearing for its betterment then all the letters should be simultaneously perceived. But can you explain when a particular letter, e. g, 'ga' is only perceived by the modified organ of hearing to the exclusion of the other letters? How do you derive the rule that imposes restriction upon our hearing? The improvement of the instrument means the exhaling of the motionless inner air. But all the letters which belong to the particular region will reap the fruit of this improvement. (Space constitutes the instrument of hearing. All the sounds which belong to that portion of the space will be heard since their common ground is affected by this act). When the screen (i. e. the drop-scene) is lifted up and the unobstructed eyes find an opportunity of seeing, the spectator beholds all the objects on the stage. Similarly, when the motionless inner air is taken out all the letters which remain in the inner region should also be simultaneously heard with our ears.

The Mīmāṁsakas hold that the organ of hearing is constituted by the space. But it is all-pervasive and partless. If somewhere some improvement is made on it then all the beings will have their organ of hearing improved. Thus all of them simultaneously hear alike all the sounds.

If it is held that the object of hearing is improved upon, then a letter or a word, which is, according to the Mīmāṁsakas, partless and all-pervasive being improved upon, should be heard everywhere. The word 'cow' which has become manifest in Madras should also be heard in Kashmeir. The Mīmāṁsakas cannot also revise their hypothesis and hold that an improvement upon the letter or the word is indirectly brought in and through its locus. Such a contention is not tenable since the Mīmāṁsakas hold that a letter or a word stands upon no locus. Even if they admit that a word or a letter finds support in the space, matters do not improve since the space is an indivisible single entity. They cannot also hold that word 'cow' is partly improved upon since it is a partless whole. The following verse has been stated by Kumārila in his Śloka-Vārttikam. The sense of the verse is this. If a letter or a word is pronounced with little effort then either we fall to hear it or when we hear it we hear it completely and distinctly. The sense of this verse is this that a letter or a word consists of no parts.

If the Mīmāṁsakas revise their hypothesis and hold that both the instrument and the letter or the word should be improved upon then this revised hypothesis should not be immune from the above two defects, viz., (1) all the letters or words should be simultaneously heard and (2) a letter or a word should be simultaneously heard from all the different spaces. The objects which are co-extensive and sensed by the one and same sense-organ are not known to be manifested by the different illuminators.

If a householder enters a room with a lamp in his hand in order to see a pot of sour milk, then the lamp reveals not only the pot but also the cakes lying on the spot adjacent to that of the pot.

In fine, if we subscribe to the hypothesis that a sound i. e., a letter, is produced but not manifested then we may soundly explain why a letter is heard only within a restricted area. Moreover, if we subscribe to the hypothesis of manifestation then we can not maintain the distinction between the loud and the low sounds. Again, we cannot explain why a sound is drowned by another. A letter is neither loud nor low since it admits of no intrinsic difference. The very act which manifests a letter has no such qualitative difference so that a letter may be presented to our consciousness as loud or low. The air which may be held to help its manifestation may be strong or gentle. But how can one grasp the quality of the air by means of the organ of hearing? If an object consists of parts then there is possibility of experiencing it differently since it is most likely that the same parts are not uniformly perceived in all cases. But if a letter admits of no parts then such an explanation does not hold good. Therefore, the hypothesis that a letter is produced is a better one.

All the Charges against the hypothesis of manifestation are answered

A reply to the criticism contained in the earlier section is as follows : The Mīmāṁsakas prefer the hypothesis that the instrument of hearing is to be improved upon to the other one. This sense-organ, being somewhat improved upon by the air, grasps a particular letter. This organ which has been thus improved upon, being accompanied by a particular set of conjunctions and disjunctions of the air with and from certain portions of the mouth, grasps a particular letter. As the Naiyāyikas hold that such conjunctions and disjunctions are able to produce letters so we, the Mīmāṁsakas, hold that they are capable of manifesting letters.

Another objection, raised by the Naiyāyikas, is this that there is no such experience as points to the hypothesis that the different letters are manifested by the different illuminators. We, the Mīmāṁsakas, give a reply to this objection with the remark "Who is this man with a thousand eyes, expressing such a view?"

Smell belongs only to the earth. All the different smells are co-ordinate attributes of earth. They are also grasped only by the same sense-organ, viz., the nose. But our experience throws light on the fact that the smell, in different cases, is manifested by the different manifestors. The smell of earth is manifested somewhere by its contact with fire, somewhere by its contact with the rays of the sun and somewhere by the sprinkling of water on it.

We, the Mīmāṁsakas, do not subscribe to the hypothesis that the taking out of the air is the only factor which makes improvement upon the instrument of hearing. If it were so then it would be merely the common manifestor of all letters. But the real improvement is something else. It is constituted by its capacity of manifesting a letter. The instrument acquires many capacities but each capacity is competent only to manifest a single distinct letter.

The Naiyāyikas take an exception to the hypothesis that the space constitutes the sense-organ of hearing and point out that if the space is held to be such an organ then all beings should have the same organ of hearing. But such a criticism is not sound because the principle of merit and demerit determines the distinction in the result. As a jar is a limiting adjunct which imposes limitation upon the sky, so there may be other limiting adjuncts which introduce difference into the space and the possibility of having a distinct organ of hearing is explained. Thus, deafness or the power of hearing is explained by means of principle of merit and demerit. The Naiyāyikas hold that the sky constitutes the organ of hearing. Therefore, the Naiyāyikas, have been paid in their own coin. The Mīmāṁsakas do not subscribe to the view that the sky alone constitutes the organ of hearing. They hold that each person has a distinct organ of hearing, otherwise the distinct auditory perception of each person cannot be explained.

Bhartṛmitra, a celebrated Mīmāṁsaka, has stated that if it is held that an improvement is made upon the letter by contact of air then the all-pervasive letter will not be benefited by it since this improvement will remain confined only within the well-defined boundary but will not go beyond it. Though an improvement cannot be made upon a portion of a letter since it is a partless substance yet a letter is heard only within a restricted area just as a universal which is all-pervasive is seen only in a limited sphere.

The Naiyāyikas shall have also to subscribe to this decisive view.

A universal is all-pervasive. But it is perceived only in an individual. Though it completely reveals itself in and through an individual yet it is not a truism that it is not perceived in and through other individuals. Similarly, though a letter is all pervasive yet it is heard only at the spot where a dhvani (a definite set of well-defined conjunctions and disjunctions) exists. We should also note that when it is heard it is heard perfectly and completely. Though it is heard at a spot yet it is also heard at other spots under similar circumstances. As the body of an individual is the manifestor of a universal so a dhvani is an illuminator of a letter. It is pointless to hold that a letter is heard if it is located upon a substance and that it is not heard if it is not located upon a substance.

As a letter is not grasped as ubiquitous and partless so the properties of dhvani, viz., dullness, sharpness, etc., appear to be the properties of a letter. In a like manner though plumpness and thinness, etc., are the properties of a body yet they are known to us as belonging to the universal. The person who has never experienced the plump cow individuals such as Sābaleya, etc., is known to perceive the universal of cow-ness as thin.

Or, the properties such as sharpness, dullness, etc., are not presented to our consciousness as those of a letter. But the consciousness of a letter appears to us to be sharp or dull since an act of consciousness simulates its manifestor.

Likewise the letters either increase or decrease in volume. But they do never eclipse one another. (In other words, the letters appear to be such because the consciousness of a letter is either sharp or dull. This derivative property of an act of consciousness is attributed to a letter. A letter always remains to be the same.)

As the dim light of a lamp is thrown into shade by the brilliant ray of the sun so the weak current of air is surpassed by the strong current of air.

Thus the above two hypotheses, viz., (1) an improvement is made upon the organ of hearing and (2) an improvement is made upon the letter are proved to be true since they are now freed from all defects. Hence, the hypothesis of the manifestation of a letter is better since a letter is proved to be eternal on the strength of recognition.

The hypothesis of the manifestation of a letter is better than that of the production of a letter since the former obeys the law of parsimony.

Sirs, let us now discuss which of the two hypothesis, viz., that of the new origin of a letter and that of the manifestation of a letter, obeys the law of parsimony.

Let us at the outset examine in detail the hypothesis of creation. The Naiyāyikas, the Vaiśeṣikas, the Sāṁkhyists and the Buddhists subscribe to the hypothesis that a letter is an effect. No body thinks of the wretched philosophers, viz., the Cārvākas, in this context.

The venerable Vaiśeṣikas agree with us the Mīmāṁsakas, in the manner of perceiving sound. A sound is produced either by conjunction or by disjunction. It, being thus produced, spreads over all directions. It goes up and down. It also proceeds obliquely. When it spreads it looks like a round Kadamba flower with its pollen on all sides. Each sound produces another similar sound at a very close quarter. Thus a sound generates many similar sounds. They, on their turn, produce other similar sounds in a similar manner. Or, as a wave produces a series of waves so a sound produces a series of sounds. A sound which is last but one of the series arises in the sky confined within the ear-walls. It inheres in the sky, limited by the ear-walls. It is sensed by the organ of hearing, i. e. the limited sky. But such a conjecture simply provokes our laughter.

The hypothesis that a sound produces another sound is a very uncommon one. A man of common sense fails to follow such a hypothesis. Two acts of consciousness are known to be causally connected. But the causal nexus is not known to hold good between the two sounds.

No body places his confidence in the hypothesis that a sound produces on all sides up and down its similar sounds at a place very close to that of a listener.

If a sound produces at all a series of sounds why does not the series continue to exist for all times to come since the abrupt exhaustion of the velocity of a sound does not take place like that of the velocity of the air. How is it that a sound is veiled when the sky is partitioned by the walls, etc. ? The inherent cause of a sound is the sky. It, being all-pervasive, exists even within the wall.

Now, the Vaiśeṣikas may contend that the sky which has no contact with a wall which envelops it is the material cause of a sound. In that case, they should furnish us with sufficient proofs.

Again, if a sound produces a similar sound then how is it that a faint sound produces a long sound? A near sound is heard to be loud but a distant one is heard to be faint.

A series of sounds cannot be compared to that of waves since a wave has size, motion and speed but a sound has none.

The Vaiśeṣikas have argued that a sound produces a similar sound because it is an attribute like a colour. Such an argument is baseless because the minor premise that a sound is an attribute involves the fallacy of material contradiction. It has not yet been established that a sound is an attribute.

A sound is never experienced as depending upon a substance. But when we perceive an attribute, viz., colour, etc., we perceive it is inhearing in a substance. Therefore, how can a sound be an attribute?

The main argument of the Vaiśeṣikas that a sound produces another sound because it is an attribute like the attribute of colour is opposed by the following counter-arguments. A sound does not produce another sound because it is a soundlike the sound which is produced within the ear-hole. Conjunction and disconjunction do not produce a sound because they possess the essence of conjunction and disjunction like the other conjunction and disjunction which do not produce sound. These counter-arguments are ready at hand. We should not dilate upon this insignificant hypothesis.

The followers of Kapila hold that the mode of the organ of hearing goes to the place where a sound is produced. It assumes the form of a sound. In other words, a sound imparts its form to the mode of the said organ. Thus the mode of the organ undergoes a change. But the mode is intermixed with the sky. Why does the near sound impress its form on the mode but not the distant one? Is there any law to govern the above change in the form of a mode? As there is no such law so a sound which is produced near Cawnpur should be heard in the distant village Gauramūlaka in Kashmir. Moreover, a sound which is produced in a partitioned area should also be heard since that mode of the organ of hearing which has no dimension cannot be obstructed by the partition walls when it goes out to reach the sound.

If the wind blows towards the organ of hearing from a sound then the sound should not be heard since the flowing wind blocks the passage of the moving mode.

But it is a fact that even a distant sound is heard if the wind blows favourably, i. e., towards the organ of hearing. It is also a truism that a near sound is not heard if the wind does not blow favourably. But if we subscribe to the hypothesis of the Sāṁkhyists then the near one will be heard but the distant one will not be heard under the above circumstances.

According to the Śāṁkhyists there is identity between a mode and a substance having the mode. The mode of the organ of hearing should be like the organ of hearing. In that case, it is co-extensive with the organ of hearing The organ of hearing is very extensive. The mode of it should also be equally extensive. In that case, do not we hear all sounds near or distant alike?

The Ārhatas (the Jainas) hold that a sound is a whole and is constituted by a number of minute particles. Thus created, it proceeds from its place of origin towards the ears of a person. Thus it is heard. It is a very nice hypothesis stated by them.

Each letter consists of parts. They are changing particles. They constitute the whole. But it is a very curious hypothesis.

These particles are never perceived. Their process of combination is consequently imperceptible. Each letter has its peculiar combination of parts. Which letter is constituted by which combination?

The constituents of a letter are very tight. They have been combined by no body. They cannot frame a whole in the shape of a letter as a very tight and impact body.

Thus, why is not the whole, viz. a letter, which is very light, deflected from its path by the blowing wind? Again, if it dashes against a tree then why is it not shattered into pieces?

How long does such a weak letter move on to reach its destination? When it enters the ear of a person how is it also heard by other persons?

If it is held that it comes out from the ear of that person and goes into the ear of another person then how will the Jainas explain the simultaneous hearing of a letter by many persons?

Now if the Jainas hold that many letters are simultaneously created by a speaker in accordance with the number of hearers then it will be pointed out that so many letters cannot be created by the single effort of a speaker. Even if we admit that each hearer has a distinct letter to hear then the possibility of the simultaneous hearing of a single letter by many persons is simply ruled out.

We shall not discuss much about the keenness of the intellect of the Digambara Jainas (the naked ones) since when they display their intellect to defend their hypothesis the critics simply laugh at their defence.

Almost all the Buddhists hold that a sound which is heard is not related to the organ of hearing. The organ of hearing has a peculiar power by means of which a sound is heard. But such a statement comes from the lips of the foolish logicians. A distinct sound is as unrelated to our organ of hearing as a sound in the close area is. But the Buddhists fail to explain why a distant sound is only heard to the exclusion of the second one. The Buddhists also violate the general rule regarding the nature of an object, viz., something becomes an object only when it becomes united with the subject. We have discussed the Buddhist hypothesis only because it does not deserve to be neglected like that of the Cārvākas.

The hypothesis of the creation of a sound as offered by the logicians of the other schools have been heard. Now, let the reader hear the hypothesis of the manifestation of an eternal sound as offered by the Mīmāṁsakas.

Whenever a speaker intends to speak something a mental activity sets in. It (mental activity) stirs up the inner organs such as the lungs, the heart, the stomach, the kidneys and the liver. As a result of their activity the internal air comes out. When the air comes out it acquires speed and motion. The passage of the air from the within is very clear. Those who hold that the air is perceptible feel the presence of the air by means of touch if they place their hands near the mouth of the speaker. But those who hold that the air is an inference may infer it from the motion of a piece of cotton placed before the mouth of the speaker.

When the internal air comes out from within, it spreads in all directions. It, at the same time, drives away all the motionless air which is an impediment to the manifestation of a sound. It reaches the articular space enclosed by the ears and thus makes a sound audible.

If the mental activity of the speaker is either great or small then the speed of the air correspondingly becomes high or low. When the air rushes out with violent speed and moves on with great force it suddenly stops like a flying arrow and cannot reach a very distant place.

The air is a mass. It is a material substance, having a limited dimension. When it moves its movement is obstructed by the other material substances encountering it on its path. For this reason when a sound is manifested within an area enclosed by the walls it is not heard by another person standing outside. The hearer imagines that a sound comes from the direction from which the air blows with speed. When a person blows conch the air manifests an inarticulate sound.

Or, though a latter is not worthy of being grasped by the ears yet the ears will have immediate experience of the universal of a sound.

In fine, we, the Mīmāṁsakas, do not indulge in idle imagination. The speed of the air is a well-known fact but not a fiction. We have only indulged in imagination regarding the improvement made upon the organ of hearing. This improvement of the organ is supersensuous. This hypothesis is based upon presumption. It is not a very strange one. It has a logical necessity.

The impartial judges hold that the hypothesis of the manifestation of a letter obeys better the law of parsimony than that of the creation of a letter.

Moreover, if we subscribe to the hypothesis of manifestation then we can explain why all letters are not simultaneously heard. There is a hard and fast rule to show that a single letter is only heard at a time. Again, recognition being a source of valid knowledge, one should hold that a letter is eternal.

The judgment "What is recognized is eternal" is not universally true because though an act of consciousness and an action are recognized yet they are not eternal. The invalidation of this generalization has been stated in the chapter on perception. Such a statement simply reveals your foolishness. A fallacy cancels the truth of an induction. But it does not interfere with the truth of perception. It becomes irrelevant if we run from one conclusion to another. We shall not take an exception to the conclusion that an act of consciousness and an action are experienced by an act of uncontradicted recognition. But if their recognition is contradicted then how can an act of consciousness and an action stand on the same footing with a sound?

The summing-up of the conclusion that sound is eternal

A sound is established to be eternal on the strength of recognition in spite of the vigilant watch and opposition of the logicians of the Nyāya and Vaiśeṣika schools. The proof in the shape of presumption has been advanced beforehand. The arguments in favour of the non-eternality of a sound have also been refuted.

The sentences which the Vedas contain are eternal. The meaning of these sentences does not involve contradiction. From the knowledge of eternal sentences it is easy to infer that letters are eternal.

The experts on the Vedic accents (the teachers of the science of Śikṣā) hold that a sound is constituted by the particles of the air. Such a hypothesis is not sound. As the hypothesis of the Jainas that a sound is produced by the changing atoms has been refuted so we may also refute this hypothesis in a similar manner.

Those who hold that all objects are transitory on the strength of the evidence of the destruction of the gross objects cannot uphold the thesis that a sound is destructible.

As the constituents of the gross objects are known to be subject to destruction so they may arrive at a false generalization that all objects are destructible. But as a sound consists of no parts so it is not destructible like a jar.

The commencement of the refutation of the thesis that sound is eternal.

We, the Naiyāyikas, refute the thesis of the Mīmāṁsakas thus. The two proofs, viz. representative perception and presumption, advanced by you in order to prove the eternality of a sound, can in no way establish the above thesis. Presumtion, put forward by you, amounts to this that a word which is pronounced to convey its meaning to others is eternal because the communication of the meaning of a word cannot be otherwise explained. But this argument is very weak since the communication of the meaning of a word may be otherwise explained. The Mīmāṁsakas hold that as a letter is recognized to be one and the same so it is eternal. They also think that in the opinion of the Naiyāyikas such a recognition reveals the resemblance of a letter to another but not the identity of a letter. They have misrepresented the thesis of the Naiyāyikas and misdirected their energy to refute a wrong thesis.

If the universal of gatva (a universal inhering in the consonant ga) is admitted to exist then everything (beginning from the ascertainment of the relation existing between a word and its meaning and ending in the communication of its meaning) will be perfectly established.

Now, the Mīmāṁsakas contend that the hypothesis regarding the existence of such universals has been refuted by them. But the Naiyāyikas urge that the above topic should be reopened since it is the vital point upon which the whole controversy revolves.

If the existence of such a universal is discarded then the communication of the meaning of a word is not otherwise possible. Besides a universal, there is no such object as is recognized. Thus, we, the Naiyāyikas, obtain victory over the Mīmāṁsakas.

On the other hand, if the universal of gatva is established then it helps to communicate the meaning of a word and explains the recognition of the letter 'ga'. Thus, the Mīmāṁsakas are defeated.

For this reason we, the Naiyāyikas, have left aside the details of discussion regarding other matters and tried our level best to establish the thesis that the universals inhering in the letters are real, i. e., they do actually exist.

The proof of the thesis that each letter is a member of the class which consists of many such letters is stated in order to establish the thesis that the members of the same class are united by a universal which is referred to by an act of recognition.

Let us discuss whether a universal belongs to a letter or not. The two acts of the awareness of the letter 'ga' are not the same. It is a fact that the letter 'ga' is numerically identical with apparently another 'ga'? But does it appear to be different owing to the distinct illuminators of a letter? Or, is it that the distinct acts of consciousness refer to the different letters i. e., ga's? Now, if each letter is numerically identical with the so-called another similar letter then the difference in its awareness is explained by the diversity of its illuminators. In that case, the assumption of the universal of a letter is absurd since it has no locii to stand upon.

If the different acts of the consciousness of a letter refer to the different individual letters then the letters which appear to be the same are really many. But if these different individual letters are presented to our consciousness as identical then we should think over the matter and try to find out the object to which the awareness of identity refers. Regarding this point, we, the Naiyāyikas, hold that the awareness of the said identity refers to a universal, e.g., gatva but not to a single letter, e.g. ga. It may be also stated in this connexion that the distinct acts of the consciousness of ga, e.g. the awareness (es) of 'ga, ga', etc. do not owe their existence to the action of the different illuminators of the letter 'ga'. If the Mīmāṁsakas urge that the different illuminators are only responsible for the appearance of difference then why is not it that the letters such as y, r, l, v, etc. are fundamentally one but they are presented to our consciousness to be different owing to the action of the diverse illuminators? If it is admitted then the differences of all letters are to be discarded and it should be accepted like the grammarians that there is only one basic letter which is a partless whole that transcends all differences.

The Mīmāṁsakas may contend that as mutual distinction of the letters, viz., v, r, l, etc. is clearly noticed by all so how can the hypothesis that all letters are substantially one be entertained? But if the different speakers, viz., a man, a he-parrot and a she-parrot pronounce the same letters then the Mīmāṁsakas may point out that the letters are the same but appear to us to be different since the manifestors of the letters in these cases are different. In the above case, there is very little chance of taking an exception to the above solution. But when one and the same speaker utters the word 'gagana' etc. how does the first 'ga' appear to differ from the second one? The reason stated above does not apply to this case. The Manifestor of the two ga's is the same.

Now, the Mīmāṁsakas may contend that though the mouth of the speaker is one and the same yet the airs which manifest a letter are different. They say "Let the mouth be one. It does not matter much". Some other thinkers hold that the mouth itself is not one since it is an aggregate of several parts. If this is the contention of the Mīmāṁsakas then the objectors may as well point out that the different airs similarly manifest the letters y, r, l, v, etc. The purport of this objection is this that the letters should not be taken as essentially different.

Now, the Mīmāṁsakas may contend, that when the letters y, r, l, v, etc. are presented to our consciousness the specific distinguishing feature of each letter is also presented to our consciousness. But when the word 'gagana' is presented to our consciousness no distinction between the first ga and the second one is detected by anybody. In this case, there are two acts of pronouncing but the letters pronounced are not different. This contention is not sound. Though there is no awareness of specific difference yet there certainly exists numerical difference. Specific difference is something other than general difference since here there is the knowledge of numerical difference.

Now, the Mīmāṁsakas contend that the individual cow designated as Śābaleya is known to be different from the individual cow called as Bāhuleya. Hence the difference existing between them is real. But the one individual letter 'ga' is not distinctly known to be different from the letter 'ga' pronounced at a different period. One 'ga' may be quickly pronounced. The other may be slowly pronounced. Such pronunciation makes no real difference. The so-called difference is only conditional.

Such a contention is not reasonable. In every individual cow the distinguishing features of the different limbs such as dewlap, hoofs, hump etc. are clearly cognised by us. Owing to their big size this distinction is easily grasped. When sesamum, rice and kulattha pulses are boiled and morsels are prepared from them one morsel cannot be distinguished from another. But there is numerical difference among these morsels since one morsel is known to be other than another. Similarly, though the one letter 'ga' cannot be clearly distinguished from another letter 'ga' yet the former is numerically different from the latter. Thus there are many ga's.

Now, the Mīmāṁsakas may contend that there is noticeable distinction among the balls of boiled rice and if this distinction is not grasped then the difference existing among the balls cannot be grasped.

But such a contention is not tenable. If the above balls of boiled articles are minutely observed then some of them are observed as quadrangular, some others as triangular, some others as round and so on. Thus each ball has its distinguishing features. These characteristic features are presented to our consciousness. But if we simply cast our eyes on them and make no effort to detect the distinguishing features then we know them to be numerically different. Thus, we bring home our point that these balls are many.

Now, the Mīmāṁsakas may further contend that the awareness of distinction is the consciousness of difference. But such a statement is not true. The reason which is behind our criticism is this. As action, e.g., the act of walking etc., consists of several moments. Each moment is very subtle. There is a fine shade of distinction which marks off one moment from another.

Now, the Mīmāṁsakas urge that if a person does not cognize the distinguishing features of an object then he has no knowledge of difference. Thus, the awareness of the distinguishing features is regarded as identical with the awareness of difference. Such a conclusion is not sound. The moments of actions like the act of walking etc. are subtle. The difference of one moment from another is detected though the minute distinctions of such moment are not detected. Now, the Mīmāṁsakas may contend that it should be assumed that the distinguishing features are cognized since the awareness of difference presupposes the consciousness of the distinguishing features.

Now, the Naiyāyikas come forward and join issue with them. They hold that the letters in the word 'gagana' are apprehended as different from one another. Thus, it may be as well assumed that the distinguishing features of the letters are detected. But they are not real. They are attributed to the letters owing to their association with the other factors. They are like the red colour attributed to crystal.

The Naiyāyikas review this answer and point out that the example quoted above is not an exact one. The red colour attributed to a piece of crystal is due to its association with lac. But the letters have innate distinguishing features in the shape of various accents, such as either udātta or anudātta or svarita, etc. The letters are always presented to our consciousness along with these distinguishing features. The letters are never cognized without having these distinctive marks. Therefore, the difference of one letter from another is natural but not accidental.

As each act of consciousness involves a necessary reference to an object such as a jar, a picture etc. but there is no such consciousness as is blank, i.e., points to no object so the acts of consciousness are many. Similarly, as each letter is marked by a distinct accent so letters are many, it is not proper to hold that consciousness is one and eternal but appears to be many as it comes in contact with many objects which are to be regarded as limiting adjuncts. The author of the Mīmāṁsā sūtra has acknowledged that an act of consciousness comes into being (vide his sūtra on perception: buddhijanya pratyaksamiti). We, the Naiyāyikas, shall afterwards refute the hypothesis that consciousness is eternal. Now, if it is held that the diversity of objects accounts for the difference in objects then the diversity of objects should also be explained. Now, if it is held that the diversity of consciousness points to the manifoldness of objects then it may be pointed out that such a proposition involves the fallacy of a vicious circle. In other words, the diversity of objects points to the plurality of the acts of consciousness but the plurality of the acts of consciousness presupposes the diversity of objects. Thus, we arrive at the conclusion that the difference of one act of consciousness from another is intrinsic, the difference of one object from another is also intrinsic and consciousness reveals it. There is no need of discussing other relevant matters for the present. As the colour 'white' is many such as brilliant white, grey white etc.—so the letters are many since the vowels are accented in three different ways (either the rising of the voice on a vowel is denoted or the falling of the voice on a vowel is denoted or the rising and the falling of the voice on a vowel are denoted). Kumārila may hold that the colour 'white' is really one but appears to be many because it inheres in different locii. If he subscribes to this view then he has lost his balance of judgment owing to the passionate love for the above hypothesis.

'The action is one', 'consciousness is one' and 'the colour 'white' is one in this world'. Such statements are made by a passionate gallant before a courtesan in her house. Moreover, if this line of argument is rigidly followed then why should not we accept the doctrine that the soul is one ? The reason behind the objection is this. Though we subscribe to the doctrine that there is one universal soul yet we can explain why the soul encased in this body is happy and why the soul enshrined in that body is sorrowful because the different bodies impose limitation upon the same soul. The path followed by the Mīmāṁsakas is not far away from the doctrine of monism. Therefore, they should no more brag of their superior logic. Now, the Mīmāṁsakas may contend that in the word 'gagana' the two ga's are not essentially different and they appear to be different because of their association with the vowel 'a'. But such a contention is not tenable because the Mīmāṁsakas hold that the vowel 'a' is essentially one and the same and admits of no difference. Again, let us cite a pair of similar words 'digaja' and 'diggaja'. In the latter word there are two g's. They are presented to our consciousness as different though the prior 'g' has no association with the vowel 'a'. We may also cite other pair of examples in which the two conjunctive consonants have the same sound but are presented to our consciousness as different. They are as follows 'samadaḥ and sammadaḥ' : 'malaḥ and mallaḥ', 'āvikaḥ and āvikkaḥ', 'patiḥ and pattiḥ', 'patanam and pattanam' etc. The meaning of the word 'digaja' is known to be different from that of the word 'diggaja' because the two words are essentially distinct from each other but not because the same consonant is pronounced twice. As the word 'diggaja' contains a larger number of letters so it has a different meaning. But it is not a fact that the words 'digaja' and 'diggaja' consist of the same number of letters but have different meanings when they are differently pronounced. Even if the word 'go' is pronounced a hundred times then it conveys only and the same meaning viz. an animal having dewlap. The expert etymologists hold that the word 'diggaja' contains two g's but do never declare that it contains only one 'g' which is uttered twice.

In the words 'go' 'guru' 'giri', 'geha' etc. though the vowels which immediately follow the letter 'g' are different yet the letter 'g' is presented to our consciousness as the persisting identical object. Therefore, the letter 'g' is one and the same object. This contention of the Mīmāṁsakas is not tenable. It has been proved by us, the Naiyāyikas, that in these words there are different g's. In the words like 'diggaja' etc. where the first 'g' is not associated with a vowel the two g's have been shown to be different. Let us make our position clear. We do not deny existence to an identical element in the different individuals, viz., g's. But we lay emphasis on the point that the individual g's possess intrinsic difference since this difference is an object of uncontradicted experience and cannot be otherwise explained. The point which we intend to bring home is this that the individual g's like the individual cows form a class. Though the individuals are mutually different yet a universal, an identical element, inheres in them. All the individual cows are one when we look on them from the standpoint of the universal of cowness. Similarly, all the individual g's are one when they are looked on from the standpoint of the universal of g-ness. But if the individuals as individuals are judged then their difference is manifest. In other words, what we intend to impress is that they possess an element of identity as well as an element of difference. Now if the Mīmāṁsakas contend that this difference is merely external i.e., an outer layer since the different manifestors explain the appearance of difference in letters then we simply repeat the argument, stated before, that the very existence of the different letters, 'y', 'r', 'l', 'v' etc. can be explained away. Moreover, the individual cows such as Śābaleya etc. are cognised by us to be different because their manifestors are distinct. But the so-called different individuals should be really one.

Now, the Mīmāṁsakas may put this question : "Which are these different manifestors which make the individuals appear as different ?" Kumārila also says to this effect. As dhvani is the manifestor of a letter so there is no manifestor of the difference of the individual cows apart from their bodies. The body of an individual cow invariably manifests the universal of cowness. Let us explain the true statement of Kumārila. In case of a letter, a letter does not manifest itself but dhvani manifests a letter. The difference, belonging to a manifestor, explains why a single letter appears to be many. But in case of individual cows etc. there is no manifestor of difference excepting the body of an individual cow. If we do not subscribe to the view that the body of an individual cow is essentially different from that of another then how can we account for the distinction of an individual cow from another? Again, we recognize a persisting element in the individual cow. This identical element is the universal of cowness. There is no such proof as goes to establish the universal of gatva (a universal belonging to the letter 'g').

The above view is not tenable. The existence of the universal of cowness like the universal of gatva is not accepted by all. It is not a sense-datum. But its existence is to be established by means of reasoning. How do we cognize the difference of an individual cow from another? The cognition of such difference is due to the specific contact of the eyes with the individual cow. If we simply look at a cow, we do not cognize this difference. But when our eyes have a special contact with an individual cow this distinction of an individual cow is perceived.

Now, the Mīmāṁsakas may contend that the mere sensing of an individual cow reveals its distinctive features. Such a contention is not tenable. When we merely sense an individual cow we know it only to be a cow. But if we perceive individual cows with their distinctive marks and express it by proposition viz., "This is Śāvaleya". "This is Bāhuleya" ete. then the contact of the eyes with the object is invariably distinct. If the first contact of the eyes with an individual cow produces such a perception as is fortunate enough to reveal its distinctive features then why has the first perception of the letter 'g' been unfortunate in this respect? In that case when the letter 'g' reaches the ears and the different manifestors of the different letters remain unknown the difference holding between the two g's, contained in the words 'gagana' and 'gaṅgā' etc., should also be directly organised. There is no need of dilating on this point.

The proof of the hypothesis that the universals such as gatva etc. belong to letters.

This is the sum and substance of the above discussion which centres round the point that each letter is a member of a class. Either one is to disregard the accepted hypothesis that the members of a class have a common property and a particular class is distinguished from another or one is to accept the hypothesis that the universal of gatva belongs to the different g's as the universal of cowness belongs to the different cows. If the existence of the universal of gatva is admitted then the universal of atva cannot but be accepted. In other words, the letter 'g' is not a single individual. But it is a member of a class which consists of many g's. Similarly, the vowel 'a' is a member of a class which subsumes many different a's under itself. All these a's have mutual distinction because some of them are presented to our consciousness as short, some other a's as long and still some other a's as prolated and so on. If one subscribes to the view that a long vowel, viz., 'a' is recognised as identical with the short vowel viz., 'a' then he should also recognise the vowel 'i' as identical with the vowel 'a' since both of them are vowels. Though 'a' and 'i' are vowels yet they are to be distinguished from each other. If this is the view of the above person then he should not conceal the distinction that separates the short vowel 'a' from the long vowel 'a'. If he agrees with us then it will be sound to hold that the meaning of the word 'araṇya' is different from that of the word 'āraṇya'. As the expert musicians follow the difference of the same sound in the different notes of gamut so the expert grammarians can only notice distinction in the same 'a' differently pronounced. It may be either accented or unaccented or as circumflexly accented. It may be pronounced either by the contracted part or by the extended one and so on. Hence they hold that the vowel 'a' admits of eighteen different kinds. The different a's possess a common character which is objectively real. It is called atva. They also express the different kinds of a's as a group of similar a's. In other words, a's form a class. Every one also understands that this division applies to sound itself. But men do not think that this division owes its existence to the variety of winds which come in contact with our vocal chord in order to utter a letter. Now, it may be contended that not only letters but also the winds condition the communication of meaning since there is an impression in the mind of the people, that the winds are only responsible for the different appearances of the same letter. If this is the contention then this impression alone should condition the communication of meaning but not letters since it is universally present whereas a letter is not so. Let us have an end of this discussion here. (The above criticism points to this that, the word 'araṇya' does not contain the vowel 'a' but according to the impression 'a' appears as 'a' under the influence of the wind. Owing to this impression we make out the meaning of the word 'araṇya'. The impression is present whereas the letter is absent. The absent letter cannot help to communicate the sense of a word. The impression, being present, does it. Hence we should hold that the impression alone conditions the communication of meaning).

In fine as the communication of the meaning of a word takes place with the help of such universals as are gatva and others so we should not assume that the letter 'g' is eternal.

Some other Mīmāṁsakas hold that the genus viz. soundness does not belong to the letters—not to speak of species belonging to letters.

When we perceive a particular and remember another particular we admit that these two particulars have an identical element which constitutes the common property since the recalling of another particular is at the root of the assumption of the common property. As on the perception of the individual cow, Śāvaleya by name, we remember another individual cow named Bāhuleya so on hearing the letter 'g' we do not remember the letter 'v'. (The purport of this statement is that the letters have no common property and that there is no scope for imagination to assume such a common property).

Now, it may be contended that whenever we hear a particular sound it is presented to our consciousness in its generic form viz. 'this is sound', 'this is sound'. Such an experience does not invariably point to the existence of soundness as the common property of all sounds. But, on the contray, the experience involves a reference to the common property in the shape of audibility. As each sound is audible so the common property of audibility belongs to all words.

Such a contention is entertained by the unwise disputants since memory alone does not determine the existence of a common property. The law of similarity is one of the guiding factors of memory. When we perceive an individual of a particular species we remember an individual of a different species. they are similar. Let us take an example. When we perceive a gavaya we are reminded of a cow. Hence, the verbal expression of a universal presupposes the uncontradicted awareness of sameness. A universal, the common element of all individuals of a class, is referred to by the awareness of the same. If an individual is cognized as possessed of a universal then such cognition does not necessarily provoke the memory of another similar individual. It (the above cognition) sometimes produces the memory in question but also fails to do so at some other times. Therefore, the universal is not a condition of memory. But similarity conditions memory. Suppose there are two similar bodies. The head of one of them is cut off. If we see the truncated body then we remember that it is similar to that body. The letters such as 'g' etc. are not similar to one another. Owing to the absence of similarity one letter being heard the memory of another letter is not awakened. It is not a truism that the memory in question is not produced because the letters do not possess a common universal.

The Sāṁkhyists hold that similarity itself constitutes a universal and a universal is not a distinct object. This view is not tenable since though cows and gavayas do not belong to the same species yet they are similar. The Mīmāṁsakas take an exception to the existence of soundness, a universal, and hold that the common idea of soundness presupposes the common property of audibility as its condition but does not refer to the universal of soundness. The Naiyāyikas review this criticism and point out that like the Buddhists, the Mīmāṁsakas should also deny existence to the universal of cowness since the common idea of cowness may presuppose the common property in the shape of capacity for performing the same acts such as carrying a load, milking etc. as its condition. But, really speaking, the conclusion that a universal does not exist cannot be maintained. Like the universal of cowness, the universal of soundness should not also be set aside.

From the above remark the universal of Brahmanhood is known to be established. It is perceived when the person perceiving it gets the proper instruction. It is not to be considered as super-sensuous because it receives the aid of instruction for its perception. When a person difinitely perceives the universal of cowness on hearing the statement "This is a cow", (he has word-intertwined experience of a cow). It is noted that he depends upon 'the instruction that the word 'cow' signifies the universal of cowness for such perception. Somebody has said that if a person ascending the peak of a hill sees an object then the object is not taken as transcendental. (Nobody holds that difficult perception is not direct). It is not sound to hold that the determinate perception of Brahmanhood as belonging to the Brahmins such as Paiṭhīnasi, Paippala, etc., is conditional since it may be as well pointed out that the determinate perception of cowness is also conditional (When we say that such and such perception of the said universal is not direct, the said universal is indicated by the knowledge of some signs which are bound up with it). Some other thinkers hold that when we see with our eyes, unaided by instructions, a person having an amiable appearance we are able to distinguish him from a Kṣatriya and recognize him as a Brāhmaṇa, therefore we require no further discussion about these side issues.

The refutation of the arguments in favour of the hypothesis that sound is eternal. The relevant matter is now going to be discussed. The sense of a word is communicated without any difficulty if it is admitted that universals such as 'gatva' etc., belong to letters. With the aid of them a word conveys its meaning without the least troubles. The Mīmāṁsakas hold that a word is pronounced with the definite object of conveying its sense to others. But if a letter, the constituent of the said word, perishes in the moment just after its utterance then the very object of pronouncing a word is defeated. Thus the Mīmāṁsakas arrive at the conclusion that sound is eternal.

This conclusion is not sound. They also hold that as a word simultaneously conveys all the individuals so it is eternal. This argument is also refuted by the above statement. The law that the relation of significance holds between a word and its meaning is established if it is admitted that the universals belong to the different letters.

The Mīmāṁsakas hold that a word being only one the suffix 'kṛtvasuc' is only attached to numeral words. (The suffix 'Kṛtvasuc' denotes the sense of—'times' in the English grammar, e.g., three times, four times, five times etc.).

The Mīmāṁsakas mean to say: When one says that a word has been five times uttered the sentence does not signify that five distinct similar words have been uttered. It conveys the sense that the word which is uttered is one and the same but the acts of utterance are different. It points to the hypothesis of the Mīmāṁsakas that sound is eternal. The above interpretation of kṛtvasuc as given by the Mīmāṁsakas is not universal since it faces exceptional cases.

The young lady of slender figure has cast side glance three times at her lover, embraced him four times and kissed him eight times. In this case each of these acts is many. Thus the suffix 'kṛtvasuc' is used even when the repetition of one thing is not conveyed by it. Now, the Mīmāṁsakas may point out that the above sentence purports to convey the repetition of the acts of kissing, etc., as the male and the female partners remain to be the same. The Naiyāyikas review the Mīmāṁsā view and hold that if a person feeds five Brahmins at a time, another five Brahmins at another time and so on then does it mean that he has fed the same five Brahmins five times ?

In a poem of a poet who displays an alliteration of the letter 'g' many ga's are noticed. The readers also say to this effect that there are many ga's.

The Mīmāṁsakas make mention of the recognition of the letter 'g'. If this recognition is held to be true then it should point to the universal of g.i.e. 'gatva' but not to the letter 'g'.

Moreover, if the recognition points to the letter 'g' then we hardly notice any distinction between this recognition and that which refers to the act of dancing or to the movements of a dramatic person or to the ordinary bodily movements. When we go to recognize a letter we know that it has passed away. Hence, how can we establish the hypothesis that a letter is undestructible ?

Though we, the Naiyāyikas, shall establish the truth of recognition in the chapter on the refutation of phenomenalism yet some other Naiyāyikas point out that there is a gulf of difference fixed between the recognition of a post and that of a letter. When we recognize a letter to be the same as was heard before we also know that it has passed away. As the recognition refers to an object which ceases to exist so it is not true.

The Naiyāyikas hold that a sound endures only for two or three points of time. So, the recognition of a sound is not at all possible because of its too short duration.

Let us bring home our point. A sound at first comes into being. Then the auditory perception of it is produced by it since an object is only grasped by such perception as is produced by it. When the above perception is produced the sound is perceived. (The sound which is now heard is other than a similar sound heard before). On hearing this sound the impression due to the previous hearing of another sound is revived. We remember afterwards that this sound was heard before. Then our organ of hearing or inner organ, accompanied by the memory of the sound, will produce recognition. Then this sound will be recognized as that sound. But whence does sound enjoy such a long life ? The Mīmāṁsakas may contend that the long life of sound will be assumed on the strength of this very recognition itself. The Mīmāṁsakas might have rightly subscribed to such a conjecture if the sound had not been known to be destroyed at the time of recognition.

Moreover, a word is not heard merely as a word. Such perception refers to a distinct word. The propositions which express these judgments of perception are as follows :—

"This is the word cow", "This is the word 'horse'" and so on. When such a word (e.g., a cow) is heard a similar word 'a cow' will be recalled in our mind. A series of such recollections will continue in our mind. With the aid of this memory a series of recognitions referring to a cow will go on in our mind. As this series of consciousness consists of successive but not simultaneous events so the word 'cow' should have a longer span of life.

The Mīmāṁsakas have cited an example to illustrate their point. They have said, "When the massive cloud covers the sky and the night is enveloped by pitchy darkness there are short-lived flashes of lightning at some intervals. Some external objects around us are revealed by them. They are also recognized instantaneously. The recognition of a word may be compared with that of the said external objects".

Such a contention is not tenable. The objects which are revealed by the flash of lightning may last long. When the objects illuminated by the flash of lightning are recognized we have no knowledge that they have been destroyed. (But, on the contrary when a word is recognized we know for certain that the word in question has ceased to exist.)

Some logicians define recognition thus :—It is such sensuous cognition as is produced by the sense-organ in cooperation with an impression and points to the identity of an object which is cognized with that which is remembered.

Some other logicians say, "The object which is now recognized was apprehended before. The past apprehension is now recalled in memory. Recognition refers to the object which is now recollected. Thus, the object is qualified by the cognition which is now remembered. Hence, it is not grasped by the external sense-organ. Therefore, the recognition of an external object such as a post is produced by the inner organ. Thus, we cannot establish the permanence of an object on the strength of its recognition.

There are two judgments about a letter. The recognitive judgment assumes the form that this letter is that letter. The negative judgment is that the letter does not exist. Both the judgments are not true. One of them invalidates the other. In this case how are we to determine which of these two judgments is true ?

The above problem is thus solved. If we hold that the judgment of recognition does not point to the identity of this with 'that'. But it refers either to the common universal (such as gatva) which is shared by the subject and the predicate or to such similarity as holds between the subject and the predicate.

Now, the Mīmāṁsakas may contend that the above negative judgment points to the destruction (the non-existence) of the manifestation of a letter but not to that of a letter. The Naiyāyikas take an exception to this suggestion and hold that the above negative judgment will be meaningless if it does not refer to the negation of a letter. Therefore, let the judgment of recognition be contradicted. Let us take this judgment to be an erroneous one. Or, the Mīmāṁsakas may urge that there is no crucial evidence pointing to the destruction of a letter. Thus, there may be room for doubt about the truth of the negative judgment. In other words, the negative judgment may also be false.

Such a criticism is not tenable. The negative judgment that a letter does not exist is also strengthened by the judgment of otherness that this letter is not that letter. It is not reasonable to hold that these two negative judgments may be otherwise explained.

On the one hand, the judgment of recognition is dependent but, on the other hand, the negative judgment is independent. In other words, the judgment of recognition presupposes the recollection of a letter for its very existence. But the negative judgment referring to the negation of a letter is not conditioned by such a recollection. Thus, of the two judgments about a letter only the judgment of recognition is invalidated by the negative one.

Moreover, a judgment of recognition does not invariably point to the conclusion that the object recognized is eternal. Let us cite examples of the recognition of non-eternal objects, viz., an action. etc. We cannot pin our faith in the truth of the hypothesis that sound is eternal since we definitely know that a sound has passed away. It should also be noted in this connection that we do not mean to say that the evidence of recognition *per se* is unreliable. In other words, we do not suggest that each and every object which is recognized is held to be eternal on the strength of recognition.

But we mean to say that as the knowledge of the destruction of a sound is true so the evidence, given by recognition about the truth of the hypothesis that sound is eternal, becomes weak.

Though an action is recognized yet it is not proved that it is eternal. Similarly, sound is not held to be eternal though it is recognized.

The Mīmāṁsakas put this question to the Naiyāyikas "Why do you cite an example in order to bring home your point?" In other words, they mean to say that the evidence of perception is final and as such a judgment of perception requires no corroboration. The Naiyāyikas say in reply that there is much truth in the objection but the Mimāṁsakas have missed the real point of the Naiyāyikas. They generally cite examples in order to convince the Mīmāṁsakas of the truth of the hypothesis of the Naiyāyikas since they (the Mīmāṁsakas) cannot follow the trend of the abstract argument of the Nyāya school (their mind being obsessed by prejudices). They have become impatient to prove the hypothesis that sound is eternal). Out of impatience they fail to draw a distinction between the argument which is good and that which is bad. They behave like a thirsty person who wants to drink everything but makes no distinction between mobile and immobile things. Therefore, there is no need of discussing the hypothesis whether an action and a phenomenon of consciousness are eternal since such a hypothesis owes its origin to their excessive fondness for another particular hypothesis.

An Objection to the hypothesis that sound is Manifested but not Created

The Mīmāṁsakas hold that as a letter is eternal so it is manifested but not created. A possible objection to the hypothesis is that the auditory perception of sound at a particular spot by a particular person cannot be explained. They apprehend this objection and give an answer to it. They hold that if an improvement is made either upon the auditory sense-organ or upon sound (i.e., the letter which is heard) or upon both of them then the restricted perception of a letter is fairly explained. The Naiyāyikas hold this explanation to severe criticism and point out that the Mīmāṁsakas simply deceive people by the explanation. The objects which belong to the same locus and are sensed by the same sense-organ are manifested by the same manifestor. There is no exception to this rule. But the Mīmāṁsakas have taken an exception to this rule and pointed out that various accents, belonging to the same locus are manifested by the different manifestor. The Naiyāyikas review this criticism and hold that these scents are grasped by the same sense-organ but do not belong to the same locus.

Now, if the Mīmāṁsakas suggest that all the different scents belong to the same locus as the earth is one then it should also be accepted that the Himalayan range and the Vindhya range belong to the same locus.

Though the earth is one and the same yet the earthen objects are not one. The above scents belong to them. As the locus of scents is not one so they are manifested by the different manifestors.

It may be held that the letters are self-sufficient and as such they stand upon no locus. Or, it may be stated that the letters stand upon the sky as their locus. In any case, it can never be asserted that the letters belong to the different loci.

Now, the Mīmāṁsakas may contend thus :—The sky is an indivisible single substance. But the Naiyāyikas divide it into many parts by an act of imagination. The imaginary parts constitute the different auditory sense-organ of the different persons. With the help of imaginary parts they explain that each person has a separate pair of ears. Similarly, we may impose imaginary division on the sky and hold that letters will find the distinct locii in the different parts of the sky. As they do not belong to the same locus so they may be manifested by the distinct manifestors.

The Naiyāyikas examine this contention and hold that the solution of this sort is not sound. The word 'cow' may have been heard in the sky which is enclosed either by the mouth of the speaker or by the ear of the listener. In that very locus the word 'horse' may be heard at present. (In other words the Naiyāyikas point out an exception to the general law formulated by the Mīmāṁsakas that a distinct word belongs to a separate locus. In the above case, though the two words are different yet their locus is one and the same). The scent which belongs to the flower of the Mādhavī creeper is not smelt in the flower of the Bandhūka tree or in that of the Madhūka tree. (In other words, the Naiyāyikas hold a brief for their hypothesis that each scent has a distinct locus).

Thus, the Naiyāyikas reassert the objections raised by them against the Mīmāṁsā hypothesis of manifestation with greater force. As all the letters belong to one and the same locus so it cannot be held that a distinct letter is manifested by a separate manifestor.

If some Mīmāṁsakas contend that an improvement may be made either upon the letter itself by means of the air or upon the auditory sense-organ or upon both even then they cannot surely maintain the required hypothesis that a distinct manifestor manifests a distinct letter.

They may argue that the invisible principle of merit and demerit is only responsible for the above hypothesis of manifestation. The Naiyāyikas record their protest against this solution with the following note. If the hypothesis that all letters are created is assumed then no reference to the invisible principle of merit and demerit is necessary. Each letter is conditioned by a distinct set of known conditions. No visible object is known to stand in the way of the creation of a distinct letter. The fact that a letter comes into being is experienced by all.

An improvement to be made upon the auditory sense-organ is nothing but the evacuation of the slowly moving air. The Naiyāyikas have already said that if the hypothesis is assumed then the letters which are intended not to be heard will also be heard. (In other words, all the letters should be simultaneously heard. No satisfactory answer to this objection is available). Now, if the Mīmāṁsakas revise their hypothesis and hold that the suggested improvement is something else than the evacuation of the slowly moving air then they assume something which is a unique object.

Again, if the Mīmāṁsakas hold that the letters are permanent, an improvement is durable and the auditory sense-organ is even lasting then the word 'cow' though unmanifest should be heard since an improvement has been made upon it and the improvement itself, the condition of perception, persists. But if the Mīmāṁsakas hold that the said improvement is transitory but not persisting then the hypothesis that sound is transitory is a better one since the transitoriness of sound is experienced.

Bhartṛmitra suggests that an improvement is made upon the auditory sense-organ. By the suggestion he merely expresses his unprecedented scholarship ! The hypothesis that an improvement is made upon the auditory sense-organ is not sound. If this improvement is permanent then an uproar should be heard (i. e., all letters should be simultaneously heard). The hypothesis will not be elaborately discussed since Kumārila himself, the famous Mīmāṁsaka, has rediculed Bhartṛmitra for it and subjected it to severe criticism. There is no need of disputation over it.

Kumārila states that a hypothesis which is contrary to that of the Naiyāyikas is to be resorted to by the Mīmāṁsakas. The Mīmāṁsakas should follow the teaching of the Vedas and hold that the auditory sense-organ is constituted by space but not by the sky. Such a hypothesis is not sound. Space is the only source of knowledge of spatial proximity or remoteness. It has got no other function to do. In all cases, the literal meaning of the Vedic sentences should not be insisted upon since they suggest something else. But a thinker who attaches too much importance to himself assumes that space constitutes the auditory sense-organ.

The hypothesis that all the sense-organs are elemental will be proved later on. Space is not an element. Therefore, it constitutes a sense-organ. Now, the Mīmāṁsakas may contend that space is as all-pervasive as the sky is and that there is no distinction between space and the sky so far as their ubiquity is concerned. The trend of this contention is that there is no bar to the hypothesis, "Space constitutes the auditory sense-organ." A reply to his contention is this that as Time and the Soul are equally all-pervasive so they might have as well constituted the auditory sense-organ. Now, the Mīmāṁsakas may defend their position with the remark that Time and the Soul do not constitute sense-organs since they have got some other functions to do. The Naiyāyikas have an easy reply to this contention. They will simply say that the same logic applies to Space. The Vedic text which has been cited in support of the hypothesis that space constitutes the auditory sense-organ purports to suggest something else. As the Vedic sentences "Let the eyes be united with the sun, and let the ears be united with the space" run so the Vedic text "Let the vital breath be united with the sky" is also real. The last Vedic sentence cannot be set aside. On the strength of this

Vedic sentence we cannot hold that the sky constitutes the vital breath which is constituted by the air. Therefore, the Mīmāṁsakas should give up the hypothesis that space constitutes the ears. The sky, enclosed by the ear-drum, etc., constitutes the auditory sense-organ. We enjoy pleasure or pain, derived from words. The invisible principle of merit and demerit accounts for such feelings. It is the cause that converts the sky into the auditory sense-organ. We, the Naiyāyikas, have stated this hypothesis at an earlier section. Now, the Mīmāṁsakas may turn up and contend in the following manner: As the Naiyāyikas hold that the restriction is imposed upon words by the invisible principle of merit and demerit so the manifestation of sounds will be determined by the same principle. (In other words, the Naiyāyikas make an appeal to the agency of the invisible principle of merit and demerit in order to explain why one hears such words as produce the feeling of pleasure or as produce the feeling of pain. The Mīmāṁsakas follow their foot-steps and hold that it is due to the working of the same invisible principle that a particular letter is manifested to the exclusion of others.) The Mīmāṁsakas ask the Naiyāyikas why do they object to the hypothesis of the Mīmāṁsakas? They say, "If sound is eternal then there will be no law of the manifestation of sound."

The Naiyāyikas try to substantiate their objection and hold that the contention of the Mīmāṁsakas is not sound. They hold that sense-organs such as eyes, etc., are not capable of grasping some possible objects and this incapacity is due to the agency of the invisible principle of merit and demerit. It is for this reason that the eyes cannot perceive darkness. But the nature of objects does never change. A cold object e.g. ice does never change its nature of being cold. We have stated before that no manifestor has been noticed to make any selection in time of manifestation. A letter is not a single unit. It is a class name. Many individual letters of the same class are directly perceived by us. (In other words, 'g' is a common noun but not a proper noun.) All the letters are not simultaneously heard by all in accordance with the empirical law of hearing. If a letter is within the field of hearing of a listener then it is heard. If it is not then it is not heard. This law is derived from experience.

If an empirical law of hearing is available then why should the Mīmāṁsakas entrust the invisible of merit and demerit with the burden of solving the problem?

The refutation of the hypothesis that a letter is manifested.

If it is held that a letter is manifested then how do you distinguish between a letter which is loudly pronounced and one which is lowly pronounced? For, let us now see whether the property of being loud or that of being low belongs to a letter or to the air. Now, if the Mīmāṁsakas hold that the said properties belong to a letter then they should admit that a letter which is loudly pronounced is distinct from that which is lowly pronounced. In that case, they subscribe to the hypothesis of the Naiyāyikas.

Now, if the Mīmāṁsakas hold that the said properties belong to the air then the Naiyāyikas ask, "How are the properties of being loud and low heard by us?" The reason behind this objection is this that the property of the air can never be heard. The Mīmāṁsakas cite an example in order to prove their hypothesis that the property of one object seems to belong to another. They have illustrated that the properties of an individual, viz., fatness, thinness, etc., are attributed to the universal which inheres in the individual. The example, shown by them is highly probable since the universal, the individual and the property of an individual are sensed by the same sense-organ. But, in the present context, the air is either sensed by the organ of touch (according to the Naiyāyikas) or supersensuous (according to the Vaiśeṣikas). But it is strange to hold that the property of the air seems to belong to a letter which is grasped by the auditory sense-organ.

The Mīmāṁsakas subscribe to an alternative hypothesis that the property of being loud or low belongs to consciousness. But it is absolutely unreasonable to hold such a hypothesis. An act of consciousness is different from another because their objects are different but not because they are intrinsically different. There is another point to add to our criticism. The Mīmāṁsakas hold that consciousness is supersensuous because it is an act. As the property of being loud etc., belongs to consciousness so it is supersensuous. Thus, this hypothesis shares the same lot with the former one, viz., the said property belongs to the air. Thus, the said property has no chance of being perceived. The property of being loud or low has been carried away by the terrible storm. It has no chance of escape. The said property does not belong to the object which is perceived. It inheres in such an object as transcends our sense-perception.

The Mīmāṁsakas may contend that if the air which manifests a particular letter is suppressed by some other air which manifests another letter then the letter is not heard. The Naiyāyikas subject this contention to severe criticism and ask even if the air is suppressed, why is the letter not heard ? The Naiyāyikas refer to an illustration which confutes the hypothesis of the Mīmāṁsakas. If the light of a lamp is subdued by the rays of the sun then is not the colour of an object perceived ?

(Now, the Mīmāṁsakas find fault with the above example and point out that as a particular letter is manifested by the particular air so a particular letter is not heard on the suppression of its manifestor.) The Naiyāyikas challenge the very assumption of the Mīmāṁsakas and say that experience does not teach that the different airs manifest the distinct letters. This point has been criticised at an earlier section.

In order to explain that the sound, manifested by the playing on conch-shell, is somehow heard the Mīmāṁsakas hold that the universal which belongs to the sound is heard but not the sound itself. The hypothesis is not sound.

The Naiyāyikas ask the Mīmāṁsakas, "Oh Mīmāṁsakas ! speak out the truth. Have you ever seen or heard that if an object is imperceptible then its common property is perceived ?"

Again, the Mīmāṁsakas hold that every sound is articulate. But the sound which is manifested by a conch-shell is inarticulate. According to the Mīmāṁsakas the universal of soundness belongs only to the articulate sound (i.e., to letters). The inarticulate sound of a conch-shell does not possess the universal. In that case, how do they perceive the universal of soundness on the locus which is the sound of a conch-shell ?

The hypothesis that a sound is created obeys better the Law of parsimony than the other one that a sound is manifested

There are two rival hypotheses about a letter. According to

one a letter is created. According to the other a letter is manifested. The superiority of the one to the other is to be determined. The Mīmāṁsakas think that the law acts better in grasping a word and its meaning and that the firstone is superior to the second. (In other words, if one frames such a hypothesis regarding a letter as requires a smaller number of assumptions in order to hear a word and understand its meaning then the proposed hypothesis is superior. If one frames such a hypothesis regarding a letter as requires a greater number of assumptions in order to hear a word and grasp its meaning then the other hypothesis is inferior.) The procedure of the Mīmāṁsakas is not sound. The Naiyāyikas say, "We should dive deep into the very root of the problem."

If the permanence of a letter is established by an independent proof then the hypothesis of the Mīmāṁsakas is correct. But if its impermanence is proved then their hypothesis is wrong. The hypothesis of the Naiyāyikas is, however, correct. It is very strange to imagine that the internal air, being extracted from within the body, drives away all the stand-still airs from all sides. Kaṇāda, in his Vaiśeṣika Sūtra, holds that the fire goes up, the air blows obliquely and the initial action of an atom and that of the inner organ owe their origin to the invisible force of merit and demerit of the individual souls. As the air blows only in an oblique manner so it cannot be satisfactorily explained how a word is heard both upward and downward.

The air does not give up its natural movement in an oblique way so long as the air blowing from another direction collides with it and makes it change its direction.

When a speaker pronounces a word with his head down the word is heard even from an upper place. And when he pronounces a word with his face turned up it is not a fact that it is not heard from below. If a word generates similar words on all sides in a circular manner like the pollens of a kadamba flower then there is a possibility of hearing a word on all sides without any reference to the place of occurrence of the basic word. But the circular movement of the air is never noticed in this world. (If the air manifests a word then the hearing of such a word is not possible from an adverse position).

If a speaker pronounces a word with his face covered up to his throat by a non-porous skin then the word is heard. But in that condition, it is not possible for the internal air to come out.

The Mīmāṁsakas also hold that the movement of the air is impeded by an obstacle in the shape of a wall, etc. The air cannot also move forward when its passage is obstructed by the non-porous skin.

Moreover, when the nine appertures of a dispeptic person are blocked the rumbling sound of the wind in the intestine is heard. In his case, from which apperture does the internal air come out? The Mīmāṁsakas may contend that the inner air comes out from the pores of the skin. The said air is very feeble. And as such it cannot drive away the external air which stands still. Again, even if the air outside blows gently, no word will be heard since though the air outside blows gently yet how can it be driven away by the inner air, being itself stronger than the internal air? The Mīmāṁsakas may contend that some other kind of the imperceptible external air envelops a word but the perceptible air which causes the Śyāma grass (a species of grass) to dance does not hide it. Such a contention is not tenable since the existence of the imperceptible air cannot be proved. Even if it is admitted that such an imperceptible air exists and conceals a word then the more powerful air will be in a position to conceal it with greater facility. (It is absurd to hold that the imperceptible air covers a word but the perceptible air does not.) Therefore, we arrive at the logical conclusion that a sound generates a series of similar sounds. Let us cite similar examples in its support. The attributes, like colour, etc., are observed by us to produce same attributes. It is also experienced that an event of consciousness which belongs to the all-pervasive substance produces another event of consciousness, an event of consciousness may occur at a particular space but it sometimes produces another event of consciousness at another space. If Devadatta takes his walk on the road then a particular event of consciousness happens in his mind at a particular spot but the resulting consciousness occurs at another spot because he moves on. (The colour inhering in threads produces the same colour in the cloth, produced by them. The threads constitute the material cause of the colour. The colour which inheres in the threads, the material cause, is also one of the causes. It is called the non-material cause asamavāyikāraṇa. Some forms of consciousness determine some other forms of consciousness. A judgment presupposes the awareness of a predicate. The indeterminate perception of an object conditions its determinate perception. But one form of consciousness is the efficient cause of another form of consciousness. It is technically called the Nimittakāraṇa. A person, say Devedatta, starts for another village. He moves on without any stop on the road. He has the indeterminate perception of a cow on the road at a particular part of the road. But as he moves on so the determinate perception of the cow occurs in his mind at another part of the road).

These examples point to the conclusion of the Naiyāyikas that a sound is created and it produces another similar sound. Now, the Mīmāṁsakas may take an exception to this conclusion on the ground that the series of the resulting sounds will be infinite, i. e., interminable. The Naiyāyikas anticipate this possible objection and try to meet it. The series of the resulting sounds terminates but does not continue *ad infinitum*. A sound is not the only cause of another sound. It depends upon other concomitant conditions in order to produce another sound. They do not always regularly assemble to co-operate with the cause. Their assemblage is controlled by the invisible principle of merit and demerit.

If this law of causation is honoured then we explain how it becomes possible that a violent sound produces a less violent sound. As the conditions of a violent sound become weak so they produce the less violent sound.

A series of waves has been cited running parallel to the series of sounds. These two series are not equal in all fours. A sound has no strength, velocity, etc. like those of a wave (Jayanta means to say that when we draw a comparison the two objects which are compared do not agree in all respects.)

The Naiyāyikas hold that if the sky is partitioned by a wall, etc. then a sound does not produce another similar sound and so on. But why does it not produce its effect? But such an objection does not affect our hypothesis. The unpartitioned sky is the material cause of a sound but not the partitioned one. The hypothesis in question is based upon sound observation. Thus, the sky under all conditions is not the material cause of a sound.

The Proof of the Hypothesis that a Sound is an Attribute

The Mīmāṁsakas hold that the hypothesis "A sound is an attribute" has not been proved. Some Naiyāyikas hold a brief for it and argue that a sound is an attribute because it depends upon a locus. The argument is not tenable. The generalisation that an object which depends upon a locus is an attribute, is not materially valid since the six types of reality may require a locus to stand upon. Kaṇāda accepts the hypothesis that all reals which are subsumed under six different types stand upon a locus with the exception of some self-sufficient substance such as space, time, atoms, etc. No body can perceive that a sound being an attribute of the sky, inheres in it. The sky being supersensuous, the attribute which belongs to it is also imperceptible

If the Mīmāṁsakas argue, "How is it that a sound is perceptible because its locus is imperceptible?" then the Naiyāyikas meet it by means of an analogical argument, "As consciousness and some other attributes of the soul are intuited through the soul, their locus, is supersensuous so a sound is perceptible".

If the Mīmāṁsakas contend that the above analogy is incorrect then Jayanta replies that there is no need of digression since the hypothesis of the Naiyāyikas will be conclusively proved at the subsequent chapter of this work.

Now, the Mīmāṁsakas may ask, "What is the proof in favour of the hypothesis that a sound is an attribute?" The Naiyāyikas may in reply hold that it is an inference based upon the method of residual. If a sound is not an attribute then there are two other possible alternatives. It is either a substance or an action. If these two alternatives are eliminated then it remains only to be subsumed under the class of an attribute since if it is not an attribute, it is impossible for it to have a universal, etc. Why is not sound a substance? Because a sound is effectuated by a single substance. A substance is either self-sufficient, i. e., caused by no substance or an effect of many substances. The sky, atoms, etc. come under the former type. The dyads, etc. are included in the latter type. A sound is an effect of a single substance because it inheres only in the sky. Hence, it is not a substance. It is not an action because it produces another sound. No action produces an effect which is subsumed under the class of an action. No body imagines that a sound is either a universal or the relation of inherence or the positive difference because the universals of being, soundness, etc. inhere in it. Hence, by the process of elimination a sound remains only to be an attribute. Thus, by an indirect method, it is proved that a sound is an attribute.

The Mīmāṁsakas contend that if a sound is proved to be an attribute then it inheres in the sky since no such attribute is seen as does not inhere in a substance and it cannot be proved that a sound inheres in the earth and such other substance. Thus, we see that if it is an attribute then it is an attribute. Hence, it is a glaring instance of the fallacy of a vicious circle. The Naiyāyikas advance the following argument in order to strengthen their hypothesis. As a sound produces a similar effect so it is an attribute. Again, it being an attribute inheres only in the sky. So, it is heard only by the ears which are constituted by the sky. The sound which is produced by conjuntion and disjunction at a place far away from the ears cannot be heard because it is beyond the reach of the ears. In order to hear it, a series of similar sounds should be assumed. If it is proved to be an attribute then a series of sounds is assumed. If a series of sounds is assumed then a sound is proved to be an attribute since as it produces a similar effect so it excludes itself from being an action. Thus, this proof involves the fallacy of a vicious circle.

The Naiyāyikas give a rejoinder to the above objections. They hold that the above two hypotheses do not involve the fallacy of a vicious circle. A sound is assumed to stand upon the sky since it is sensed only by the auditory sense-organ. As it is an attribute so it produces a similar effect. It has also been conclusively proved that the auditory sense-organ is a part of the sky. We, the Naiyāyikas, shall also prove that all sense-organs grasp only those objects with which they come in contact. Again, if a sound does not inhere in the sky then it cannot come in contact with the auditory sense-organ. As an object which is not united with the sense-organ is not perceived so we infer that a sound inheres in the sky. A remote sound is not heard. In order to explain that it is somehow heard we assume that a sound produces another similar one. We do not hold that a sound produces a similar effect because it is merely an attribute. Thus the fallacy of a vicious circle does not vitiate our hypothesis.

Some hold that a sound is assumed to rest upon the sky because it is an effect of the sky. Again, if it is assumed that sound inheres in the sky because it is an effect of the sky then this hypothesis involves the fallacy of a vicious circle as stated before.

Some logicians hold that a sound stands upon the sky because it is an effect. The Mīmāṁsakas subject this view to severe criticism. They hold that if it is assumed that a sound rests upon the sky because it is an effect then this hypothesis just like the above one involves the fallacy of a vicious circle. A sound stands upon the sky because it is an effect. It is an effect because it rests upon the sky. If it rests upon the sky why is it an effect of the sky ? A sound which inheres in the ears is only heard ? For this reason, a series of sounds is to be assumed. (A series of sounds implies that the first sound produces a second one and the second one generates a third one and so on. These sounds constitute a series. We hear some sound when a remote one is at the basis of it. In order to explain this perception it is assumed that a sound produces another sound. A remote sound does not inhere in the ears and a sound which does not inhere in the ears is never heard). The Naiyāyikas give a reply to the above objection. They say that the conclusion that a sound is an effect is not arrived at by the above process of reasoning. A sound is determined to be an effect because the difference of a sound from another and its destruction are direct and in a determinate manner fit in well with the hypothesis that a sound is an effect. The Naiyāyikas lay emphasis on this point only but one should not think that they use it as a logical ground of the said hypothesis. There is no need of subtle discussions on this point.

Some other logicians hold that a sound is other than an

action because it is perceived. The conclusion that no sound is an action is drawn because it is perceived. But this conclusion is not drawn because it generates a similar effect. Therefore the hypothesis does not involve in the least the fallacy of a vicious circle. Thus, by all means, a sound is proved to be an attribute by means of an inference which is based upon the method of residual. But Kaṇāda holds that no attribute inheres in an attribute. How will the Vaiśeṣikas explain the Judgments "The sound is great, etc." ? The Judgment, based upon sound experience, is that the sound is very loud. This judgment cannot be set aside. Therefore, the sūtra of Kaṇāda should be explained in a different way. Kaṇāda means to say that no attribute is qualified by a similar attribute. Thus, the above hypothesis suffers from no defects. Therefore, a sound is an attribute of the sky.

As the qualities, *viz.*, will, hatred. etc., are proved to be attributes of the soul by means of a logical process based upon the process of elimination so a sound is proved to be an attribute of the sky.

The Mīmāṁsakas put forward counter-arguments to negate the Nyāya-hypothesis. One of them is as follows :

A sound does not produce a similar effect because it is a sound. The argument is not strong since the minor premise cannot draw the conclusion.

A sound may be heard if the hypothesis that a sound produces a series of sounds is subscribed to. This hypothesis obeys better the law of parsimony than that of the Mīmāṁsakas who hold that a sound is manifested.

We, the Naiyāyikas, welcome the negative criticisms which have been directed against the hypothesis of the Buddhists, the Sāṁkhyists and the Jainas.

If it is held that a sound is an effect then it is fairly explained why a particular sound, e. g., a particular letter or a particular word is heard to the exclusion of the other ones. But if the hypothesis that a sound is manifested is subscribed to then it is hard to explain why a particular letter is only manifested. (The reason behind our criticism has been stated before). Therefore, the conclusion that a sound is nothing but an effect is conclusively proved. The author of the Nyāya-sūtra has also said to this effect. The Nyāya-sūtra runs thus:—"A sound is non-eternal since it owes its existence to a cause; it is sensed by an external sense-organ and it is used like a created object."

The reason 'Ādimatvāt' (having a cause) implies that conjunction and disjunction produce a sound but do not manifest it. It implies that a sound is destructible (non-eternal). Hence, the reason that a sound closely follows an effect is not fallacious. The reason that a sound is perceptible implies that the perception of a sound is only possible in a restricted manner. A particular person can only hear a particular sound at a definite time. (The exact meaning of the term 'aindriyakatva' is that a sound is the possible subject of the judgment of perception which results from its sensing). The term may mean that the different individual letters, belonging to the same class, are perceptible if they are differently pronounced and heard by the different listeners. The above two reasons point to the conclusion that a sound is destructible. The Mīmāṁsakas hope against hope when they try to refute the above conclusion on the strength of recognition. The fantastic hope is also removed by the above arguments.

The reason 'kṛtakavadupacārāt' (on account of its use as an effect) implies that a sound is destructible like pleasure, pain, etc., since the distinction between sharp and mild sounds is drawn and the suppression of a sound by another sound is admitted. The author of Nyāya-sūtra shows another reason in support of the above view. His sūtra runs thus: 'Since a sound is not cognized before its utterance and no veil which may cover it is noticed' (2.8.19.). He purports to convey by means of this sūtra that a sound is not cognized because it does not exist. The stand-still air cannot envelop a sound since an object, having limited extension, can only envelop another such object but cannot veil an object having unlimited extension like the sky. A sound is not by its very nature a transcendental object like the sky. Therefore, as it is experienced to be short-lived so it exists only so long as it is required for its perception. It is not unreasonable to hold that a sound does not endure long. The author of the Nyāya-Vārttika has advanced a proof to substantiate the thesis that a sound is impermanent. He argues that a sound is impermanent since it as a member of a class is perceived by the external sense-organ like a jar.

The Mīmāṁsakas point out a fallacy in the above argument. They hold that all universals are characterized by universals. As two universals co-exist in the same locus so one is characterized by another. The argument of the critics is absolutely unreasonable since it is well-known that the universals and some other objects do never possess a universal. The two universals, viz., pṛthivītva, ghaṭatva (a universal belonging only to earth and another belonging to all earthen jars) co-exist in a jar. But it cannot be held that the universal of ghaṭatva is characterized by the universal of pṛthivītva. Therefore, the argument, put forward by Uddyotakara, is free from all defects.

The criticism, directed by Kumārila against the thesis of the Naiyāyikas, is as follows : He holds that the marks, viz., the possession of a universal, perceptibility, etc., indicate alike both eternal and non-eternal objects. But he who puts forward the above marks to establish the thesis that a sound is non-eternal is not adept in the art of logic. This is the statement of one who is not conversant with the rules of Nyāya logic.

Kumārila himself advances some reasons in order to prove his thesis that a sound is eternal. But the reasons are not conducive to the above conclusion. The word 'cow' which was uttered yesterday is identical with the word 'cow' which has been uttered to-day since the awareness of the word 'cow' reveals one and the same word 'cow'.

An act of awareness has, however, competence only to reveal a real object. But it has no such power as to reveal an object as eternal or non-eternal.

Kumārila holds that some reasons are not competent enough to prove the thesis that a sound is non-eternal. But he himself advances similar reasons to draw the conclusion that a sound is eternal. But is it not strange to do so ?

The reasons which have been advanced in support of the thesis that a sound is eternal are very weak. Therefore, the Mīmāṁsakas cannot but hold that a sound is an effect, i. e., non-eternal. The Mīmāṁsakas have shown eloquence, repeating the words of the Vedas. But such eloquence has no scope in the sphere of logic.

We, do not subscribe to the view that every existent object is transient. Therefore, we cannot say that a sound has only instantaneous being. The Mīmāṁsakas hold that gross objects are only destructible. They mean to say that composite substances are only gross objects and imply that a sound is not destructible, not being a gross object. This view also stands cancelled.

The objects such as a jar, etc. are gross and stable. Their destruction depends upon that of their minute parts. A sound is unstable by nature. Hence, its destruction takes place. Again, it is a gross object.

If the Mīmāṁsakas revise their thesis and hold that a sound is transient then how should they previously assert that a sound is eternal ? If they hold that the former opinion is based upon some other argument then that argument must be found out. But it is useless on their part to stick to the dogmatic traditional view with high regard for it.

There is no need of elaborately discussing this topic. Discard the hypothesis that a sound is eternal. One who is conversant with the rules of logic should accept that a sound is non-eternal. A sound is an effect since the omnipotent and omniscient god Śiva, having moon on his forehead, is the author of all letters.

The end of the third chapter of Nyāyamañjarī.

ĀHNIKA IV

The Vedas are the work of a person

Thus we have proved that all letters partake of the character of an effect. Anything articulate, viz., a word, constituted by letters, a sentence, etc., owes its origin to a person who is its author. Thus the authorship of a person with regard to words, sentences, etc., is established.

Even if we admit that the words are eternal then it seems to us to be highly probable that a sentence is composed by a person since it is a combination of words. Hence how can we say that the Vedas are eternal, i.e., they have not been composed by a person ?

All the orderly arrangements are composed by an agent. The Vedic sentences are such an orderly arrangement. Therefore they are composed by an agent. The major premise is materially valid. The sentences of Classical Sanskrit Literature are composed by an agent. They serve as a positive instance. The reason, put forward by us, possesses all the five conditions requisite for a sound reason. The above reason is also strengthened by an ancillary argument. Hence it should not be held that the reason in question does not belong to the subject of inference. Let us cite a few Vedic sentences, viz. Śanno devīrabhiṣṭaye, etc., and examine them. Each of these sentences is an orderly arrangement of words containing accents properly distributed and other signs of arrangement. We directly know that the reason in question belongs to the Vedic sentences referred to.

The reason in question is not contradictorily related to the major term since it belongs to the positive instances such as the epic Kumāra-sambhava. It is a truism that the said epic is the work of an author and that it contains the orderly arrangement of words. The reason in question is not doubtful since an orderly arrangement does not belong both to the objects which have an author and to the objects which have no author. No orderly arrangement is noticed in the sky which has no author or in the sky-flower, etc. having no author.

The presence of the reason in question is not contradicted by some other sources of true knowledge. It has not been definitely proved either by perception or by the Vedas that the Vedas have no author.

The reason in question is not suspended by a forceful counter-argument. Just as when we perceive the common property of the two things but not their distinctive marks a doubt arises in our mind in the form "Is it a man or a post ?". If one puts forward a reason to prove that the Vedas have an author and another person advances a counter-reason to prove that the Vedas have no author then no decision is reached. But no such counter-argument has been stated.

In order to prove that atoms are non-eternal if one argues because it has limited extension then the generalisation is wrong. There is no relation of invariable concomitance holding between the middle and the major terms. Such an objection does not apply to the syllogism in question. An arrangement is invariably effectuated by an author. As smoke owes its existence to fire and points to it so an arrangement owes its existence to an agent and indicates its existence. Therefore, the reason in question is sound and conducive to the conclusion.

The refutation of the thesis that the Vedas are eternal

The Mīmāṁsakas appear on the field and oppose the thesis of the Naiyāyikas. They hold that the argument of the Naiyāyikas is counteracted by another argument. Therefore, the above mark is not convincing. The counter-argument, put forward by the Naiyāyikas, is as follows :

When one studies the Vedas he sits at the feet of his preceptor in order to learn them as we do now. The very phrase "The study of the Vedas" denotes the learning of the Vedas from a preceptor by a pupil (who receives all the words of the Vedas in their proper order from the mouth of the preceptor and gets them by heart). The learning of the Vedas in such a manner is called Vedādhyayana. The very word 'Vedādhyayana' points to the thesis that the Vedas are eternal. (If somebody is the author of the Vedas he has not learnt them from his preceptor. If he does not learn them from his preceptor then he is not a competent teacher. In order to make the study of the Vedas possible the series of the teachers of the Vedas must remain uninterrupted i.e., beginningless. Thus there is no author of the Vedas).

The argument is not sound. An argument like the above one does not draw a conclusion. Only from the meaning of the word 'adhyayana' it is not reasonable to arrive at the conclusion that the Vedas are eternal. The above reason is fallacious. We can also hold like-wise that the Mahābhārata has no author i.e. it is also eternal. He who studies the great epic of Bhārata learns it from his teacher. He has also learnt it from his teacher and so on *ad infinitum.* The study of the Mahābhārata implies the learning of it from a competent teacher like the study of the same epic at the modern age.

Now, the Mīmāṁsakas may contend that there is a piece of uncontradicted recollection that the Mahābhārata has an author. If this is their contention then it may also be held that the lord of all beings (Prajāpati) is truly remembered by all as the author of the Vedas. Now, the Mīmāṁsakas may defend their case with the remark that the Vedic mantra which refers to the authorship of Prajāpati has no literal meaning. It represents an allegory since the literal meaning involves contradiction. In the above mantra it has been stated that the four Vedas, the four castes and the four stages of life have been created by Prajāpati.

The Naiyāyikas say in reply to the above contention that the reference to the authorship of the son of Parāśara contained in the Mahābhārata may have as well some other purpose to serve. It does not purport to convey that Vyāsa has composed the Mahābhārata.

As the Mīmāṁsakas hold that the Lord of all beings is extolled in the Vedic mantras which involve references to him so the Naiyāyikas may as well say that the son of Satyavatī, i.e., Vyāsa, has been eulogised in the verses which refer to him.

Now, the Mīmāṁsakas may contend that no body has direct acquaintance with the fact that God has composed the Vedas. In reply to this it may be pointed out "Have your ancestors seen Dvaipāyana Vyāsa who was born in an island with their own eyes ?"

If the Mīmāṁsakas press their point saying that they possess unmistaken memory of tradition that the son of Satyavatī has composed the Mahābhārata then the Naiyāyikas may argue that there is a popular and unflinching belief which is widely accepted that Prajāpati is the author of the Vedas.

The Mīmāṁsakas continue to argue. They say "Oh Sir; why do you deflect from the right path, being deceived by the rumour current in the circle of carters and such other persons who are devoid of the power of discretion ?" The Naiyāyikas may retort that when one is advised by his parents to do something small he undertakes it out of his implicit confidence in their advice. But if one performs a Vedic rite which entails an expenditure of a huge sum and demands a lot of troubles to undergo without remembering the advisor then he surely commits a great blunder. One cannot reasonably take action upon the words of the Vedas if the author of the Vedas is not remembered by him just as one cannot attach any importance to a mutilated book containing poems of great and small poets. In any case the author should be recollected. One cannot suggest that the continuity of the Vedic tradition might have been broken in the past so the author of the Vedas could not be remembered. Just as we cannot remember the name of the founder of a deserted old well as well as a garden not visited by persons. Therefore, the author of the Vedas must be remembered. The Mīmāṁsakas join issue with the Naiyāyikas and hold that the author of the Vedas is not only remembered but also cannot be recollected. Memory is always based upon experience. Nobody has an experience of the author of the Vedas since there is no creation of the world. Even if it is admitted that the author of the Vedas exists and that He is not visible as He is incorporeal.

Even though we assume that God is corporeal and that He is visible in the beginning of creation yet nobody sees Him compose the Vedas.

Though we admit that the people see Him reap the Vedas yet a doubt arises in their mind whether or not He has composed the Vedas or He reads the Vedas composed by somebody else.

Or, if we hold that God reads the Vedas written by somebody else then a fresh doubt appears in our mind whether or not he has really composed the Vedas. Such a doubt points to the suggestion that the Vedas are eternal.

If nobody directly knows that God has composed the Vedas and everybody makes an appeal to memory as the source of the knowledge of God, then the series of recollections, handed down from one generation to another, is really unfounded. It looks like a row of blind men in which one blind man is following another.

One holds that the sages have mystic intuition of God as the author of the Vedas. But we, the Mīmāṁsakas, do not subscribe to this view. How can we follow the steps of the Naiyāyikas since we do not place our confidence in their assumption?

If it is held that the Vedas themselves declare that God is the author of them then it is a glaring instance of circular reasoning. The Vedas are the source of true knowledge because God is their author. Again, we truly know that God is their author since the Vedas are the source of true knowledge.

(Now, the Mīmāṁsakas assert their conclusion in the light of the above negative criticisms). The Naiyāyikas have arrived at an erroneous conclusion since they have based their view upon the Arthavāda portion of the Vedas. They have failed to distinguish the arthavādas from the mantras which are an embodiment of injunction since they have failed to study the Vedas in their proper order. They have not dived deep into the character of the Vedic mantra. They have taken only a superficial view of the mantras. Nobody really recollects the author of the Vedas. Thus we hold that the Vedas have not been composed since we do not remember the author of the Vedas who must have been remembered by us. We do not put our reason in the proper syllogistic language. Hence, the charge that the middle term does not belong to the minor term should not be levelled against the above argument. The exact middle term is that it is that the author of which is not remembered (The syllogism runs thus : All the works the author of which is not remembered are such as have no author. The Vedas are such a work. Therefore the Vedas are such as have no author).

A review of the above thesis is as follows : The Mīmāṁsakas have recourse to such a path as does not obey the rules of logical discipline. They have abandoned the reason which was put forward at the outset. They have at first tried to establish that the study of the Vedas pre-supposes an instruction from a preceptor by means of a reason. The implication of this argument is that the Vedas are eternal. Now, they advance another reason "being a work the author of which is not remembered". Let this reason be accepted. We shall not take the Mīmāṁsakas to task because they have recourse to another reason. The Mīmāṁsakas have raised an important point which is not to be set aside as a minor one. Do they intend to establish the conclusion that the Vedas have not been composed by means of an independent reason "being a work the author of which is not remembered?" Or, do they intend to counteract the reason "being an arrangement of words", put forward by us? It is not logical to hold that a syllogistic argument supersedes another such argument. It cannot be proved that like perception and verbal testimony an inference sets aside another inference. If two syllogistic arguments are equal in strength then they will contradict each other because of their equal strength. If they are of unequal strength then that which makes an argument weak will also invalidate it. In that case it is superflous to assume that an inference is set aside by another inference. The Mīmāṁsakas may hold that they have put forward the counter-argument in order to set aside the reason offered by the Naiyāyikas. But such a statement is contrary to reasoning. The two reasons which point to the two properties contradictorily opposed to each other cannot be simultaneously applied to the same substratum—the subject of inference. Therefore, in this case, one of them is surely fallacious. All the objects of the world cannot have two such parts as remain incompatible with each other. Therefore one of these two reasons is surely fallacious. As it is fallacious so it cannot draw the conclusion, which is expected of it. Therefore, no purpose will be served if the opponents put forward a reason to cancel another reason. If a counter reason is simply advanced the syllogistic argument which it intends to contradict does not come out to be fallacious. There is no such fallacy as is called "Viruddha-avyabhicārī". (The term in question denotes that syllogistic argument is fallacious if another true reason being advanced, contradicts the conclusion of the above syllogistic argument). We shall prove the absence of such a fallacy in the subsequent section. We shall also show that whenever a counter argument is put forward in order to contradict a syllogistic argument the fallacy of Prakaraṇa-sama is not committed. But the fallacy of Prakaraṇa-sama takes place if the reason which is really a source of doubt, the marks of its distinction remaining unobserved, is advanced. Hence, if one intends to find fault with the reason advanced by his rival then he should take the trouble of examining whether or not the said reason belongs to the subject of inference, i.e. the minor premise is materially valid. He should not make wild conjectures to find out the counter-reason.

Now, let us see which of the above two reasons fails to draw the conclusion. The two reasons are as follows :— (1) being an arrangement of words and (2) being that the author of which is not remembered. The decision on this point is this. The reason "being an arrangement of words" is competent to draw the conclusion since nobody has ever seen that the words arrange themselves without being arranged by a person.

Oh revered sirs: Oh great men who move in the circle of experienced persons ! have you ever seen or heard in this world that the words in a sentence combine themselves by their inherent power ? If it is held that the words contained in the Vedas get themselves combined by their innate nature then why do not the threads which make up a cloth spontaneously combine themselves ?

In the sentences, viz., "Śan no devīrabhiṣṭaye", "Nārāyaṇaṁ namaskṛtya", "Astyuttarasyāṁ diśi devatātmā" etc., the arrangement of words is the same. But if we hold that in some of these sentences the words have been arranged by a person and that in other sentences they have been arranged by no person then the source of such a differential treatment is only traced to a great confusion of mind. Those who indulge in such a conjecture should have also held that smoke is sometimes produced by fire and that it is not also sometimes produced by fire.

Now, the Mīmāṁsakas make the following ironical remarks, viz. "The Vedas have become equal in rank with the Kumārasambhava of Kālidāsa ! Alas the Naiyāyikas, the foremost believers, have established the authority of the Vedas !"

"No need of derision", "Say the Naiyāyikas in reply to the above remarks. The Vedas resemble the epic 'Kumāra-sambhava' only in the arrangement of words but in nothing else. If we (the Naiyāyikas) say this much then they do not deserve to be laughed at for this only. Does not soundness belong to the Vedas alike as it does to the sound produced by conch-shell? Does not existence inhere in the Vedas as it does in all the objects? The works of the poets like Kālidāsa etc. bear the stamp of their author on their face. But the Vedic works are entirely different from them. When the Vedic works are learnt by us we discover the marks of uniqueness inherent in them.

There are uses of words, verbs, prepositions etc. in the Vedic literature. But there is much novelty in their use. The Vedic works contain laudation, condemnation, the story narrated by a single person, the story narrated by two or more persons and other matters not to be found in Classical Sanskrit Literature.

Each Vedic Saṁhitā (a collection of Vedic verses) admits of various recensions. The matter which has been discussed in one recension of a particular Vedas is not to be found in another recension of the same Veda. Such a diversity of forms and matters is not to be found in Classical Sanskrit literature.

Thus, the students of Vedic Literature form their opinion from its uncommon character about the Vedas that the Vedic works have not been composed by an author. Therefore, the Mīmāṁsakas drink the cup of glory in this world.

We, the Naiyāyikas, join issue with the Mīmāṁsakas and refute their hypothesis. Let the Mīmāṁsakas drink the cup of glory or a cup of milk or medicated clarified butter in order to remove the dullness of their intellect. But there is no mistake in our hypothesis that the Vedas have been composed by an author.

The combination of parts of a jar is different from that of parts of a mountain. Still the combination of parts is due to the activity of an agent, i.e., it presupposes the existence of a person who combines the parts. Similarly, the arrangement of words, etc., in the Vedas is different from that of words etc. in a book of the classical period. Though the arrangement is different yet there is no doubt about the fact that it is due to the activity of an author.

We have got something to say regarding this matter. We have elaborately stated it at an earlier section. Now we say this much only that as the arrangement of words in the Vedas is a class by itself so one should infer that the author of the Vedas is necessarily an extra-ordinary person. But it becomes absurd to deny the existence of God. We have already stated this view. Nobody disputes to admit that the great works of Kālidāsa and other great poets which have an aesthetic appeal have been composed by an author. It is also experienced that each of these works has its distinctive mark.

The poetic expressions of Kālidāsa are as if dipped by nectar, besmeared by sandal paste and polished by the moonbeams. Though the sentences of Bāṇa Bhaṭṭa consist of long compounds yet they have charmed the circle of poets, rousing emotions as they do. Similarly, in each literary work some diversities are noticed. The very nature of the Vedas suggests that the Vedas have no author because nouns, verbs etc., have been strangely used in them. It is indeed a novel argument which has merely verbal significance. If you have implicit confidence in the characteristic feature of the Vedas then why do you not apply your attention to examine the other characteristic feature of them, viz., the narration of the created objects? The Vedic sentences which involve references to the created objects run thus:—"Babara, the son of Pravahaṇa desired", "Kusura Vinda, the son of Uddālaka, desired, Oh Pūruravas ! do not give up your life" etc. Now, the Mīmāṁsakas may contend that they are created in each cycle of new world. Hence they are eternal in this sense. Then, the Naiyāyikas may as well say that the Vedas are different in each emergence of the new world. It has been stated that after the expiry of each Manu era the fresh Vedas are composed.

If we frame the hypothesis that the Vedas are eternal seeing the characteristic features of the Vedas then the said hypothesis is only based upon pure imagination but is not established by a proof.

If we try to explain away the created objects mentioned in the Vedas then the explanation is not reliable. The students of Vedic literature in course of its study come across many terms which denote created objects. Therefore, the Vedas are not eternal. Therefore, the reason 'being an arrangement of words' is not impotent to draw a true conclusion. But the counter-reason 'non-remembrance of an author' is incapable of drawing the conclusion since it has not been proved that the author of the Vedas is not remembered. Even if it is admitted that no author of the Vedas is remembered then the non-remembrance of such an author does not necessarily point to the absence of an author since it may be otherwise explained. The composition of the Vedas having taken place in the remote past the author of the Vedas is not remembered. As the author of the Vedas is distinct from all other persons so he has no definite body. Consequently, nobody can remember Him as that particular person who has composed the Vedas as we do remember Pāṇini or Piṅgala as an author of a particular work. It is not true that God does not exist since inferential and verbal knowledge point to His existence. The Mīmāṁsakas argue that the Vedas are eternal because the Vedas have such an author as is not remembered. The rule of inference is that the reason must belong to the subject of inference. The reason in question is definitely subjective. In other words, the person who is going to infer can only know whether or not the reason belongs to the subject of inference. It is impossible for all persons to determine whether or not the reason in question belongs to the subject of inference. How do you know that all persons do not remember the author of the Vedas ? You do not intuit the mind of all persons. If you had done so you would have been omniscient. You cannot arrive at a generalisation based upon an analogical argument, viz. "As I do not remember such an author so all other persons do not remember him." Thus, such a generalisation is too wide. Therefore the reason "Being that the author of which is not remembered" is truly unknowable. Again, if we do not remember the author of the Vedas then the zeal for performing the Vedic rites on the part of the intelligent persons will gradually fade away since an advice without an advisor is impossible. Even if we admit that such an advice is a possibility then we cannot place our confidence in it since the source of its validity has not been determined. (We have rather positive apathy for sentence which is self-caused, i.e., which does not come from the lips of a speaker, not to speak of any regard for it). We have stated before that the truth of a sentence is not asserted if it does not merely involve self-contradiction. As the respectable persons have absolute reliance upon the trustworthy persons so it is possible that they unhesitatingly observe the Vedic rites. Thus the non-remembrance of an author cannot be logically taken as a counter-reason of being an arrangement of words.

The said reason advanced by the Mīmāṁsakas does not independently prove that the author of the Vedas does not exist. It really amounts to the non-apprehension of the author of the Vedas. Such a view is not tenable since the author of the Vedas is an inference. What is inferred is also known. The Mīmāṁsakas may contend that the inferential knowledge of the author of the Vedas is not logically tenable because it has been contradicted by the non-remembrance of the author of the Vedas. But such a contention is a glaring instance of vicious circle since if the said non-remembrance is established then the said inference is contradicted and if the said inference is contradicted then the said non-remembrance is established. The Mīmāṁsakas may point out that the establishment of the truth of the said inference suffers from the same defect. The truth of the deduction depends upon the truth of the major premise in question, i.e., induction. The truth of the said inference does not depend upon the contradiction of the truth of the said non-remembrance.

The Mīmāṁsakas say that the above reason does not directly prove the absence of authorship of the Vedas. But they do not believe in the existence of transcendental objects like god, etc. They ask their opponents to furnish them with the proof with regard to the hypothesis that the Vedas have been composed by a person. As the opponents cannot supply with such a proof so non-remembrance enforces on our mind its resultant knowledge that the author of the Vedas does not exist. The Naiyāyikas say in reply to this argument that such a conclusion might have been accepted if there had been no inference. We have already stated that the Vedas have an author because they possess an arrangement of words.

The Mīmāṁsakas have said that the origin of the Vedas cannot be traced to a person. Such a statement is not fair. When we perceive a new curtain, etc. how do we determine the existence of a weaver who is beyond the ken of our vision ?

We infer the existence of a weaver who has made a cloth, etc. from the object which has been created by him. Similarly, we infer the existence of the author of the Vedas from the arrangement of words contained in them (the Vedas).

A soul cannot advise others if he does not possess a body. Hence we can assume that God sometimes has a body. As He has no permanent body so He is not remembered like the other authors, viz., Vyāsa etc.

As a poet who belongs to our age is known as the author of a particular poem by his contemporary fellows so God will also be known as the author of the Vedas by his contemporary fellows.

As the misapprehension regarding the poem that it has been composed by some body else but not by the said poet is removed so the erroneous knowledge about the authorship of the Vedas will be also dispelled.

It has been stated in connection with the definition of perception that a transcendental object which is inferred by us is perceived by the sages.

Thus we see that perception and inference are the two main sources of knowledge about the authorship of the Vedas. I memory is held to be the source of such knowledge then it has the chance of being discredited.

Hence, in order to repudiate the hypothesis that God is the author of the Vedas, memory which has been taken as the only source of such authorship by the opponents has been discredited on the ground that it is based upon the Arthavāda section of the Vedas. Such a criticism is pointless. We have already indicated how perception and inference threw light on the authorship of the Vedas.

The Mīmāṁsakas have stated that the hypothesis of the Naiyāyikas involves circular reasoning. The Vedas are the source of true knowledge because they have been composed by omniscient God and God exists because the Vedas point to His existence. But the critics misrepresent the hypothesis of the Naiyāyikas. The objection raised by them, is not fair. The Naiyāyikas have given an answer to this charge at an earlier section. God as the creator of the universe is an inference. The Vedas simply strengthen the said conclusion. The Naiyāyikas do not hold that the Vedas are the only source of God, the creator of the universe. It has been stated before that the creator of the universe is inferred from the earth, etc.—the created objects.

The author of the Vedas is the creator of the earth and such other objects

Does the creator who has fashioned this earth compose the Vedas ? If this question is put to us then we answer this question with the remark "Oh yes". Now the opponents may urge "What is your proof?" Our answer to this question is as follows :

Omniscient God is competent to construct such a huge universe full of diversities — a universe where the different sorts of beings enjoy the fruits of their action.

The person who knows each action of each being and the fruit of such an action can only compose the Vedas which are nothing but an embodiment of instructions regarding actions and their results. Hence we assume that nobody but God composes the Vedas.

If the assumption of a single person serves our purpose then why shall we assume a second person as the author of the Vedas ? We find no sufficient reason for assuming many persons, entrusted with the different functions.

In the matter of the creation of the universe we subscribe to the hypothesis that there is only one God. No purpose is served if we hold that there are two or more creators of the universe. Suppose there are two Gods. Now, if their will is concordant then one of them is redundant. Again if their will is discordant then one of them is sure to undermine the work of the other creator. In that case, one of them ceases to be God.

The hypothesis of the plurality of Gods is not at all satisfactory. If the will of many gods is perfectly concordant then the hypothesis of the plurality of gods is absolutely meaningless. He whose will is inviolable makes up his mind to reward or to punish a being. What He desires turns out to be true by means of His majesty. How can the other Gods help in this matter of inflicting punishment or awarding a reward ?

Let us assume many gods. If their will is discordant then two opposite wills cannot simultaneously materialise. Hence, he whose will is frustrated cannot be God. If one God desires that a particular person shall be a king and another God desires that he shall be killed then how can these two conflicting desires simultaneously take an effect ?

If the first desire of making one a king is fruitful then the second one of killing him will be frustrated. If the second one materialises then the first one will be baffled.

Thus we have established that there is only one God who creates the universe full of diversity.

All the Vedas have been composed by one and the same author

As the creator of the universe full of diversity is one so the author of all the Vedas is God who is one. No proof can be put forward in support of the hypothesis that many gods have written the Vedas. The assumption of many gods simply violates the law of parsimony.

Now, an objection is raised against this hypothesis. How do you arrive at the conclusion that one God has composed all the Vedic works ? Why have not many treatises been composed by the different authors ?

The above objections, raised by the opponents, against the said hypothesis, have been met thus.

All the Vedas have the same author because the same well-connected subject-matter has been taught in all the Vedas. Suppose a principal rite has been enjoined. All its relevant accessory rites have been advised by the Ṛg-Veda, the Yajur-Veda, the Sāma Veda and the Atharva-Veda. As all these accessory rites contribute towards the completion of the principal rite so they are held to be connected with it. (To perform any Vedic rite the assistance of the four different priests is absolutely necessary. The priest who exclusively follows the Ṛg-Veda is called 'hotṛ'. The priest, following only the Yajur-Veda, is called 'adhvaryu'. The priest who is only in concern with the Sāma-Veda is designated 'udgātṛ'. The priest who deals only with the subject-matter of the Atharva-Veda is called 'brahmā'). The priests perform the duties of a hotṛ according to the Ṛg-Veda. The priests discharge the duties of an adhvaryu-priest in accordance with the Yajur Veda. The priests execute the duties of an udgātṛ according to the Sāma-Veda. The priests complete the duties of a brahmā according to the Atharva-Veda. The subsidiary actions which have been stated in the different recensions of the Vedas such as Paippala etc., are necessarily implied for the completion of the main action. They say that all the minor actions, taught by the different recensions of the Vedas, point to one and the same main action. We shall decide this matter at subsequent section not far off.

As the subject-matter of Vedic literature indicates that it represents an inter-related system united by a common purpose so how can the Vedic literature be composed by the different persons having cross-purposes?

If this is the argument of the Naiyāyikas then how is it that a foot of a verse is composed by a single poet and the other feet are composed by the other poets? (The main point in this objection is this that a single poem represents a whole the different parts of which are composed by the different poets. In spite of the diversity of authors the poem maintains the unity of an idea. Similarly, the Vedic literature may represent a single system of ideas or actions though it has been composed by the different authors).

An answer to this objection is as follows. The second poet reading the foot of a poem composed by the first poet grasps the intention of the first poet and composes the other feet following the idea of the initial poet. Otherwise if the idea of some portion of a poem composed by a poet does not agree with that of the other portions of the same poem then it becomes an incongruous poem like the literary product of Viśva Vasu. But if the ideas, expressed by the complete poem form a consistent whole then it is a piece of certainty that the idea of the first poet has been realised by the poem.

Now, in case of the Vedas if we hold that there are other gods who follow the intention of the first god then the intention of one god constitutes the key-note of the Vedas and there is no need of assuming other gods. Thus, we arrive at the conclusion that God is the author of all the different recensions of the Vedas. The opponents also admit that the naming of the different recensions such a Kāṭhaka, etc. may have been after the name of the celebrated teachers of the particular subject. Moreover, the various branches of a tree spread out in the different directions. All leaves, flowers and fruits do not belong to a single branch. But they belong to a few branches. Similarly, the Vedas which teach the details of the subsidiary rites branch off in different recensions.

As all those branches of a tree develop from a single tree so the origin of all the recensions of the Vedas is traced to God, the best of all persons.

The creator of the universe who has immediate knowledge of merits and demerits of each soul and of the various degree of their maturity has given a code of instructions which has universal applications. It is reasonable to hold that He has composed the Vedas.

All persons pin their faith in the words of the Vedas because they believe that the Vedas have been composed by eternal and trustworthy God who is possessed of all excellent virtues. No intelligent person will place his confidence in the veracity of the Vedas because they have been composed by no author. We have discussed this point at an earlier section.

Thus, the hypothesis that the Vedas presuppose an author as they contain an arrangement of words and sentences has been proved.

The determination of the relation holding between a word and its meaning

The Mīmāṁsakas hold that the man-made relation of denotation does not hold between a word and its meaning. They strongly assert that a word has an innate power of conveying an object just as the power of burning is inherent in fire. A person simply learns that this word has the power of conveying this object from the use of an experienced old man. What will a person do in this matter? Such a view is not logically tenable. If a convention that this word denotes this object is not set up by a person then a word cannot convey its meaning.

Now, the Mīmāṁsakas contend that as no relation subsists between a word and its meaning so why is it discussed at all whether or not the said relation is dependent or independent of a person? The relation holding between a word and its meaning is not that of conjunction which obtains between a plum and a small reservoir of water. The said relation is not that of inherence which subsists between threads and a piece of cloth. The said relation is not also perceived to be either of them. No other relations which are based upon any one of these two relations are also possible. It has been stated that a word is heard as belonging to the mouth but an object is seen on the ground. The relation between a word and an object is not an inference. When we utter the words "razor, a sweet ball, etc." neither we experience a cut in our mouth by a razor nor the filling up of our mouth by a sweet ball. An object, denoted by a word, does not belong to the place where a word is uttered. Similarly, a word does not belong to the place where an object exists. The word and the object, denoted by it, do not co-exist because the locus, the instrumental cause and efforts, the conditions of a sound, are not perceived where the objects such as a jar, etc., exist. The Mīmāṁsakas also point out that the Naiyāyikas themselves deny the truth of the hypothesis that a word is more pervasive than the object conveyed by it.

The Naiyāyikas give a reply to the above objections. They say "We do not admit that the relation of conjunction holds between a word and the object meant by it". The Mīmāṁsakas put the following question to the Naiyāyikas : Is the above relation that which obtains between a cause and an effect or that which holds between the conditions and the conditioned or that which subsists between the locus and the object located?" "None of these relations holds between them", is the reply given by the Naiyāyikas, The Mīmāṁsakas remark that this admission amounts to this that there is no relation whatsoever between a word and the object meant by it. The Naiyāyikas reply that it is not a truism that there is no relation between a word and the object denoted by it since a word invariably expresses an object as smoke points to fire. The Mīmāṁsakas question "Does the relation of the pervaded hold between a word and the object? The Naiyāyikas reply "No. If we subscribe to the view then verbal knowledge will be inferential". The Mīmāṁsakas ask "What is this relation that holds between a word and the object denoted by it?" The rejoinder of the Naiyāyikas is that this relation is a conventional one. The Mīmāṁsakas question, "What is a convention?" The Naiyāyikas answer that a convention is an act of will which determines that this word will denote this object. In other words, a relation between a word and an object is fashioned by an act of will. Such a relation is called a conventional one.

The Mīmāṁsakas raise another question viz., "If the Naiyāyikas subscribe to the hypothesis of convention then why do they refer to the hypothesis of the relation of conjunction holding between word and its meaning and refute it ?" They further point out that the hypothesis of such conjunction is highly reasonable from the stand-point of the grammarians since they hold that the relation of identity in difference holds between a word and its meaning. (But the Naiyāyikas have no reasonable ground for suggesting such a hypothesis in order to criticize it). The Naiyāyikas hold that the meaning of a word is conventional. Such a view is not tenable since the convention is set up by a human being and no law is imposed upon the external objects by the mere will of a person. The Naiyāyikas may contend that God's will being inviolable, the conventional meaning of a word is possible. If this is their contention then why should not an object convey meaning just like a word). But the will of a person cannot upset the law of nature. Let us take a concrete example. A person has no desire for knowing fire. He sees smoke. Though he has desire for knowing water yet he cannot but infer fire in spite of his adverse desire. In case of smoke and fire the relation of concomitance holding between smoke and fire is natural. But in order to discover this relation repeated observations of the co-existence of smoke and fire are necessary. Similarly, the relation of denotation, (technically called the power of communicating the exact meaning) holding between a word and its meaning, is a natural one but is not made by any person. But in order to ascertain the power of communication of a word we are to depend upon the usages of the experienced senior persons or upon the traditional meaning of the adjacent word. Now, a question arises in our mind with regard to the hypothesis of this natural relation. The relation which obtains between light, the illuminator, and the object, illuminated by it, is natural. No body is conscious of this relation when he sees an object illuminated by light.

If this is the case, what is the necessity of knowing the relation of denotation through the usage of the experienced persons? In other words, whenever a word is heard why does it not directly convey its meaning? Such an objection does not affect the above hypothesis. A word is merely an indicator. The nature of an indicator like smoke is this that it (an indicator) reveals the object to be indicated by it to a person only when he knows the relation obtaining between them (the indicator and the indicated). The competence of this relation and such other factors are included in the conditions of perception. They are not necessary factors of verbal knowledge. The power of communication belonging to a word is as natural as is the power of revealing which belongs to a lamp. A word conveys its meaning by means of this power. It does not communicate its meaning by means of its conventional relation.

The Mīmāṁsakas contend that a convention is nothing but the determination of a particular relation holding between a word and an object meant by it. In other words, a convention implies that this word denotes this object but nothing else. Thus a convention is only a piece of knowledge. A piece of knowledge belongs to the soul. It does neither belong to word nor to an object denoted by the word. Hence, it cannot constitute a relation obtaining between a word and its meaning. The Naiyāyikas hold that the said convention has been set up by God. Does God bestow such authority upon the senior persons or upon the traditional meaning of the adjacent word? Now, a question arises in our mind with regard to the hypothesis of this natural relation. The relation which obtains between light, the illuminator, and the object, illuminated by it, is natural. No body is conscious of this relation when he sees an object illuminated by light.

If this is the case, what is the necessity of knowing the relation of denotation through the usage of the experienced persons?

In other words, whenever a word is heard why does it not directly convey its meaning ? Such an objection does not affect the above hypothesis. A word is merely an indicator. The nature of an indicator like smoke is this that it (an indicator) reveals the object to be indicated by it to a person, only when he knows the relation obtaining between them (the indicator and the indicated). The competence of this relation and such other factors are included in the conditions of perception. They are not necessary factors of verbal knowledge. The power of communication belonging to a word is as natural as is the power of revealing which belongs to a lamp. A word conveys its meaning by means of this power. It does not communicate its meaning by means of its conventional relation.

The Mīmāṁsakas contend that a convention is nothing but the determination of a particular relation holding between a word and an object meant by it. In other words, a convention implies that the word denotes this object but nothing else. Thus a convention is only a piece of knowledge. A piece of knowledge belongs to the soul. It does neither belong to a word nor to an object denoted by the word. Hence, it cannot constitute a relation obtaining between a word and its meaning. The Naiyāyikas hold that the said convention has been set up by God. Does God repeatedly make it at the dawn of creation for each person wherever each person utters it ? Or, does He frame it once for all persons in the beginning of this world ? Even if it is admitted that the said convention is repeatedly created for each person then does the convention which is repeatedly set up become a new one or remain the old one at all instances of utterance ? If it is held that a new convention is set up each time then how do we know that a convention helps to communicate the meaning of a word ? If the power of communication is transcendental then what is the good of setting up a new convention ? That which has been done before is being done again. It is not reasonable to repeat again what has been done.

An object may be made known again and again but it cannot be created more than once. A word may be uttered by the different persons. Is the relation obtaining between a word and its meaning in each case made different or identical ? If the relation is made distinct in each case, how does a word communicate the same meaning ? How does the word 'cow' signify an animal having dewlap? How does the word 'horse' mean an animal having manes ? If the relation is held to be one and the same then the relation which has been created cannot be re-created. The relation is brought to light but not created. The Naiyāyikas may hold that the relation between a word and its meaning has been once created by God in the beginning of the creation of the world.

Such a contention is not sound. It is highly improbable to imagine such a period of time since it is illogical to cherish a belief in the existence of an age when there is no verbal transaction. Thus we arrive at the conclusion that the relation holding between a word and its meaning is eternal and is learnt from the people. But the said relation cannot be created. The defect which undermines the hypothesis that the relation is created does not affect the hypothesis that the eternal relation is learnt since the second one is based upon sound reasoning. It is within the range of our experience that the inexperienced boys learn from the use of the experienced old persons that this word signifies this object and so on. These experienced old persons were also young. They learnt the meanings of words from the other old persons. These old persons learnt it from the other old persons at their young age and so on *ad infinitum*. Thus there is no beginning of this world.

Moreover, if the hypothesis that a word is eternally related to its meaning is denied then how may it be distinguished from winking or signalling by hand, since it depends only upon convention and lacks intrinsic power of expression? In that case, a word will be as good as the lashings of a whip or piercing with a hook or beating with a sharp instrument. The popular view is that a meaning follows from a convention. If we subscribe to the hypothesis that a convention determines the meaning of a word then all words would be reduced to the state of arbitrary ones, coined by us just like the word 'Yadṛcchā'. If we go so far as to accept this hypothesis then the words like cow, horse, etc., will have no definite meaning.

Now, the Mīmāṁsakas anticipate the possible objections to be raised by the Naiyāyikas and meet them thus. The relation between a word and its meaning is established only by convention because a word does not uniformly signify the same meaning in all countries. In the Sanskrit text the word 'jāti' has been used. It purports to convey a country. In a particular country a word conveys a definite meaning. In some other countries that very word does not convey the above meaning. But it signifies something else. Let us take an example. The word 'caura' signifies a thief. It has been employed by the people of the southern countries to denote rice. Such different meanings of the same word speak in favour of the hypothesis that the relation obtaining between a word and its meaning is set up by our convention. If the said relation were eternal then such a change in the meaning of a word would have not been possible. The above objection is not tenable. Each word has power of expressing all possible meanings, i.e. is competent to denote all objects. In a particular country a particular word is employed to denote a particular object. When we bear a word the relation of which to an object is not known we cannot make out its meaning since a doubt about its denotation arises in our mind. We are at a loss to determine the exact meaning which it purports to convey. Again if we hold that a word has no power of expressing its meaning then, on hearing a word, no doubt as to its meaning should arise in our mind since a conventional relation has not been established between it and its meaning. The meaning of a word which has been accepted by the Aryans should be accepted by us but the meaning of a word which has been accepted by the non-Aryans should be disregarded by us. Therefore, the relation subsisting between a word and its meaning has not been created by human beings. It is eternal. The hypothesis that a relation between a word and its meaning is established by convention is not based upon strong reasons. Hence, a human being has no hand in fashioning this relation.

The refutation of the hypothesis that the relation between a Word and its Meaning is eternal

The refutation of the above hypothesis is as follows. It is unreasonable to hold that the relation between a word and its meaning is eternal. A word and its meaning are within the reach of valid source of knowledge such as perception, etc., but their relation as a distinct entity is not cognized in a similar manner by any proof.

Now, the Mīmāṁsakas may contend that the very power of expressing a meaning has been stated as constituting the relation between a word and its meaning. This being the nature of this power it has only a dependant existence. Having such existence how can it be cognized like an independant whole ? Such a contention does not hold good since the existence of a subtle power apart from a cause and its auxiliary conditions has been refuted. This power is not perceptible since it is not cognized like a substance. It is not also an inference. It is a truism that a cause is inferred from an effect. But if one tries to infer the above power from an effect then it may be pointed out that the said effect may be brought about by a cause other than the power in question. On the contrary, though one assumes the hypothesis of power yet the hypothesis of the said relation remains unavoidable. If the relation between a word and its meaning had not existed then the meaning of a word would not have been ascertained. If the said relation is established then the meaning of a word is determined only by means of it. Thus the assumption of an eternal relation becomes redundant. Now the Mīmāṁsakas raise an objection against the hypothesis of conventional relation. They say, "As convention is a creation of human will and the force of will is irresistible so the converse of the relation should have held between a word and its meaning." Such an objection is not reasonable. If the hypothesis that a word has the power of expressing a meaning is denied then can a word be competent to denote a meaning ? Now, the Mīmāṁsakas raise another question, viz., "If the power of expressing a meaning is denied to a word then how is a word competent to signify a meaning?" An answer to it is as follows. The word 'ga' which contains the universals such as gatva, autva, etc., in proper succession is entitled to be denotative. But the object which is meant by it is expressible. Let us make our point clear by means of an illustration.

A Vīraṇa (a kind of grass) is a substance. There are also substances which do not belong to the class of Vīraṇa. Of all substances Vīraṇas alone produce a mat because the universal of vīraṇatva inheres in them. The other substances cannot produce it. It has been stated that the power of producing an effect does not belong to it. The Sāṁkhyists hold that an effect in its potential form belongs to its cause. Thus an effect has pre-natal existence. But you do not subscribe to this view. Though the Naiyāyikas do not subscribe to the hypothesis of Śakti (the power of producing an effect) yet the inherence of a particular universal being the determinant of naming the relation of denotation will never change its direction. In other words, the object which is named will never play the part of a name. Therefore, the relation which holds between a word and the object denoted by it is other than the power of expression. The said relation is not that of universal concomitance holding between smoke and fire. Whenever the relation of universal concomitance holding between smoke and fire is cognized we also know that smoke does not exist at a spot where fire is absent. But whenever the relation of denotation holding between a word and its meaning is apprehended we also come to know that this object is known from this word. This is the final lesson on the relation of denotation which we learn from experience. We have already stated that verbal knowledge is different from the inferential one because the former one pre-supposes the knowledge of the relation of denotation. There would be no doubt about the truth of the hypothesis that a word reveals an object by its power innate in it, if the word is not uttered either by a mistake or negligence it reveals the intended object just as a lamp illuminates an object.

The Mīmāṁsakas hold that though the power of revealing an object is innate in a word yet the word reveals its meaning only when the relation between them like that between smoke and fire is known. The Naiyāyikas remark that as these two cases are not parallel the illustration is not exact. Smoke has no inherent power of revealing fire though it is by nature an invariable concomitant of fire. Thus if such relation obtaining between smoke and fire is not known the knowledge of fire does not follow from the perception of smoke. But the Mīmāṁsakas assume that a word has an inborn power of revealing its meaning. If this power is natural then why should verbal knowledge depend upon the relation of denotation holding between a word and its meaning. The Mīmāṁsakas say "We know a word to be a revealer only when we understand that a word produces knowledge. But we fail to make out this character of a word only on hearing it". The Naiyāyikas give a reply to this contention. As many times as we hear a word and know that this is a name and this is the object named so many times we make out the meaning of a word heard by us. Thus the efficacy of the relation of denotation has been stated by it. Without the efficacy of the relation of denotation a word cannot convey its meaning. The power of expressing a meaning is not inherent in a word.

The Mīmāṁsakas have taken an exception to the hypothesis of the Naiyāyikas on the ground that a conventional relation partaking of the nature of consciousness, belongs to the soul but does neither belong to a word nor to an object meant by it. Such a criticism is not sound. Though consciousness does not find a locus in them (a word and its meaning) yet they may be related to it as an object.

The Mīmāṁsakas have criticised the hypothesis of the Naiyāyikas thus: If a word communicates its meaning only by means of its conventional relation then a word will be better in no way than the piercing of a hook or the lashings of a whip. It that case, a word is redundant. Such a criticism is only superficial. If the power of conveying a power in itself conveys a meaning, why does not the word do? If the power of conveying a meaning were inherent in a word then we should have held that the power itself conveys a meaning but not the word. If the Mīmāṁsakas argue that the power is merely a condition of conveying a meaning whereas a word is the cause of such conveying then the Naiyāyikas will also simply meet the objection with the remark that the same logic applies to the hypothesis of the Naiyāyikas. In other words, a word is the cause of communicating its meaning but the conventional relation is merely the condition of such communication.

As smoke depends upon the knowledge of universal concomitance in order to indicate fire so a word depends upon the knowledge of the relation of denotation in order to communicate its meaning. In spite of this dependence none of them (smoke and a word) ceases to be a cause.

Moreover, popular usage bears an evidence to the truth of the hypothesis of conventional relation e.g. Devadatta has said 'Learn this meaning from this word'. An ordinary person talks like this. Therefore, the hypothesis of conventional relation should be accepted. It is the conventional relation which alone explains why a particular word conveys a different meaning in another country.

The Mīmāṁsakas hold that each word is capable of conveying all sorts of meanings. In different countries some words are restricted to particular meanings by usage. Such a hypothesis does not convince one that a word communicates its meaning since the dilemma whether or not a word is identical with its meaning cannot be solved. We cannot hold that the said power is different from a word because the former is never cognized as different from the latter. If we admit that the said power is identical with a word then all the different powers belonging to a word should also be identical. Now, the Mīmāṁsakas may contend that the different powers are inferred from the different effects. Such a contention is not tenable. How can one account for the diversity of effects as due to the difference in powers? The variety of effects may also be otherwise explained. The different conditions may explain the diverse effects. If it is held that all words are capable of conveying all meanings than a word should communicate different meanings. The Mīmāṁsakas may contend that though each word admits of different meanings yet a word is restricted to a particular meaning by means of conventional relation. That is why a word does not simultaneously convey all meanings. If this is the contention of the Mīmāṁsakas then the hypothesis of power inherent in a word should yield place to that of conventional relation. There is no need of assuming so many powers.

The Mīmāṁsakas hold that when a word is heard the listener is at a loss to ascertain the exact meaning since many meanings flash in his mind. Such a doubtful state of mind leads one to assume that a word has various powers. Such a view is not sound since many powers inhering in a word cannot explain the above doubt. The above doubt arises in one's mind because universals belonging to letters, the constituents of a word, play an important part. Let this view be discussed. A word is constituted by many letters each of which has a particular universal. It signifies a meaning. But if none of its constituents conveys a meaning then how can a word, an aggregate of letters having no meaning, convey a meaning? This question, remaining unsolved in our mind, raises the above doubt.

The Mīmāṁsakas have also said that the meaning of a word is that which is conveyed by it used by the Aryans but the meaning of a word which has been accepted by the non-Aryans is not a real one. They will simply take an oath to prove their thesis. In other words, the thesis is not based upon sound logic. It is not a fact that a word which has a peculiar meaning in the non-Aryan country communicated no meaning. It is not a truism that the meaning of a word which has been accepted by the non-Aryans is contradicted. It is also not true that the meaning of a word, accepted by them, produces doubt in the mind of the people.

Why will the meaning be not a real one? The Mīmāṁsakas may argue that the meaning of a word current in the Aryan country contradicts its meaning, current in the non-Aryan country. Then we ask them "Why does not the latter contradict the former?" In order to solve the above difficulty we shall rather hold that some words like the word "akṣa" admit of alternative meanings. The scope of the concurrent alternative meanings will be cut down by the delimitation of areas. In one province one of the alternative meanings will be fixed up. Another meaning will hold good in another province and so on. In other words, the scope of each of the alternative meanings will be well defined and fixed up. The Mīmāṁsakas themselves have learnt the meanings of the words 'pika', 'tāmarasa', etc., from the non-Aryans. In the section of Aveṣṭi, i. e., Rājasūya they have explained the word 'rājya' following the footsteps of the non-Aryans. We shall refrain from discussing minor details. Let us turn our attention to the point at issue. The relation of denotation i.e., the relation holding between a word and its meaning, is constituted by convention. It is reasonable to subscribe to this view. We should also bear in mind that a word denoting a universal has no fixed meaning. The word 'cow-ness' does not invariably signify the universal belonging to all cows. It may mean something else.

The Mīmāṁsakas take an exception to our hypothesis on the ground that whenever a person utters a word he establishes each time a new convention. But they have missed our point. They have criticized such a hypothesis as has not been accepted by us. We hold that God has created a convention once for all in the beginning of creation. The meaning of all words has not been arbitrarily determined like the word 'yadṛcchā'. The meanings of some words have been fixed up by us according to our sweet will. These words bear a close resemblance to the word 'yadṛcchā'. We have proved that the creation of this universe has a beginning. We have also put forward irrefutable syllogistic proof in support of the thesis that God exists. We two (the Naiyāyikas and the Mīmāṁsakas) differ in this that on the one hand you (the Mīmāṁsakas) hold that the relation of denotation is eternal but on the other hand we (the Naiyāyikas) hold that the said relation as fixed by God is the same till now. But you hold that not only the relation of denotation is ascertained but also the power of expression inherent in a word. We hold that the relation of denotation is exclusively grasped. As a meaning is conveyed by this word, this is a denotative word but no information about the innate power of a word has been received. We shall also cite that their relation is specifically mentioned. This much may be admitted that as a meaning is conveyed by a word, this is a denotative word. When a person learns the use of words from the usage of persons adept in the use of words he knows only this that this word conveys this meaning. But he knows nothing about the innate power of a word.

With this much knowledge about a word we are in a position to say that a word communicates its meaning to one. The knowledge of the relation of denotation, being the invariable condition of verbal knowledge, we are not justified in assuming the inherent power of a word. Hence, the relation holding between a word and its meaning is not eternal. Therefore, the thesis of the Mīmāṁsakas that the denotative relation is established by three kinds of proof is not accepted by the Naiyāyikas.

It is a truism that the meaning of a word is learnt from the behaviour of an experienced person who commands and that of another such person who carries out the same from the knowledge of the object denoted by it when it is brought and perceived. It is also true that a listener rightly infers from the movement of the experienced person who has been employed that he has obeyed the command of his employer. But it is not true that the power of expression which rests upon a word and its meaning is a presumption. We have already stated that the knowledge of the power of expression is not necessary for the communication of the meaning of a word. Therefore, the determination of the relation of denotation is due to two kinds of proof but not three. Therefore, as a word has no innate power of expression and lacks eternal relation to its meaning so the verbal usage has been introduced by God who has established a relation between a word and its meaning by His sweet will. The use of words is not beginningless. It owes its existence to God.

Now the Mīmāṁsakas raise an interesting problem. If God sets up the relation between a word and its meaning and communicates it to men then He does it by means of sentences. These sentences consist of words. These words should also be significant. How are they known to be related to meaning? if they are so related then how is their meaning communicated to others by means of a different set of words? The meaning of these words is not known to persons whom God teaches. Hence if we hold that God has connected words with their meanings then there will be a *regressus ad infinitum* to communicate the meaning of a word by means of a never-ending series of sentences consisting of words of unknown meanings. Thus even if we admit that God has created the relation of denotation between a word and its meaning we must hold in order to render its communication possible that He teaches men by means of such words as have been known to be significant by the usage of the experienced predecessors. If a word is known to be significant by means of usage then what is the good of admitting the existence of God or of admitting the relation of denotation as created by God? Thus, the hypothesis that the relation of denotation is eternal is better. A reply to these objections is as follows :—

The good self has learnt to discharge his weapon but does not know the target to be aimed at. These objections are applicable to us if we create the said relation. But they do not apply to God, the omniscient being. God who has created the infinite universe by His mere will for the fruition of the diverse unrequitted actions has superexcellent skill in teaching which lies beyond the ken of our imagination.

Our imagination fails to conceive of the creation of this Earth and such other objects by a mere act of will. God does so. Therefore it is not at all difficult for God to create the relation of denotation and to communicate it. There may be counter-arguments which disprove the existence of God. If the existence of God is once established then the counter-arguments regarding the relation of denotation have no scope. We have already put forward irrefutable arguments which prove the existence of God. As we do not create the relation of denotation so we should not be taken to task.

Men like us, i. e., imperfect beings having limited knowledge, initiate little boys into words, their meanings and their mutual relation by pointing their finger-ends to the yonder objects.

Hence, the verbal transactions of the old persons constitute the means of throwing light upon the relation of denotation introduced by God. Thus when one learns the relation of denotation noticing the transaction of the experienced persons he understands the meaning of words, i. e., these words communicate these ideas. Though the relation between a word and an object denoted by it is not eternal yet the former does not remain unrelated to the latter. On the strength of the relation of denotation set up by God the uncontradicted knowledge of the meaning of a word follows from a word. We have already discussed this point. There is no need of dilating upon it.

Therefore, as it is reasonable to hold that God has created the relation of denotation which subsists between a word and its meaning and between a sentence and its meaning so the hypothesis that God is the author of the Vedas is sound.

The Vedas are a source of valid knowledge because they have been composed by God

The Mīmāṁsakas take an exception to the above hypothesis.

They object to it with the following remark. The Vedas are a source of valid knowledge because they have been uttered by a trustworthy person but not because they are eternal. If the Naiyāyikas argue that the Vedas are a source of valid knowledge because they have been uttered by a trustworthy person then how do they know that the reason belongs to the subject of inference, i.e., the minor premise is materially valid? When one infers that the hill is fiery because it is smoky he perceives smoke to be present in the hill. Similarly, we cannot perceive the character of being uttered by a trustworthy person to be present in the Vedas. As the Vedas consist only of words so they can be only perceived with our ears. The proportions of letters having 'probateness' etc., are sensed with ears. They are perceived as proportion of a letter. But the character of being uttered by a trustworthy person is never perceived as the property of a letter. We cannot also establish by means of an inference that the said property belongs to the Vedas since there is no mark which points to the conclusion. The Vedas are held to be a source of valid knowledge because they have been uttered by a trustworthy person. But one fails to prove that the Vedas have been uttered by a trustworthy person since no reason is available. Such being the state of our knowledge how can we say that the Vedas have been uttered by a trustworthy person. This is the sum and substance of the objections, raised by the Mīmāṁsakas against the Nyāya-hypothesis. A reply to the above objection is as follows. There is no need of twisting sentences. We have already shown the way by means of which it has been proved that the said reason belongs to the subject of inference.

It has been elaborately proved that a sound is not eternal and that every arrangement of letters presupposes an author since it partakes of the nature of an arrangement of letters.

It has also been proved that there is an omniscient creator of all effects. We should assume such a cause as satisfactorily explains an effect. We shall also show that the Vedas contain no such theme as is contradicted by perception. The defects pointed out by the critics such as mutual contradiction, tautology, etc, will be answered.

The efficacy of injunctions, praises, condemnations, Vedic

mythology and incantations will be shown. No iota of the contents of the Vedas is superfluous.

All such assumptions, viz., the Vedas are the evolute of Śabda Brahman, etc., as oppose the hypothesis that the Vedas have been composed will be refuted.

If all matters which we intend to prove are proved to the hilt then what else remains to determine that the Vedas have been composed by a trustworthy person (an omniscient being). If all the contents of the Vedas are proved to be true then it may be boldly asserted that the Vedas have been composed by a trustworthy person.

The Mīmāṁsakas raise a dilemma whether or not the above hypothesis is established by perception or by an inference. The Naiyāyikas meet it with the remark that the above hypothesis is established by perception. All the syllogistic arguments, viz., "All arrangements of letters are composition" "The Vedas are arrangements of letters. Therefore the Vedas are composition" and the negative criticisms which refute the hypothesis of the rival schools discharge the function of an accessory condition. They have contribution towards the framing of the premise that the Vedas have been uttered by a trustworthy person. The major premise that all true sentences are uttered by a trustworthy person is based upon sound observation. We can cite the sentences of the Āyur-Veda (the science of life) as a positive instance. Observing the works we arrive at the generalisation, viz., "What is stated by a trustworthy person is true". The efficacy of some medicinal herbs and roots, viz., pippali, patola, mula, etc., has been narrated in the Āyur-Veda. When they are used by a diseased person the desired result follows from them. The drinking of milk and churned sour milk has been prohibited in order to ameliorate the diseased condition of the person by the science of life. The truth of such statements is directly observed by us. We know that there is perfect accordance of these statements with facts. But these statements are true because they have been uttered by a trustworthy person. The truth of the generalization "What is stated by a trust-worthy person is true" is directly grasped by us. Similarly, the truth of mantras is cognized by us. In cases of scorpion-bites or snake-bites or the taking of poison some mantras (magic formulas) are recited to heal the persons. The persons affected get themselves immune from poison. When a person is seized by an attack of epilepsy —a dreadful demon, he is cured of this disease by an application of magic formulas. When evil clouds which hurl thunderbolts at random hover above the cornfields, the danger of crops is averted by the recital of mantras. The efficacy of mantras has been repeatedly observed by us. The trust-worthy persons are the preceptors of these persons who are expert in driving away the evil spirits, thunder-bolts, etc. Thus, the truth of the above generalization is also verified in these cases.

Now, a question arises in our mind, viz., the Āyur-Veda is true because it accords with facts which are perceived by us, How do we say that the Āyur-Veda is true because it has been uttered by a trustworthy person ? The truth of the above generalization is not convincing. The said criticism is not sound. We may perceive the accordance of the said science with facts and determine its validity thereby. But we do not explain how it acquires its validity. The genesis of its validity is to be traced to the utterance of a trust-worthy person. The efficacy of this science is tested by perception. Thus it is directly known to be true. But if the metaphysical aspect of its truth is discussed then we hold that it has become true because it owes its existence to such a cause as has excellent property. We have already discussed this aspect of the problem. We have noticed that the statements of deceitful person. viz., 'there are such and such objects on the banks of a river, etc., do not accord with facts. Hence, we strongly re-assert our hypothesis that a statement is true because it has been uttered by a trust-worthy person. The source must be perfect otherwise the effect of an impure cause cannot produce true knowledge. Perception may help to ascertain the truth of a statement but does not impart truth to it. Therefore it is sound on our part to hold that what is uttered by a trust-worthy person, is true. The above generalization has been verified in the Āyurveda and other cases. The relation of universal concomitance which subsists between the utterance of a trust-worthy person and truth is grasped by us.

The method in question is not sound since it is beyond our powers to know that the said works have been composed by a trustrworthy person. By the application of the joint method of agreement and difference we come to know that the statements contained in the Āyur Veda are true but we do not know them to be true because they have been composed by a trust-worthy person. The statements which are verified by the application of the joint method of agreement and difference are only known to be true. Let us take for example the statement about marbyllion, etc. The statement to which the method in question does not apply is said to be untrue. The statement that one who uses somarāji lives a thousand years illustrates our point. If we assume that the Āyur-Veda has been composed by a trust-worthy person then we should hold that it has been partially composed by a trust-worthy person and partially composed by an unreliable person. Such a proposition is not reasonable. But it is forced on them who hold that the Āyur-Veda has been composed by a trust-worthy person. Because the truth of the Āyur-Veda cannot be verified by the application of the joint method of agreement and difference. Does the person who frames the above proposition make an experiment on himself in order to verify the truth of the Āyur-Veda ? Or, does he do it on some-body else ? If he makes an experiment on a person other than himself then does it universally hold good or does it hold good on a particular person at a particular time and place ? In any case the path in question is beset with insurmountable impediments. It is impossible for a person to know during the span of his life to know all diseases, their causes, the conditions of their aggravation, the conditions of their ameliorations, medicines, their various combinations, their proper doses, their strength, efficacy and assimilation and their varying strength in relation to the changing place, time and bodily conditions of a person. The impressions of the experiment made in the past life are not in this life.

The people are innumerable. The diseases are endless. The action of metals, herbs and other substances, having various properties, upon the animal bodies cannot be numerically counted.

A man cannot cross the ocean in the shape of the science of medicine even if he tries to do it for lacs of yugas.

A particular substance which cures the disease of a person,

having a particular constitution, is conducive to his ill-being when it is chemically combined with other substances.

A substance having medicinal property produces an effect on a person but does nothing on another person. Let us take a concrete case. If one takes marbyllon, purging takes place. But if a person who suffers from constipation owing to the wind-troubles takes the above medicine, his bowels do not move.

If a person drinks sour milk in autumn then he gets fever since the secretion of bile at that time is excessive. But if he drinks it during the rainy season then he is cured of fever since the conditions of his system are then different.

There is not the slightest sign to know the universal healing property of a medicinal substance so that if it is known as holding good in a particular case then it may not be known as holding good universally.

The person who is capable of knowing the details of every thing should be omniscient since his powers are infinite. His existence should not be controverted, raising counter-arguments.

Now, the Mīmāṁsakas take an exception to the above hypothesis that God is the author of all works. They hold that the science of medicine has not been composed but is only remembered like the science of grammar and the like. Those who intend either to abridge or to elaborate a pre-existing science are known as the author of a science such as Caraka and others. But they are not omniscient persons. The science which has been handed down to us from time immemorial should not be taken as imperfect as it has come down to us through the ignorant persons. The science is perfect because it has a sound basis to stand upon. As the science of grammar is based upon the usage of a connoisseur so the truth of the medical science hinges upon the joint method of agreement and difference. The grammar of Pāṇini and others based upon the pre-existing uses, is incorrect if it finds fault with the uses of the expert. It is wrong because it undermines its own basis. Similarly, some critics hold that a statement of the medical science is not to be taken as true if its truth is not verified by the joint method of agreement and difference. If the conclusion of the medical science is contradicted by the joint method of agreement and difference then it is wrong.

The above criticism does not hold good. The joint method of agreement and difference cannot constitute the basis upon which the existence of the medical science rests since it has been discussed that the truth of every topic cannot be determined by the experimental method, having limited scope. If you hold that Caraka has composed his medical treatise, having ascertained all the properties of all substances recorded in it by the joint method of agreement and difference then we strongly assert that such glorification of the joint method of agreement and difference has been discredited. We have made a number of experiments only on a portion of the medical science till today, applying the joint method of agreement and difference. On noticing the result of these experiments we are able to ascertain the truth of that portion of the said science since there is perfect consilience between a claim and its fulfilment. We assume the truth of the entire science since the truth of its portion has been established by the experimental method. Thus as we have a belief in its truth so we act upon its advice. Hence, the joint method of agreement and difference does not constitute the basis of the medical science. If a science is nothing but a record of experiments then all of us would have written works on science. The hypothesis that all sciences are without a beginning like the Vedas is not sound. We all rightly remember that Caraka is the author of a medical treatise as we do recollect that Kālidāsa is an author. Our memory of the authorship of Caraka is never challenged. One cannot also hold that the medical science has no origin since it is transmitted through memory only. If this hypothesis is true then why does the question that it passes through a band of ignorant people arise at all ? The basis of the medical science suggested by you, cannot be accepted since your hypothesis has been refuted. Therefore, an omniscient person is the author of Āyur-Veda.

The advice of an ignorant person is of no use. So we should assume the Caraka and others are well acquainted with the contents of their work. Is there any proof which points to the hypothesis that they have directly known all these objects ? A reply to this question is as follows. As the joint method of agreement and difference has its limitations so all matters discussed by Caraka are beyond the reach of inferential knowledge. We shall show later on that it is not reasonable to conjecture that all contents of his work have been borrowed from the Vedas like the law-book of Manu because all the so-colled basic works have not been composed by a single author. If somebody else is held to be a pioneer in this matter then why is Caraka open to blame ? We cannot think of the service of an analogical argument to solve this problem. Presumption is not a distinct source of knowledge. The truth of the medical science cannot be challenged because the truth of many medicines prescribed by it has been repeatedly corroborated by the method of residues since Caraka and others directly knowing space, time, persons and the different conditions of their body, have ascertained the efficacy of all medicinal substances in their relational character. If this is so then why are the prescriptions containing Somarāji etc. falsified ? If such prescriptions do not prove their efficacy then it has been stated that the medical science is partially true. The above defect does not invalidate the medical science. A prescription does not prove its worth if a medicine is not properly administered or a person taking it is not particular about direction of its constituents may be defective. The Mīmāṁsakas speak highly to the Vedic rites. The injunctions enjoining these rites are also open to the same defects.

Suppose, you perform the Vedic rite Kārīrī but rain does not fall. 'Now what is your opinion of the judgment about the injunction enjoining the Kārīrī sacrifice ? Is it partially true? Now, you may argue that the injunction is true but the failure of rain is due to some defects in the performer, etc. A similar argument can also be advanced in favour of the truth of the medical science.

A secular action which does not yield a result is defective. But a rite enjoined by the Śāstras, though unfruitful, is not so. This is the note of the Mīmāṁsakas. But the conditions which baffle the fruition of an action are held to be the same.

Good results are sometimes observed on the application of some medicines. The persons who use them become very strong and long-lived. Therefore, the science of medicine has been composed by a trustworthy person. It has no other sources. Thus the Vedas which are productive of similar results have been surely composed by the trustworthy persons.

Hence the generalisation "What has been stated by a reliable person is true" has been applied to the Āyur-Veda and found to be true. In order to vindicate the truth of the above generalisation the author of the Nyāya-Sūtra states that the statement of a trustworthy person admits of two kinds because it points to perceptible and transcendental objects. When a trustworthy person makes a statement about a perceptible object his statement is verified. We discover that the relation of invariable concomitance holds between the statement of a trustworthy person and truth. By means of induction we arrive at the conclusion that the statement of a trustworthy person about transcendental objects is also true. Therefore, the works containing the mantras, etc., owe their truth to a trustworthy person, their author.

The Mīmāṁsakas take an exception to this view. They argue that no omniscient sage is ever found out to be the author of the medical science. If it is seen that the contents of a medical treatise are true because its author is omniscient then the illustrations such as the Āyur-Veda, etc., have been vainly mentioned. But it is a truism that the medical treatise of Caraka and others are held to be based upon works having intrinsic truth. Nobody believes that such works are true because they have been composed by the omniscient persons. How is it that such medical treatises have been cited as instances which corroborate the extrinsic truth of the Vedas ?

The Naiyāyikas meet the above objection, raised by the Mīmāṁsaks. They say that the generalization "the statement of a trustworthy person is true" has been distinctly verified and found to be universally true when it has been applied to the statements of the Āyur-Veda, etc. The Material validity of the major premise has been clearly stated in the earlier portion of this section. Similarly, the material truth of the minor premise has also been proved. The syllogistic argument is contradicted neither by perception nor by verbal testimony. It is not also set at naught by another syllogistic argument. The middle term fulfils all the five conditions which are required for drawing a true conclusion. Therefore, it correctly draws the conclusion.

If the Vedas are held to enjoy intrinsic truth then we cannot cite a parallel case in support of this view. We are not aware of a single case which we assert as true unless we believe that the person who has made the statement is reliable.

As there is unshaky confidence in the truthfulness of the author of the Vedas so the Vedas have right, backed by reason, to induce persons to perform Vedic rites and difficult sacrifices which involve a heavy expenditure of money etc. If the Vedas are simply free from contradiction, they cannot induce persons to such actions. No need of further discussions. The hypothesis, suggested by the Mīmāṁsakas is not acceptable. Therefore the Vedas are the source of valid knowledge because they have been uttered by a trustworthy person.

The method of Ascertaining the truth of the Vedas as suggested by the Mīmāṁsakas

Some other philosophers prove the veracity of the Vedas in a different manner. Two sets of thinkers, belonging to the two different schools of thought, contest the authority of the Vedas. One of them believes in the existence of the next world. The other set does not believe in the existence of such world. We should prove the immortality of the soul, etc., by means of syllogistic arguments, meet the arguments of the said non-believers and establish the existence of the next world. Those who believe in the existence of the next world hold that the diversities, noticed in this world, viz., some are happy, some are unhappy and so on, are exclusively due to differences in their actions in the past. Actions do not come into being if they are not performed. If they do not come into being, they are as unreal as the sky-flowers are. How will they bring obout results, viz., happiness, misery, etc. ? Therefore one cannot but subscribe to the hypothesis that good or bad actions have been performed. If one does not know the nature of an action, he cannot perform it. Which act will a poor fellow undertake as he knows nothing about it ? As actions can be done only when their nature is completely known. What is the source of its knowledge ? Sense-perception is not capable of throwing light on such actions as lead to transcendental ends such as Heaven etc.

An action is not also an inference. By the joint method of agreement and difference the causal relation subsisting between the act of eating and the feeling of satisfaction is established. But by the same method we fail to establish the causal relation holding between a sacrifice and heavenly bliss. As we cannot otherwise explain the diversities of this world so we infer the existence of different conditions in order to explain them. The knowledge of the diverse conditions being vague one cannot be guided by this light to perform an act. It has been stated to this effect.

We should definitely know that virtue or vice brings about the particular result. If our knowledge is indefinite, does it help us in any way ? The services of an analogical argument may be thought of in this context. But it is of no use. Though the common people advise one another regarding actions to be performed yet it is un-reasonable to hold that they should know actions which lead the performer up to heaven. Those who advise people without knowing the nature of actions are not trustworthy. The persons who are ignorant of the scriptures cannot properly know actions because there is no sufficient reason in support of their knowledge. If we suppose that the knowledge of actions is handed down by the preceding generation to the succeeding one then it will only amount to this that a batch of blind men is led by another batch of such men. Therefore when the believers in the existence of the next world will perform actions which are fruitful in the next world they should at first learn from the scriptures the efficacy of each action. The scriptures in question are the Vedas. Thus every body accepts the veracity of the Vedas. In other words, the Vedas have intrinsic truth.

Now, an objection may be raised against the above solution. A person will be initiated into the mystery of action conducive to either virtue or to vice by means of popular ideas. No knowledge of the Śāstras is required. The popular definition of virtue or of vice is this: what does good to us is virtue and what does disservice to us is vice. In other words, what is good is virtue and what is evil is vice. Vyāsa has also said to this effect. Nobody including even the untouchable Caṇḍālas depends much upon the Śāstras in order to know virtue or vice.

The above view does not hold good since the popular view which is not based upon a sound basis is not true. The popular view is nothing but an uninterrupted series of remembrances of the view in question. Memory owes its origin to some form of true knowledge but does never arise independently. Hence, its source should be traced out. It is neither based upon perception nor upon similar sources of true knowledge. Therefore the popular view must be based upon the Śāstric doctrine. As the popular views of a particular subject are many and incompatible with one another so people do not place their confidence in a popular view if it has an independent origin. It is not logical to define that virtue is good and vice is evil since the above definition does not apply to the muttering of incantations and to the drinking of wine. (The muttering of incantations does no palpable good to us. The drinking of wine in moderate doses does no palpable injury to us). Again, one may derive pleasure from the sinful act, viz., the illicit connection with the wife of a preceptor, etc. Hence, the definitions in question do not apply to all cases. Hence, the Śāstras should be taken as the only source of virtue and vice.

Can we know the following details from a popular view? Such and such sacrifices produce these results. The recitation of such and such mantras yields such and such results. This person is entitled to this act. These are the subsidiary rites which are to be performed in order to render the principal rite complete. This is the proper place where a rite is to be performed. These are the priests who are competent to perform an act. Therefore we should gather all the necessary information about a distinct act from the Śāstras. The Śāstras in question are nothing but the Vedas. We have already expressed this view. Therefore, the validity of the Vedas stands above all disputes. This is what we have got to say.

If the above thesis is presented in this manner, the view that the world has no beginning is forced on us. As our knowledge of the Vedic rites does not commence from a particular date so the Vedas should also be accepted as eternal. If we subscribe to the above thesis then the standpoint appeals to our reasoning, viz., the Vedas are intrinsically true because they are eternal. In that case, we cannot hold that they are true because they have been composed by a trustworthy person. Therefore the path adopted by us in order to prove the validity of the Vedas, is the sure way to the establishment of their validity.

We do not subscribe to the hypothesis that the world has no beginning. There is divergence of opinions regarding the hypothesis according to which there will be simultaneous destruction of the whole universe. All compositions partake of the character of an effect. Therefore, God has composed the Vedas in the beginning of this world.

The world owes its existence to God. But the creation and the destruction of the world go on in a cyclic order for ever. The world process does not start on a particular date. Men may be enlightened on the rituals from the different Vedas in the different cycles of creation.

Now, the Mīmāṁsakas may put a question to the Naiyāyikas viz., "Is there any proof which establishes the hypothesis that the Vedas are different in the different cycles of creation"? The Naiyāyikas give an answer in this effect : "Oh intelligent thinkers; is there any proof regarding the oneness of the Vedas in every cycle of creation ?" When the whole world is destroyed at the end of creation the Vedas necessarily meet their destruction. God alone survives. He may either compose the new Vedas or may recollect the old ones. We may subscribe to any one of these two hypotheses. But it is a truism that God who has half-moon on his forehead enjoys absolute independence in this matter. The Vedas with the dawn of creation are presented to the consciousness of God who is without a second. They cannot be different from those that were composed. God has no memory as He always intuits all objects. The hypothesis that the Vedas have been composed is immune frcm all defects. In fine, the sage Akṣapāda has written an elaborate treatise on logic in order to convince the people that the Vedas impart true knowledge because the Vedas have been composed by a trust-worthy person. He has also pulled up ignorance, the source of all sophistry, by the roots.

An objection to the validity of the Atharva-Veda

Some critics raise an objection in this manner the Ṛg Veda, the Yajur Vedas and the Sāma Veda teach us interrelated subject-matters. Hence we infer that these three Vedas have been composed by the same author. They are the source of valid knowledge as it is an inference that they owe their existence to one and the same author. But the Atharva Veda is entirely different from the above three Vedas since it has no concern with the religious rites mentioned in them. For this very reason it cannot be a source book of the religious rites. Even if we accept the hypothesis that the Vedas are the highest authority and their validity is intrinsic then we arrive at the conclusion that the Atharva Veda does not enjoy the same validity along with the other three Vedas since it enjoins some actions which are not included in the three Vedas. The Ṛg Veda, the Yajur Veda and the Sāma Veda enjoin the biggest religious acts such as the Soma-sacrifices Jyotiṣṭoma etc. Instructions regarding these sacrifices have been given in the different recensions of the Vedas. The Brahmins who are well-versed in these three Vedas can only take part in the observance of these rites. Therefore, the Vedas which enjoin such religious acts are only valid. The Atharva Veda is not so. The popular view throws some light on this topic. The science which renders a distinct service to the people admits of four-fold division, viz., the science of logic, the three Vedas, the body of Vocational training and Political or Economic science.

Śruti and Smṛti bear evidence to the above view. The passages quoted from the Taittirīya Brāhmaṇa, the Śatapatha Brāhmana and the Nārāyaṇa Upaniṣad corroborate this view. The relevant portion in the passages is that they refer only to the three Vedas. The Saṁhitā of Manu strengthens this view. The Saṁhitā says that one should observe the vow of celibacy for a period of twelve years in order to study the different Vedas. A Vedic student should reside in the house of his preceptor for 36 years. and read the three Vedas viz., the Ṛg Veda, the Yajur Veda and the Sāma Veda. He should thus observe the vow of religious study. Manu has also stated in his section on funeral ceremony that one who performs funeral ceremony should earnestly feed Brāhmaṇas who have made a complete study of the Ṛg Veda, the Yajur Veda and the Sāma Veda together with the corresponding Brāhmaṇas and the different recensions of the Vedas. Manu makes mention only of those Brāhmaṇas who have made a complete study of the three Vedas as entitled to the funeral feast. But he does not make mention of the Brāhmaṇas who have studied the Atharva Veda. Nay, in some cases, prohibition is noticed. A Brahmin who is well-versed in the Atharva Veda should not be invited to do this and that act.

A reply to the said objections

Some thinkers answer the objections, raised in the previous sections, in the following manner. Let us suppose that the Atharva Veda has no efficacy in the Vedic sacrifices. But how can its efficacy in the other rites be set aside ?

The rites mentioned in the Atharva Veda are performed in order to counteract the influence of the evil stars or to augment prosperity or to put one's enemy to an end. In order to observe these rites the assistance of a priest is required as the services of Hotṛ Adhvaryu and Udgātṛ are requisitioned in connection with the performance of sacrifices prescribed in the three Vedas. The priest, proficient in the Atharva Veda, is called 'Brahman'. This Veda is the only authority on the above rites.

The objections raised against the authority of the Atharva Veda are not sound. The sage Bādarāyaṇa holds that the Vedas are the independent sources of valid knowledge because they do not presuppose the other sources of knowledge for their validity. Jaimini has shown the way to ascertain the validity of the Vedas, following the foot-steps of Bādarāyaṇa.

Akṣapāda and Kaṇāda have established the validity of the Vedas by means of a different method. The Vedas are true because they are God's words. Akṣapāda holds that the Vedas are true like Mantra and Āyur Veda because they have been composed by a trustworthy person. If we follow any one of the above methods then we see that each of them equally leads to the validity of the four Vedas. Even if we make a thorough search, we find the least difference in the Vedas. Can any body say embracing the standpoint of the Mīmāṁsakas that the three Vedas are eternal but the Atharva Veda is not so because the author of this Veda is remembered ? Can any body hold from the standpoint of the Naiyāyikas that the three Vadas have been composed by a trustworthy person but the Atharva Veda has not been so composed ? Hence as the method of determining the validity of the Vedas is the same so the four Vedas are equally true, being treated by the same logic. It is well known that all manners and customs of discriminating persons belonging to the four castes and the four different stages of life on this Earth, encircled by the four seas, are based upon the four Vedas. Therefore, no body should suspect the validity of the Atharva Veda. The manners and customs of all people residing in the land of the Aryans are based upon the Vedas and upon the laws of Smṛti but not upon the caprice of individuals. The Vedas and Smṛti declare that the four Vedas stand on the same level of authority. Many sentences of the Atharva Veda find a place in the Ṛg Veda, the Yajur Veda and the Sāma Veda. Let us illustrate the point in question. The Śatapatha Brāhmaṇa makes a reference to the Atharva Veda. It discusses the topic of horse-sacrifice. When it enlightens the rites to be observed on the third day of horse-sacrifice it refers to the mythological stories to be narrated in connection with the performance of the Pariplava sacrifice. In this context a sentence that it is that Atharva Veda is found. The Chāndogya Upaniṣad makes mention of the Ṛg Veda, the Yajur Veda and the Sāma Veda and also of the Atharva Veda as the fourth one.

Now a question arises in our mind. In the Chāndogya Upaniṣad, History as well as the Purāṇas have also been mentioned as the fifth branch of study. What is your exact question ? Do you suggest that story as well as the Purāṇa should be the fifth Veda ? Or do you suggest that the Atharva Veda should not be the fourth Veda ? As the Atharva Veda is qualified by the adjectice "fourth" so it comes down to the level of history and the Purāṇa but does not go up to the level of the Vedas. Why does this suggestion appear in your mind ? If you think that the adjective "fourth" assigns a subordinate position to the Atharva Veda then as in another place it has been said that the three Vedas were created so the adjective 'three' being applied to the Vedas, the three Vedas should also be thrown into the shade. If you argue like this that the counting of the Atharva Veda along with History and the Purāṇa is at the root of its subordinate position then we point out that such an argument is baseless since all the Vedas have been counted along with them.

The Śatapatha Brāhmaṇa commences a topic with the remark that the Ṛg Veda is the vital breath of Brahman and completes it with the statement that a Brāhmaṇa well up in the Atharva Veda is equal to Brahman. It has been stated in the Chāndogya Upaniṣad that the rays of the sun, collected on the north, are his veins through which honey flows. The mantras seen by the sages, Atharva and Aṅgiras are bees that produce honey. The Taittirīya Upaniṣad says that besides the sheath known as Prāṇamaya there is another inner sheath called Manomaya. It makes a number of statements of this sheath. In this connection it remarks that the Yajur Veda constitutes its head, the Ṛg Veda its right wing, the Sāma Veda its left wing, the Brahman its soul and the Atharva Veda its tail. The Taittirīya says "To face the east is better for the recitation of the Ṛg Veda, to face the south is better for the recitation of the Yajur Veda, to face the south is better for the recitation of the Sāma Veda and to face the west is better for the recitation of the Atharva Veda. In the Śatapatha Brāhmaṇa the following statements about the holy study of the Vedas are found. It commences with the statement that the mantras of the Ṛg Veda are the five mid-day oblations of milk unto gods. In this context it has been stated that the mantras of the Atharva Veda are the oblations of omentum to be offered to gods. He who studies the Veda everyday with this knowledge pleases gods with the offer of the oblation of omentum. Gods, being satisfied, incur his pleasure. The mantras of the Taittirīya Saṁhitā throw some light on the meaning of the above statement. O Fire ! a person proficient in the Atharva Veda, has kindled you from Puṣkara. In the above mantras we find the word 'Atharva'. It is not the name of a particular sage. Such an interpretation does not stand to reasons since similar words, found in the other Vedas, may shake our confidence in the truth of the Vedas. We have cited passages from the Saṁhitās, Brāhmaṇas, Upaniṣads etc. in order to prove the authenticity of the Atharva Veda.

We shall now place quotations from Smṛtis before our readers in support of the validity of the Atharva Veda. Manu says 'One should recite the Āṅgirasa Śruti from the Atharva Veda in connection with an act intended for killing some body (abhicāra). Manu uses the term 'Śruti'. He gives it a status equal to that of the three Vedas.

Yājñavalkya enumerates fourteen sources of knowledge. He says that Purāṇa, Logic, Mīmāṁsā, Smṛti and six branches of the Vedas and the Vedas are the fourteen sources of knowledge and laws. Using the term 'Vedaḥ' he says that the Vedas are four but not three, otherwise the number 'fourteen' cannot be filled up. In another Smṛti work the number of the Vedas has been clearly stated. The auxiliary sciences, the four Vedas, Mīmāṁsā, the science of Logic, the Purāṇa and Dharma Śāstra constitute the fourteen branches of study.

It has also been stated in another law book that there are fourteen sources of knowledge, viz., Purāṇa, Dharma Śāstra, Mīmāṁsā, Logic, the four Vedas and the six auxiliary sciences.

Śātātapa also says :

The person who has little knowledge of the Ṛg Veda, the Sāma Veda, the Yajur Veda and the Atharva Veda and the six auxiliary sciences (Vedāṅgas) and gives an expression to his knowledge is regarded by us as a great man.

In another Dharma Śāstra it is stated that the council of the learned men consists of five scholars of whom the four members are Vedic-scholars (each scholar is proficient only in one of the four Vedas) and the fifth one is well up in the Dharma Śāstra. Śaṅkha and Likhita hold that the council of the learned men consists of ten members. The qualifications of them are as follows: the first four ones are well-versed in the Ṛg, Sāma, Yajur and Atharva Vedas, the fifth one is well up in the six auxiliary sciences, attached to the Vedas, sixth one is adept in the Dharma Śāstra, the seventh one is proficient in Mīmāṁsā, the eighth one is a sound Naiyāyika, the ninth one practises the religious vow of life-long celibacy and the tenth one embraces the rite of Agnihotra. Vālmīki holds that the said council is constituted by the four Vedic scholars and a scholar of Dharma Śāstra. Among the persons who purify their clan the following persons have been mentioned, viz., persons adept in the four Vedas, persons well up in the six auxiliary sciences attached to the Vedas, person who observe some particular rites and recite some particular Sāma-hymns, and the students of the Atharva Veda. All these statements of many authors of Dharma Śāstras point to the thesis that the Vedas are four in member.

The authors of the other branches of study are noticed to hold a similar view. The great Patañjali, the author of the most elaborate bhāṣya, gives priority to the mantras of the Atharva Veda among his illustrations, viz., "Śanno devīrabhīṣṭaye etc." In the topic on the eternality of the Vedas, Śabara, the commentator on the Mīmāṁsā sūtras, has mentioned the different recensions of the Atharva Veda. In the topic on the different recensions of Vedas as he has made references to the various recensions of the Vedas other than the Atharva Veda so he has also mentioned the two recensions of the Atharva Veda, viz,. Maṇḍuka and Paippalāda and discussed many points regarding them. In the concluding portion of this topic he has clearly written that the different Vedas do not teach different rites. A particular rite which is taught in the Ṛg Veda is not different from the same rite taught in the Atharva Veda. Those who are well-versed in the Vedas, Smṛti, the tradition of the good people and usages have no chance of entertaining a doubt about the truth of the said conclusion.

Now, the objector may contend that he does not say that the Atharva Veda is not true. But he holds that it is distinctively other than the three Vedas. Not only the three Vedas are other than the Atharva Veda but also there is mutual distinction among the three Vedas themselves. The Yajur Veda is distinct from the Ṛg Veda and the Sāma Veda. The Rg. Veda is distinct from the Yajur Veda and the Sāma Veda. The Sāma Veda is also distinct from the Ṛg Veda and the Yajur Veda. Such a distinction does not amount to a defect. It is in the nature of all positive objects, as a book consists of words, conveying their meanings, which are all things. They are not identical. Do they lose their own nature on this account. (If the Vedas are not identical, they do not lose their significance).

The objector revises the character of his objection and holds that the phrase "The Atharva Veda is other than the three Vedas" signifies something else. It means that the Atharva

Veda does not give any advice with regard to an act which is somehow connected with the three Vedas. This is what is meant by the phrase "The Atharva Veda is other than the three Vedas."

Such an interpretation is not tenable. Because in the Atharva Veda there is provision for many sacrifices such as Iṣṭi (a sacrifice which is performed only by the four priests and the performer of the sacrifice), Paśu (a sacrifice which is concluded by a single day), Ahīna (a soma sacrifice which lasts for many days), Satra (a soma sacrifice which is performed by many persons one after another) etc. When we perform a sacrifice all the Vedas play the same important part in it. The Vedic Jurisprudence holds this view. The objector may contend that the three Vedas, viz., the Ṛg Veda, the Yajur Veda and the Sāma Veda play the same important part in performing a Vedic rite but not the Atharva Veda since in a Soma sacrifice the Ṛg Veda supplies with the duties of a Hotṛ priest, the Yajur Veda with those of an Adhvaryu priest and the Sāma Veda with those of an Udgātṛ priest but the Atharva Veda does nothing.

This is a wrong statement of facts since the Atharva Veda supplies with the duties of a Brahman priest. The Gopatha Brāhmaṇa says to this effect. The lord of all beings intending to perform a Soma sacrifice asked the Vedas "Whom should you invite as a Hotṛ priest ?" Raising this point he suggests that a Brāhmaṇa proficient in the Ṛg Veda is to be invited as a Hotṛ priest since he is conversant with the duties of a Hotṛ priest; a Brāhmaṇa well-up in the Yajur Veda is to be invited as an Adhvaryu priest because he is acquainted with the duties of an Adhvaryu priest; a Brāhmaṇa skilled in the Sāma Veda, is to be invited as an Udgātṛ priest because he is thoroughly aware of the duties of an Udgātṛ priest and a Brāhmaṇa who is a sound scholar of the Atharva Veda is to be invited as a Brahman priest. Making the above suggestions he has said again "If you do not appoint such persons as Hotṛ, Adhvaryu, Udgātṛ and Brahman then the sacrifice will be spoiled." Therefore one should appoint a scholar of the Ṛg Veda as a Hotṛ priest, a scholar of the Yajur Veda as an Adhvaryu priest, a scholar of the Sāma Veda as an Udgātṛ priest and a scholar of the Atharva Veda as a Brahman priest. Moreover, if there is a deficiency in a sacrifice, it will be made good by the influence of the Atharva Veda. If an inauspicious element creeps into a sacrifice, it will be converted into an auspicious element by the influence of the Atharva Veda. If something becomes worn out in a sacrifice, then it will acquire a new life by the influence of the Atharva Veda. Completing the Soma sacrifice the institutor of a Soma sacrifice should drink the remaining portion of Soma juice from the sages "Bhṛgu and Aṅgiras" i. e. the priests well-versed in the Atharva Veda.

The Atharva-veda constitutes the Trayī

The persons who are well-versed in the Atharva-Veda only read the above Vedic passages which refer to the Atharva-Veda but the scholars of the three Vedas do not come across such Vedic sentences. The students of the three Vedas read the following Vedic passages. They declare that the Ṛg Veda helps to discharge the duties of a Hotṛ priest, the Yajur Veda assists to discharge the duties of an Adhvaryu priest and the Sāma Veda renders assistance to discharge the duties of an Udgātṛ priest. But which Veda does help us to render the service of a Brāhmaṇa priest ? They say in reply that the duties of a Brāhmaṇa priest may be fulfilled by the knowledge of the three Vedas. The Vedas also subscribe this view that the scholars of the Ṛg Veda, the Yajur Veda and the Sāma Veda respectively discharge the duties of the Hotṛ, Adhvaryu and Udgātṛ priests. The duties of a Brāhmaṇa priest are performed by the essence of three Vedas. In other words, there is no need of inviting a scholar of the Atharva Veda to discharge the duties of a Brahman priest.

An answer to the above objection is as follows. It is not a fact that we have not read the Vedic sentences referred to by you. But the above sentences signify that a Brahmin who is well-versed in the Atharva Veda is Brahman. If you put a question to us "Why do you say like this ?" then listen to our reply. There is no such distinct book as goes by the name "trayī" (triplet). Though the collection of the Ṛg Veda, the YajurVeda and the Sāma Veda is loosely called trayī Collection yet it has space enough to include other mantras. The collection includes other books and is designated as the triple Vedas, viz., the Ṛg Veda, etc. Each of them has become fruitful by helping to discharge the duties of a Hotṛ priest, etc. The collection of the three Vedas has become fruitful since each unit included in it has fulfilled its own mission. As all these three units equally share the credit of realizing ends so there will be no discriminatory treatment among these units with regard to the realization of ends. When a collection is analysed into its units the unnoticed mantras which represent another unit are only presented to our consciousness. A whole is distinct from its parts. But unlike a whole a collection is not distinct from the units which are included in it. These units, i.e., the three Vedas, have got their definite duties to discharge. If the three Vedas have to discharge the duties of a Brahman priest in addition to their own duties then will they be able to bear such a heavy burden ? We say "No, it is not a heavy burden. The three Vedas jointly advise the duties of a Brahman priest. But none of them is the triple Vedas. The Atharva Veda alone is the triplet. As the Ṛg Veda, the Yajur Veda and the Sāma Veda are included in the Atharva Veda so the Atharva Veda having helped to discharge the duties of a Brahman priest, the three Vedas jointly perform them".

Now, another problem arises in our mind. If a person who reads the three Vedas discharges the duties of a Brahman priest then are not the duties of a Brahman priest fulfilled by the triple Vedas ? Our answer is in the affirmative. But we intend to clarify our answer in the light of the principles laid down by the Vedic jurists, i.e. the Mīmāṁsakas. There is a Vedic passage which states that sacrifices and animal sacrifices other than Jyotiṣṭoma and Darśa-cum-Pūrṇamāsa should be performed for the realization of a single end but Jyotiṣṭoma and Darśa-cum-Pūrṇamāsa sacrifices should be performed for the fulfilment of all ends. But if one performs Jyotiṣṭoma or Darśa-cum-Pūrṇamāsa sacrifice only once then all his ends are not simultaneously realized. In order to accomplish another object the performance of the said sacrifice should be repeated. In the section on Yogasiddhi a principle has been laid down to interpret the above Vedic passage. According to this principle though the fulfilment of many ends has been apparently suggested by the above passage yet a single object is only accomplished by the performance of any one of the above sacrifices. Similarly, when one prepares himself to discharge the duties of a Brahman priest he can think of taking the assistance of a particular Veda only but not of the triple Vedas since a particular Veda renders help to him but not the three Vedas.

Now, another question crops up in our mind. The Vedas other than the Atharva Veda are identical with the triple Vedas. The Atharva Veda is also identical with the triple Vedas. If the above statements are true then the Atharva Veda should not be distinguished from the three Vedas since all the Vedas have the same character. An answer to this question is this. Each of the three individual Vedas which constitutes the triplet has its distinct designation. None of them bears the name of the correction of the three Vedas. There is a Vedic sentence "Trayyai vidyāyai śukraṁ tena Brahmatvam". It requires clarification. The fourth case-ending has been attached to form Trayyai and Vidyāyai. It has been used in lieu of the sixth case-ending. The term "śukra" signifies essence (sāra). Thus the above sentence means that the duties of a Brahman priest are discharged by the essence of the three Vedas, viz., the Ṛg Veda the Yajur Veda and the Sāma Veda. The three Vedas cannot be the essence of themselves. Again, the essence of the three Vedas cannot be absolutely different from the three Vedas. Hence the essence of the three Vedas is the Atharva Veda. Thus the Atharva Veda is an embodiment of secret doctrines. The term 'Atharva,' signifies 'a mystic'. It has been stated in a particular recension of the Atharva Veda that the Atharva a Brahman priest discharged his duties by means of the Atharva Veda which is an essence of the three Vedas. For this reason the Atharva Veda is not distinct from the three Vedas. All the Vedas extend their hands to perform a Vedic rite prescribed by any of the Vedas. 'All' has not been used in a restricted sense. All the Vedas signify the four Vedas but not the three Vedas. So the Atharva Veda has been mentioned as the Brahman Veda in the earlier and the later parts of the Brahmaṇa. The actual text mentions the four Vedas, viz., the Ṛg Veda, the Yajur Veda, the Sāma Veda and the BrahmaVeda.

We shall now give only the sense of the Vedic texts quoted

by Jayanta. In a sacrifice a Brahmin versed in the Atharva Veda should be appointed as a Brahman priest. Otherwise the said sacrifice remains imperfect.

A Brahman priest should be properly honoured. A Brahmin, proficient in the Atharva Veda, is equal to Brahman, the Śabda-Brahman. The acts prescribed by the Atharva Veda are the articles by which he is honoured. The four Vedas participate in the Vedic rite. The food which is prepared by the Brahman priest is known as Brahmaudana. This name has been given by the Vedas themselves. When a Vedic rite is celebrated the priests known as Hotṛ, Adhvaryu, Udgātṛ and Brahman should be entertained with a hearty feast. The acts, prescribed by the Atharva Veda, constitute the integral part of the Soma sacrifice too. The Sāma Veda eulogises the Atharva Veda since the acts, prescribed by the Atharva Veda, remove the possible defects in a sacrifice. It has been stated before that the acts, prescribed by the Atharva Veda, make up deficiency, remove evils and mend all defects in a sacrifice by their influence. For this reason we hold that a Brahmin, well-versed in the Atharva Veda, is Brahman. In other words, his powers are as unlimited as those of the Absolute are. The sound scholars have elaborately discussed this matter and logically established this conclusion in other works. Therefore, the point in question has not been very elaborately discussed in this book.

Some invite our attention to the statements "No body should have connection with a Brahman who has exclusively read the Atharva Veda". We have no regard for it since it is a statement of the Kalpa Sūtra and moreover is contrary to the spirit of the Vedas. If the above statement would have been a Vedic sentence then it had been interpreted in the light of the proper context. Most probably it has bearing only upon a particular Vedic rite. When that particular Vedic rite will be performed no scholar of the Atharva Veda should be appointed as a priest. It is an unconditional general statement then a conflict between the two Vedic sentences becomes inevitable. These two contradictory statements must be reconciled. We have cited Vedic sentences which accept the Atharva Veda as one of the Vedas. The prohibitive sentence suggests that the Atharva Veda falls outside the scope of the Vedas. The Vedas cannot blow hot and cold in the same breath. Therefore, the prohibitive sentence must have a restricted meaning. A scholar of the Atharva Veda should not be appointed as a priest in connection with an act where his sacrifices are not required.

Another objection has been raised against the inclusion of the Atharva-Veda in the Vedas proper. It has been said that the mantras of the Ṛg Veda are loudly recited, the mantras of the Sāma Veda are loudly chanted and the mantras of the Yajur Veda are very lowly recited but nothing has been stated about the Atharva Veda. This objection is not sound. The characteristic features of mantras have been shown but those of the Vedas have not been pointed out. All the Vedas admit of two broad divisions viz., Mantra and Brāhmaṇa. The mantra part of the Vedas has two sub-divisions viz., prose and poetry. The mantras of the Yajur Veda are prose. Those of the Ṛg Veda are metrical. But those of the Sāma Veda are not only metrical but also melodious. The mantras, judged from this point of view, admit of three divisions. Jaimini, having classified these mantras, defines them. The definitions given by him run thus. The mantras in which feet are arranged only in accordance with the sense are called Ṛg mantras. The mantras which are musical are Sāma mantras. The remaining ones are Yajur mantras. Thus he classifies the mantras under three divisions. These characteristic features such as loudness etc. do not belong to the entire Vedas admitting of two broad divisions viz., mantras and Brāhmaṇas. The three types of mantras already mentioned are found in the Atharva Veda. These characteristic features belong to them. The term 'trayī' owes its origin to the threefold division of the mantras. Two statements viz. (1) "The Atharva Veda is the Trayī" and (2) "It is superior to other branches of knowledge" will not be contradictory. The Atharva Veda is included in the Trayī because it contains the mantras of the Rg. Veda, the Yajur Veda and the Sāma Veda. But it has at the same time a distinct individuality because it represents its subject-matter in its own peculiar manner. Some other thinkers suggest that the Atharva Veda is the Ṛg Veda because the mantras of the Ṛg Veda abound in it, a small quantity of the Yajur mantras is found in it and no musical mantra of the Sāma Veda is noticed in it. We may accept this suggestion as it involves no contradiction.

Those who hold that the term 'Veda' applies to the three Vedas but not to the fourth Veda cherish a strong hatred against the Atharva Veda. The usage of the experienced teachers stands as a proof in this matter. This is the Veda. This is the Brāhmaṇa. When these sentences are uttered the listener makes out the meaning of the term 'Veda' as representing the four Vedas. When a student says before some learned scholars that he has studied the Veda they ask him "Which Veda has been studied by you?" He replies that he has studied the Atharva Veda. Nobody condemns him with the remark "The book which has been studied by you is not the Veda". Some critics hold that the term 'Veda', pure and simple, does not denote the Atharva Veda. The former requires a prefix to signify the latter. The same remark equally applies to the other Vedas as we say that this is the Ṛg Veda or the Yajur-Veda or the Sāma-Veda. The term 'Veda', pure and simple, also applies to the three Vedas. The same term is also equally applicable to the Atharva Veda. We say that Bharadvāja has studied the four Vedas. Atharva Veda does not stand on the same footing with the Āyur-Veda. Hence it would not be looking down upon as the inferior Veda. It has been stated that the Vedic injunction relating to the study of the Vedas touches the four Vedas without any distinction.

The law books also say to this effect.

Yājñavalkya has said :—

If a person who has been invested with the sacred thread reads everyday the Atharva Veda to the best of his capacity then he pleases gods with the gift of omentum and the departed ancestors with the gift of honey and clarified butter.

The knowledge of the Vedas and the art of performing sacrifices are handed down through the traditional chain. The same law applies to all the four Vedas. We shall no more discuss this point. The four Vedas enjoy the same level of dignity and sanctity since they are equally valid, become alike the object of holy study and constitute means to the realization of human ends.

Primacy of the Atharva Veda

If you do not get satisfaction without knowing the sequence of the Vedas then we say that the Atharva Veda is the first in order of time. The mantras of the other Vedas and the syllable 'om' signifying the Absolute have subsequently emerged. A passage of the Veda points to this direction. The passage runs thus. Brahma ha vā. . . . akṣaramudakrāmat etc. It clearly shows that the syllable 'om' manifested itself in the mind of Brahman at a later period when he had become fatigued with the study of the Atharva Veda. The three great mantras, viz., om bhuḥ svāḥā, om bhuvaḥ svāhā and oṁ svaḥ svāhā and the well-known musical note called Bṛhatī have sprung up from the Atharva Veda. A boy who has been invested with the sacred thread in accordance with the injunctions laid down in the Atharva-Veda may study the other Vedas. But a boy who has been invested with the sacred thread in accordance with the injunctions laid down in the other three Vedas is not entitled to read the Atharva Veda because he has not been initiated into the study of the Atharva Veda. It has been stated in a law book that one who has been ceremoniously initiated into the study of the Atharva Veda is entitled to read the other three Vedas but one who has been ceremoniously initiated into the study of the other three Vedas is not entitled to read the Atharva Veda. Those who stick to the belief that the three Vedas are only authoritative perform expiatory rites, prescribed by the Atharva Veda, when they commit any blunder in performing a Vedic rite. Thus we see that the Atharva Veda is superior to the other three Vedas.

Some scholars have cited a verse from the Saṁhitā of Manu in order to establish the exclusive authority of the three Vedas. A religious student, being ceremoniously initiated into the study of the Vedas, should study the three Vedas for a period of 36 years, residing at the house of his preceptor. Another alternative injunction is found in the 3rd chapter of the Manu-saṁhitā. One should observe the vow of absolute celibacy for a period of 12 years in order to study a single Veda. He should observe it for 24 years if he studies the two Vedas. He should do it for 36 years if he studies the three Vedas. There is also another injunction in another Śruti work that one should observe the vow of celibacy for a period of 48 years if he studies the four Vedas. This injunction has not been dishonoured by men of culture. Some may think that it admits of a different interpretation that it applies only to the study of the three Vedas. It purports to enjoin that a religious student should observe the vow of celibacy for a period of 16 years in order to study each of the three Vedas. Such an interpretation is not sound since it comes into conflict with the initial injunction and also becomes fruitless. Hence, the alternative injunction points to the study of another Veda. The scope of this injunction is not restricted to the choice of the length of time, i.e., the period of 12 or 16 years for the study of a single Veda. The Second interpretation of the injunction is disregarded since it comes into conflict with another Vedic injunction. One should institute the sacrifice of Agnihotra when his hair does not turn grey. In other words, one should embrace the life of a householder during his youth. But if one is to practise the vow of celibacy for a period of 46 years after the sacrament of upanayana then his hair will turn grey. At an advanced age his entry into the married life becomes meaningless. The alternative injunctions regarding the study of the Vedas have been suggested in order to avoid the possible conflict between the two Vedic injunctions stated above. Therefore the discussion which revolves round the determination of the number of years for the study of the Vedas is not dependable The injunction of the law book that one should observe the vow of celibacy for 16 years in order to study each of the four Vedas cannot be honoured. Manu's prescription for the study of the three Vedas does not imply the bare denial of the study of the Atharva Veda. The injunction, given in Manu's law book that one should study the three Vedas, has a positive import. It enjoins one to read the three Vedas. The three Vedas may be other than the Atharva Veda. But it does not import a bare denial. It does not purport to convey that one should not read the Atharva Veda. There is no proof positive which points to bare denial. Manu's injunction concerning the study of the Vedas demands that a student should observe such and such vow in order to study the three

Vedas. The three Vedas have not been specified by him. It has not been clearly stated that one should observe this vow in order to study the Ṛg Veda, the Yajur Veda and the Sāma Veda.

In Manu's chapter on Śrāddha ceremony it has been enjoined that a Brahmin should be respectfully entertained with a feast in a Śrāddha ceremony. It has been stated that the invited Brahmin should be proficient in the three Vedas. In that sentence there are three adjectives viz., Veda-pāraga (one who has gone from one end to the other end of the Veda). Śākhāntaga (one who has made a complete study of one recension of the Veda) and Samāptiga (one who has made the complete study of the Veda). If we try to find out the inner significance of the three adjectives then we come to learn that a Brahmin who has studied only one of the three Vedas (the Ṛg Veda, the Yajur Veda and the Sāma Veda) is not entitled to the above invitation. But if a Brahmin who is born in the family keeping up the tradition of the study of the Atharva Veda, reads only a portion of the Atharva Veda, he becomes a paṅkti pāvana) purifies the row of Brahmins with whom he dines). As the purifier of a row he is entitled to invitation in such a feast. A partial study of the Atharva Veda confers upon a student the honour of being the purifier of a row. If one holds that a Brahmin who is a scholar of the Atharva Veda does not deserve invitation in such a feast then he goes against the spirit of the Śāstras.

The Brahmins who have properly read some portion of the Sāma Veda or some portion of the Ṛg Veda or some portions of the Ṛg Veda and the Yajur Veda are allowed by the Śāstras to be invited in a feast to be held on the completion of Śrāddha ceremony. This injunction seems to us to be the second alternative in order of importance because the first injunction declars that Brahmins who have made the complete study of the Veda should be invited in a feast to be held on the completion of Śrāddha ceremony. This injunction has no negative import. It does not purport to convey prohibition, the exclusion of the Atharva Veda from the Vedas.

We have proved to the hilt that the Atharva Veda is one of the Vedas. But the author of the Tantra-vārttika makes such remarks about the Atharva Veda as shows that he acknowledges it to be the Veda only out of compassion. It seems to us that he is either afraid of the critics of the Atharva Veda or cherishes a hatred against it or is in the dark about it. He holds that though it is assumed that the Atharva Veda is not useful to the Vedic rites in general yet its efficacy in some Vedic rites cannot be ignored. Such remarks do not make an appeal to us. In the former and the latter parts of the Brāhmaṇa attached to the Atharva Veda various types of sacrifices have been enjoined. They are as follows :— Iṣṭi (a sacrifice demanding the services of the performer of the sacrifices and four priests only), Paśu (a sacrifice in which animals are slain), Ekāha (a sacrifice which lasis for one day only), Āhīna (a kind of Soma sacrifice which lasts for many days) and Sattra (a kind of Soma sacrifice which is performed by the co-operation of many persons).

An objection may be raised against the validity of the Atharva Veda that if injunctions enjoining these sacrifices are found in the other Vedas then why does the Atharva Veda contain similar injunctions in itself? The objection has been very fair and nicely put ! We may also put this question to the objectors that if these injunctions are found in the Atharva Veda then why do the other Vedas accommodate them? Moreover, we fail to understand the real target of your attack. But we have said that you are not competent to rebuke either of them. It is not a fact that strange Vedic rites for averting evils, augmenting prosperity and killing enemies are not found in the other Vedas because a Śyena sacrifice (as a hawk preys upon other birds etc.) results in killing the enemies of the performer of the sacrifice) but strange Vedic rites have also been prescribed by the Yajur Veda. Therefore all the Vedas enjoy the same dignity and are similar so far as their contents are concerned. There none of the Vedas can claim distinction. The Vārttikakāra (Kumārila) states that the rites prescribed by the Atharva Veda are observed only by a priest who has the designation of Brahman. This statement is not correct. He holds that the functions of the Vedic priests are two-fold, viz., Vaihārikī vṛtti and Pākayajña vṛtti. When many priests co-operate to perform a Vedic rite the co-operative activity of the priests is called vaihārikī vṛtti. The Dharma-Sāstras hold that the rites for averting evils etc. should be done by the Brahma priest alone. Therefore Kumārila has stated like a man in the street that as the Vedic rites prescribed by the three Vedas are performed by Hotṛ, Adhvaryu and Udgātṛ priests so the peculiar rites, prescribed by the Atharva Veda, are performed only by the Brahma priest. The remark that the rites, prescribed by the three Vedas are performed only by their own priests clearly indicates the breach of impartiality on his part for all the four Vedas. The Vedic rites cannot discriminate between the priests proficient in the three Vedas and those well-versed in the Atharva Veda since one and the same Vedic rite has also been instructed by all the Vedas. In order words, each Vedic rite is well connected with all the Vedas. Hence all the Vedas have the same authoritative power. But those who do not care to atone for their sin arising from despising the Veda can differentiate a particular Veda from the other Vedas. Those who are morally good do not think in this way. We refrain from discussing this point to a greater length.

The equality of the four Vedas (the concluding portion).

As the four Vedas like the four arms of Viṣṇu are possessed of excessive majesty of the same quality so they are eulogised by the worthy praises and yield various objects coveted by the different persons. As Lakṣmī, the goddess of fortune, repudiates the stigma that she is fickle by nature and firmly clings to the four hands of Viṣṇu so truth, fortifies itself by refuting the charges of falsehood attributed to the Vedas by the contesting parties and rests upon the four Vedas. The tree in the shape of the Vedas has four stumps. Its different branches and off-shoots are mutually connected. The utility of the Vedas is well known in the different societies of human beings. The Vedas have become very vast because of the growth of their branches (in different directions). The Ṛg Veda is represented by twenty one recensions, the Yajur Veda by a hundred recensions, the Sāma Veda by a thousand recensions and the Atharva Veda by nine recensions. Each stump of the Veda tree spreads forth branches which are very charming by their flowers and fruits in the shape of charming compositions. As birds perch upon branches, adorned with flowers and fruits and drink their honey so the people of the twice-born classes read the different recensions of the Vedas and enjoy the sweetness of their composition.

A discussion on the validity of Tantra, Āgama, etc. Some raise the following question :— Do you establish the validity of the Vedas in this manner ? If the question is answered in the affirmative then can you prove the validity of Tantras and other Āgamas in the same manner ?

Why do you put a question like this ?

If the first question is answered in the affirmative then the framer of the question has got nothing to say. With regard to the second question the objector himself solves the problem in a definite manner. In his opinion all the other Āgamas should be taken as erroneous since they involve mutual contradictions.

Now a question is put to the person who raises the question. The question runs thus :—"Dear Sir ! when you put this question which Āgamas are before your mind ?" "Do you think of the Purāṇa, History and Dharma Śāstras ? Or, do you think of the Āgamas of the Śaivas, the Pāśupatas, the Pañcarātras, the Bauddhas, the Jainas and of the other sects ?" We shall subsequently discuss the problem of the validity of Āgamas of the Śaivas and others. Some critics come forward and say that the Dharma Śāstras, written by Manu and others, are absolutely true because they give us advice on rituals cast in the Vedic mould to be performed by us. They also hold that there is no necessity of discussing the problem of validity. They further add that the above Śāstras derive their validity from the Vedas. The contents of these Śāstras have no chance of being untrue because there is nothing to contradict them. All the Vedic scholars till now observe rites, prescribed by Manu, with perfect confidence in him.

He cannot subscribe to the hypothesis that the authors of these Śāstras, having visualised the contents of their works have recorded them because they cannot perceive dharma which is transcendental, being itself potential but not actual. It is not reasonable to believe that Manu and others have been taught by some other persons to compose their works. There is no proof to establish the hypothesis that the supposed teacher was able to know the transcendental objects. If there is proof in favour of his knowledge then has Manu committed any offence not to acquire such knowledge ? If we hold that the works of Smṛti are not based upon a sound basis and assume that they are based upon a series of instructions then they will be inevitably a memorandum of instructions for ignorant persons. It is unfair to assume that Manu and others have imparted instructions to us with the motive of deceiving us since there is nothing to contradict their instructions. Moreover, all good people acknowledge the works of Manu and others as an authority. We have already discussed this point. Eliminating all the possible hypotheses we stick to the last hypothesis that the works of Manu and others should be based upon the Vedas. The Vedas are the proper and competent source of them. Kumārila also says to this effect. No person is known to be infallible. The words of a person are sure to deceive us by their misdirection. An assumption must be based upon the solid rock of facts. If it is far away from facts then it is not convincing. Again, we shall have to make a minimum number of assumptions if we hold that Smṛti is based upon the Vedas.

There is a divergence of opinions among those who hold that the works of Manu and others are based upon the Vedas. Some hold that the works known as Smṛti are based upon such Vedic injunctions as are inferred from the known mantras and arthavādas. Some other thinkers hold that they are based upon such recensions of the Vedas as are scattered here and there. But still another band of thinkers hold that they are based upon such recensions as have been obsolete. No useful purpose will be served if we scrutinize the three rival hypotheses and prove that one of them is the most appropriate one. But if we are true to our reasoning power then we shall assume by all means that they (Smṛti works) owe their existence to the Vedas, the perennial source of truth but not to other sources since there is no proof advanced in favour of the truth of these sources. Again, if these works, 'Smṛti' which is well-known in this world will be significant. But if we hold that the works of Manu and others like the Vedas contain laws derived from perception then the designation 'Smṛti' loses its significance. Moreover, if the works on Smṛti are based upon the Vedas then in case of disagreement between them and the Vedas with regard to a subject matter it will be reasonable to hold that the decision of the latter will prevail upon that of the former. In case of the Vedas the decision which they express is authoritative because their foundation has been proved to be firm. But in case of law books the decision which they express is not authoritative since its basis is yet to be discovered. We are to find out a passage from the Vedas which will confirm the decision given by Smṛti. Whenever one exerts his mind to recollect a passage from the Vedas which constitutes the basis of the Smṛti text the Vedic passage which contradicts the conclusion of the Smṛti text flashes before his mind. How can one assume that the said Smṛti text has a corresponding Vedic passage as its basis ? In other words, as there is no contradiction in the Vedas so the two conflicting Vedic passages do not exist. Kumārila says to this effect. A proverb runs thus :—"How can an ass carry a load which was carried before by a horse?"

Some other thinkers suggest that in cases of conflict between the Vedas and Smṛti it is reasonable to give an option. In other words, one may either abide by the decision of the Vedas or by the decision given by Smṛti. This is the sure way of solving the above problem. There are two types of the Vedas viz. the Vedas which are directly heard and the Vedas which are inferred are called Smṛti. As the two types of the Vedas have no beginning so one cannot contradict the other. So Śruti and Smṛti are nothing but the Vedas living and dead in our memory. Therefore, it is not fair to assume that mantras and arthāvādas constitute the basis of Smṛti since the Vedas which are being inferred are eternal.

Now, a fresh question which arises in our mind runs thus:— If you do not subscribe to the hypothesis that Smṛti is the source of true knowledge because it is based upon the Vedas then how can you restrain the free thinkers from propagating the view that Smṛtis which are not affiliated to the Vedas are also true ? A reply to it is as follows. The views of the poor thinkers have already been refuted. Jaimini has refuted the above view in his Mīmāṁsā-Sūtra "Api vā kartṛ-sāmānyāt pramāṇam anumānaṁ syād iti". (1.2). The phrase "kartṛ-sāmānyāt' denotes 'having the same right'. The persons who are entitled to perform the Vedic rites enjoy the privilege of performing rites prescribed by Smṛti. We have learnt from experience that he who sips water with the utterance of mantra (performs a Smṛti rite) but he who strews kuśa grasses on the sacrificial altar performs a Vedic rite. But those who follow the dictates of the non-affiliated Smṛtis are not entitled to perform Vedic rites. Hence, the Smṛti works of Manu and others are held to be the source of true knowledge but not the non-affiliated Smṛtis.

Let us now discuss the hypothesis that the law books, composed by Manu and others, are the source of true knowledge because they are based only upon the Vedas but not because they derive their truth from the other sources of true knowledge. We shall now criticise it. You loudly proclaim the hypothesis that Smṛti is true since it is based upon the Vedas. There is a mystery behind this proclamation. You cannot tolerate the view that the principle of merit and demerit is intuited by the transcendental perception of the sages. Such an attitude of your mind is illogical. As God has been proved to be the creator of everything and lord of all beings, omniscient and compassionate so the transcendental perception of the sages who enjoy divine grace is competent to have the direct knowledge of Dharma. It is absolutely distinct from the normal perception of the ordinary people. The existence of such transcendental perception has been proved by us in the chapter on the definition of perception. Therefore we have established the point that the Dharma-Śāstras, written by Manu and others, may as well derive their truth from the transcendental perception of the sages.

The Mīmāṁsakas have raised an objection against the hypothesis of the transcendental perception of Dharma that Dharma cannot be perceived since it has only a potential being but is not an event in time. Hence they hold that the Vedas are the ultimate source of knowledge of the transcendental objects. This view has been refuted. As God perceives the Agnihotra sacrifice and such other sacrifices as virtuous acts so the sages like Manu and others will be able to apprehend directly rites like Aṣṭakās etc., as virtuous acts. It is superflous to know whether or not virtue has an actual being or a potential being. Now, an objection may be raised against the above hypothesis that the Vedas and the Dharma Śāstras are based upon perception. The implication of the above hypothesis is this that God has perceived the sacrifices like Agnihotra etc., as virtuous acts. If this is the implication of the above hypothesis then God's omniscience is at fault since He is unacquainted with the rites like Aṣṭakā etc., as virtuous acts. Or He may be called cruel since He does not communicate it to others though He is directly acquainted with it. The above objection does not impair the hypothesis in question. There is no doubt about the hypothesis that God is omniscient. But He does not directly instruct everything. He directly teaches some subjects and gets the teaching of subjects done by others. The persons who are the mouthpiece of God are the blessed sons of God. They acquire such intuitive capacity as enables them to be an instructor only through his grace. The Vedas also declare that the sages like Manu and others have intuited Dharma. It is also recorded in the Vedas that the sages who intuited Dharma revealed mantras in order to initiate the ignorant persons into Dharma.

Now, a problem arises in our mind. It runs thus. As the Vedas and the Dharma Śāstras are based upon perception, so if a conflict arises between the Vedas and the Dharma Śāstras then one is at liberty to exercise his option, i.e., he may accept either the decision of the Vedas or that of the Dharma Śāstras. In that case, as an injunction of the Vedas cannot contradict another injunction of the Vedas though one is clearly opposed to the other so there will be no contradiction between the Vedas and the Dharma Śāstras. Let us take an example from the Sāma Veda'. It has been enjoined that a Vedic song is to be sung loudly (the song is to be set to the tune Bṛhat Sāman). It has also been enjoined that the same song is to be sung lowly (the song is to be set to the tune Rathantra Sāman). The one and the same song cannot be sung both loudly and lowly. Therefore there is contradiction between these two injunctions. But these two injunctions being equally strong one cannot invalidate the other. Therefore in such cases the performer is permitted to exercise his discretion. He may exercise his free will to sing loudly or lowly. There is no distinction between the eternal perception of God and the transcendental one of the sages so far as their validity is concerned. But a distinction which exists between these two perceptions is this that God's perception is eternal whereas the perception of the sages is an event in time. But this distinction makes no material difference in the nature of their validity. In the above matter our final opinion is as follows : In case of a conflict between the injunction of the Vedas and that of Smṛti as both of them are based upon the Vedas so the problem of the conflicting injunctions is solved and we arrive at the conclusion that in such cases it is optional on the part of the person enjoined to obey either of them. We may solve the problem in a different manner. We hold that the scope of these two conflicting injunctions should be so well defined that there will be no room for conflict. Some restriction will be imposed upon the range of each injunction so that one injunction will not encroach upon the field of another injunction. Thus the so-called irreconcilable conflict will be satisfactorily solved. The sound Vedic scholars assert that there is no illustration of conflict between the Vedas and Smṛti. Thus as the Dharma Śāstras are based upon the perception of the trustworthy persons so they are true. Some authoritative persons say that the Purāṇas are the fifth Veda. It has been stated that History and the Purāṇas should supplement the Vedas since the Vedas apprehend that the ignorant persons will lay blame on them.

We have no dogmatism in this matter. We may agree with the Mīmāṁsakas in this point that Smṛti is true since it is based upon the Vedas and the Purāṇas are also true since they like Smṛti are based upon the Vedas. By all means the six sources of knowledge, viz., the four Vedas, Smṛti and the Purāṇas, furnish us with the instructions of the proximate means to human ends. The six auxiliary branches of the Vedas headed by grammar supply us with the key to open the store-house of knowledge. They remain always subordinate to the principal branches of study and being rightly applied, become helpful to their understanding. But they do never directly teach Dharma. No new instructions can be had from the Kalpa-sūtras.

They simply inform us of the proper order of the disorderly many subsidiary rites as means to a principal act. Mīmāṁsā is a discursive work which determines the meaning of a Vedic sentence. Nyāya Śāstra purports to establish the truth of the Vedas. We have discussed this topic in our introduction to Nyāya-mañjarī. In fine, we say that these fourteen sources of knowledge are regarded as authentic. Some of them initiate us into the proximate means to human ends and the rest teach us the remote means to human ends. This view is agreed on all hands.

The demonstration of the authenticity of the Āgamas of the Śaiva, the Pāñcarātra and such other Schools

Various other Āgamas are noticed by us. They generally admit of two types. Some Āgamas are absolutely opposed to the Vedas, viz., the Āgamas of the Buddhist school. The other Āgamas are not opposed to the Vedas. But they teach new rites which have been suggested by them. The Āgamas of the Śaiva school illustrate the second type of Āgamas. Of these two types we hold that the Āgamas of the Śaiva school are authentic since we find reasons neither to entertain a doubt about the truth of knowledge, derived from these Āgamas nor to contradict the truth of knowledge, derived from these Āgamas nor to contradict the truth of such knowledge by other true judgments. It has been established by the Dharma Śāstras and inference that these Āgamas have been composed by God. We cannot imagine that they owe their origin to greed, delusion and such other sinister motives. Some doctrines of the Śaiva system of thought are in perfect agreement with those of some sections of the Vedas. Thus there is no scope for entertaining the hypothesis that these Āgamas bear the stamp of sinister motives such as greed, delusion, etc., on their face. They do not challenge the authority of the Vedas since they do not discard the caste-system etc., accepted by the Vedas. Reasons which have been advanced in support of the authenticity of the works of Manu and such other persons are not applicable to vindicate the truth of the Āgamas of the Śaiva school. But still it is reasonable to hold that they are true. If we carefully examine the doctrines of these scriptures then we find that they are saturated with the teachings of the Upaniṣadas which point to final emancipation.

Kṛṣṇa-Dvaipāyana and others—the leaders of the Vedic scholars, approve of the authenticity of the Āgamas of the Śaiva school, etc. But this approval of the authenticity of the Pañcarātra school is also hinted at since there is nothing to discredit the truth of the scriptures of this school.

Lord Viṣṇu has been declared to be the author of the said scriptures. He is none but God. God who is the eternal cause of the whole world has infinite majesty. He creates, preserves and destroys it. As He discharges three distinct functions, viz., creation, preservation and destruction so three designations, viz., Brahman, Viṣṇu and Śiva, are given to Him. In the Vedas there are repeated references to the hypothesis that Rudra is only one without a second; and Viṣṇu strides over this world. It is also stated that Rudra is Viṣṇu. As they are held to be in charge of creation, preservation and destruction so the ways and means of worshipping them have been prescribed in the Vedas. In the scriptures of the Śaiva and the Pañcarātra schools the different methods of worshipping them have been given. Such a difference does not imply that the scriptures of these schools are in conflict with the Vedas since the methods of worshipping God are merely optional. Hence their authenticity should not be challenged since they have been composed by the trustworthy persons and are not opposed to the Vedas.

The scriptures of the Buddhists are not authentic

No man of culture approves of the authenticity of the scriptures of the Buddhist schools since these scriptures which prefer to teach the means of final emancipation really embody lectures on misconduct. It is a plain fact that the Buddhist scriptures are not affiliated to the Vedas. We learn from them that they have advised to abandon all manners and customs arising from duties prescribed for the different castes.

The Buddhist saints who are indifferent to the worldly pleasures are addicted to animal slaughter. So their conscience is clouded. Hence their scriptures are not true.

They generally induce persons to do such acts as are prohibited by the Vedas. Whose speech will not falter to declare that the scriptures are true?

Though it is a very rare phenomenon that few persons sometimes obtain mysterious control over some departments of Nature, following the said sinful path yet this success is compared to the enjoyment of creature comforts, derived from killing a Brahmin. This success will result in hellish tortures.

Sins which arise from indulging in prohibited acts are never remedied. The inevitable result of them is to suffer in inferno in the future.

The defenders of Buddhism may argue in favour of the truth of the Buddhist scriptures that Buddha and such other saints, the authors of these scriptures, are trust-worthy persons since they have become omniscient practising meditation. How do you meet this argument? It is refuted thus. No book can pass as a work of a trust-worthy person unless and until an authoritative person recommends it to be so. He approves of the authenticity of the Vedas, the Purāṇas and the Dharma Śāstras which closely follow the teachings of the Vedas and those of some Āgamas that are not hostile to the Vedas. But he does not recommend the truth of the Āgamas of the Buddhist school. How will these Āgamas be accepted as works of the trust-worthy persons? The motive behind the composition of these texts may be clearly stated. Ignorance, greed and such other motives play an important part in their composition. With this remark the Buddhists who challenge the authority of the Vedas should be excluded from the list of the trust-worthy persons (āptas). The Buddhists review this stand and say.

"Who is an authoritative person? What is his appearance? How much is the number of such persons? What is his conduct? Answer these questions." Moreover, in order to establish the truth of their scriptures the Buddhists hold that Buddha is a trust-worthy person. They may also add that they have got their own authoritative persons and their number is roughly a hundred crores. How can you refute this view? The refutation of this view is as follows. The stages of life are well-known in the land of Āryas. The second question is "What is his appearance?" Does this question amount to this? How do his hands and feet look like? Or, how do his head and neck look like?

(Our simple answer is this that all his limbs bear a close resemblance to those of a human being). The number of these authoritative persons is so vast that it is beyond the scope of human calculation. The authoritative persons who adhere to the laws of caste-system and the duties of four stages of life are as old as the Vedas are. Those who believe in the truth of their Āgamas are also loyal to the above tenets of the Vedas.

The wicked Buddhists, restrained by the influence of the Vedas, avoid the touch of Cāṇḍālas. If they bid a long farewell to caste-system then how does the touch of a caṇḍāla contaminate? the other saviours in the name of initiation into the mystic intuition of incomprehensible Reality commit sinful acts such as the taking of prohibited food, unchartered debauchery etc. But they being afraid of the great persons who honour caste-system, do everything behind a screen but not in broad day-light. But if they have unflinching confidence in their scriptures then why do they behave like a thief? Thus they cannot claim that they have got hundreds of millions of great men as their own. But the great men who adhere to caste-system etc., discard such Āgamas as are hostile to the Vedas but do never join hands in their praise.

Whenever a man of good conduct touches a saviour he takes an ablution and washes his cloth with water. The Buddhists have no social intercourse with them. Almost every body follows the dictates of the Vedas. An Āgama, non-affiliated to the Vedas, is a trick to mislead people.

The voluminous work, known as the Vedas, fortunately is possessed of such unique wealth of contents that the authors of Āgamas non-affiliated to the Vedas envy it. When they vindicate the truth of their Āgamas they follow the method of the Vedas to express their ideas. As they try to dive deep into the subject-matter of the Vedas they import Vedic ideas in their Āgamas here and there. They consider their works to be pure by the touch of the Vedas. The lamp of the truth of the Vedas becomes bright as it were in their heart. As no Āgamas other than the Vedas stand the test of the good opinion of the great men so they have not been composed by the trust-worthy persons.

It has been declared that the system of logic has been written to establish the validity of the Vedas. If the task is done by the approval of the great men then what is the necessity of composing the said logical system. Enough of these superficial objections! There are a few heretics who contradict the veracity of the Vedas accepted by the great men. The weapon in the shape of logic is hurled against them in order to counteract their arguments. Therefore the truth of the scriptures stated before is established. But the works which are not affiliated to the Vedas are not true.

The hypothesis that all Āgamas are authentic since they have been revealed by the trust-worthy persons

Some thinkers accept the veracity of all Āgamas since the truth of knowledge imparted by them is neither contradicted nor doubted. They imagine that all Āgamas like the Vedas have been composed by the trust-worthy persons. These Āgamas teach us both secular and transcendental matters. Their teachings on secular matters are found to be correct. (But the verification of their doctrines with regard to transcendental objects is not possible. This remark applies to the Vedas as well). An objection has been raised regarding the Āgamas that all Āgamas, having discordant voice should invalidate one another. It is met thus. All Āgamas are equally true since they have been composed by trust-worthy persons. One Āgama cannot cantradict another Āgama since a weak spot is noticed in none of them. The content of one Āgama is contrary to that of another. The said contrariety is negligible. All the sentences of the Vedas are held to be true. They exhibit such contrary character. The touch of the head of a person, the drinking of wine, the killing of a cow etc. have been enjoined by some Vedic injunctions. But the just opposite acts have been enjoined by some other Vedic injunctions. Moreover, the Āgamas are not really opposed to one another since they do not disagree in pointing out the goal of human life.

The Āgamas are many. The roads to the goal of life, they prescribe, are also many. But they all converge upon the same goal of life as many rivers carrying different currents of water flow into the same ocean.

In all the systems of thought final emancipation has been declared to be the only ultimate goal of human life. But they differ from one another in selecting various forms of knowledge as ways and means to that end. But many of them agree together to declare that the object of such knowledge is the soul. Those who hold that the discriminating knowledge between Puruṣa and Prakṛti leads to final emancipation express the view that Puruṣa should be distinguished from Prakṛti. Those who preach the doctrine that the soul does not exist make a show of refuting the existence of a soul. But they believe in the existence of pure consciousness (consciousness which is not mixed up with feelings, passions, desires, impressions etc.). This consciousness has its independent existence, i.e., it is not a by-product of matter. It does not rest upon another object as its locus. Such consciousness is a substitute for the soul. The only difference lying between these two hypotheses is this that the soul is static but a series of phenomena of consciousness is dynamic. The Buddhists also hold that this series of consciousness is infinite, i.e., does neither begin nor meet with an end. All the different systems agree in accepting the two principal tenets, viz., the knowledge of Reality and final emancipation. (They all believe that the knowledge of Reality is the proximate cause of realising the ultimate goal and the cessation of all sorrows is the final goal of human life. Let each Āgama prescribe its own distinct rite. One Āgama may advise its followers to wear matted hair and besmear their bodies with ashes. Another Āgama may prescribe to carry a stick and a water-pot. Another Āgama may teach its followers to remain naked. But do these diverse teachings suggest that the Āgamas are at war with one another? Do not the Vedas enjoin the different ways of attaining Heaven? Hence though the Āgamas hold contrary views yet this opposition does not contradict their validity. Now, an objection is raised against this solution. How do you correctly know if Kapila is omniscient then Sugata is not omniscient. Again, if both of them are omniscient why do they hold contrary views? Such an objection is met thus. If they are unanimous in major topics then their difference in minor matters may be easily overlooked. But sometimes the very existence of difference invalidates a work. If an Āgama instructs a rite which loudly denounces other Āgamas then such condemnation does not amount to their invalidation since condemnation does not logically determine invalidation.

The Āgama of a particular sect prescribes to take food from the skull of a dead person. We entertain a doubt as to the validity of the Āgama because it prescribes such a rule. Such a doubt arises in our mind since we are familiar with the teachings of the other systems of thought, have framed a habit of thinking in that direction and possess deep-rooted impressions of the contrary teachings. In other words, we have formed a peculiar angle of vision. From that point of view we find fault with the above prescription. But we do not dive deep into the merits of the question.

But, on the contrary, persons who possess calmness of mind and have compassion for every creature entertain a doubt about the validity of the Vedic injunction prescribing animal slaughter. Let one's heart trouble, thinking of the killing of enemies enjoined by the Vedas since carnage is its end and personal gain is its motive. The killing of animals has been prescribed as a means to an end (a subsidiary rite) in connection with a few sacrifices such as Agni-soma etc.

We learn from the Vedas that the killing of animals is useful to the completion of the sacrifices mentioned above. People undertake such actions, being inspired by the Vedas. A compassionate person entertains a doubt, even in such cases, about the validity of such injunctions. They say "If animal-slaughter is a religious act, which act will be an irreligious one ? The truth of the Vedas is not discredited in spite of the inclusion of such disputed injunctions. Similarly, the other Āgamas will also be held to be true though they contain certain matters which do not find universal acceptance.

A hostile remark has been made against some procedures of the other Āgamas which advocate the attainment of perfection. It has been stated that though one attains communion with Śiva yet he will be punished in the future because he has done prohibited acts. Such criticisms are not fair since these acts have not been prohibited by the Āgamas in question. Though the said acts have been prohibited by the other Āgamas yet they may be taken as optional ones. If they are proved to be the means to the ultimate goal of a human being then how can it lead to a pit-fall ?

Or, we may assume for the sake of an argument that the act which has been prescribed by a particular Āgama and at the same time condemned by the other Āgamas may be productive of evil consequences in the future. Still, an Āgama is not invalidated because of its prescription of such an act just as the truth of the Vedas is not questioned though they contain injunctions enjoining Śyena sacrifice and its like. All these scriptures prescribe acts, considering the mental get-up of the followers with an eye on educating them in accordance with capacity. The injunction that one should perform Śyena sacrifice, intending to kill an enemy points to a deeper meaning. The injunction contains the (significant class-name) 'abhicāraḥ' (intending to kill enemy). The said epithet signifies that the person who transgresses the prohibition that one should not kill an animal is directed to perform Śyena sacrifice. The person who is entitled to Śyena sacrifice will commit a sin because he will kill his enemy by means of this sacrifice. The Vedas will not be discredited because they enjoin such acts. It has been stated in the Śabara Bhāṣya that some injunctions enjoin such acts as produce good results in the next life some other injunctions enjoin such acts as bring about prosperity in this life and some other injunctions enjoin such acts as yield evil consequences. It is not irrational to enjoin different acts according to the capacity of the different persons to be directed by injunctions. One who covets death is enjoined to perform the Sarvasvāra sacrifice. One who longs for a long life is enjoined to perform the Kṛṣṇala caru sacrifice. Such prescriptions do not invalidate the Vedas.

In the Buddhist scriptures caste-system has been refuted. This refutation is significant. It suggests that the Buddhists extend their favour to all and take pity upon all. The good-will and the softness of heart of the Buddhists have been praised. The refutation of caste-system purports to convey the good qualities of the heart of the Buddhists. The abolition of caste-system should not be literally taken. There is a rule in the Buddhist scriptures that a sick man or a man of very low birth should not be admitted to mendicant orders. It is, therefore, reasonable to hold that all the Āgamas are true since they have been composed by the trust-worthy persons such as Kapila, Sugata, Arhat and such other personages.

God is the author of all Āgamas

Some other thinkers suggest that God who is the ruler of this Universe is the real author of all Āgamas. He has direct experince of the various degrees of maturity of actions of all creations. He enters into their feelings and sees that there are several roads to final emancipation. He takes into consideration the capacity of each person, determined by his previous actions and instructs him the proper way to the final goal. He assumes various bodies by virtue of His transcendental powers and goes by different names. The epithets 'Arhat', 'Kapila' and 'Sugata' apply to God who is self-identical. If one assumes that there are many mniscient beings than he violates the law of parsimony.

Lord Buddha is the son of Śuddhodana. How can he be God? Revered Kṛṣṇadvaipāyana has given an answer to this question.

Whenever there is a degeneration of religion and irreligion prevails upon the earth I assume a body.

The body of Buddha has been procreated by Śuddhodana but not his soul. Therefore, the great teachers of religion hold this view that Lord Viṣṇu comes down upon this earth as an incarnation of divine law.

If the Vedas and the other Āgamas have one and the same author, why do not the other Āgamas command the same respect from the great personages? It is a truism that they do not honour the other Āgamas as much as they do the Vedas. Because God is directly aware of the subconscious mind with its tendencies of a few persons, chalked out a path for them, and blessed them with His instructions. Innumerable persons derive immense benefit following the royal road, prescribed by the Vedas. For this reason, their regard for the Vedas is very high but that for the other Āgamas is limited. If all of them owe their existence to the author why are they at war with one another? The Vedas themselves furnish us with the required answer. We may cite a large number of Vedic instances which represent irreconcilable views. Therefore, all the Āgamas are true since they have been composed by God. The other thinkers hold that all the Āgamas are true because they rest upon the Vedas as their foundation. We should not hold that Manu's law-book is reliable because it has been composed by a trust-worthy person since to err is human, the words of a person sometimes mislead us and a hypothesis should be based upon facts. We shall make minimum assumptions if we hold that the said book is based upon the Vedas.

This argument applies to all Āgamas. The Vedas which are believed to be the basis of Manu's Law-book are not known to us. If the upholders of this hypothesis hold that they are to be inferred then we may as well say that the Vedas which constitute the basis of the other Āgamas are also to be inferred.

Now, the Mīmāṁsakas may argue that as the preformer of the Vedic rites and that of the rites, prescribed by Smṛti literature, are one and the same person so the Vedas which are supposed to constitute the basis of Manu's Law-books are inferred. But those who obey the dictates of the other Āgamas do not perform the Vedic rites. So we cannot infer that the other Āgamas are based upon the Vedas. Hence how can we infer that the Vedas constitute the basis of the other Āgamas ?

The above argument does not refute the hypothesis that the other Agamas are based upon the Vedas. If a person who observes Vedic rites is identical with him who performs acts preseribed by Smṛtis then this identity does not determine the validity of Smṛtis. This shows that the Vedic rites may be blended with those of Smṛtis.

It is not a truism that an act which is not correlated to a Vedic rite is not derived from an authentic source. The duties of the different castes and the different stages of life are not discharged by one and the same person. Are they not derived from an authentic source ? As the said duties are derived from an authentic source so an act which is not correlated to a Vedic rite is also derived from an authentic source.

It may be argued that as a person who follows the path of the other Āgamas does not perform the Vedic rites so the other Āgamas are based upon a source which is distinct from the Vedas. The argument does not hold good. There is nothing to contradict the hypothesis that the Agamas are based upon the Vedas since they contain no error—no defect.

If it is held that the authors of the other Āgamas have direct experience of the contents of their works by transcendental perception then this assumption does not obey the law of parsimony. The recensions of the Vedas are infinite. The Āgamas in question may draw their materials from any of the Vedic works. It is highly logical to hold that they are based upon the Vedas.

Now if it is assumed that the Agamas in question are based upon the Vedas, why do the Mīmāṁsakas who are well-versed in the Vedas cherish hatred against this assumption ? Our reply to this question is this : "Just approach the Mīmāṁsakas who bear a grudge against the other Āgamas to find out an answer."

Why do the Mīmāṁsakas cherish hatred against cow-slaughter which has been clearly prescribed by the Vedas ? The alleged incompatibility holding between the Vedas and the other Āgamas has been refuted. As the Vedic literature is infinitely large so it is difficult to establish the said discrepancy.

Do you think that a fraction of Vedic literature, which being committed to memory is current among us constitutes the whole of it ? How do you know for certain that the views which we do not accept do not correspond to those to be found in the other branches of the Vedas ?

The Sāṁkhyas hold that Prakṛti is constituted by three guṇas, viz., Sattva, Rajas and Tamas. A germ of this hypothesis is noticed in the Vedic literature. The verse 'ajām ekāṁ lohita-śukla-kṛṣṇām etc.' points to it. The Buddhists hold that the sages live only on the air. It is a repetition of the Vedic conclusion that the realisation of consciousness as the ultimate reality is the goal of life. The Vedic scholars notice the germs of a few customs such as putting on red cloths, besmearing the whole body with ashes, using the skull of a dead man as a pot and so on in the Vedic literature.

Though the followers of some Āgamas do not perform the Vedic rites like the adherents to Manu's Smṛti yet those Āgamas are the source of true knowledge since they are based upon the Vedas. Hence all the Āgamas should be treated as Smṛti.

Manu in some places teaches the duty of an individual. Such teaching is not the product of his imagination. He closely follows the Vedic texts. Everything has been given in the Vedas. The Vedas are the store-house of all knowledge.

The mention of the name of Manu is by way of illustration. The names of the other authors of Smṛti should also be taken into consideration. Gautama, Yama, Āpastmba, Samavrta, Kāṭhaka and others should also command our respect. Similarly, the same treatment should be accorded to Arhat, Kapila, Sugata and such other persons. The verse which offers eulogy to Manu should be interpreted in such a catholic spirit.

Now, a fresh problem arises. If we are so generous in our attitude towards the Āgamas then the works of the materialists should be accepted as authentic. A germ of the materialistic doctrine is noticed in the Vedic literature. The body is nothing but our soul. It is constituted by the gross elements. It perishes with the decay of elements. No consciousness persists after the destruction of a body. No soul is immortal from this point of view. The continuity of consciousness is absurd. If the materialistic philosophy is taken to be true then the safety of all Agamas will be assured.

The solution of this problem is as follows. No duty has been prescribed by the materialistic system. It is purely dialectical in its character. No work of this system is entitled to the designation of Āgama.

The materialists may contend that their work embodies duties. One should pass his days in happiness as long as he lives. It is no advice since our instinct prompts us to seek after pleasure. An advice in this matter is useless. One should not follow the round of duties prescribed by the Vedas. One should not place his confidence in the teachings of the Vedas. What has been taught by the materialists has been refuted.

The materialistic philosophy is based upon the prima facie view stated in the Vedas but not upon the conclusive views of the Vedas. In the Bṛhadāraṇyaka Upaniṣad the concluding portion of the doctrine of soul runs thus:—"I do not intend to mislead you, misrepresenting the doctrine of soul. The soul is imperishable. It has a short-lived contact with a body". Therefore the books on materialism do not represent an independent point of view since they embody the superficial view of things, stated in the Vedas in order to be refuted. As the above view is confuted by the concluding portion of the Vedas so it should be absolutely disregarded. But it will be improper on our part to assume that the views represented in the other Āgamas are based upon the prima facie views, stated in the Vedas since no corresponding counter-conclusions are noticed in the Vedas. Therefore, all Āgamas are authentic since they are based upon the Vedas.

The proving of the hypothesis that a particular Āgama is not authentic

Now, a fresh problem arises in our mind. If the validity of all Āgamas is thus established then a new book which I write may be accepted as authentic within a few days. The reasons which have been stated above are also applicable to it.

The book which is very old is reported by some cunning fellows as a new one.

The Āgamas are held to be authentic if they satisfy the following conditions :

(1) They must attain celebrity among the circle of the great persons.

(2) They must be accepted by a large number of men of good conduct.

(3) Though they may have been recently composed yet they should not instruct such conduct as appears to be unprecedented.

(4) The greed of money should not be the motive of their composition.

(5) They should not preach such doctrines as cause anxiety to others.

Any and every treatise should not be considered to be an authentic one. Shall we accept 'Kuṭṭinīmatam' (a book written by Damodara Gupta) in which advice has been given by a senior prostitute to the junior ones as an authentic one ?

Let us cite an example of bad conduct under the name of religion. So goes the rumour that some designing persons introduced a festival known as Nīlāmbara vratam (a black curtain festival). They used to hang up a curtain. Behind the screen a large number of men and women used to mix freely with one another and to enjoy promiscuous relation with no regard for moral codes. The king Śaṁkara Varman, conversant with the essence of religion, stopped it as he knew it to be something unprecedented. But he did not stop the real religious practice of the Jainas and others.

In fine, we arrive at the conclusion that the Vedas are true as they have been composed by a trustworthy person. They have been so composed that no defects which have been ascribed to them by the philosophers of the rival schools belong to them. Thus validity has been firmly assured of them. The other Śāstras are true since either they are based upon the Vedas or they have been composed by the trustworthy persons. We may apply any of these two reasons to prove the thesis. But under no circumstances one can point out defects in the Vedas on the ground that the Vedas are not based upon a source book.

An objection to the validity of the Vedas

Veracity does not belong to the Vedas unlike health which is the property of a sound body. The body of the Vedas suffers from many defects such as falsehood, etc.

One who is desirous of getting animals should perform the Citrā sacrifice. One who intends to get a son should perform Putreṣṭi sacrifice. On the completion of these sacrifices the performer does not invariably obtain the result. Therefore the injunctions, prescribing Citrā sacrifice and its like, are false.

The defender of the truth of the Vedas meets the objection thus. What is the meaning of the first injunction. The sentence proposes to import that he who intends to get an animal should perform the above iṣṭi. We are to prove that one obtains animals just after the conclusion of the said iṣṭi. Then why are not the injunctions prescribing the Citrā sacrifice, etc. true ?

In the injunctions, viz., "One should perform a sacrifice as long as he lives". "One should offer libation as long as he lives" nothing is stated about the prolongation of the life of the performer of a sacrifice since life is not the result of such actions. Similarly, as animals do not result from the Citrā-sacrifice so desire for animals should qualify the performer of the sacrifice. When one knows for certain that he cannot gain animals by means of the said sacrifice he may not perform the sacrifice. We shall discuss this matter later on. Reflecting on the nature of an action we come to know that a result which a sacrifice is proclaimed to yield will follow it in close succession since an effect is seen to follow from an act in immediate succession. Some say that an act should produce its effect during its lifetime since when our limbs are pressed we enjoy pleasure. One who undertakes to perform a sacrifice does so under the impression that the feeling of want which pains him will be removed at once. The act of sacrifice, being an act, will perish after sometime. Such being the nature of a sacrifice how can it yield the so-called effect in the remote future ? Some argue in the following manner. When an act had existed it did not yield its result. When the said result is produced the act does not exist. In that case how can we causally connect a sacrifice with the result ? How will a sacrifice yield the result, having perished at the time of its fruition ? Moreover when the said result is obtained in some other time some other tangible causes are noticed to condition it. A sincere service, rendered to the owner of animals, is the tangible cause of getting animals. As such a visible cause is noticed so no person of clear understanding will subscribe to the hypothesis that a sacrifice like Citrā, etc., the result of which is not tangibly established produces the said result. Thus we hold that the injunctions which prescribe sacrifices like Citrā, etc., are false.

We cannot pin our faith in the truth of the Vedic injunction which prescribes sacrifices like Citrā, etc., since they do not yield the promised result. Similarly, we are not convinced of the truth of the other Vedic injunctions prescribing Agnihotra sacrifice and others.

The injunctions which prescribe Agnihotra, etc., are false since they are part and parcel of the Vedic sentences like the Vedic injunctions enjoining sacrifices like Citrā, etc. They are not held to be true because there is no agreement between a promise and its fulfilment. It should also be noted that there is also discrepancy between an injunction and its result in case of the Vedic injunctions "One who deserves to have a son should perform the putra-iṣṭi-sacrifice".

Sometimes, we notice just the opposite of what has been stated in the Vedas (A person who has undertaken the sacrifice of Agnihotra should preserve the fire kindled at the time of his marriage ceremony as long as he lives. The fire is preserved in a pot. After his demise, the pot, containing the said fire, is taken to the cremation ground. His funeral pyre is set to fire only by means of this preserved fire. If this fire is not available the dead body of the performer of an Agnihotra sacrifice will not be burnt). In the Vedas the collection of the pot, containing the preserved fire, has been enjoined. Having given instruction relating to the above act the Vedas declare that this dead person, the performer of Agnihotra sacrifice armed with the instrument of sacrifice, goes to heaven. What is the meaning of the demonstrative pronoun 'this' (eṣaḥ), used in the Vedic text? If it is held that 'this' signifies the soul then it has only a secondary meaning since the soul is a transcendental object. The soul does not wield the implements of a sacrifice, viz., a wood-knife, a pot-sherd, etc. Therefore the pronoun 'this' signifies the body. But the body does not go to heaven since the body is reduced to ashes. This state of the body is opposed to its going to heaven. Thus the result, declared by the Vedas, is reversed. The Vedas are not true since there is no agreement between a promise and its fulfilment and there is a reversal of the declared result.

The Vedas are false since they involve inner contradiction. There are three injunctions in the Vedas, viz., (1) "One should offer libation after sun-rise", (2) "One should offer libation just before sun-rise", and (3) "One should offer libation in the early morning, i. e., long before sun-rise". Having prescribed these three periods of time of offering libation they (these hours of libation) have been prohibited by artha-vādas which condemn such libations at these periods. If one offers libation after sun-rise then the dog called Śyāva licks the content of his libation. If one offers libation long before sun-rise, Śabala licks the content of his libation. If one offers libation just before sun-rise then the dogs Śyāva and Śabala lick the content of his libation. The defenders of the Vedas cannot hold that these are nominal artha-vādas having nothing to import. The reason behind our statement is this that a praise amounts to an injunction and condemnation indicates a prohibition. As a praise and an injunction have the same meaning to import so condemnation and prohibition imply the same sense.

The defenders of the Vedas may argue that when one condemns something he does not do it for the sake of mere censure but when he condemns something he does it for praising something else. Such a contention is not tenable. The specified periods of time have been prohibited. No hour remains in order to be praised by this censure. Therefore the Vedas are false since they impart incompatible instructions, i.e., they involve contradiction.

The Vedas are false since they contain repetition. (The hotṛ priest utters a Vedic mantra in order to kindle fire. This mantra is called Sāmidhenī. Or, the hotṛ priest places faggots on fire uttering a Vedic mantra. This mantra is called Sāmidhenī. These Sāmidhenī mantras are eleven in number. Each mantra has its distinct designation). The first one of these Samidhenis is called the prathama ṛk. The last one is called the uttama ṛk. It has been enjoined that the prathama ṛk is to be repeated three times and the uttama ṛk is also to be repeated thrice. If these mantras are recited thrice, such a recitation amounts to repetition. As the Vedas prescribe to read out a mantra again and again so they are open to the charge of repetition. If the single recitation of a mantra bears fruit then the thrice recitation of the mantra is redundant. Therefore the Vedas are not true since they contain false statements, involve contradiction and encourage idle repetition.

The author of the Nyāya-sūtra says to this effect. In case of Putra-iṣṭi-sacrifice the Vedas make a false statement. When they enjoin the offer of libation they involve contradiction. When they advise to utter a mantra again and again they expose themselves to the charge of repetition. The Vedas are not true since they suffer from these defects.

A reply to the charge of the falsehood of the Vedas.

The above problem is solved thus. Gautama says that it is not true that the Vedas are untrue since they do not fulfil the promise held out by them. He further adds that the result is not obtained because there may be some defects in the sacrificial act itself or in the institutor of the sacrifice or in accessaries of the sacrifice. The critics of the Vedas hold that the Vedas are not the source of true knowledge because they make a false declaration of results. But it is not a fact. As it has not been established. The false declaration of results is proved by the experience of the absence of results. The latter is not an invariable concomitant of the former. It is seen that though the Vedas are not false yet the expected result is not obtained. Do you think that the result is not obtained because the Vedas are false ? Or the expected result does not occur because there are some defects somewhere in the conditions of a sacrifice. There is no crucial instance on either sides. Now the critics may contend that as the result does never immediately follow from a sacrifice so the result is not experienced because the Vedas are false. They further add that the said defects in the performer of a sacrifice is not responsible for the non-appearance of the expected result. Such a contention is not sound. Our experience teaches that if the Kārīrī sacrifice is well-done then there is instantaneous rainfall. It is not a case of accidental coincidence. The causality of the said sacrifice has been stated by the Vedas. It has been verified by the joint method of agreement and difference. Some sacrifice yields secular results like a son, etc. If we reflect on the nature of these results then we come to know that these results cannot be produced at once. A son does not fall from the sky like drops of rain. The union of a man with a woman is one of its necessary conditions. So a son is not born just after the completion of a sacrifice. It is also seen that somebody receives a gift of animals just after the completion of a sacrifice. Let us cite an example. Our grandfather desirous of owning a village performed a sacrifice known as Saṁgrahaṇī. He obtained the village of Gauramūlaka just after the completion of the sacrifice.

Now, the critics raise another problem. Let the acceptance of a gift be the tangible cause of getting an animal, etc. Let the union a man with a woman be the cause of begetting a son. Is there any necessity of postulating a sacrifice as a cause ? Do not argue in this strain. Though the tangible conditions assemble yet the effect is not produced. When the sacrifice is performed the result follows. Thus we arrive at the definite conclusion that the union of a man with a woman accompanied by the performance of a sacrifice is the cause of begetting a son.

Moreover, when all persons wait upon their preceptors, read

the books upto the end with equal attention the result differs in degree. Therefore it is not reasonable to hold that the tangible conditions are only responsible for the result. Now, the objectors may contend that the very nature of the tangible material causes is responsible for the difference in the result. Such a hypothesis will be refuted later on. A condition over and above the tangible ones must be assumed.

Some thinkers hold a similar view and say that a sacrifice and an injunction enjoining it are to be included in the list of conditions. There are cases when sacrifices are performed without any defect but no result in the shape of getting a son or an animal, etc., follows even in the remote future. In such cases it is to be assumed that a powerful unrewarded action persists from the previous birth and counteracts the fruition of the present action. The sacriptures also lend their support to this hypothesis. If an action does not sometime yield its result then unrewarded merit or demerit lingers to prevent its result. The author of the Nyāya-Sūtra illustrates the counteractive agents of an action citing various examples. But he does not believe that these defects constitute the exclusive counteracting agents. It is not responsible to hold that the Vedas are not true since the result does not follow in close succession. They may yield results after some lapse of time. When they do not yield results some factors such as defects in the performance or counter-acting agents may be responsible.

Moreover, the Vedic injunction concerning Citrā sacrifice signifies that one obtains animals if he performs it (Citrā sacrifice). But there is no proof in favour of the suggested meaning that the result of the said sacrifice follows in immediate succession. The present time comes only within the scope of perception. The injunction enjoining Citrā sacrifice suggests that the result will occur at an indefinite period of time. Perception cannot contradict such an injunction since the subject-matter of an injunction does not fall within the province of perception.

Kumārila Bhaṭṭa has said to this effect in his Śloka-Vārttika. If the result of an enjoined act does not follow in close succession the injunction in question is not invalidated thereby since it does not refer to say fixed period of time within which the result of the act will be produced (i.e. obtained).

The objector has stated that if we reflect on the nature of an act then we come to know that the result of Citrā sacrifice should follow in close succession. They also put forward an analogical argument that whenever one presses his limbs he feels pleasure arising from it. But this is the analogical statement of an ignorant person since no result of an ordinary act should be logically compared to that of an act enjoined. An ordinary act yields a particular result but an enjoined act also produces a different result. In case of cultivation an improvement upon land is the result of the act of tilling. The wealth of harvest is the result of an act enjoined by a sentence. When do you find an injunction with regard to cultivation ? Such an injunction is found in the science on agriculture, or, we learn it from the experts. Or, we learn it from the joint method of agreement and difference which is a substitute for an injunction. (If we cultivate we get harvest and if we do not cultivate, we do not get harvest. Thus one should cultivate in order to grow harvest.)

There are some secular injunctions current among the people. Let us take an illustration of such injunctions, viz., one who is desirous of getting a salary should cook food in another person's house. The act of cooking is enjoined by the above injunction. The result, produced by the act, is rice. But he who obeys the injunction gets salary which is its result. A law which governs all acts is this that an effect follows an act in close succession. But in the above illustration there is no definite temporal sequence between an injunction and its result. One who obeys the above popular injunction does not necessarily get the result i.e., salary just after the completion of the enjoined act. In a sacrifice the immediate result of the act of offering an oblation to fire is a change in the nature of an article offered. A person who massages the limbs of another person irregularly gets the reward of his service. There are secular injunctions such as one should wait upon a king with a view to owning a village etc. There is no law regarding these injunctions that a result regularly follows from such an injunction at a definite period of time. Prescriptions of medicine have been instructed by the

Āyur-Veda (medical science). If one follows any such instruction and takes medicine then he does not instantaneously get its result. But it requires an interval of time to get it. Thus there is no proof with regard to the hypothesis that every act produces its effect in close succession. It is generally said that if a person performs a particular sacrifice then he very quickly obtains animals. Such a statement has been made in view of the mental condition of a person who has been suffering from taking bad food for a long time and is in need of animals. But it is not logically sound. A person who performs the said sacrifices wishes to have the result. But there is no logical certainty about the speedy result.

If the desire of the person or that of his priest is very strong then he gets the result in this life. But the result of a sacrifice is not instantaneous like that of an ordinary act. There are certain acts which bear fruits in this phase of life but take time to produce them. If one desires to possess holy effulgence then he should be invested with the holy thread at the age of five. But the boy does not possess holy effulgence as soon as he is invested with holy thread. But after a lapse of time he acquires it. Similarly, the other rites which are performed for acquiring manly vigour etc., share the same lot. As there is no hard and fast rule that acts which are enjoined yield immediate result so the result of such an act being not immediate the injunction concerned does not become invalid. If an act enjoined does not bear its fruit even after a long interval of time then some defects or demerits of the institutor stand in the way of its fruition. We have already made this point of view clear.

A reply to the objection against the validity of the Vedas from another standpoint.

Some other thinkers do not approve of the incompleteness of a Vedic rite due to a defect in the performer of the rite etc. They hold that if a sacrifice does not yield its result in this life then it will do so in the next life. As a purposive Vedic rite is completely observed with an eye upon each of its details so it is not fair to assume a defect in it. So we assume that the result is obtained in the next life.

We assume that there are three kinds of Vedic rites, viz., (1) some acts produce results in this life, (2) Some other acts bring about irregular results and (3) the rest acts bear fruits in the next life. Among them the Kārīrī sacrifice yields its result in this life. When famine breaks out and the whole country is tormented with excessive heat owing to the scarcity of rain the Kārīrī sacrifice is performed.

Rainfall is the result which it aims at. Rainfall is anxiously expected by all since it pleases all. So rain should come down instantaneously. The actual wording of the Vedas is noticed thus :—If it rains then the Vedic rite will be completed with rain-drops. But if it does not rain on the day of performance then libation should be offered on the next day. Sacrifices like Jyotiṣṭoma etc. bring forth fruits in the next life. The very nature of the fruit speaks for itself that it will be effectuated in the next world.

Paradise is happiness beyond comparison. Or, it is a place where such happiness is enjoined. A person having this body can neither enjoy such happiness nor enter that land of bliss. The sacrifices like Citrā etc. produce irregular results. We may obtain the result of the Citrā sacrifice, viz., animals in this life or in the next life. We should also note the following in this connection. We see that some persons who have not performed the Citrā sacrifice obtain animals. If it is held that the gaining of animals is due to tangible causes such as service, the acceptance of gifts etc., then with the break-down of the causal relation subsisting between the said sacrifice and the gaining of animals the materialistic view should be embraced. If we stick to the hypothesis that we gain animals by means of a sacrifice then we should determine which rite helps us to do so. We are sure that if one performs such rites as bestow on him holy effulgence, etc., he does not gain animals thereby. He has not performed the Citrā sacrifice which helps him to gain animals in this life. If he had performed the said sacrifice in the previous birth then he must have obtained the result in that life since it has been admitted by them that the Citrā sacrifice brings forth its result in the same life. Now our opponents should explain "How does he gain animals ?"

Now, the opponents may contend in the following manner. They take their stand upon the authority of Gautama's law-book and quote a passage from his book to suit their purpose. Some persons who performed the Jyotiṣṭoma sacrifice and such other sacrifices in the previous birth enjoyed some portion of their fruits after their demise. Merits arising from such acts have not been exhausted. On the strength of stored-up merits they gain animals. Gautama says, "When persons belonging to four castes and four different orders of life discharge their respective duties prescribed by the scriptures they enjoy heavenly bliss after their death. When the stock of merits giving heavenly bliss is exhausted they are again born on this earth owing to the influence of remaining merits. Now, they become distinguished scholars, are noted for their good conduct and acquire immense wealth etc." We are not able to follow the meaning of this passage as given by you.

A Vedic rite produces a particular result but cannot bring forth another result since an act and its result are causally connected.

For this very reason the above passage of Gautama's book does not refer to a particular Vedic rite. It refers to many such rites. On the basis of this reasonable assumption we should interpret the passage of Gautama. Persons, belonging to different castes and orders of life, have performed many Vedic rites. Among these rites they enjoy the fruit of Jyotiṣṭoma after their death. The other Vedic rites viz., Citrā etc. do not produce result at that time. When merit arising from Jyotiṣṭoma becomes exhausted the turn of other sacrifices such as Citrā etc. comes up. Merit arising from them has been held up so long. It finds an opportunity of producing its effect. The performers of Citrā sacrifice take their birth marked by distinction, on this earth, in order to enjoy its fruit. This is the inner meaning of the passage of Gautama. Hence the ownership of animals in this life is due to the performance of Citrā sacrifice in the previous birth. Such ownership is neither due to actions other than Vedic ones nor due to the other Vedic rites. As Citrā sacrifice irregularly produces its result so the result of Citrā sacrifice is not invariably produced in this life. The Vedas, containing injunctions, are not false since if the result of Vedic rites is not seen in this life, they will produce their result in the next life.

A reply to the above reply

We answer the points, raised by the rival school and directed against us, in a serial order. Do the Vedas clearly state the threefold division of the Vedic rites ? Or, do you grasp it, examining the nature of Vedic injunctions? Or, do you discover it, reflecting on the nature of the result of such injunctions? Or, do you exercise your sweet will to establish such division? Of these suggestions the first one is not tenable since there is no clear statement indicating the three-fold division of injunctions. The Vedic injunctions run thus :—One who is desirous of rain should perform Kārīrī sacrifice; one who desires heaven should perform Jyotiṣṭoma sacrifice; and one who expects to gain animals should perform Citrā sacrifice. This much has only been stated in the Vedas but nothing more. The Vedas do not declare that such-and-such rite yields its result in this life, such-and-such rite brings forth its result in the next life and such-and-such rite irregularly produces its result. The function of an injunction is to induce a person to a good action. The subjunctive mood in which a verb, contained in the Vedic sentence, is used implies that it should be done in response to his desire. But an injunction does not induce a person to an impracticable action. It induces a person to a practicable action. If the desired object is not realised then an injunction does not prompt one to undertake such an action. A person undertakes such a sacrifice as leads to the desired goal. An injunction implies that the causal relation subsists between a sacrifice, the meaning of a verb, and its result. But an injunction does not imply whether the result which the institutor of a sacrifice intends to have will immediately happen or not. But if we closely examine the nature of the result of a sacrifice then we know that heaven is realised in the next life but not in this life. But, it does not point to the realisation of the result in the next life. The result of Citrā sacrifice viz., the gaining of animals does not immediately follow the sacrifice. A person may cherish a wish to classify results but it has no effective power. We cannot ascertain the meaning of the Śāstras by means of our arbitrary will. There is no proof in support of the three-fold division of results.

The argument which has been put forward to prove the

thesis that the result of Citrā sacrifices takes place at an irregular interval may be easily applied to the result of Citrā sacrifice which invariably yields result in this life. The Citrā sacrifice brings forth its result in this life but there is no certainty about the time of its occurrence. Kumārila has said in his Śloka-Vārttika that Citrā sacrifice produces its result in this life but nobody can accurately predict the time of its fruition. It is not a fact that the god of cloud does not send down rain if the Kārīrī sacrifice has not been performed today. Why do you not postulate that the Kārīrī sacrifice performed in the previous birth, is responsible for rainfall ? Therefore, let the Kārīrī sacrifice be irregular in yielding its result.

The objectors may contend that the statement "It is not a fact that the god of cloud does not send down rain if Kārīrī sacrifice has not been performed today" purports to convey that the rainfall in question is due to merit. They prove their point thus. If there is a plenty of harvest, people are happy. The enjoyment of happiness in due to merit. Therefore merit alone accounts for the said rainfall. If this is the drift of the above contention then they should as well say that one will gain animals without performing Citrā sacrifice. One derives much pleasure from drinking milk, sour milk etc. The enjoyment of such pleasure is due to merit. Such merit will alone help him to gain animals. For this purpose the performance of Citrā sacrifice is not at all needed. Rice depends upon Kārīrī sacrifice and the gain of animals depends upon Citrā sacrifice. Let one gain animals and have rainfall due to merit alone since the pleasure derived from taking rice mixed up with sour milk is effectuated by merit. Now, the Mīmāṁsakas may contend that the Vedas distinctly mention that the gain of animals is due to the performance of the Citrā sacrifice. Hence merit, arising from any good action, produces an enjoyment of pleasure but does never account for the gain of animals. If they argue like this then it may be pointed out that the Vedas distinctly declare that Kārīrī sacrifice brings forth rain. In that case merit arising from any good action will not explain rainfall. (The draft of this discussion is that the result of Kārīrī sacrifice appears irregularly. If the Mīmāṁsakas accept it then they should discard their thesis viz, the three-fold division of Vedic rites).

The Mīmāṁsakas may contend that the deep reflection on the meaning of the Vedic sentence "If one performs Kārīrī sacrifice today but it does not rain then he will offer libation tomorrow etc." makes us understand that rain which results from Kārīrī sacrifice takes place in this life. If this is their contention then on the absence of such a direct statement, e.g., "One who wishes rain should chant the hymn seen by Saubhari etc.", the Vedic rite should produce its result in the next life. Moreover, if the secular character of a result is determined only by the authority of the sentence "One should offer libation to-morrow" then the obvious secular character of the result of a Vedic rite, not based upon such an authoritative Vedic sentence, will cease to exist.

If the secular character is asserted of rain because it is to be enjoyed in common by many then the same logic applies to the result of Citrā sacrifice, viz., animals. The perfomer of a sacrifice is not necessarily a selfish person since he has been advised to feed his sons and daughters, guests and servants etc. before he takes his meal. But we admit that rain does service to a greater number of people. No need of comparison.

Now, the Mīmāṁsakas argue that rain is secular because men long for its speedy setting in, but the same logic applies to animals since they are also coveted in a similar manner. When men are oppressed by excessive heat owing to the absence of rain they long for its speedy arrival. When people pass their days in anxiety, being afflicted by the scarcity of food they also long for animals in a similar manner. In fine, we suggest the following. He who bestows drinking water gets satisfaction in return, i.e., he never suffers from the scarcity of water. He who gives food enjoys endless bliss. These instructive words of a sage point to the thesis that merit is the condition of bliss in general. It is also implied that if Kārīrī sacrifice is not performed rain may come down and if Citrā sacrifice is not performed animals may be gained. If this implied meaning is accepted one does not enter the fold of the Cārvākas since it is never stated that a result does not follow from a Vedic rite. The accepted moral law that a vedic rite and its result are causally connected is not at all violated.

The problem why Kārīrī sacrifice does not occasionally produce its result has been solved. If a Vedic rite though thoroughly performed does not become fruitful sometimes then unrequited demerit which is in store for the performer of the rite from the previous birth counteracts its fruition. The scriptures also lend their support to this solution. Hence, one should arrive at the conclusion that Kārīrī sacrifice irregularly gives its fruit. The above-mentioned demerit cannot create a perpetual hindrance. When it is requited it must terminate. When demerit which stands in the way of the fruition of Kārīrī sacrifice wanes, i. e., when the obstacle is removed Kārīrī sacrifice surely becomes fruitful. Again, Kārīrī sacrifice may not produce its result in this life owing to the presence of an obstacle. But it cannot decay without bringing about its result. It will most probably yield its result in the next life. So it cannot but be irregular in producing its effect. In this manner we approve of the hypothesis that the other sacrifices like Citrā etc. are also irregular in producing their result. When Citrā sacrifice is performed perfectly well but its result is not obtained it is assumed that demerit hinders its fruition. Citrā sacrifice agrees on all fours with Kārīrī sacrifice with the only exception that Kārīrī sacrifice is capable of producing an instantaneous result. Similarly, we explain the nature of other sacrifices which are performed by persons longing for the spiritual lustre of a Vedic scholar, undissipated semen, food, a village etc. Therefore, we should accept the literal sense of the above-quoted passage of Gautama's Dharma-śāstra. The Mīmāṁsakas have stated that if a purposeful Vedic rite is performed along with all its subsidiary rites then there is no possibility of its being defective. Such a statement is really illogical. Even though a person sets himself to perform a sacrifice accompanied by all its subsidiary rites yet defects may unwittingly creep in through inadvertence. The author of the Nyāya-bhāṣya has exhibited that such inadvertence admits of various types. Therefore the former way of solving the problem is better.

The determination of the meaning of the term Dharma from the standpoint of the Naiyāyikas

The objectors have joined issue with the believers in the efficacy of sacrifices and said "How do the sacrifices bring forth results since they do not endure when the so-called results appear?" Such an adverse criticism is not fair. Though a religious act does not endure till the appearance of the expected result yet the institutor of the act acquires invisible potentiality arising from it (the term "saṁskāra" stands for adṛṣṭa but not for impressions).

This invisible potentiality which is produced by a religious act is an attribute of the individual soul like the other ones, e. g., consciousness, etc. It persists in the soul until the result appears.

As consciousness is generated by the contact of the soul with the sense-organs, etc., so invisible potentiality arises from the performance of sacrifices and similar religious acts.

Consciousness is short-lived but unlike it invisible potentiality lasts till the appearance of the result of Vedic rites. If one does not subscribe to this hypothesis then the causal relation between a religious act and its result cannot be established. As the thinkers of the other schools admit that impressions condition memory so the Naiyāyikas hold that invisible potentiality which determines the appearance of the said result will also belong to the soul.

This invisible potentiality admits of two kinds, viz., merit and demerit. The invisible potentiality which arises from a sacrifice or from a similar pious act is called merit but the unseen potentiality which springs up from sinful acts such as the killing of a Brahmin is called demerit.

The finding of the different meanings of the term Dharma and the refutation of these meanings

The followers of Kapila hold that the specific mode of Buddhi which is part and parcel of inner organ is colled adṛṣṭa (invisible principle of merit and demerit). The Jainas suggest that the changing substance entitled puṇya is called Dharma. The Buddhists hold that tendencies which tend to form habits and reside in Citta (the inner organ) are called Dharma. The older section of the Mīmāṁsakas assert that a new thing which emerges from the performance of pious acts such as a sacrifice, etc., and goes under the title 'Apūrva' is Dharma. According to Śabara the religious acts themselves are Dharma. The followers of Prabhākara preach that a mandate which is signified by an injunction is called Dharma. The view of the Sāṁkhyists that a specific mode of Buddhi is Dharma and that of the Jainas that the changing substance is known as 'puṇya' stand refuted as their fundamental tenets have been refuted. As the existence of the soul will be established so it should be held that Vāsanā belongs to the soul but not to Citta. Therefore, the Buddhist hypothesis is not sound. The existence of Apūrva which steadily persists, being unsupported during the time intervening between the performance of a sacrifice and the attainment of heaven cannot be proved. So the hypothesis of the early Mīmāṁsakas is not tenable. Some Mīmāṁsakas hold that the pre-non-existence of the effect of a sacrifice or the force of a sacrifice is denoted by the term 'Apūrva' but such a meaning is not tenable. [There is a misprint in the textbook. 'Agni-śabdena' is a misprint. It should be 'Apūrva-śabdena'.] The Prabhākaras hold that a mandate which is signified by a Vedic injunction is denoted by the term 'Apūrva'. Such a meaning is not tenable. This view will be refuted later on. He who performs a sacrifice is called a pious man (a man who is possessed of dharma). So, the term 'dharma' has been employed in the sense of another term which denotes a sacrifice and such other good acts. Hence, the final import conveys that a sacrifice is the meaning of the term 'Dharma'. Such a decision is not tenable. A sacrifice, being short-lived, cannot produce its effect after a long time. Hence, the terms 'sacrifice' and 'dharma' are not synonymous.

Even the people at large say that dharma (merit) springs up from the performance of good acts such as a sacrifice, charity, etc. This popular view gets the support of an age-long tradition which gives evidence to the proposition that the performance of good acts begets merit inhering the soul.

We should interpret the Vedic illustration "Yajñena Yajñam ayajanta devāḥ", etc., as referring to dharma. Dharma, being a lasting attribute of the soul, is capable of producing an effect even after a lapse of long time. In fine, dharma which is a potentiality is a durable attribute of the soul, encased in a human body. This attribute may easily produce an affect in the future. Hence, the Vedas do not tell a lie when they prescribe Citrā sacrifice which does not produce an instantaneous effect.

In a Vedic sentence we find a reference to the institutor of a sacrifice, armed with the sacrificial implements. The truth of this sentence is contradicted by perception since the body of this person is reduced to ashes. Such a charge against the truth of the sentence in question is baseless. The demonstrative pronoun 'this' refers to the soul to which the identity with the body has been attributed.

The soul may go to heaven since the verb 'to go' has been used in a secondary sense. 'To go' conveys the meaning of enjoying. It is quite possible for the soul to enjoy heavenly bliss. When we say that the soul is born or that it is dead we use these sentences in a secondary sense. We purport to convey that the soul has been united with a body or that the soul has been separated from a body. Similarly, when we state that the soul goes to heaven we mean to say that the soul enjoys heavenly bliss. As the soul is all-pervasive so it has no motion. The soul is an agent because consciousness, conation and volition inhere in it. Its agency is not determined by its activity. We shall discuss this point later on. When we say that the institutor of a sacrifice is armed with sacrificial implements we purport to convey that he possesses them. The relation of ownership subsists between him and the implements in question. We should not think that these implements are conjoined to the soul since all souls, being all-pervasive, are conjoined to them. In that case these would have no distinction to mark off the soul in question from the rest. Therefore it will be better for us to suppose that the relation of ownership holds between the soul and the implements in question. Though the souls are all-pervasive yet the particular soul will be distinguished from all other souls since none but the soul in question possesses the above implements. It is adequately proved that the relation of ownership subsists between the soul and the above implements.

In fine, the charges of falsehood, etc., levelled against the Vedas, are baseless.

The Vedas are immune from inner contradiction, etc.

It has been pointed out that the Vedic injunction concerning the time of pouring libation to fire suffers from inner contradiction. The three different hours of such offerings have been prescribed with regard to the three different acts of pouring libation. One has got to select the hour of pouring libation. He should never transgress the hour once selected by him.

If one selects any one of these three hours and dishonours his selection by violating it then he becomes an object of censure. Thus injunctions and prohibitions are not contradictory as their spheres of application are wide apart.

When the repetition of the Vedic mantras is necessary, being due to significant regulation it does not amount to the defect of tautology since the Vedic mantras are not repeated for nothing out of caprice. The Vedas distinctly declare that the number of kindling verses (sâmidhenī) should be fifteen. The mantra "I strike the enemy who hates us and whom we hate in return with this thunderbolt, having fifteen sharp edges" has been given in the Vedas. In this context there are only eleven kindling verses given in the Vedic text. We cannot get the number fifteen if we do not repeat the verse. The mantras must be repeated. But there is no definite ruling in this matter. The absence of a rule will surely lead to a chaos. In order to bring the situation under law and order, a restriction is imposed upon the repetition of mantras. The rule of repetition runs thus : The first and the last mantras should be read out thrice. Hence as the repetition in question has got a definite purpose to serve so it does not suffer from the defect of tautology.

If the repetition of a mantra is fruitless then it will be open to the charge of tautology. But in the present context the repetition of mantras is not fruitless. Hence the charges of inner-contradiction, falsehood, repetition, etc. do not detract from the absolute validity of the Vedas.

The sage Gautama, being determined to vindicate the validity of the Vedas, discusses the meaning of the Vedic sentences in his own work since he thinks that such a discussion is a means to the justification of the validity of the Vedas.

An objection to the validity of the Vedas since they contain arthavādas (praises, condemnations, mythological stories, etc.)

The objectors continue their negative criticism thus : Though you are adept in the art of logic yet you have not been able even today to remove all the defects to which the Vedas are exposed.

Let us reaffirm defects which belong to the Vedas. He wept. As he wept so he acquired the epithet 'Rudra'. The lord of all beings heated his own fat. Then he poured libation of the same into fire. But a goat came up as a result of this deed. Gods became confused when they had come to know about divine worship. Are these arthavādas literally true ? Or, do they advise us to discharge some duty ? Or do they play the part of a means to an end which has been referred to by the Vedic injunctions containing verbs in the subjunctive mood ? In any case, they are encircled by inconsistencies on all sides. If one holds that arthavādas contain a record of events which happened then such a statement is contradicted by other proofs. Thus the Vedas cannot save themselves from the charge of untruth as they contain such matters as are contradicted. There is no proof in support of the correctness of statements about weeping, the heating of fat, confusion, etc.

Moreover, the artha-vādas such as the inner organ is prone to theft, everybody tells a lie, etc., inform us of such matters as are contradicted by other proofs. It is a truism that everyday does not naturally tell a lie and that the inner organ of everybody is not prone to theft.

Moreover, smoke has been seen during the day as rising from fire but the brightness of fire has not been seen. For this reason the brightness of fire is seen at night but not smoke. This is another instance of arthavāda the subject-matter of which is contradicted by perception since the above two objects are perceived when they come in contact with the sense organ.

Let us cite another instance of arthavāda the content of which is contradicted by perception. It states "We do not know whether we are Brāhmaṇas or not". When we perceive a man we recognise him to be a Brāhmaṇa provided that this act of perception is strengthened by proper instruction. Some arthavādas also come in conflict with the scriptures. Let us illustrate our point. Who knows what exists or does not exist in the next world. The Śāstras instruct that heavenly bliss results from the performance of Jyotiṣṭoma sacrifice and so on. Is this result impossible in the next world ?

Let another instance of arthavāda be cited. This sentence makes an assertion about the Trirātra-Brāhmaṇa seen by Garga. The face of a person who knows this Brāhmaṇa looks very beautiful. But nobody's face looks more beautiful if he knows the Brāhmaṇa. The truth of the arthavāda in question is contradicted by perception.

There is also an arthavāda which indicates the futility of some other Vedic rites. The text of the arthavāda is as follows : One fulfils all his desires if he pours final libation into fire. He who performs the Paśu-bandha sacrifice conquers all the worlds. He who performs the horse sacrifice conquers death, gets rid of all sins and of the sin which arises from the killing of Brāhmaṇa. He who is acquainted with the text dealing with the horse-sacrifice gets all these benefits. If the pouring of final libation alone is sufficient to fulfil all desire, if the conquest of all worlds is only possible through the performance of the Paśu-bandha sacrifice and if the knowledge of the text dealing with the horse-sacrifice confers on us the full benefit of the performance of the horse sacrifice then what for are these instructions regarding the performance of the other Vedic rites ? The Vedic rites which have been instructed in the Vedas should sink into insignificance though one is to take a lot of cares and troubles to perform them since the same results are obtained by means of the other easier methods.

Let another example of arthavāda be cited. Fire should be kindled neither on earth nor in the mid region nor in the sky. The kindling of fire has been prohibited in a roundabout way. It is impossible to kindle fire either in the mid-region or in the sky. Is the denial of kindling fire in either places significant ? The sentence which purports to prohibit the kindling of fire on earth should be taken as the universal prohibition of the kindling of fire since the kindling of fire is only possible on earth.

Let another illustration of arthavāda be quoted. The institutor of a sacrifice is (the kuśa grass strewn over a sacrificial altar) and the sacrificial post is the sun. How can we accept the truth of such a sentence ? Sentences like this directly refer to such things as are contradicted by our perception. The performer of a Vedic rite cannot be the kusa grass and the sacrificial post cannot be the sun. (The performer of a sacrifice is a man but not grass. We learn this from our perception. The sacrificial post is a log of wood but not the sun. We gather this from perception). Therefore such sentences are not literally true. We cannot prove them to be so.

Now the defender of the truth of arthavādas may suggest that these arthavādas oblige us to do something. Such a suggestion is not logically sound since the acts which are indicated by the arthavāda are not practicable. He (the lord of gods) wept. As he wept so he acquired the epithet 'Rudra' from the weeping. Now let us assume an act which may be indicated by this sentence. If we are to assume we should assume like this : So goes the story that Rudra wept. Other persons should also weep following his example. But we cannot entertain such a suggestion. Weeping means the shedding of tears arising from sorrow due to the separation from dear and near ones. One cannot weep because the Śāstras instruct him to do so. The lord of all creatures heated his own omentum and poured it into fire. So should other persons follow his example, heat their omentum and pour it into fire. Such an act is impracticable. Who can pour his own omentum into fire after having heated it ? If this act is done after whose performance would a goat immediately go up to the sky ? Gods were bewildered. Therefore others should be bewildered. Such an instruction cannot be worked out. Nobody can create his own state of bewilderment at the instance of the Śāstras. We cannot frame injunctions from these artha-vādas. Therefore, the second alternative suggestion is not sound.

Now, a third alternative suggestion has been forwarded that the implied meanings of arthavādas are means to a principal act which has been expressed by a distinct injunction. The third suggestion is not also possible since it is not easily possible for something to be a means to an obligatory act. An Arthavāda may act as an accessory to an injunction if it prescribes or to gods having bearing upon the main obligatory action. Let us cite an instance in order to clarify the point in question. There is an injunction, viz., "One should perform the Agnihotra sacrifice". There are other injunctions, viz., "One should pour the libation of sour milk into fire", "One should pour the libation of milk into fire", etc. These injunctions are called 'viniyogas' (A viniyoga is such an injunction as enjoins the means to an obligatory action). The latter injunctions supply us with articles which are required for the performance of Agnihotra sacrifice. Thus these injunctions become subsidiary ones whereas the principal one is that which enjoins the Agnihotra sacrifice. There are other injunctions, viz., "One should offer offerings in the evening to the lord of all beings and to the god of fire. These injunctions reveal the nature of gods to whom an offering is to be made. Thus they become subsidiary to the injunction which prescribes the Agnihotra sacrifice. This service cannot be rendered by arthavādas. The arthavādas in question do not prescribe minor acts which directly or indirectly feed the main act. The minor duties have been enjoined by the following injunctions, viz., "One should pound Brīhis", "One should sprinkle water on Brīhis", etc. Thus we see that the arthavādas in question render no help to any injunction.

Now the defenders of the truth of arthavādas may contend that arthavādas are helpful to injunctions since they induce the intelligent persons to perform obligatory duties and encourage them. Such a contention is not tenable. Some good selves hold that our implicit confidence in the eternality of the Vedas encourages one to undertake an obligatory act prescribed by the Vedas. But the Naiyāyikas assert that as a person has unflinching reverence for the author of the Vedas so he feels encouraged to take up a Vedic action but he feels no necessity of being induced for this purpose. If a person does not move to do on hearing the injunction that one who longs for such and such results should perform such and such acts then he will never budge an inch though temptations are held before him in order to induce him to take up the above actions. This is the shortcut criticism of the truth of arthavādas. The above three hypotheses fail to establish that the words which constitute the arthavādas have no self-consistence. Therefore as the arthavādas which constitute a portion of the Vedas are contradicted so the whole of the Vedas is untrue.

Now the defenders of the truth of the Vedas may contend thus : The portion of the Vedas which is contradicted by the other sources of valid knowledge may be admitted to be false. But why do you apprehend that the whole of the Vedas is untrue ? The critics give a fit rejoinder and hold that as the arthavādas bear a resemblance to the other parts of the Vedas so we disbelieve the truth of the other parts of the Vedas. According to the Mīmāṁsakas the Vedas which do not contain arthavādas are not found out. Therefore, the Vedas, being intimately connected with arthavādas, are false. Let us discuss the problem of the point of view of the Naiyāyikas. If it is clearly grasped that God is not truthful in some cases then how can it be firmly believed that He is veracious in other cases ? Therefore, the net result is that the Vedas as a whole come under untrue knowledge.

A reply to the objection against the veracity of the Vedas since they contain artha-vādas.

Our reply to the above objections is as follows. In the majority of cases artha-vādas are so syntactically connected with injunctions that they form a single sentence. A person who is desirous of prosperity should kill a white goat, standing in the south-west quarter. The god of the air is very speedy. The first of these two is an injunction. The second one is an artha-vāda. Though the sentence signifying praise does neither point to a Vedic rite to be performed nor anything relating to it yet it makes a statement about the injunction in question. Thus, it becomes a predicate of the injunction. The injunction and the artha-vāda construct a single sentence. The artha-vāda "Vāyur vai kṣepiṣṭha etc." purports to make an assertion of the sentence containing 'bhūti-kāmaḥ' as the last word. Why do these two sentences construct a single sentence ? The reason behind the supposition is this that words which constitute these two sentences imply mutual syntactical relation.

Now, a fresh question appears in our mind. By the sentence containing the word 'bhūti-kāmaḥ' as the last word a rite to be performed has been enjoyed. The learner has completely understood its meaning. There is no incompleteness from the syntactical point of view. Wherein lies the necessity of the other sentence, viz., 'Vāyur vai kṣepiṣṭha etc. ? Now it may be replied that the second sentence contains a praise of the rite communicated by the first sentence. In other words, what has been prescribed by the former sentence has been recommended by the latter one.

Now, a question re-appears in our mind. Is not the recommendation superfluous? It matters little whether praise is bestowed on the rite or not since the rite always remains the same but acquires no new character if it is recommended. Such an objection against the utility of an artha-vāda does not hold good. When words denoting praises are constructed with a sentence embodying an injunction to complete it such a complete sentence becomes significantly injunctive. If a sentence is simply used in the subjunctive mood, having no words of praise in it then does it not enjoin ? If no words of praise are found near about an injunctive sentence then a sentence in the subjunctive mood surely enjoins. But, on the contrary, if there are words of praise found near about an injunction then the sentence, expressing a command, shall contain the words of praise as its essential components, otherwise it shall not express a command since our experience teaches us to think so. If words expressing praise are syntactically connected with a sentence denoting a command then we are to see according to the grammatical rule whether there is a split in the sentence. In obedience to the rule we hold that these words denoting praise and the words which constitute an injunctive sentence are put together to express a complete idea. Our experience records its evidence in favour of such construction. If words which constitute a sentence express no correlative meaning then such a sentence should be given up or it should be split up into two or more sentences. Therefore, words denoting praise are not superfluous.

Now, another fresh question appears in our mind. It runs thus : If injunctions disunited with praise are competent enough to prescribe rites, why are praises attached to injunction?

Our answer to this question is this. According to the Mīmāṁsakas, the Vedas are not to be taken to task. According to us God is above all reproaches. When the Vedas are recited to us we understand them but we do not compose them. For the better understanding of injunctions the function of the artha-vādas has been pointed out. It is a truism that artha-vādas are not means to a Vedic rite like minor injunctions which prescribe accessories such as articles of worship, gods and other minor details which contribute towards the completion of a principal rite. Still nobody can prevent them from their efficacy in revealing the significance of such injunctions. Thus, they help us to maintain the veracity of the Vedas but do not throw light on the subject-matter of the Vedas. When the performers of sacrifices listen to bare injunctions they find little interest in them. Hearing such injunctions the spirit of prospective sacrificers for whom they are meant droops down. But on hearing the artha-vādas which contain the praise of these acts the sinking spirit is cheered up. One should perform the sacrifice 'Sarvajit'. It is a simple injunction—not associated with an artha-vāda. When we hear it do we feel much regard for it? But when we hear the associated artha-vādas such as 'Gods performed the Sarvajit sacrifice in order to win all objects and to conquer all. Every body who performs it conquers all' we cherish much regard for the rite in question. This law also holds good in worldly transaction. If persons listen to the injunction: 'This cow should be purchased' then are they induced to purchase the cow? But if they hear at the same time the praises of the cow, viz., 'This cow gives much milk. Her milk is substantial. She is very noble. She has a calf. All her calves are living etc.' then they are tempted to purchase her. If one simply asks his own experience, he will understand the efficacy of praises, i.e., artha-vādas. For this reason, some jurists assume artha-vādas where there are injunctions, i.e., injunctions not associated with artha-vādas just as they in some cases guess injunctions from artha-vādas. It has been stated that an injunction and praises always co-exist as the latter ones have bearing upon the rite in question. This statement is based upon the sound practice of jurists. An injunction is inferred from an artha-vāda (i.e. a praise) if a syntactical relation is discerned between) a sentence containing praises and a sentence embodying a mandate. But no injunction is inferred from an artha-vāda if such relation between it (artha-vāda) and an iniunction is not known to us.

In the light of the above decision we shall not assume the injunction "One should weep" from the artha-vāda "He wept etc." The objector has unfairly made an adverse criticism. In this case the syntactical relation of the artha-vāda with another injunction has been directly suggested. There is an injunction "Silver should not be paid as sacrificial fees in Barhiṣ sacrifice." The subordinate position is occupied by the artha-vāda in question (i. e., "He wept" etc.) in the above paragraph. The full text runs thus : Rudra had wept. His tears which tickled down on the ground became silver. He who pays silver in Barhiṣ sacrifice will experience a sad scene of weeping in his house within a year. Hence, silver should not be paid in Barhiṣ sacrifice. There runs the injunction that one should slay a big sheep, placing it in proper place, in honour of the lord of all beings. Its remaining portion is that the lord of all beings let out his own fat. In order to exhibit the excellence of the libation of fat, it has been stated that as soon as the libation of fat had been poured into fire the goat went up in the sky. It is merely a praise. The sun is rice, boiled in milk, known as 'Prāyaṇīya'. There is an injunction concerning 'Prāyaṇīya'. Its concluding portion is that gods were perplexed to find out the sacrificial ground and their obscurity was removed by the above-mentioned milk-boiled rice just as the sun, rising up, removes the bewilderment of persons. Thus, in all cases, the sentences containing artha-vāda (praise etc.) are to be taken as the concluding portions of injunctions.

Why do you say that the incidents referred to by artha-vādas are not true? The incidents are that silver sprang up from the tears of Rudra and that a goat went up in the sky when the sacrificial altar had been bright on the pouring of Prajāpati's own fat into it. Our reply to the charge of falsehood is that the artha-vādas are not false.

The deep meaning of these sentences (artha-vādas) is true since the literal meaning of these sentences has not been purported to be conveyed here. An artha-vāda simply suggests that some work should be done or that some work should be avoided. These two meanings of artha-vādas will be clear to us if we reconsider their significance. It should also be noted that when we know some incidents we feel fascination for or hatred against some works but the knowledge of these incidents does neither propel not repel us. Therefore; such knowledge should be disregarded as it becomes insignificant, having no useful purpose to serve. Love and hatred are the two motive forces which stir up a person. They are really signified by artha-vādas. For this reason when a person takes the meaning of an artha to his heart, he either moves to do something if he feels fascination for it or refrains from doing it if he feels hatred against it. Therefore, artha-vādas are truly significant.

Rudra did not weep. Why do you tell the story of his weeping. The story is allegorical. It purports to convey a meaning through a metaphor. It relates an attribute. The attribute of silver bears a resemblance to that of tears since both of them are white. Silver is as impure as tears since silver is supposed to be an effect of weeping . The possession of the same quality suggests the causal relation subsisting between them. Thus the story has been introduced in order to condemn the use of silver in the said sacrifice. Similarly, in a sacrifice which requires animal-slaughter the libation of fat has been recommended. In order to make this recommendation strong the story that the lord of all beings has heated his own fat to pour libation into fire has to be interpreted. In order to praise rice, boiled in milk, called the sun, the story that gods, having taken their seat in the sacrificial altar, were bewildered, has been narrated.

But the Naiyāyikas told that as the powers of God are infinite so there will be no absurdity if it is believed that the story is literally true. We may believe that silver sprang up from the tears of Rudra, the lord of all beings heated his own fat, a goat went up after the libation of fat, and gods were bewildered when they had taken their seats on the sacrificial altar. If these stories are true, is there any harm? By all means the artha-vādas in question are true.

The statement that the inner organ is a thief and the organ of speech is a liar refers to the functions of these organs. As the inner organ conceals its own nature so it is called a thief. As the organ of speech indulges in exaggeration so it is called a liar.

Smoke emanating from fire has been noticed during the day but not the flame of fire. The flame of fire is seen at night but not its smoke. The artha-vāda sentence purports to convey a special meaning. The smoke, being voluminous, is seen from a distance but the flame, being slender, is not perceived. The flame of fire increases in volume at night. So it is perceived from a distance. Smoke, being covered by darkness, is not seen at night. This statement has been made to serve a special purpose in the evening and to praise the sacrificial fire in the morning.

The artha-vāda sentence "We do not know whether we are Brahmins or not" apparently reveals a doubt about one's Brahmanhood in order to praise the act of purifying one's lineage with the utterance of mantras. (This act is so edifying that it makes the attainment of Brahmanhood doubly sure). The act of consecrating one's lineage with the utterance of incantations is so meritorious that even a non-Brahmin becomes a Brahmin if he observes it. Another artha-vāda sentence "Who knows whether the effect will happen in the next world or not" purports to eulogise in act the result of which is tangible.

The artha-vāda sentence "The face of one who knows it shines" embodies the praise of learning. The face of a teacher shines when it is looked at by the admiring students. In another sentence that he gets all the objects longed for the word 'all' does not denote all the objects in the universe without any restriction. It should be interpreted with reference to the universe of discourse. It signifies all covetable objects appended in the list of the effects of the Aśvamedha-sacrifice. The statement that he who reads the text of the Aśvamedha-sacrifice gets the same reward simply glorifies the said sacrifice.

One should kindle fire at a spot having placed gold beneath it. In order to recommend this act the kindling of fire in the sky or in the mid region or on Earth has been prohibited. One should not kindle fire at a spot where gold has not been kept inside. The injunction does not mean to say that fire should not be kindled on Earth.

The statement that the sacrificial post is the sun purports to convey that the sacrificial post, painted with bright colours and anointed with clarified butter, looks like the sun because a ceremony has been stated to be performed, viz., the Kuśa grasses should be spread over the sacrificial altar in its honour since the contribution of both of them towards the completion of the sacrifise is of equal importance. People do not always use words in the primary sense. They also employ words in the secondary sense. Our experience testifies to such usages. In the Vedic literature the words will also be similarly used. Thus, with regard to Vedic rites if one worships the household fire reciting the ṛks, sung in honour of Indra then he commits no violation of rule. Thus, artha-vādas which embody either recommendation or condemnation are the source of valid knowledge since they are syntactically combined with the corresponding injunctions to form a single unit. Similarly artha-vādas which narrate the Vedic rites differently performed by the different persons and record the mythological stories are to be similarly combined with the corresponding injunctions.

In some cases, gaps of injunctions are filled up by an artha-vāda. Thus they (artha-vādas) not only help the better understanding of injunctions but also supplement the observance of Vedic rites. Let us give an illustration. Those who sit the whole night acquire distinction. But the performance of a sacrifice at night has not been prescribed by the injunction in question. We learn it from the artha-vāda attached to it. We learn only from an artha-vāda that person is entitled to perform a sacrifice at night. Jaimini in his Mīmāṁsā sūtra (phalamatraiva nirdeśāt) has also said to the effect. The sūtra expresses this idea that if an injunction does not enjoin an action and the artha-vāda, associated with it prescribes an action then the action should be duly performed since an artha-vāda supplements an injunction. Those who seek after name and fame should perform a particular sacrifice at night. We grasp the sense of the complete injunction only through the medium of the said artha-vāda.

When a doubt arises in our mind about the meaning of an injunction the doubt is solved by the accompanying artha-vāda which supplements it (the injunction in question). The injunction is that one should make an offering of sand anointed with oily substance. Is it clarified butter or oil or fat ? When a doubt spreads over our mind the artha-vāda which is associated with the above injunction comes to our rescue. It helps us to solve the doubt. It says that clarified butter is a luminous substance. From it we learn that one should offer sand anointed with clarified butter.

The sentences which contain praise or censure become the source of valid knowledge as they, being combined with injunctions, become units of thought. In some cases, they produce valid knowledge. And in some other cases, they inform us of some duties.

The Naiyāyikas have declared the super-power of God. The incidents which have been narrated in the artha-vāda section of the Vedas are true. This section does not suffer from an exaggeration of facts. In other words, what the artha-vāda section says is literally true. Therefore, the artha-vādas do not depart from the path of truth. (The word 'varma' is a misprint. It should be vartma).

The literal truth of artha-vādas cannot be logically maintained in all cases. The sentences, e.g., "The sacrificial post is the sun" etc. are not literally true. The primary meaning of such sentences should not be insisted upon. The secondary meaning of these sentences should be taken into consideration. If they are thus interpreted then there is no scope of inconsistency.

An objection to the Validity of Mantras

Mantras are now examined in detail. Do mantras assist injunctions by revealing their meaning ? Or, do they render service to injunctions by their mere recital ? If we consider the case of mantras from these two points of view, the validity of mantras remains the same. If this be the case then what is the use of such discussion ? This system of logic does not undertake the task of interpreting the Vedas. The task of establishing the validity of the Vedas has been exclusively embraced by it. In that case, the proposed discussion is fruitless. The objection is not baseless. But if mantras do not purport to convey any meaning, they cease to be the source of valid knowledge as no meaning is made out of them. In that case the truth of the Brāhmaṇa portion of the Vedas is not substantiated since it loses all its significance, being an ally of mantras. If the above hypothesis is accepted then the Vedas become deprived of their utility of revealing rites. One may contend that a sentence which produces doubtful or erroneous knowledge is a source of untrue knowledge. Such a contention is not tenable since the sentence which conveys no sense is also a source of false knowledge.

Those who hold that mantras have no meaning defend their position in the following manner. When a Vedic rite is performed the meaning of all mantras which are recited at the time of its performance is not considered to be helpful since instructions have been given only to recite the mantras but not to remember their meaning. One recites the mantra "uru prathasva" and expands a sacrificial cake. If the mantra were helpful to the expansion of the said cake by conveying its meaning then why has the reciter of this mantra been instructed as an accessory to the expansion of the cake ? If a person, having a pair of eyes, moves only when he is led by another person then it is clearly understood that he cannot see with his eyes. As in this case the statement that he cannot see is unnecessary so in the above case the recitation of mantra would not have been useless if its meaning is essential. A priest recites the mantra 'Agnīdagnīn vihara' and carries fire from one place to another. The mantra requires no explanation. A mantra renders its assistance to a Vedic rite only by its recitation. Some service which it renders by its recitation is not seen. Still it is assumed. The order of words which is noticed in a sentence cannot be altered. So it is suggested that mantras should not convey their meanings where they are applied. When a person recites a mantra he does not change the order of words which constitute it. If a mantra renders its service by conveying its meaning then the maintenance of the order of the constituent words of a mantra will become futile since if we recite a mantra violating the order of the constituent words then there will be difficulty in understanding its meaning.

The mantras do not purport to convey any meaning since it is seen that some mantras absolutely fail to convey their meanings. Let us illustrate a few such mantras. The first of them is this 'Catvāri śṛṅgā trayo asya pādā dve śīrṣe sapta hastāso asya. Tridhā baddho vṛṣabho roravīti maho devo martyān ā viveśa'. If this mantra is significant then an animal which has four horns, three feet, two heads and seven hands should be referred to by it. But there is no such animal in this world as is required for the sacrifice in question. Therefore, the mantra conveys no meaning. The second illustration also points to the conclusion that mantras purport to convey no meaning since an inanimate object is commanded to behave like an animate object. The mantra runs thus :—'Auṣadhe trāyasva enam (Oh medicine protect this person.)' But medicine does not understand that it has been employed to protect him. Another example is this :—'Hear, Oh slabs of stone !' (Śṛṇota grāvāṇaḥ). This meaning is absurd since unconscious slabs of stone are never employed to listen to something. Moreover, the mantra 'Aditir dyaurantarīkṣam' (Aditi is the sky, she is the mịd region)'. Similar mantras are full of contradictions. How can Aditi who is the sky be the mid-region? There are some mantras the meaning of which is not at all intelligible. How can these mantras render some service to a rite by communicating their meaning? The mantras which convey no meaning are as follows:

(1) 'Amyaksāta Indra ṛṣṭiriti'
(2) 'Śṛṇyeva jarpharī turpharītu'
(3) 'Indraḥ Somasya Karaketi ca'

Moreover, mantras do not purport to convey any meaning since they have one of the two ends to realise, viz., (1) to produce merits or (2) to convey a meaning. If words are not uttered, they cannot convey their meaning. Thus the recital of mantras, being obligatory, renders its assistance to the completion of a sacrifice. Therefore it should not be assumed that sole purpose of the recitation of a mantra is to convey its meaning.

Establishing the hypothesis that mantras are valid we shall now refute the above hypothesis that mantras have no meaning. Do mantras convey no meaning? Or do they convey their meaning without being restrained by any condition? Or, is it your point that their meaning is not intended to be conveyed like the number 'one' of a sacrificial cup though the communication of their meaning is governed by a set of conditions? It is not sound to hold that they (mantras) convey no meaning since when persons who are adept in the meaning of words hear the mantra 'Barhir deva sadanaṁ dāmi (I cut the kuśa-grass, the seat of gods)' they understand its meaning. Their own experience bears witness to such understanding. In other words, if they ask their own consciousness, they will find an answer in the affirmative. One cannot hold that the meaning of a mantra is unconditionally grasped. As the constituent words determine the meaning of a sentence constituted by then in classical Sanskrit Language so words determine the meaning of a sentence in Vedic Language. It is not a truism that their meaning is not learnt since words which are used in classical Sanskrit Language are also used in Vedic Language. These words denote the same meaning. It is highly probable that the meaning of words is learnt from verbal transactions. Now though mantras may communicate their meaning yet it is not possible to hold that they do not purport to convey their meaning like the number one of a sacrificial cup since there is no reason behind the said non-intention. There is a Vedic sentence which refers to a sacrificial cup. There are other sentences which clearly determine their number. In a Soma sacrifice soma juice is divided into many shares and is proportionately deposited on the different cups since it is the recognised duty to place offerings on such cups. All cups uniformly contain such juice. When a mantra says 'Pour soma-juice into a cup', it does not purport to convey the singleness of the cup. It purports to convey the case-ending of the cup but not its number since the number has no significance. Let us now turn our attention to the mantra already referred to. The mantra "Barhir deva sadanaṁ dāmi" throws light on such articles as are required for a sacrifice. These articles must get the sanction of an injunction. So they have been previously known to us. A man refreshes our memory and helps to remember the essential articles. Thus, when we perform a rite with the aid of mantras it does some good to us. Therefore, one cannot hold that mantras do not purport to reveal articles which are essentially required for a sacrifice. Therefore, it is not fair to state that mantras should only be recited but their sense should not be grasped. There are some mantras which are only muttered. Among these mantras the Pavamānī is included. There is an injunction with regard to it that it should be muttered. The injunction prescribes only muttering. So the knowledge of the meaning of this mantra is not required. When can it be done? But if the injunction 'One should mutter' is conspicuous by its absence then we cannot disregard the meaning of a mantra which is being presented to our consciousness and is being needed for the performance of a rite.

Now, the objectors may contend that if on the strength of the injunction 'One should mutter' it is held that a particular mantra, dedicated to Viṣṇu, does not purport to convey any meaning then on the strength of the injunction 'The Vedas should be read' it may be as well pointed out that one is only to get the Vedas by heart but not to grasp their meaning the learning of which has not been emphasised. This point has been elaborately discussed in the other works on philosophy. But if we re-open the problem and discuss it in a detailed manner then we shall expose ourselves to the charge of garrulity since we overdo a minor issue. We shall not make a mountain of molehills.

It has been stated that if the very recital of a mantra is conducive to an end then its meaning is not to be insisted upon. In this connection we point out that we indirectly know from its sense that the mantra 'uru prathasva' is conducive to the expansion of a sacrificial cake. If this be the case then the injunction which reveals its conduciveness should be superfluous since it says over again what has been known. The sense which follows from a mantra and is grasped by us cannot be set aside. Now, the problem is : 'Is the mantra superfluous?' No, it is not superfluous. But it is iterative. Or, the above mantra is not an injunction. But it is an artha-vāda. In other words, it has a secondary meaning. The act of expansion augments the prosperity of the institutor of a sacrifice. It increases his children and animals and thereby augments his prosperity. In some cases, the instrumentality of mantras has been enjoined e. g., when one is to handle a sacrificial ladle he is to recite four mantras. Similarly, the instrumentality of mantras is to be noticed in the mantras 'Agnīda agnīn vihara' etc. (From āhavanīya fire some portion is carried off to establish gārhapatya fire).

It has been said that the recital of mantras is efficacious

but not its sense; the order of words in a mantra admits of no change of place. This statement does not stand to reasoning. The Mīmāṁsakas hold that the Vedas are eternal. Hence, the order of words in a mantra is unalterable. Kumārila has said that the order of words in a mantra is unalterable. Kumārila has said that if the order of words is changed then objections arise from many points of view. We, the Naiyāyikas, hold that God is the author of the Vedas. Have the students of the Vedas the liberty to change the place of words? Our conclusion on this point is this that the order of words in a mantra cannot be changed for the expression of a particular meaning intended by a person like the order of sentences in a Brāhmaṇa work.

An imaginary meaning of the mantra 'Catvāri Śṛṅgā etc.' has been apprehended. Such an apprehension is based upon sheer ignorance. It praises the act of sacrifice. It has a secondary meaning. The clause 'Catvāri Śṛṅgā' points to the four Vedas. The clause 'Trayo' asya pādāḥ' indicates the three acts of pressing the soma juice. The clause 'Dve Śīrṣe' suggests the husband and the wife who perform a sacrifice. 'Sapta hastāsaḥ' refers to seven metres. The phrase 'Tridhā baddho' implies that the procedure of a sacrifice is recorded in Mantra, Brāhmaṇa and Kalpasūtra. The predicate 'Vṛṣabha' signifies that a sacrifice fulfils all desires. The verb 'roravīti produces an impression that a sacrifice resounds with the chanting of stotras and the recitation of Śāstras.

The clause 'Maho devo martyān ā viveśa' suggests that the act of sacrifice is the best of all duties and has become current on this earth. The implication of the whole sentence is the praise of a sacrifice as we praise a river when we say that she has her breasts in the shape of a pair of curlews, rows of teeth in the shape of swans, a tuft of hair in the shape of moss and her cloth in the shape of kāśa flowers.

As a conscious being is ordered so an unconscious being has been ordered by the command 'Oh, medicine ! protect this person'. This command is means for the Praise of medicine. The sentence 'Śṛṇota grāvāṇaḥ', is an eulogy of prātar anuvāka. It is a miraculous act by the influence of which slabs of stone can even hear. The sentence 'Aditir Dyauḥ Aditir antarīkṣam' is metaphorical. Hence it involves no contradiction. There is a similar usage in our popular language, viz., 'You alone are my mother, you alone are my father, you alone are my sister and you alone are my brother.'

It has been stated that the meaning of some mantras remains unintelligible to us. An answer to this objection is that a reader is to blame. There are various ways and means of understanding the meaning of the Vedas. In spite of them if a person fails to make out the meaning of the Vedas then he does not make a serious attempt at the proper understanding of such meaning owing to idleness. Therefore, the Vedas should not be taken to task for this failure to understand. We may make out the meaning of the Vedas by the same method as we adopt to understand the meaning of the sentences of Brāhmaṇas. The first and foremost method is the usage of the experienced persons since the same words are used in Vedic and classical languages and they convey the same sense. The words which are found in classical Sanskrit Language are found in Vedic Sanskrit Language. These words have the same meaning.

Let us take a few illustrations to bring home our point. The Vedic sentence "Agnir vṛtrāṇi jaṅghaṇat" (fire dispelled darkness). But in the Vedic sentence the word 'Agni' contains cerebral 'ṇa' but in classical language the word 'Agni' has dental 'na'. Let us illustrate another Vedic sentence "Uttamā vai devagāvo vahanti" (The divine cows carry the piece of wood by which fire is kindled). Let us illustrate another Vedic sentence 'vanaspate hiraṇyavarṇa pradivaste artham" (Oh gold coloured lord of trees ! I receive from you the objects longed for by me). With regard to the above illustration some apprehend that words which have been used in Vedic sentence are different from the similar words found in classical Sanskrit language and that they do not convey the same meaning. In the face of this misapprehension if we examine these words with close attention then we recognise them to be the same. But we admit that slight changes are only noticed in the Vedic words. These words denote the identical meaning which they convey in classical language. These words admit of the same derivation. As they are derived in classical language so they are derived in Vedic language. Generally, the popular meaning of a Vedic word is accepted. But when the popular meaning of a word comes into conflict with that of it, determined by the scholars, the latter meaning is accepted as an authoritative one. In the Vedic sentences, viz., (1) 'yavamayaścaruḥ', (2) "Vārāhī upānahau" and (3) "Vaitase kaṭe Prājāpatyaṁ sañcinoti" the words 'yava', 'varāha' and 'vetasa' respectively stand for barley, a boar and cane in accordance with convention of the cultured scholars. They do not respectively signify Priyaṅgu, a black vulture and a black-berry. If there is no such convention to ascertain the meaning of a few words then we resort to the convention of the Mlecchas (those who speak in non-Sanskritic language in order to communicate their ideas). These words are 'pika', 'nema', 'Tāmarasa'.

If the convention of the Mlecchas is not available then we should find out the signification of a word from the original root with the aid of Nigama, Nirukta and Vyākaraṇa. The two words 'jarpharī' and 'turpharī' are in dual number. They have been used in the hymn, dedicated to the twin gods 'Aśvins'. With reference to the context their etymological meaning is not hard to find out. They signify the sources of preservation and destruction respectively. Thus they are names of Aśvins. In this way we should explain other difficult words. For this reason, we should not stick to the idea that mantras do not purport to convey a sense.

Mantras, revealing their senses, render assistance to a sacrificial rite. But they do not help a rite by their mere recitation like the muttering of a mantra. Thus mantras do not independently render service to a rite. But the validity of the Vedas, the ocean of nectar in the shape of human ends, cannot be detracted on that ground.

An objection to the validity of the Vedas as they contain names of rites

We now refer to a few Vedic sentences, viz., (1) 'One should perform udbhid (that which comes into being) sacrifice', (2) 'One who desires animals should perform Citra-sacrifice', (3) 'One who longs for heaven should perform Agnihotra sacrifice', (4) 'One who seeks to kill his enemy should perform Śyena sacrifice' and (5) 'One who aspires after the celestial kingdom should perform Vājapeya sacrifice'. Do these sentences prescribe means by which sacrifices are performed? Do Udbhid, Citrā, Agnihotra, Śyena and Vājapeya constitute the means to an end, viz., sacrifice? Or are these terms proper names of a few sacrifices? What is the necessity of this scrutiny? If it is held that these terms serve both the purposes then the validity of the Vedic sentences will be called in question. For this reason a thorough examination into the character of these sentences is necessary. If you hold that these sentences prescribe means with words 'Udbhidā' (that which comes into existence), etc. like the other sentences, viz., 'One should perform a sacrifice with corns' 'One should perform a sacrifice with the libation of sour-milk', etc. Do they inform us of a few specific articles by which sacrifices are to be performed? If this suggestion is accepted then there should be other Vedic sentences which will prescribe the very act of sacrifice — the end. If the act of sacrifice, i.e., the end, is not known then there is no scope for the prescription of means. The injunctions, viz., (1) "the offering of sacrifice unto Fire should be made with eight pot-sherds" and "One should perform Agnihotra sacrifice" are distinct ones which throw light on the act of sacrifice, i. e., the end. When the end is revealed to us the means are communicated to us by means of other subsidiary injunctions, viz., (1) 'One should perform the sacrifice with corns' and (2) 'One should perform the sacrifice with the libation of sour milk'.

Now, a question arises, viz., 'Why do you look out for different sentences as principal or subordinate injunctions?' Let us suggest that the single sentence 'One who aspires after heavenly kingdom should perform Vājapeya sacrifice' prescribes a sacrifice and at the same time demands that wine should constitute its means. Is this interpretation open to criticism? Yes, why is it not so? If you hold that the above sentence has two independent predicates then it cannot retain its unity. Then it should be split up into two independent sentences. One of them signifies that heavenly kingdom is to be attained by means of a sacrifice. The other one signifies that the sacrifice should be performed by means of wine (vājapeya).

The sentence, once uttered, cannot communicate the two senses suggested by our opponents.

Now, the two sentences, suggested by our opponents, contain the same verb 'Yajeta'. As the verb remains identical so it is syntactically connected with the two sentences. One who aspires after heavenly kingdom should perform a sacrifice and should do it by means of wine. In both sentences the verb remains the same. There will be no change in its character. Such a defence does not hold good. In these two sentences the verb which appears to be the same differs in essence. In the first sentence a sacrifice is enjoined because it is not at all known to us. In the second sentence a means to the sacrifice is prescribed because the sacrifice is already known to us since the prescription of a means is not at all possible if the act to be done is not known beforehand. The injunction which prescribes a means amounts to this that a sacrifice is to be done by such-and-such means. The sacrifice in question becomes the goal as it is known before. It is the substantive in the sentence. But in the sentence heavenly kingdom is attainable by a sacrifice. Heavenly kingdom is the goal. A sacrifice is a predicate. This predicate is not an accomplished fact. It is to be done. It occupies subordinate place in the sentence in question. Therefore, the sacrifice in question has contrary characters in the two sentences. The same verb cannot be syntactically connected with the two sentences. In that case it should be characterized by the irreconcilable contrary characters. He who aspires after heavenly kingdom should perform a sacrifice. In this sentence the predicate 'should perform a sacrifice' has a distinct meaning. He who should perform a sacrifice should do it with wine. In this second sentence the predicate of the first sentence is no more a predicate. It is an adjunct of the subject. So it has a distinct character of its own, (There is a gulf of difference fixed between these two characters.)

If we hold that the injunction 'One should perform a particular sacrifice with wine' prescribes only a means then the act of performing a particular sacrifice must have been learnt from another source. Therefore, the very act of performing a particular sacrifice, being already known, is not an object of valid knowledge since novelty is the criterion of knowledge. Therefore, an injunction prescribing only a means is not true. In order to avoid this defect of the said injunction the hypothesis that the above injunction prescribes the act bearing the title 'Vājapeya' is resorted to. If our opponent argues in this manner then the injunctions 'Udbhidā Yajeta', etc. become clearly superfluous. As soon as it is stated that one should perform a sacrifice, it is learnt that this act bears the title 'Vājapeya'. (As the injunctions referred to do not contain the names of sacrifices so they involve repetition and hence are superfluous). Now, as some sentences of the Vedas being superfluous, cease to be authentic so we do not continue our belief in the veracity of the other sentences of the Vedas. (The import of this topic is that the name of a sacrifice is not revealed by a Vedic injunction).

An answer to the objection that Vedic sentences relating names of sacrifices are not true

Our reply to the above problem is as follows : If it is held that the above injunction prescribed only a means then, of course, it suffers from the defect which has been pointed out by you. We think that those injunctions prescribe acts of sacrifice not known before and designate them. This alternate suggestion appears to us to be better. Let us prove the point in question. The root 'to sacrifice' (yaj) denotes a sacrifice. It is instrumental to the ultimate result, i. e., heavenly bliss. The term 'Vājapeya' is a case in apposition with sacrifice. Hence it takes the third case-ending. There are two types of instrumental cases, viz., (1) the pre-existing instrumental case and (2) the instrumental case which will come into being. In this case a sacrifice which is an instrumental case will come into being. When it comes into being it becomes instrumental to the result. Now, the instrumental case itself is an effect. It is produced. As it is a case in apposition with the meaning of a root so it takes the second case-ending in some cases. "Agnihotraṁ juhoti" is an instance of this type. In other words, an object itself, being effectuated, becomes instrumental to the ultimate result. When the character of being an effect is emphasised it takes the second case-ending. A verb in Sanskrit grammar contains two parts, viz., (1) a process and (2) a result. The result is as good as an object. We say 'cooks'. We may express it more explicitly, viz., 'He does cooking'. The root to cook included cooking in its meaning. It may be used as an objective case.

Now, a fresh question arises in our mind. As a means is prescribed by an injunction so the designation of a sacrifice should be enjoined since what has not been stated cannot be known. If this be the case then the injunction which furnishes us with designation of a sacrifice will be exposed to the same charges as are levelled against a guṇa vidhi (an injunction prescribing a means). Such a criticism is not sound. The Vedas do never state that this rite should have this designation. But we learn that this name applies to this rite because the name is significant, admitting of derivation. As this sacrifice helps us to gain animals so it is called Udbhid. A sacrifice which is performed in honour of Prajāpati (the lord of all beings) is called Prājāpatya. Various articles such as sour milk, honey, clarified butter, paddy and water, are instrumental to this sacrifice. As various articles are required for the completion of the Prājāpatya sacrifice so it is called 'Citrā'. The rite in which a libation is poured into fire in honour of Fire is called Agnihotra. As a hawk descends with a sweep and catches its prey so this sacrifice assists one to destroy his enemy. Hence from the above praise the sacrifice acquires the title of Śyena (a hawk). The word 'Vāja' means food or drink. The sacrifice which provides us with drink is called Vājapeya. Thus we arrive at the conclusion that the above words are nothing but proper names of sacrifices.

If these words constitute names of sacrifices then it is apprehended that they will be superfluous. But such an objection is not fair. Some distinguished scholars meet this objection with the remark that though the words 'Vājapeya' etc. are names of sacrifices yet they are significant since they reveal the names and the results of sacrifices. This act of sacrifice is designated by this name. From this designation we learn that a substance and a deity are its means. It is also learnt later on that the act is conducive to heaven. Hence, in some cases, names such as Vājapeya etc. denote sacrifices without violating the rules of the science of Vedic exegeses. Some Vedic injunctions furnish us with the names of sacrifices together with their means, viz., gods, articles etc. Let us cite a few examples. The first example is this "Āgneyo aṣṭakapālo āmāvāsyāyām paurṇamāsyām cācyuto bhavati iti". (The offering of food prepared on eight pot sherds to the god of fire on the days of the new moon and the full moon is fruitful.)

(Jayanta does not explicitly discuss the point in question. It requires an elaborate discussion. The word 'Āgneya' should be explained. Is it merely the name of a sacrifice like the word 'Agnihotra?' Or, does it signify something more? The word 'Agnihotra' does not indicate the deity to be honoured since there is a Vedic text in that section which supplies with the required deity. But in the Vedic sentence, quoted above, there is no such word as reveals the deity to be worshipped. Moreover, the taddhita suffix attached to the word 'Agni' indicates that Agni is the deity of this sacrifice. Hence, the above injunction supplies us with both the deity and the article to be offered and throws light on a sacrifice not known before along with its name 'Āgneya'.)

Let us now discuss the second example. It runs thus, Etasyaiva revatīṣu vāravantīyamagniṣṭomasāma kṛtvā paśukāmo hyetena yajeteti (one who is desirous of obtaining animals should sing a collection of Ṛgmantras containing the syllable 're' set to the tone of Vāravantīya, replacing agniṣṭoma, in honour of the god of fire).—Tāṇḍya mahā Brāhmaṇa).

(Jayanta does not discuss the point at issue. It should be elaborately discussed. The injunction in question throws light on a new act of sacrifice. This sacrifice is not Agnistut. The injunction also supplies us with the result of this sacrifice together with the means of performing it. The setting of the said ṛcas to the tune of Vāravantīya is the required means.)

We shall not enter into the elaborate discussion of the knotty points of the other branches of study. Our point is this that the truth of the Vedas is not challenged if the Vedas reveal the names of sacrifices. Therefore, by all means, the validity of the Vedas is established.

Jayanta says "I have elaborately discussed all these points in order to establish the veracity of the Vedas. At the same time I implore you all not to take it amiss. I do not do it out of my conceit of scholarship that I have been a sound scholar of the Mīmāṁsā literature.

The meaning of the Vedic words will be grasped if they denote only rites to be observed

The Vedic sentences which contain injunctions, praises or censures and mantras and reveal names of sacrifices have some utility as they point to rites to be performed. Our experience emboldens us to make the above remark. Therefore we should subscribe to the view that the Vedas are true only when they reveal some obligations. (This is the view of the Mīmāṁsakas).

Tne Naiyāyikas criticise this hypothesis thus :—Do the Vedas turn to be untrue if they signify already existing objects? On the strength of the above hypothesis will a large portion of the Vedic lore which points to such objects be set aside and neglected? The task before the logical treatise of the Nyāya school is to establish the truth of the Vedas *per se*. Some express their opinion in this matter that the truth of the Vedas lies in expressing rites to be performed. The logic behind this statement is as follows. When the meaning of a word is grasped a word communicates its meaning. The meaning of a word is learnt from the employment of words by an experienced man. An experienced person uses such sentences as refer to some acts to be performed. He says in the following manner : "Bring water. Fasten this cow with a cord. Go to a village". The boys who listen to these statements of the experienced person learn the meaning of the words from these mandatory sentences and their execution. The experienced persons employ such sentences with the definite purpose of relating an end. The statements about existing objects do neither persuade nor dissuade persons. Therefore, these sentences serve no purpose. Hence, these sentences are not worthy of being used. The words of which the meanings are not known cannot communicate their meanings. The words which fail to communicate their meanings are not true. Words which remain unrelated to a verb fail to convey any meaning. Therefore, we should use a sentence which contains a verb. A verb denotes an act to be performed. But proper and common nouns denoted such objects as do already exist. If a word which denotes an existing object and a word which signifies an act to be performed are uttered together then the former is employed to convey the meaning of the latter. Hence, a complete sentence purports to convey an act to be done. Therefore, a sentence is not valid if it conveys only an accomplished fact or a pre-existing substance as its meaning. A sentence is true if it points only to an act to be performed. A sentence which refers to an accomplished fact or a pre-existing object is not true. As an accomplished object is already known so it is capable of being known by some other valid forms of knowledge. If a sentence reveals such an object then it does not reveal an unknown object as it depends upon another source of knowledge for the knowledge of the object in question. In other words, its information is second-hand but not first-hand. Hence the piece of knowledge which discovers the object at first is valid. But the sentence which reveals it is not true. In this case, the said sentence only awakens the memory of the object. Those who are inclined to stick to the hypothesis that verbal knowledge is true should admit that the import of a sentence is an act and an act only.

The demonstration of the hypothesis that the knowledge of the meaning of a word is possible if it denotes an accomplished fact or a pre-existing object. Let us review the above hypothesis and arrive at a conclusion. Addressing the Mīmāṁsakas Jayanta says "You hold that the import of a sentence is an act to be performed, and that the relation of denotation holding between a word and an accomplished fact cannot be detected. But it is not reasonable to subscribe to such a hypothesis. How do you say that this word denotes an accomplished fact? A word does not convey its sense to a person who does not know its meaning. It is strange to hold that a word conveys its sense but its meaning remains unknown. All our worldly transactions are not conducted only by such words as denote existing objects. People also learn the meaning of such words. A person points his finger to a yonder object and says that this is the name of this object. At that time though no instruction is given to do something yet a person is informed of the meaning of a word. It may be contended that an instruction is imparted to this effect that one should learn this meaning from this word. Therefore a word refers to an act to be done. Such a contention is not tenable since there is no verbal instruction to this effect that one should learn this meaning from this word. It is only heard that this is the name of the object. But nobody hears that this meaning should be learnt. It may be again contended that the statement 'This is the name of this object' implies that one should learn this meaning from this word. Such a contention does not hold water since a sentence cannot communicate such a sense as has not been expressed by adequate words. None can entertain such a suggestion since if the sentence 'This word is its name' is competent enough to produce the perfect knowledge of the listener then it is useless to hold that the knowledge of the object should be fashioned in this manner. It demands to ignore logic of facts. Therefore such a demand is absurd since it is superfluous.

When one comes to know the power of the denotation of words which denote only acts to be performed he makes out only the meaning of a sentence consisting of such words. (This is the view of the Mīmāṁsakas). This hypothesis is not tenable. But by the joint method of agreement and difference the meaning of each constituent word is distinctly known and thereby its power of denotation is grasped by us. If one possesses the deep-rooted impression of the knowledge of the power of denotation of words then he surely understands the meaning of the sentences in a poem which is composed by a modern poet and which relates to existing objects. Therefore, words which denote existing objects are not to be discredited with untruth on the ground that their meaning is not detected. Knowledge which is produced by a word denoting an existing object is neither erroneous nor doubtful. As other sources of knowledge, e. g., perception etc. produce valid knowledge so a sentence referring to an existing object may generate true knowledge.

The Mīmāṁsakas have stated that a sentence which implies an effect to be produced is a source of valid knowledge since it reveals such a meaning as it is not grasped by other sources of valid knowledge. They have also stated that if a sentence makes an assertion about an existing object then it is not a source of valid knowledge as it depends upon other sources of valid knowledge. This view is not tenable. If all sentences purport to convey only an effect to be produced then they cannot induce a person to do something. We have discussed this point already. We shall also discuss this point in the subsequent section on the meaning of a sentence. If a sentence makes an assertion about an existing object then it depends upon another source of valid knowledge. But such a dependence imparts validity to it. Now, the meaning of the phrase, 'dependence upon another source of valid knowledge' should be clarified. Does it mean that the word which denotes an existing object depends upon another source of valid knowledge at the time of its coming into being? Or, does it mean that the object denoted by the word is capable of being grasped by another source of valid knowledge? These two meanings of the phrase are too wide to be accepted. If it is held that a word is not a source of valid knowledge as it depends upon another source of valid knowledge for its appearance then the validity of an inference is undermined since it depends upon perception etc. for its coming into being. It has been stated that the three types of inference are based upon perception.

If a word which denotes an existing object is invalid because the object is capable of being grasped by other sources of knowledge then all sources of valid knowledge such as perception etc. turn out to be invalid since it has been already proved that a particular object is grasped by many sources of valid knowledge. Moreover, there are sentences both Vedic and classical in the imperative mood such as 'Read', 'Fasten this cow with a piece of rope', 'Go to a village' etc. Though these verbs have been used in the imperative mood yet they do not by themselves induce a person to an action. By the joint method of agreement and difference he ascertains that they are conducive to his well-being and instrumental to the avoidance of his adversity. Being thus convinced he proceeds to do something. Thus these sentences are only formally but not really injunctive since a verb in the injunctive mood embodies a mandate or a command which independently stirs an inactive person to adopt a course of action. These so-called injunctive sentences really imply repetition of something already established. Thus those who hold that a sentence implying an effect to be performed is only a source of valid knowledge must admit that all injunctive sentences used by the people at large should not be a source of valid knowledge.

Some thinkers hold that if sentences embodying an assertion about the existing objects persuade or dissuade people then they should be taken as good as injunctive or prohibitive ones. But they are really obtruse. We have already pointed out that though a sentence contains a verb in the injunctive mood yet it loses its significance and comes out to be such a sentence as records the repetition of something already established. They suggest that the above sentences should be imagined to be injunctive though verbs in the injunctive mood are not given in them. Is a better example of their dullness required? A verb in the injunctive mood is not necessary for persuading a person. A person moves to do something on hearing a sentence when he ascertains by the joint method of agreement and difference that the sentence shows the way to human end or when he has implicit confidence in the person who utters it. It should also be noted in this connection that ordinary sentences purport to convey the intention of a speaker but not an act to be performed.

When a person hears a man-made sentence he determines that the speaker knows the content of his sentence thus, otherwise, he should not have said like this. But the Vedic sentences which have been composed by no author exclusively point to acts to be performed. Such a hypothesis is not sound. The hypothesis that the Vedas have no author has been refuted. It has been proved on the contrary that God is the author of the Vedas. We have also established that a sentence, composed by a person, does not imply the intention of the speaker. The intention of an author does not constitute the meaning of his sentence. In the sentence, 'Oh Devadatta! drive away the black cow with a stick' there is no such word as points to the intention of the speaker. It is unreasonable to hold that a sentence implies a sense which is not denoted by a word in it. The Mīmāṁsakas may contend that as the meaning of the sentence 'Go and swallow poison' is determined from its purport so the meaning of every sentence will be ascertained from its purport. The purport of the sentence is to dissuade the son of the speaker from taking meal in another's house. The meaning of this sentence is the intention of the speaker. The intention is of course revealed to us from the purport of the sentence. Thus the drift of this contention is that the intention of the speaker is the meaning of his sentence. But such a contention is not tenable. The purport of a sentence does not flash in our mind if it completely disregards the primary meanings of words contained in it. Hence, the intention of a speaker cannot be based upon the purport of his sentence. Therefore, the intention of a speaker cannot be conveyed by a sentence. How does a listener understand the intention of a speaker from his sentence ? Our answer is that his intention is inferred from the sentence uttered by him. An orderly arrangement of words is an effect. This arrangement is not possible if a person does not will to do it. Whenever one notices an arrangement of words he infers that it has been conditioned by the will of a person. When he knows the meaning of a sentence he infers to this effect 'as the speaker knows so he intends to communicate his knowledge.' A mere colourless intention which has no reference to the meaning of a sentence cannot be inferred since such an intention is the natural gift of all living beings. We cannot say that this meaning has been intended unless and until the intention takes a concrete shape, being focussed upon the meaning of a sentence. Such a qualified intention cannot be guessed if we do not know the meaning of a sentence. If the primary meaning of a sentence is not learnt at the outset then the sentence cannot convey the intention of its speaker as its sense. If it is held that the ordinary sentences signify intention but not external objects then none can know the relation of denotation holding between a word and an external object. In that case none should make out the meaning of a sentence. There is no need of further discussion. Therefore it is not reasonable to hold that words which only enter into syntactical relation with a word denoting an act to be performed rightly communicate their sense.

It has also been stated that there should be no such sentence as does not involve a reference to a process since if a process is set aside then a sentence cannot retain its self-completeness. The inflexion attached to a verb denotes a process (an act to be performed). Like a noun it does not signify an existent object. When we utter together two types of words denoting pre-existing objects and a process, words which denote pre-existent objects are employed with a view to expressing a process, i.e. something to be effectuated. This hypothesis is not tenable. The sentences viz. 'You are blessed with a new born son', 'Your daughter (virgin) is big with a child' etc. make one happy and sad. They do neither persuade us to do something nor dissuade us from doing something. The words contained in these sentences have no syntactical relation to a process, words which denote pre-existent objects are employed with a view to expressing a process, i.e., something to be effectuated. This hypothesis is not tenable. The sentences viz. 'You are blessed with a new born son', 'Your virgin daughter is big with a child' etc. make us happy and sad. They do neither persuade us to do something nor dissuade us from doing something. The words contained in these sentences have no syntactical relation to a process. But in worldly transactions similar sentences are copiously used. Now the opponents may contend that the above two sentences imply 'Be happy' and 'Be sad'. Thus they purport to do something. Such an interpretation is not tenable since no such words which denote an act to be performed (a process) are heard in these sentences. It is useless to imagine the presence of such words. None is happy if he is advised to be happy. No body prepares his mind to be happy in response to such an advice. One moves for the means which is conducive to pleasure but none sets up for the result itself. A person feels happy as soon as he hears that a son has been born to him. We have got another point to add. A person enjoys sleep with his body covered with an upper garment. During his slumber his body is bound by a piece of rope to make a fun of him. When he wakes up he suddenly imagines that he was wrapped by the coil of a snake and does not properly open his eyes out of fear. In this plight if the sentence 'You have been tied by a piece of rope' reaches his ears then in spite of its denoting an accomplished fact it becomes a source of true knowledge. In this case it is superfluous to imagine that the above sentence purports to convey 'Don't cherish fear', i.e., something to be done since as soon as he believes in the statement that he has been bound by a piece of rope his fear disappears. Therefore the above advice is fruitless. Let us cite a few examples. The sentences, viz., 'There is a terrible poisonous snake on the road', 'There is a precious gem on this spot' etc., point to pre-existent objects. They are not untrue. It is not reasonable to make out prohibition and injunction as their meaning. They do not respectively suggest 'Do not go by this path' and 'Go by this way and come by a gem' since words denoting persuasion and dissuasion are not heard in them.

The Mīnāṁsakas may contend thus :—As the speaker makes a statement after mature deliberation so he makes no superfluous statement. For this reason the advisory words such as 'Do not go', 'Go by this path', etc., have flashed in his mind but owing to some reasons such as indolence etc., he has not uttered them. Such a contention is not tenable. As the speaker is an intelligent person so he should make only a statement of facts. The listener realising the meaning of the sentence either moves toward the object or turns away from it. All listeners have no common purpose to serve. Therefore one and the same advice should not be given to all. If the listener is a snake-charmer then he welcomes the path, inhabited by snakes. With regard to the second it does not apply to him since as he, having realised the Absolute, has neither attachment for worldly objects nor hankering after wealth so the gem in question is considered by him as a rejectable object. Which advice will be given to whom ? In other words, no advice has universal application. But if a statement of facts is made then love and hatred may act as the spring of action of a listener and he may proceed towards an object or turn away from it. Therefore an intelligent person makes a statement of facts and should employ neither injunction nor prohibition.

Some Mīmāṁsakas hold that all speakers should always make such statements as advise their listeners to this effect that they should properly understand the meaning of these statements since statements whice involve no injunction should not be made. This hypothesis is not tenable. A person who knows the relation of denotation obtaining between a word and the object denoted by it makes out the meaning of the same whenever he hears it. It is not advisable to issue a mandate to make out the meaning of a sentence as one's own duty. If a person does not make out the meaning of a sentence then does he realise that it is his duty to do it?

The Mīmāṁsakas further contend that if in a sentence there is no such word as denotes an act to be brought into being then remaining words are not mutually connected since if the word denoting an act to be generated requires them (those words) then they are mutually connected, otherwise, they are not connected. Therefore all sentences purport to convey an act to be brought into being, an act which requires them to be so connected. It is seen that in sentences which are statements of facts words mutually connect themselves and communicate a connected meaning.

Words in sentences which are statements of facts do not lack mutual connection like those in the famous sentence 'Ten pomegranates etc.' If a word denoting an act to be brought into being were the pivot of mutual connection among all other words in a sentence then a sentence which is the statement of a fact and which contains no such word as denotes an act to be brought into being would not have communicated a connected meaning. It has been shown that all the sentences referred to before by way of illustrations convey well-connected meanings. Moreover, in a sentence which contains a verb in the injunctive mood all other words are noticed to be mutually connected. How will the Mīmāṁsakas explain this? If the mutual connection of words denoting facts is determined by the requirement of a word denoting something to be brought into being then the mutual connection of them (those words denoting facts) cannot take place.

The Mīmāṁsakas may further contend that the relation of all words in a sentence at first centres round a word denoting an act to be performed and later on the syntactical relation of all words is determined in the light of the principle adopted in connection with the interpretation of the sentence 'One should purchase Soma plant in exchange of a red, brown-eyed and one-year-old heifer'. In case of such a defence we regret to point out that they should admit that the mutual connection of words takes place because the word denoting an act to be preformed requires it (such connection). If they admit the act above suggestion then as in the sentence 'One should purchase Soma plant in exchange of a red brown-eyed and one-year-old heifer' the third case-ending is attached to the stems denoting substances and qualities and thereby they are considered to be fit for purchase so they are at first detected to be connected with the act of purchasing and afterwards the mutual connection subsisting between the substance and its qualities is grasped. But the third case-ending attached to stems cannot condition the mutual relation of the stems mentioned above since it points only to the subordinate position of a substance and qualities in the above context. The mutual connection of words takes place even in the absence of the third case-ending, e.g., 'The cloth is white'. Therefore we arrive at the conclusion that the hypothesis that the requirement of an act to be performed conditions the mutual connection of words is based upon pure imagination but not upon sound observation.

The rule that when a word denoting an existing object and that denoting an act to be performed are used together in a sentence the first object expresses itself as subordinate to the second one is not universally true. We find an exception to this rule in the Vedic sentence 'One should sprinkle water on sacrificial paddy. Let us explain the drift of the above argument. A sacrificial cake is the proximate condition of a sacrifice. Rice is the stuff of which a cake is made up. We get rice, unhusked paddy. In order to unhusk paddy water should be sprinkled on it. The sprinkling of water is the act to be performed. But the act in question is subordinate to paddy. Therefore the above rule does not hold good. We need not refer to this example since it finds a place in the section on New and Full Moon sacrifices where no pains have been spared to demonstrate that an act to be performed is their goal.

Let us cite another example, viz., 'the soul should be known.' In this case the act to be performed has been instructed as subordinate to the existing object. No cardinal duty to be discharged by us has been instructed since no result yet some result is suggested to us per instruction. But no such result can be imagined in this way as there is no definite instruction. The knowledge of the soul does not prompt us to any action. We hear many praises about the knowledge of the soul. There are mere praises. They cannot help us to imagine the result of the knowledge of the soul. For this reason if one knows the soul then he becomes the soul who stands above all sins and other imperfections. If one realises the perfect soul then he does not suffer from the sorrow of hankering after other objects since the soul itself is the highest goal of life. The soul is an existing substance but not an effect to be brought into being. After the realisation of the soul the men of settled conviction should exert themselves to dispel the basic ignorance about the soul. This is the finding of the learned scholars.

The Mīmāṁsakas may contend that the sentence 'The soul should be known' is injunctive since it enjoins one to acquire the knowledge of the soul. Thus, the knowledge of the soul is a duty which is to be done. Such a contention is not tenable. The knowledge of the soul is not fashioned by our will. It is the true knowledge of an object. The true knowledge of an object is determined only by the object. The verb 'jñātavyaḥ' has been used in the passive voice because the verbal suffix 'tavya' is used to emphasise the position of the objective case as a principal part of speech in a sentence. Thus the objective case in question is such as implies the preferential connection with the verb 'to know'. Thus the knowable object comes out to be the soul itself. Thus the above sentence purports to convey the soul as its sole meaning. An injunction cannot exert its influence upon the soul since a result cannot be enjoined. Kumārila has also lent his support to the above view that a suffix which denotes an injunction enjoins to do an action but not to realise a result. In other words, the sphere of an injunction is limited. The word denoting means falls within it but a result falls outside it. Knowledge is really a means: So it may be enjoined. But Jayanta points out that the knowledge of an object culminates in the object itself. It moves toward the object which is an end in itself. The culminating point of the knowledge of the soul is the soul itself. The soul cannot be enjoined. But no injunction regarding the knowledge of the soul is possible.

The instructions regarding the procedures of acquiring the knowledge of the soul, viz., Yama (non-violence, celibacy, non-possession of property etc.) Niyama (Purity internal and external, indifference, self-content etc.) and other such methods have the realisation of the soul in view. The realisation of the soul takes place through the cancellation of the world of names and forms which is an imaginary superstructure upon the solid rock of reality. The above methods are means to an end. The supreme end is the soul itself. Hence, all the changing processes are subordinate to the Soul, the self-sufficient eternal object.

The Vedāntins hold that apart from the injunctions prescribing the methods of acquiring the knowledge of the soul, viz., Yama, Niyama, control of breath, withdrawal of sense-organs from the sense-objects all injunctions enjoining sacrifices such as Jyotiṣṭoma (a Soma sacrifice) etc. are means to the realisation of the soul. The soul alone is the highest end of human life. The other ends which are effectuated do not endure. The Absolute, being uncaused, is not subject to destruction. It transcends beginningless Nescience. As it enjoys immutable existence so it is the summum bonum of human life. Our interest shifts from some objects to someother objects when we realise the unsubstantial character of the former ones. Thus it is a sort of slow pilgrimage towards the Absolute by means of the negation of a section of worldly objects. As a person starts with the process of negating worldly objects slowly so he gradually qualifies himself to realise the soul. Therefore, all injunctions are means to the realisation of the soul.

Manu has also said to this effect :—

This human body is made fit for realising the Supreme soul if one observes the following prescription, viz., the study of the Vedas, the observance of the vow of abstinence, morning and evening offer of libation to Fire, the study of the three Vedas, the paying off of the three obligatory debts, the performance of five great sacrifices during the period of life of a house-holder and the performance of other sacrifices.

The great savants say that the Vedas are the source of true knowledge if they reveal an eternal object. The Vedas should reveal both eternal and non-eternal objects. If they reveal all objects alike, they do not become untrue thereby.

It does not suit our purpose if we hold long discussion on the subject, viz., which portion of the Vedas is authoritative on acts to be performed and which one is authoritative on the eternal objects. We have spared no pains to maintain the validity of the Vedas and have done it ungrudgingly.

We have discussed all relevant matters to establish the validity of the Vedas. We have not gone beyond the bounds of relevancy. We shall now discuss some other topics which are in high favour with all. Kindly listen to them if your intellect is not over-fatigued.

The End of the Fourth Āhnika of Nyāya-mañjarī

ĀHNIKA V

Introductory

Homage be paid to God who is the sincere friend of all, the saviour of the oppressed, the comforter of the miserable and the fulfiller of hopes of those who have completely surrendered themselves to him.

Now, the hypothesis that as the meaning of a word is unreal so the relation of denotation which subsists between a word and its meaning is going to be refuted. Significant aggregate of letters admits of two kinds, viz., a word and a sentence. As the meaning of a sentence presupposes that of a word so the meaning of a word is at first discussed.

A word is of two kinds, viz., a noun and a verb. Prepositions which prefix a verb, indeclinables and prepositions which are used independently of a verb but govern a case-ending are declared to be included in nouns. A part of speech is that word to which 'sup' or 'tiṅ' inflexions are attached. The author of the Nyāya-Sūtra holds that a part of speech is that word to which inflexions are attached.

The meaning of a verb with the proper inflexion attached to it will be discussed when the meaning of a sentence will be taken into consideration since the meaning of a verb furnishes us with the key to unlock the sense of a sentence.

Now, the meaning of a noun is as follows. The inflexional nouns admit of four kinds. They are called parts of speech. Some nouns denote universals. They correspond to common nouns. Some of them denote attributes. They are abstract nouns. Some of them denote particulars. They are proper nouns. And some of them denote motion or activity. They are called verbal nouns. A common noun, viz., a cow, denotes a particular characterized by a common feature belonging to all members of a class. The Naiyāyikas hold that a particular is a substance to which a universal belongs.

A particular is a substance to which an attribute or an activity belongs. This substance has a form which is constituted by the arrangement of its parts, e.g., dewlap, etc. The universal of cowness is the common feature which is shared by all particular cows such as Śābaleya etc. Now, a question arises in our mind, viz., 'How does the noun 'cow' denote only the locus of the Universal of cowness to the exclusion of a particular cow and its form?' It puzzles us. We cannot follow the conclusion of the Naiyāyikas. If we are to discuss this problem then we shall have to hold a long discussion. We shall discuss it later on.

An objection against the acceptance of a universal

A universal is not a sense-datum. It is a matter for discussion. As its existence cannot be proved so it is non-existent like the horns of a hare. How can the locus of a universal be the meaning of a word? A universal cannot be perceived since an act of perception reveals only an exclusively particular point of reality which does not endure through the past and the future times.

A universal rests upon many similar locii. Its essence is constituted by its belonging to such locii. The comprehension of such an essence presupposes the knowledge of similarity which is due to the act of comparing these locii. Thus, the comprehension of a universal is not immediate as it has a relative being. Perception is immediate. It presupposes no prior knowledge for its existence. How can perception reveal a universal?

Unless all locii of the so-called universal are compared and known to be similar a universal which belongs to all particulars as their common property cannot be known. Hence the knowledge of a universal has a dependant character. Perception immediately results from the sense-object-contact. It involves no reference to the past and the future times. It is independent of all prior knowledge. How can it discover universals. Judgments, which follow it in close succession, being constructed by our imagination, cannot reveal real objects. Even if a universal is the object of a judgment, it has only an imaginary being but no real existence. An inference or verbal knowledge cannot establish the reality of universals since they reveal imaginary objects but no real ones. We shall explain in a different manner from the Buddhist point of view how a person comes across a real object when he proceeds towards it after having inferred it. A particular is not different from a universal since their distinction is not apprehended. If we place a blue lotus, a myrobalan, and a melon fruit on our palm then their difference is at once detected. But a universal and a particular are not different since they are not differently perceived. A universal is not different from a particular since the space occupied by a particular, is not grasped to be different from that occupied by a universal. Spaces, occupied by the different objects, are grasped by us as different, e.g., the space, occupied by a jar, is different from that occupied by a piece of cloth since they are different. As no spatial difference is noticed between a universal and a particular so they are not different. A universal is not different from a particular since a universal is not cognised if a particular is not perceived. If an object is different from another object then the cognition of one does not presuppose that of another. Let us take an illustration. A jar is different from a piece of cloth. The former is cognised independently of the latter. But a universal is never cognised if a particular is not cognised. Therefore a particular is not different from a universal.

The locus of a Universal is logically untenable.

A universal rests on a particular. If a particular is not grasped then a universal remains uncognised. Such a contention is not tenable since the suggestion that a universal rests on a particular is not at all tenable. Does a universal wholly rest on a particular (say a body)? Or, does the former partially rest on the latter ? We shall solve the problem at the outset. None of these two replies is satisfactory. If a universal wholly rests upon a distinct particular then it resides there completely. And as such it should be exclusively perceived there. There is no chance of cognising it at another locus. Again, if a universal rests upon a particular partially then a universal does not wholly rest on a particular. In that case, how can we recognise a particular cow as a cow ? Moreover, a universal is a partless whole. As such it consists of no parts. Hence, the different particulars cannot share it part by part. If a universal wholly rests on a particular locus then it cannot wholly rest on another locus since an object which completely occupies a particular space cannot occupy another space in the same manner without being born again. Thus it is difficult to solve the problem of locating a universal on a suitable locus since no suitable locus is to be found out. The Buddhist fail to follow the hypothesis of the Vaiśeṣikas that a universal inheres in all the particulars of a class. The Vaiśeṣikas define the relation of inherence thus:- It is such a relation as subsists between the container and the contained which are inseparably connected and is a source of the judgment that one rests on another. Now if two objects are inseparable from each other then how does the relation of inherence subsist between them ? If an object keeps itself apart from another object then a relation takes place between such a pair of objects, e. g., a plum fruit and a reservoir of water or a male and a female. If the two objects are inseparable then they are one with each other. As there is no difference between them so how can they be related to each other ? In other words, a relation pre-supposes two terms but one-term-relation is an absurdity. Thus with regard to the two inseparable objects we cannot say that one of them rests on the other.

The Vaiśeṣikas may contend that though substances and attributes do not exist apart yet they are united by the relation of inherence. There is no sense in this contention since an object having an attribute cannot be distinguished from an attribute. An object having attributes cannot demonstrate its separate entity from attributes such as colour etc. But it is strange that the Vaiśeṣikas wish to draw a distinction between a substance and its attributes.

Moreover, the Vaiśeṣikas have drawn a distinction between the eternal Yutasiddhas and the non-eternal Yutasiddhas. According to their texts the word 'Yuta-siddha' is a conventional one. They say that the eternal atoms are Yutasiddhas since they move independently. Their absolutely independent character is proved by their free movement. The distinct entity of the two non-eternal objects depends upon their inherence in the separate substrata. Let us illustrate this point.

A piece of cloth is distinct from a jar since the former inheres in threads and the latter inheres in pot-sherds. Threads are distinct from pot-sherds. Therefore, a piece of cloth is distinct from a jar. But a jar always depends upon pot-sherds. Hence, a jar is not (yuta-siddha) independent of pot-sherds. The eternal substances like an atom are always independent. But non-eternal substances are relatively independent. Hence the word 'yuta-siddha' admits of the two shades of meaning. Again, the Vaiśeṣikas hold that the all-pervasive substances, e. g., the sky etc. have no mutual contact. Such a hypothesis is not accepted by all. It is their own affair. The Vaiśeṣikas should only abide by this decision. But the others will not be bound down by it. The objects which exist independently of one another (yuta-siddha) may be distinguished from one another. They may come into being independently of others. Their mutual difference may be cognised by us. This is the import of the term 'yuta-siddhi' used in the Vaiśeṣika literature. The above meaning of the term 'yuta-siddhi' throws light on that of the term 'ayuta-siddhi'. Its meaning should be contrary to that of the term 'yuta-siddhi'. Thus the term 'ayuta-siddhi' means non-independence, and non-difference. Thus the two objects which are said to be ayuta-siddha cannot be related to each other. Thus, the relation of inherence holding between parts and a whole should be discarded.

Kumārila Bhaṭṭa has also said to this effect. If the substratum of a universal does not come into being beforehand and does not stand unrelated to a universal to be located upon it then it cannot be united with a universal. If the independent existence of the substratum of a universal at the initial stage is admitted then the assumption of a yuta-siddhi becomes illogical. The Vaiśeṣikas admit that an atom comes into contact with the two ubiquitous substances such as the Sky and Time. But such an assumption owes its origin to mere idle imagination. We shall not discuss the minor details of the Vaiśeṣika system. Therefore, it is not reasonable to hold that a distinct relation subsists between a universal and its substratum.

But the logicians, adept in the art of reasoning, hold that the relation holding between a universal and its substratum is that of rūpa (character) and rūpin (object characterised). This hypothesis is not sound.

What does the word 'rūpa' convey ? Does it mean an attribute like whiteness etc. ? Or, does it signify the form of an object ? Or, does it stand for the nature of an object ? If it conveys an attribute such as whiteness etc. then a universal should belong neither to the colourless air and to the internal organ nor to an attribute and to an action. If it means the form of an object then a universal should not belong to the formless objects such as an attribute etc. If it stands for the nature of an object then a universal becomes identical with the substratum of a universal since the nature of an object is never cognised as different from an object. There is only verbal difference between the nature of an object and an object but there is no material difference between them. Moreover, what is this rūpa, Is it a substance? Or, is it a property of a substance? Or, is it a distinct substance? We have alrealy pointed out that it is not a distinct substance. It is not property of a substance since the property of a substance is not presented to us as distinct from the substance itself. If it is held that the property of a substance is identical with the substance then the so-called relation between them has no logical justification for its existence. We have already discussed the point. The Vedic scholars even after mature thinking cannot clearly define the relation holding between rūpa and rūpin and distinguish it from the relation of conjunction or from that of inherence. It is merely a verbal device. New terms have been only used. But there is no new object corresponding to it. There is no need of continuing this topic any more.

Moreover, does a universal wholly occupy all spaces? Or, does it wholly belong to all particulars only? It is omnipresent then a white horse should be presented to us as a horse. An elephant should be grasped by us as a camel and so on. If the above hypothesis is subscribed by them then the overlapping of universals becomes inevitable. This amounts to a logical crisis. The upholders of the hypothesis may contend thus : As a group of particulars can only manifest a particular universal so there will be no overlapping of universals though all universals are omnipresent. The body of an animal consists of many limbs. A mutilated limb should manifest a universal. Each limb should have manifested the said universal. The universal should be perceived in each limb of the body of a particular animal. But it is not so perceived. Moreover, a universal is a partless whole. As such it cannot be held that the particular part of a universal is manifested by the particular limb of the body of a particular animal. Moreover, there is nothing to determine that the universal of cowness pervades the entire body of a particular cow. Again, if the body of a particular animal be the manifestor of a universal like a lamp then the universal cannot belong to the body which is its manifestor. (An object which is manifested by a lamp cannot belong to a lamp). On the contrary, we discover a law from our experience that an object which is not perceived everywhere is not omnipresent. For this reason we arrive at the conclusion that the universal of cowness cannot be all-pervasive. But if it is held that a universal belongs to the body then we admit that the above criticisms do not apply to this hypothesis. But it does not stand above all criticisms. If a calf is born today we cannot recognise it as a cow. The reason of this non-recognition is as follows. When the calf was in the womb of a cow it did not possess a body at the earlier stage of embryonic life. No universal belonged to it at that stage. As soon as it had been born, a universal came to reside in it. A universal cannot be transferred from its place of residence to some other place since it remains inactive all through. Even, if it is admitted that a universal comes from some other place then how is it that it does not desert its old place of residence ! When it comes over to a new place it does not come piece meal. Again, it does not partially reside in its substratum. In other words, how can it wholly occupy both the places old and new ? A series of such fresh problems will crop up. They will give a rude shock to this hypothesis.

Kumārila Bhaṭṭa holds that a universal is an entity and is both identical with and different from its locus, i. e., a particular. Every object is presented to our consciousness as possessed of two characters viz., specific and generic. We distinguish, an object from all other objects because of its specific character. We also comprehend all objects as one because of its general property. An object cannot produce these two different ideas in our mind if these two characters do not belong to it. If an object is exclusively particular then it cannot produce a general idea in our mind. If an object is merely universal then it cannot produce an idea of distinction or exclusion in our mind. One cannot suggest that one of these two ideas is erroneous as it is constructed by our imagination. The ideas of generality and particularity (uniqueness), produced by an object, are never contradicted. So these ideas are not erroneous. Those who hold that they are not true commit a mistake.

Let us compare an instance of error with the double ideas produced by an object and mark their difference. When we take the rays of the sun for water the rays of the sun are not presented to our consciousness. The character of water replaces that of the rays. But the idea of particularity does not present that of generality. The idea of generality does not also present that of particularity. There is no opposition between these two ideas. There is only co-ordination between them. These two features are simultaneously presented to our consciousness. But in case of the indeterminate perception of an object these two features are not presented to our consciousness as distinct.

The hypothesis, propounded by Kumārila, is not based upon sound logic. Kumārila himself has stated that an object possesses mutually incompatible characters. In the face of such a statement we restrain us from being vociferous in pointing out his defects. In other words, as he has exposed his own defects so we are not to point out his mistakes.

Kumārila's hypothesis amounts to this : What is universal is particular; What is one is many; what is eternal is non-eternal; and what is is not. He says something which nobody has experienced. He may say so. But it does not sound well. Some philosophers hold that as contrary characters are experienced in an object so there is no opposition. Such a statement is not tenable. Nowhere such contrary characters are noticed in an object. In other words, no object possesses general and particular characters. Our experience does never reveal the general character of an object. Under the influence of various imaginations men, being confused, entertain the above hypothesis. Let them dwell in the domain of error. But it is a truism that an object cannot have different characters since every object has only one character but the other character is imaginary. The judgment which refers to a persistent element should not be taken as true by the sound logicians.

An exclusively particular is immediately sensed by us. It involves no reference to other objects. A particular which excludes itself from all other objects is only real. Thus the specific character is only real. But its general character is not real. It is a construction of our imagination.

Without examining the character of our experience whether it is true or not, it will be wrong on our part to admit that an object has two-fold character since we experience the double characters of an object.

If we entertain a belief in the non-existence of an object then only on the strength of this belief we cannot hold that the knowledge of the said object is false. But this knowledge should be tested by the canons of logic by the sound thinkers.

No object, having many characters, is grasped by an indeterminate perception. How can a character which is held to be common to many particulars be cognised to be such without making a reference to other objects? In other words, if we do not compare an object with other objects, perceived by us, we cannot find out the common element.

A universal resides in many particulars. If these particulars are not recognised, a universal, belonging to them, cannot be grasped. But sense-knowledge cannot recognise it.

Those who hold that a universal is sensed do not know well the character of sense-knowledge. With the purpose of advocating monism they do not admit that particulars are only sensed. As particulars are only sensed so universals are not objectively real, i.e., they do not belong to particulars.

Concepts are Possible Even if Existence is Denied to Universals

Now, if existence is denied to universals, how do you explain a common idea, i.e., a concept, viz., 'a cow' as referring to particular cows such as Śābaleya etc.? Such an idea is merely constructed by our imagination. It does not owe its origin to objectively reals. Our opponents hold that universals are objectively real. A common element belongs to these universals, viz., existence etc., since all universals are accepted to be designated as universals. In other words, the common element of universality belongs to them. The so-called common element is due to some other factors. It is subjective but not objective. Oh long-lived one! If you say so then some factors may be easily found out and the concept 'cow' which is shared by every judgment referring to a particular cow will take the place of the universal of cowness. In other words, there are no universals which are held to be objectively real. The concept 'cow' explains everything which the universal of cowness is supposed to do.

Now a question may be put to the Buddhists. What is the character of this Upādhi ? The Buddhists reply that an upādhi is the rendering of the same service. As a particular cow carries load, service, i.e., from the pragmatical stand-point, all cows considered individuals render a distinct service. Being afraid of perceiving difference all objects are taken as one. As there is a distinction between the service of a cow and that of a white horse so there is no such noticeable difference between the usefulness of syrup and that of molasses. Now the Naiyāyikas raise a question that though the difference between the second pair of objects is not much yet they do not perform the same function. The Buddhists reply that as they look alike so they are taken as one. The Naiyāyikas press their point and say that they do not look alike. The Buddhists give a rejoinder to this question thus : What you say is true. But people ordinarily judge that all kinds of molasses produce the same effect. Being guided by this impression they hold that they look alike i.e. they neglect their difference of forms. Though we perceive their difference yet we judge them all as a cow. So they are taken as the same. We neglect their differences and take them as one. Similarly, all kinds of molasses are taken as one. This answer has been given by a section of the Buddhists.

As in the subsequent stage of judgment they are taken to be one so the perception of differences at the primary stage of knowledge is overlooked. As the judgments which follow the distinct perceptions of individual cows are similar so we assume that these individual cows possess an identical element.

In fine, the Buddhists say that an upādhi is the source of similar judgments. For this reason, a universal does not actually exist.

The Naiyāyikas join issue with the Buddhists and hold that if the existence of a universal is denied then how does one go to employ words and infer ? Because one cannot employ a word if he does not know the relation holding between a word and the object denoted by it and one cannot infer if he does not know the relation of universal concomitance obtaining between the probans and the probandum. If a word denotes only an individual object then it is not possible to know the relation of denotation subsisting between a word and its meaning. Again if the relation of universal concomitance holds between a particular probans and a particular probandum then we cannot draw a conclusion since deduction presupposes generalisation. Do you know the relation between all words and all particular objects denoted by them ? Do you know all the relations of universal concomitance which hold between all individual pairs of probans and probandum.

We cannot know all such relations since individual objects which belong to different times and spaces are infinite in numbers. Hence all objects of the world are beyond the range of our experience. We cannot select a representative individual and discovering the relation of denotation or that of universal concomitance can serve our purpose. If we do so, we are liable to commit a fallacy. Suppose we know that this word denotes this particular object and this probans is universally connected with this probandum. When this word is heard some other particular object may be signified by it. Similarly, when the probans in question is seen some other probandum may be inferred. So we are liable to commit a fallacy.

We have learnt that this word conveys this particular meaning. But we also learn that the word in question also conveys another individual meaning. In case of inference, a probans sometimes points to some other individual probandum. But if we do not know that the relation of denotation holds between this word and this particular object and that the relation of universal concomitance obtains between this particular proban and the particular probandum then the word cannot signify the object and the probans cannot point to the probandum in question. The sum and substance of the argument of the Naiyāyikas is that the hypothesis of a universal is necessary for the possibility of verbal and inferential knowledge.

The Buddhists meet the above objection thus : The objection, raised by the Naiyāyikas, would have been pointed if the probans and a word had been related to an exclusively particular real. According to the Buddhists the meaning of a word and the probandum are constructed by our imagination. As they are not real objects so the Naiyāyikas do not squarely solve all problems concerned.

The Naiyāyikas raise a deeper objection against the above superficial solution. They urge that if the relation of denotation does not belong to a word which is sensed by all and if the relation of universal concomitance does not belong to a probans which is also sensed by us then as the processes of verbal and inferential knowledge involve the fallacies of regressus ad infinitum etc., so nobody will betake himself to these processes of knowledge to communicate his idea or to prove something.

Now let us clearly state the objection raised by the Naiyāyikas against the Buddhist hypothesis indicated above. In order to follow the import of a statement one should be conversant with the convention that the constituent words denote these meanings. In other words, verbal knowledge presupposes the knowledge of the meaning of words. If the meaning of a word is only an inference then verbal knowledge presupposes inferential knowledge as its necessary condition. A syllogistic argument consists of propositions. Each proposition consists of terms. The meaning of each term should be grasped. But its meaning is an inference. Again, this inferential knowledge presupposes verbal knowledge. Verbal knowledge, again, depends upon inferential knowledge. The inferential process consists of propositions. Each proposition is constituted by terms. The meaning of each term is to be ascertained. The meaning of a term is an inference. Again, the same processes are to be repeated. Thus, verbal knowledge will surely lead to a regressus ad infinitum. Moreover verbal knowledge presupposes inferential knowledge as its condition and inferential knowledge presupposes verbal knowledge as its condition. So, it is a glaring instance of circular reasoning. In case of inference induction is an indispensable condition of inferential knowledge, i.e. deduction. Again, induction presupposes deduction as its invariable condition. The second deduction also presupposes induction and so on ad infinitum. It is an instance of regressus ad infinitum. Moreover, induction presupposes deduction and deduction presupposes induction. So it is also a glaring example of circular reasoning.

The Buddhists meet this objection with the remark "Do not argue like this. Why do not you follow our stand-point ? We have repeatedly tried to impress our point of view upon your mind. Verbal and inferential knowledge refer to imaginary objects. As concepts do not point to real objects so the above objections do not affect our position.

The vindication of conceptualism a negative general image.

The Naiyāyikas subject the Buddhist hypotheses to apoha (a negative general image) to severe criticism. They point out that if concepts do not refer to a real common element then inferential and verbal knowledge should be declared null and void. The Buddhists say in reply to this objection that concepts surely refer to a common element but this common element is not objectively real. What is this unreal common element ? It is an exclusion of the other of itself. Non-non-A is the common element of A. It does not belong to the external world. A concept refers to such an object. When a negative image is cognised the knower imagines that it belongs to the external world.

Words denote these negative general images. For this reason the Buddhists hold that a word denotes the exclusion of the other of the object denoted by it. This hypothesis amounts to this that concepts do never refer to real objects. If you ask "why" then our answer is this that perception is the super-excellent source of knowledge and that there is such part of a real object as will be revealed by the other sources of knowledge on the failure of perception.

The function of conceptual knowledge is to negate the other futures which may be wrongly attributed to an object. The mother-of-pearls is mistaken for silver owing to the similarity of their properties. In order to negate silverness attributed to the mother-of-pearls the services of a true judgment that it is not silver are required. Similarly, though a particular cow, viz., Śābaleya, etc. is completely grasped by our indeterminate perception which is free from imagination and is non-erroneous yet the otherness of a cow may be attributed to her due to some conditions. In order to cancel the attributed character the judgment that this is not a non-cow is necessary.

But no judgment like this can grasp the real nature of a cow since she has been previously cognised. Now the objectors may contend that an object is characterised by various characteristic features. Some of them have not been grasped by the earlier perception. They are now grasped by the judgments. Such a contention is baseless. A thing-in-itself may be characterised by various characteristic features. If a characteristic is not grasped then it will remain undetected for ever since it is impotent to characterise its substantive. The characterization brought about by the characteristic features is not different from the thing itself which is characterized. So whenever a thing which is characterized by these characteristic features is grasped all the characteristic features are grasped. As the complex character of a thing-in-itself is a given fact so the said function of judgments to know a particular characteristic feature is futile. This is the view of a section of the Buddhists.

A thing-in-itself has many characteristic features which are adjectival in their character. These adjectives have power to mould it. The change which is imparted to it is identical with itself. This change is effective. Whenever the thing-in-itself is apprehended it is cognised along with its changed form. Hence, if a particular characteristic feature of the thing-in-itself remains uncognized then it amounts to this that the changed thing-in-itself with all its adjectives has not been grasped. How is it possible? The transformed character of the thing-in-itself does not remain uncognized. In fine, this is the conclusive portion of the Buddhist hypothesis.

The refutation of a negative general image (*apoha*)

Kumārila Bhaṭṭa has measured his swords with the Buddhist hypothesis that a word denotes a negative general image. The sum and substance of Kumārila's critical remarks may be put thus : The word 'apoha' denotes an exclusion. An exclusion is negation. No negative object is independently grasped like a jar. So it should have been mentioned as a dependent object. Now, it should be found out what is the locus of the said exclusion, i.e., negation. An exclusively particular real cannot be the locus of the exclusion in question since it always stands unrelated to imagination. Subspecies like Śabaleyatva, etc., cannot be the locus of the exclusion of the other of a cow since it is only excluded by the exclusion of the other of Śābaleyas only. If the Buddhists accept the above suggestion then a cow cannot be logically distinguished from the exclusion of the other of Śābaleyas. In other words, we fail to draw a distinction between a cow and non-non-Śābaleya since Sābaleya is only not non-Śābaleya. Other cows such as Bāhuleya, etc., are non-Śābaleya but they are not non-cows. Or, if the Buddhists hold that the exclusion of non-cows belongs to all individual cows then this thesis does not stand to reasons since if all cows are not comprehended then the exclusion of non-cow is not at all grasped. All individual cows are countless as they occupy different spaces and times. For this reason all individuals of the cow-class cannot be put together by a hundred years. Hence the exclusion of non-cow cannot exist as a logical entity apart from all individual cows. Therefore we should think of a new exclusion of non-cow which is a common property of all individual cows and which wholly resides in each individual cow. Now if we are frank in our expression of idea then we should hold that cowness is the locus of the exclusion of non-cow. If we admit the existence of cowness then why should we take the trouble of assuming the concept of the exclusion of non-cow ? Moreover, our point of criticism will be missed if you think that the exclusion of non-cow cannot be admitted since it has no locus to stand upon. You should note the point of criticism that such an exclusion cannot be admitted because there is no possibility of knowing all individual cows simultaneously. According to the Buddhists the words such as 'a horse', etc. do not signify a positive object. They all convey negative meanings. The meanings are grasped as negative objects. The Buddhists will adopt the same procedure to comprehend the exclusion of the other of these objects. The same criticism holds good in every case and sets at naught their hypothesis. Therefore in no case a concept can point to a negative general image. Indeterminate perception, according to the Buddhists, is such awareness as is not associated with imagination. But this piece of awareness cannot be communicated to others. Thus, all the worldly transactions should come to a stop.

Moreover, all words such as Śābaleya, etc., denote negative meanings. They cannot be distinguished from each other. And as such they will be considered as synonyms.

Now, the Buddhists may argue that there will be no difficulty in distinguishing one 'apoha' (a negative general image) from another since all such images possess marks of distinction. Such an argument will not hold water since they cannot be mutually distinguished. If they had been mutually distinguished from one another then they would have been reals like exclusively particular points of reality. Now, the Buddhists may counter-charge the Naiyāyikas with the following remarks that all words denoting universals should also be taken as synonyms as all universals stand for generality. Such a counter-charge does not make an appeal to reasons since these universals are positive objects and are accepted to be many, being mutually different. But as apohas are merely negative in their character so they are not mutually different. Now, the Buddhists may adopt a new line of defence and hold that, these apohas will be mutually different since the locii such as a white horse and Śābaleya, etc. on which they stand possess marks of distinction. Such a defence is not tenable since it has been shown that the said locii cannot contain apohas. Again, if the Buddhists hold that an apoha which stands upon a particular locus is different from another apoha which has another locus to stand upon then apohas should be treated as particulars and be marked off from one another. If they admit them to be such then apohas should lack the character of being general. Now, the Buddhists may adopt another line of defence and hold that apohas may be distinguished from one another on the strength of their function of negating different objects and the words denoting apohas will not be synonyms. Such a defence is not sound since such a distinction is indirect, being based upon negative function. The distinction which the objects to be negated possess cannot be transferred to apohas since the objects to be negated are not presented to our consciousness as positive ones but the other of a particular object. The said other has not a definite shape since all the others are not grasped by us. As the other in question is vague so the exclusion which negates it is also indeterminate. Moreover, some objects which are marked by otherness are very remote and lie beyond the reach of our knowledge. In that case how is the exclusion of such others at all possible ? If the 'other' has not a distinct character then the exclusion of the other becomes incomprehensible. Let us take an example to illustrate the point at issue. The exclusion of non-cow lacks a distinct character since the term 'non-cows' denotes everything excepting cow. Therefore it is a vague term. An exclusion of non-cow is also indefinite in its character since it is impossible to comprehend the full extent of non-cow.

Even if we admit the Buddhist hypothesis that apohas differ if the objects to be negated are different then apohas will be taken as identical when the objects to be negated are the same. Let us take two terms for the better understanding of our point of criticism, viz, 'a cow', and a 'horse'. Now we are to determine the meaning of these two terms by the exclusion of their other. The meaning of the term 'cow' is to be determined by the exclusion of non-cow (other than a cow). And the meaning of term (horse) is to be fixed up by the exclusion of non-horse (other than a horse). 'Non-cow' and 'non-horse' comprise within their denotation many objects such as elephants, etc. in common. Only horses do not fall within the denotation of non-horse and cows remain outside the denotation of non-cow. The term 'cow' excludes only horses as the distinct object to be excluded and the term 'horse' excludes only cows as the distinct object to be excluded. These two objects constitute the mutual differentia of the above two terms.

We should also bear in mind in this connection that the objects denoted in common by the terms 'non-cow' and 'non-horse', form the majority. In this case if the Buddhists hold that the terms 'cow' and 'horse' are different since the objects excluded by them are different then it may be at once pointed out to them that they convey the identical meaning since the majority of objects excluded by them are identical. We have already shown that the term 'cow' excludes only horses over and above the common objects which are excluded by the term 'horse'. Similarly, the term 'horse' excludes only cows besides the common objects which are excluded by the term 'cow'. Considering the objects which are excluded by the terms 'cow, and 'horse' the major portion of them is the same. If we seriously judge the negative meanings of these two terms then we should arrive at the decision that their negative meanings are identical. Now, the Buddhists may argue that as the negative meaning of the term 'cow' contains a horse as its distinctive element so it is definitely determined. Such an argument is not convincing. The term 'lion' also excludes a horse. Hence a lion might be taken as a cow.

Now, the Buddhists may take up a new line of defence. If they hold that the term 'cow' denotes only an exclusion of non-cow but does not make mention of a horse as the distinct object to be excluded then they make a wrong statement since each and every item which falls within the denotation of non-cow is incomprehensible, the range of denotation being infinitely large. There is no reason of placing them together under a single collection since the objects which are comprised within the denotation of non-cow such as horse etc. do neither occupy the same space nor coexist.

Now, the Buddhists may press their point that the reason behind the assembling of all objects denoted by the term 'non-cow' rests with the term itself. If this is their contention then it is really deplorable since the positive meaning of the term 'cow' is at first determined and then the meaning of the term 'non-cow' is grasped as it is a correlative term, involving a constant reference to the object to be negated (excluded) by itself. If the positive meaning of the term 'cow' is already established then is there a reference to non-cow for the finding out of the meaning of the term 'cow' at all necessary? Is there any necessity of excluding non-cow? But for the proper understanding of the meaning of the term 'cow' the Buddhists have pleaded for the negative process.

Now, we see that without having recourse to the negative process the meaning of the term 'cow' is comprehensible. If this is so then the hypothesis of non-cow is gratuitous. The Buddhists may argue in favour of their hypothesis of an apoha that a particular cow is only an established fact but not the universal of cowness. Such an argument is not tenable. A particular is a point of reality. It cannot be communicated to others by means of a word. The Mīmāṁsakas haves tated that if a universal is a necessary assumption for the understanding of the meaning of a term then the attempt at the framing of the hypothesis of an apoha is futile.

Now, the Buddhists may contend that the apoha 'non-non-cow' denotes all cows without an exception. Such a hypothesis involves an irrefutable fallacy of circular reasoning. If the meaning of the term 'non-non-cow' is understood then that of the term 'cow' is grasped and, again, if the meaning of the term 'cow' is intelligible then that of the term 'non-non-cow' is comprehensible. In fine, the critics hold that as an apoha is incomprehensible so it is impossible to distinguish one apoha from another by means of a reference to difference in the objects negated by them. Do we negate particulars of a class by means of an apoha? Or, do we negate a whole class in an abstract —a general character, i.e., a universal? Nobody can negate a particular of a class since a particular transcends the scope of the conceptual process of negating. Moreover, no particular is denoted by a term. Now, if the Buddhists hold that the object to be negated bears a general character then though it is negative in its character yet it must be admitted to be generic at the same time. Why do you hold that an apoha is the negation of a negation? Are you not aware of the import of the phrase 'the negation of a negation'. When one negation cancels another negation the resultant of this counter-negating process is a positive object. Thus the meaning of a word is not negative. It is a positive object.

Now, another question flashes in our mind. It is this : Does the exclusion itself of the objects to be excluded such as a horse, etc., differ from them? Or, does it become identical with them? If the Buddhists hold that the said exclusion has a specific character by means of which it distinguishes itself from the objects negated then it will be accepted as a positive object. One cannot characterize a negation. Hence, no verbal transaction is possible with it. One can only make a statement about a positive object and communicate it to others. If the

Buddhists say that an apoha is possessed of a specific character, i.e., a mark of distinction then it is surely a positive object since a positive object is only predicated and communicated to others by means of a proposition. If the Buddhists hold that an apoha and the object negated by it are one and the same thing then the term 'cow' and 'non-non-cow' should be synonymous since both these two terms denote negation. Moreover, if a term denotes merely an exclusion (apoha) then the proposition that this lotus is blue will lose all its significance since the relation of identity holds between the subject and the predicate and the relation of identity cannot be maintained in this case. A negation cannot predicate another negation. Two distinct negative terms cannot point to the same object. There is no such real object as is referred to by the two negations as their substratum. Though the Buddhists hold that the points of reality which are exclusively particular are objectively real but they transcend denotation. No other objects are real. Hence the relation of negation with reality is not at all possible. Moreover, the Buddhists deny existence to the relation of denotation which holds between a term and the object denoted by it.

As the negative meaning of the words 'existent' and 'knowable' is impossible to find out so they do not denote 'apohas'. Nobody is aware of an unreal object as other than an existent object and of an unknowable object as other than a knowable object. If the objects to be excluded are necessarily presented to our consciousness then they must be taken as existent and knowable. Thus the term 'existent' and 'knowable' can exclude neither non-existent and unknowable objects nor existent and knowable objects. What is beyond the reach of our consciousness cannot be negated. Therefore, the Buddhists cannot hold that the object to be excluded has an imaginary being since if the object to be excluded is a construction of our imagination then the object to be excluded ceases to be unreal and unknowable but becomes knowable.

We should also examine the meaning of the word 'apoha'. It will certainly mean the exclusion of non-apoha. What is the nature of non-apoha? (If every word denotes an apoha then non-apoha is certainly unknown something). If the Buddhists say that non-apoha is not at all possible then why is it not possible? If it does not exist then what remains to be negated? Therefore, the word conveys no meaning. How do you account for the negative particles 'not' (nañ), etc.? In the sentence "It does not exist" what is the meaning of the particle 'not'. How do the preposition and a group of indeclinables (conjunction etc.) known as nipāta denote apoha. It is difficult to establish that a verb denotes a negative meaning. In the sentence "He cooks" the verb 'cooks' cannot have a negative meaning.

Now, the Buddhists may revise their thesis and hold that only common nouns denote apoha. All words do not denote apoha. The Mīmāṁsakas ask 'How do they explain words other than common apohas' then how will the Buddhist reconcile revised thesis with their initial proposition that all words denote apohas. Why do the Buddhists cherish so much hatred against the view that common nouns denote universals which are not conceptual? Words other than common nouns are either meaningless or denotative of concepts. Let common nouns share the same lot. Why do the Buddhists mark an exhibition of their ignorance propounding the thesis that words denote apohas?

The Buddhists hold that a sentence signifies mere conceptual knowledge, i.e., agreement or difference between coucepts. They flatly deny that a sentence points to the meanings of words mutually related. Very well, let words denote concepts. Why do they insist upon propounding the thesis that words denote apohas?

(In this connection we shall refer to some other points which have not been explicitly mentioned by Jayanta. The 'negative' particle 'not' broadly denotes two meanings, viz., emphatic denial and bare denial. If the negative particle 'not' denotes an apoha then these two meanings cannot be made out. The word 'nipāta' requires an explanation. A word which does not convey its own meaning which is not associated with that of a verb as identical with that of another word in a sentence is called a nipāta. Its meaning is also distinct from that of inflexions. A nipāta may admit of many meanings. The nipāta 'ca' admits of three meanings. It may convey the sense of 'and' or that of 'only' or that of 'because'. If the nipāta 'ca' denotes an apoha then many sentences containing 'ca' will be meaningless. Prepositions which are affixed to verbs and are devoid of independent meanings are called upasargas. They cannot denote apoha. A verb in the active voice denotes an activity of its agent (its nominative case). If it denotes an apoha then there will be no relation between the verb and its nominative case).

Denunciation of the hypothesis of universals and advocacy of the hypothesis of apohas

The Buddhists now review the criticisms of apoha, offered by the Mīmāṁsakas. The Mīmāṁsakas have made those remarks as they are innocent of the views of the Buddhists.

If an apoha is a positive object and belongs to the external world then the cobwebs of your arguments rightly entangle the Buddhists. But an apoha is not so as the Mīmāṁsakas think of it. But, according to the Buddhists, an apoha is an inner object since it is a form of consciousness. Now, if it is an inner object then what will be the fate of your arguments, demonstrated by proposition ? In other words, your arguments will be pointless. Does it mean that an apoha is that awareness of an object which includes the object in itself ? Such a statement is not exact. An apoha is neither inner nor outer but it is distinctly other than both consciousness and its object.

Now, the Mīmāṁsakas raise a question and ask, "If something is neither an internal nor an external object then it should be unreal. How do the Buddhists hold that the meaning of a word is such an unreal object, viz., an apoha ?"

A reply to the above question is as follows. The Buddhists say, "As we have not appeared on the scene with the intention of establishing the reality of meanings of words so how do you frame a charge in this manner ? As it belongs neither to the inner world nor to the outer world so it is held to be unreal and imaginary. Now, you may ask, "What is its exact character ?" Our reply is this that it is referred to by a judgment which is a construction of our imagination and that it is merely a vague form which is attributed to knowledge. The Mīmāṁsakas ask—if an external object does not stand in front of a perceiver then the form of which object is referred to by a judgment as its predicate ? We beg to point out in reply to the above question that the suggestion of the Mīmāṁsakas does not hold good that the form of a sensible object is only referred to by a judgment as its predicate. The reason behind our reply is as follows. An object which is exclusively particular is sensed by us. But when we have a true sense-perception of an object it is not presented to our consciousness as excluded from all other objects. We have stated before that an object as excluded from all objects is referred to only by a judgment of perception. Or, as a judgment of perception judges about the image of a point of reality so it fails to reveal a real object, i.e., an exclusively particular but reveals only an exclusion."

Now, the Mīmāṁsakas raise a strong objection against the above solution, offered by the Buddhists. They point out that as an exclusion and the object which is excluded by it are identical so an exclusion and a point of reality which is excluded from all other objects are one and the same object. Thus they draw the conclusion from the above premises that judgments of perception refer to points of reality as they refer to an exclusion. They remark that judgment of perception should enjoy the same status as an indeterminate perception, i.e., pure sense-perception. The Buddhists give a reply to this objection. They hold that such a remark is baseless. Judgments of perception do never refer to the points of reality. An exclusion which is referred to by a judgment of perception is not real. But it is merely an imaginary form which is attributed to the subject of a judgment. If the said exclusion were real and belonged to the point of reality then the above objections would have been true. But the exclusion in question is not so. This point has been made clear already.

Some objectors raise a new objection against the above conclusion of the Buddhists. They say that an awareness of exclusion involves three factors, viz., it refers to the object which is excluded, to those objects from which it is excluded and to the objective ground of exclusion. As a judgment of perception which is held by the Buddhists to refer to exclusion does not reveal these three factors so how can it be a judgment about exclusion ? The Buddhists meet this objection. They hold that the above objection will hold good if the perceiver of exclusion expresses his judgment of perception in the proposition "I behold the object as excluded from all other objects."

But the corresponding proposition does not assume the above form. Therefore, the objection, raised by some objectors, does not hold good.

The Mīmāṁsakas press forward their objection. They hold that it is unreasonable to hold that judgments refer to imaginary forms. But the reasons which have been advanced by the Buddhists in favour of the hypothesis that a judgment refers to an exclusion are inconsistent. If the Buddhists admit the truth of the above finding then why do they indulge in sophistry and mystify apoha ?

The Buddhists meet this objection and solve the problem thus: The determinate perception of a cow follows in the wake of its indeterminate perception. It refers to its class-name, viz., cow and to its universal, i.e., cowness and to such other features. The perceptual judgment of a cow is expressed by the proposition that this is a cow. Similar judgments also refer to a negative form which excludes the object in question from others. Thus the proposition 'This is a cow' assumes the form 'This is not non-cow.' But the proposition 'This is a cow' does not assume the form 'This is other than a horse, a cat and such other objects.' This judgment of perception does not refer to the point of reality. There is no real object such as a universal in this world. For this reason an exclusion from others than the object in question is referred to by a judgment of perception. The above reasons indicate that a judgment has only a passing reference to the negative form. This is what the Buddhists say. This statement does not mean that an apoha is the direct object of perception.

Now, the Mīmāṁsakas urge their point in criticism against the Buddhists thus: According to the Buddhists what is perceptible is other than non-perceptible and is also other than its homogeneous objects. This is the true character of a thing-in-itself which is sensed by us. An object which is referred to by a judgment is presented to our consciousness as other than its heterogeneous objects. But a thing-in-itself is never presented to our consciousness in such a manner. A judgment involves a necessary reference to an exclusion from non-objects. But it does not involve a reference to an exclusion from homogeneous objects. But no regulator which determines the cognate character of knowledge is discovered. Oh, intelligent one ! do not entertain the thought that judgments which are constructed by our imagination are not determinate. What determines an object distinguishes it from all homogeneous and heterogeneous objects. This distinction is presented to our consciousness. If such two-fold distinction is revealed by imaginary knowledge then it becomes determinate knowledge in all respects. In that case, all other forms of imaginary knowledge and words should point to such well-defined objects. But it is not a correct statement of facts. If the above view is true then why does the image of a cow, produced by the word 'cow' distinguish a cow from heterogeneous objects but not from homogeneous objects ? Words and judgments, constructed by imagination, have the same import. For this reason, it is held that words denote an exclusion from objects other than itself, i.e., a negative image—an apoha.

The negative image in the form that this is an exclusion of all other than this is constructed by our imagination and is attributed to the image of the thing-in-itself. As it is an attribution so it does not belong to the external world. As it is not a form of consciousness so it does not belong to the inner world. For this reason you take this apoha as negation which belongs to the external world. And as you are a fool so you talk yourself hoarse, finding fault with the hypothesis of apoha without rhyme or reason. An apoha is undoubtedly referred to by a judgment. But a judgment which judges about a positive object or about a negative object does not judge about apoha. An apoha is judged by a distinct type of judgment. Hence it is neither a positive object nor a negative one. (This hypothesis of apoha has been propounded by Kamala Śīla in his Tattva-saṁgraha. The commentator holds that an apoha is not a positive object as its form does not belong to the outer world. It is not negation since it is determined as a real object. T.S.p. 361). It is presented to our consciousness as distinct from both positive and negative objects, determinate in its character and similar to external objects. It is not reasonable to hold that these three features belong to any external object. When a judgment has a positive predicate the copula implies the relation of identity. But if a judgment has an apoha as its predicate then the relation of identity does not reasonably hold between the subject and the predicate since the relation in question has no scope there. Moreover, in a negative judgment an apoha cannot be identified with negation since an apoha is determined as a real object and its identification with negation is self-contradictory. When a cow is perceived and judged that this is a cow but not a horse, an apoha has a well-defined character. There is a cow but not a horse, an apoha haś a well-defined charaeter. There is no element of indetermination in it. We cannot determine an object without negating other objects. A judgment which involves an apoha must have a necessary reference to an exclusion from all other than itself. It becomes impossible to determine an object if exclusion does not come to its aid. If it is impossible for exclusion to extend its help to determination then our knowledge enters into the sphere of a doubt. If a doubt envelops an object then it will be never determined. If externality is denied to an apoha then the different judgments which refer to the same apoha will be an idle repetition of the initial judgment referring to the apoha in question. In order to avert this difficulty an apoha should be considered as an external object. Even if we subscribe to this amended hypothesis, the possibility of such repetition is not ruled out. Therefore, an apoha should not be taken as an external object. Therefore, the original hypothesis that an apoha is neither external nor internal stands to reasons.

An apoha is neither an external object nor an internal object. It has got only an attributed form. It appears to be an external object. If it does not bear the stamp of exclusion on the face of it then it will not be similar to an external object. Our experience is the ultimate result from which we can trace back the hypothesis that judgments of imagination refer to exclusion.

Though all words such as a cow, a horse, etc., are employed *ab initio* to denote positive objects yet the logicians settle their meanings that they are employed to point to the exclusion of all other than themselves. According to these logicians it has been stated that the interpreters of words accept the negative meanings of words after much deliberation but the employers of words do not do it. The negative meaning of a word is called an apoha. It is neither internal nor external. It is something different. It is an ascribed form. As it is fashioned by the shadow of exclusion so it is called a negating object, i.e., an apoha. This view is based upon the hypothesis that an unreality is presented to consciousness. Or, an imaginary image is only a from of consciousness. It is a mere idea having no object to represent. The distinct shape of each idea is fashioned by variety of impressions though its distinct individual character is not due to difference in real external objects which are supposed to produce the different ideas. As ideas appear as external objects so all our worldly transactions are carried on by means of them. As they carry the stamp of exclusion on their face so they discharge the function of negative. This view presupposes the externalisation of our consciousness.

Now, some objectors raise an objection against the above solution of the problem. The upholders of both hypothesis, viz., the presentation of unreality to our consciousness and the projection of consciousness to the external world agree to the proposal that judgments do not refer to the real objects. How do we carry on transaction with the real objects? The Buddhists say in reply to this that when the things in themselves such as grasses etc. are sensed by a person he feels no desire for taking hold of them since desire at the root of volitional reaction and motion is not provoked by pure sense-perception. If you ask 'Why', then we submit what we have got to say. The external thing-in-itself is bereft of a name, a universal etc. A name or a universal is a construction of our imagination. It is an attribution. The real thing-in-itself seems to be identical with the imaginary object. Let us explain how this identification takes place. After the sensing of the real thing-in-itself, the sensible object, a judgment having a name, a universal, etc. as its predicate follows in the wake of it. The perceiver thinks that he has acquired the true knowledge of the thing-in-itself. In other words, he fails to detect his own mistake and believes that he knows the real object.

The reason behind the identification of the thing-in-itself, the sensible object, which is beyond the reach of imagination with the imaginary object which is possessed of a name, universal, etc. is nothing extraordinary. We are firmly impressed with their identification because the determinate perception of an object closely succeeds its indeterminate perception, i.e., pure sense-perception. Being misled by the quick succession of events of perception the perceiver forgets the momentary character of a thing-in-itself and believes that he knows the sensible object. This wrong identification is at the root of his movement. The sum and substance of the Buddhist hypothesis is that the identification of a sensible object with an imaginary one supplies us with the key-note of the movement of the percipient. Non-discrimination of the difference of the sensible thing-in-itself from the imaginary object which is endowed with a name; a universal, etc. is responsible for the identification of the one with the other. If this account of the Buddhists is taken to be true then does the ascertainment of the non-difference of the two said distinct objects amount to their identification? When we mistake the mother-of-pearls for silver as we fail to distinguish between them so we cannot merely assert that they are different. Similarly, we are not in a position to assert that sensible object is different from the imaginary object. The determination of the non-difference of the two events of perception presupposes the simultaneous presence of the said two perceptions as its condition. But when pure sense-perception takes place the determinate perception of the imaginary object is conspicuous by its absence. Therefore, pure sense-perception cannot condition the said determination of non-difference. The determinate perception of the imaginary object cannot produce the above determination of non-difference since a judgment of perception cannot refer to the sensible thing-in-itself. For this reason, it is stated that owing to the non-apprehension of difference between the two objects the person who judges an object moves for it. The thing-in-itself, a sensible object, which has practical efficiency is also found out since all the subsequent events are causally linked up with the sensible thing-in-itself. The thing-in-itself is the source of pure sense-perception which generates determinate perception. Movement follows in the wake of this determinate perception. This is what the Buddhists mean to convey.

A perceiver senses the thing-in-itself which is at the root of all sorts of perception. Though the subsequent judgment of perception propels him to bring the objects of perception yet he gets at the real object when he obeys the dictates of his determinate perception. Let us cite an example to illustrate the point in question. Suppose there is a gem inside a bamboo-stick-box. This gem emits its rays through the intervals of the sticks. A man mistakes the rays for a gem. He moves for it. He is crowned with success. In other words, he gets at the real gem. But if there is no real object at the root of his perception then an illusory judgment becomes his motive force which sets him in motion. He becomes disappointed when he moves for it. Suppose, a person mistakes the flame of a lamp for a gem. He proceeds to have it at the instance of his illusory perception. His hopes are baffled. But if a thing-in-itself is at the root of one's perception then he who is innocent of the real nature of things thinks that he has seen the real object by means of his determinate perception not referring to the real object and has got at the object when he has acted in accordance with the finding of the said perception. This impression of the person is not based upon the true knowledge of a real object. (A judgment is not true apprehension. Pure sense-perception is true. As it is not mixed up with imagination so it does not impel one to action. A judgment of imagination can only prompt one to an action). The Buddhist logicians hold that an object referred to by a judgment is not real and that an object which is real is never referred to by a judgment which impels a perceiver to activity. When a perceiver perceives an imaginary object and believes it to be real he moves towards it. From the above discourse it is clear that the Buddhists should interpret the determination of an object in terms of the non-discrimination of difference between a real object and an imaginary one. Thus, the perceiver identifies the real object with the imaginary one, moves towards it and gets at the real object. So we say that an ordinary person transacts his worldly business in this way. On the other hand, a critical thinker has got to carry on his worldly transactions like a common man.

An image which catches a likeness of exclusion is designated as an apoha. It is held by the Buddhists as the meaning of a word. But as an ordinary man cannot adequately analyse the content of his awareness so he mistakes an apoha for a universal.

All the laws which govern the location or non-location of universals upon their locii, (i.e. their complete or partial standing upon their locii) equally apply to apohas. But there is a sharp distinction between an apoha and a universal. It is this that an apoha is unreal.

Though all drugs have the same specific property yet all of them cannot cure alike diseases, viz., fever, etc. But a particular drug can do it. Similarly, though all particulars, having no universals to mark off, are theoretically capable of producing the same effects yet distinct particular produces a distinct effect. The Buddhists mean to say that the Naiyāyikas postulate universals on the basis of the assumption that a distinct class of particulars produces a distinct class of effects. This assumption is superfluous. But it should be assumed that the capacity of producing the same effect does not belong to all particulars. The positive aspect of this assumption is that a distinct particular produces a distinct effect.

According to the Buddhists though an apoha is unreal yet it is not true that it cannot be characterized by adjectives, etc. Therefore, the Naiyāyikas should not subscribe to the hypothesis that the meaning of a word is a universal, or the form of an object or a particular.

The proof of the reality of universals

The above objections against the reality of universals are thus met with. Does an apoha get the preferential treatment at your hand because a word does not denote an external object such as a universal, etc., owing to its non-existence or because experience testifies to the existence of an apoha ? We find no reason to pick a quarrel with you on the point whether an apoha is experienced or not since you hold that an apoha is experienced by you. This does not imply that a universal does not exist. As you hold that a distinct thing-in-itself is an object of pure sense-perception which is neither a doubt nor an error so we hold that a universal is an object of non-erroneous perception.

Is it a royal edict that the initial perception is only connected with the thing-in-itself but the subsequent perception is not so connected ? Or, let the initial perçeption be the source of true knowledge. But how do you say that it reveals only its characteristic feature but not its generic character ?

We shall not kill our time in detecting the content of pure sense-perception since pure sense-perception is very short-lived. On the one hand, you hold that sense-perception reveals only the peculiar trait of an object but, on the other hand, we state that perception reveals also the generic character of a thing. If we go on disputing like this then how shall we settle matters ? It will not be settled by one taking one's oath since an affidavit has no jurisdiction over this matter. Consequently we should take into consideration the working of perception which extends over a longer period and solve the problem on its finding. In other words, we should accept the existence of generic character as sense datum. In this context if you hold that the first sense-perception reveals only individual features then how does a judgment of perception refer to its generic character ?

The Buddhists cannot hold that the judgment in question is a piece of verbal knowledge but not a piece of perceptual knowledge. Verbal knowledge is always caused by the knowledge of a word. The name of an object plays no part in producing its determinate perception. Even if the name remains unknown the determinate perception of an object takes place. The perceiver is directly aware of the generic character of the said object. Let us illustrate the point in question. A Deccanise while perceiving a series of similar fleeting things has discovered a common element which is equally shared by the past and the present things. He has perceived a persisting common element. If a person who is innocent of the relation of denotation, i.e., does not know the name of a new class of objects, sees many strange objects at a place then he sees their generic and specific characters.

Moreover, whenever the four fingers of a person come in contact with the eyes of a person he sees them and understands their common and peculiar features. If this is so, how do you say that the individual trait of a thing is only visualised ? Moreover, a person saw as individual cow called Śābaleya in the past. At a later period he sees another individual cow Bāhuleya by name. Experience says that he remembers Śābaleya which was seen before. (We cannot explain the remembrance of Śābaleya if no common property belongs to these two individual cows. It is unreasonable to hold that a common element is not grasped. How can we remember an individual on beholding another individual which is entirely different from the first?

As a person remembers an individual cow seen before on beholding another individual cow so we think that he has seen a common property which belongs to both of them. We shall also add that even if we behold another individual cow, i.e. other than the seen one then we recognise it that it is that cow. We have also proved that this piece of recognition is true. We shall discuss this point at a greater length when we shall refute the doctrine of universal flux. So we hold that the persisting common element is referred to by the judgment of recognition. As our perception reveals the mutual difference of individuals so the said judgment does not refer to individuals since they cannot be identical.

If we place some paste of sesame seeds or of pulse seeds by the side of heaps of sesame seeds and pulse seeds then we do not see with our eyes individual seeds in the paste. But we grasp with our sense-organs the common element belonging to the seeds and the paste. Therefore when we have an indeterminate perception of an object we perceive both the characters, specific and generic. Hence it is not wise to deny existence to universals. At the stage of initial perception the common and the peculiar traits of an object are presented to us. Hence the generic and the specific properties are real.

Now, the Buddhists may ask the Naiyāyikas : 'Is the generic property sensed in the form that this is common?' The Naiyāyikas also put this question to the Buddhists: 'Is a thing-in-itself also sensed in the form that this is different?' Though a universal is sensed by us yet it is not recognised as such, i.e. as a common element. At that stage our apprehension of a universal is not determinate. We are not aware of our apprehension because the substantive is not cognised in an expressible form. If we sense a universal but fail to introspect our sensing then we firmly assert that we have failed to acquire a distinct apprehension of the individuality of a thing-in-itself. But it is a matter of great regret that the Buddhists distinctly apprehend the exclusive character of a thing-in-itself by means of pure sense-perception.

The Buddhists ask, 'How can you know a universal as a common persisting element ? How are all individuals to which a universal belongs as their common property cognised ?' The Naiyāyikas give a retort to the Buddhists thus : 'How is an exclusion grasped ? As you are aware of all objects excluded from the thing-in-itself in question so we are conscious of all objects which are subsumed under the same class.' In other words, the method of apprehension is the same, i.e., the Buddhists and the Naiyāyikas have got to face the same difficulty.

The Buddhists contend that a thing-in-itself can never be sensed as devoid of both specific and generic characters. They also add that if the Naiyāyikas hold that it can be done then they should define the object of indeterminate perception. The Naiyāyikas hold that when an object is indeterminately perceived it cannot be expressed in a proposition. In other words, as this apprehension is not determinate so there is no clear-cut distinction between a subject and a predicate. How can it be expressed in a proposition ? But the perception which is generated by this determinate perception bears evidence to both the characters of an object. It reveals its individuality (i. e. specific character) and a universal (the generic character — the persisting common element). Therefore those who are thoughtful admit that each real object has two characters, unique and common.

These two (the Sautrāntikas and the Vaibhāṣikas) who hold that things-in-themselves have only one character, i.e., they have merely peculiarity, are great fools.

The refutation of objections against the Realīty of universals

One of the main objections raised by the Buddhists against the reality of universals that two incompatible characters cannot co-exist in the same locus at one time is not tenable. In this case no incompatibility subsists between a universal and the individuality of a thing-in-itself since no such incongruity is known to us. Let us take an example of opposition existing between the two judgments having the same object. When we mistake a piece of the mother-of-pearls for silver we cannot cognise the yonder object in the form that this is the mother-of-pearls and silver. But when one of the predicates is contradicted we cognise the other predicate. But in the present case such a contradiction takes place. (Let us explain the argument of Jayanta Bhaṭṭa). Suppose there is a yonder object, say, the mother-of-pearls. Its specific character is not observed by us. We attribute silverness to it. We cognise it in the form that this is silver. When this judgment is contradicted we are able to cognise it in its true character. Here the yonder object cannot be both the mother-of-pearls and silver. The individuality of a thing-in-itself and its generic character (a universal) are not incompatible with each other. They, without contradicting each other, co-exist in one and the same individual. Let us cite an example of such co-existence of the two characters in the same locus. A jarness and earthness co-inhere in an individual jar. A jar is a member of the jar-class. So it has the specific character of jarness. It is also an earthen pot. Hence it has got the generic character of earthness. So specific character and generic one co-exist in the same locus. These two characters are not incompatible with each other. Similarly, the peculiar trait of an object is not necessarily incompatible with its generic character. We are to reply upon the evidence of our perception for our decision in this matter. It cannot be formally decided that individuality is incompatible with the generic character). Because whenever there is contradiction between two predicates, one predicate is presented to our consciousness, contradicting the other one. In the present case there is no such contradiction between peculiarity and generality. So there is no need of assuming such contradiction between them. If we behold light and darkness as compresent in the same locus then who can say that one is incompatible with the other ? But as their compresence in one and the same locus at the same time is not observed so they are held to be incompatible with each other. But as individuality and generality are not observed to be incompatible so they are not incompatible.

Moreover, the awareness of the individuality of an object does not falsify that of its generality. The apprehension of the individuality of an object does not prevent the appearance of that of its generality and *vice versa*. The sum and substance of this verse is that there is no opposition between individuality and generality.

Kumārila in his Ślokavārttika has said to this effcct. An object has variegated colour. We may show one of its colours which we intend to do. Similarly, if an object has two characters then these two characters are noticed in it. Hence, we determine that the relation of identity-in-difference holds between an object and its characters. (Kumārila means to say that the universal as an abstract one is different from an individual. Hence, a universal is both identical with, and different from, an individual).

Therefore, in this manner as the relation of identity-in-difference has been determined to exist so let us subscribe to the hypothesis of Kumārila and hold that every object in this world has two characters, peculiar and generic. But we think that Kumārila, the great, dreading the cob-webs of sophistry in the shape of the problem of relation existing between an individual and a universal, has admitted the truth of the hypothesis of the relation of identity-in-difference. Let us take no notice of it. We feel no necessity of criticising it.

We hold that a universal is not identical with the individual to which it belongs and that it is different from an individual which possesses it but still the individual is its locus. The Buddhists in their treatises have recorded many problems regarding the relation of a universal with an individual. All of them will be solved by the majestic influence of perception. Perception alone will negate all the arguments of the Buddhists against the possibility of relation between an individual and a universal. (We see with our own eyes that a universal stands upon an individual. So a universal must be somehow related to an individual, the locus of it. But a universal consists of no parts. It is absolutely partless. It cannot partially stand upon its locus. It simultaneously inheres in all locii. We learn all these facts from perception. Hence, the logic chopping of the Buddhists is thoroughly meaningless).

The Buddhists have stated that as the mutual difference existing between a lotus flower and a myrobalan is noticed so no difference of a universal from an individual is observed by us. (The implication of this argument is that an individual is non-different from its universal). We have met this argument thus : 'The awareness of a universal is different from that of an individual. (The implication of this answer is that if they were identical with each other then they would not have been presented to our consciousness as different. The same object is not presented to our consciousness in a different manner). The second argument of the Buddhists against the distinct identity of a universal is that as a universal does not occupy a space distinct from that of an individual so they are not different. Let us clarify the objection raised by the Buddhists. A jar is different from a piece of cloth because a jar is sometimes seen at a place where a piece of cloth does not exist though they may sometimes co-exist in the same locus. But a universal does never keep itself apart from an individual, its locus. We never see it exist separately. Therefore, a universal is not distinct from an individual, the locus of the universal in question. The argument is not cogent since we cannot perceive a universal if an individual, its locus, is not perceived. As a universal always finds its locus in an individual so a universal, unrelated to an individual, is not observed. It is not a truism that a universal-in-itself is not seen because it does not exist. As a universal stands upon an individual, its locus, so it is not noticed at a spot where an individual does not exist. Do not think for this reason that a universal is not distinct from an individual.

The third objection raised by the Buddhists against the distinct identity of a universal that as the relation subsisting between a universal and an individual, its so-called locus, is not logically tenable so a universal is non-different from an individual, its locus. We give a reply to the objection thus : A universal wholly stands upon each of its locii. You may contend that if a universal wholly stands upon a particular locus (an individual) then it should not be noticed in another locus (another individual). Then we say by way of reply that whom shall we chastise for this ! It is a fact that it is also perceived in other individuals. How shall we conceal its perception from you ? A universal has no parts. How can we say that it partially exists in the different individuals. You may ask, "Does a universal stand upon some other locus ?" We answer your question with the remark : 'Your logical acumen is wonderful. You demand that an example is to be given in every case as we cite an instance to strengthen our syllogistic argument.'

If you ask : "What is the name of this relation ?" then we can this much say that it inheres in its locus but we do not know its proper name. We have also got to submit something in this context that the relation which subsists between two inseparable objects is called inherence. The Buddhists also join issue with the Naiyāyikas and hold that the relation of inherence which holds between two inseparable objects has been discarded since it has been proved that it involves logical contradictions. A reply to this objection is this that the relation of inherence cannot be dispensed with. The two objects which are held to be inseparably connected with each other cannot be taken as identical since the awareness of one is different from that of another and the difference in awareness cannot be explained if the corresponding object is not different. The two objects which are held to be different on epistemological grounds do not occupy different spaces. (Let us cite examples to illustrate the above point of view of the Naiyāyikas. A piece of cloth inheres in threads. A jar inheres in its parts, i.e., pot-sherds. A piece of cloth does never exist apart from threads. But threads exist independently of a piece of cloth. A thread inheres in its minute parts. But a piece of cloth does not inhere in them. A jar always inheres in pot-sherds. It can never exist apart from them. But a pot-sherd inheres in its parts. A jar does not inhere in them (these parts of pot-sherds). Though the parts of a whole can exist independently of a whole yet the whole cannot exist independently of its parts. Hence, as both the whole and its parts cannot exist independently of one another so they cannot be held to occupy distinct spaces. We cannot also hold that a piece of cloth identical with threads, its constituents and that a jar is identical with its parts, viz., pot-sherds). In such cases, where the two objects occupy the same space but are distinct from each other a distinct relation subsists between them as they are presented to our consciousness as related. This is called the relation of inherence.

The above relation holds between a whole and its parts and a substratum and its attributes. We shall prove later on that a whole is different from its parts and the substratum of attributes is different from its attributes. In these two cases as they occupy no separate spaces so there is no doubt about the fact that they are inseparably connected.

The Buddhists take an exception to the relation existing between an individual and a universal on the ground that if the individual does not come into existence independently of its relation with its universal then it cannot be related to a universal since a relation presupposes its relata. If a relatum does not exist, a relation cannot take place. If the Naiyāyikas admit that an individual exists prior to its relatedness then it is a case of relation which subsists between the two separable relata. Thus the thesis of the Naiyāyikas that the two relata are inseparable does not stand to reasons. This point has been answered by the great teachers of the Vaiśeṣika system. They hold that whenever an individual comes into existence it becomes related to its universal. We do not give this answer simply following the convention of our school. But we say this because uncontradicted experience lends its mighty support to it. Only on the strength of our own convention we do not hold that no ubiquitous substances are related to one another. We say this because it is impossible for them to be united with one another by a tie of relation. One cannot come in contact with another because there was no inter-space between them. The relation of conjunction takes place only when one comes in contact with another with which it has not been united. An ubiquitous substance inheres in none since it is self-sufficient. We have no experience as to the truth of the hypothesis that an omnipresent substance stands upon another such substance. We feel no need of stretching out this point.

The relation which holds between a wreath and a piece of thread, between the neck of an animal and a piece of rope and between such other objects is different from that which holds between an individual and a universal and between an attribute and a substance, etc., since a universal and an attribute, etc. have no parts. Again the Buddhists have pointed out an defect in the hypothesis of the relation of inherence that the existence of the relation of inherence in its relata cannot be rationally explained. This defect does not attract our notice. Moreover, they have put forward a dilemma, viz., either a universal is omnipresent or it exists only in its individuals and subjected the hypothesis to a severe criticism. The dilemma is not strong enough to smash this hypothesis. Experience is omnipotent. We honour the evidence of experience and frame a hypothesis in the light of our experience. In other words, our suggestions or conjecturs are based upon sound observation.

We admit that all universals wholly inhere in every locus, i.e., in every individual without an exception. In other words, all universals are omnipresent. But a universal is not perceived in every locus since a distinct individual is the manifestor of a universal but is not available in every place.

It is a well-known order of things that a particular individual manifests a distinct universal. There is no exception to this rule. Whenever the particular individual is perceived at a spot the universal manifested by it is also perceived there.

A universal is omnipresent but is not perceived everywhere. Whenever an individual which manifests a universal exists there the universal menifested by it, is also perceived.

Is there any proof that a universal occupies other spaces and does not solely inhere in individuals subsumed under a particular class? The universal of cow-ness has not been seen at a spot. If an individual cow is brought there the said universal is also perceived there.

As one can drag a body but not the soul so one can bring an individual cow to a spot but not the universal of cow-ness along with it. So, you will be compelled to admit that the universal of cow-ness existed at a spot where an individual was absent. Whenever a distinct individual is seen a universal is also manifested. For this reason, if a universal is once manifested at a spot then it will not be perceived there at other times (i. e., when an individual which manifests it will be absent from the spot). The manifestation of a universal takes place at the spot where a distinct individual is perceived. So, a universal is not seen at a spot where its manifestor does not exist.

Though the universal of cow-ness is shared by all individuals yet some thinkers hold that the class of individual cows is the special locus of it. So, the calf which sees the light of day today is cognised as a cow since everybody recognises it to be such.

Whenever an individual is born it becomes united with a universal since the union with a universal and the birth of an individual takes place simultaneously. A universal does not reside in its locus before the beginning of the locus. A universal does not come to its new locus from an old one. But the material cause from which the locus of a universal comes into being enforces its union with a universal. If one questions : 'How does it take place ?' then he finds fault with the cause of another effect. In other words, he does not follow the operation of the law of causation.

Now, we put a question to you. A bull is tawny brown. A cow is black. She eats green grass. The pair procreates a white calf. How does an event like this take place ?

As an individual in which a universal finds its locus is not perceived if it does not possess attributes such as colour, etc., so if a locus does not possess attributes such as colour, etc., then a universal, located upon it, is not perceived. If we frame a hypothesis of universals in the manner described above then how does a series of contradictions indicated by our objector affect it ?

If we subscribe to the hypothesis of an exclusion from non-cows in lieu of the universal of cow-ness then it does not silence serious questions. How does a calf (a thing-in-itself) which is born to-day become excluded from non-cows ? In other words, if a calf is excluded from non-cows as soon as it is born then it becomes also united with a universal as soon as it is born.

In fine, we beg to submit the following : You should give up the tendency of demonstrating your skill in destructive criticisms. You should follow the track of universal experience of the world of real objects. Then you should suggest such types of real objects as are not exposed to blemishes. You should follow the right way of thinking. Do not be impervious to reason and unreasonably obstinate.

As our experience of a particular remains ever uncontradicted so our experience of a universal does never meet with contradiction. It has been already stated that the concept of a universal involves no contradiction. As we cannot deny existence to a particular so we cannot deny existence to a universal. As we perceive a particular with our sense-organ so we perceive a universal. Hence, we cannot hold that a universal is a creation of our imagination. A universal is not an inference. We do not infer it from an effect. If we had subscribed to this view then we would have been taken to task since an effect may be otherwise explained. As a universal is directly cognised so the above objection is absolutely baseless. If a logician holds that the idea of continuity or persistence is due to a distinct power but not due to a universal then what is this distinct power? Is it eternal or non-eternal? Is it dependent upon or independent of a particular? Is it sensed by us? Or, is it transcendental to our sense-organs? If we deny existence to a universal then the above problems arise in our mind and press for their immediate solution. Considering all these aspects of the problem the distinguished logicians subscribe to the hypothesis that a universal exists without diving deep into the matter. This is merely a superficial account of the hypothesis of a universal.

Now, a fresh problem arises in our mind. As the Naiyāyikas hold that distinct universals such as the universal of cow-ness etc. stand upon distinct groups of individuals so the Buddhists may as well hold that some individuals of a particular group produce a common idea i. e., some individual cows produce the idea of cowness and that all individuals of a group are not required to produce it. This alternative suggestion does not hold good since the distinct character of an idea is only explained by a distinction in the character of its corresponding object. If they hold that the conditions of the said idea being different, the idea is different then the Naiyāyikas may as well say in reply "You are agreeable to assume a distinct condition. But why do cherish hatred against assuming a distinct object viz., a universal?" If you admit the truth of the general law that a distinct idea has a corresponding distinct object then existence cannot be denied to a universal.

Now, the Buddhists take an exception to this view. They hold that though a universal does not stand upon other universals yet they produce a common idea. Why are the Naiyāyikas partial to universals? In other words, the Buddhists find out an exception to the above general law and challenge its truth. The Buddhists advance another argument to disprove the hypothesis that a word denotes a universal. They argue thus:—Suppose there are fifty objects of the same kind. We count them one after another as one, two, three, four and so on up to fifty. But if you hold that the number belongs to a universal but not to an individual then you are to count each one of them as fifty. This is absurd. Hence, the hypothesis of a universal has no justification. If the idea of an army without noticing elephants, horses etc. or that of a forest without noticing certain kinds of trees such as dhava, khadira (catachu) etc. arises in our mind then it turns out to be a false one. On this ground shall we hold that the idea of a jar shall also be wrong? Let us clarify the above argument of Jayanta. We employ the words 'army', 'forest' to signify their proper denotation. If we see a crowd of men and call it an army then the word has been wrongly used. Similarly, if we see a row of trees in a garden and say that this is a forest then the word 'forest' has been wrongly employed. The ideas conveyed by these words are also erroneous. In some cases, if we wrongly employ a word then it does not mean that in every case we wrongly use a word. Similarly, if some ideas are wrong then it does not mean that every idea is erroneous. If a judgment is contradicted then it is false. If one holds that a universal belongs to the universal of existence then the proposition is false since no universal belongs to a universal such as the universal of existence. "The genesis of a false judgment is traced to some conditions. They are responsible for the attribution of a predicate to a subject. But the idea of cowness cannot be framed by means of individual cows with the help of some conditions. This is merely a very short statement of arguments in defence of the hypothesis of a universal.

Kumārila has said to this effect :-

As existence belongs to the different objects so it is called a common property of all of them. Or, as it produces the same idea so it is called a common property.

Now, the Buddhists say that as the different individuals have got the same practical efficiency so it seems to us that they possess a common property. As they serve the same purpose so they produce in our mind the idea of oneness. The drift of this argument is this that without assuming a universal the idea of oneness may be explained. No doubt you have stated a rival hypothesis but it does not stand upon sound logical ground since the basic hypothesis that the different causes have the same practical efficiency has not yet been established.

The Buddhists have also stated that concepts are identical since the causes of them are always the same. Such a statement is not logically sound. A concept it not the joint product of many sense-perceptions. But each concept follows in the wake of a sense-perception. Hence one concept is different from another concept. Thus concepts are many. Concepts have no distinct part to play so that they may make the impression that they are the same. How do the Buddhists know that they are identical ? The identity of concepts is not sensed since sensible objects are only sensed. The identity of concepts is not a sensible object. The Buddhists may hold that the identity of concepts is established by means of a distinct concept. The Naiyāyikas will also point out that the above solution is not satisfactory since all concepts point to an imaginary object only or they cognise the form of an imaginary object only. But they are not competent enough to grasp their identity or distinction. Now, they should argue like this. All concepts reveal such forms as cannot be mutually distinguished. Hence they are held to be one. Suppose, an individual cow the 'Śābaleya' is sensed. This sense perception produces a concept. It reveals the general form of a cow. Another individual cow is sensed. The second sense-perception also produces another concept. But this concept does also reveal the same form. As these concepts fail to reveal a distinct object so the objects which are revealed by concepts cannot be distinguished from one another. Hence, though sense-perceptions which produce concepts are different yet concepts present themselves in such a manner that the distinct identity of their causes cannot be traced. Sense-perceptions, having lost their marks of distinction, become fused into one.

The above argument is not convincing. As concepts are fleeting phenomena of consciousness so they are mutually distinguishable, But the distinct character of forms which they reveal are not made out. Is the form of a concept distinct from a concept itself ? Or is it identical with the concept itself ?

This question should be answered at first. If it is distinct from a concept then it is nothing but a universal in a different name. But the Buddhists may contend that a universal is real whereas the form of a concept is unreal. Hence, the form of a concept is distinct from a universal.

Such a contention is not tenable, since no sound argument has been advaneed to negate the reality of a universal. Again, if it is held that the form of a concept is identical with the concept itself then these forms are mutually different as these concepts are and they cannot be unified. In that case how can the fusion of antecedent sense-perceptions into one be justified? Oh fool! you do not admit the existence of a universal. But when you have been asked 'How do the similar concepts arise?' You have said 'Because sense-perceptions produce the same effect. viz. similar concepts'. None but a mad man can give an answer like this. Hence it is foolish to state that phenomena of consciousness which produce identical phenomena of consciousness are identical.

The Refutations of the Hypothesis That a Concept Points to the Exclusion of its other

The Buddhists have an incoherent statement to establish the hypothesis that concepts point to and words denote the exclusion of their other. They hold that proofs other than perception are not so powerful that they will discover properties of an object, non-sensed by perception. Hence concepts and words function to negate the other forms attributed to the real image of an object. For this reason concepts refer to and words denote the exclusion of their other. Such a defence is really insignificant.

An object which has been sensed in every possible way cannot be held to be not perceived. The logicians of the Nyāya school hold that knowledge which reveals what has been known is also true. If the doctrine of universal flux is refuted then it is not unreasonable to hold that an object which has been already grasped by us at a particular point of time and space may also be known to us in a different place and at a different period of time. Moreover, the Naiyāyikas hold that a substratum possesses a good number of properties and all of them are not simultaneously perceived by a person. Some of its properties are grasped by a particular proof. Some of them will be detected by a different proof and so on. A substratum is one. But it acquires various properties, capacities being accompanied by various accidental accessories. These properties or capacities according to a substratum are secondary ones. Why will a substratum change its identity every moment because of its changing aspects ?

Or, suppose, if a substance is grasped in its entirety by an act of sense-perception and then is determined again by a number of perceptual judgments then will these judgments be futile ? Can we conjecture on this account that determinate perception points to some thing which remains outside the scope of sense-perception ? Certainly, we cannot indulge in a conjecture like this. Suppose, the thirst of a person has been quenched. Hence, the lunar orb is of no use to him. Can we therefore imagine that the lunar orb is silver ? It is a wild goose chase. In other words, we cannot imagine that concepts point to the exclusion of their other. And thus we arrive at the conclusion that concepts point to and words denote real external objects which are not mere exclusions from their other. If this conclusion is accepted then we see nothing wrong with criticisms offered by Kumārila Bhaṭṭa.

In order to meet the charges brought by Kumārila against the hypotheses of Apoha the Buddhists have revised their original theses and made a new suggestion that concepts point to an image having imaginary form which is tinged by the rejection of real exclusion. They also hold that words also denote such an imaginary image. We cannot carry on worldly transactions with such an image.

What is known by the name of a concept is conciousness. It is stainless by its very nature. It does not become impure without coming in contact with something else. The existence of some colouring matters must be postulated in order to tinge it. They may be either internal impressions or external objects.

If it is held that the colouring matter which tinges consciousness is neither internal nor external then it is a great artful dodge engineered by the cunning fellows. Only objects truly characterize consciousness since impressions, being effectuated by the consciousness of objects, cannot characterize consciousness.

Thus consciousness must be characterized only by objects though they may exist in a distant place. But an imaginary object which exists nowhere cannot characterize consciousness. It is merely an idle conjecture. The form of an imaginary object cannot be attributed. Judgments which follow senseperception in quick succession re-do the work of sense perception. They cannot create objects which are excluded. The Buddhists may hold that they refer only to exclusion. The Naiyāyikas take an exception to this view. They point out that as all sensible objects are other than their homogeneous and heterogeneous objects so both sense-perception and determinate perception should refer to exclusion. Why should the judgment of perception only refer to an exclusion ? The Buddhists may argue that if both types of perception refer to an exclusion then the judgments of perception should be futile as they simply repeat the work of sense-perception. Such an argument does not hold good. If the Buddhists hold that judgments of perception are true but futile owing to the fact that they merely refer to the known objects then the Naiyāyikas may agree with them in this point of criticism. The Buddhists may also hold that these judgments point to some other objects in order to free them from the charge of being futile. This much they may be allowed to hold. But the Naiyāyikas have no faith in the Buddhist thesis that the judgments of perception only refer to the exclusion from the heterogeneous objects but not to that from the homogeneous objects.

As there is no distinction between the exclusion from the heterogeneous objects and that from the homogeneous objects so the hypothesis that judgment of perception only refers to one of these two types of exclusion does not hold good. If judgments of perception refer to both types of exclusion, i.e., from the homogeneous and the heterogeneous objects then they should reveal only particulars like sense perception. If this be so then we shall not be able to communicate that a word denotes a class of objects, on inductive conclusion and so on since the relation of denotation, universal concomitance, etc. presuppose universals as their terms.

Thus verbal knowledge, inferential knowledge and so on should go to hell. If the said exclusion is an external object then the destructive criticisms, offered by Kumārila, will threaten the Buddhist hypothesis like thunder. If concepts are internal phenomena then they cannot characterize consciousness. If they are neither external nor internal objects then they are merely empty words, Have such objects some degrees of reality or not? If they are absolutely unreal objects such as the horns of a hare they have no practical efficiency. We shall follow the path already chalked out to refute the presentation of unreal objects and criticise the hypothesis in question from that standpoint. A real object should be either internal or external. Hence, the new path, devised by the Buddhists, in order to escape from the charges laid down by Kumārila. is perilous. Hence one should postulate objects corresponding to his judgments. If concepts refer to external objects then it is reasonable to hold that they are related to existence or non-existence imported by some other words. When we hear a word, viz., a cow, the awareness of a universal flashes in our mind. But the universal is not presented to our consciousness as related to existence or non-existence. It requires some sort of relation to existence or non-existence for its complete determination, That is why some other words are employed. The essential feature of an object is its everlasting property. It does not change. If the essence of an object is determined then it excludes itself from that of another object. A jar is always a jar. It does never hecome a piece of cloth. But from the above remark we cannot hold that a concept merely refers to negation, i. e., an exclusion. No need of dilating upon this point.

The Concluding Portion of the Proof of a Universal

All such transactions take place with regard to external objects. How do the Buddhists explain the movement of a person for an object? They say in reply that a perceiver moves for an object because he identifies a sensible object with a conceptual one. What is the character of this identification? If they hold that the identification in question stands for the non-detection of difference between a sensible object and a conceptual one then this state of mind resembles that of a person who has fallen into a swoon. If the Buddhists hold that an object which has not been determined inspires movement then it is a sensible object. In that case, an apoha (an exclusion of heterogeneous objects) has got no function to play. The Buddhists may hold that concepts are presented to our consciousness in their negative character. In that case when a perceiver goes near an object why does he with his mental powers unimpaired move for it?

If the Buddhists hold that a conceptual object appears to one as a sensible one then it is a case of illusion but not that of non-discrimination. An illusion having no ground does not take place. Moreover, this knowledge is not contradicted like the mistake of the rays of the sun for water. As there is nothing to contradict it so it is not an illusion.

Why do you say that one comes across an external object when he is propelled by a mistake just like a person who gets a gem, being misled by its rays ? Suppose, a person mistakes rays of a gem for a gem moves for it and acquires it. Similarly, why do the Buddhists say that when a person is guided by the light of a concept and moves for an object he gets an external object. It is consistent with the canon of logic that a person gets an external object because the judgment of perception is true. That is why the Naiyāyikas incline to discuss the topic that a word denotes an individual, its form and a universal.

If the existence of external objects is established then the Buddhists who disregard the distinction between imaginary and independently real external objects are put to silence. Now the meaning of the word 'cow' is discussed. The subject matter of our discussion is 'Does it stand for the form of a cow or its universal ?'

Subject of inquiry : The meaning of a word such as a cow etc.

When is the meaning of the word 'ākṛti'? It denotes the form of an individual i.e. the organisation of limbs of an individual. Those who follow the foot-steps of Jaimini hold that the word 'Ākṛti' denotes a universal. But the Naiyāyikas do not accept the said interpretation since in the Nyāya-Sūtra a distinction has been drawn between jāti and ākṛti.

Jaimini in his Mīmāṁsā Sūtra negates the rival view and holds that ākṛti denotes a universal since the form of an animal is useful in a sacrifice but if a universal were absolutely different from a form in the above case, it would be absolutely useless. Śabara, the commentator on the Mīmāṁsā Sūtra, sticks to the same interpretation since he says that a universal which is characterised by the form of an animal i. e. the arrangement of its limbs viz. dewlap etc. is useful in a sacrifice. Kumārila has elaborately explained this point in his Śloka-vārttika.

Kumārila says : A universal is ākṛti. The etymological meaning of the word 'ākṛti' is that it is such as determines an individual. A universal determines an individual. Therefore a universal is denoted by the word 'ākṛti'. A universal is the common property of all individuals. It is the source of the idea of oneness i. e. a general idea.

The author of the Nyāya-sūtra holds that the primary meaning suggests that a form is distinct from a universal. Hence he is of the opinion that the word 'ākṛti' denotes the form of an individual but not a universal. An ordinary person also holds that the word 'ākṛti' signifies an orderly arrangement of limbs of an individual. Merits reside in him who has a beautiful form. Hence, the word 'ākṛti' primarily denotes the orderly arrangement of limbs.

We should now discuss whether the form of an individual is denoted by a word or not. Like the followers of Jaimini we should not disregard 'ākṛti' which is also one of the possible meanings of a word viz. an individual, a form and a universal.

The establishment of the hypothesis that a word denotes only an individual.

These who hold that an ākṛti is one of the meanings of a word have stated, "It is well known to all that the meaning of a word is ascertained by the two methods viz. the use of a word by a speaker and the understanding of its meaning by a listener. Let us explain, the condensed statement. An experienced person employs a word to communicate his idea since it is significant. He employs the word 'cow' to convey a particular sense. A listener grasps the intended meaning from the word. The meaning which he understands is that of word. The experienced persons use the word 'cow' in order to convey a definite meaning. The listeners make out the exact meaning from that word. The meaning which they grasp is that of the word 'cow'. The experienced persons do not employ the word 'cow' to signify an animal having manes. But they intend to mean an animal having dewlap etc. Hence it is clear that the word 'cow' signifies a particular form. The word 'cow' is used to mean such an object as is sensed by us. The form of an object is perceptible. Our sense-organs point to the fact that the form of a cow is distinct from that of a horse. There is no doubt about the truth of the statement that the form of an object alone distinguishes the object itself from another. If the perceptible object constitutes the meaning of a word then the form of an object should be its meaning. The form of an object should be indirectly related to actions such as the act of sending etc. through the medium of an individual. This is the sum and substance of the thesis put forward by those who hold that the form of an object constitutes the meaning of a word. The above hypothesis does not stand the scrutiny of reasoning since the form of an object varies in every individual. It is not possible for one to know the relation of denotation holding between a word and all forms of all individuals belonging to a class. Does the said relation hold between a word and a few forms or between a word and all forms? Can the ākṛtivādins solve this dilemma? If they hold that the above relation holds between a word and a few forms then as the word also signifies those forms to which it is not related so the knowledge of these forms conveyed by it is false. If the word is related to every form then an infinite number of relations is to be postulated. The word 'cow' does not denote a particular form viz. the form of Śābaleya since it also denotes the form of Bāhuleya which excludes that of Śābaleya. We cannot find out a single common form which belongs to all individual cows scattered over the three worlds and relate it with a word since the individual forms are infinite in number. For this reason we cannot hold that a word denotes the form of an individual. Moreover, the form of an object is not related to an action such as the act of sending etc. An individual is taken from one place to another but not its form. (The form of an individual is nothing but the different conjunctions of its limbs. It is an attribute. So it is not at all related directly to an action).

On hearing the sentence "Bring a cow" an intelligent person does not bring an object which bears the form of a cow viz. the picture of a cow or an earthen cow.

Let us now examine the hypothesis that a word denotes only a universal. Now the following question is put to the upholders of the above hypothesis. According to them a universal is all-pervasive. If one says "Bring a cow" then why does he not bring an earthen cow ? The universal of cowness as well belongs to an earthen cow, being itself ubiquitous. A reply to the above question is as follows : When one says, "Bring a cow" why does not the listener bring an elephant ? Because a universal is all pervasive. Now, the upholders of the above view raising the above problem solves it in the following manner: Though a universal is present everywhere yet it is not presented to our consciousness as such. No individual can manifest all universals. A particular individual manifests a particular universal. This answer is not satisfactory. We regret to point out that it is only an animal, having dewlap, etc., which manifests the universal of cowness. That is why when we say "Bring a cow" an earthen cow is not brought since an earthen cow does not manifest the universal of cowness. Moreover, as an earthen cow bears the stamp of a cow so if one says "Bring a cow" then he who holds that a word denotes only a universal cannot prevent the listener from bringing an earthen cow. Another point may also be added to the list of criticisms directed against the above hypothesis. If a word denotes only a universal then the proposition "A cow is white" becomes meaningless. The above proposition does not accord with the order of reality. The colour 'whiteness' qualifies the object denoted by the word 'cow'. If the word 'cow' stands for the universal of cowness then the relation of identity which holds between a noun and an adjective cannot hold between the colour 'whiteness' and the universal of cowness. The colour 'whiteness' does not belong to the universal of cowness. Those who hold that the relation of identity holds between a noun and an adjective should say that the colour of whiteness is related to an individual which the said colour belongs to. The upholders of the hypothesis that a word denotes only a universal subscribes to the view that the relation of identity holds between a noun and an adjective. Therefore, they should accept the hypothesis that a word denotes only an individual.

If an individual constitutes the meaning of a word then some sort of relation may be established between an individual and an act to be performed by the dictate of the Śāstras. If a universel is the primary meaning of a word then the relation of denotation is easily grasped. If a form is the meaning of a word then it is related neither to an action nor to a word. Why does an ākṛti (a form) constitute the meaning of a word? We should now determine which of the two, viz. a universal or an individual constitutes the meaning of a word. The upholders of the hypothesis that a word denotes only an individual say to this effect.

An individual should constitute the primary meaning of a word if we take into consideration the consistency of the meaning of a word with injunctions governing the performance of the Vedic rites. If a universal is denoted by a word then injunctions with regard to cutting, killing, sprinkling, etc. become irrelevant since nobody can cut, or kill or sprinkle a universal. Moreover, there are injunctions which enjoin thus: "One should make a gift of 6 articles, of 12 articles, of 24 articles, etc." In these cases the number six, etc., cannot be connected with a universal. If we do so, it will be repugnant to the actual order of things. If an individual is denoted by a word then the meaning of a word fits in well with an injunction. Hence, only an individual constitutes the meaning of a word. There is another point in favour of this hypothesis. In a sacrifice if an animal is offered to a deity but it manages to escape then an injunction runs to the effect that another animal of the same class, having the same colour and age, should be slain. If a universal had been the primary meaning of a word then the killing of another animal would not have been possible. Another animal which has been brought now possesses one and the same universal. Hence, it cannot be qualified by the word 'another.'

But if an individual is the primary meaning of a word then the animal which has been brought will be well described as distinct from that which has fled. But if a universal is the meaning of a word then the universal, belonging to the animal which is being brought, being identical with that belonging to the former one, the adjective 'another' will not be applicable. Hence, an individual constitutes the meaning of a word.

If an individual is denoted by a word then the bringing together of animals, the increase of number, their reduction of number, the killing of them and the relation of ownership, etc., are consistently explained.

This meaning is not well conveyed if it is held that an individual is the secondary meaning of a word. If the straight path is available one should not go by a curved one.

We shall also establish the point that though a word conveys an individual yet it has also secondary power of expressing a universal. Thus the apprehension of assuming an infinite number of relations and that of misrepresenting objects will disappear.

Moreover, some other logicians (the Naiyāyikas) admit that words denote perceptible objects. A universal is not the only object which is perceived. Therefore you must admit that an individual is only conveyed by a word. Whenever a listener hears a word he knows only an individual.

The followers of Jaimini do not subscribe to the hypothesis that a word denotes only an individual. The criticism offered by them is as follows : The primary meaning of a word is either a mere individual or an individual characterized by a universal. A mere individual does not constitute the meaning of a word since no speaker employs a word to denote any individual and no listener hearing the word 'a cow', understands any particular cow. The upholder of the hypothesis may modify his view and hold that the word 'a cow' denotes an individual cow, characterized by the universal of cowness which is the common property of all cows. In this case, the word 'a cow' denotes the universal of cowness but not an individual cow. If you ask 'why' then listen to our argument. If a word merely denotes an individual then we cannot employ it to convey another individual. If we convey a particular individual by a particular word and employ it again to express another individual then we shall hold that its meaning is a common property, shared by all individuals but not a particular individual.

Now, the upholder of the above hypothesis defends himself thus 'As another individual is also nothing but an individual so the word 'a cow' has been employed to express an individual but not a universal. Such a defence does not hold good. If the word 'a cow' is employed to express a mere individual then it should also be used to convey a particular white horse since it is an individual. Now, the upholder of the above hypothesis may argue that the word ('a cow') is employed to convey only that meaning which it has been found to be employed to denote. In other words, nobody employs the word 'a cow' to convey a white horse. Hence it does not denote a white horse. The argument may be met thus. Nobody has used the word 'a cow' to convey a new born calf since it has not been found to be employed in that sense. For this reason, our acquaintance with the usage of words does not justify the hypothesis that a a word denotes an individual. It is not also possible to learn from usage that the said word denotes each and every individual. If we subscribe to the hypothesis that a word denotes only a particular then on hearing the word 'a cow' we should determine that this is only a particular cow but not that this is also a cow. We cannot employ a word at our sweet will if there is nothing to regulate its meaning. Therefore, if a word is employed to convey a particular object then there should be some regulating factor to determine its employment. Now it may be said that the word 'a cow' is employed to convey an individual which the universal of cowness belongs to. In other words, the universal of cowness regulates the use of the word 'a cow'. Let us examine the solution in question. Does the universal regulate the employment of the said word, being itself known or unknown? It cannot regulate, remaining unknown since if it could then the word would become too wide to denote any and every object. If it is held that the universal of cowness is known from the word 'a cow' then we point out that the word 'a cow' is at the outset related to the universal of cowness by the relation of denotation since there is a well-accepted rule that a qualified object is not at all known if the qualification is not grasped.

Now, the upholder of the above hypothesis may say in his defence that the word 'a cow' imparts the knowledge of an individual cow as a substantive and that of a universal as a predicate. Such a defence is not tenable since a word is brought to bear the great burden. A word will not be saddled with so heavy a load but there is no other alternative left to them for the explanation of the presentation of an individual. Do not think "we are concealing the awareness of an individual though it is conveyed to us. We are also concealing the awareness of a universal though it is presented to us". Universal experience bears witness to the presentation of both objects. The power of conveying both objects viz., an individual and a universal is too heavy a load for a word. The awareness of any one of them points to that of another. If we accept this suggestion then does the word 'cow' denoting a universal indicate an individual or does it signifying an individual point to a universal ? When one is to choose between these two alternate suggestions he arrives at the conclusion that a word denotes a universal since a universal, qualifying an individual, is firstly presented to our consciousness. When a universal is conveyed by a word the awarness of an individual follows from it. Thus, the hypothesis that a word has power of expressing both objects is not accepted.

Well, as we know from the word 'daṇḍī' (a clubman) both the substantive and the predicate so on hearing the word 'cow' we shall also understand that the individual cow is a noun and the universal of cowness is an adjective which qualifies it. For this simple act of communication does it carry a heavy load ? Our criticism is as follows. The example, cited by the upholders of the above thesis, has no bearing upon the point in question. The word 'daṇḍī' is derived from a stem with a suffix attached to it. Hence it may carry both senses. The stem in question is 'daṇḍa'. It denotes an adjective. The suffix 'in' which is attached to the stem has the sense of possession. It denotes a noun. But the same logic does not apply to the word 'cow'. In the above example the word 'daṇḍī' does not denote an adjective and the word 'daṇḍa' does not denote a noun. In other words, the word 'daṇḍa' is not a single word. It consists of two elements which are as good as two words. But in the case of the word 'cow' which has been compared it is a non-composite word which consists of no parts. It stands for either a noun or an adjective. If it denotes a noun and has got to convey the sense of an adjective then it may do it on receiving the aid of some other sources of knowledge. But it has no innate power of expressing an adjective. But if the word 'cow' denotes only an adjective then it may point to its noun since the universal of cowness which is an adjective does not stand unsupported. As it must stand upon a locus so it helps to infer the said locus. We are not to blame if we say like this. Everybody knows that when a word is pronounced an individual is presented to our consciousness. Now, a doubt arises in our mind—is an individual directly communicated to our mind by a word or, is it known to us by the medium of a universal? The distinction between these two cases of knowledge is not perceived by us. The problem in question is to be solved by means of an argument. We are to take a lot of troubles to prove that a word simultaneously denotes two meanings viz. a noun and an adjective. We do not also know that it successively conveys two senses viz., it conveys the first meaning at the outset, stops for sometime and then conveys the second meaning. If there is no word to denote an individual. But we know for certain that the knowledge of a universal is due to a word. The Naiyāyikas do also admit that a judgment presupposes the awareness of a predicate as its antecedent condition. Kaṇāda has also stated thus:—The colour 'whiteness' inheres in a substance. When we know that the said colour is in a substance we know that the substance is white. The awareness of the white colour inhering in a substance and the judgment that the substance is white are causally connected.

Well, as the word 'daṇḍī' conveys the sense of a noun as well as an objective so from the word 'cow' we shall be able to learn an individual cow as a noun and the universal of cowness as its adjective. But why do you say that it would be a heavy load on the part of the word 'cow' to convey these two meanings ? A critic points out that the example in question is mismatched. In the above example the word 'daṇḍī' consists of two parts, viz., the stem and the suffix. As it admits of two parts so one part conveys the noun and the other one communicates the adjective. The word 'daṇḍa' constitutes the stem to which the suffix 'in' having the sense of 'matup' suffix, has been attached. The stem denotes an adjective and the suffix stands for a noun. The word 'daṇḍī' does not denote an adjective and the word 'daṇḍa' does not denote a noun. But here the word 'cow' is a single one. It may convey either a noun or an adjective but cannot convey the both. If it is to convey an adjective while conveying a noun then it should receive the help of another source of knowledge since none can aseume that the word 'cow' has power to convey both the noun and the adjective. But if the word 'cow' denotes only an adjective then the universal of cowness which is an adjective cannot stand unsupported. It must have a support to stand upon i. e., requires a noun to qualify. The metaphysical logic casts its shadow upon the science of grammar. It conveys a noun by implication. If we hold this view, we do not violate the logic of grammar. Every body knows from his own experience that whenever a word is uttered an individual is presented to our consciousness. We have no conclusive direct knowledge that an individual is directly communicated to us by a word but not implied by a universal. Consequently, a doubt arises in our mind, viz., either an individual which is a noun is conveyed by a word or it is implied by a universal, the meaning of a word. The doubt in question is to be solved by means of logical discussion. It is a very difficult task for us to carry out that a word denotes both a noun and an adjective as its primary meaning. Moreover, no experience of us bears an evidence to the hypothesis that a word denotes a meaning at the outset, stops for sometime and then denotes another meaning. Our experience says that the awareness of an individual is produced by that of a universal even if there is no word to convey the noun. Hence the awareness of an individual is generated by the medium of a universal. The source of the knowledge of a universal is a word. This is the final conclusion we arrive at.

You, the Naiyāyikas, have also admitted the truth of the hypothesis. Kaṇāda says "The colour 'white' inheres in a substance. If we are aware of the fact that the colour 'white' inheres in a substance then the judgment that the substance is white is framed. There is casual relation existing between the awareness of the white 'colour' inhering in a substance and the judgment that the substance is white."

It has been stated that as the verbs, viz., to cut, to kill, to sprinkle etc., are related to individuals so an individual constitutes the primary meaning of a word. The statement is fallacious since in some cases verbs are also syntactically connected with verbs. An example is as follows:—The Vedic text "one should prepare fire in the shape of a hawk" is the example in question. It may be contested that an individual is only subservient to a Vedic rite, i.e., an action since a universal, a formless being, cannot be serviceable. Such a contention does not hold good. The reason behind the above criticism is as follows. In the above rite a hawk is not mentioned as instrumental to it just as an animal is referred to as instrumental to a Vedic rite in the Vedic text 'paśunā yajeta'. The designation of a Vedic rite as fire is the title of this section. The wording of this text purports to convey that a hawk should be constructed after observing a few rites. A real—a bird hawk cannot be created by observing a few rites. We also remember what has been stated in the chapter devoted to the naming of fire. It has been stated that a hawk cannot be created by piling bricks. But fire is so prepared that it assumes the form of a hawk. Hence a universal is subservient to a rite but not an individual. Now, it may be contested that the resemblance of fire to a hawk will be constructed. Such a contention does not hold water since resemblance is not a thing to be done. What is similar to a particular hawk is also dissimilar to another hawk. Hence, dissimilarity accompanies resemblance. The objection that a universal being formless, is not subservient to a rite is baseless. Though an attribute and an action are formless yet their efficacy in connection with the performance of some rites it acknowledged. Let us cite an example. One purchases a red cow. One offers libation into fire going round it. We shall also prove that a universal is also indirectly related to an action since an individual is implied by a universal. Hence the verbs, viz., to cut, to kill, to sprinkle etc. are indirectly related to a universal.

A rite which is practicable by means of an individual, implied by a universal, is said to be practicable by the universal itself just as an action which is performed by the body and the sense-organs is asserted to be done by the soul that dwells within the body.

Let us clarify the example quoted above. The soul is the enjoyer of the fruit of all actions. It is the doer of all actions. But as it is formless so it gets everything done by means of its associated body and sense-organs. It cleans the twigs of a fig-tree carefully, observes the sacrificial ghee, and does such other things through the instrumentality of its body and sense-organs. Thus it becomes the agent of an action, i.e., a doer. Similarly, a universal performs an action through the help of an individual and becomes instrumental to an action.

Hence the Mīmāṁsakas hold that a universal is instrumental to an action. But it performs its action through the acvitity of something else just as the formless and static soul becomes the doer of an action.

A few rites which require the service of a individual for its completion have been cited. They are as follows. One should make six gifts. If an animal dedicated to a god in a sacrifice runs away then another animal bearing a close resemblance to it should be killed. A universal is instrumental to these rites through the medium of an individual. Following the same line of thinking growth, reduction and aggregation etc., may apply to universals. Again, if we hold that a word denotes a universal then the relation of denotation holding between a word and a universal is easily cognised. If a word denotes an individual then it should be admitted that a word denotes an infinite number of individuals. (All individuals belonging to a class are denoted by the same word. Hence, the power of denotation belonging to a word is infinite. Again if it is held that a Word denotes only an individual then a word is wrongly used since it is employed to convey an object which it does not denote. There are the possible defects which vitiate the hypothesis that a word denotes an individual. The hypothesis in question is not exposed to them.

It has been also objected that a word denotes a perceptible object and that a universal is not the exclusive object of perception. The sum and substance of this objection is that a word cannot denote a universal only.

This objection has been met by Kumārila, the author of Ślokavārttika. He holds that a concrete object having various properties is the object of our perception.

Kumārila in his Śloka-vārttika raises a prima facie objection, viz., if a perceptible object has various properties then why should a word denote a universal only? He says in reply to it that a word cannot denote an object having various properties. All words denote objects, having a direct reference to a universal.

There is not a single word which is logically conceived as competent to denote an object having various properties. It is not also easy to grasp the relation of denotation holding between the word and the object having various properties. Thus, we should restrict the power of denotation and hold that a word denotes only a universal which is one of the various properties of an object. This hypothesis stands upon sound logic. Hence, a universal is the only primary meanig of a word. This is the essence of the hypothesis that a word denotes only a universal.

The Refutation of the Hypothesis that a Word Denotes a Universal

The above hypothesis is going to be refuted. A universal does not constitute the primary meaning of a word (i.e. pada) used in a sentence. A pada is the combination of letters with an inflexion attached to it but is not a mere stem. The law of grammar holds that a stem and an inflexion express their meanings which are mutually related. When an inflexion such as the second case-ending etc., is attached to a stem the meaning of an inflexion is presented to our consciousness derived from a word as a substantive and that of a stem denotes a universal then the meaning of an inflexion cannot be related to a universal. A universal cannot be a case. It has got no gender masculine, feminine or neuter. Moreover, it cannot be marked with a number such as 'two', 'three' etc.

Now, the upholders of the above hypothesis may contend that all these difficulties will be solved because an individual is the secondary or implied meaning of a word. The Naiyāyikas join issue with them and point out that the above solution is not satisfactory. A word is once uttered or employed. It partially expresses a meaning by its primary power and then again conveys a different meaning by its secondary power. The secondary meaning, conveyed by it, is related to case, number and gender and is presented to our consciousness. This order of the presentation of a meaning in its relational character is not borne out by our experience. (A word once uttered completely expresses its meaning. It does not gradually convey its meaning. Such an expression of meaning goes against the grammatical law).

It will be improper on our part to relate the meaning of an inflexion with a universal. It looks like a contradictary injunction that one should wet with fire. As the meaning of an inflexion is related to a male so the meaning of an inflexion is related to a universal through the medium of an individual. Though the relation is not direct yet why will not it be logically tenable? When an inflexion conveys its meaning it does it as related to the meaning of a stem, viz., a universal. But it is not the aim of an inflexion to convey its meaning as related to the secondary meaning of a stem since if it does so, there will be no uniformity in conveying the primary meaning of a word. The Mīmāṁsakas hold that as it is impossible to establish a relation between the primary meaning of a word and that of an inflexion so the meaning of an inflexion is related to an individual. Such a defence is not tenable. A soul is logically called the author of an action since it has consciousness, volition etc. But a universal is eternally static and is in no way related to a process. So in grammar a universal is never used as a case. Hence how will the meaning of an inflexion be related to a universal ? It can in no way be related to a universal.

The number such as one, two, etc., is said to be syntactically related to a universal. But the former does not belong to the latter. The number belongs to such a substratum with which it is not syntactically connected.

No body experiences that a number is indirectly related to a universal through the medium of an individual. If a number is not related to an individual at first then it is logically absurd for it to be related to a universal. Such a gradual development of knowledge actuated by the necessity of removing inconsistency is not experienced.

An individual which is the generator of an action, is marked off by a universal and is qualified by a number etc., is denoted by a word. A universal does not constitute the primary meaning of a word.

The Mīmāṁsakas have held that a universal is directly related to a Vedic action. They cite an example, viz. 'One should arrange fire in the shape of a hawk.' In this case the form of a hawk has been mentioned. There is no reference to a universal. Hence a universal is not directly subservient to an action.

The Mīmāṁsakas have said that the pile of bricks containing fire does not bear a resemblance to a particular hawk since if it is similar to one hawk then it may be as well dissimilar to another hawk. The argument of the Mīmāṁsakas is not convincing because the universal of hawkness is formless and it is highly inconsistent to hold that the said pile is similar to a universal. It is as good as to say that it is similar to the sky. The example in question does no service to them. It simply represents their evading spirit.

There are many other verbal usages such as 'Give a cow' etc., in which an individual having the universal of cowness is syntactically connected with the verb 'to give'. So the learned men hold that the primary meaning of the word 'cow' is only an individual possessing the universal of cowness.

A word primarily denotes one characterized by a universal. It is not logical to hold that the meaning of inflexion is at first related to an individual and then becomes related to an individual and then becomes related to a universal. If we hold this view then the process of denoting a meaning by a word involves much complication and becomes round about. So this view is not correct.

If we subscribe to the view that the primary meaning of a word is an individual characterized by a universal then the use of cases in apposition finds justification. If we do not subscribe to this view then the co-ordination subsisting between a subject and a predicate cannot be explained.

So, a word denotes the possessor of a universal. Now, the Mīmāṁsakas raise an objection to this hypothesis. What is the exact meaning of the word ('tadvān' having that) ? The literal meaning is that this has that. The demonstrative pronoun 'this' stands for a near individual. Hence the meaning of the word amounts to an individual having a universal. If it denotes particular then the hypothesis is open to the same charge that a word has an infinite power of conveying meaning and has unjustifiably wide denotation, i.e., it denotes objects which fall outside the sphere of its denotation. But as there is no word to denote a universal so a universal cannot be used as an objective. If the opponents hold that a word denotes both an individual and a universal then they load a word with the heavy burden of conveying two distinct objects. We have already discussed this point.

The Naiyāyikas meet this objection thus. The etymological meaning of the word 'tadvān' is that this has that. But will the demonstrative pronoun 'this' not stand for a distinct particular such as 'śābaleya'. Moreover it does not denote all individual cows in the universe. But it stands for any individual cow, the substratum of the universal of cowness but does not mean a distinct individual cow such as śābaleya. As the word 'tadvān' denotes the substratum of a universal, e.g., the universal of cowness, so the relation of denotation holding between the word 'cow' and all individual cows is grasped by us. Again, as the common property of the meaning of the word 'cow' is the universal of cowness so the above charges that a word has infinite power of denoting objects and has unjustifiably wide denotation become pointless. Again, we do not admit if a word does not denote noun without denoting its adjective. So we do not overburden a word with the weight of its meaning. As we simply grasp the relation of denotation holding between a word and the locus of a universal so how much is the weight of meaning on the part of a word is to carry. There are a few charges which are levelled against some hypothesis viz. if a universal is not distinct from its locus then a word cannot denote both an individual and a universal etc. But they do not effect our hypothesis since all these objections are squarely met with.

Moreover, perception does not reveal a universal only. A universal is a property of its substratum viz. an individual. Perception reveals both, viz. an individual and a universal. When a word is employed to denote an object of perception how is it that it denotes only a universal? Therefore we arrive at the conclusion that if a word is employed to denote an object as is perceived then a word should also mean the same object. There should be perfect coordination between the meaning of a word and the content of an act of perception.

Now, the Mīmāṁsakas raise an objection against the above solution. They point out that a substantive and a predicate are not simultaneously perceived. The Naiyāyikas even do not admit such a perception. The direct awareness of a predicate and a judgment are causally related to each other. Hence, the sense perception of a universal takes place at first. Hence a word should also denote a universal at the out-set. Therefore, it has a reference to a universal for the relation of denotation informs of it. Hence, the primary meaning of a word is a universal but not an individual.

The Naiyāyikas say in reply to the above objection. It is not a truism that a predicate is only perceived but not the substantive. Both the subject and the predicate are perceived. Whenever a universal is perceived the sense-object contact in the shape of conjunction cum inherence is required. For this reason whenever a sense-organ senses a universal it senses an individual, the locus of a universal. We do not say that an individual is only perceived and its substratum is an inference. If we think with the Mīmāṁsakas then we should admit that our sense organ senses an attribute but the substance which possesses it is an inference. But there is no such provision in the logical code of the Mīmāṁsakas. Hence we hold that the substratum of a universal is also perceived. As there is perfect co-ordination between the meaning of a word and the content of perception so it is not logical to hold that a word denotes only a universal.

Kumārila has stated that a word is always employed with the main purpose of conveying a universal, the element of an object since if we hold that a word denotes only an individual then we are to admit that a word has infinite power of denoting innumerable individuals and when it conveys its meaning it transcends its power of denotation. But we are not to face the difficulty of meeting all these objections if we hold that a word denotes the locus of a universal. Therefore we should not impose limitation upon the meaning of word, subscribing to the hypothesis that a word denotes only a universal. The Mīmāṁsakas may further contend that a word and the corresponding perception of its meaning do not refer to the same object. If we admit that they do so then the knowledge derived from a word will be identical with that derived from sense organs. But it is a fact that these two pieces of knowledge are not identical. The reason behind their non-identity is this that when we perceive an object we grasp all its specific features but when we know an object through a word we do not have such a detailed knowledge. Hence, the distinction of verbal knowledge from perceptual one is established. The same opinion has been expressed by an expert thus:—"A man who has been burnt differently feels the actual contact of fire with his body." In other words, the knowledge of the meaning of the word 'burning' is entirely different from the actual experience of burning The drift of the expert opinion is this that there is a gulf of difference existing between perceptual and verbal knowledge. Its underlying suggestion is this that a word denotes only a universal.

Now a question arises in our mind. It challenges the truth of one of the previous conclusions reached by the Naiyāyikas. If verbal knowledge is widely different from perceptual one then how will they stick to the hypothesis that the different pieces of knowledge, derived from various sources of knowledge in some cases point to one and the same object? In other words, how will they explain the hypothesis of Pramāṇa-samplava? An answer to the above question is as follows. The objection, raised against the hypothesis of pramāṇasamplava, has already been met. Though we admit that there is a gulf of difference existing between perceptual and verbal knowledge since the former one reveals all the details of the specific character of an object and the latter one does not do it yet these two pieces of knowledge refer to the same object as they refer to the same substratum. Again, ever if we refute the hypothesis of Pramāṇa-samplava then it does not follow that a word denotes only a universal but not the substratum of a universal. Moreover, if it is admitted that a word denotes only a universal then the word 'a cow' and 'cowness should convey the same meaning. There should be the judgment that cowness is white like the judgment. "A cow is white". The suffixes 'tva' 'tal' etc. conveying an abstract property should only signify the meaning of the stem to which they are attached like the word 'cāturvarṇya'.

If the Mīmāṁsakas think that the word 'cow' denotes the universal of cowness but implies an individual then it is contrary to reason to hold that the word 'cowness' (gotva) which has been derived from the word 'go' with tva 'suffix', denoting an abstract property, attached to it exclusively denotes a universal. A universal, detached from an individual, is never found out.

If you hold that when the word 'cow' is heard the universal of cowness is known as associated with the universal of cowness but when the word 'cowness' is heard a universal-in-itself is only known. If you hold this view then you come round our path. If it is held that a universal having a locus to stand upon is denoted by a word then it amounts to this that a word denotes the locus of a universal, otherwise, a universal having a locus to stand upon cannot be asserted. When we intend to express only a universal as independent of its locus we use words ending in suffixes viz. tva, tal etc. Patañjali in his Mahābhāṣya has said as the concrete objects are denoted by nouns so nominal suffixes such as tva, tal etc. are attached to these nouns. Let us explain with reference to a familiar example. A universal belongs to a 'cow'. The word 'cow' denotes a concrete individual. It consists of two parts viz. (1) a class-character, the specific character of all individuals belong to the class of cow and (2) exclusively particular. The word 'cowness' is employed only to express its class character. The nominal suffix 'ness' is attached to the noun 'cow'. The word 'cow' is employed since the universal belongs to it. The above remark of Patañjali gives evidence to the hypothesis that a word denotes the substratum of a universal. We have already stated that in the preposition "A cow is white" the relation between the subject and the predicate is squarely explained if we subscribe to the hypothesis that a word denotes a concrete individual. i.e. an individual possessing a universal. A concerte individual stands for a representative individual.

The Proof of the function of a Word to Denote an Individual

The Mīmāṁsakas hold that a sentence, in the subjunctive mood, does not refrain from conveying its meaning until and unless all the minor details which are necessary for the principal act are expressed. Similarly, you are to admit that a word does not completely convey its meaning until and unless it expresses an individual. As a word signifies an individual by the uninterrupted process of conveying its meaning so an individual is also included in its primary meaning.

The Mīmāṁsakas hold that words in a sentence always reveal their meanings as interconnected with one another. These words do never convey their meanings in an isolated manner. Therefore, they should say that a word reaches the culminating point to convey its meaning when it communicates a particular. Moreover, universals do not get themseleves inter-connected without a reference to particulars. The Mīmāṁsakas cannot also hold that the disconnected universals are communicated to us by their denotative words since according to them words do never present disconnected objects as their meanings to our mind. As the word 'Gaṅgāyām' in the sentence 'Gaṅgāyām Ghoṣaḥ' (there is a village of cowherds on the banks of Ganges, the river) indicates a place, adjacent to the flowing river 'Ganges', on the strength of its secondary meaning so the word 'cow' in the sentence "A cow is white" does not mean as individual cow by means of its secondary meaning. This criticism is quite clear from our experience.

The meaning of a word is learnt if we carefully understand the meaning of the said word noting its usage by the experienced persons. We learn from the usage that words like cow etc. signify concrete individuals i.e. substract of universals.

The author of Nyāya-sūtra says that the meaning of a word consists of an individual, a universal and a form. In the above sūtra there is a particle 'in'. It has been given in the Sūtra in order to determine something. What does it determine ? It determines the selection of a particular meaning as a principal one from the meanings according to the merit of a particular case. Though a concrete individual constitutes the meaning of a word yet in some cases the universal plays the important part and a particular occupies a subordinate position. Let us cite an example "A cow should not be injured." It is universal prohibition. This prohibition applies to all cows. In some cases an individual plays the most important part and the universal sinks down into a subordinate position. Let us cite examples viz. "Untie a cow", "enchain a cow" etc. In some cases, a form occupies the central position, a particular has a subordinate place and a universal is conspicuous by its absence. Let us cite an example viz. cows from powdered rice should be prepared. If we use sentences in order to create mere forms then universals do not belong to earthen cows and similar objects though the universals are all pervasive. The absence of universals from such objects has been already established. Hence, the meaning of a word is a concrete individual. It is impossible for a few words to denote universals. They merely denote particulars. Words like the sky etc. constitute examples of such cases. There are proper nouns such as Ḍittha etc. which are well known as names. They stand for individuals since objects which they mean are devoid of universal. So, a word like Ḍittha is called a dravya-Śabda (the name of a substance).

Those who hold that a universal belongs even to an individual which admits of imaginary distinctions should also hold that a universal resides in the individual known as Ḍittha since there are several individuals designated by the name Ḍittha'. Why are you so opinionated ? As there exists no such universal as skyness so there exists no universal as Ḍitthatva. There is no scope for the wise to indulge in pure imagination with regard to this topic.

There are a few abstract nouns. They signify only attributes characterized by species which exclusively belong to them. There are some other abstract nouns which stand for attributes but imply substances by their secondary sense since in some categorical propositions a term denoting a substance is used as a subject and a term, denoting an attribute, is used as a predicate and a copula which stands for the relation of identity unites them.

Words like scent, sound, taste etc. signify only attributes having specific characteristic features. They never imply substances. The proposition that a lotus is scent is never used. Scent is never used as a predicate which is asserted of a lotus since no body says that rice is scent and a mango is taste. There are some words such as Śukla etc. which signify attributes but imply substances. It is seen that in order to convey a white substance the word 'white' is only used. But when we associate with the word 'white' with the word 'attribute' the word 'white' does not imply a substance as its power of implying a substance is restricted. These words like words having suffixes indicative of abstract qualities (whiteness etc.) exclusively denote attributes. A horse has white colour. Whiteness is in a horse. White colour and whiteness denote one and the same thing.

There are two kinds of verbal nouns. Among verbal nouns some denote nominative case of a verb, some objective case, some instrumental case, some other cases. But some verbal nouns exclusively denote verbs. The above ones refer to a verb at the outset and then signify a substance which is connected with it. The word 'pācaka' (a cook) is an example of the first type of words. Though the connection with a verb is not directly noticed yet it has capability of being connected with a verb. The experts noticing such capability use such words.

When we use words like pācaka (a cook), lāvaka (a cutter) etc., we do not mean to say that a cook is cooking and a cutter is cutting. We call a person a cook or a cutter even when he does not cook or he does not cut. We have noticed usages even in the absence of a verb.

A verbal noun of course denotes a verb. But it does not denote it as a process which is in the making. It denotes it as an accomplished fact. There is no reference to the different stages of an act which precede and succeed. A verbal noun which is derived from a root in the passive voice with a suffix attached to it has a double character. It looks like a substance as well as like a verb. When it represents the verbal character it does not mean that everything has been done and nothing remains to be done. So it has been said that it looks like a verb.

The first step towards the understanding of a word is that the one of its use and its primary meaning are not one and the same thing. Let us take an example viz. the word 'pācaka'. The act of cooking gives us the cue of its use. The nominative case of the act of cooking is its primary meaning.

There are a few words which are derived from a root in the passive voice with kṛt suffix attached to it. The cue of their use is identical with their primary meaning.

Thus we have stated the primary meanings of nouns. But we shall discuss the meaning of verbs later on.

We learn from the general usage and from the passing acquaintance (with a few illustrations) that prepositions, indeclinables and nouns admit of various meanings. In most cases prepositions are prefixed to verbs. There is a general rule that some indeclinables become prepositions when they are prefixed to verbs. Some prepositions are annexed to nouns e.g., pravayaḥ. It means one who has advanced in age. Other prepositions modify verbs and determine their meanings in various ways. The above view has been expressed by some thinkers.

When a root is prefixed by different prepositions it admits of various meanings. If the root ḥr is prefixed by the preposition 'vi' then it amounts to the root 'to play'. If it is prefixed by the preposition 'ā', to eat becomes its meaning. If it is preceded by the preposition 'sam', it is identical with the root 'to kill'. If it is proceded by the preposition 'pra', it signifies the act of beating. If it is preceded by the preposition 'pari', it is synonymous with the root 'to give up'.

Sometimes we see that a preposition, preceding a root cancels its meaning. Let us take an example viz., prasthita. (started). The primary meaning of the root 'sthā' (to stay) is to stop all motion. When it is prefixed by 'pra' it expresses the sense of going. An adverb should not contradict the original meaning of the root which it is expected only to modify.

An abjective which characterizes a noun but does not mar its sense is a true adjective. This is our view. An abjective does not repudiate the meaning of its noun.

Whenever a preposition is connected with a verb it brings

about a change in the meaning of the original root. As it does so it becomes an adverb. Though a root acquires the power of conveying various meanings, being associated with a preposition yet it being thus associated, conveys a definite meaning. The function of a preposition is this that it channelizes the meaning of a root. But it does not permit a root to express any meaning in an unrestricted manner. For this reason a preposition is an adverb.

We shall not discuss the point either a preposition denotes a meaning or indicates it since it is irrelevant to the issue in question. By the joint method of agreement and difference the meaning of a word it ascertained. If a root is preceded by a preposition then it conveys a certain meaning but if it is not preceded by the same it does not convey the same meaning. Do the prepositions denote a meaning ? Or do they indicate it. We shall not enter into this discussion, There are a few indeclinables such as 'ca' etc., which express the sense of conjunction. There are a few prepositions which are used independently of verbs. An example of the type of prepositions is this "Bṛkṣam prati dyotate". The meaning of such prepositions will be determined by usage and common sense. This topic requires no futher discussion.

Some thinkers hold that this word conveys this meaning. Or, if a particular meaning is communicated by a particular word the meaning is denoted by it. There are persons who have the power of understanding but cannot make out the meaning of a word. In order to make them understand we quote a few examples. We have said something to establish the validity of verbal knowledge. In other recondite works the nature of a word and its meaning have been elaborately discussed. We feel no necessity of discussing the same topic over and again since the subject-matter is very extensive. Now, we find leisure of discussing other topics. When we have established the existence of universals we have said that words are related to external objects. In the meantime by this little endeavour our labour has been crowned with success.

The Finding of the Meaning of A Sentence.

We have ascertained the meaning of a word. We just now

discuss the meaning of a sentence. The scholars hold diverse views on this topic.

The Rival Hypotheses on The Meaning of a Sentence.

(1) Some logicians hold that a sentence cannot refer to external objects. It refers to ideas in their non-relational character. Though the ideas are not mutually related yet they appear as external objects standing in relation to one another. (2) Some other logicians hold that the relation which takes place among the meanings of words in a sentence is real but not imaginary. A sentence refers to external objects. (3) A different batch of logicians holds that a sentence refers to the exclusion of the contrary of its apparent meaning. When we say that it is white we mean thereby that it is not black. (4) Another sect of logicians conjectures that a sentence without taking the risk of being denied points to the relation holding among parts of speech, and holds that their meanings are arranged in order of their position viz. principal and subordinate and that the principal act which is accomplished with the help of accessory case-endings is signified by a sentence. (5) Some other logicians suppose that a sentence signifies the operation of an agent directed toward an end, it is known as the meaning of the verb 'karoti' and it is also designated as bhāvanā. The optative suffix liṅ denotes a particular kind of operation. It is called śābda-bhāvanā. It has an injunctive force in it. It impels a person to activity which is directed towards an end. It is also called an injunction. (6) Someother logicians point out that if the liṅ suffix denotes the above two meanings then it violates the law of parsimony and suggests that a sentence signifies an injunction. The injunction should be performed. It impels persons to activity. The followers of this school of thought are divided in their opinion. (a) The first batch of disciples admits that the suffix liṅ impels persons to action since they are aware of its impelling force. These disciples also hold that the other function of the suffix liṅ is not presented to our consciousness. The view that a sentence prescribes the performance of any act enjoined or not is too weak to maintain. Therefore an act which has been enjoined should be observed. (b) Someother disciples subscribe to the view that when we understand something as

our duty we also make out that the scripture orders us to discharge it. Hence, an injunction impels us to discharge our duty. A person engages himself in fulfilling his duty when he knows it to be such since when a man knows that it is his duty he moves for accomplishing it. (7) Some other logicians hold that a new enterprise is denoted by a sentence. So, these different hypotheses are at variance with one another. Let us see which one is correct.

The View that a Sentence Denotes an Idea :

Some logicians hold that no real external object is denoted by a sentence since if a real external object is denoted by a sentence then is it different from the meanings of its constituent words or not? One cannot say in the affirmative since the difference of the meaning of a sentence from those of its constituent words is grasped by no body. In the sentence "Gauḥ śuklā ānīyatām" (a white cow may be brought) the constituent words are 'gauḥ', 'śuklā' and 'ānīyatām'. The word 'gauḥ' stands for a universal. The word 'śuklā' denotes an attribute viz. whiteness. The word 'ānīyatām' signifies an act. Is the meaning of a sentence identical with that of each word or with the collective meaning of all words? This problem is to be solved at the outset. Nobody will say that the meaning of a sentence is identical with that of each word since no body grasps the meaning of a sentence in this way since the meaning of the word 'gauḥ' alone cannot constitute that of the above sentence. It is not also possible to hold that the collective meaning of all words constitutes that of a sentence since the collection of the meanings of the words is not possible. How does the collection take place? Does it occur because the different meanings exist? Or, does the apprehension of their meaning combine them? We cannot say that the meanings of the different words combine together because they exist since all objects which are denoted by words exist but no body comes across a distinct sentence which refers to all of them. Therefore it is difficult to ascertain a definite and distinct meaning of a sentence. The objects, denoted by words, are not combined by means of their ideas or awareness since ideas of objects or their awarenesses do not simultaneously arise in our mind. When we form the ideas of an object the idea of another object is conspicuous by its absence. Thus the simultaneity of two ideas is not possible. Moreover the letters which constitute each word are the real means to the appearance of the idea of an object corresponding to a word. These letters do not simultaneously come into being and co-exist. Therefore, how will the collection of objects, denoted by words, be possible through ideas?

Moreover, do all the meanings of words which assemble together constitute the meaning of a sentence, being themselves related to one another or not? We cannot say in the negative since a cow, a horse, a man, an elephant and so on are not seen to constitute the meaning of a sentence since they remain unrelated to one another. It is also difficult for one to establish the relation between two objects since the relation between the two objects presupposes their correlation. But an object does not refer to another one since they are unconscious. Ideas are also not correlative since they have only momentary existence. They cannot also unite objects with a tie constituted by themselves. For this reason a relation cannot constitute the meaning of a sentence. The objects or their ideas are not mutually related since the reason behind their non-relation has been stated before.

If we follow the above reason then the hypothesis that the negation of the contrary is the meaning of a sentence will also be refuted. (A cow cannot produce the judgment that she is not a horse). The idea of an object cannot convey the negation of its opposite since this hypothesis is not logically tenable (The ideas enjoy momentary existence. Hence, they are not competent enough to convey such a judgment as its meaning). Kumārila has also said to this effect.

In the sentence "A cow is white" if the word 'cow' denotes all sorts of cows viz. white, black, red etc. and if the idea of a cow produces that of white then the idea of white can negate the idea of non-white or can relate itself with that of a cow.

Though the idea of white has a reference to that of a cow yet no relation subsisting between them (these two ideas) is grasped by us.

Kumārila has also subjected the thesis to the same criticism. Though there is correlation between the two ideas or objects yet no relation subsisting between them is grasped by us. A relation is really significant if it is one of the following ones viz. the causal relation, conjunction, inherence etc. No such relation is detected by us. If it is held that co-existence is one of such relations then it may also be pointed out that it is too wide (Kumārila means to say that as the idea of white co-exists with many other ideas so the said relation will also take place between the idea of white and any other idea).

In some cases, adequate words do not denote the relation which subsists between the meanings of words. Hence, it is no better then non-existent. In a sentence which conveys either the identity of one object with another or the relation holding between two objects no word is found to denote either of them. Hence, neither the said identity nor the relation is the meaning of a word. If they are not conveyed by words then they cannot be the meaning of a sentence. Again if a word is given in the sentence to denote either of them then confusion becomes worse confounded. Does the sentence. "The white cow be brought the relation" convey any sense ? Hence the hypothesis that a sentence points to external objects as its meaning is absolutely absurd. Hence, an idea which appears to be the relation of the external objects may be the meaning of a sentence. The people transact all their worldly business by means of it.

This is the sum and substance of this hypothesis.

The Refutation of the Hypothesis that an Idea is Conveyed by a Sentence:

The above hypothesis is not logically tenable since the existence of external objects has been erewhile established. An idea which appears to be the relation of external objects cannot be the meaning of a sentence since having established the reality of external objects we have commenced to bestow our consideration upon the meaning of a sentence. Now, we have no time to discuss the hypothesis that the meaning of a sentence is nothing but an idea. The upholders of the above hypothesis say that the meaning of a sentence is not the aggregate of the meanings of its constituent words. Very well, let us put a question to them. We ask them to give an answer. If one utters the word 'a cow', it produces an idea in our mind. Again if one utters the sentence "Bring a white cow," it also produces an awareness in our mind. Do the word and the sentence produce in our mind the same idea? or, do they produce different ideas? If you answer the first question in the affirmative then you say something which is contrary to our experience. But you may say that these two ideas are different. They are not different if their corresponding objects are not different. So, you will be compelled to admit that the objects referred to by these two ideas are distinct. Thus, the object conveyed by a sentence is distinct. It constitutes the meaning of a sentence. If a word denoting an attribute or a verb is only uttered along with the above noun i. e. a cow then a distinct meaning is conveyed by the two words combined. The expert grammarians hold that when the volume of the meanings of a word increases it is called the meaning of a sentence. Again, it is not a fact that the relation holding among the meanings of words is not presented to our consciousness. When we employ a sentence "A cow' a horse, a man and an elephant exist", the meanings of its constituent words are presented to our consciousness as unrelated to one another. In other words, they are independently presented to our consciousness. But when we employ the sentence "let a white cow be brought" the meanings of its constituent words are not presented to our consciousness as unrelated to one another. We shall elaborately discuss later on how a relation presents itself to our consciousness and what is the means of its presentation. In fine, we arrive at the conclusion that a sentence communicates an external object to us but not an idea. In other words, its meaning is objective but not subjective.

Though a sentence refers to an extra mental object yet one should not hold that it conveys merely a negative sense in the shape of the negation of the contrary of its predicate since the meaning of the sentence referred to is presented to our consciousness as a positive object and the above negative sense presupposes the relations holding between the meaning of its constituent words. (Let us now clearly state the above hypothesis and its criticism. The sentence "The cow is white" conveys the sense that the cow is not black. 'Black' is the contrary of 'white'. When we say "The cow is white" we do not assert the predicate 'white' of the cow. But we simply negate the contrary of the predicate. The critics point out that the proposition "The cow is white" consists of the main terms viz. 'cow' and 'white'. The first one denotes the subject and the second one denotes the predicate. If the relation which subsists between the subject and the predicate is not presented to our consciousness then the above negative sense will not be presented to our consciousness. If we do not know that the cow is white then we cannot understand that she is not black. If we know that whiteness inheres in the cow then we are in a position to grasp that blackness does not inhere in it. The knowledge of the absence of blackness presupposes the presence of whiteness).

When the word 'cow' is used it produces an awareness of all cows. If the word 'white' is syntactically connected with the word 'cow' then it excludes the connection of the word 'black' with the word 'cow'. Therefore, you cannot hold that a sentence conveys only the sense of an exclusion. The very knowledge of the relation of the predicate with the subject throws light upon the exclusion of the contrary of the predicate from the subject. When we know that the meaning of the term denoting the subject of a proposition is related to that of the term denoting its predicate, we grasp the complete meaning of the said proposition, i. e., a sentence. When we understand the complete meaning of a sentence the exclusion of the contrary of white, viz., the black, etc., may be implied by the same sentence. If such an implied meaning takes place, let it take place. But on account of this implied meaning we cannot hold that a sentence conveys only a negative sense. i. e., communicates the exclusion of the contrary of its predicate.

The Demonstration of the Hypothesis that a Sentence Conveys Something Which is to be Accomplished Because of its Importance

From the above criticism it is clear that a sentence conveys a positive sense and the meaning of a sentence is other than our ideas. Now, some thinkers hold that a sentence points to something which is to be done. They purport to convey the following idea. The meanings of words constituting a sentence have mutual reference. Their mutual relationship creates an atmosphere which renders their mutual reference favourable. Hence, it is the current view that the meaning of the constituent words of a sentence, being related to one another, form the meaning of a sentence.

The meanings of words are not mutually related if they are not arranged in the relation of the principal and the subordinate. We are to determine which one of them is principal and which ones are subordinate. If a verb does not find a place in the sentence then a sentence cannot be used since a verb being not uttered, the requirement of a listener is not fulfilled. In cases of worldly transactions in order to satisfy the requirement of a listener a sentence is employed. We also make out the meaning of vedic sentences as we do in cases of ordinary sentence used in mundane transactions. From a verb we know that an object which is to be accomplished is its meaning and that the object consists of parts standing in the relation of prior and posterior in time. We also learn that a verb does not communicate the sense of an accomplished fact. In a sentence there are words denoting accomplished facts and a word which signifies an object to be accomplished. Let us now discuss their mutual position in a sentence. Does a word which stands for an accomplished fact occupy the principal position? Or, does a word which signifies an object to be accomplished occupy the principal position ? Having bestowed due delibertion on the matter we learn that accomplished facts are taken as means in order to realise the object to be accomplished. An object to be accomplished should be done and hence it occupies the superior position. It is the meaning of a sentence. It is not distinct from the meaning of a verb.

Whenever we are aware of an object to be accomplished by us it points to the means which are required for its realisation. An object to be accomplished is directly related to some of these means, i.e., some means are proximate. Some means are indicated by words which do not occur in the sentence. Some means are pointed by some other sentences. Some means are revealed to us by passages occurring in other contexts. Some means render their indirect assistance to realise the object to be accomplished. Some means are abandoned by the object to be accomplished though they stand in close proximity but lack capacity. Though some means stand in a remote place yet the object to be accomplished attracts them since they are capable of bringing it about. An act (an object to be done) which is performed by a host of objects denoted by case-endings rendering proximate or remote help to it is the meaning of a sentence.

[On hearing the injunctions such as "One should sacrifice", "One should make gifts," "One should pour libation," "One should study the Vedas" and so on a person who is impelled to action knows that this action should be performed and he performs it. The word which reveals qualifications for a person wishing to perform an action implies the agent who is required for the performance of an action. Thus it makes us understand that an agent has usefulness in his action. It purports to convey that this person is the agent of this particular action and this action is to be completed by this person. In that case an agent forsakes its principal position in a sentence since an agent is a means to an action but not vice versa. An agent is also known to us the executor of an action. A sentence also advises a person to this effect that he should do this. If you ask "Why does a person perform an action?", then our rejoinder is that the sentence which enjoins a person to do is regarded by him as the valid source of knowledge. One has been ordered by the injunctive sentence, "One should perform this action". If a person who has been thus ordered does not perform the prescribed action then he will transgress an injunction, i.e., an obligatory duty. One discharges his duty because he has conviction in the validity of the scriptures. A man who does not covet for the fruit of an action performs an action because he is goaded by the habit of performing actions. This habit strengthens his attitude of indifference towards the worldly objects. This attitude being confirmed, he gradually negates the reality of all worldly objects. Thus, he acquires the highest qualification for realising the Absolute. As he qualifies himself so he acquires a deep insight into the subtle truth. The highest qualification, acquired by him, enables him to grasp the summum bonum of life. If we are to discuss this matter then we are to prolong this topic to a greater length. Let us cut short this discussion for the present. The drift of this section is that as an action plays the most important part in a sentence so it is the meaning of a sentence. Jaimini says "That which does for another is śeṣa (subsidiary). A substance, the attribute of a substance and the consecration of a substance occupy a subsidiary position in a sentence. But a sacrifice, its result, viz, heaven, etc., and a person who enjoys the result are not regarded as śeṣa." The inner significance of Jaimini's sūtra is that a substance, the attribute of a substance and the consecration of a substance render a service to an action but an action assists none. In other words, an action is an end in itself but not a means to an end. Thus it is not subsidiary.

The Demonstration of the Hypothesis that a Sentence Points to the Result of an Action Since the Fruit of an Action is Superior to the Action Itself:-

The criticism of the above thesis is as follows. Why does an action occupy the principal position in a sentence ? Does it occupy such a position by its intrinsic nature ? Or does it acquire the position by verbal authority ?

If we think over the problem from the realistic point of view then we find the superiority of the fruit of an action. No intelligent man undertakes a fruitless action.

Though a person is enjoined by the Vedas or directed by his superiors or commanded by his king to do an action yet he does not betake himself to it when he is not confident of his success. A dullard carries out the order of his superiors either in order to avoid a slap or in order to gain a sweet-meat. In other words, a fool indiscreetly undertakes an action either out of fear or out of greed.

The Mīmāṁsakas re-examine their criticism and hold that they will not decide the question of superiority from the realistic point of view but from the linguistic point of view. They attach the highest authority to the verbal knowledge. The knowledge which is communicated to them by words is taken as valid. Let us take an example, viz., a king's servant (rāja-puruṣa). If the actual order of things is taken into consideration then a king occupies the most exalted position, being the ruler of the world. The wretched person who serves him earns his livelihood obeying his will. But if the superiority is decided from the linguistic point of view then the servant occupies the superior position in the compound word. The reason is that in a tatpuruṣa compound the sense of the last member predominates.

Similarly, in case of the above injunctions viz. "One should sacrifice", "One should make gifts", "One should pour libations" etc. an action has been emphatically enjoined. The sense of an action predominates in those injunctive sentences. But one who is desirous of heaven should sacrifice. Now why the clause "Who is desirous of heaven" has been given ? Does it not point to the fruit of an action ? Let the question of superiority be settled. An agent has been mentioned for the purpose of an action. In other words, an agent is a means to an end. The end is an action. But if an action is done and a result is produced in the natural order of things then let the result be produced. Let an agent put forth his energy for the fruition of his action. But the above injunctive sentences do not attach prominence to the fruit of an action. The statement that if an action is performed then the result itself follows is significant. What is the significance of the word itself? It purports to convey that an action is not a means to an end, viz., the result of an action.

The above contention of the Mīmāṁsakas is not logically sound. If they interpret the injunctive sentence "Svargakāmo Yajeta" in the above manner then it will be difficult syntactically to connect the word "Svargakāmaḥ" with the verb 'yajeta'.

The Mīmāṁsakas meet the objection with the following remark. The word in question denotes the subject of the sentence. A subject is a means to an action but not vice versa. The critics point out that the word 'svarga-kāmaḥ' does not stand for the subject. It refers to one who qualifies himself for the enjoyment of the fruit of an action. But nobody is known to be desirous of heaven from his very birth so that he may be engaged in the action as an agent. The literal meaning of the word "Svarga-kāmaḥ" is either of the following two. A man who has a longing for heaven is called 'Svarga-kāmaḥ.' Or, a man who wishes for heaven is called 'Svargakāmaḥ'. The two senses of the above term clearly state that a person who has set his heart upon heaven is Svargakāmaḥ.

Now, let us discuss how heaven, the object of desire, is syntactically connected with the verb. Does it render visible or invisible help to the verb ?

Heaven does not visibly assist the verb :

The sentences, viz. "Sandal is heaven," "Damsels, sweet sixteens, are heaven" imply the identity of heaven with substances like Sandal, damsels, etc. Hence the word 'heaven' denotes a substance. Jaimini holds that if substances are related to the object of a verb then they, assisting the object of a verb, are related to the verb. As sour milk and other such objects, being an accessory matter, render assistance to an action so heaven indirectly contributes its help to the action in question. Desire, also, has its contribution in this matter because it exercises influence upon the collection of materials which are a means to the action in question. Thus it benefits an action. The benefit which such desire renders to an action is visible since a person moves for collecting materials, being induced by such desire.

The view in question is not sound since the word 'heaven' does not denote a substance since it denotes bliss but not a substance. The very sandal is not heaven to a person who is afflicted with cold. But it is said to be heaven by him who is oppressed by the heat of summer. The very lady is designated as heaven by an erotic person. But she is not so to a person whose passion has subsided. Thus heaven invariably denotes bliss but not a substance. As heaven is not a substance so it is not a means to action. Some thinkers imagine that the peak of the gold-mountain is heaven since no other place is an abode of infinite bliss. Such a place is not a means to the said action since nobody can have an access to it and the articles like sour milk etc. are not available there.

Heaven does not render invisible help to an action :

If one imagines that our inner organ is an ocean and concentrates his mind upon this imaginary object then he acquires merit and thereby benefits an action. Similarly, desire for heaven will generate merit and through this invisible result help the act of sacrificing. Such an assumption is far-fetched. Heaven is infinite bliss. Bliss is not a means to an end. But everything else is a means to bliss which is an end in itself. Hence, heaven is not a means to a sacrifice. But a sacrifice is a means to heaven. Thus as the above sentence does not enjoin a means to a sacrifice so the word 'Svarga-kāmaḥ' (one who desires heaven) is not syntactically connected with the verb since it does not communicate an agent. If you ask, "How is it connected with the verb ?" then we say that the word stands for one who enjoys the fruit of an action.

Who enjoys the fruit of an action ? He who is entitled to own the result of an action enjoys it. He who is capable of producing an action has right to enjoy its fruit. Now, the Mīmāṁsakas may contend that the agent of an action is only entitled to enjoy its fruit. They suggest that an adhikārin is a kartṛ. In other words, the word 'Svarga-kāmaḥ' stands for an agent. The word 'svāmī' suggests an agent but does not denote a person. In order to be the owner of the result of an act the person must possess capacity. A person does not acquire the right of ownership simply because he happens to be an agent. The relation which holds between an action and a person is not distinct from that which subsists between a case-ending and a verb. (This is the contention of the Mīmāṁsakas) (The Naiyāyikas reply). A person knows at first that it is his duty and he is capable of discharging it. Thus a person, being aware of the ownership relation, enters into the case-relation. In other words, he is conscious of the case-relation afterwards.

Now, the Mīmāṁsakas raise another point against the above decision. They say "You do not deny existence to the case-relation as the upholders of the thesis that a word denotes only a universal refuse to believe the awareness of an individual. But how will you prove that the case-relation is subsequently presented to our consciousness ?" Some thinkers give an answer to this question. They hold that the person requires no further qualification, viz. his distinct relationship with the verb since he has been already mentioned as qualified. A person who possesses the requisite qualifications of an agent viz. capacity etc. becomes the agent of an action.

If a person does not possess such qualifications then he has no right to enjoy the fruit of an action. For this reason, we hold that a person who possesses the requisite qualifications is the real agent. Mere agency does not confer upon a person the right to enjoy the fruit of an action. Thus a person who desires heaven acquires the said right. If he performs an action with the purpose of attaining heaven then he thinks "Let heaven be my enjoyable object. How can I attain heaven, and being prompted by this aspiration longs for heaven as his goal. Hence, the performer of a sacrifice is mentioned as one who desires heaven. If that action does not lead to heaven then an opposite idea is presented to our mind viz. he desires heaven but performs a sacrifice. He longs for one thing but does another thing. Such a critical attitude of our mind may develop. Therefore, if it is not admitted that an action is a means to one's desideratum then a person who desires heaven cannot engage himself in that action. If a person is not entitled to an action then he can in no way be connected with it. So when one deserve the fruit of a sacrifice he who desires heaven goes to perform a sacrifice. The title does not accrue to a person if the causal relation does not subsist between the act of sacrifice and heaven. Hence, we must admit that heaven is the end and the act of sacrifice is a means to it. Therefore an action, being a means to its fruit—the end, cannot maintain its principal position in a sentence. We cannot hold that the sentence which contains a verb signifying this action purports to convey the action as its meaning. Jaimini has also said to this effect :— "When an action is performed in order to realise an object an action occupies a subordinate place, being itself accessory.

Say, 'Which action is the meaning of a sentence?' Do you say that the act of sacrifice, the meaning of the root 'yaj', is the meaning in question ? Or, do you say that the said action is conveyed by a suffix attached to the root ? Of these two suppositions what is conveyed by a root is a means to the object of desire. Hence, the action which is conveyed by a root occupies a subordinate place. This position has been already made clear. The meaning of a suffix becomes that of a sentence when it is presented to us only as a means to the meaning of a root and the object of desire. In no other way it is presented to our consciousness. Our rival thinkers also approve of this hypothesis. Hence, we hold that no sentence purports to convey an action as its principal meaning. We believe that this view is shared by all.

As a person is more important than the result to be attained so he may be the meaning of a sentence :

Let us now follow the logical development of the above two hypotheses. Why do you say that a result is signified by a sentence ? Why do you discard the hypothesis that an action is the meaning of a sentence ? The reason is that it occupies a subordinate place. This logic applies to the case of a result also. A result is also subordinate to a person since it serves the purpose of a person. Heaven is not attained by itself. A person endeavours to attain it. But everybody desires all objects as they are to be enjoyed by him. As they are desired by a person so they do not occupy a principal position in a sentence, Jaimini has stated that a result is also not prominent since it serves the purpose of a person. Now, the logical conclusion which is suggested by the above discussion is this that a person who performs a sacrifice should be the meaning of a sentence. He uses freedom and leans upon none. The Mīmāṁsakas point out that the above conclusion is not satisfactory. A person is also used as a means. He is engaged in consecrating posts made up of fig trees. The height of a post made up of fig tree is measured by that of a person. Thus a person is required to some action. Jaimini also holds that a person is a means to an action.

The refutation of the hypothesis that an action or a person is signified by a sentence :

If we admit the authority of Jaimini then we are in a fix. We do not know what we shall do. Let us clearly state the problem. One acts in order to have a result. A result in its turn serves the purpose of a person. The aim of a sacrifice is also to complete an action. If the wheel of prominence revolves in this fashion then which of them will occupy the principal position in a sentence ? Which will be the meaning of a sentence ?

Our answer to the above problem is as follows. A person is not the meaning of a sentence since there is a divergence of opinion regarding the hypothesis that a person is signified by a verb—not to speak of the hypothesis that a person is signified by a sentence. Why do you say that the agent, i.e., the performer of an action is not signified by a verb ? According to the rule laid down in Pāṇini's, grammar a lakāra (a verb in all its tenses) signifies an agent. Why shall not we hold that an agent is signified by a verb ? What is the meaning of the term (lakāra) ? Pāṇini enjoins that when the present tense of a verb is to be indicated lakāra assumes the form of laṭ. When an agent is to be communicated the suffix 'śap' is attached to it. A verb takes an inflexion in the second person when it is syntactically connected with a pronoun standing for the second person. A verb takes an inflexion in the first person when it is syntactically connected with the first person, a pronoun indicating the first person. A verb takes an inflexion in the third person when it is syntactically connected with the third person. The inflexions which indicate the third person are 'tip', 'tas', and 'jhi'. In order to indicate the plural number of a person the terminal inflexion which is attached to a verb has a definite form. To indicate the dual or the singular number of a person the terminal inflexion, attached to a verb, has a distinct form. Thus, each number has been distinctly indicated by a separate sentence. The sūtras which enjoin cases, number and case-endings should point to syntactical unity as they all refer to one and the same substantive. The sentence "One person cooks" has been interpreted by the authorities on grammer thus: As the number of the nominative case of the verb (to cook) is singular so the terminal suffix 'tip' is attached to it. If there are two nominative cases of the verb (to cook) then the terminal suffix 'tas'is attached to it. If the nominative cases of the verb (to cook) are more than two then the terminal suffix 'jhi' is attached to it. Thus it is clear that the number of the nominative case is conveyed by a verb with a suffix attached to it but not the nominative case. Hence, how is it that the nominative case of a verb, i. e., an agent, is conveyed by a verb ? There is no need of elaborately discussing the subject matter of another science. Therefore, a person who performs an act is not the meaning of a sentence. The result produced by a verb, is not the meaning of a sentence since the dilemma that a result is either an accomplished objcct or not cannot be solved. If a result is an accomplished fact then the designation does not properly apply to it since it has been mentioned non-accomplished object of desire.

The Proof of the Hypothesis that Bhāvanā is the Meaning of a Sentence

If an accomplished fact is not a result then a result is to be brought into being. In that case, we cannot imagine that a result cannot be produced. Therefore, the Mīmāṁsakas propound the hypothesis that an activity is the meaning of a sentence. This activity or process leads on to a possible result. Hence, it is bound up with past, present and future times.

The Determination of the Nature of an Activity :

What is a bhāvanā, i. e., a process. A bhāvanā is that which brings into being an object to be produced. The result, viz., heaven etc., is to be produced since it comes into being. Whatever comes into being is also brought into being. Our experience teaches that whatever comes into being is the nominative case of the verb, 'to be'. Whatever is eithcr eternal or unreal does not come into being. Kumārila Bhaṭṭa says to this effect in his Śloka-vārttika. (An object which does not come into existence or which endures for ever cannot be created like the sky-flower or the sky.)

Heaven and such other objects which are objects of our desire are other than the sky and the sky-flower. For this reason such objects may be created. A bhāvanā is an activity of the agent towards a course of action which terminates in a result. It signifies that it causes one to come into being. This idea is expressed by a causal suffix attached to the verb, 'to be'. The heaven is the nominative case of the non-causal verb 'is'. The nominative case of the original verb becomes the objective case of the same verb with the causal suffix attached to it. The bhāvanā denotes the activity of an agent who causes something to come into being. A person brings into being heaven which is to come into being, by means of his own activity. The very activity which produces it (a result) is called 'bhāvanā'.

Now, the propounders of the hypothesis that a sentence signifies an action put a question to the framers of the new thesis. They suggest that the so-called activity of a person is nothing but an action. This activity is not distinct from an action. It is not a class by itself. Hence, the hypothesis that a sentence points to an action has not been refuted. This suggestion creates a new problem. An answer to this problem is as follows: Any and every action is not a bhāvanā, i.e., the activity of an agent. Bhāvanā is the activity of an agent. But it is distinct from all visible sacrificial acts which are done in an order of time, viz., prior and posterior. Some of these acts are previously performed and the others are subsequently performed. All these acts are arranged in due order of time. A bhāvanā is distinct from the aggregate of the sacrificial acts thus arranged. The activity of an agent is experienced by us as distinct from such sacrificial acts taken both singly and collectively.

A bhāvanā (the activity of an agent) is not to be produced by any one of those acts. It does not produce only one of those acts. But it produces all acts which are produced and which, at the same time, produce other acts. This activity is distinct from all acts and cases and is communicated to us by a word. (This is the sense of the above verse). Let us critically examine an example. A verb in the subjunctive mood, viz., 'yajeta' has been illustrated. If we analyse the word 'yajeta', we find that it consists of two parts, viz., a verb (the root yaj) and a suffix, indicative of subjunctive mood. The root 'yaj' signifies the act of sacrifice etc. The suffix, attached to the root, communicates an injunction which has an impelling force and the number of agent etc. But the activity of an agent which is distinct from processes, denoted by a root, and is called bhāvanā is not conveyed to us by a suffix. Pāṇini recognises no such inflection like the suffix indicative of the subjunctive mood as points to the activity of an agent. Hence, the activity of an agent does not constitute the meaning of a sentence.

An answer to the above question is as follows. If one minutely observes the import of verbal communication then he understands that the activity of an agent is also conveyed by a verb. Let us now leave aside the verbs in the subjunctive mood. If we carefully examine the verbs in the present tense then we shall see that from the verbs 'yajate' etc. we unmistakably guess the activity of an agent. As we grasp the act of cooking etc. from the verbs, 'cooks', 'goes' etc. so we make out the activity of an agent which is invariably connected with all these acts. Though the act of cooking and such other acts come into being and cease to exist yet the knowledge of the activity of an agent remains unaffected. When nominal suffixes are attached towards 'Upagu' etc. the resultant words are 'Aupagavaḥ', 'Kapatavaḥ', 'Aupamanyavaḥ' etc. These words convey as well the meanings of suffixes attached to the basic word. The lifting up of a weight and the taking down of a weight are implied by such suffixes. Similarly, an additional meaning viz. the activity of an agent is observed to permeate through the original meaning of a verb.

Moreover, when one intends to explain the meaning of a verb viz. 'cooks' he explains it thus :—One does the act of cooking. The act of cooking becomes the object of the transitive verb 'does'. In Sanskrit language the meaning of pacati is expressed in the form 'pākam-karoti'. The word 'pāka'—the meaning of the root 'pac' gets the second case-ending. This case-ending points to the fact that pāka is the object of 'karoti.' The word 'karoti' (does) represents the activity of an agent. The terminal inflexion, attached to the root, points to the activity of an agent. We have already stated that the word 'karoti' stands for such an activity.

When the question 'what does Devadatta do?' is put, two sorts of answer are given by the two speakers. One says that he does cooking. Another person holds that he cooks. These two answers purport to convey the same thing. Otherwise the inquirer would not have grasped the answer. Thus the two words "pākaṁ karoti" (does cooking) convey the same meaning as is conveyed by the single word "pacati" (cooks). The meaning of the root 'to do' is grasped by us as distinct from that of the root 'to cook'. The distinct meaning which is conveyed by the root 'to do' is called 'Bhāvanā' (i.e. the activity of an agent).

Some critics join issue with the above thinkers and hold that a terminal inflexion, attached to a root, does not convey an activity which is distinct from the number of an agent etc. and is other than the meaning of a root. If a distinct activity had been grasped then the verb 'karoti' (does) would have conveyed it. The verb 'karoti' consists of two elements viz. (1) the basic root (kṛ) and (2) the terminal inflexion attached to it. These two elements cannot present to our consciousness two distinct meanings.

A reply to the above criticism is as follows : The thesis has not been properly grasped. If one uses two words viz. 'pākaṁ karoti' then the sense which is conveyed by the inflexion attached to the first 'kṛ' is different from that conveyed by the inflexion attached to the second (kṛ). But if we use the word 'pacati' then the inflexion attached to the root 'pac' conveys the same sense as is denoted by the inflexion attached to the first (kṛ).

Nobody disputes that the number of an agent and such other things are expressed by these inflexions. Thereby we should not deny the presentation of an activity as noted above.

The activity which is conveyed by 'karoti' cannot be somehow communicated by any other word. Words which denote distinct verbs only convey also such an activity. All words do not communicate it. Which are the distinct words pointing to such an activity? Oh yes, there are such words as we shall now mention.

All transitive verbs, having terminal inflexions, point to the activity of an agent. The verbs like yajeta etc., having proper inflexions attached to them, indicate the said activity. There are a few verbs which are intransitive. When suffixes are attached to them they assume forms like the words 'bhāva', 'bhāvanā.' and 'bhūti'. The sufflxes 'ghañ', 'lyuṭ' and 'kti' have been attached to the root 'bhū' (to be). The resulting words denote existence or being but not an activity. There are some words which denote rites but not verbs. Let us illustrate them. The words like Śyena Yāga etc. exemplify them. The words like Śyena etc. are proper names of some Vedic rites. This point has been proved before. But there are roots of transitive verbs viz., yaj, dā, 'hu' etc. When we use them in sentences we attach proper terminal inflexions to them. These terminal inflexions having synthetic character, indicate the actual mood of a verb viz., the subjunctive mood etc. Verbs, having been employed in proper forms, express the activity of an agent. Let us illustrate few verbs employed to convey the activity of an agent. They are 'yajeta', 'dadyāt, 'juhuyāt' etc. As the above meaning, viz., the activity of an agent is expressed by a verb in the causal form (bhāvayet) so it is also distinctly expressed by the verb 'karoti'. One cannot say that the said activity is not conveyed by the verb 'karoti', (The printed text-book seems to us to be incorrect. We suggest two corrections here, viz.

bhāvayet itivat and nānuraktena. We are following the Banaras edition of Nyāya-mañjarī p. 308 lines 25 and 26). But when the verb 'karoti' is not associated with other acts such as the act of sacrificing etc. it cannot be employed to signify the said activity. Therefore the distinct words such as yajati etc. communicate the activity of a person known as bhāvanā which is to be brought into being. Thus the existence of bhāvanā is proved.

Some thinkers hold that bhāvanā is a distinct type of activity and is an internal activity of the soul. It is distinct from the outer motion known as spanda (vibration).

Some other thinkers hold that bhāvanā is conation which belongs to the soul. When it appears the soul gives up its inactivity.

This conation effectuates sacrifice, libation etc. Everybody admits that it is distinct from the acts such as sacrifice, libation etc.

Though conation is an attribute of the soul yet it is not similar to the attribute of ubiquity etc. The soul is directly aware of its existence because it bears upon acts such as sacrifice, libation etc.

Another sect of thinkers holds that as a universal belongs to all individuals of a particular class but does not belong exclusively to a particular individual so the universal verb which is shared by all distinct acts such as sacrifice, libation etc. is called bhāvanā.

As cowness belongs to all individual cows viz., Śābaleya etc. as their common property and each individual cow e.g. Sābaleya etc. has its specific property so an activity in general belongs to all acts, viz. the act of sacrifice etc. as their common feature and each act has its specific feature e.g., the act of sacrifice has its peculiar form. The common activity is called bhāvanā. As the universal of cowness, isolated from all particulars, e.g., Śābaleya etc. cannot be presented to our consciousness a pure common activity dissociated from all particular activities, cannot be presented to our consciousness. This common activity is always presented to our consciousness as associated with other particular activities. The absence of pure common activity is not proved because of its such association. The pure soul is never experienced. It is always experienced as associated with pleasure, pain etc. the specific attributes of the soul. But such an association with attributes does not disprove the existence of the pure soul. This being the case, when a question 'what is he doing?' is put with regard to an unknown specific act an answer is given viz., 'he cooks', he reads book etc. As it reveals the specific nature of an act so it is appropriate. Though 'bhāvana' is an act in general yet it is not a universal like the universal of cowness or the universal belonging to an act. If it were an acomplished fact that it would not be enjoined.

Moreover, in cases like the following 'One should sacrifice'. 'One should make gifts', 'One should pour libation' etc. a consecutive series of non-specified activities is presented to our consciousness. Such a series of activities is enjoined. Such non-specified activities as are denoted by roots and are capable of being performed constitute bhāvanā. From this stand-point one may hold that a bhāvanā is denoted by a root. One may argue that a bhāvanā does not constitute the meaning of a root since the verbal nouns such as pāka (cooking), dāna (giving) etc. do not communicate a bhāvanā. The defender of the views may also counterargue that a bhāvanā should not also be denoted by a suffix because verbs like 'bhavati' etc. do not convey it. (We get the verb 'bhavati' by attaching a terminal inflexion to the root bhū.). In fine, we say that we need not make much of accurately settling the point in question. It is our confirmed opinion that a bhāvanā is conveyed either by a root or by a suffix.

A Bhāvanā Consists of three Factors:

A bhāvanā is communicated to us either by a root or by a suffix. But it relates to three subjects of urgency (1) viz. what is to be achieved (2) by which means it is to be achieved, and (3) how is it to be realised. The first subject of inquiry is what is to be achived. This inquiry is answered by word 'svarga-kāmaḥ' (one desirous of heaven). What is to be achieved? 'Heaven' is our answer.

Now, a doubt arises in our mind. The word 'svarga-kāmaḥ' points to an agent but not to an end. Therefore, the above solution does not satisfy us. The above doubt may be solved thus. It is a truism that the said word points to an agent. But here the statement purports to convey heaven. Heaven denotes bliss par excellence. It is an end in itself but not a means to an end. Heaven is desired as an object to be achieved. Hence it falls on the side of a desirable object. We mean to say that heaven is to be achieved. If the word 'svarga-kāmaḥ' literally signifies one who desires heaven then it is clear that heaven is to be achieved. If one admits that the compound word 'Svarga-kāmaḥ' is an example of the Bahuvrīhi compound then it points to the fact that heaven is to be achieved. If we carefully examine the force of an injunction then we see that an injunction points to the above conclusion.

When one is aware of the end that he should achieve heaven he enquires. "By which means is heaven to be achieved ?" This inquiry is satisfied if it is held that heaven is achieved by a sacrifice. Thus a sacrifice is related to heaven. Now, a question arises in our mind viz. no word such as yāgena is given in the injunctive sentence. He means to say that there is no such explicit statement as shows that one should attain heaven by means of a sacrifice. But it is given that one should sacrifice. ('Given' is equivalent to 'heard'.) The complete verb consists of two parts viz. (1) the root and (2) a terminal inflexion. It is said that the terminal inflexion in the subjunctive mood denotes a bhāvanā (the mental activity of an agent). Now, the remaining element is the bare root. Now if a kṛt-suffix is attached to this root then the word 'yāga' is framed. If the third-case-ending is joined to this word then we get the word 'yāgena'. Now, the question is "How can the bare root 'yaj' convey the sense of inflexional word 'yāgena' ?" The problem is solved thus:— Oh longlived one: You do not take an exception to the hypothesis that a bhāvanā is denoted by a suffix or an inflexion. Thus you should also agree to accept that a bhāvanā also relates itself to a sacrifice. A bhāvanā refers to a sacrifice (yāga) in such a manner as fulfills its requirements. If its requirements were not fulfilled then it would not have referred to a yāga. If the root 'yaj' fulfills the requirement of an instrument then it becomes capable of being related to a bhāvanā. In this manner the root 'yaj' is related to a bhāvanā. The meaning of the root 'yaj' does not convey the sense of the third-case ending. Hence, let the third case-ending be not attached to the root 'yaj'. But owing to the force of expression belonging to a word the root 'yaj' conveys a yāga as an instrumental case. If you ask, "Owing to the power of denotation of which word does the root 'yaj' convey the above meaning, i.e., the meaning of yāgena ?" then we answer that owing to such power belonging to an inflexion in the subjunctive mood an inflexion which conveys a bhāvanā the above meaning is conveyed. There is no royal mandate to the effect that the instrumentality of an object is conveyed only by the direct mention of the third case-ending. A subjective inflexion denoting a bhāvanā suggests the sense of the third case-ending. We along with the critics accept the above view. Therefore, why do not the critics accept the view that in the sentence "one who is desirous of heaven should sacrifice" heaven is the object to be achieved.

Or, when from a verb the meaning of a root is known as an object to be achieved, the second case-ending signifies that the associated object is to be achieved.

Now, a doubt arises in the mind of the objectors. If the above solution is final then the meaning of the root is identical with the object which is to be accomplished. In that case, the root 'yaj' will answer the question what is to be achieved ? It should fall on the side of what. If you ask what is to be performed then the answer is a sacrifice. Again, a sacrifice requires an instrumental cause for its completion. What is its instrumental cause ? A sacrifice should be causally connected with Brīhis (a kind of paddy) determined in another Vedic sentence The meaning of the root 'yaj' should not be taken as an instrumental cause. The inflexion which is attached to the root denotes an activity to be brought about. This activity is directly directed towards an object which is close at hand. It is its natural course of direction. If it does not concern itself with an object and if it is taken to relate itself with an instrumental cause which is remote then the activity does follow the proper channel of direction. Therefore the said activity should not be connected with an instrumental cause.

An answer to the above objection is as follows. The syntactical relation as suggested by the objector would have been accepted if the word 'svarga-kāmaḥ' had not been given in the injunctive sentence. As it has been given in the sentence so the meaning of the root 'yaj' should be taken as an instrumental cause but not as an object. If you ask 'why' then our reply is this. The object which is to be achieved is heaven. Therefore, the root 'yaj' does not signify an object to be achieved. But it signifies an instrumental cause which helps the coming into being of an object. The reason behind our statement is this. Heaven is an object of desire. It is pleasure itself. As the world 'heaven' conveys no other sense so it, being nothing but pleasure in itself, is worthy of being achieved. When we long for an object to be achieved heaven alone attracts attention as an object longed for. So a sacrifice, conveyed by the root 'yaj', does not represent itself as such an object. Heaven requires an instrumental cause for its coming into being. The instrumental cause in question is a sacrifice. Thus, a sacrifice has been determined as an instrumental cause. A particular sacrifice, Jyotiṣṭoma by name has been again mentioned as an instrumental cause. Therefore, it is reasonable to hold that the sacrifice, conveyed by the root 'yaj', is identical with Jyotiṣṭoma. Thus, Jyotiṣṭoma and such other proper names become designations of sacrifices.

There are a few designations of rites which give evidence in favour of the hypothesis that a sacrifice itself is an object to be achieved. Let us cite an example viz. "Agnihotraṁ juhoti (one should perform the Agnihotra homa)." The example, cited by the objector, does not affect our hypothesis. Though the meaning of the root superficially appears to be the object to be accomplished yet a deep insight into the construction of the sentence reveals that the said homa, called Agnihotra, is really an instrumental case; otherwise the compound word 'Savarga-Kāmaḥ' will have no syntactical relation in the sentence. We have already cleared our position. In some Vedic sentences the names of sacrifices are used as an objective case e.g. 'Agnihotraṁ juhoti'. In some other Vedic sentences the names of sacrifices are used as an instrumental case e.g. 'Jyotiṣṭomena yajati' etc. Therefore 'yaji' should be syntactically related as an instrumental case. Thus we establish the point that a sacrifice is a means to an end but not an end-in-itself. This is what is meant by the statement that a sacrifice is the instrumental cause of a sacrifice.

It has been stated that the proximity of the root 'yaj' to its inflexion indicates that the meaning of the root is the object to be accomplished. Such a statement is contrary to reasons. Two words are mutually related in a sentence by a particular relation if they are determined as fit to be related in such a manner. When such fitness for being mutually related is logically ascertained, ground for mutual relation to be held between the two terms is prepared. In the absence of such fitness, mutual relation between two terms cannot take place. Heaven is a fit object to be achieved and a sacrifice which is denoted by the root 'yaj' is fit to be its instrumental cause. We have already stated our view.

When one learns that a person should achieve his object longed for by means of a sacrifice a desire springs up in his mind how to perform a sacrifice. Now, he connects the system of means mentioned in the injunctive sentence and in other sentences with the sacrifice in question. The means mentioned in the sentence enjoining a sacrifice is that one who performs a sacrifice with a view to acquire animals should sing a song consisting of the Revatī Ṛks set to the tune Vāravantīya—a song sung in the Agniṣṭoma sacrifice. The means mentioned in other sentences are as follows :— One should unhusk paddy with pestle and mortar', One should grind rice'. One should offer twigs to fire and 'One should worship fire'. Our conclusive view is that these means possess visible and invisible efficacy. They almost in every case give an answer to the question 'how'. When a visible benefit is made one is to think such acts as the act of pounding etc. This act has a direct influence upon the meaning of the root i.e. the rite to be performed. A subsidiary action which contributes towards a sacrifice in an invisible way renders indirect benefit to it e.g. the twigs of a sacred tree. (If one makes an offering of twigs to fire then he gets benefit in the next world. Hence, it renders an indirect service to the sacrificer. But if we do not pound rice then we cannot prepare cakes from rice. So its service is tangible. The two terms 'sannipatyopakāriṇi' and 'ārādupakāriṇi' have been used by

Jayanta in senses contrary to those of these two terms used by the modern authors of philosophy.

When an end, means to it and an act—the triparte elements of a sacrifice are mutually related a sacrifice becomes fit to be performed. The fitness which it acquires is called bhāvanā. If a bhāvanā takes place then an injunction and a prohibition become fruitful.

There are two injunctions, viz. (1) 'One who desires heaven should perform Darśa and Paurṇamāsa sacrifices' and (2) 'One who longs for heaven should perform Jyotiṣṭoma sacrifice.' These two injunctive sentences are to be interpreted in the light of the principle laid down before. The meaning of the first sentence is this that one is to achieve heavenly bliss by means of Darśa and Paurṇamāsa sacrifices and he shall have recourse to the subsidiary actions such as the establishing of sacred fire, etc.

An objector may find fault with this hypothesis and argue against it thus. If this is your hypothesis why do you think that an injunction is inevitably necessary ? You have said that when verbs are used in the present tense they signify the activity of an agent. Then why do you assume a verb in the subjunctive mood ? Now you may contend that 'We assume an injunction i.e. a verb in the subjunctive mood either in order to demonstrate the causal relation holding between a sacrifice and heaven or in order to persuade one to undertake an action or to dissuade him from doing it. But due consideration being given to requirement, fitness and proximity though a verb is used in the present tense yet it pointing to the activity of an agent throws light on the causal relation subsisting between the act of sacrifice and heaven even without the aid of an injunction. Now the upholder of the above hypothesis may contend that assumption of an injunction is necessary because it supplies us with the impelling force i.e. an injunction goads us to undertake a rite. Such a contention does not hold good since the movement of a person depends upon his will. If a person knows that a sacrifice is a means to heaven then he who desires to attain heaven moves for it i.e., adopts the adequate means but he who has no such desire does not move to do anything. How does an injunction help him in any way ? An injunction can neither fetter the legs of an unwilling person with an iron chain nor tie down the hands of such a person with a piece of rope. A person desires to avoid the sphere of prohibition which includes the drinking of wine, the killing of a Brahman etc. because he knows these acts to be evil ones and desists from committing them. Hence neither an injunction impels one to undertake an action nor prohibition prompts him to retard from an action. Therefore, it is illogical to assume the hypothesis of an injunction or that of a prohibition for the purpose of movement or otherwise.

The determination of the character of an injunction (vidhi)

We do not know what is the definition of an injunction (vidhi). Some thinkers say, 'An injunction causes a person to move—a person who has not moved but does not reveal what remains unknown since the second definition is too wide."

Yes, we have heard the verse which contains the definition of an injunction but fails to ascertain what is exactly the mover of the unmoved. Even the great savants of learning entertain a grave doubt as to the exact characterization of a mover. Does the suffix which is symbol of the subjunctive mood cause one to move ? Or, is the sense of the suffix, presented to our consciousness, a mover ? Or, does the operation of the awareness of the sense of the suffix give us an impetus ? Or, is the result of an action a mover ? Or, is the ascertainment of an exact means to the desired goal an impeller ? Or, is an attachment for the desired goal a motiff ? As there are so many rival hypotheses on the point at issue so the true character of a mover is not determined. Hence, we fail to grasp an injunction. You have said 'What is the need of having recourse to an injunction ?' We have got something to say in this matter.

This is the super excellent power of an injunction which unites a sacrifice, the meaning of the root 'yaj', with heaven with such a tie as holds between a means and an end.

If one holds that the sentence "svargakāmo yajeta" (One who desires heaven should sacrifice) has no injunctive force and the word 'svargakāmaḥ" points only to the agent then this statement is inconsistent like the statement "The white colour is the Hotṛ priest". If the sentence is not used in the subjunctive mood then the verb 'yajeta' cannot syntactically relate itself with heaven as its object since heaven occupies a subordinate place in the sentence, being the first member of the compound word 'svarga-kāmaḥ' and is very remote from the suffix which stands for the actual verb. According to the natural order of words given in the sentence a sacrifice should have been the objective case since a sacrifice is practicable and is constituted by consecutive parts. It is only through the favour of an injunction that the relation of a means to an end between a sacrifice and heaven is revealed to us; otherwise, we could not have known it. Therefore, we must assume a sentence in the subjunctive mood.

How does an injunction indicate the relation of a means to an end ? It reveals the relation in this way. A suffix representing the subjunctive mood, normally induces a man who has implicit confidence in the result of a rite to undertake it. When a person listens to an injunction which commands him to pursue non-human end, his interest flags since he has no regard for the ideal. When a person moves for performing a rite, being prompted by an injunction the injunction, apprehending some limitation in its persuasive force settles the question that heaven—the human end, is an object to be accomplished and a sacrifice is its means. The persuasive force of an injunction is demonstrated as it throws light on the end and its means.

An exception has been taken to the above hypothesis with the remark, 'If a person does not move to undertake a Vedic rite though an injunction points to heaven as the end of human life then how can an injunction exercise its persuasive force ? Such an objection is baseless. An injunction does not set a person to motion like the air. The air sets conscious or unconscious objects in motion. But an injunction only induces one who is endowed with consciousness. The inducement of a conscious person by an injunction makes him feel that he has been led to an action by the injunction. Such an awareness cannot be produced in the mind of a person if an injunction does not reveal the goal of an action. When the goal is brought to light the complete knowledge of a Vedic rite is produced. When the true knowledge of a Vedic rite dawns on a person he is persuaded by an injunction conforming to the path of proof to undertake a Vedic rite. If a person does not undertake an action owing to his idleness etc. or owing to the absence of need then let him not undertake it. But an injunction has done its duty because it has stimulated the listener to the effect that he has been inspired by it. The awareness of inspiration is onething and the volitional reaction in the external world is another thing.

An injunction is at the root of the knowledge of the causal relations holding between a sacrifice and the goal of a person. This knowledge owes its origin to the awareness of the first inspiration set up by an injunction.

If one listening to an injunctive sentence 'One should sacrifice', feels the inspiration but does not comprehend the causal relation indicated above then the injunction does not become complete in itself. For this reason, it is said that the said causal relation is hinted at by the awareness of inspiration. In case of prohibition on listening to a prohibition that none should kill a person he is not prevented from perpetrating an evil deed, however prohibited it may be, unless and until he realises that the said act is intrinsically evil. Therefore, an injunction is significant even if an act is prohibited like an enjoined one. Hence, an injunction must be resorted to.

The question 'Why has an injunction been resorted to?' appears to us to be similar to that raised by Simple Simon. We do neither follow injunctions nor avoid prohibitions of the modern age. We are not the authors of the Vedas. But we simply learn them. We learn from the Vedas the sentence in the subjunctive mood that one who is desirous of heaven should sacrifice etc. The well-defined meaning of such an injunction is that heaven is an end to be achieved and a sacrifice is a means to that end. Such a meaning is not supplied to us by an act of imagination. It is conveyed to us by the suggestive power of an injunction. Therefore we should have recourse to an injunction.

The definition of motif

It has been objected that an injunction is hard to grasp because springs of action have not been determined. An answer to this objection is as follows. The result of an action cannot be a motive since the result of an action is open to a puzzling dilemma, viz. it is either a pre-existent object or a non-existent one. If a result already exists then nobody tries to bring it about. Again, if a result is non-existent then it is unreal like the horns of a hare. As such it cannot logically act as a motive since a motive of this type has never been experienced.

If you say that a result which is desired is a motive then it may be as well said that the very desire constitutes the motive of an action but not the result. Our desire for obtaining a result may be excessive. But if the means to an end is not determined then nobody can reasonably undertake an action. A man who desires heaven does not simply make a show of an action in order to attract a large number of audience. The exact means to the real good should be his spring of action. The people also behave in this fashion when they transact worldly matters. They learn from the medical treatises written by the great physicians that the myrobalan fruit remedies a few diseases. When they fall a victim to these diseases they use it. Considering that food appeases hunger hungry person sets to take food. Therefore what is conducive to the well-being of a person is his motif.

The above hypothesis is not sound. Does a means to the well-being stimulate one's activity, being itself known or unknown? A means which is not known as such does not stir our activity. If a person does not learn the medicinal properties of a myrobalan fruit from any source whatsoever, then he, being ill, cannot use it as a remedy. Therefore source of the knowledge of a means is really a mover. How do we know that the means in question leads to the end in question? When the means and the end are tangible we know them in their true colour by the joint method of agreement and difference. When the end is invisible the means to this end is learnt only from the verbal authority. Therefore, an authoritative word excites our inclination for a work. Such a word by itself (i. e. if its sense is not properly understood) does not set up our activity. If it had done so then it would have behaved like the wind etc. If a word, being itself not properly grasped, makes us move as the wind, or a demon or a bad king does, then a man should undertake a work whenever he hears a word but does not understand its sense. Such a conjecture is absurd. For this reason, a word impels to action when its sense is thoroughly grasped. Inflexions indicative of subjunctive mood, cannot impel a person to undertake a work simply revealing the motif of an action. A word is distinct from other sense-organs viz. the eyes etc. since it communicates its meaning. In spite of this distinction it is the instrumental cause of the knowledge of its meaning which it conveys. An instrumental cause is such as does something. A cause cannot produce its effect if it does not operate. It must be operative. The inflexion, indicative of the subjunctive mood, does not merely effectuate consciousness but also gives an impulse to work. We know it from our experience. When one makes out the sense of liṅ (an inflexion, indicative of the subjunctive mood) he is seen to undertake a work. The operation of liṅ is responsible for this movement. The operation of liṅ is called Śābda-bhāvanā. It denotes an injunction i. e. a command. It gives an impulse to wotk.

The Two Types of Bhāvanā

Sentences, used in the subjunctive mood, communicate two kinds of bhāvanās viz. Śābda-bhāvanā and Ārthabhāvanā.

Of these two Ārthabhāvanā is the activity of the agent which causes something to come into being but not denoted by the uninflected verb i. e. by the basic root. Something comes into being. The activity of an agent is directed towards it. It belongs to an agent. When heaven, the nominative case of the verb 'to come into being', becomes the objective case of the verb, belonging to the sacrificer, the process, denoted by the second verb, is called "Ārthabhāvanā". It has been already explained. The process or operation which belongs to a word or to its constituent element and induces a person to undertake a sacrifice is called 'Śābda-bhāvanā'. The suffix or inflexion, indicative of the subjunctive mood, denotes another type of Bhāvanā (an energy which propels one to bring something into being). It is known as 'Śābda-bhāvanā'. This view has been expressed in the Tantravārttika by Kumārila.

When one listens to a sentence containing the verb 'sacrifice' in the subjunctive mood (i.e. one should sacrifice) he makes out its two meanings (1) that it is his duty to perform the sacrifice and (2) that he has been induced to do it. Hence as the suffix or the inflexion, indicative of the subjunctive mood, communicates one's own obligatory duty to be discharged so it expresses an inducement to discharge it. Therefore, Kumārila, the author of Tantra-Vārttika holds that a sentence in the subjunctive mood points to the above two types of bhāvanās i.e. Ārthabhāvanā and Śābda-bhāvanā.

Therefore, the activity of an agent towards a course of action is called Ārthabhāvanā. The operation of a word is also known as Śābdabhāvanā. These two bhāvanās are presented to our consciousness. As the operation belongs to a word so it is called Śābda-bhāvanā. If the operation which belongs to a word remains unapprehended then it does not assist the communication of sense. Hence, this bhāvanā is denoted by a word. Kumārila has said to this effect that the Vedic liṅ denotes Śābdabhāvanā by its primary denotative force and assists to communicate the meaning of a Vedic sentence in the subjunctive mood.

A Śābda-Bhāvanā Requires three Constituent Elements

A Śābda-bhāvanā, being, itself a bhāvanā, requires three elements like an Ārthabhāvanā. The three elements are as follows:—(1) What is to be accomplished i.e. the end is to be realised; (2) the instrument by which the end is accomplished; and (3) the manner or process in which the action is performed. These three constituent elements should be shown. The three elements of Śābda-bhāvanā are as follows: (1) The inclination of a listener for an obligatory duty falls under the end of Śābda bhāvanā. This point has been explained before. The function of an injunction is to impel a person to an action. The primary meaning of an injunction is Śābda-bhāvanā. The inclination of a person is roused by an injunction. Therefore, an injunction aims at the rousing of the inclination of a person. Śābda-bhāvanā discharges the function of an instrumental cause or a means which operates to bring an enjoined person into relation with an action. In other words, owing to the instrumentality of Śābda-bhāvanā an inclination for undertaking an action is evoked. Likewise in case of Ārthabhāvanā, the attainment of heaven is due to the instrumentality of a sacrtfice. With regard to the working of Śābda-bhāvanā it may be said that an inclination for performing an action is called up in the heart of a person when an obligatory duty is thoroughly determined.

Śābda-bhāvanā which is denoted by an injunctive word is the instrumental cause of the inclination of a person for a certain action. The manner of performance is fulfilled by the operation of recommendatory passages bearing upon an injunction. The listeners are not inspired to undertake actions when they listen to bare injunctions. But when they listen to various praises of such actions contained in the recommendatory passages, they become very much pleased at heart and are inspired to undertake actions enjoined by injunctions. Thus these recommendatory passages increase the intensity of inclination. Hence the operation of recommendatory passages fulfills the procedure of Śābda-bhāvanā. The aim of Śābda-bhāvanā is to rouse the inclination of an agent for an action. Words which communicate an obligatory duty are the instrumental cause. Mandatory passages supply one with the procedure of performance. Thus, Śābda-bhāvanā which consists of three essential elements is verily an injunction.

The Determination of Relation Holding Between an Injunction and Bhāvanā :

If it is held that Śābda-bhāvanā itself is an injunction then an objection may be raised against the view that it is a logical impossibility to establish unity in the different meanings of words constituting a sentence. (The sense of this objection is as follows. If an injunction implies Śābda-bhāvanā and a verb denotes the inclination of an agent then the meaning of a sentence cannot be communicated. How does a sentence communicate its meaning ? If the meaning of a word is presented to us as syntactically related to that of another word in a sentence then the presentation of mutually related meanings is called verbal communication. An inflexion, indicative of the Vedic subjunctive mood, denotes Śābda-bhāvanā in the capacity of an injunction. The same inflexion denotes the inclination of an agent in the capacity of a verb. These meanings, being denoted by the same word, are presented to us. Hence, the mutual relation of these two meanings, presented to our consciousness, cannot be called the verbal communication of the meaning of a sentence.) The above objection does not hold good since both the meanings are presented to our consciousness as mutually related as the presentation, of the two meanings by the same suffix, indicative of the subjunctive mood, constitutes the connecting link. Kumārila in the chapter on sentences of his Ślokavārttika has said to this effect. As an injunction and a bhāvanā are communicated to us by the same suffix so their mutual relation is at first determined and then they are related to the meaning of the basic root.

An injunction excites the activity of an agent towards a course of action. Kumārila has rightly said that an injunction enjoins an agent to direct his own activity towards a course of action. Now, an objector raises an objection 'How does an injunction relate itself with a bhāvanā?'

Now the Vārttikakāra himself has admitted that the mutual relation between an injunction and a bhāvanā is presented to our consciousness before their relation with the meaning of the root of a verb. Though an inflected word denotes the senses of both the root of a verb and the suffix attached to it yet it is to be admitted that the meaning of the root of a verb constitutes the primary material and along with it the two meanings of the liṅ suffix, viz., an injunction and a bhāvanā are presented to our consciousness as an appendage. Therefore, the activity of an agent is related, to an injunction without being directed towards a course of action. It, being directed a course of action, is not related to an injunction. But an agent, having his activity not directed towards a course of action, cannot perform a duty. The activity of an agent is complete when it involves three essential elements, viz., (1) it is in pursuit of an end; (2) it requires the aid of an instrumental cause; and (3) the manner of procedure is also given. When an agent is possessed of such an activitiy he is capable of performing an obligatory duty; otherwise, he is not. But an injunction does not relate itself with a complete activity. If it remains unrelated to a complete activity then how does an agent direct his activity towards a sacrifice and adopt the proper means to realise his end?

An answer to the above objection is as follows. It is a truism that an injunction does not know how to relate itself with the activity of an agent directed towards an end, viz., sacrifice etc. But as an injunction and the activity of an agent are denoted by one and the same suffix so the injunction in question communicates its relation with the bare activity of an agent. When a bare activity is excited in an agent an injunction cannot fulfil its mission. It does not relax its efforts. But it waits for the fulfilment of its mission. It behaves like a bridegroom who has been wedded to a girl who is below her teens. As he patiently looks forward to her adolescence and for the buddihg of her beauty in each limb with his hands stretched, so the injunction tarries unless and until the activity in question takes a concrete shape, having enriched itself with all details, i.e., an agent engages himself in the actual performance of an obligatory duty. Kumārila has said in his Śloka-vārttika to this effect.

Though an injunction(Śābda-bhāvanā) relates itself with such an activity of an agent as has not been connected with other factors yet it does not remain in situ, being thus related since it lacks the moving force.

An injunction prompts an agent to an obligatory duty. But the activity of an agent does not become effective unless and until it is in close touch with its three elements.

An injunction comes into being but does not exercise power unless and until a bhāvanā (the activity of an agent) without depending upon others excepting an injunction becomes efficient.

The activity in question requires an end and such other requisite objects for its fruition even if the required objects are supplied by another injunctive sentence. It intends to establish its relation with such a subject-matter as has been referred to by another context. It is also desirous of establishing relation with the meaning of the root of the verb in question like the archetype. It also intends to establish a relation with a subject-matter implied by another such subject-matter. Such is the uniformly profound power of the verbal authority.

The method of interpreting an injunction in due order has been instructed by the great interpreters of the Mīmāṁsā. If we are to understand the meaning of a sentence referring to the activity of an agent then we are to pursue the method of interpretation and to unfold its meaning by degrees. A bhāvanā constitutes the meaning of a sentence. If it remains understood in a sentence then the blank place of the bhāvanā should be filled up and the import of the bhāvanā should be made out. A bhāvanā, being associated with many subsidiaries such as many species, attributes, substances, act. etc, assumes diverse forms. But we understand the meaning of a sentence from a sentence by one and the same method.

In every case the operative ending is attached to the root of a verb and hence the activity of an agent (ārthībhāvanā) constitutes the meaning of a sentence. The said bhāvanā is qualified by many subsidiaries, viz. various attributes, species etc. It is referred to by a judgment. Though a judgment refers to various objects yet it points to a unified whole. Just as a picture contains diverse lines of various colours but they represent a single form.

(As the listener of an injunction has had direct experience of the principal acts of a sacrifice and their subsidiary ones so when he listens to the injunction 'One should sacrifice' a picture of main acts and subsidiary ones is painted in his heart since he posesses impressions arising from the said experience. When the contents of a sacrifice are thus arranged he becomes inclined to perform a sacrifice. When an agent moves to perform a sacrifice the above described judgment arises in his mind.

The concept of a bhāvanā is the result of a long drawn process of thought. It gradually unfolds itself. The bhāvanā itself is a complicated process rendered complete by its accessories. Let us take an example of a long-drawn process viz. the act of cooking. This act continues for sometime and consists of many acts. We commence from pouring water into a cooking pot and putting rice into it and end in the boiling of rice which is independent of other acts. The whole series of acts is known as the single act of cooking. The main act of cooking consists of several minor acts such as pouring water, placing rice inside the pot, stirring the content by waiving ladle, the extraction of gruel etc. These acts extend over a long period of time. Similarly, verbal knowledge is one which commences from the knowledge of the meaning of a word and ends in the knowledge of the meaning of a sentence.

Some say 'The knowledge of a knower dawns with the knowledge of the meaning of a word. It blooms like a flower having the knowledge of the meaning of each constituent word as its petal. Then it develops into the form of a fruit in the shape of the knowledge of the meaning of a sentence. We need not hammer on this point any more.

Thus the meaning of a sentence goes under the name of Bhāvanā. It is the activity of an agent. It is directed towards heaven, sacrifice etc. But the activity which prompts one to do something is called Preṣaṇā. It constitutes the primary meaning of the optative ending attached to the root of a verb. Or, it is the function of an injunction. Everybody denominates is as an injunction.

An examination of the hypothesis that śābda-bhāvanā constitutes the meaning of a sentence :

Some other thinkers do not subscribe to the above hypothesis. They point out that śābda-bhāvanā is the activity which belongs to a word, is produced and denoted by it. When a word denotes and produces śābda-bhāvanā does it do, being itself inactive ? Or, does it produce a process, having recourse to a distinct activity ? If the propounders of the hypothesis answer in the negative then they will be compelled to admit that a word should directly communicate its meaning without the aid of an intervening process and the assumption of an intermediate process is redundant since it produces a process, unaided by another process. If they say in the affirmative, then the hypothesis is open to the fallacy of regressus ad infinitum. They should also devise ways and means of solving the problem. But it is a hard nut to crack. We have already elaborately discussed in the chapter on the definition of proofs in general that there is no distinct process excepting the vibration of elements. The reiteration of the same topic is superfluous. The same line of thinking should be followed in this case.

With regard to the process of a word which is said to be created and denoted by it a few questions arise in our mind. Does a word firstly denote a process and then produce it ? Or, does it at first bring about a process and then denote it ? Or, does it simultaneously produce and denote a process ? It is illogical to hold that a process is denoted when it has not come into being. Nobody christens his son when he is not born. Moreover, in that case, a word is not related to its meaning. Again, a word does not simultaneously produce and denote a process since the non-production of a process precedes its denotation and the hypothesis requires toil and trouble on the part of its propounders to be demonstrated. The alternative suggestion that a word creates and then denotes a process is not also tenable since as it does not endure long so it finds no opportunity of communicating the process after having created it.

How will the weak optative suffix in the presence of strong bulls carry a very heavy load? How will it express an agent, and the number and the activity of the agent? How will it produce an efficient force belonging to a word and communicate it? It can hardly bear the burden.

Another point deserves our special attention. How does an injunction which goes under the name of Sābda-bhāvanā relate itself with the activity of an agent—the import of a sentence?

An answer to this question has been already given. It has been replied that as an optative suffix denotes both word-efficient force and the activity of an agent so they enter into the relation of being denoted by one and the same suffix. Now, the objector points out that though the relation of being denoted has been stated yet the crux of the problem has not been touched. The activity of an agent towards a rite is known as Ārthī bhāvanā. It is the principal meaning of a sentence. An end, an instrumental cause and the manner of performance are invariably required by the activity of an agent. The words such as 'svarga-kāma' etc. fill in with all the requisite elements. The meanings of these words render assistance to the activity of an agent as subsidiary elements. But word-efficient force fills up none of the requisite elements of the activity of an agent. Hence, it is not subservient to this activity. Two principal objects such as a jar and piece of cloth or two principal acts such as the act of cooking and that of reading are never noticed to be mutually related as principal and accessory matters.

Now, the upholder of the hypothesis may contend that an ārthī bhāvanā is subordinate to a śābda-bhāvanā since the activity of an agent is conducive to the subject-matter of an injunction bearing the title of śābda-bhāvanā. If this is the contention then the objector points out that an injunction should be the import of a sentence but not the activity of an agent since the letter is subsidiary. Therefore, the assumption that an optative suffix denotes two principal meanings is not appreciated.

The hypothesis that Śābda-bhāvanā and Ārthībhāvanā are mutually related because they are denoted by one and the same suffix is not sound. The words 'Akṣa', 'Pada', 'Māsa' etc. admit of various meanings but the different meanings of each word are not known to be related to one another on the above ground. Moreover, in order to serve which purpose do you hold that the same suffix denotes the above two bhāvanās? An answer is given to this effect. When we hear the optative suffix the ideas of the object to be accomplished and prompting simultaneously flash in our mind. Two distinct acts of knowing do not take place in our mind. These two contents are not apprehended by the single act of knowing. If this is the case then let only one meaning be denoted by the optative suffix. If it has only one meaning then the question of the mutual relation holding between the two meanings needs no discussion. And the optative suffix is not saddled with a heavy load.

A mandate is denoted by a sentence

Now, we take for granted that the meaning of an optative suffix is one and the same. But if the said suffix communicates both duty and inspiration then it carries the same heavy load as before. What may be the meaning of the optative suffix which is both duty and inspiration ?

An answer to the above question as given by Kumārila is as follows. It is not a heavy task for an optative suffix to convey the same meaning as follows from it. The meaning of a sentence which no proof other than the optative suffix comes forward to convey is known as a mandate. (This mandate is nothing but an inspiration). Kumārila explains his point of view. Every body agrees to the point that the meaning of a word is learnt from its usage. A general rule is noticed that in order to communicate, the sense of a sentence is used since the above rule gets the sanction of usage. Among these sentences let us take into consideration such sentences as involve the verb 'yajeta'. In these sentences we shall take no notice of the meanings of words other than the said verb since if the meaning of a verb is known then the meanings of other words will gather strength in order to render assistance to the meaning of the verb. Let us now discuss the meaning of the verb 'yajeta'. From the above discussion it follows that the verb 'yajeta' denotes inspiration. The meaning is detected by the application of the joint method of agreement and difference. When we hear other words we have no knowledge of inspiration. But when we have the word 'yajeta' we have knowledge of inspiration. Thus we conclude that we cannot take an exception to the above meaning of the verb 'yajeta'. In other words, it is proved that the verb 'yajeta' denotes inspiration.

If we discuss the meaning of the verb 'juhoti' etc. then we see that the verbal terminations, indicative of the present tense, the present perfect tense etc. denote the continuity of an act, the cessation of an act etc. but not inspiration. A root in general does not denote inspiration since such a meaning is not invariably denoted by it. Hence, it is logically sound to hold that an optative suffix denotes inspiration. What is the exact nature of the said inspiration ? When this inspiration takes place and works within the heart of a listener he feels that he has been enjoined to discharge particular duty. Such an inspiration goes under the title of injunction. Pāṇini, the great grammarian, recollecting the old tradition of grammar, prescribes that an optative suffix denotes injunction. When a sacrifice, the meaning of the root 'yaj' or the activity of an agent is mentioned no inspiration is communicated to us. In a nutshell an injunction itself is nothing but an inspiration. When a verb viz., 'yajate' (one sacrifices) is used in the present tense it conveys a sense to us. But when the same verb is used in the optative tense viz., yajeta (one should sacrifice) it conveys a distinct sense since in this case the relation between an inspiration and the person who is inspired to do something is communicated. Now, a question arises in our mind. Does not the above illustration convey the relation between a sacrifice and its agent ? An answer to the above question is this : It is not a truism that the said relation is not conveyed. But it is also a fact that the relation between an inspiration and the inspired is at first conveyed. We hold that when a person is inspired he prepares himself to do an act.

When a person is prompted to do an act how is he prompted? Does he feel an abstract inspiration? No, he is prompted to do a concrete act, viz., he is inspired by the sentence that he should perform a sacrifice. The said inspiration has direct bearing upon a concrete act. In other words, the abstract relation between an inspiration and the inspired is not distinctly conveyed. There is much truth in your statement that the performer of a sacrifice is prompted to do it as an agent of the act. But when the performer of a sacrifice is prompted to do it the relation between an inspiration and the inspired is held to be distinct from that which holds between the agent of the act of sacrifice and the act itself. Thus, the person who institutes a sacrifice has double relations. On the one hand, he is related to the act of sacrifice and on the other hand he is related to inspiration. He looks like the King's cow having double relations. She is related to the King. She is also related to her milk. She who is related to the King is related to milk. She who is related to milk is related to the King. Similarly, a person will be related to prompting and to the act of sacrifice. A person who is prompted does an act and the person who does an act is prompted. This is the sum and substance of our hypothesis.

Now, an objection to the above hypothesis arises in our mind. Inspiration has no double characters since prompting itself is an act. When a person is induced to do something that which induces is called a prompter. Hence prompting itself is nothing but an act. Thus the relation holding between prompting and the person who is induced is nothing but the relation of a person with an act. This objection would have been true if the meaning of the optative suffix had been the actual mover like the air etc. An injunction is said to be the mover in the sense that it produces the awareness "I have been inspired to do it". It simply communicates an inspiration but does not actually inspire a person to do an act. Thus, the relation holding between inspiration and the inspired is distinct from the particular case relation, i.e., the relation subsisting between a nominative case and a verb.

An awareness is nothing but an act. That which produces an awareness is the nominative case. Thus, the relation in question is that between a nominative case and a verb. In other words, the relation holding between inspiration and the inspired is not a distinct one. This objection does not hold good, since, the distinction between a cause and a mark is well-known. In this case, we, the Mīmāṁsakas, have tried to prove that the relation subsisting between the institutor of a sacrifice and the act of sacrifice is an instance of that which holds between a nominative case and a verb and that the said relation is distinct from that existing between inspiration and the inspired. We have also established that they are distinct from each other. The Naiyāyikas say that they do not preclude the Mīmāṁsakas from assigning any name to the distinct relation in order to mark its distinction. Let the relation between inspiration and the inspired be a distinct one. How do you know that it is at first apprehended ? A person undertakes an obligatory duty when he knows that he has been ordered to do it. It is seen that he performs a sacrfice when he is induced by his teacher. When one listens to the Vedic injunction 'One should perform a sacrifice (yajeta)' he realises at first that he has been ordered to perform it. And afterwards he performs a sacrifice. Hence, the relation between inspiration and the inspired flashes at first in our mind but that between a nominative case and a verb is presented next to our consciousness. For this reason the meaning of the optative suffix is known at the outset. It is known as an inspiration. It is a mandate. It is denoted by a sentence in the optative mood.

Now, an objector raises an objection that as sentences in the imperative mood and in the optative one are used to convey invitation etc. as well so how does an injunction convey merely a mandate ? The Mīmāṁsakas give a reply to this objection that all the distinct senses conveyed by them are not essentially distinct from a mandate and that their minor differences are due to their association with adventitious elements. According to the varying degrees of importance of the performance of rites a verb in the imperative mood or in the subjunctive one conveys different shades of meaning, viz., inspiration, solicitation etc.

But every shade of meaning gives us an incentive to work. It has been stated by the grammarians that the optative and the imperative suffixes denote an incentive since none of their senses is dissociated from the above sense.

The meaning of the causative suffix is different from that of the optative suffix :

The incentive which is conveyed by the imperative suffix etc. is presented to our consciousness as distinct from that conveyed by the causative suffix. The causative suffix is prescribed when the activity of a causer is to be conveyed. The said activity moves the agent to do something. When an incentive is to be conveyed the imperative suffix is prescribed. Hence, the meaning of the imperative suffix is identical with that of the causative one. Thus, he who says 'Do this, do this' causes another to do this. This is the sum and substance of the objection raised by an objector. The above objections are not tenable since they produce different forms of awareness in our mind. The sentences 'Let him do. He should do' communicate a particular meaning to our mind. But the sentence 'He causes him to do' conveys a distinct meaning. The activity of a causer is denoted by the causative suffix. But the activity of a mark is denoted by the imperative suffix. The activity of a causative agent is in concern with an activity which has commenced. This is the exact meaning of the causative suffix. But in case of the imperative suffix the sense is contrary to that of the above one. In case of the causative suffix a person commences an act and another person causes him to do it. But in case of the optative suffix a man is prompted to do an act by means of an incentive and when he has moved to do it he experiences the performance of an act. Thus there is a great gulf of difference fixed between them. When we use a verb in the causative form a person causes one who is doing something to do it. But when we use a verb in the optative mood an incentive is given to a man who has capacity for discharging a duty. An immobile object which has no capacity for discharging a duty is not stirred. With regard to the lord of trees it is not enjoined 'You should perform a sacrifice.' Since an immobile object has no such capacity. A Brahmin who is inspired by an injunction to perform a sacrifice has not yet commenced to perform a sacrifice. With regard to the institutor of a sacrifice an injunction 'One should perform a sacrifice' is not enjoined. But it is only enjoined with regard to one who has not as yet commenced to perform a sacrifice. Thus, the meaning of the causative suffix is in all respects different from that of the optative suffix.

If verbal proof is the only source of a command how is a command communicated to us as the meaning of such and such word ?

Some thinkers raise an objection to the above hypotheses. They point out that according to the hypothesis the optative suffix may have a distinct meaning but no proof other than the suffix itself reveals it. Now the trouble is 'How can one know that the optative suffix conveys the said meaning?' Our reply to this question is as follows. Though the verbal command or incentive is known to us only by the source of verbal knowledge yet it is easily proved that the knowledge of the relation of denotation which holds between the optative suffix and the command is acquired. When we listen to the sentence in the optative mood viz. 'One should sacrifice' 'One should give', 'One should pour libation' etc. an injunction is presented to our consciousness. How do we admit that this injunction is communicated to us by the optative suffix ? An answer to this question is that from the usage we determine that the optative suffix denotes the above sense. When an experienced person listens to the sentence 'Go and read' it is noticed that he makes haste to act accordingly. We have also learnt from experience that the responsive activity of the listener is due to the grasp of the sense conveyed by a word. Suppose, a person perceives a delicious fruit such as a mango etc. and has definitely known by the joint method of agreement and difference that it is conducive to pleasure. Now if he longs for it, recollecting its conduciveness to pleasure then he gets by it and relishes. Such a desire is an attribute of the soul. It is introspected like the soul. The soul is an object of self-consciousness. We cannot exhibit it to another person. On that ground it cannot be held that no discussion about the soul is possible. The hypothesis that the soul is intuited by nobody is not tenable. A third person can introspect his soul by means of self-consciousness. The desire which leads to the enjoyment of a fruit is an attribute of the soul. It can only be introspected. It is not a truism that the said desire transcends our knowledge. When the said desire is introspectd by a person he moves for its enjoyment. When we see that another person moves for doing something we infer that the listener of the injunctive sentence has the knowledge of the incentive or the command conveyed by the injunctive sentence.

It is our experience that when we hear the optative suffix etc. we feel an inspiration but when we do not hear such a word we do not feel such inspiration. Thus we determine the meaning of the said suffix by the joint method of agreement and difference. This is our solution to the above problem. Everybody may know it from his own experience that whenever a listener hears the optative suffix he is aware of an incentive to work. But when a person hears the optative suffix for the first time he does not become aware of the incentive to work. The said inspiration can be made known to us by no other proof. The meaning of the verb 'kurvat' can only be communicated by the verb 'kuryāt'. But no other proof can reveal the meaning of the said suffix. In the face of such a conclusion those who hold that the optative suffix without any reference to the knowledge of the relation of denotation communicates an incentive to duty by its own intrinsic force lack the courage of conviction. Hence, we should disregard them and take no interest in their views.

If you hold that no word excepting the optative suffix conveys a command then how is it that word 'niyoga' conveys a command and the meaning of the word should fall outside the scope of all proofs other than the verbal one? Oh Sir ! a command cannot be communicated to us by the derivation of the word 'niyoga'. Its etymological derivation is this:—The root ,Yuj' has the indeclinable 'ni' as its prefix and 'ghañ' as its suffix. The above derivation is resorted to only to explain the form of the said word. As the command is conveyed by the verbs 'yajeta' etc. so it is communicated to us by no other words. Hence the Mīmāṁsakas hold that 'Dharma' is revealed by no proof other than the verbal testimony. The function of the optative suffix is command (niyoga). It is nothing but the obligatory duty itself. It is revealed only by the verbal testimony but by no other proofs. It is not reasonable to hold that the optative suffix conveys an operation which prompts one to perform an obligatory duty. It communicates an obligatory duty which is the meaning of a sentence. Some Mīmāṁsakas hold that the Vedas purport to convey only objects to be accomplished but not existent realities.

A niyoga prompts one to perform an obligatory duty by its verbal force.

The hypothesis in question like that of the Bhāṭṭas suggests that an injunction has got two parts to play. It plays the role of a mover and that of a rite to be performed. Oh long lived one ! you behave like a person who has become incoherent owing to the influence of sleep since you have held that a mover is not different from a rite to be performed. You boldly assert that a niyoga is a mover and is also a rite to be performed. How do other thinkers suggest double characters of a niyoga ? They cannot entertain this suggestion. When a niyoga expresses its verbal import it is a mover. When it is comprehended from the side of its meaning it is a rite to be performed since an injunction points to an act to be performed. When a person says 'I carry out the order of my preceptor I execute the royal mandate' why does he perform an act—the content of an injunction ? If this is the question then we give the following answer. An order has no concrete shape like a jar and hence it cannot be worked out. We are to work out the content of an order, i. e. the object to which the said order points. When a preceptor orders his pupil 'You should carry a kind of wooden water-pot' he thinks that he has obeyed the order of his preceptor by carrying a water-pot. When a king orders his officer 'Go to the fort' he thinks that he has executed the order of the king by going to the fort. Therefore, a niyoga (an order) is nothing but an act to be performed.

A fresh question arises in our mind. There is a verbal usage to this effect 'I do this by royal order'. This shows that the said order points to the act to be performed. The above objection does not hold good since some thinkers point out that in the above example the said order is to be carried out and the third case ending in 'rājājñayā' signifies that he has been directed by the king to do it.

A Niyoga Stirs Our Activity When Its Sense Is Grasped.

But other thinkers of the Prabhākara school hold that the verbal aspect of an injunctive sentence implies the obligatory duty to be discharged and that the sense of an injunctive sentence points to it (the said sentence) as a mover. The intrinsic nature of niyoga (an embodiment of command = an injunctive sentence) is the state of an act to be performed. But as they very niyoga induces the man ordered to discharge his duty so it is called a mover. A niyoga reveals itself as an obligatory duty in such a manner that it has not also abandoned its nature as a mover. It also acts as an inducer without forsaking the character of being an obligatory duty. The import of the verbal aspect of the suffix does not overburden the optative suffix as Kumārila does.

An Injunction Having no Reference to an end acts an Inducer:

The very niyoga which is conveyed to us by the very words constituting an injunction is "yajeta svarga-kāmaḥ". It is presented to our consciousness as characterized by two concomitants. The root 'yaji' expresses one of these two concomitants viz., the act to be performed. Another compound word 'svarga-kāmaḥ' suggests the second concomitant viz., the person who has right to perform a sacrifice and enjoys its fruit. If it is made out that a sacrifice is a means to heaven then it is established that a person who is desirous of heaven has right to perform a sacrifice. Thus, it amounts to this that only a person, desirous of heaven, performs a sacrifice and the path, already chalked out, is to be followed to establish syntactical relation between a sacrifice and one desirous of heaven. But we do not think that an injunctive sentence induces a person to perform a sacrifice because it exhibits the fruit of the enjoined sacrifice. If such a view is held then the independence of an injunction is at stake. An injunction is not so weak that it cannot induce a person to perform a sacrifice till it does not exhibit the fruit of the action enjoined. If we do not admit the truth of the hypothesis that an injunction independently induces a person to perform a rite then injunctions such as 'One should perform a sacrifice as long as one should live etc.' should not induce a person to activity. Very well, a question is now put to you viz., 'Are these injunctions 'One should sacrifice as long as he lives' etc. absolutely fruitless ?' The Mīmāṁsakas say 'We answer in the affirmative'. They admit that these are fruitless. The reason behind this admission is this. An injunctive sentence does not require a fruit for its completion. But an injunction 'One should perform a sacrifice' requires two essential elements for its completion. The two factors are at follows. 'What it to be performed' and 'Who will perform it' are required by an injunction. These two elements are related to sacrifice as an injunction requires them. If this is the case then the above injunction 'One should sacrifice so long as he lives' its import is that a living person is enjoined and the obligatory duty is to perform a sacrifice. Then the fruit of this injunction will be assumed after mature consideration. It is not mentioned in the scriptures. What is the function of an injunction in case of the injunction 'One who desires heaven should perform a sacrifice ?' Does it hint at the right to perform a sacrifice of a person who desires heaven ? No, in this case an injunction expresses only a command. If we do not subscribe to this view then the mention of the word 'svarga-kāma' loses all its significance. The injunction in question purports to convey that heaven is the goal and a sacrifice is a means to its attainment. The word 'svarga-kāmaḥ' has not been inserted in the injunction to serve the useful purpose of exhibiting the result of this sacrifice. Therefore an injunction does not function to stir movement for the attainment of goal. But the desire for the attainment of goal is the cause of movement. Some authoritative persons hold that a desire for the attainment of goal is the real motive which drives a person to action and an injunction lacks the driving force since an injunction completes its mission, vindicating the relation of means to its end. But it does not concern itself with the actual performance of a Vedic rite.

Hence, as the Śyena sacrifice is a sinful act so in that case it has been shown that a person who desires to kill his enemy by means of the Vedic mystic-rite has right to perform the Śyena sacrifice. The use of participle (Śatṛ suffix) in abhicaraṇa justifies the above interpretations of the Vedic passage "Syenena abhicaran yajeta." In this case, the Vedic passage does not induce him to undertake the Śyena sacrifice. The person does not make out from the passage that the killing of an enemy is his duty. But he does not simply know the means to the killing of his enemy. The scripture simply gives him instruction with regard to the more means of slaughter. The said injunction does not influence him to perform the Śyena sacrifice since the strong desire to kill his enemy drives him to perform the said sacrifice. Therefore, the word 'beneficial matter' has been put in the definition of Dharma (Duty) in order to exclude sinful deeds such as the Śyena sacrifice etc. from duty. The definition of Dharma is this: Any matter which serves a useful purpose and is laid down by Vedic injunction is Duty.

When the qualification of a person is determined by his desire of some fruit the scriptural passages induce him to adapt such procedure of performance as is a necessary means to a rite. The author of the Mīmāṁsā Sūtra has said to this effect that the scriptures enlighten merely a sacrifice. In case of the verb 'yajeta' a sacrifice, the meaning of the said verb is known to be a means to heaven. But when a sacrifice is known to be a means to heaven the manner of procedure is not known. Hence, at that time scriptural passages alone induce a person to adopt procedure of performance since there is no desire of some fruit which may act as a motive. Therefore, the killing of an animal which takes place in connection with the performance of a rite dedicated to Agni and Soma is not a sinful act. In that case the killing of an animal is one of manners of performance. The prohibition that one should not kill animals is a general rule. The general rule extends its jurisdiction over all matters without encroaching upon the sphere of a particular rule. As the killing of an animal is one of the subsidiary actions of the rite dedicated to Agni and Soma and is laid down by the Scripture so the general rule which prohibits animal-slaughter cannot declare it to be a sinful act.

An Injunction Induces a Person to an Action Without Referring to its Fruit

Now, a fresh problem arises in our mind. It is this that when a person betakes himself to perform the Śyena sacrifice he is induced by scriptural passages since instigation which is the function of an injunction constitutes its differentia from other proofs. It is not a truism that an injunction throws light only on the relation between a means and an end like the joint method of agreement and difference since an injunction is nowhere obstructed in its normal function of instigating person to actions expressly stated by the Vedas. Similarly, in case of the injunction "One should perform Śyena sacrifice" the movement of a person for the action is likewise instigated. (The main purport of this objection is to controvert the Mīmāṁsā thesis that Śyena sacrifice is a sinful act). The above problem is thus solved. The instigation of an injunction consists in producing the judgment "I (the listener) have engaged myself in such and such action." It is a true reflection on the characteristic feature of an injunction since an injunction uniformly behaves in all cases viz. in case of Śyena sacrifice, the means par excellence of killing an enemy or in case of the manner of performance or in case of a sacrifice dedicated to Agni and Soma. Though in the matter of external worldly activities the compelling force of an injunction remains intact yet if desire of some gain and similar other motives over and above aninjunction induce a person to an action then the power of instigation belonging to an injunction stands neutralized as it remains neutral in fore-sacrifices which are required as a means to the animal cake-offering.

Let us clarify the above Vedic example. The preparation of an animal cake is a subsidiary rite of the Agnisoma sacrifice. When a cake is prepared in connection with the main sacrifice fore-sacrifices are performed. When its subsidiary rite is to be observed i.e. an animal-cake is to be prepared or independent fore-sacrifices to be observed ? The conclusive answer on this point is that no fore-sacrifices are to be observed when an animal cake is prepared. Hence, it has been said that the injunctive function i.e. the power of instigation remains inactive

In the case of the neutrality of the power of instigation the prohibitive law ' None should kill an animal" exerts its influence. But if, inevery case, the power of instigation, belonging to an injunction, remains unimpaired then Śyena sacrifice is in no way distinct from Jyotiṣṭoma sacrifice since as a prohibitive passage exerts no influence upon the undertaking of Agnīṣoma sacrifice so it does not stand in the way of one's first move for Śyena sacrifice. It may be objected that in the case of Jyotiṣṭoma sacrifice the enjoyer of the fruit of the said sacrifice does not transgress the prohibitive passage by his enjoyment since heaven is not a forbidden fruit. But in the case of Śyena sacrifice 'as the killing of animals is prohibited so he who enjoys the fruit of Śyena sacrifice transgresses the prohibitive passage. Such an objection does not hold good since when a person acquires the right to perform Śyena sacrifice the enjoyer of its fruit does not transgress the prohibitive passage. In other words, the force of the injunction which governs Śyena sacrifice remains equally strong. So, the said prohibitive passage becomes powerless with regard to the said injunction. Therefore, the fruit of Śyena sacrifice is not affected by the prohibitive passage. The enjoyer of the fruit of Śyena sacrifice commits no sin.

Now, the old Mīmāṁsakas solve the above problem thus. They hold that an injunction does not instigate a faithful listener to produce a result with the mandate "Bring about this result"— they say that an injunction induces such a person to undertake a rite with the advice "perform this". They also state that when the person has right to perform an action the prohibitive passage "None should kill an animal" exerts its unimpaired influence upon him. In other words, Śyena sacrifice is a sinful act. The critics subject this view to a serious criticism. They say "Oh long-lived one : you have entered into our views. If an injunction does not induce a person to bring about the result of an action as he desires it then it should not also instigate him to adopt its means. An injunction reveals only a means to an ignorant person since an injunction establishes only what has not been previously established. It has been stated that the person knows that he should do an act but does not know the exact means. In the case of Śyena sacrifice one knows that he should perform Śyena sacrifice in order to kill his enemy. But if the means of killing his enemy is not prohibited by the scriptural passage then it is to be admitted that the person who performs Śyena sacrifice does not transgress scriptural prohibition. Kill your enemy with the magical practice of Śyena sacrifice. Thus we arrive at the conclusion that Śyena sacrifice is the means of killing an enemy. In other words, if one performs Śyena sacrifice he does not transgress scriptural prohibition. We need not unnecessarily prolong this discussion. In the case of a qualification based upon desire of some fruit an injunction does not require a result. But the rule is that a result is the means of acquiring the proper qualification to perform a rite.

A prohibitory injunction expresses turning off, having no reference to sin

Though the prohibition of animal-slaughter has been settled by the scriptures yet the person who is qualified to kill his enemy has been laid down by the same scriptures. Hence, we cannot assume that a prohibited act, viz., the killing of an enemy, gives rise to some sort of sin.

Even if we assume that the said act, viz., Śyena sacrifice produces evil consequences such as hell, etc., then the said Śyena sacrifice does not get the sanction of an injunction. But the injunction which prescribes Śyena sacrifice should not be so dishonoured.

An injunctive sentence always requires these two necessary factors, viz., (1) a rite and (2) a person qualified to perform the rite. When these two factors are supplied an injunction becomes complete in itself but requires no other additional factors for its completion.

In the case of Śyena sacrifice a person who is in a fit of rage and ready to kill his enemy is qualified to perform it. The result of this act is the killing of an enemy towards which the qualified person is directed.

The determination of the subject-matter of prohibition

We cannot till now make out what is the import of a prohibitive injunction. The verbal terminations denote activities directed towards an end. The basic roots to which they are attached denote acts to be accomplished. According to the Mīmāṁsā doctrine roots reveal something to be accomplished in a consecutive series. A negative particle denotes negation which is not accomplished in a consecutive series. Hence, it does not constitute the subject-matter of an injunction. The negative particle is not construed with verbal termination called liṅ. So, negation is never implied by an injunction since the said verbal termination is not attached to the negative particle. But it (the verbal termination) is attached to the root 'han'. The act of killing cannot be enjoined by an injunction since if it had been implied by an injunction then it would have been dharma (duty). Moreover, such an injunction will be meaningless. There is no necessity of an injunction which prescribes killing since men have natural propensity for doing it. The meaning of the root 'han' (to kill) as qualified by the meaning of the negative particle is not enjoined by an injunction since the meaning of the negative particle does not qualify the meaning of the root 'han' (to kill) in the manner in which an adjective qualifies its corresponding noun.

In the case of the injunctive sentence "He offers an oblation with sour milk" sour milk has logical ground to qualify the offering of an oblation since it is the instrumental case of such offering. But it is not reasonable to hold that the meaning of the negative particle modifies the act of killing because the very act of killing itself is negated, i.e. the very act ceases to exist.

A mere human effort does not constitute the subject-matter of an injunction since such an effort does not owe its origin to an injunction, i.e., it comes into existence independently of an injunction. An effort which is qualified by the meaning of the negative particle does not form the subject-matter of an injunction since the negative particle does not logically qualify it as it does not modify the act of killing.

As words 'non-Brahmin', etc., purport to convey emphatic denial, i.e., they convey the sense of some positive objects determined by negation so 'non-killing' implies emphatic denial but not bare denial. If this is so then it will be employed to denote a positive act other than the act of killing. Now, what will be the meaning of the sentence "He shall not kill" ? It will certainly imply that he shall do something else. If this meaning is admitted then what is the specific nature of the act ? We cannot make out any sense of 'shall not kill' if its meaning is carefully examined. If it is said that non-killing implies any act whatsoever other than the act of killing then such a view is not tenable. Any and every act is not incited by an injunction. Such acts owe their origin to natural propensities not inspired by injunctions. Hence, an injunction becomes unnecessary. If a man lives then he surely does something, viz., either he reads or walks or eats something.

Now, a new hypothesis may be put forward for our consideration. The negative particle has no connection with the subject-matter of an injunction. But it is connected with the authoritative voice of an injunction. It sets at naught the authoritative voice of an injunction. So, it is called as non-proof (Pramāṇābhāva). A person who is bent upon killing is dissuaded from it. It is implied by the negative particle that it is not one's duty to kill.

The above view is not tenable. According to the settled rule of syntax a verbal termination indicative of optative tense (liṅ) is construed with the root 'han'. It is the character of an injunction that it instigates a person to an act. The negative particle which denotes denial stands by it.

An injunction bends towards it. Though it bends towards it yet if the former is construed with the latter then the characteristic feature of the former, viz., the property of instigation will be destroyed. It is the invariable nature of the negative particle that it implies the negation of an object with which it is construed. If one intends to construe the negative particle with an injunction then the sentence implies that there is no such injunction as enjoins killing. If the upholder of this thesis contends that it is a desirable contingency then the inevitable result which follows in its wake is that killing is not conveyed by an injunction.

The upholders of the above hypothesis argue in the following manner. In the case of the injunction "He offers an oblation with sour milk" the offering of an oblation is established by some other passages. In other words, it is not an originative injunction. The Mīmāṁsakas of the Bhaṭṭa school hold that the injunction lays its emphasis upon sour milk since sour milk, being the instrumental case of the said offering of an oblation, qualifies it. So, following the line of the above argument, the Prabhākaras may take this stand that an injunction with regard to killing is meaningless since natural propensities prompt men to kill. The prohibitive injunction contains the negative particle in it. If the negative particle finds a place in a sentence but has no part to play then it should be meaningless. In order to solve this riddle why do not you admit that the injunction points at negation?

Now, the objectors raise an objection. They hold that the word 'Karma' denotes an action. In the above case the offering of an oblation of which sour milk is an instrumental case has been enjoined. Therefore, considering it from the side of its result the offering of an oblation is enjoined by an injunction. But it is not proved by any proof. But in the case of the prohibive injunction that he shall not kill, the negative particle cannot be logically construed with any word as the word "sour milk" is construed with the offering of an oblation since the nature of the negative particle is to negate. Such a criticism does not hold good. The negative particle assumes the dignity of an adjective (a qualifier) because it dissuades one from the act of killing. When we hear the root 'han' as modified by the negative particle the discussion from the act of killing is conveyed to us.

Sour milk is the instrumental case of the offering of an oblation in the above case. It is an accomplised thing. Though it qualifies the offering of an oblation and becomes thus related to it yet the offering of an oblation does not give up its character of being an action. Similarly, though the meaning of the root 'han' is known as related to negation, the meaning of the negative particle yet the qualified meaning is presented to our consciousness as arranged in the relation of being prior and posterior. When we hear the word 'a-Brāhmaṇa' an accomplished thing other than a Brāhmaṇa is conveyed to us. But when we hear the sentence "He shall not kill" it does not imply an accomplished thing. Therefore the injunctive sentence "He shall not kill" enjoins an action, viz., dissuasion from killing.

Or, negation will be related to the verbal termination indicative of liṅ (optative mood). Pure optative verbal termination denotes an instigator. But if the negative particle is attached to it then it, being thus qualified, denotes dissuading something. This is the primary meaning of a word. Who is to be brought to book for this finding ?

Optative verbal termination is not attached to the negative particle because the negative particle is not a root. Verbal terminations in all tenses and moods are attached only to roots but not to other words. In the fitness of things the meaning of the verbal termination is construed with negation, the meaning of the negative particle. As they are related so the boiled down meaning does not imply that there is no such injunction as enjoins killing. In the case of prohibitive injunction "He shall not kill" it does not induce a listener to an action. But it does not mean that he is dissuaded from all action. He is only not induced to the act of killing. If one does not subscribe to this view then the listener will be indifferent to all sorts of actions. We shall no more criticise our rival hypothesis. Thus in the case of prohibitive injunction such an injunction has to essential factor, viz. (1) the action which is enjoined is arranged in relation of being prior and posterior and (2) negation is related to an injunction. Thus its connection with the two anubandhas is established.

Thus when the implication of an injunction is fully discussed a person shall assume the result of a rite prescribed by the Vedas according to his imaginative power. Therefore, a rite enjoined by the Vedas should depend upon its result.

Why shall a person dissuade from an evil deed without the threat of sin ? He may not of his own accord dissuade from it. So, prohibitive injunction lays down his dissuasion.

If a person is excessively fond of killing animals then he does not turn away from it though he knows that animal slaughter is productive of great evil. If this be the case then why will a prohibitive injunction prescribing dissuation be invalid ?

An injunction may yield a result or not. A person may be inclined for killing or not. An injunction shall remain steady in its own function. Its function cannot be interfered with.

It has been repeatedly said that an injunction operates to produce the knowledge of instigation. That is when one listens to an injunction he feels that he should do the act prescribed by the injunction. Therefore, an injuncton is never unsuccessful in its mission.

If an injunction does not depend upon the result of an action then why does a person assume the result of actions such as Viśvajit sacrifice etc. of which no result has been directly expressed by the Vedas ? Moreover, if there is no mention of a fact or which is essentially required for a sacrifice, viz., a person who is qualified to perform a sacrifice then a person, qualified to perform a sacrifice, is assumed, otherwise an injunction ceases to be an injunction. As the same rule uniformly applies to all sacrifices so it is assumed that a person who desires heaven is qualified to perform a sacrifice. This assumption is part and parcel of an injunction. Do not think that the said assumption is of human origin. The Vedic scholars hold that it is a portion of the Vedic sentence. In fine, they say that the assumption of qualification is that of a relevant matter which is useful to a sacrifice. It is not the assumption of a result. The assumption of a qualification is not identical with that of a result. An injunctive sentence conveys the mandate of a sacrifice together with the assumption of two useful matters bound up with a sacrifice, viz. the qualification of a sacrificer and the result of a sacrifice.

A mandate is called the meaning of a sentence owing to its importance. Though other matters, such as a sacrifice etc., are revealed by it yet they occupy a subordinate position since they become an object of our experience as the sphere of the working of a mandate. But the mandate itself occupies the main position in a sentence since it is presented to our consciousness as strengthened by various rites and their causal factors having tangible result and being implied by its intrinsic power. If it is held that the main thing is that which is accomplished then we shall say that a mandate is that which is accomplished. If one holds that an end occupies the most important place then this hypothesis is not disproved. But it is also to be noted that an end is to be realised and its realisation depends upon a mandate. Hence, a mandate occupies the principal position. But a sacrificer who is enjoined to perfom a rite occupies a subordinate place. (As a mandate presupposes a person who is ordered so such a person finds a place in the sentence.) A mandate constitutes the meaning of injunctive sentence since it occupies the principal position in a sentence.

The fourfold division of a mandate

Injunctions admit of four kinds since this division is based upon the analysis of our corresponding experience into the four different types. Of these four kinds let us cite example of the originative injunction. The illustration is that he shall perform Agnihotra sacrifice. It conveys nothing but the origination of Agnihotra sacrifice itself.

The illustration of the injunction of connection of the main rite with its accessory ones runs thus. The injunction:—"He shall sacrifice with sour milk" implies the connexion of the accessories such as sour milk etc., with the main rite which has been conveyed by the originative injunction "He shall sacrifice with milk".

The example of the injunction of qualification is that he who desires heaven shall perform Agnihotra sacrifice. When the rite is revealed by it the person who is qualified to do the rite is known in and through the said rite.

This is only to be stated about the injunction of the due order of performance that all things useful in a sacrifice are known only when a rite is performed in due order up to its end. It is an offshoot of the injunction of qualification. The example of the injunction of qualification is its illustration. The above-mentioned injunction "He who desires heaven shall perform Agnihotra sacrifice" illustrates it also.

In some cases single injunctive sentence illustrates four different kinds of injunction. In those cases each kind of injunction does not require a distinct sentence for its illustration. The illustration is as follows :—In Agniṣṭut sacrifice a group of hymns, known as Vāravantīya and sung in honour of Agni, is to be inserted into the Ṛk verses called Revatī. The said sacrifice is to be completed by the subsidiary rite, being commenced with the recitation of the above verses. A person who desires animals shall perform this sacrifice. [A person who desires animals is qualified to perform the above sacrifice.] In the above instance, the injunction of origination, that of connexion of the subsidiary rite with the main one, that of qualification, and that of performance in due order have been illustrated. The different kinds of injunctions are guessed by us from the diversity in the nature of actions themselves. The very injunction leads one to infer the adequate means for the completion of the sacrifice denoted by the basic root. For this reason the injunction in question is called the determinant of the second injunction. Let us illustrate it. The injunction of appointing a preceptor is implied by that of the study of Gāyatrī mantra by a Brahmin lad to be invested with sacred thread.

The different forms of injunction

In some cases, if a thing is got in order to realise another object then an injunction does not imply another similar thing which is a helpful means to an action, laid down by the Vedas. Let us illustrate our point. A young she-calf one year old is taken to a sacrificial place for sale and is purchased and got. The dust clinging to the hoof of such a calf is required in a certain sacrificial rite. Though the above calf has come there for some other purpose but not for the said purpose yet another calf should not be brought there for taking dust. The injunction gives such a decision in this matter. In a context an injunction which brings together all matters to be collected is called Grāhaka vidhi.

In a particular context though an injunction refers to many matters yet it does not include a particular rite viz., twelve upasads (12 libations in an ektype sacrifice of the Archetype Jyoti toma). Noticing their excellence they are included in this context from another context. The injunction of connection of the accessory rites with the main one includes within itself an injunction. It is called an injunction within a viniyoga.

The Different Forms of Injunction

In some cases even in spite of the absence of the evidence of an applicatory injunction settling connection between a subsidiary act and its principal injunction which indicates the connection of the single number of an animal as subsidiary with the seizing of an animal as its principal one is called upadāyaka. Let us take an illustration: One should sacrifice with an animal (paśunā yajeta). The singular number of the third case-ending attached to paśu does not enjoin that the number of the said animal should be one. It simply enjoins that an animal, the meaning of the basic stem (paśu), should only be taken into consideration since the number one of the animal has been already enjoined. The number one has not been enjoined here because the said number has not been mentioned in the injunctive sentence. An animal should be seized but numberless animals should not be seized. There is no reason to discard a number which has been mentioned before. In other words, the number one of the animal should not be given up. Therefore, the import of the entire argument is that the number one belonging to the animal is to be taken as subsidiary to the principal act, viz., the seizing of an animal.

An injunction which prescribes an offering to Sūrya is ectypal. As it draws all manners of performance belonging to archetypal rite towards its own rite so it is called 'codaka,' i.e., the rule of transfer.

The conclusion that an injunction is the meaning of a sentence

In fine, manifold efficacies of the only Lord Injunction, the meaning of the optative mood, have been shown since his body is endowed with the power of instigation. We shall no more discuss the subject-matter of the Mīmāṁsā literature, the theatre of intellectual feats of the great leaders of thought. An injunction of the above description constitutes the meaning of a sentence.

All the characteristic features of an injunction have been discussed in the work of Jaimini - a work consisting of twelve chapters. All the details about an injunction have not been discussed by us, apprehending the danger of making this treatise cumbrous.

Only the panoramic view of the problem of injunction has been presented in its due order. The great thinkers differ from one another in the above-mentioned meaning of a sentence.

The establishment of the hypothesis that the knowledge of an end is the motive of one's action

It has been stated that a sentence conveys an injunction which is presented to our consciousness by him, etc, and the injunction itself is an act to be accomplished and an embodiment of instigation. Though it may be so yet we do not grasp it to be distinct from human activities which are being experienced by us.

An act is apprehended by us to be such as leads us on to an end because it is that which is to be accomplished and which stirs our movement. But if an injunction is other than an act then it cannot partake of the above two characters of an act.

The Mīmāṁsakas have already shown that the relation which subsists between an act and an agent is distinct from that holding between the director and the directed. An injunction constitutes the second relation. The said contention of the Mīmāṁsakas does not stand to reasons.

The verbs 'should do' etc. purport to convey no instigation which is other than an act itself.

The Mīmāṁsakas raise an objection to this effect. Do the verbs, 'does' and 'should do' etc., convey the same sense ? Oh long-lived one ! your knowledge of etymology is novel. I see. We do not hold that the senses, conveyed by these two verbs, are not different from each other. The verb 'does' communicates to us an act which has commenced and persists in the present time. But though it conveys an instigation yet it does neither cause one to move for it nor indicate that one should do it.

If it is communicated to us as a director then why does not it cause us to do it ? It should have caused us to do it. As it contains an element of instigation in it so it acts as an instigator. It is a truism that the said act is presented to our consciousness as an instigator. But in reality it does not act as an instigator. It is only a verbal practice to say "I obey the order of the king". The sentence does not convey the instigation "I should obey the order of a king" (i.e., I am under the obligation of obeying the order of a king). The sentence "I obey the order of a king" implies that to obey the order of a king is an act which is accomplished by me.

An order is that which is known to be carried out by others. He who obeys an order does not think that it should be carried out. But a ruler who makes an order thinks that it should be carried out. If it is not admitted then one is to follow the order of any and every person. Though a sentence conveys instigation yet intelligent persons do not undertake an action, hearing sentences, uttered by young boys, or insane persons etc.

No body cares to obey the order of a king from whom nobody apprehends danger if it is disobeyed and from whom no body expects the fulfilment of their desire if it is obeyed. If one listens to a sentence containing a verb in the present tense and expects some result form it then he acts in accordance with it though the verb has no verbal termination indicative of the optative mood. The sentence "One recovers from taking myrobalan" proves the thesis.

There is no distinction between the sentences "One who desires recovery should take myrobalan" and "One recovers from taking myrobalan" as to their prompting force.

In fine, the people arrive at the logical conclusion by the joint method of agreement and difference that an end induces a person to an action but not an injunction.

In the above matter such a conclusion may be entertained. In ordinary worldly transactions a person may undertake an action out of desire for fruit or in accordance with the intention of a director. In these cases an end is the remote or indirect cause of movement. The origin of the Vedas cannot be traced to a human being—a speaker. So, when a person listens to the sentences of the Vedas he undertakes an action, being inspired by the knowledge of instigation. But if a person listens to the sentences of a mad man containing verbs in the optative tense, he does not feel that he is inspired by them to do something. Even if he feels inspiration and undertakes an action, his action does not yield the promised result. So, the above sentences are disregarded as incoherent talks. But in the case of the Vedas as a person hears the injunctive sentence "One should sacrifice" so he feels inspired to undertake the enjoined act. There is no reason to set his inspiration at naught. Hence, he engages himself in undertaking the enjoined act. The Vedas are not the source of invalid knowledge because the author of the Vedas is not a director. It has been stated before that as the truth of the Vedas is self-evident, so they discharge all the functions of true knowledge. Some thinkers hold that the Vedas owe their origin to an author. A person who has desire for fruit undertakes an act in accordance with the intention of the said author. Though this hypothesis suggests a possible answer to that of the Mīmāṁsakas yet we do not insist upon it since if we entertain the said hypothesis then we alter our course of discussion. But we express the following point of view as our own. As the feeling of inspiration establishes one's movement for an action so the compound word 'Svargakāmaḥ' should be interpreted in a different sense, following the footsteps of Badari. (It has been suggested that desire for fruit does not stir one's movement). Let the compound word simply qualify a person when a person as qualified for a particular rite is selected.

If the above view is accepted, we take no exception to it. But we object to the supposition that supreme bliss is an end since it is gratuitous. Now, one may argue that if supreme bliss is not an end then the compound word 'Svargakāmaḥ' cannot be an adjective of a sacrificer. The import of this argument is this that the result of an action is the end to be realised. If we arrive at the conclusion that the result of an action is our goal then we cannot but hold that an end prompts us to action owing to its intrinsic power. This hypothesis gets the support of the popular opinion. Moreover, it knows no exception. So there is no reason why we should discard it and subscribe to the conjecture that the feeling of inspiration prompts us to an action.

If you admit that an order points to a result then the result itself occupies the principal position in a sentence. As the order itself becomes subordinate to it (a result) so the conclusion that an order is the primary import of an injunctive sentence is contradicted.

Now, the Mīmāṁsakas contend thus:- The meaning of an injunction like the meaning of a root, is not a means to the result. If it had been a means then it would have been a subsidiary. But as a result is implied by the meaning of an injunction so it is held that an injunction is meant for a result. The intrinsic character of an injunction is to be a prompter. If you subscribe to this hypothesis then let the meaning of the root 'yaj' be the object to be accomplished. In that case why do you say that an order, the meaning of an injunctive sentence, is an object to be accomplished ? Now, the Mīmāṁsakas may contend on the basis of the current verbal practice that an order is completed when a sacrifice, the meaning of the root 'yaj' is performed. There runs a verbal usage "I am completing the order of my master."

If this is their contention then our counter-argument runs thus :- If the meaning of a root completes both an order, the meaning of an injunctive sentence, and a result then the sentence in question is open to the charge of syntactic disunity. (If a sentence refers to two independent substantives then the splitting up of a sentence into two is inevitable).

Moreover, owing to the acceptance of the hypothesis that the meanings of all constituent words of a sentence are interrelated an order is known as connected with its subject-matter. In the present context an order of a sacrifice is made. So a sacrifice is apprehended as the raison d' etre of an order.

Now, if we assume that an order is carried out by a sacrifice, the meaning of the basic root then we admit that an order becomes a means to an end, viz. the result. Thus, as it is an accessory matter serving the purpose of another so it is not the principal import of a sentence. This point has been discussed before.

Now, it may be suggested that a sacrifice completes two things viz., an order and a result. An objection arises in our mind viz. "Does it simultaneously or successively complete them ?" It is not capable of completing them simultaneously. If it had such capacity then they would have been identical.

One may not see an order since it is conveyed only by a verbal statement. But why will not one see that it is completed along with the ultimate result viz., heaven, animal etc ? Let the second alternative suggestion of successiveness be admitted. Is an order at first completed and does the completion of the said result follow it ? Or, does the completion of the result precede and is a result completed afterwards? If it is held that an order is completed at the out-set then why should a man move for accessory matters which are means to a sacrifice ?

Just as by performing fire-sacrifices a mandate concerning Darśa and Paurṇamāsa sacrifices is completed but the enjoined matter which remains unfinished is completed in accordance with the direction of the Śāstras as a sacrificer may also move for the completion of the accessory matters of a sacrifice in conformity with the direction of the Śāstras even after the execution of an order.

The Mīmāṁsakas may contend that it is a desirable contingency. If this is their contention then we say in reply "O Mīmāṁsakas ! as the activities of a human being are directed towards the attainment of the highly desired end owing to his natural appetites so they do not come within the province of injunction. Hence, you contradict your own statement when you hold that sacrifices like Śyena sacrifice etc are sinful acts.

If the Mīmāṁsakas contend that the result is at first established and the order which concerns it is completed then the inadmissible logical consequence that the result, being established before the completion of the said order, should be visible becomes inevitable When a sacrifice has been duly performed the promised fruit viz., a son, animals etc., is not tangibly obtained. If it is held that though the result remains inevitable yet it is established then such a conclusion is absolutely mysterious.

Some Mīmāṁsakas contend that a sacrifice, the meaning of the root, completes an order through the operation of the unimportant intermediate process viz., the establishment of heaven etc. This contention also stands refuted. The reason is as follows.

As the minor operation of fire, viz., the act of blazing, at first, takes place before its main operation in the shape of the act of cooking so the minor operation, viz., the establishment of heaven, should be at first experienced. But this logical consequence is inadmissible. Now the Mīmāṁsakas contend thus : He who desires heaven intends to enjoy celestial bliss by means of a sacrifice. So it is learnt from the texts that an order, the meaning of verbal termination indicating optative mood should be at first executed. Now, if the said order is completely carried out then we are given to understand by verbal authority that the result, viz., heaven, has also been produced. The establishment of heavenly bliss will be certified by experience in the future: Such a contention does not stand to reasons. We do not experience, heaven is twice established by means of the two distinct sources of knowledge. The first proof of heaven is furnished by verbal knowledge and the second one is offered by our experience. We fail to make out what is the genesis of the hypothesis that heaven will be established in the future by means of experience.

The act of sacrifice is short-lived. It does not endure in the future. You (the particular sect of Mīmāṁsakas) do not admit the existence of transcendental result in the shape of some power etc. arising from a sacrifice.

You hold that the words 'apūrva' and 'dharma' denote an order by means of their secondary meaning. But an order does not endure long like power or like an impression belonging to the soul. Is an order an embodiment of instigation ? Or, is it a result itself ? What do you say ? Let an order be either of them. But none of them lasts long. The above hypothesis leads to an inadmissible logical conclusion. If an impression that obedience to such an order brings up the result takes hold of the mind then an order implies a result. But an order is never empty. It is directed towards an object which is to be accomplished. It is characterised by the object. It is obeyed because it has a concrete shape. An act is not accomplished if the necessary conditions do not assemble and the requisite intermediary processes do not make their contribution. Hence, an act implies them all. Similarly, an order cannot be executed if the person who is duly qualified to perform the act is not mentioned. Hence, an order implies such a person. When an order is qualified by the implied person it points to the result of an act. Hence, the result of an act is assumed. But an injunction does not require a result. But the above statement does not stand to reasons.

If a thing does not come into being without being conditioned by another thing then the latter should be implied by the former. But though an injunction implies a person duly qualified to perform an act yet it cannot be held to imply the result of an act.

As soon as a person touches an impure caṇḍāla he becomes instantaneously impure. Similarly, a person, desirous of heaven qualifies himself to perform an act by his mere desire for heaven. Therefore, the assumption of such a person is not arrived at by implication. Hence, how can the implication of such a person be that of a result ?

Now, the Mīmāṁsakas may contend that a person who is desirous of heaven is known only by an inference to be duly qualified to perform a sacrifice. He is not a qualified person if he cannot manage to attain heavenly bliss by dint of his own act. The solution of the problem as offered by the Mīmāṁsakas is not satisfactory.

It depends upon the will of a person to do an act. Scriptural passages themselves cannot do an act. A person who desires heaven is only directed to perform a sacrifice just as a living person is only directed but not a dead one. The drift of this argument is this that the assumption of a duly qualified person is mechanical but not inferential.

Our experience says that an object, longed for, is our goal. Let us take an example to illustrate our point. A person who desires cure shall take myrobalan. In this case the taking of myrobalan is our end. Similarly, in the ease of a Vedic rite enjoined by the passage "A person who desires heaven shall sacrifice" heaven is our goal, O gentle one; how have you found out that the same law applies to secular matters to determine the goal ? The goal is discovered when we either reflect on the primary meaning of a word denoting the qualified person or discuss the intrinsic character of an injunction.

The meaning of a word is such. Or this person desires it to be so. Why do you think in this way ? It does not come within the province of an injunction. O long-lived one ! If you think that it follows from the intrinsic nature of an injunction then why do you heap censure on Kumārila Bhaṭṭa, because he holds that a permanent obligatory rite yields a result ? No adjective has been given to the agent of an optional rite or to that of an unconditionally obligatory rite in order to distinguish him. All persons who may be living or desirous of heaven are equally qualified to perform optional or such obligatory rites. The drift of his argument is this that as it goes without saying that the agent of an optional rite is living, so it goes without saying that one who desires heaven is the agent. The same rule applies to a categorically obligatory rite.

The influence of an injunction upon an insect is the same. An injunction does not instigate an intelligent person to perform an act, being threatened with the fear of being fruitless.

Now, the Mīmāṁsakas raise an objection to the above suggestion that a standing obligatory rite bears a fruit. In the case of an optional rite it has been directly stated that the goal of this act is heaven but in the case of a standing obligatory rite no such goal has been directly mentioned. On the strength of which authority has an end of such an obligatory rite been assumed ? The Naiyāyikas give a reply to this objection. They hold that it is the very injunction which leads us to such an assumption. The mention of heaven is of no use to us if an injunction does not require it. An injunction attracts an unheard fruit in the shape of heaven and requires it as its essential element just as it appropriates the fruit mentioned in the passage. "He has become possessed of streams of clarified butter". Hence an injunction is the sole authority in the matter whether an action bears a fruit or not. We shall disregard the suggested authority whether the fruit is heard or not. If a standing obligatory rite bears no fruit then we shall hold that both optional and permanent rites alike shall bear no fruit.

In the light of discussions concerning an injunction it will not be inconsistent to hold that if a person performs any prohibited action then he gets punishment in the shape of sufferings in hell.

A person with his conscience clouded by unbearably oppressing hatred considers the slaying of a Brahmin to be his duty since he thinks that the said act is conducive to pleasure. A person has also believed that alcoholic drinks are also conducive to pleasure since he is a confirmed votary of Epicurus. If an injunction does not inform that the above acts are conducive to suffering but not to pleasure then how can it turn a person away from the sinful acts ? Hence, he should admit that a permanent obligatory rite yields a result viz., the destruction of accumulated sins like the removal of sin of omission and that a prohibited action leads to sufferings in hell. If we do not admit it then we fail to establish what is duty and what is contrary to duty.

Moreover, if the performance of prohibited acts does not generate sin then the slaying of a Brahmin is not a sinful act-not to speak of Śyena sacrifice. Thus the term 'artha' in the definition of dharma becomes meaningless.

If the Mīmāṁsakas hold that a person moves for the means owing to his natural propensities but observes the procedure of performance, being inspired by the scriptural passages then their view is not sound.

Because means, unaided by the manners of procedure, cannot produce the intended result viz., heaven. The learned scholars are of an opinion that a means, aided by the procedure of performance, is really a means par excellence.

The division of the conditions of a sacrifice into two different heads viz., (1) Karaṇa (means) and (2) Itikartavyatā (manners of performance) is a very minor one. But if a sacrifice is performed with the completion of all its subsidiary actions then and then only it leads to the desired goal. But if a single subsidiary action is omitted then the sacrifice does not produce its result. Therefore, if we are to perform an optional rite then we must be particularly mindful of the performance of all subsidiary rites without an exception. This is the teaching of the Vedas. Hence, one should move for the manners of performance out of mere desire for the attainment of goal as he does for the means.

If in both cases pure desire of result is the sine qua-non of his movement then the killing of an animal in connection with the sacrifice dedicated to Agni and Soma should be considered as a sinful act just like the Śyena sacrifice.

Moreover, it has been stated by the Mīmāṁsakas that in the case of an optional rite the operation of an injunction amounts to the relation of a means to an end holding between a sacrifice and its result. The above statement is not correct. The reason is as follows. The relation subsisting between an injunction and a sacrifice is that of the inducer and the induced. A sacrifice is presented to our consciousness as a subject matter of an injunction. But the desired result is not known to us as a means to heaven. Again, if it is held that the only operation of an injunction is to reveal causal relation then the view virtually leads to the conclusion that an injunction enjoins that this is the means and that this is the end. In that case an injunction should give up its own intrinsic character of inducing one to movement one who has not as yet moved for an action.

There is a well-known saying that an injunction has four different modes. But its basic character of being an instigator underlies all of them.

An injunction at first communicates its incentive to an enjoined rite and then informs that the above act is an obligatory duty. A person who is induced to perform this rite scrutinizes his duty minutely.

On listening to the verbal termination indicative of the optative mood the listener feels inspiration and then apprehends that a sacrifice is a means and heaven is an end and the relation holding between them is that of a means to an end. Now, the Mīmāṁsakas take an exception to the above suggestion and point out some defects in it. In the case of an optional rite a person, instigated by an injunction, proceeds to perform a rite. This is the sum and substance of the said suggestion. But if some body does not undertake an action then he shall commit the sin of omission since he has transgressed an injunction. Such an objection does not hold good. A person who desires heaven is qualified to perform a rite. But one who has no such desire has not requisite qualification to do it. Let us take an example to illustrate our point in question. A Vaiśya should recite a group of verses. But if a Kṣatriya does not recite those verses, he does not commit the sin of omission. But the person who desires heaven undertakes to perform a rite, being induced by an injunction. If one admits that movement for a means owes its origin to desire then his activities for manners of procedure of performance will be held to be due to desire also since he has moved for it, being inclined to render assistance to the said sacrifice. Thus, an injunction should be defunct in all matters. It is needless to discuss this question any further.

Moreover, how do you hold that an injunction is the import of a sentence since a meaning is ascertained from usage ?

The Mīmāṁsakas have said the following: One has direct experience that his voluntary activities spring from his desires. So it is natural for him to infer that such activities of another person also spring from his desires. Such an inference is not justifiable. One cannot be conscious of his own inspiration since there is nothing to reveal it. An instigation is not self-luminous like its own consciousness. If the Mīmāṁsakas contend that the awareness of instigation is self-luminous then we ask them 'what is its cause ?' Its cause is to be found out by scrutiny. If the Mīmāṁsakas hold that the optative mood communicates it then we point out that this view is not tenable. When a listener hears an injunctive sentence how has he learnt that the optative mood denotes instigation ? As one is aware of the fact that his own activities are preceded by the awareness of instigation so it is an inference that the activities of another person are preceded by the awareness of instigation. Thus we shall understand that verbal terminations, indicative of optative mood, communicate instigation. But one should very carefully think over the question 'How is he aware of instigation when he learns the meaning of a word or of a sentence ?' If the Mīmāṁsakas hold that he knows it from another source of valid knowledge then we say 'O Mīmāṁsakas ! get up and discuss no more since your pet hypothesis that instigation is communicated only by the verbal source has been disproved.'

We have previous experience that a wood-apple and such other fruits are conducive to pleasure. Hence, whenever we see them we move for eating them. It has also been settled that desire of pleasure is the motive of our activity. There is no other motive which prompts us to activity. Some thinkers have said to this effect that worldly transactions are due to desire which is based upon recollection since everybody is aware of his own desire for fruits.

Some thinkers other than the Naiyāyikas assume that a sentence communicates instigations. We, the Naiyāyikas, take no exception to it. But it is also true beyond the shadow of a doubt that desire for a fruit is the real motive in such cases.

If the fruit of an action induces a person to take upon himself an undertaking then the objections, raised before, will be met.

If the earlier statement is true then how can one say "I am pouring libation at the instance of my preceptor ?" Let us set aside such a popular remark. In the above case the preceptor does not induce him to action. But the desire of gaining good or that of avoiding an evil is the prime condition of his movement. Hence, it is reasonable to hold that the fruit of an action is the real motive. Our experience bears witness to the truth of this hypothesis.

Moreover, some other thinkers have suggested that the intention of a director is the prompter since nobody undertakes an action at the instance of a person who has not won the former's heart by his personal charms. But if the fellow is captivated by his personal charms then he reads the intention of his idol from the latter's browbeat, etc., but not from his words and takes up an action.

The hypothesis is not sound. The said person undertakes an action, inferring the intention of his director since he believes that if he acts up to his director's intention then he will be able to look after his own interest. He does not undertake an action with the consideration. "Let my director be pleased". But if the pleasure of his director is the source of his own pleasure then he may desire the pleasure of his director as the source of his own pleasure. He does never undertake an action only with a view to bringing about the pleasure of his director. Lord Buddha himself who was bent upon doing good to all embraced altruism as his own interest since to render service to others was his self-interest. Hence one's own pleaure is the motive. If the Mīmāṁsakas hold that the intention of the director induces one to an action then they should admit that there is no director in the Vedas since they say that the Vedas have not been composed by an author. Therefore, there is no chance of knowing the intention of a director. As there is no possibility of guessing the intention of a director so nobody should move for the Vedic rites. Hence, the fruit of an action is the only motive.

The Mīmāṁsakas have raised a few objections against the said hypothesis. They have put forward a dilemma to invalidate it. Is the fruit an accomplished fact or not? They believe that this riddle cannot be solved. So, the hypothesis is not logically tenable. The above argument is not fair since the fruit of an action prompts us to action since it is an object of our desire. If the unaccomplished fruit of an action is our motive then why is not an unreal object our motive? The Naiyāyikas say by way of reply that an object which is absolutely unreal like the sky-flower cannot be our motive.

A man desires pleasure or cessation from pain but nobody longs for a purely imaginary object like the sky-flower.

Those who hold that love is the motive have in their mind the view that the object, longed for, has the prompting force since love is a form of desire.

Some thinkers hold that an object which is conducive to our welfare instigates us to action. This hypothesis is not fair. The reason behind our criticism is this that we do not move for an object which we do not long for though it is conducive to our welfare.

Now, the Mīmāṁsakas contend that a person who is in need of something does not move for an indefinite object. But he moves for an object which he definitely knows to be conducive to welfare. Hence, the determination that this means will surely lead to goal is the real motive. This is true. But if the knowledge of the sure means and the desire of fruit assemble then the latter should be called motif. Because movement for an object springs from desire. Conation is another name for inner activity resulting in bodily movement. The followers of Kaṇāda hold that conation is the effect of desire. Conduciveness to welfare determines the acceptability or the otherwiseness of an object but does not stir movement. It has been also suggested that conduciveness to welfare which is intimated by efficient force is the motive. The distinct mention of this motive is not logically tenable. Efficient force consists of three elements. When we apprehend its distinct feature we determine that the relation of means to its end holds between a sacrifice and heaven, the two elements of bhāvanā (efficient force). It should not be held that the activity as characterized by these two elements is conducive to welfare. As bhāvanā has not as yet come into being so its property, viz., conduciveness to welfare, cannot come into existence. If a cow is not born then the universal of cowness does not belong to its limbs, viz., dewlap, etc. If the three elements are not fulfilled then the activity of a person, called bhāvanā, does not come into being.

Some hold that a word, indicative of optative mood the sense conveyed by it, constitutes the motive. This hypothesis has been already refuted.

An injunction by its intrinsic character does not stir our movement. If one admits that an injunction prompts us to activity when the causal relation between a sacrifice and heaven has been established then the end turns out to be an instigator in spite of the absence of his verbal admission.

Some hold that an injunction is the real instigator since it reveals the end. The view is not tenable. If this is the view then an injunction is no better than perception, etc.. and the unique character of an injunction is done away with.

He should be informed that if an injunction conveys a fruitless act then it loses all prestige. Even an ignorant person does not undertake a fruitless act.

Does any intelligent man set to a fruitless work ? Now, the Mīmāṁsakas contend that there are some persons who do not undertake an act even though they are informed of its result. The Naiyāyikas say in reply (to this contention) that it matters little if they do not undertake such a work. The reason is this that an injunction does not cause one to do an act. But we have stated before that an injunction does not inform. The Mīmāṁsakas further contend that it may inform of an act though it does not reveal its result. Is there any obstacle to such information? The Naiyāyikas review this contention and point out that such an injunction does not serve the purpose of an indicator to all. If it goes to inform an intelligent person then he is not well-informed in the absence of the declaration of a result. There is no need of talking much about it.

So, the result of an action—the object of desire, is the real motive, the author of Nyāya-sūtra has thus composed his sūtra. 'yamartham adhikṛtya', etc.

The concluding portion of this topic

Hence, neither an injunction nor liṅ—the verbal termination indicative of the optative mood, is the cause of the volition of a person. Even bhāvanā, the denotation of liṅ—the verbal termination indicative of the optative mood is not capable of producing volition. Conduciveness to welfare which belongs to a rite prescribed by the Vedic injunction cannot bring about such volition. It is not also logical to hold that fondness is the cause of volition. So, the author of Nyāyasūtra, who has clear thinking, has stated that an end which is the object of desire is the cause of volition.

The determination of the meaning of a sentence.

The opponents of the Nyāya school say, "Refuting the rival hypothesis you have established that an end is the final cause of volition. Now, as you are intolerant of other's views so you yourself say what is the meaning of a sentence. Gautama holds that a motive is that for which a person moves. Thus he has shown that an end has prompting force. An intelligent person knows an object by the source of valid knowledge. He takes hold of it if it is worthy of taking and rejects it if it is rejectable. When a person is inclined either to take it or to reject it he makes an effort in that direction. This effort is called pravṛtti, When this effort reaches its goal, i.e., the actual taking of an acceptable object or the discarding of a rejectable object taking place the effort becomes fruitful, i.e., it is crowned with success. As Vātsyāyana makes the above remark so he has hinted at the hypothesis that the desire for fruit stirs our movement. So, following his foot-steps we have also subscribed to the above hypothesis.

But neither the author of Nyāya-sūtra nor his commentator has hinted at the meaning of a sentence in any place. The purport of this statement is 'Why do the Naiyāyikas seriously discuss the problem at all? An answer to the question is this that this branch of study has a distinct subject-matter of its own. The Nyāya branch of study is the science of logic but not the science of grammar.

If this is the case then why has the Sūtrakāra discussed the meanings of words, viz., a particular, a universal and the form of a particular? This question is highly reasonable. The author of the Nyāya sūtra has taken steps to vindicate the validity of verbal knowledge. In order to do so he has had to silence his opponent who has loudly declared that words have only imaginary meanings.

If this is so then the truth of verbal knowledge will not be established unless and until it is held that a sentence denotes external reals. Therefore, an effort should be made in this direction. You have said the right thing. The author of the Nyāya-sūtra thinks that steps which he has taken to establish the real meanings of a word have been in the right direction to propound the meaning of a sentence. For this reason he has not given us instruction that the meaning of a sentence is distinct from that of a word. Hence, it is his intention that the meanings of words constitute the meaning of a sentence. For, will the Mīmāṁsakas accept the hypothesis that the meanings of words constitute the meaning of a sentence ? The Naiyāyikas say in reply 'Oh yes, by all means'. They also mention in this connection that many meanings of words constitute the meaning of a sentence but not a single one does it.

Now, some remarks may be made by way of criticism. It has been suggested that many meanings of words constitute the meaning of a sentence. But they are nothing but meanings of words. The meaning of a word can never constitute that of a sentence since a word communicates its meaning in its universal aspect but never does it in the particularized aspect. But a sentence always communicates a particular meaning. A particular is one thing and a universal is another thing. It has also been stated in another place that a sentence conveys an additional meaning. Therefore, the meaning of a sentence is distinct from that of a word and the meaning of a word is another than that of a sentence.

A solution to the above criticism is as follows. O long-lived one : You have not followed the real purport of our statement that many meanings of words constitute the meaning of a sentence but not the single meaning of a word constitutes it. What we have meant to say is this that the mutual relation of word-meaning constitutes the additional meaning of a sentence. As this relation takes place so an extra meaning has been asserted.

If a word does not denote a particular object then the mutual relation of word-meanings is not explained, it is stated that a sentence points to particular objects. But the relation in itself (i.e., isolated from the relata) does not constitute the meaning of a sentence since it has not been communicated by a word. Let us take an example, 'Let a white cow be brought'. Among the constituent words of a sentence no word which denotes a relation is heard. Even if we admit that a word denotative of relation is heard then it has syntactical connection with no word of the sentence. Does the sentence 'Gauḥ śuklā ānīyatām saṁsargaḥ' (Let a white cow be brought—relation) convey a meaning ? Hence, the mutually related meanings of words constitute the meaning of a sentence but not their relation in its isolated form. This idea has been expressed in the sentence 'Vyatisaktato avagater vyatisaṁgasya' (The meaning of a sentence is communicated by the mutually related meanings of its constituent words). As threads produce a distinct whole, viz., a cloth or as sticks produce mattress, a distinct whole, so a distinct whole in the shape of the meaning of a sentence is not produced by the meanings of its constituent words. No such distinct whole is apprehended by us. A universal, an attribute, and an action are presented to our consciousness but a whole is never presented to our consciousness. Hence, a distinct whole, constituted by the meanings of words, is not the meaning of a sentence. So, the author of Nyāya-sūtra has not given the idea of the meaning of a sentence as something distinct.

Now, another point deserves clarification. A relation among meanings is not possible if they are not arranged as principal and secondary ones. If many meanings occupy principal positions in a sentence then none actually enjoys the principal position. In a sentence many meanings may occupy a secondary position. For this reason many secondary meanings should qualify a principal meaning which thus becomes qualified. The qualified meaning which occupies the principal position should be the meaning of a sentence. A judgment which is produced by a sentence refers to the qualified object. The drift of the above statement is that a sentence has a distinct meaning of its own. The Naiyāyikas point out that the above statement is true but still mutually related meanings are only presented to our consciousness. They also hold that no distinct object is constituted by these mutually related meanings. When these meanings are mutually related to one another we admit that the primary or secondary position is distributed among them. But the same position is not uniformly occupied by the certain type of meanings in all cases. If the uniformity of position had been always maintained by a particular type of meanings then it would have been always declared as the occupant of the principal position. In some cases an action occupies the principal position and the case form of a noun becomes subordinate to it. Let us take an example 'One should sacrifice with Brīhis'. In some cases, the case form of a noun occupies the principal position and an action becomes subordinate to it. Materials denoted by a noun, are known to be the object of desired action. Let us take an example 'He sprinkles Brīhis'.

In some cases, an action occupies a secondary position but a material occupies the principal position. But in some cases, a material occupies a secondary position but an action occupies a principal position. Reflecting on the purport of a word the position of the meaning of a word is determined.

In fine, as the position of the meaning of a word in a sentence cannot be settled in a definite manner so it is better to hold that meanings of words which are mutually related constitute the meaning of a sentence. There is no divergence of opinion about the hypothesis that some relation is communicated by a sentence.

Those who hold that a mandate or a bhāvanā or an action constitutes the meaning of a sentence admit that the mutually related meanings of words constitute the meaning of a sentence.

Now, another point invites our attention. As relation is conveyed by a sentence so mutual exclusion is also communicated by it. When the sentence 'Let a white cow be brought' is heard, black, cows etc., are excluded from the meaning of 'a white cow'. It has been said that mutual exclusion is not the meaning of a word. Hence, mutual exclusion is not conveyed by a sentence as its meaning.

Now, if the Naiyāyikas argue in this way then relation is also denoted by no word in a sentence. There is much truth in this criticism. Though the said relation is not denoted by any word yet it is not true that it is not implied by it. How is it that what is not meant by a word is implied by it ? This point will be clarified in the subsequent chapter. But mutual exclusion cannot be thus implied. Thus a difinite conclusion is arrived at that the mutually related meanings of words constitute the meaning of a sentence.

Or, the meaning of a single word, which occupies the principal position and which is qualified by the meanings of the other words of a sentence, occupying the secondary position, constitutes the meaning of a sentence. One should admit the truth of this hypothesis on the strength of the experience that a sentence produces a single judgment.

The establishment of the hypothesis that an end is the meaning of a sentence

It is not very easy to determine what is the single meaning of a sentence. If the pitcher containing coronation water is to be given to any one of these meanings then it may be given to an end since no word is uttered without any purpose.

In some cases an end is directly stated by a word. In some other cases an end is indicated by the context. In some other cases an end is suggested by discussion. The net result is that an end is the ultimate goal which is pointed to in every case.

All case forms of nouns produce an action. An action produces a result, i. e., an end. But a result produces no other result. Hence, a result is only conveyed by a sentence since it occupies the principal position.

A question still arises in our mind. An end is for the benefit of a person. But an end is not an end in itself. Hence, a person should occupy the principal position. Such a hypothesis should not be entertained. An end itself is happiness, so it cannot rest unsupported. It finds its support in a person since happiness is an attribute of the soul. Though the soul is said to be the substratum of happiness yet it does not mean that a person enjoys the principal position since the very person in whom happiness inheres makes an effort to obtain happiness. A bhāvanā is an activity which is directed towards an end.

A mandate cannot induce a person to undertake an action if there is no end to realise. These points have been discussed before.

The hypothesis that an action in itself which involves no reference to an end is the meaning of a sentence has been refuted.

Hence, as an end is an object to be realised without an exception and as all actions, etc., are directed towards it, so it is desirable that an end is the meaning of a sentence.

The Mīmāṁsakas raise an objection to the above conclusion. The goal of an action is heaven, etc. The objects like heaven, etc., are by their intrinsic nature pre-existing things. Hence, they cannot end into relation with case forms of nouns. Case forms of nouns cannot be related to pre-existing things by such relation as holds between any cause and an effect. Now, the Naiyāyikas may contend that they may be related through the intervening action. The Mīmāṁsakas raise another question. The end is related to an action. The case forms of nouns are also related to an action. What is the difference between case forms of noun and an end ? The case forms of nouns are related to an action which is a means. But an end is related to an action as an object to be realised. An object is accomplished by an action. An action is not produced by an end, i.e., an object. Hence, it is established that an end occupies the prominent place.

As the meanings of words, being mutually related, constitute the meaning of a sentence so the author of Nyāya-sūtra, taking note of it, has not said that a sentence conveys a distinct meaning, i.e., a meaning which is other than those of words.

Or, owing to the prominence of its position an end is asserted to be the meaning of a sentence. Sound thinkers make an attempt at establishing the hypothesis. It is well known to all that an end has been taught by the author of Nyāya-sūtra as the motive.

The refutation of the hypothesis that the vibration of the soul (udyoga) is the meaning of a senteuce:

Some thinkers hold that when one listens to the verbal termination in the optative mood a distinct type of activity (udyoga) arises in the soul. This udyoga constitutes the meaning of a sentence. But we are absolutely in the dark about its characteristic feature. What is this activity of the soul? There are nine attributes of the soul viz., consciousness, pleasure, pain, desire, hatred, volition, merit demerit and impression. They only constitute its specific attributes but none else. Either consciousness or volition or any one of desire and hatred is the so-called activity of the soul since other attributes cannot be thought of to be so. If consciousness is held to be the activity of the soul then the hypothesis is the same as that an idea is the meaning of a sentence. Thus no new hypothesis has been suggested. Again, if volition is the action of the soul then udyoga is another name for bhāvanā. Now, if it is either of the two, desire and hatred, then the meaning of a sentence is either desire for pleasure or desire for the avoidance of pain. This is the hypothesis of the Naiyāyikas. There is nothing new in it. Or, if the activity of the soul as suggested by the Bhāṭṭas is the vibration of the soul then it is bhāvanā only and nothing else. If it is held that mandate which is to be carried out by a listener is udyoga and it instigates him to an action then it is nothing but an injunction (niyoga). Udyoga and niyoga convey the same sense since they have been derived from the same root. Their difference in form lies in this that the different prepositions have been prefixed to the same root. They do not mean different objects.

There is no need of this unheard chapter on udyoga. It is only known to the persons mentioned in the Mahābhārata.

It is not known to persons like us.

The refutation of the hypothesis that a sentence conveys knowledge

Some thinkers hold that a sentence conveys knowledge. This hypothesis has been already refuted since its parallel hypothesis that a sentence conveys the knowledge of relation has been refuted.

Pratibhā is surely a form of knowledge. It is produced by a sentence. But it is not denoted by a sentence. Just as the awareness of colour is produced by eyes. But colour is not an object of them (Hence Pratibhā is not the meaning of a sentence).

The upholders of the above hypothesis argue thus :—As an external object does not exist so a sentence denotes only the knowledge of an object. The argument does not hold good since the existence of an external object has been proved. When the sentence that a tiger has come is uttered different emotions arise in the minds of courageous and timid persons. If they know for certain that a real tiger has come then these mental changes take place owing to their innate tendencies. But if they have the mere idea of a tiger then such actual emotions do not occur. It is a fact that when a person learns from a sentence that a real tiger has come emotional change takes place in his mind. But the mere knowledge of a tiger does not bring about such a change. If the upholder of the above hypothesis contends that the external object does not exist at that time then our reply to the contention is that it is a deceptive one and that it will not accord to the object denoted by it. But it is also to be noted that it points to something which has no external reality. When a real external object, say a female, appears before us different mental reactions occur in our mind in accordance with our innate tendencies. Some (ascetics) consider her to be untouchable dead body. Some (sensuous persons) take her as an enjoyable object. Some beings (tigers etc) think of her as an edible object. The different subjects have different forms of knowledge. Similarly, when different persons have grasped the meaning of the sentence that a tiger has come, different mental reactions take place. The brave persons are encouraged to hunt it. The timid ones are cowed down with fear. Such mental phenomena occur. But their appearance does not imply that a sentence denotes knowledge. Or, you may say that a sentence implies knowledge from the pragmatic point of view. If you like, you may subscribe to this view. But on no account the hypothesis that a sentence denotes knowledge or a word denotes an idea is true. Now, the upholders may contend that though knowledge is not denoted by a sentence yet it will constitute the meaning of a sentence like the relation of objects. An answer to this contention has been given. The mutually related objects constitute the meaning of a sentence but not the mere relation of objects. In this case too, the objects which are presented to our consciousness constitute the meaning of a sentence but not the knowledge of objects. Moreover, there is no hard and fast rule that the objects, denoted by sentences, must belong to the present time like the objects of perception. It has been argued that as sentences point to past or future objects so they denote knowledge since objects are not present. The argument is not tenable since though sentences indicate past or future objects yet they point to such objects as have been proved to be real. It is superfluous to hammer this point into their head.

In fine, the meaning of a sentence is objectively real. It is not a creation of our imagination. Even if it is held that a few words have imaginary meanings then it is to be admitted that these words are related to objects. The charge of falsehood levelled against verbal knowledge on the ground that external objects do not exist has been refuted. Thus we arrive at the sound conclusion that verbal knowledge is true.

ĀHNIKA VI

An introductory discussion to ascertain the real nature of a word

The objector raises a question that the problem of the validity of verbal knowledge has not been as yet solved since the source of the knowledge of the meaning of a word and that of a sentence has not been determined.

The Naiyāyikas say in reply that they solve it thus:- Is there any difficulty to solve the problem ? If an event follows in quick succession an antecedent one then the latter is the cause of the former. When one listens to a word or a sentence he is aware of the meaning of a word or of that of a sentence. Hence a word and a sentence condition the knowledge of the meaning of a word and that of a sentence respectively.

What is a word ? And what is a sentence ? As assemblage of letters is called a word. A collocation of words is called a sentence.

The above definitions are not satisfactory since the real assemblage of letters is a fiction. If it is so then how will letters assemble to constitute a word ? If the formation of a word is impossible then a sentence which is said to be the collocation of words is far more impossible. Again, letters cannot denote a meaning since the problem, 'Do letters singly or collectively convey a meaning ?' has not been squarely solved. Hence the objectors hold that there is another word which is distinct from letters. It is called sphoṭa. This name is significant because it communicates its meaning.

Now, the Naiyāyikas may say 'Let it be so, and let a sphoṭa which is other than letters convey a meaning. What is the harm to us ?' The objectors point out 'Why is it not a source of trouble to them ?' The Naiyāyikas hold that a word or a sentence is a source of true knowledge because its author is a trust-worthy person. But a sphoṭa, being eternal, does not owe its existence to a trust-worthy person. They have proved that a word which is a collocation of letters is non-eternal. But such a collocation of letters is not a source of valid knowledge since it fails to convey a meaning. But the word viz. sphoṭa which communicates a meaning is not non-eternal. Hence, it has not been effectuated by a trustworthy person. Hence the Naiyāyikas have troubled themselves in vain, adopting a wrong track. For this very reason the Naiyāyikas have got to prove by all means that non-eternal letters convey a meaning and that hypothesis of a sphoṭa is to be refuted.

Now, the argument of the Naiyāyikas is as follows : Let us take an example viz. the word 'gauḥ'. When the letters 'g' etc. are presented to our consciousness we are aware of a meaning. But if they are not presented to our consciousness, we have no knowledge of its meaning. Hence the letters 'g' etc. are competent to communicate a meaning. Again, they are called sound since they are grasped by our auditory sense-organ. Hence, we should not assume a word designated as sphoṭa since it is neither perceived nor inferred nor presented to our consciousness.

The Refutation of the Hypothesis that Letters Convey a sense

The objector, i. e., the upholder of the hypothesis of sphoṭa reviews the above criticism and says "How will your hypothesis stand ? All your hopes are shattered . How do the letters convey a sense ? If the letters viz.'g' etc are to communicate a meaning then do they convey it singly or collectively ? A letter cannot singly convey a sense since when a letter is singly heard no sense is made out. The collocation of letters is an impossibility. Even if it is assumed that a collocation of letters takes place then does it convey a sense, itself remaining unknown or being known" ? According to the Naiyāyikas letters do not coexist when they are not cognised since it has been proved that sounds pass away like a dream.

Though the Mīmāṁsakas hold that a sound is eternal yet all letters from 'a' to 'z' coexist. Hence it is very difficult to determine that a definite collocation of letters expresses a precise meaning.

Now, the Naiyāyikas may contend that letters do not effectuate consciousness like the eyes etc. If they had done so then their unknown coexistence would have been enough to produce consciousness. But as letters serve as a mark so they indicate another object when they themselves are present and known like smoke etc. Hence when they are presented to our consciousness their assemblage is a necessary condition. But such a collection of letters is an impossible feat. Are the letters which constitute an assemblage uttered by a single speaker or by many speakers ? Now, if it is held that the said assemblage is of such letters as are uttered by many speakers then a great uproar takes place. Letters being drowned in that uproar, their individual distinction is hard to discern. Under these circumstances you will think of assemblage or non-assemblage of such letters. Even though we admit that letters anyhow assemble yet such an assemblage does not convey a sense. Now, if letters are pronounced by a single speaker then it is noted that they are uttered with the help of different organs of speech. They are pronounced successively but not simultaneously. Hence, the order of succession of the appearance of letters invariably takes place since the succession of letters has not been given up. If such succession is admitted then a single letter should convey a sense. But our experience contradicts the above conclusion. Therefore, as the assumption of the assemblage or the non-assemblage of letters has no logical significance, letters do not convey a sense. The same criticism holds good with regard to the phenomena of consciousness, produced by letters. The events of consciousness, produced by consecutive letters cannot simultaneously take place. If each letter successively produces an event of consciousness the awareness of each letter should convey a sense.

Again, the upholders of this view may further contend that the last letter of a word with the aid of impressions due to the awareness of its antecedent letters conveys a sense. Such a contention is not logically sound. The reason behind this criticism is as follows. An impression revives the recollection only of that object the consciousness of which has produced it (the impression). But it cannot produce the consciousness of another object. If they hold that the said impression will recall the memory of all antecedent letters in due order and communicate its meaning then such a defence does not hold good. If one admits it then he should also admit that different forms of consciousness simultaneously take place since like the memory of all letters antecedent to the last one the knowledge of denotation should also be assembled at this time, following the experience of the last letter. Otherwise, there is no room for the knowledge of denotation. And for this reason the simultaneity of consciousness happens to take place. There is no sufficient reason to hold that the recollection of all antecedent letters and the knowledge of denotation successively come into being. If the contenders insist on the point that these events of consciousness successively occur then at the time of the appearance of the knowledge of denotation the memory of antecedent letters passes away. In that case will the memory of antecedent letter render its assistance to any body ? Now they ask 'why ?' We point out that different impressions recall distinct memories but do not revive such recollection as simultaneously refer to many letters.

Now, the defenders may contend that there will arise a recognitive judgment having a reference to past and present letters and the letters referred to by it, will communicate a meaning. They simply hope against hope since there is no such condition as favours the appearance of the above judgment. The sense-organ is not capable of grasping past letters, an impression does not reveal a present letter and a sense-organ and an impression do not co-operate to produce a judgment which refers to both past and present letters. Because when an impression is revived by the perception of a concomitant object and such other objects it produces only memory but nothing else. Its capacity for producing memory is only known to us. It does not render its assistance to sense-organs by its operation to produce a judgment which refers to letters.

Again, if letters had been held to communicate a meaning then thev would have conveyed the same sense though their order had been inverse. Now if they hold that letters require a definite order for the communication of meaning then they should also think of the problem whether the order of letters is distinct from letters or not. If the order of letters is not distinct from the letters themselves then the letters, in spite of their interchange of place, remain the same. Then, why do not they convey a sense, having a mutual change of place? If the order of letters is distinct from letters themselves then something distinct is admitted to denote a meaning. In that case, the critics express their wish to come over to this side (the side of defenders).

Now, the defenders of the former hypothe is persist in arguing to uphold their view thus :—A word is known to convey a particular meaning by means of verbal usage. A word is used by a person and it communicates a meaning. Then the number and the order of letters which constitute the word are observed. We notice that a person uses a word and it conveys this meaning. At that time we observe the definite number of letters which constitute the word and the particular order in which the letters are arranged. We also learn from the verbal usage that the same member of letters arranged in the same definite order will convey the same sense. This is our final conclusion on this point. What is the good of chopping logic?

Kumārila has also said to this effect :—As many letters, arranged in a definite order, are known to convey a particular meaning so many letters, arranged in that very order, convey the same sense.

The upholders of the hypothesis of sphoṭa say in reply that they should now discuss the point as to how one learns the meaning of a word from the verbal usage of another person. If one learns that another person understands the meaning of the word in question then he understands that the word conveys the same sense. When he reads the apprehension of meaning of another person he observes which letters convey which sense in which manner. As he has observed so the same number of letters arranged in the same order will communicate the same scenes to him. Hence, the path of the communication of meaning as constructed by letters is very difficult to understand.

As long as questions, viz. How many letters communicate a meaning? Which are they? In which manner do they convey a sense? are not put to you, you go on saying that so many letters point to a meaning, they are such and such and they convey a sense in this way.

Sphoṭa is an inference

From the trend of the above arguments we arrive at the conclusion that letters by no means convey a meaning. But it is also a fact that when letters are uttered they communicate a meaning. This knowledge of the meaning is an event in time. This event cannot take place if there is no cause par excellence to account for it. Hence, we hold that the cause par excellence is sphoṭa.

The knowledge of meaning is an effect. Let its cause be inferred. Or, let it be an instance of negative inference. Or, let it be a case of presumption. By all means one is to accept the knowledge of meaning as an effect. On the strength of anyone of the above arguments a cause par excellence of the said effect is to be assumed. We suggest that the cause par excellence in question is sphoṭa.

It is a partless whole. It is eternal. It consists of no consecutive elements. Hence, defects which have been mentioned to undermine the hypothesis that letters convey a meaning do not affect the hypothesis that sphoṭa conveys a sense. Hence, sphoṭa denotes a meaning. It has been said that a meaning is communicated by a word (śabda). The fifth case-ending has been attached to the stem 'śabda' (a word). Such a usage is highly appropriate. In other words, 'sabda' is the basic stem. It stands for sphoṭa.

Now, the upholders of the above hypothesis may contend that the word 'śabda' denotes letters and these letters convey a sense. Even if their contention is admitted, they cannot reasonably explain why the fifth case-ending in singular number has been attached. If the above contention is true then the usage should be that words communicate a meaning but not a word does it. If a word is taken as synonymous with a sphoṭa then it becomes appropriate to hold that a word conveys a meaning. Thus the case-ending in singular number and the basic stem are appropriately used.

Now, the upholders of the rival hypothesis take an exception to the said conclusion and argue that the word 'śabda' does not denote sphoṭa. But it stands for letters since word 'sabda' denotes audible sense-data. Letters are such sense-data. The import of this argument is that sphoṭa is not denoted by the word 'śabda'. The argument does not hold good since the universal which belongs to all śabdas is also audible but lacks the practical efficiency of a śabda. Moreover, though the inarticulate murmur of the spring is audible yet it cannot communicate a meaning like a śabda. Hence, what communicates a meaning is a śabda. A sphoṭa-śabda communicates a meaning. But letters do not convey a sense. For this reason, sphoṭa alone deserves to be denoted by the word śabda.

Now, the upholders of the rival hypothesis raise another objection that if what points to another object is śabda then smoke, a substance, which indicates another object should be taken as śabda. The defenders of the sphoṭa hypothesis say in reply, "Do not say this. When we hear at the commencement of a statement 'Atra Gauḥ' many objects are presented to our auditory sense-perception. Let us discern at the out-set what is a śabda among them. We come to a decision that what communicates a meaning is a śabda. If this conclusion is established then there is no room for the doubt that smoke and such other substances are śabdas.

Now, the upholders of the rival hypothesis advance a fresh argument in favour of their hypothesis and point out that if letters are present then a meaning is communicated and that if letters are not present then a meaning is not communicated. They make the critical remark 'How is the communication of a meaning causally connected with a sphoṭa?' 'The defenders of the sphoṭa hyphothesis give a reply to the above criticism. What is not an invariable, unconditional and immediate antecedent is not a cause. If an object invariably, unconditionally and immediately precedes an event then the former is the cause of the latter. Letters do not invariably, unconditionally and immediately precede the communication of meaning. How is it that they do not precede in such a manner? Letters manifest a sphoṭa at the out-set. Then a sphoṭa communicates a meaning. The communication of a meaning does not immediately follow the hearing of letters. The manifestation of a sphoṭa takes place. The immediate antecedence of letters is thus contradicted. Therefore letters are not the cause of the communication of a meaning. A sphoṭa really communicates a meaning. But the people mistake that letters have communicated a meaning,

The manifestation of a sphoṭa by letters

Now if it is held that a sphoṭa is manifested by letters then where are those riddles which beset the hypothesis that letters communicate a meaning ? The riddles are as follows. Do letters singly manifest a sphoṭa ? Or, do letters collectively manifest a sphoṭa ? Kumārila Bhaṭṭa has raised a few problems as to the manifestation of a sphoṭa by letters.

Those who hold that the apprehension of letters conditions the manifestation of a partless sphoṭa are not immune from the above questions. Śabara, the great commentator has also raised a question that if impressions due to the experience of letters are assumed then an invisible agency is postulated. But he has solved the question thus: In order to get rid of such an assumption if a sphoṭa is postulated then two such assumptions are made. We are to assume the very invisible impression and over and above it a sphoṭa—a distinct thing, is to be assumed.

The defenders of the sphoṭa hypothesis meet the above objection thus: They hold that the above criticism does not affect their hypothesis. The above riddles do not arise with regard to the manifestation of a sphoṭa. If the critics ask 'why' then the reply is as follows. A band of thinkers defends the hypothesis in this way. When the first letter is heard a sphoṭa is manifested. The second letter and the rest ones are not to be taken as superfluous since they make an improvement upon the manifestation of a sphoṭa. Let us cite a parallel case. Those who test a gem do not clearly grasp its true character at the first sight. Though the true character of the gem is not clearly manifested at that time yet it clearly reveals itself to his mind when it is repeatedly examined.

Similarly, in this case too when the first letter of a word is heard a sphoṭa is manifested. Though its manifestation takes place yet the speaker will employ the other letters in order to make the said manifestation much more vivid and distinct.

Inarticulate sounds manifest a sphoṭa

Some other followers of the sphoṭa school hold that inarticulate sound (dhvani) is the only manifester of a sphoṭa. The essence of a dhvani consists in the air. These airs in the shape of dhvanis manifest a sphoṭa which is partless. When a sphoṭa is manifested it comes in contact with the organs of speech viz. palate etc. which are the source of letters. Afterwards this very contact acts like a limiting adjunct. It eclipses the real character of a sphoṭa and makes it appear as one having many parts such as letters etc. As the air is constantly flowing so dhvanis pass away after they have been pronounced. They manifest the imaginary forms of a sphoṭa. Our experience teaches that a thing appears to be what it is not when it becomes associated with a limiting adjunct. Let us take an example to illustrate our point. When one looks at his face through the different media such as a sword, a gem and a mirror, his face appears to be dark, long etc. The same musical note assumes various forms when it is manifested by the various musical instruments such as a lute, a flute, a small drum, a big drum etc. For the reason stated above letters are mere appearances but not real. Moreover, they do not manifest a sphoṭa. Therefore, how can the above riddles, viz., 'Does a letter singly manifest a sphoṭa ?' 'Do letters collectively manifest a sphoṭa' etc. exert their influence upon the hypothesis in question.

The appearance of letters is due to association with limiting adjuncts. These letters have only imaginary forms. The upholders of the rival hypothesis say, 'It is observed by the joint method of agreement and difference that letters condition the communication of meaning.' On the basis of this observation they also hold that the assumption of a sphoṭa involves two assumptions. They say in reply to the above objection, that if they admit the existence of a sphoṭa, they make no assumption not to speak of double assumptions.

In fine, a sphoṭa conveys a sense and letters are not the invariable condition of communicating a sense. They are to be taken as superfluous for this purpose. This conclusion which is arrived at is incontestable.

The Perceptibility of a sphoṭa

Moreover, the logicians of the Nyāya school of thought take delight in argumentation. In order to please them we have shown that a sphoṭa is an inference. But we do not really subscribe to this hypothesis. Our conclusive view is this that a sphoṭa, being perceived by our auditory organ, is a percept.

Some critics have made an adverse comment on this hypothesis. They remark that the sphoṭa-vādins persue a hide and seek policy with regard to sphoṭas and letters. Though letters are perceived yet they are held as not perceived since they are unlucky. But though a sphoṭa is not perceived yet it is held as perceived since it is lucky.

The sphoṭa-vādins give the following rejoinder to the above criticism. They point out that they do not say that letters are not perceived. But they hold that though letters are non-existent yet they are presented to consciousness through the influence of a condition. They mean to say that a sphoṭa appears as a letter when it is associated with a dhvani. Let us take a parallel case. A face appears to be long etc. when it is looked at through a reflecting glass. A single individual sound in the shape of a sphoṭa is presented to our consciousness. It is absolutely partless. It is presented to our consciousness as a single entity, e. g. a word and a sentence. But letters are not presented to our consciousness when we are aware either of a word or of a sentence. The consciousness of a universal does not refer to individuals to which the universal belongs. The awareness of a whole does not refer to parts in which the whole inheres. The consciousness of a word or that of a sentence is not illusory just as the presentation of an army or of a forest as a single unity. Many individual soldiers are presented to our consciousness and they are taken as a single unit, viz. an army. Many trees are perceived and are taken as a single unit, viz. a forest. But we do not perceive many letters and take them as a single word. Similarly, we do not perceive many words and take them as a single sentence. The oneness of a word or of a sentence is not a construction of our imagination since it is not contradicted by a sound experience. Now, our critics may suggest that the awareness of the oneness of a word or of a sentence is also an appearance since it is conditional. A word appears as one since it produces the knowledge of a single object. A sentence appears as one since it produces a judgment which refers to a single object in the shape of a relational whole. Thus, the awareness of the oneness of a word or of a sentence is conditional.

The sphoṭa-vādins say in reply to this criticism, 'How does the communication of a single object take place?' The awareness of the meaning of a word or of a sentence presupposes the consciousness of a word or of a sentence. If the unity of the awareness of the meaning of a word or of a sentence conditions the unity of the consciousness of a word or of a sentence then this solution involves the irrefutable fallacy of a vicious circle. Similarly, the unity of the consciousness of a universal or of a whole may be as well held to be conditional. But the Naiyāyikas meet this charge with the remark that the consciousness in question is true since it is a piece of uncontradicted experience and is beyond the shade of a doubt, the sphoṭa-vādins may also point out that they may also put forward the same argument in favour of their hypothesis.

Therefore, the consciousness of a word refers to a pada-sphoṭa and the consciousness of a sentence refers to a vākya-sphoṭa. The sphoṭa is thus perceived. A pada-sphoṭa communicates the meaning of a word. And a vākya-sphoṭa communicates the meaning of a sentence.

The proof of a vākya-sphoṭa

The critics open their criticism thus. If a sphoṭa-śabda is partless then a sentence is also a sphoṭa but nothing else. As such it should not consist of parts, viz. words. Again, if the sphoṭa-vādins hold that a sentence consists of words as its part then words should also consist of parts in the shape of letters.

The sphoṭa-vādins say in reply to the above criticism : Our heart leaps with joy on hearing the above remark. We think that the lamp of conscience of the long-lived one will be kindled. You will take our point of view and think aright when you will be initiated into it. You are under the sway of illusion that different letters exist. But they do not really exist. A sphoṭa, being associated with various dhvanis, appears as different letters. In order to enlighten you we have shown before that a pada-sphoṭa is partless. But really speaking, a pada-sphoṭa does not constitute the part of a sentence. A sentence is partless. It conveys a meaning which consists of no parts. As a word is partless so a sentence is also partless and a word does not constitute its part.

Some other thinkers also hold that as a word does not belong to a sentence as its part so the meaning of a word does not belong to the meaning of a sentence as its part. A sentence and its meaning are partless. If one imagines that a sentence consists of parts then an absurd conclusion will be inevitable.

Let us clearly state our argument. Suppose, a sentence consists of parts. Words constitute its parts. Letters constitute the parts of a word. A letter should also consist of parts. These parts should also consist of parts. An unending series of parts will go on. There will be no resting place of our imagination. Owing to the regressus ad infinitum no solution will be arrived at.

If you stop the process of vivisection into parts on reaching letters then why should you not stop it at a sentence? The consciousness of the meaning of a sentence is like an integrate whole which admits of no division. Such an awareness can only owe its existence to such a sentence as is individual. Those who commence verbal communication learn the usage of language together with its import from the uses of the experienced ones. The experienced ones do never employ words unnecessarily since mere words do not play an important part in a verbal transaction. A sentence renders a useful service in such transaction, if one is initiated into the use of a sentence. A sense is definitely grasped from it. What appears to be part of a sentence is nothing but an appearance. The meaning of a sentence is also an indivisible whole. It admits of internal diversity like a man-lion. A man-lion is a class by itself. It is neither a man nor a lion. Similarly, the meaning of a sentence is distinct from that of words like sweet drink etc. As sweet drink has its separate existence it is distinct from sugar, fragrant Nāgakeśara and peppercorn, as a picture is distinct from vermilion, red Arsenic, lac etc. as a mixed tune is distinct from gamut, so a sentence is distinct from words and the meaning of sentence is distinct from those (the meanings) of constituent words.

The Unreality of parts of a Sentence

If the above account is true then how do we think that words are parts of a sentence ? In reply to the above question we say that such a division of a sentence into parts is merely imaginary but not real. Now, you may contend that parts of a sentence are not merely imaginary since words being syntactically related to a sentence their meanings are seen to be related to the meaning of a sentence. The contention is not tenable since if from the words kūpa, sūpa and yūpa a letter, from each word is taken out and a word is framed then no sense is made out. Again, if one merely follows another then the latter should not be the cause of the former. A cloud of dust follows an elephant, a horse etc, It is generally held that the elephant, the horse etc. are the cause of the cloud of dust. Similarly, the cloud of dust is seen to follow a row of ants. Hence, a row of ants should be held as the cause of the cloud of dust (The sense of this argument is that mere sequence does not help to determine the relation of causality holding between the antecedent and the consequent events. Similarly, the causal relation does not hold between the meaning of words and the meaning of a sentence though the latter is preceded by the former).

Hence words which consist of the two elements, viz., the basic element and the suffix are not real. We also imagine that they have meanings. The imaginary meaning of these words is resorted to as the condition of the meaning of a sentence. But such a meaning is never noticed as a real existent object like a Śāla tree (a kind of teak tree). It is also seen that even an imaginary object is a means to the realisation of a real object since false snake-bite and the like effectuate actual death. The alphabets of our scripts are not real letters which we pronounce. But they help us to make out the real sense of a sentence. You cannot contend that these alphabets are real. They are essentially lines but not letters. Being lines they cannot convey a sense. If we take a line to be the letter 'g' then it conveys a meaning. It enjoys a real existence as a line. In that capacity it fails to convey a meaning. It is not real in that capacity in which it conveys a meaning. In other words, the alphabets are real in the sense of lines but lines they convey have no sense. They enjoy imaginary existence as letters. But they convey sense as letters. Thus, an imaginary object may be the condition of a real event.

Those who subscribe to the view that words are constituted by letters hold that parts of words, viz., the basic element, the suffix etc., do really exist since they are presented to our consciousness as such and are the source of the communication of the meaning of a word. The sphoṭa-vādins join issue with them and hold that the above contention is not sound. The etymological derivation of a word admits of so many diverse ways that it is difficult to find out all of them. Let us take an example, viz., the word 'bhavati'. Sometimes the derivation of the word has been given thus :- the root 'bhū' constitutes the basic element. Sometimes the suffix 'kvip' is attached to the word 'bhava'. Thus the noun 'bhava' is converted into the verb 'bhava'. Verbal termination is attached to it. The complete word 'bhavati' is thus framed. Thus we see that in order to derive a word we have recourse to various tactics, viz., pratyaya, ādeśa, āgama, guṇa, vṛddhi and the dropping of a letter, etc., Thus, the process of derivation is very conflicting. There is no straight way of derivation. Is the splitting up of a word into two elements, viz., the basic element and the suffix real? This is the basic element and this is the suffix. This division of a word into two parts is purely imaginary.

In order to determine the meaning of a sentence the meanings of words have been selected by imagination and held apart. Bhartṛhari in his Vākyapadīyā has said to this effect. Some specialists in Etymology have drawn out words from partless sentences by their pure imagination and divided them into two, four or five classes. This division resembles the splitting up of a word into two elements, viz., the basic element and the suffix.

Moreover, if these words had been real then they would have been presented to our consciousness in their unalterable forms. But their forms are alterable. (They mislead listeners.)

Sphoṭa Enjoys the Status of the Absolute

Now the critics of the doctrine of sphoṭa raise a problem. As the sphoṭa-vādins hold that letters are not parts of a word and words are not parts of a sentence so the clauses are not to be held as parts of a complex sentence. For this very reason complete sentences included in the chapter of a book should not enjoy real existence. And for the same reason the chapters of a treatise should have no reality. Is it the very reason at the root of the conclusion that the śāstra aims at teaching one indivisible truth without the second ?

A rejoinder to the above criticism is as follows. If you seriously desire to know the essence of our doctrine then, O good sir, you may follow it. Śabda is the Absolute. It is the One without a second. Various tendencies of thought arise from the beginningless Nescience. It eclipses the One and distorts it. It makes the Śabda Brahman appear as different meanings. A meaning has no separate existence apart from its denotative word. Therefore, the distinction holding between a word and its meaning is purely imaginary. Everybody takes shelter in Nescience as a real means to true knowledge. The real essence of everything in this universe is śabda since every form of consciousness is interpenetrated by. There is no such form of consciousness as is not associated with verbal expression. It has been stated by Bhartṛhari in his Vākyapadīya (1.125). The essence of consciousness is the state of being intermingled with words. No piece of consciousness can be dissociated from verbal expression. If any piece of consciousness ceases to be associated with words then it cannot reveal its content, viz., the subject and the predicate. Because a judgment expresses the distinction between the subject and the predicate only in and through the medium of verbal expression. Hence consciousness is indissolubly associated with the verbal expression.

The above verbal expression (vāk) has been duly divided into three classes, viz., (1) Vaikharī, (2) Madhyamā and (3) Paśyantī. Of these three the first form of Vāk is the totality of all manifest letters. The manifestation of these letters such as 'g' etc. is due to a number of conditions such as the different limbs, viz., the throat, the palate etc., the vocal organ, and the different efforts of the inner air in successive orders. The contact of our body with the vocal organ is called vaikhara. The vāk which is manifested in the place of such contact is known as vaikharī. Some other thinkers have also subscribed to this hypothesis.

The vāk which assumes the form of letters is called vaikharī. The assumption of such a form is due to the operation of the vital breath of the speakers. But the manifestation of letters takes place when the said air blows over some particular limbs in a distinct manner.

The second form of vāk consists of a series of inarticulate sounds only grasped by our internal organ. We come across a group of common letters which may pass for a noun or for a verb. There is no mark of distinction. In other words, there is a series of letters. We may arrange these letters in different groups. The first groups of letters may be presented to our consciousness as nouns and verbs. The same letters which constitute (nouns may constitute) verbs if they are included in the different groups of letters. Thus, the same letters constitute both nouns and verbs. Hence, words have no definite form and character. As their forms vary so they have imaginary being. Hence they are not real. As their character is ever changing so we cannot make out the sense of a sentence spoken to us by a speaker. Let us take an example "kālena dantināgāstvam", and analyse it into words that are supposed to constitute it. The above sentence gives out two senses. In order to suit the sense words are different. Though the above sentence is split up into different sets of words in conformity to the different senses yet the letters remain the same. The sentence may give the following meaning "You have come on a dark elephant" (kālena kṛṣṇena dantinā hastinā āgās tvam). Shall we accept the above meaning and arrange words accordingly ? The sentence may also give the following sense that elephants roar or snakes hiss in time. Words which constitute the sentence are as follows :—(Kāle samaye nadanti śabdāyante nāgāḥ kariṇaḥ phaṇino vā). Or, shall we accept the second meaning and arrange words accordingly? Hence, as there is no rule for the division of a sentence into words so this division of words and their meanings is imaginary but not real.

The upholders of the hypothesis that a sentence is constituted by words may contend that the splitting up of a sentence into words with their proper meanings will be settled in accordance with the first meaning which a sentence conveys. In reply to this contention it may be said that if this is admitted then why shall we make arrangements for splitting up a sentence into words? When the sense of a sentence has been gathered what is the good of splitting up a sentence into words? Moreover let us take two examples, viz., dadhyatra and madhvatra. In these two cases though the vowel 'i' in dadhi and vowel 'u' in madhu are not visible yet they conveysense as we all know. Hence the division of a sentence into words and the division of a word into letters are not real. Therefore, we arrive at the true conclusion that a sentence admits of no parts and that a part-less sentence conveys a sense which admits of no parts. It does not consist of manifest letters which are grasped by the auditory sense-organ. Such a form of Vāk is called Madhyamā. Some other thinkers also hold a similar view. The form of Vāk which entirely depends upon the function of our intellect and having transgressed the operation of the vital breath flows on in a successive series is known as Madhyamā. The form of Vāk which is self-luminous consciousness and whose flow in a series of successive events is not noticed is called Paśyantī. Some other thinkers have also contributed to a similar view.

The form of Vāk which realises its identity with inner consciousness and has given up its march in a series of flowing events for good is eternal and very subtle. It is called Paśyantī.

As the subject matter under discussion is very lengthy, we shall not hold elaborate discussion on it since such a discussion will surely interfere with the elaboration of the relevant topic. In the present context the above account of the said thesis will suffice. The people employ sentences in order to transact all verbal intercourse with others since words and letters fail to render the above service. A sentence is not a whole consisting of parts. Hence the distinction which holds good between a whole and its parts does not apply to a sentence. A sentence admits of no parts. It conveys its sense as a partless non composite thing. The meaning which it conveys is also partless. Clauses (i.e. incomplete sentences) are also worthy of being employed since our verbal transaction is accomplished by them. Hence, we do not deny existence to them. But this procedure owes its origin to the state of ignorance. Let this path of verbal transaction continue to exist as it is seen. But when true knowledge will dawn all these hypotheses will be falsified. But no verbal transaction can be conducted by means of mere words and letters since mere words and letters are never employed. Under these circumstances we do not consider it to be wise to hold that words and letters enjoy real existence.

In fine, Vākya-sphoṭa is indivisible one. It admits of no changes i.e. successive states. It conveys a meaning which is similar to it in every respect. But all these letters are very short-lived by their intrinsic nature. They absolutely depend upon imagination for their existence. They do not constitute one of the necessary conditions of communicating the meaning of a sentence. Therefore, there is no need of discussing this topic to a greater length.

An Introduction to the Refutation of Sphoṭa

The refutation of the sphoṭa-hypothesis is as follows. How do you postulate the hypothesis of existence of a sphoṭa ? What is your basis? Do you admit the existence of sphoṭa on the strength of an inference ? Or, do you do it on the stronger evidence of perception? You cannot establish the existence of a sphoṭa by means of an inference since the letters which are arranged in a definite visible order convey a meaning, being thus arranged.

The Establishment of the Hypothesis that Letters Convey a Meaning

The Sphoṭa-Vādins raise an objection to the above solution. They hold that dilemmas have been put forward. These dilemmas clearly indicate that letters neither singly nor collectively convey a meaning. Therefore, the thesis that letters convey a meaning has been refuted. An answer to this argument is as follows. The said criticism is not sound. The dilemmas, advanced by the critics, are specimens of bad logic. When letters stand apart, without being related to one another they individually convey no meaning. But when they are united with one another to form a collection they collectively convey a meaning.

The possibility of the collection of letters has been gainsaid because they appear successively. Such a criticism is not sound. Though letters come into being in succession yet they conjointly produce an effect. There are several instances which show that the succeeding phenomena form a collection and conjointly produce an effect. As three slabs of stone which are simultaneously placed on an even spot keep a vessel on them so it is seen that all morsels of food taken one after another conjointly make one effect, viz., the feeling of satisfaction. If one of these morsels is left out then such satisfaction does not arise. Hence, this satisfaction is the conjoint effect of all morsels of food. But none can swallow up all morsels of food at a time. Though morsels of food are successively swallowed up yet their collection takes place. In connection with the various forms of Soma sacrifice the number of repetitions of the recitation of a particular Anuvāka (a group of hymns) varies. If the recitation of the said Anuvāka is not repeated as many times as has been prescribed then the enjoined fruit is not obtained. Even if the number is less by one, the fruit will not accrue to the performer of sacrifice. Hence in the Vedic literature the conjoint action of the successive acts has been acknowledged. So in the secular matters we have also seen that the successive phenomena mutually co-operate to bring about an effect. In other words, the combination of successive phenomena takes place to achieve a common end. Let us quote another example from the Vedas to illustrate our point of view. Darśa sacrifice (a sacrifice to be performed on the day of new moon) and Pūrṇa-māsa sacrifice (a sacrifice to be performed on the full moon day) are mutually connected as the Dvandva compound conveying the sense of conjunction indicates. In other words, the combination of these two sacrifices has been admitted. These two are main sacrifices. Each of them has many subsidiary sacrifices known as Āgneyas (dedicated to Agni) and others. The subsidiary sacrifices of the one are to be performed during (the dark fortnight). And the subsidiary of the other ones are to be performed during (the bright fort-night) day. Hence, the successiveness of these acts is unavoidable. In spite of their successiveness they are observed to render assistance to the main act. Similarly, the Vedic priest presses Soma creeper and extracts juice out of it in order to offer it to Indra and Vāyu and separately does the same act for the twin gods Aśvins. When he repeatedly presses Soma creeper to draw out juice for Indra and Vāyu he recites only a single mantra. The first series of acts of pressing Soma creeper done for Indra and Vāyu is an instance of joint action. The second series of acts done in honour of Aśvins follows the first one. Hence, these two acts take place successively. But the first series of acts which is a combined one and the successive second series of acts conjointly render an assistance to the accomplishment of the main act. Hence, the collection of successive phenomena is not incompatible. Thus, though letters appear successively yet they will combine themselves to convey a meaning.

The refutation of the hypothesis that a sphoṭa is an inference

The sphoṭa-vādins raise a few objections to the above solution offered by the rival party. They say 'We admit your statement about several swallowings of morsels and repeated recitations of hymns in connection with the various forms of Soma sacrifice since they conjointly produce an effect and successively come into being. It is also noticed by all that they gradually produce their effect. Now, the Naiyāyikas put a counter question to them. If your statement is correct then do you observe that Āgneya sacrifices and such other sacrifices gradually produce an effect ?' The Sphoṭa-vādins say in reply to this question, 'We hold that they bring about minor Apūrvas. We also hold on the strength of the authority of the Vedas that when all the minor sacrifices viz., Āgneya etc. will be completely performed the main Apūrva will be accomplished.' Now, the Naiyāyikas take an exception to this solution and raise a few questions. An Āgneya sacrifice is a process. It consists of several short-lived acts which are successive. Does each constituent act of Āgneya sacrifice gradually contribute something towards the appearance of the minor Apūrva, the ultimate result of Āgneya sacrifice ? Have you got an experience of such contribution ? Do minor Apūrvas individually produce parts of heavenly bliss ? They cannot produce such parts since the main act remains unperformed as yet. Therefore the collection of minor Apūrvas has got no important part to play. But they play some insignificant part to bring about the ultimate result. Their efficacy is not denied since the main sacrifice will be defective without their performance. Now, the Naiyāyikas turn their attention to their main thesis and say, "It is not a fact that we cannot show that letters contribute something towards the communication of meaning as the minor Apūrvas have a little contribution towards the main sacrifice." If you ask "What is the effect of these letters?" then we say in reply "Either the perception of each letter will be the effect produced by each letter or the impression of each letter due to such perception will be its effect."

Now, the Sphoṭa-vādins take an exception to the above solution of the Naiyāyikas and point out that the relation which obtains between parts and a whole does not subsist between the two sets of minor sacrifices and the main sacrifice. The Naiyāyikas say in reply that though the said relation does not hold yet the above two sacrifices contribute their useful quota towards the completion of the main sacrifice. They also point out in this connection that the part-and-whole-relation is hard to establish between the minor Apūrva and the main Apūrva. It is also to be noted that words, i. e. parts of speech, clearly play an important role as parts of a sentence. They communicate the meanings of words. These meanings constitute parts of the meaning of a sentence. In this respect, they stand above all criticism. Let us now compare and contrast the mode of operation of the different letters with that of the different acts cited as examples. The act of going is not a long process. It comprises within itself a series of transient acts. When we say that a man goes to a village from a particular place he slowly moves towards it. Each constituent act perceptibly contributes something towards the realisation of the final goal. Similarly, each swallowing of morsel brings about satisfaction to some degree. In this way, the minor sacrifices gradually help towards the realisation of the final end, the ultimate result of the main sacrifice. In all these cases, the final result is gradually achieved. But letters do not contribute towards the gradual communication of the sense of a word. In spite of this contrast letters produce their impressions and memories since they are vividly perceived. As they produce these effects so the main object, viz., the communication of the meaning of a word, is actualised. Hence, there is no exception to contribution on the part of letters towards the slow but progressive realisation of the main object. In other words, letters behave in the same way like the examples quoted above. But there is a bit difference in the mode of operation of these letters. A word consists of a few letters. Among them all the antecedent letters excepting the last one are past when they render service. But the last letter bodily exists at the time of rendering an assistance to the communication of the meaning of a word. In the manner just stated the collocation of letters conveys the sense of a word just as the imaginary momentary acts bring about the ultimate result. The adjective imaginary requires an explanation. These acts have real existence. But they are short-lived. When the actual result is brought about they cease to exist. In that case, the causal relation cannot hold between them and the ultimate result. (So Jayanta holds that their presence is imagined).

Though these letters are successively perceived yet a recognitive judgment of inner perception like an introspection will arise. It will refer to all the letters. It will help to communicate the meaning of a word. Suppose, a few objects have perished and have been perceived one after another. Still, our experience says that there arises a recognitive inner perception which refers to all those past objects. Let us cite an example. Devadatta ate a hundred mangoes. No body can deny existence to this judgment. It is not also an instance of doubtful knowledge. It is not also an erroneous judgment which is contradicted by a subsequent judgment. If a copulative judgment of this sort is not assumed then many verbal usages based upon the similar judgments should be discredited. The judgment in question refers to past letters, the objects of recollection and to the last letter which is an object of present perception. Thus it refers to both types of letters existent and non-existent. Hence one cannot but admit that it has a peculiar form. Or, if the said judgment arises after the passing away of the last letter then it refers only to non-existent letters. And as such it has no peculiar form. This judgment alone conditions the communication of the meaning of a word. Therefore, the vicious dilemmas, viz., 'Do letters singly convey the sense of a word or not ?', 'Do letters collectively convey the sense of a word or not?' etc. are now pointless.

Now, the Sphoṭa-vādins raise another point by way of criticism. They hold that if the said letters are serially presented to the above copulative judgment then this judgment is no better than the perception of each discrete letter. In that case, though all letters are presented to this copulative judgment yet the collocation of all letters cannot help the communication of the meaning of a word. But if all letters are synthesised by the said judgment like a bunch of flowers then the order of succession of all letters being not referred to by the judgment, these letters should condition the conveying of the sense of a word though they are arranged in a reverse order.

The Naiyāyikas meet this objection thus : A mere copulative judgment does not condition the communication of the sense of a word. The required judgment which immediately follows the perception of letters arranged in a distinct order of succession causes the communication of the meaning of a word. This judgment is not the presentation of letters merely arranged like a bunch of flowers.

If this is the case then how do you entertain a doubt about the arrangement of letters in a reverse order? Again, if the said judgment were the presentation of letters like a bunch of flowers then there would have not arisen the question of the order of arrangement reverse or non-reverse i.e. actual since in a bunch of flowers no order of the arrangement of followers is followed. This copulative judgment which refers to a definite number of letters follows in close succession to the antecedent acts of perception caused by these letters. The acts of perception reveal the serial order of the said letters. Hence, how can the reversal of the serial order of these letters take place ? These letters which are grasped by the first experience follow a definite serial order. They being arranged in that very order are referred to by the successive copulative judgment. These letters as presented by the copulative judgment make way for the communication of the meaning of a word, constituted by them. Hence, our hypothesis suffers from no defect.

Another alternative suggestion may be possible. Śabara, the authoritative commentator on the Mīmāṁsā Sūtras, has described that the last letter of a word accompanied by the impressions of its previous letters, convey the sense of a word, constituted by them. All letters communicate the meaning of words, constituted by them in the same manner.

We have already said what we should say now with regard to this subject-matter. We have stated that an impression does not produce the knowledge of the meaning of a word. It simply revives our memory. This is what our experience teaches. Now a question arises in our mind, Viz., 'It is a royal mandate that an impression shall produce memory only?' An answer to this question is this that it is the mandate of logic but not that of a king. An impression is not a distinct substratum. When we carefully know an object and repeat its knowledge with all seriousness the traces of knowledge are called an impression which can revive memory only. It is only inferred from its effect, viz., recollection. It is not perceived. It is a kind of faculty. It is not possible for an impression which itself is an after effect of knowledge to be able to generate the new knowledge of an object. Can it produce an effect other than that for which it has been postulated? An impression which revives memory owes its origin to the apprehension of an object. If one holds that an impression generates the apprehension of an object, he speaks of a novel type of impression. It is very difficult on our part to find out the cause of such an impression. Really speaking, we find none. Therefore, an impression cannot be the cause of the apprehension of an object.

The above argument is not sound. A person who possesses the impression of a letter arising from apprehension is seen to apprehend an object. Thus a saṁskāra (impression) is not merely such a faculty as exclusively generates recollection. It is an attribute of the soul. It is called vāsanā : (It is the residuum of an apprehension like the fragrance of a flower which has been removed). It is capable of producing the apprehension of an object just as it generates memory. In every case, we say whatever is in accordance with experience. Our experience is the source of true knowledge. On the strength of our experience we admit that an impression is competent to produce memory. Our experience also teaches that the knowledge of an object arises from impression. Letters and their apprehension have almost simultaneously taken place. No other sound is presented to our consciousness. We shall ask our opponents to consider this aspect of the above problem. The knowledge of an object takes place in our mind. We cannot say that such an event occurs without any cause. As it cannot happen without any cause so it necessarily implies its cause. An impression is the cause par excellence of such knowledge. Thus, the knowledge of an object, depending on impression like memory, suggests that the impression is the cause.

Now, a question arises, viz., 'What is the cause of an impression?' This is a foolish question since it is well-known that an impression owes its origin to the apprehension of an object. Some logicians say 'It is natural law that the vivid apprehension of an object produces impression which is the cause of memory.'

Now, a fresh question arises in our mind. How does an impression which generates memory effectuate the apprehension of an object? The sense of the question is that the apprehension of an object is presentative in its character. Hence, how can an impression bring it about? If it is effectuated by an impression then it will be representative. There is no hard and fast rule that an impression shall produce memory only. The apprehension of an object produces a special kind of impression. When the apprehension of an object of a particular type comes into being and no adequate cause is found out to account for its existence it is said that such an apprehension owes its existence to this type of impression. Various types of effects are explained only on the assumption of diverse types of causes. This hypothesis is based on the solid rock of experience.

We are not wedded to an opinion that an impression is the direct cause of the knowledge of the meaning of a word. It is a remote cause. It will produce such knowledge through the medium of memory. Let us explain the second hypothesis. A word generally consists of a few letters. All its constituent letters are not simultaneously pronounced. When the last letter is pronounced almost all antecedent letters have passed away. When the last letter is heard the memory of the past ones is recalled by their impressions. Thus, we may have the knowledge of the meaning of the said word through the instrumentality of letters which areremembered and of the letter which is apprehended. Thus we see that this hypothesis suffers from no defects.

Now, the Sphoṭa-vādins raise a fresh problem. The letters of a word which are now past have not been simultaneously presented to our consciousness. They have been gradually heard by us. Thus the impression of each letter has been generated by the experience of each letter. As memory depends upon the efficacy of an impression so each letter should be separately remembered. Thus all letters shall be consecutively but not simultaneously remembered. This being the possible course of events, all letters are not simultaneously recollected. Thus as the combination of letters is not possible so all defects, stated before, vitiate the hypothesis in question.

The Naiyāyikas meet the above objection thus. They hold that the above defects do not vitiate the said hypothesis. As letters successively appear so they are consecutively experienced. These successive experiences gain strength and produce such an impression (i.e. work out such a qualitative change in the soul) as simultaneously recalls all letters which have been previously experienced in memory. Let a parallel case be cited to bring home the point in question. Gold is kept in a closed vessel. It is repeatedly heated. Repeated heatings bring about a qualitative change in gold. Thus several acts which gradually take place cumulatively produce an effect. Thus, an impression (a new type comes into being). The logical conclusion of the above hypothesis is that impression brings forth another well-developed impression. If the Naiyāyikas subscribe to this hypothesis then they assume something transcendental i.e., something which cannot be corroborated by visible facts. The Naiyāyikas join issue with their critics and emphatically assert that it is not transcendental. The very study of the Vedas presupposes such an impression. The reading of the Vedas is an act. As such it is short-lived. If the critics do not subscribe to the result of the cumulative readings of the Vedas that an impression begets another then the first reading of the Vedas being not distinct from the last one a student cannot be able to get an Anuvāka of the Vedas by heart in spite of his life-long study.

Now, the Sphoṭa-vādins sum up the arguments of the Naiyāyikas and say, "There are two alternatives before us. We are to accept any one of them. Either we are to admit that an impression effectuates another impression or we are to admit that an impression is responsible for the knowledge of the meaning of a word. Any way we are to assume transcendental causality. Now, may we ask why do you take an interest in the hypothesis of impression and why do you take an aversion to the hypothesis of sphoṭa ? Please state the reasons for your partiality and aversion". The Naiyāyikas say in reply that the proper answer has been given by the celebrated commentator mentioned before (i.e., Śabara). He has pointed out that if a sphoṭa is assumed then one is to make two assumptions, viz., a sphoṭa and an impression.

Now, the Sphoṭa-vādins contend thus: 'We are not required to make double assumptions. An impression of the ordinary type is not a novel object. It is a well-known object which is admitted by all. Therefore, we make no new assumption. We have not allowed an impression to go beyond its normal activity. We firmly stick to the hypothesis that an impression exclusively produces memory. But you, the Naiyāyikas, have allowed an impression to transgress its normal law. We have not followed your foot-steps.'

The Naiyāyikas give an answer to the above charge. They say to the Sphoṭa-vādins, "How is that you have not allowed an impression to go beyond its normal activity ? You also admit that there is an impression that revives the memory of all letters at a time. The very same path which is adopted by letters to reveal the meaning of a word is also followed by them for the manifestation of a sphoṭa. You assume the hypothesis of an impression but over and above it you postulate the hypothesis of a peculiar sound. Thus, both of us agree to accept the hypothesis of impression. But we do not subscribe to the view that the only function of an impression is to revive memory. But we have only allowed an impression to transgress its limit and to produce the knowledge of the meaning of a word. But you have ab initio put forward the hypothesis of the world of a new pattern. You have postulated sphoṭa—a class of transcendental sound. You also assume that the said sphoṭa is distinct from letters and it is partless. How is it that your assumption does not suffer from cumbrousness ?"

Kumārila has also subjected the said hypothesis to a severe criticism. He says, "The Sphoṭa-vādins assume that a sphoṭa exists and distinguishes itself from letters. A word consists of parts. Hence, they should also postulate that a sphoṭa is partless. Hence, the assumption of impression which plays a necessary part in the production of the knowledge of the meaning of a word has no part to play in the manifestation of a sphoṭa." (Sphoṭa-vāda, Sl. 94). Kumārila's criticism in a nut-shell is this that the assumption of impression, on the part of the Sphoṭa-vādins. is superfluous.

The Naiyāyikas press the Sphoṭa-vādins hard. They review the arguments of the Sphoṭa-vādins. The Sphoṭa-vādins have held that when the initial letter is presented to our consciousness sphoṭa has become manifest and when the subsequent letters are known to us the awareness of the sphoṭa becomes distinctly vivid. They also cite an example. They hold that the manifestation of sphoṭa is like that of gem. The said example is not appropriate. Gem consists of parts. Hence all minute parts are not discovered by its first perception. Subsequent acts of perception reveal them. In this case subsequent acts of perception have some important part to play. But a sphoṭa is partless like a letter. Hence, the initial letter reveals it in its entirety. What part will the subsequent letter play ? A letter being partless, the partial manifestation of a letter is not possible. Similarly, a sphoṭa is not partially manifested since it is partless.

Kumārila has also said to this effect : 'If a letter is pronounced in a low voice, it is not heard at all. If it is loudly pronounced, it is distinctly heard. The whole of a letter is heard and nothing remains to be heard afterwards. The same rule applies to a sphoṭa. Either it is entirely known or it is not known at all.' (Sphoṭa-vāda Śl. 17).

The Sphoṭa-vādins have cited a second example in order to establish their hypothesis. They hold that though a group of Vedic hymns or a verse is presented to consciousness on its being heard for the first time yet it is very clearly and vividly known when it is repeatedly heard. Similarly, though a sphoṭa is manifested by the first letter of a word yet it will be more vividly revealed by the other letters. The example, cited by them, bears no resemblance to a sphoṭa since it is absurd to think that a group of hymns or a verse consists of no parts. Some parts are letters and some other parts are words. The first awareness fails to grasp them all. When they are heard again and again they are retained and are clearly and distinctly known to us. Thus the distinct knowledge of a group of hymns or a verse refers to its parts. But a sphoṭa is partless like an individual letter. Hence the awareness of a sphoṭa knows no different degrees of vividness. It remains always the same. Therefore, the example in question is not appropriate.

The refutation of the hypothesis that a sphoṭa is manifested by a dhvani.

Those who hold that dhvanis manifest sphoṭas but not letters are not sound judges. They prefer this view because they think that they can avoid the very dilemma which besets the hypothesis that letters manifest a sphoṭa. The dilemma in question has been referred to in the last section. Though dhvanis which are very slow give rise to audible letters yet they fail to manifest sphoṭas. Again when we wish to pronounce words very quickly words thus pronounced, convey no meaning since letters, contained in each word, are not distinctly grasped. The drive of this criticism is this that if dhvanis had manifested sphoṭas then both slow and fast dhvanis would have alike manifested sphoṭas.

Now, the upholders of this hypothesis may contend that dhvanis, in order to manifest sphoṭas, hold up indistinctly pronounced letters with the help of organs of speech and the air just as we keep down a sword, a dirty mirror etc. which exhibit a distorted image of a face such as the dark complexion, the unusual length etc. The above contention is not tenable. There is no justifiable cause for the appearance of such letters since the letters good or bad are presented to our uncontradicted experience. But a sphoṭa which is distinct from letters is never presented to our consciousness. If one holds that an object which is not experienced exists and an object which is experienced does not exist then he talks like one who says that horns exist but a hare does not exist. The new path which has been adopted by you is not less cumbersome. Śabara, the commentator on the Mīmāṁsā sūtras, has rightly remarked that if sphoṭas are assumed then two assumptions are to be made viz. dhvanis and sphoṭas are to be postulated. Moreover, the letters are assumed to manifest a sphoṭa which will also follow them to communicate the meaning of a word. In other words, the hypothesis of a sphoṭa has in no way an advantage over the hypothesis that words communicate meanings. Hence there is no need of postulating the hypothesis of a sphoṭa.

The other thinkers i.e., the Mīmāṁsakas, hold that as letters survive even after their presentation to consciousness so they communicate meanings without requiring the help of impressions. But we do not subscribe to this hypothesis since letters are transient. It is illogical to think that letters persist to exist even after their presentation to consciousness. According to our training we know that letters communicate meanings. They do their function as they have been observed before to do it. Kumārila has also said to this effect :

"As many letters, arranged in a particular order etc."

This hypothesis has been viewed with disfavour by the Sphoṭa-vādins. They ask "How many letters, being arranged in which particular order, do convey meanings ?" We are poor fellows. We shall not be able to give the right answer. Please ask your own consciousness. It is a very trifling objection. We should not think much of it. You have also said that either letters may communicate meanings even if they violate the temporary order of their arrangement or if the said order of letters is necessarily required then a sphoṭa should be the temporary order of letters. Such a suggestion is not sound. A temporary order is nothing but the different strokes of time. A sphoṭa cannot be identical with the different strokes of time. The temporary order of letters does not independently communicate a meaning. Again, the temporary order of objects other than that of letters does not also communicate a meaning. But such an order, belonging only to letters, communicates a meaning. Kumārila has also discussed the problem thus :-

There are two alternative suggestions viz. (1) Does the mere order of letters (i.e. not the letters themselves) convey the said sense ? Or, (2) do the letters arranged in an order of succession convey it? Though these two alternative suggestions are possible yet the second one is the true hypothesis. In other words, the letters arranged in an order of succession but not the mere order of succession convey the sense of a word. The order of succession which belongs to the letters thus arranged renders its assistance to them to communicate a meaning. There is no need of logical demonstration to establish it since the said order of succession is nothing but the property of the said letters. Hence, the very letters which have been noticed to convey a particular meaning, being arranged in a particular order of succession, will also convey the same meaning, being arranged in the same order. Thus, a sphoṭa is not an inference. We do not infer it as we do a cause from an effect. It is not also a presumption. We do not presume the hypothesis of a sphoṭa in order to explain the knowledge of meaning. So we establish our point.

The refutation of the hypothesis that a sphoṭa is perceptible.

The sphoṭa-vādins have also argued that as it is generally admitted by usage that a meaning has been communicated by a single śabda so the usage in question points to the hypothesis of sphoṭa. Such an argument is not sound. If letters communicate a meaning in accordance with the law stated before then the above usage holds good.

Now, the sphoṭa-vādins take an exception to the above solution. The word 'śabda' does not denote an impression (saṁskāra). In this world it is not well-known that the word 'śabda' denotes an impression. No body can prove by means of any method that the said word denotes an impression. A person, ignorant of the meaning of a word, learns the meaning of a word when he is instructed by another person in its meaning. If the word 'Śabda' signifies an impression then it is never noticed that the impression, belonging to a person, generates the knowledge of another person. No body can detect such a causal relation since an impression is a transcendental object. Now, the critics of the Sphoṭa-vādins may hold that the word 'śabda' stands for letters. Now, a question arises in our mind. Does the word 'śabda' mean each individual letter or an aggregate of letters? If it signifies each individual letter then the word 'śabda', should communicate no meaning since an individual letter conveys no meaning. Moreover, it should not denote an aggregate of letters since the word 'śabda' is a class name, i.e. a common noun. If we use proper names in the dual or plural number then a common noun in the singular number cannot be used as a case in apposition with either of them. Verbal usage like the following is never seen. Verbal usage "Yajñadatta and Devadatta are a man", "Dhava, Khadira and palāśa are a tree" etc. is conspicuous by its absence in the literature. Similarly, the verbal usage that 'g', 'au' and 's' are a Śabda is never seen.

Now, the critics may contend that as the word 'forest' denotes a collection of trees so the word 'Śabda' signifies a collection of letters. As the verbal usage that a forest is trees is seen so the usage that a śabda is 'g', 'au' and 's' will be appropriate. Such a contention is not tenable. The above example illustrates the relation of identity in difference, holding between the subject and the predicate. In certain cases, we notice identity. But there are also cases which clearly indicate difference. A collection is held to be identical with the objects collected under it. Some verbal usages point to this direction. But there are some other usages which point to the fact that there is difference between a collection and the objects collected. The examples, viz., the forest of mangoes and the forest of wood-apples, clearly indicate their difference. But there is no single instance which refers to the difference of a Śabda from letters. The verbal usage, viz., this is a Śabda of 'g' 'au', etc. is conspicuous by its absence.

Again, you may contend that the word 'forest' points to the identity of the aggregate of objects with the objects included in the aggregate since a verbal usage that the mango trees are nothing but a forest is noticed. A sentence that the letters 'g' etc. are nothing but a Śabda will also be put to use. But such a verbal usage is not noticed. Again, we distinguish the mango trees etc. from a forest. We do not employ the word 'forest' if we intend to convey a particular mango tree. It is well-known that words 'forest' etc. are nouns of multitude. If this is so then one may in a figurative sense think of the identity of the meaning of the word 'forest' i.e., an aggregate of trees with the particular trees such as a mango tree etc. Thus, the sentence that mango and other trees are a forest may be employed. But, in the above case, the letters 'g' etc. cannot be distinguished from a Śabda. So we never use a sentence that this is a Śabda of letters 'g' etc. Therefore nobody can even in a secondary sense think of the identity of the particular letters 'g' etc. with 'Śabda' which denotes the multitude of all letters. Thus, those who hold those letters are Śabda cannot fairly justify the usage that Śabda communicates a meaning.

Now, the critics of sphoṭa-vādins give a reply to the above criticism. They hold that they should not bother to discuss the problem whether the word 'Śabda' may be appropriately or inappropriately employed to denote the individual letters 'g' etc. It matters little if it exactly denotes such letters. It is also of little importance if it does not exactly denote such letters. The reason behind our remark is this that mere verbal usages current in the world do not establish the existence of things. O rival thinkers—Sphoṭa-vādins : the authors of sciences of philology also corroborate our thesis. The grammarians hold that a verb denotes an action. But they do not hold that sphoṭa, represented by a verb, denotes an action. Even if we take into consideration the practice of the authors of several sciences then the existence of a sphoṭa which is not based upon sound proof cannot be admitted. Can we identify popular usage with any proof ? We have already refuted the thesis that a sphoṭa is an influence. We shall also prove that a sphoṭa is not perceived. A sphoṭa lies beyond the range of other proofs. Therefore the Sphoṭa-vādins take vain pride in citing the popular usage "A Śabda communicates meaning to us". They should forget it.

If we uphold the thesis that a letter communicates a meaning then the said popular usage stands justified. The reason is as follows. The last letter accompanied by the impressions of the preceding letters conveys meaning. If this is the thesis then the use of singular number in the word 'Śabda' is logically tenable since the letter in question is a Śabda and has singular number. The thesis that letters, referred to by a recognitive judgment, communicate meaning suffers from no defect since the word 'Śabda' is not employed here to denote such letters as are individually taken into consideration. Let us take a concrete example e. g., the word 'gauḥ'. The collection of letters 'g', 'au' and 's' which is not other than the word 'gauḥ' communicates a meaning. A word which denotes a collection has singular number. It may be used as a predicate of a subject which has plural number. (In Sanskrit grammar there is no hard and fast rule that the subject and the predicate of a proposition should have the same number. So, the proposition that such and such letters are 'śabda' is quite appropriate. Here, the word 'Śabda' denotes a collection of letters. It has singular number. It may be predicated of the subject, such and such letters. Moreover we come across verbal usages like the following, "The vedas are the authority on this matter" etc.). Moreover, the mention of the statement, "We make out a meaning from Śabda" is highly illogical on the part of the Sphoṭa-vādins. The word 'Śabda' does not denote 'sphoṭa'. In other words, sphoṭa does not constitute the primary meaning of the word 'śabda'. No linguists are seen to employ the word 'Śabda' to denote a sphoṭa as they are noticed to use it in the sense of a letter. The Sphoṭa-vādins may contend that Śabda is defined as the indicator of an object. This contention is hardly tenable since the definition is too wide. Smoke which points to fire should also be denoted by the word 'Śabda'.

Now, the Sphoṭa-vādins, having reflected on the problem from its initial stage, may revise the said definition and hold that Śabda is such as being audible indicates an object. (This definition shows an improvement upon the previous one since it does not apply to smoke and similar other indicators. None of these objects is audible. Hence, the defect of being too wide is overcome). But this definition is not applicable to a sphoṭa since a sphoṭa is not audible. Moreover, some portion of the definition is superfluous. The definition should be like this "What is audible is Śabda". This amended definition is competent enough to distinguish Śabda from all other objects. Hence, the shorter definition is logically sound. The definition in question should not consist of two elements necessary and superfluous. Letters are only audible but no other objects. Therefore letters are only Śabda. A sphoṭa is not Śabda. Kumārila has also directed his criticism against the sphoṭa-theory thus.

Letters independent of one another are distinctly grasped by our auditory sense-organ. Neither the constituent factor of a letter nor a sphoṭa is presented to auditory sense-perception."

Now, an objection may be raised against the above definition. If the definition of Śabda is this "What is audible is Śabda" then it also becomes too wide since it applies to the universal of existence (sattā). The above objection is not tenable. The intended difinition is this "What is only audible is Śabda." The adverb 'only' which denotes exclusion has not been appropriately given since śabda is not exclusively heard by means of ears. Ears require the co-operation of manas (the internal organ) to hear Śabda. Hence, no purpose is served by the above exclusion. Such an objection is not tenable. The intention of the said exclusion is to distinguish the instrument of this sense-perception from all other such homogenous instruments. Thus, the definition implies that the sense-perception of Śabda is produced only by ears but not by such other sense-organs. Hence, eyes etc. are only excluded but not the internal organ viz., manas. Even if the amended definition is accepted then it remains still too wide since it is applicable to the universal of Śabda. Such an objection does not hold good. This defect will be easily mended if the clause 'is possessed of a universal' is added to the definition. Thus, the complete definition of Śabda is as follows :

"What is audible and is possessed of a universal is Śabda". (This is the correct definition of Śabda. It suffers from no defects. The universal of Śabda possesses no universal. Hence, the definition does not apply to it). The trend of this discussion from its very beginning requires the further qualification as has been proposed just now. This definition will not be too wide even if it applies to the thundering of clouds or to other inarticulate sounds since they all belong to the class of sound. Vātsyāyana, the author of Nyāya-bhāṣya, has stated that sound admits of two kinds viz., letters and inarticulate sound. The definition, "What is the indicator of an object is sound" is not a correct one. We have stated it before. We shall now controvert it and assign our reasons. Suppose an articulate sound reaches our ears. We are still ignorant of the relation of denotation. Hence, the above sound carries no sense. As it communicates no sense, it ceases to be sound since according to the said definition every sound points to an object. When the relation of denotation has been known to us after some time the same thing again becomes sound since it conveys now a sense to us. Therefore the above definition is not universal.

Again, we do not follow your intention behind the procedure of determining the true character of sound. Why do you imagine the identity of śabda with universal, attributes, actions etc. i.e., objects denoted by words ? Why does this misgiving arise in your mind ? Why do you refute the imaginary identity ? We fail to appreciate the value of your useless attempts. Why do you raise absurd propositions and refute them ? We have well understood that words are distinct from their meanings. Therefore what is audible is Śabda (sound). But a sphoṭa is not audible. Hence, those who hold that letters constitute words, sentence etc. and convey a meaning can only justify the popular view "We make out a sense from a sound (Śabda)". Hence the popular view goes in favour of the varṇa-vādins but does not favour the sphoṭa-vādins. This is our conclusion.

The sphoṭa-vādins join issue with the Varṇa-vādins. They raise an objection "Why do not you admit that a sphoṭa is audible ?" They also state that every body is aware of the fact that sound produces an awareness of common element which finds expression in the verbal sign 'a word, a sentence etc.' But they also point out that the auditory sense-perception produced by a sound, does not refer to letters. Such a hypothesis is not logically sound. The reason behind our criticism is as follows. Whenever we perceive individual cows, viz., Śābaleya, Bāhuleya etc. we recognise a common property in each of them and name it as the universal of cowness. Similarly, if we had recognised a word or a sentence in every letter then we would have admitted that a word or a sentence is a type of common property which belongs to every letter. But, as a matter of fact such an awareness does not occur to our mind. Let us illustrate another type of common property which belongs to each of its constituents. A piece of cloth is made up of threads. It inheres in each thread that constitutes it. When we have the first perception of a piece of cloth we perceive the whole without having the discriminative krowledge of its constituent factors. Similarly, do we hear a word or sentence without attending to each constituent letter one after another ? If we had heard a word or a sentence as a distinct whole without having the distinct auditory perception of each of its constituent letters then we would have gladly accepted the thesis "A word or a sentence stands on the same footing with a piece of cloth." As a piece of cloth is constituted by its parts so a word or a sentence is not framed by its parts. A word or a sentence does not inhere in letters. It is not a common whole which is shared by all letters. We do never grasp it as a whole at a time.

Now, the Naiyāyikas refute the thesis of the Sphoṭa-vādins. They state that the thesis of the Sphoṭa-vādins that if the word 'gauḥ' (a cow) is repeatedly heard then a persisting same element is perceived. They now criticise it and point out that the perception of a persisting same element owes its origin to an adjunct, viz., a single vowel. But if words consist of many vowels, e. g., Devadatta etc. then many letters are but slowly perceived by us. Thus, when a peace of cloth is presented to our consciousness its parts are not cognised as separate from its whole. Hence, when a word or a sentence is presented to our consciousness a same identical object is not grasped like a universal or a whole.

Now, the Sphoṭa-vādiṇs contend that consciousness which arises from the generic form of a word but not from its specific form is called the awareness of Sphoṭa. Now, the Naiyāyikas ask, "Do you hold that the universal of sound (soundness) is same as Sphoṭa ? They point out, you cannot answer in the affirmative: A Sphoṭa has a distinct entity. It is not identical with the universal of sound. A universal is called common property (sāmānya) because when a particular is perceived another particular of the same class is remembered. When we see a particular cow, called Śābaleya we remember another particular cow, named Bāhuleya. But, in the present case, if the letter 'g' is presented to our consciousness, the letter 'au' is not remembered. Hence, Śabdatva is not a universal. It is also to be noted that when letters, words and sentences are presented to our consciousness they all produce similar consciousness. This consciousness points to the same object, viz., the fact of being a sound. Therefore, a sphoṭa is nothing but a sound in general.

The critics of the Sphoṭa-hypothesis join issue with the Sphoṭa-vādins and subject the above suggestion to a severe criticism. They point out that some thinkers of the sphoṭa-school, being apprehensive of the existence of a sphoṭa, have hesitated to identify a sound in its generic character with the universal of sound. They have concealed the real thing and mystified it. But their apprehension has been misplaced. It is a truism that the universal of sound is not a sphoṭa. When each letter is cognised it is presented to our consciousness as a sound. A letter is not a sphoṭa. The consciousness of each letter refers to two elements—universal and particular. The universal element is constituted by the universal of sound, i.e., soundness. The above consciousness refers to no other common element. The piece of consciousness which is expressed in the verbal form 'sound' refers to the universal of sound but not to a sphoṭa. Jayanta has also conclusively proved the hollowness of the thesis that when a particular of a class is grasped by one another particular of the same class is necessarily remembered. Therefore, a sphoṭa is not referred to by such consciousness as is expressed by the term 'a sound'. Similarly, the awareness of a word and a sentence does not involve a reference to a sphoṭa. It has been rightly said that the knowledge of words and sentences bears the stamp of sameness because they conjointly produce one and the same effect. It resembles the knowledge of a forest or an army. It is a piece of knowledge which simultaneously refers to many objects. A sphoṭa does not bear a resemblance to a universal. Their distinction has been noted before.

The Sphoṭa-vādins hold that a word is presented to consciousness as identical with a sentence because they conjointly produce the same effect, viz., the communication of the same meaning. Such a hypothesis involves the fallacy of a vicious circle. The communication of the same meaning is at the root of the awareness of the identity of a word with a sentence. Again, the awareness of the identity of a word with a sentence is the source of the communication of the same meaning. It is not fair to overlook the above fallacy. It has been stated before that the aggregate of letters remembered and perceived helps to communicate the meaning of a word. It is not a universal rule that the knowledge of identity of a word with a sentence brings about the communication of a meaning. Therefore, how does the hypothesis of the critics involve the fallacy of a vicious circle ?

The Sphoṭa-vādins may now contend that if a word is not identical with a sentence then how is it that the consciousness of an object, denoted by a word, forms an integral part of a judgment, expressed by a sentence? The assumption that a word and a sentence are identical is a foolish one. If objects are identical or different then and then only their corresponding acts of consciousness are identical or different. If two objects are different, the corresponding acts of consciousness are identical but if the former two are identical then the latter two are also identical. It is a long-standing hypothesis that the acts of consciousness which refer to the same object are identical. It is not a law of Epistemology that if the conditions of acts of consciousness are different then the acts of consciousness are distinct from one another and if the said conditions are the same then the acts of consciousness are identical. Let us take an example. The conditions of the acts of perception of one and the same object, viz., the eyes, light and inner organ are different but they, in spite of their difference,generate such acts of perception as refer to the same object. If acts of consciousness are the same then the objects referred to by them should be the same But one cannot subscribe to the view that several acts of consciousness are same because one and the same word has produced all of them. If different judgments are similar then the object referred to by them is one and the same. But we should not think that they all are similar because they have been produced by one and the same sentence. Many consecutive letters convey an object as their meaning. But they do not point to the identity of a word with a sentence. The grammarians who are under the sway cf illusion think of the identity of a word with a sentence as a current view. Their illusion lies in their assumption that a word and its meaning are identical. We have established with strong argument that a word is absolutely different from its object. Our very experience contradicts the attributed identity of a word with its meaning. Hence, we do not accept such a theory. Therefore, we do not feel the necessity of discussing this subject. In fine, we say that a sphoṭa is not established by perception.

The Refutation of the Hypothesis that a Word or a Sentence is partless

A judgment refers to a unified whole of objects which are mutually related to one another. Two judgments will differ if their objects are different; and two judgments are identical if they refer to the same object. As these two epistemological rules are honoured, there is no inner difference in the meaning of a sentence. The object referred to by a sentence, should have its abstract identity. The critics admit that the relational object which constitutes the meaning of a sentence is a unified whole. But they point out at the same time that though the said object is a unified whole yet it admits of parts. But those who hold that a sentence conveys a partless whole have no sound theory of knowledge.

The question whether a part exists or not is highly impertinent. But sound thinkers should discuss the problem whether the meaning of a sentence consists of parts or of no parts.

In every sentence a word is distinguished from the sentence itself and the meaning of a word is differentiated from that of a sentence. If in a sentence its parts and their meanings are not distinctly grasped then the sentence remains unintelligible to us. Hence, in every sentence its parts and their meanings are presented to consciousness with their distinctive features. Now, the Sphoṭavādins may contend that a sentence and its meaning are partless and if they are grasped by us as having part then this knowledge is illusory. Such a contention does not hold good since a judgment which is contradicted is illusory but if it does not meet with contradiction, it is not illusory. One cannot pass his judgment on a piece of knowledge as illusory at his own sweet will. An illusion is not baseless. There must be some ground for its falsehood. The Sphoṭa-vādins should mention some ground for its falsity. They may say that the knowledge of a sentence having parts is false because it bears resemblance to an illusory judgment. The critics point out that they fail to detect a false judgment which it resembles.

If a sentence is well known as having parts and if another sentence having no parts, appears as consisting of parts owing to its resemblance to the first one then the knowledge of the second sentence may be called illusory. Now, the sentence in question is partless. It appears to be possessed of parts owing to its likeness to a sentence having parts. If the Sphoṭa-vādins argue in this way then they must admit that there is a sentence which has parts. But they do not make such an admission since they hold that all sentences are partless. Even in the body of a man-lion the two parts maintain their distinction and are presented to consciousness as distinct. Hence, a man-lion is not the instance of a partless whole. Hence, it must be admitted that there are parts in a sentence. In a picture the colour of red Arsenic is distinguished from that of vermillion. In a drink the taste of each ingredient such as Nāga-kesara etc. is distinctly felt. In different forms of music the different notes of a scale are distinctly heard. Therefore, these are not illustrations of partless wholes. Now, the Sphoṭa-vādins may cite a new type of illustration, viz., the awareness of a picture etc. The critics admit that such awareness is partless. They also point out that the knowledge of the meaning of a sentence is also partless since every form of consciousness is partless. But an object which is referred to by our consciousness and which is either an illustration or is illustrated is only possessed of parts. Hence, a sentence and its meaning are not partless.

Let the second thesis of the Sphoṭa-vādins be examined. From the usage of the experienced persons the relation of denotation obtaining between a word and its meaning is learnt but not that holding between a word and its meaning. We cannot express an idea by means of a word. The above thesis is not tenable since in order to know the relation of denotation holding between a sentence and its meaning the meaning of a word cannot be dispensed with. If a man is acquainted with words and their meanings then he can even make out the meaning of a sentence newly constructed. If by means of insertion and elimination the meaning of a word is not grasped then each sentence being an indivisible unit the number of sentences will know no limit. In that case one is to know the meaning of each sentence. As such it will be absurd to know the meaning of a sentence. In order to know the meaning of a sentence we must admit that a sentence is divisible into words and each word has its meaning.

The Sphoṭa-vādins have also stated that mere words are never employed and words, for this reason, enjoy no real existence. Such a thesis is not tenable. Let us cite a concrete case in support of our criticism. When a big complex sentence is employed, subordinate clauses are not independently used. Hence these clauses which constitute the said complex sentence turn out to be unreal. Now, the Sphoṭa-vādins may contend that these clauses are real in order to render the said complex sentence significant. Such a contention does not hold water. The Naiyāyikas will also hold that words are invariably employed in order to do the same function, i.e., to make the said sentence expressive. There are a few sentences the meaning of which is obtained through the context. Even, in these cases, words play an important part since they are uttered to convey such matters as are beyond the reach of a context: [The text is very corrupt in this paragraph. In order to have a consistent meaning we have made necessary corrections. We ask our readers to be careful and request them to examine our corrections. Now, the Sphoṭa-vādins make another suggestion in favour of their thesis. When a boy gets by heart a book he does not realise the result of his study. Similarly, when a sentence is read out one may not realise the distinct indiv duality of letters or words. In the face of this suggestion the Naiyāyikas strongly assert that letters and words must have a necessary place in a sentence just as parts of a chariot occupy a necessary place in the chariot though they cannot discharge its function. Now, it may be contended that parts of a chariot are necessary because they render some other service which a chariot cannot do. The Naiyāyikas say in reply that letters and words will also be capable of doing something which a sentence cannot do. The parts of a chariot make a partial contribution towards the function of a chariot. Do letters or words make any such contribution ? Yes, letters or words also make a partial contribution towards the function of a sentence. Some letters of a sentence are significant by themselves. Therefore, letters and words are not creatures of our imagination. They enjoy reality.

The Sphoṭa-vādins have also raised an objection that as words constitute parts of a sentence and letters are elements of a word, so letters should have also parts. Such an objection expresses the unprecedented scholarship of the said objectors. A jar is a whole consisting of parts. On that ground one cannot hold that an atom should consist of parts. One determines the nature of an object through cognition and non-cognition. An object possesses only such nature as is revealed through cognition. An object does not possess such nature as is not presented to our consciousness. Parts of a sentence and a word are cognised but those of a letter are not presented to our consciousness. Kumārila has also said to this effect.

If a letter is slowly uttered, it is not at all grasped. If it is distinctly uttered then it is grasped in its entirety. Kumārila means to say that if a letter had been a whole consisting of parts then some of its parts would have been grasped sometimes. He also states that nobody should postulate a whole having parts if its parts are never cognised. Therefore, letters are partless wholes. Therefore, it is a foolish statement that a letter should have also parts like a word or a sentence. Letters have no parts.

A sentence and its meaning are relational wholes because if the constituent words are present then the sentence in question is significant and if such words are absent then the sentence in question conveys no sense. If the same logic is applied then the conclusion that a word consists of parts is arrived at. It is also understood that the stem of a word and its suffix are real. These parts of a word are not merely imaginary. In the inflectional words 'vṛkṣam' 'vṛkṣeṇa' etc. the stem has the same meaning but the case-endings are different. In the inflectional words 'vṛkṣam', 'ghaṭam etc. the stems have different meanings though the case-ending has the same meaning. In those cases the meaning which a particular word denotes is expressed by it (the word). The above conclusion has been unmistakably established. How can one say that these parts are unreal ?

The Sphoṭa-vādins have argued in favour of the reality of a

sphoṭa that though the words 'kūpa', 'sūpa', 'yūpa' etc. contain many similar letters yet they do not convey the same meaning. They draw the conclusion from the above premise that the possession of the same letters does not help to communicate the meaning of a word. The drift of this argument is that the letters, contained in a word, do in no way contribute towards the communication of the meaning of the word. Such a conclusion is contrary to reasons. Every word has its fixed meaning. The mere presence or absence of similar letters does not help to convey a meaning which a word does not denote. If only similar letters had determined the meaning of a word then the words 'kūpa' etc. would have conveyed the same meaning. But a word conveys only the same meaning as is denoted by it. A word which is not denotative of a meaning does not convey it. Our experience points to the conclusion referred to just now. Now, by the joint method of agreement and difference we determine that this word denotes this meaning. If, in a particular case, the constituent letters of a word are similar then it will not be reasonable to enforce the conclusion that in other cases all constituent letters are similar though some of them are not so. (Jayanta means to say that in words 'kūpa', 'sūpa' and 'yūpa' the letter 'u', 'p' and 'a' i.e., the 2nd, the 3rd and the last one are similar but the initial one of each word is different. Hence, one cannot hold that all letters are similar. (Therefore, the above words do not convey the same meaning.) If a heap of dust moves along with a row of ants then the latter is not the cause of the former. With this remark the Sphoṭa-vādins take an exception to the hypothesis of the Naiyāyikas. (They mean to say that though a meaning is related to a word yet the constituent letters of the word do not contribute towards the communication of the same meaning.) Such an objection is pointless. Sometimes a heap of dust is raised by the hoofs of horses. It is also noticed that a row of ants is rendered motionless by such a heap of dust. Hence, one cannot arrive at the conclusion that a group of letters does not condition the communication of the meaning of a word. We do not definitely know the exact cause of the above heap of dust since it may be raised by horses or by young camels or by elephants. If a condition is wrongly stated of the above effect, viz., the heap of dust then the critic may find fault with the above suggestion. But still it is unmistakably true that the said heap of dust has been raised by many animals since heaps of dust which have been raised either by horses or by camels or by elephants are similar. Therefore, animals have raised the above heap of dust.

The Sphoṭa-vādins have argued that as the words like 'aśva-karṇa', etc., have lost the sense of their constituent words (aśva and karṇa), so the other compound words may also imitate them. In other words, they suggest that the formation of compound words is futile. They hint at the hypothesis that words have no parts. (The word 'aśva' means a horse and the word 'karṇa' denotes an ear. But the word 'aśvakarṇa' denotes a species of tree. Thus, the meaning of the constituent words 'aśva' and 'karṇa' do not contribute towards the meaning of the compound word 'aśva-karṇa'. They generalise that all words are partless.) Such a hypothesis does not stand to reason. The word in question finds a place in the list of such words as convey conventional meaning only. The constituent words do not express their true meaning. A compound word in the above context expresses a distinct meaning. This is the law which governs the meaning of a word. According to this law the meanings of the components of a compound word have gone to the background. Accordingly, the meanings of the constituent words have been given up. If, in a particular context, the meanings of the constituent words have no part to play then it does not follow that the component terms of words like aśva-karṇa, etc., will never convey their meanings. The words 'aśva' and 'karṇa' convey their sense when they remain either compounded or uncompounded. But if the compound word formed by them expresses a conventional meaning then its constituent words lose all their significance. Let us illustrate the point that the components of the compound word 'aśva-karṇa' are significant when they do not form a compound word. Ride a horse (aśvamāroha). There is an ear-ring on the ear (karṇe kuṇḍalam). The words 'asva' and 'karṇa' are also expressive of meaning when they are compounded. The compound word 'aśvakarṇaḥ' is expressive of its meaning, viz., the ear of a horse. Thus, we see that component words which constitute a compound word are not absolutely meaningless.

The Sphoṭa-vādins have also stated that the analysis of a word into its elements is not logical since the interpreters agree to differ from one another with regard to the said analysis of a word. Hence, the division of a word into a stem and a suffix does not hold good. This criticism is not sound. As a person places his confidence in the statement of the authoritative persons, so the illustration "tri-muni Vyākaraṇam" admits of an analysis. This analysis gets the approval of Pāṇini. So it is true but not imaginary. In many details of analysis the interpreters agree. They only differ from one another in vikaraṇas (signs of the different classes of verbs), etc. Such differences are insignificant. Therefore, the analysis of a word into its stem and suffix is really true. One cannot suggest a novel analysis by mere imagination.

The Sphoṭa-vādins have also offered another criticism which points to the difficulty of analysing a sentence. They cite an example "kālenadantināgāḥ" in support of their criticism. There are two sentences "kālena dantināgāḥ" and "kāle nadanti nāgāḥ". But it is very difficult to find out the constituent words of these two sentences since letters which compose these words are the same. Such a criticism does not stand to reason since difference between the two words constituted by the same letters is detected by their varying accents. A section of grammar deals with accents. So, it is not difficult to learn words with their proper accents. Let us take an example 'sarāmaḥ'. It may be a verb or two distinct words (a pronoun and a noun) or a compound word. If it is a verb (sarāmaḥ-we go) then its accent is different from that of a noun. If the word 'sarāmaḥ' stands for two words, viz., 'saḥ' and 'Rāmaḥ' then words and their accents are different. If it is a compound word denoting one co-existing with Rāma then the word itself and its accent are also different. The contending party will also be able to note these differences. Hence, it is easy to understand the analysis of a sentence.

The Sphoṭa-vādins have also stated in continuation of their criticism that in the examples "Dadhyatra", "Madhvatra", etc. the original words have undergone euphonic changes and do not retain their original forms. How is it that they convey their meaning though they are not perceptible in their original forms? Such a deviation from their original form is not open to a serious defect. These two words have only undergone partial changes since they are recognised. The above defence has been offered by a section of logicians.

The other logicians hold that the words 'Dadhi' and 'Madhu' respectively end in vowels 'i' and 'u'. Though they respectively end in 'y' and 'v' yet they will convey the same sense as is denoted by the original words. This is the teaching of the science of grammar that the words 'dadhy' and 'madhv' will respectively convey the same meaning as is respectively expressed by the words 'dadhi' and 'madhu'. Hence, the words, in spite of their euphonic changes, will convey their meaning. No defect will arise from the said euphonic change. Let us stop here since it is fruitless to prolong such discussion.

We, the Naiyāyikas, have got something more to add in this connection. If words are merely imaginary then why do the ancient servants take so much pain to explain the growth of the consciousness of words? The critics think that imaginary objects are also means to the real things. They cite examples in order to prove their hypothesis. They hold that false snake-bite and similar imaginary events bring about the effects of actual ones. If the examples are critically examined then we see that, truly speaking, false snake-bite is not the cause of the state of unconsciousness. It is the apprehension of taking poison that is the cause of such state. An apprehension is a form of consciousness. It is not true that consciousness does not produce an effect. Moreover, an act of consciousness is not an imaginary object. Thus, a cause produces an effect. The drift of this argument is this that words are real.

The Sphoṭa-vādins also state that scripts are false but produce the consciousness of the real objects. It is a foolish statement. Written letters are nothing but lines drawn on writing materials. These lines in themselves are not false. When they are taught by the trustworthy teachers such as khaṇḍika, a reputed teacher mentioned in the ancient literature, the disciples receive proper training and have deep-rooted impression of these scripts. When they see these lines they infer letters. They have been initiated into the relation of invariable concomitance holding between scripts and letters. Hence, whenever they see scripts they infer letters. When a boy, thus initiated, reads written scripts he at first infers letters and later on grasps the meaning of words. Therefore, imaginary objects are not means to real ends. Why does one mistake a line for a letter ? The reason behind this mistake is this that one sees probans but takes it to be probandum in a figurative sense. Examples in support of this view may be cited. We measure a quantity of fried barley powder with a certain weight. We say that this is such and such weight (say prastha). The letter 'g' is inferred from a particular line. We hold that the particular line is the letter 'g'. If our opponents do not subscribe to this view then an ignorant person who is innocent of scripts should make out a sense out of lines, i.e., a written word since lines which pass under the namse of unreal letters exist. But, as a matter of fact, such a person gathers no sense from the above lines. Therefore, one grasps the meaning of a word after having inferred letters from lines. One is habituated to such inference. The different processes of inference occur in the subconscious mind since they take place very quickly. The intervening time-gaps between these processes are beyond the range of knowledge. If one does not subscribe to this hypothesis then he cannot explain how a sense is gathered from a few lines. As words and their meanings are real so a sentence and its meaning are not partless wholes. This is our final conclusion. You have embraced the path of concealing the constituent words and the constituent letters of words of a sentence but tried to point to Śabda Brahman as the only reality. We shall discuss this topic in a detailed manner later on.

You have admitted the three broad divisions of a sentence. We agree to differ from you in this point. We admit the existence of Vaikharī vāk only since Vaikharī vāk is well known as a sentence (Vaikharī—articulate).

The vāk which has been designated by you as madhyamā is nothing but the mental resolution. It is a form of consciousness. It is not a division of a sentence. An act of consciousness which is expressed in language and refers to its corresponding object does not give up its own character, i.e., the characteristic feature of consciousness.

The form of vāk which is called Paśyantī bears the title Indeterminate perception. The Naiyāyikas consider it to be so. All forms of consciousness are not invariably associated with words. In other words, all sorts of consciousness are not necessarily associated with words. When an act of consciousness which reveals an object comes into being, it may be or may not be so associated. But an act of consciousness which is not so does never fail to reveal its object even if its name is not known.

The concluding portion of the refutation of the Hypothesis of Sphoṭa

Let us now refrain from the discussion about the Absolute and discuss the point at issue.

The letters which are objects of our distinct awareness are not imaginary. They constitute words which make up a sentence. They are conditions of the comunication of meaning. A sphoṭa which is distinct from letters is not presented to our auditory perception. A sphoṭa which has been undermined by ill luck cannot convey a sense.

The meanings of words condition the meaning of a sentence

Thus the hypothesis of a sphoṭa being refuted the hypothesis that letters convey the meaning of a sentence comes to the forefront. Some critics take an exception to it. They say, 'Let letters convey the meaning of a word. But they are incapable of conveying the meaning of a sentence'. Now, an objection arises in our mind. It is this 'How is the meaning of a sentence conveyed? In order to meet this objection they suggest that the meanings of words which constitute a sentence help to convey the meaning of the said sentence. They explain the raison detre of their hyphothesis thus. Letters exhaust all their powers when they convey the meaning of a word constituted by them. No power is left to them to convey the meaning of a sentence. But the power of word-meanings remains unexhausted to communicate the meaning of a sentence. Hence, they convey the sense of a sentence. The potential energy of letters is assumed by us by means of implications. As we cannot otherwise explain the communication of the meanings of words so we assume that letters have potential energy to convey the meanings of words. But the communication of the meaning of a sentence does not necessarily require letters as its condition. Hence, we should not assume the hypothesis that letters have potential energy to convey the meaning of a sentence.

Another point of criticism flashes in our mind in this context. Do letters bring about one and the same impression in order to convey the meaning of a word and that of a sentence? Or, do they produce the two different sets of impressions in order to perform the above two effects? A verse which contains the above point runs thus: How can one and the same impression bring about two diverse effects? It is well understood that letters produce no new impression other than the known one.

As we can explain the communication of the meaning of a sentence in a different manner so there is no justification for the assumption that one and the same letter produces the different types of impressions. In the case of words when the last letter is perceived by us it is not very difficult for us to recollect its antecedent letters in their proper order since they have not passed away long ago. But in the case of a sentence, as some of the antecedent letters ceased to exist long before so it is very difficult to remember them in their due order. Hence, it is impossible and unprecedented to hold that such letters are recalled in memory and combined to form a sentence. Moreover, though words which compose a sentence are uttered at intervals yet they are experienced to convey the sense of the said sentence. In this case there is no chace of the recollection of the antecedent letters. For this reason letters do not contribute towards the communication of the meaning of a sentence. Another point may be added to the criticism in question. If letters are to convey both the meanings of words and sentences then do they do it simultaneously or successively? Now if these letters are uttered only once then it will be unreasonable to hold that they simultaneously discharge both functions since they are incapable of doing them (functions). If it is held that they sucessively convey the above two meanings then it will be unreasonable to hold that they convey the meaning of a sentence at first since the meaning of a sentence is never observed to be conveyed if the meanings of its constituent words are not known.

Now, the upholders of the above hypothesis may contend that letters convey the meanings of words at first and then convey the meaning of a sentence. But it is a matter of great regret that letters unnecessarily redouble their efforts to convey the meaning of a sentence since the meaning of a sentence is communicated as soon as the meanings of its constituent words are conveyed. Words fully exhaust their capacities in order to convey their meanings. Therefore, it is established that the meanings of words communicate the meaning of a sentence.

Moreover, it is learnt by the joint method of agreement and difference that the meanings of words precede the meaning of a sentence. A person who inattentively listens to words and fails to grasp their meanings does never comprehend the meaning of a sentence. But though a person does not listen towards yet he is acquainted with the meaning of a sentence provided that he is in a position to know the meanings of words through some other sources of knowledge.

One who sees the white colour of an object and hears sounds of neighing and trots knows that a white horse is running. But if a person is not acquainted with the meanings of words then he is never observed to comprehend the meaning of a sentence.

The above view has been presented by Kumārila in Ślokavārttika (Chapter on a Sentence verse 358). He intends to convey that a person beholds from a long distance the white colour of an object. He fails to identify it.

Then he hears its neighing. He infers from the sound that it is a horse. He also hears the sound of its trots. He also infers its motion. The said white colour is an attribute. Horseness is universal. The said motion is an action. They cannot float in the air. They require a locus i.e. a substance to stand upon. The coordination of an attribute, a universal and motion is possible since they are capable of being mutually related. Their mutual relation is well-indicated by the sentence, 'A white horse is running.' Words which constitute the above sentence are not presented to his consciousness. But the meanings of such words have been gathered by sources of knowledge other than auditory perception. The knowledge of the meanings of words contributes towards that of the meaning of a sentence. But the meaning of a sentence is never grasped without comprehending the meanings of words.

The knowledge of the meaning of a sentence invariably presupposes that of the meanings of words but does not necessarily presuppose that of words. Therefore, the knowledge of the meaning of a sentence cannot be effectuated by that of words.

The critics raise another point against the above hypothesis. The awareness of the meaning of a single word fails to condition the knowledge of the meaning of a sentence. Moreover, the totality of the awarenesses of all words which constitute a sentence does not invariably precede the knowledge of the meaning of a sentence. In some cases, such conditions assemble. Therefore, the relation between the said condition and the conditioned is not universal. The antecedence of the said condition is accidental and hence variable. Its variableness i.e., non-universality is a defect which prevents the awareness of the totality of meanings of all constituent words from being the condition of the knowledge of the meaning of a sentence.

Such an objection is not sound. The first part of the said objection is pointless since the upholders of the above hypothesis do not contribute to the hypothesis that the consciousness of the meaning of any single constituent word conditions the knowledge of the meaning of a sentence. On the other hand, they take share in this view, i. e., they deny the causality of such a condition. Though the condition viz., the totality of the awarenesses of all meanings of constituent words is variable i.e., non-universal yet the causal relation which has been pointed out to be defective is not really so. The reason behind this defence is this that the meanings of words do not require the help of the knowledge of universal concomitance to indicate the meaning of a sentence. Hence, the said defect of variableness which invalidates a mark takes no effect on it. The knowledge of the meaning of a sentence is not an inference. The canons which govern sound processes of reasoning do not apply to it. Though the meanings of all constituent words are not armed with the knowledge of universal concomitance yet they become combined with one another, taking into consideration mutual requirement, proximity and material non-contradiction (yogyatā). The mutual combination of the meanings of all words constitutes the meaning of a sentence. The meaning of a word, being related to those of other words, is equivalent to the meaning of a sentence. Thus, as the meaning of a sentence is conveyed through the agency of the meanings of constituent words so the knowledge of the meaning of a sentence is not a piece of verbal knowledge. Such a conclusion may be anticipated but does not turn out to be true. Words play an important part in bringing about such knowledge at the out-set. Hence, the knowledge of the meaning of a sentence is verbal. Words communicate their meanings. The consciousness of such meanings is followed by the knowledge of the meanning of a sentence. Therefore, the conclusion that the knowledge of the meaning of a sentence is verbal is free from all defects. Śabara has also said to this effect. He holds that words complete this task by communicating their meanings. As soon as the meanings of words are presented to consciousness, they generate the knowledge of the meaning of a sentence.

The Refutation of the Hypothesis that the Meanings of words Communicate the Meanings of a sentence

Let us now examine the hypothesis proposed in the precedent section. Meanings of words do not convey the meaning of a sentence. But a sentence conveys its own meaning. Then reason behind the above remark is as follows. It is well-known that this is the meaning of a sentence. Nobody says that this is the meaning of words. It is imagined that a word is a collection of letters, such a word which is no better than the collection of letters conveys its meaning. Similarly, a sentence which is an imaginary collection of words will also communicate its meaning.

Now, the upholders of the hypothesis under criticism may contend that there is no such sentence as is a collection of words and is distinct from the so-called constituent words. These words themselves are equivalent to a sentence. And they satisfy an obligation when they communicate their own meaning. It has been stated before that they exhaust all their power by fulfilling the above duty, and become absolutely impotent to convey the meaning of a sentence. This argument does not stand to reason since the meanings of words have also completed their task and have nothing to do. How do they fulfil an obligation ? They have completed their task by producing their own knowledge.

Now, the upholders of the hypothesis in question may contend thus : "Words have fufilled their obligation as they completely convey their own meaning. It has been stated that they convey the meaning of a sentence over and above their normal duty. To convey the meaning of a word is one thing and to convey the meaning of a sentence is another thing. How can a word discharge twofold duties which are distinct by their nature ? But our hypothesis does not suffer from this defect since the meaning of a word, having produced its own consciousness, does not engage itself in discharging some other duty. Hence, the meanings of words should convey the meaning of a sentence." The critics point out that the above contention is not logically tenable. The reason behind their criticism is as follows. The last word of a sentence has not fulfilled its mission as it has not some other task. The last word of a sentence, being benefited by the recollection of its antecedent words, is called a sentence. Some say that the meaning of the last word, being mutually related to the rest of its antecedent words, is known as the meaning of a sentence. Hence, the meaning of a sentence is conveyed only by a sentence.

Now, the contenders have taken an exception to the above suggestion. They put a few questions to the critics. Let us discuss some of them. Do words discharge double functions, viz., the communication of its own meaning and that of the meaning of a sentence on the strength of recollection which is due to a single impression ? Or, do they do these two duties by means of different impressions ? Let us clarify the purport of the questions. The knowledge of the meaning of each word produces an impression. One type of impression is represented by it. Another type of impression is produced by such knowledge as refers to the aggregate of all words, constituting a sentence. The well-known accepted principle is this that the diversity of effects points to the heterogeneity of their causes. In order to explain a particular effect a transcendental impression is assumed. If effects are different in their nature then many diverse transcendental impressions will be assumed in order to explain them. (Thus we see that the above questions are not hard nuts to crack. No gratuitous assumptions are made. The assumption of the two types of impressions is necessary. Such an assumption offers an answer to the above questions.)

The defenders of the hypothesis in question have also stated that it is impossible to recollect letters, passed away long ago. Such a statement is not logically sound. We may somehow imagine that as letters are contents of the knowledge of a word so words may be contents of the knowledge of a sentence. We shall immediately discuss this supposition.

Let us now turn our attention to another problem, viz., 'Do letters convey the meaning of a word and that of a sentence simultaneously or successively ?' We answer this problem thus. Letters discharge their function in this order. They convey the meaning of a word at first. Afterwards they convey the meaning of a sentence. Now, the upholders of the hypothesis under discussion may contend that the solution, offered by the critics, amounts to this that the meanings of words point to the meaning of a sentence. The above remark of the defenders in question is not logically tenable. The meaning of a word is an object of knowledge. It cannot be included in the source of knowledge. Moreover, the difference of the meaning of a word from that of a sentence is not absolute. Hence, the relation between an indicator and the indicated, which holds between smoke, accompanied by the relation of universal concomitance, and fire and between a lamp, unaccompanied by the relation of universal concomitance and the colour, does not obtain between the meaning of a word and that of a sentence. If the defenders of the above hypothesis judge it impartially then they will realise that an object cannot be both the illuminator and the illumined. Hence, their verbal statement that the meanings of words point to the meaning of a sentence is empty but not founded upon the rack of solid facts. If they contend that nature divides them into such two halves then they behave like the disciples of the Buddhists who hold that one and the same phenomenon by its very intrinsic nature plays the part of a mark and the object marked.

Now, the defenders of the hypothesis in question may contend thus : Words denote universals. A sentence points to a particular. There is a great gulf fixed between a particular and a universal. As a universal is not cognised without the medium of a particular so a universal points to a particular. Hence, a universal plays the part of an illuminator and a particular is illumined by it. As there is a real difference between an illuminator and the illumined, so a universal differs from a particular. The implication of the above contention is this that their suggestion is logically sound and they do not follow the foot-steps of the Buddhists in order to defend the above hypothesis.

Let us examine the above solution. We all accept the conclusion that there is a real difference between the meaning of a word and that of a sentence. But we also submit the following by way of criticism in this connection. If words which constitute a sentence cease to function then no meaning is conveyed by them. Just as the eyes do not reveal an object when they cease to function. Hence, the suggestion of the defenders, "As smoke and such other objects which are knowable objects point to fire and other objects so the meanings of words which are knowable objects point to the meaning of a sentence" does not hold good. Words, conveying their own meaning, are capable of communicating the meaning of a sentence. Why do you not follow the text of your own school. Kumārila has said to this effect.

When words function to communicate the meaning of a sentence as their main task they also convey their own sense which invariably precedes the final meaning just as a bundle of faggots emits flame in order to boil some articles of food. The sense of this statement is that words, having communicated their own meaning, convey the sense of a sentence.

The secondary operation of a cause does not interfere with its main operation. Words have two kinds of power to convey their meaning viz., (1) the power to convey the primary (etymological) meaning and (2) the power to express the inner meaning. Words exhaust their first type of power to communicate their own meaning. The second type of power is fully applied to express the meaning of a sentence.

Though words have fulfilled their mission, to some extent, communicating their own meaning yet they have not as yet completed their main task for which they have assembled. Thus, the knowledge of the sense of a sentence will not fail outside the scope of verbal knowledge. If words do not operate at all in order to convey the meaning of a sentence then the knowledge of such meaning does not surely come under the jurisdiction of verbal knowledge. If it is admitted that the knowledge of the meaning of a sentence is verbal because of its causal connection with the knowledge of words then one should also hold that it is also a piece of auditory sense-perception since it is indirectly connected with the auditory sense-organ. Let us now examine the critical remark of the defenders of the hypothesis under discussion. If they hold that the meaning of a sentence is communicated when words have completely ceased to operate then we fail to understand which kind of proof will effectuate the knowledge of the meaning of a sentence. The knowledge of the meaning of words is not perceptual since the meaning of a sentence is supersensuous.

The knowledge of the meaning of a sentence is not inferential since the propounders of the said hypothesis themselves have said that it is not an inference and elaborately refuted the affirmative view. Again, this knowledge is not verbal since words have completely ceased to operate. Universals are not known without particulars. Hence, a universal points to a particular. The drift of this line of argument is that the meaning of a sentence is known through presumption. Do the upholders of the said hypothesis say it in the affirmative ? If they say so then the very meaning looks like dharma which is revealed only through presumption. Such a conclusion is neither sound nor acceptable to you. Thus, the meaning of a word turns out to be the seventh source of true knowledge. Such a conclusion is not acceptable to you. Therefore the meanings of words do not determine the knowledge of the meaning of a sentence.

The defenders of the said thesis have stated that the joint method of agreement and difference reveals that the meanings of words are the source of the meaning of a sentence. Something may be stated on this point. The meaning of a sentence is not an independant reality. It is nothing but the meanings of words in their relational character. The meaning of a sentence is possible only when the meanings of words constitute it. There is no doubt about it. But the knowledge of the meaning of a sentence cannot be causally traced to the meanings of words. Words communicate the meaning of a sentence since words have not ceased to operate. When a man remains inattentive he does not listen to words since he, being attentive, says shortly after. "I have not heard your words as my mind was otherwise engaged. Please repeat them." If words had not conveyed sense then he would have made out the meaning of words, having recollected the words but would not have made a request to repeat them for his hearing. Therefore, the knowledge of the meanings of words lies at the root of that of the meaning of a sentence. But the meanings of words do not convey that of a sentence.

The defenders of the said thesis have said "One, seeing the white colour and hearing the neighing sound, comes to know that a white horse is running." They have made an observation in this connection that the said judgment is derived from the meaning of words but not from words. Such a conclusion is not convincing. Do we not see a white cow move ? Does no sentence convey the sense that a white cow moves. When we perceive her to move the resulting judgment that a white cow moves is a percept. The judgment in question is not the meaning of the sentence that a white cow moves. The judgment that white horse is running is deducive in its character just like the syllogism that there is fire on the hill. If a judgment flashes in our mind but a sentence is not heard before then we cannot say that the said judgment is the meaning of a sentence.

There is no need of prolonging this discussion.

The concluding Portion of the above Topic is that a Sentence Conveys its own Meaning

By means of an imaginative synthesis letters are combined into words and a sentence. Thus letters, having assumed the forms of words and a sentence, convey the meaning of words and a sentence. Therefore, the knowledge of the meaning of a sentence is not produced by the meaning of words. Such knowledge owes its existence to a sentence which has not ceased to operate.

How do letters constitute a word and a sentence ?

What is the hypothesis according to which letters constitute a word and a sentence by an imaginative synthesis and convey their sense ? Jayanta refers to it in order to solve the problem thus :—

The ancient teachers of the Nyāya school have framed the following hypothesis. At the out-set the initial letter is presented to our consciousness. When this consciousness passes away an impression which is produced by it survives. Then the second letter is grasped. The awareness of the second letter coupled with the impression of the first letter produces a more effective second impression. Afterwards the third letter flashes on the mind. The awareness of the third letter accompanied by the two previous impressions produces a more powerful impression of the third letter. As long as the last component letter of a word is not cognised, the inner process of framing impression will go on in this way. When the last letter is apprehended a strong impression is generated. An act of recollection recalls all antecedent letters in memory. The apprehension of the last letter passes away at the third moment of duration of the said recollection. Hence, the apprehension of the last letter is on the point of destruction at the second moment of duration of the said remembrance. The last letter which is an object of apprehension is on the verge of destruction and the group of letters which are recalled in memory constituted a word. Then the knowledge of the initial word produces an impression. Afterwards in accordance with the procedure of letters the knowledge of the second word arises in the mind. The knowledge of the second word coupled with the impression of the first word produces a very strong impression of the second word. Then, according to the order of apprehension, impression and recollection, the knowledge of the third word takes place. All the impressions previously strengthened and the knowledge of the third word cooperate to produce a more powerful impression. Thus, the modus operandi will continue unless and until the knowledge of the last letter flashes in our mind. The very powerful impression which comes into being immediately before the knowledge of the last word revives the memory of all antecedent words since the impression which is made strong immediately before the knowledge of the last word becomes exceptionally strong. The collection of words which consists of letters and one of which is known and the remaining ones are recalled in memory passes under the name of a sentence.

A sentence, having thus come into being, communicates its own meaning. One must admit that an impression produces another impression and an impression has skill in producing such impression. If one does not subscribe to this hypothesis then in all cases, the repetition of an act will become futile.

The Refutation of the above Hypothesis Regarding the Constitution of words and Sentences by letters

The critics take an exception to the above hypothesis and point out the following defects in it. They hold that the said solution is not satisfactory since if it is admitted then the simultaneity of the two acts of consciousness should be accepted. They, now substantiate their charge. As antecedent words are recalled in memory just after the presentation of the last word to our consciousness so the relation of denotation holding between a word and its meaning will also be at that very point of time recalled in memory since the meaning of a word will not be cognised if the relation of denotation is not remembered. Again, if the meaning of constituent words is not grasped then the meaning of a sentence will not flash in our mind. And without the remembrance of the relation of denotation the meaning of a word is not presented to consciousness. When we employ words to convey objects of every day occurrence the listener follows us without being consciously aware of remembering the relation of denotation holding between words and their meanings. Memory also subconsciously or unconsciously helps us when we infer an accustomed object. The inference of such an object is not preceded by the conscious process of recollecting the relation of universal concomitance. But one is compelled to admit that the relation of universal concomitance is somehow remembered. Similarly, we should also assume that the relation of denotation is subconsciously or unconsciously recalled in memory. The reason behind this assumption is this. An inhabitant of the cocoanut island who is absolutely innocent of the relation of denotation obtaining between a word and its meaning cannot make out the meaning of a word. As the apprehension of the relation of denotation has happened before so the recollection of the said relation renders the useful service. Therefore, the recollection of words antecedent to the last one and that of the relation of denotation simultaneously take place just after the presentation of the last word to consciousness. Thus the simultaneity of the two acts of consciousness unavoidably occurs.

Now, the defenders of the above hypothesis may contend that the remembrance of the antecedent words follows that of the relation of denotation. Thus, they try to evade the charge of simultaneity. The critics point out a fresh defect in the present solution. If this is their contention then they will admit that at the time of the recollection of the antecedent words the meaning of words flashes in their mind. Thus, the simultaneity of the two acts of consciousness takes place in another form. They cannot say "The meaning of words does not flash in the mind."

The reason is this that if all the conditions of an effect really assemble and the obstructive element is conspicuous by its absence then the appearance of the said effect cannot be prevented. Now, in order to face the charge of the simultaneity of the two acts of consciousness the defenders may suggest that the remembrance of all antecedent words will succeed the knowledge of the meaning of a word. If this is their contention then the sentence in question will surely be bereft of the last word since the auditory perception of the last word has passed away at that time. Let the point in question be clearly stated. When the relation of denotation obtaining between antecedent words and their meanings is recalled in memory the perception of the last word is on the point of destruction. And when the meaning of words is presented to consciousness the said perception of the last word has passed away.

The Refutation of the above hypothesis Regarding the constitution of words and sentences by letters

Now, the defender may argue in his defence that the last word continues to exist though it is no more presented to our consciousness. We say only by way of criticism, "May the elaborate system of Logic be safe !" (The critics suggest that such an admission contradicts all accepted hypotheses and invalidates the system of logic itself.) Again if it is held that the last word is not presented to consciousness though it persists then we simply put this question to them viz. "What service it render, thus persisting ?" He may say in reply to the question that it will be presented to our consciousness again. We put another question to him. The question is "What is the source of the second consciousness?" If the auditory organ once suspends its function then it does not resume its work. At least we have no knowledge of such working of the auditory sense-organ. Nobody has direct knowledge of an external object in and through mere introspection. The inner organ has no direct access to an external object. When it receives the aid of an external organ it is able to be aware of an external object. If the consciousness of the last word re-appears anyhow then the charge of the simultaneity of the two acts of consciousness stands irrefutable.

Moreover, all these antecedent words are mere empty sounds and as such they continue to exist as sounding brass and a tinkling symbol. Such unintelligible sounds, being remembered, convey no sense. What benefit do we derive from their recollection ? Now, if you (the upholder of the thesis under criticism) hold that those words along with their meanings are recalled in our mind then in every case the simultaneity of the two different acts of consciousness will be inevitable since an act of consciousness will surely be crossed by an act of remembrance, i.e., the remembrance of the relation of denotation. Therefore, the hypothesis of this type is highly inconsistent.

A Revised Hypothesis that Letters Constitute Words and Sentence in Another Way

Some interpreters represent the process of the word-building in a different manner. All letters are combined in a single unit to form the first word. The first word, thus formed, is presented to our consciousness at the outset. Then the relation of denotation is recalled in our mind. When the said relation flashes in our memory the consciousness of the first word is on the eve of destruction. During this state of crossing the antecedent act of consciousness, referring to the first word, produces another event of knowledge which points to such meaning as is denoted by the first word. Afterwards, the knowledge of the said meaning produces an impression. Then following the order of events stated above, the consciousness of the second word comes into being. Then, the relation of denotation holding between the second word and its meaning is recalled in our memory. The consciousness of the second word is on the eve of destruction at that time. At this stage of its life the immediate antecedent consciousness of a word, in co-operation with the remembrance of the relation of denotation, produces the knowledge of the meaning of the second word. The meaning flashes in our mind as determined by its own denotative word. The knowledge of the meaning of the second word, in co-operation with the impression of the knowledge of the meaning of the first word, makes a stronger impression. Now comes the turn of the formation of the third word. A few letters which consecutively follow one another are combined into a word. Thus, the third word is revived. It is presented to our consciousness. Again, the relation of denotation which obtains between the third word and its meaning is recalled in our memory. Again, the consciousness of the third word on the verge of its destruction, assisted by the memory of the relation of denotation, produces the knowledge of the meaning of the third word as determined by the third word. This knowledge in co-operation of its antecedent impression, strengthens the existing impression. Thus, the process of the growth of knowledge goes on unless and until the last word of the sentence is presented to our consciousness and its meaning is communicated. At last, the awareness of the last word produces the knowledge of its own meaning as determined by the denotative last word. Afterwards, the antecedent strong impression produces a judgment of memory which refers to all meanings as determined by the past words. The said judgment of memory and the judgment which refers to the meaning of the last word point to all words as determinant of their contents. The collection of words, thus revealed, constitutes a sentence. The meanings which are presented to our consciousness as denoted by these words constitute the meaning of the sentence in question. Thus, a collection of words and their meanings some of which are recalled in memory and some of which are directly experienced constitutes a sentence and the meaning of a sentence respectively.

The Review of the Alternative Hypothesis

The alternative hypothesis does not stand to reasons. When the meaning of the last word is known by us the last word is also presented to our consciousness as its determinant in the capacity of a denotative word. The word in question is undoubtedly one of the conditions of the knowledge of the said meaning. There is no divergence of opinion regarding the view in question. If the word is cognised, no body can deny existence to it. The word cannot cognise itself. It must be an object of some kind of cognition. Let us now define the exact nature of this cognition. What is its cause ? The cognition in question does not owe its existence to the auditory sense-organ. The first apprehension of the last word is perceptual. The perception in question is auditory. The auditory sense-organ, having produced the above perception of the last word, has become inactive with regard to the same effect. As it has been inactive so it cannot de novo produce that cognition which points to a word as a determinant of some meaning. We cannot directly introspect an external object with the help of our inner organ. If an external object had been directly introspected then all the words first, second and so on would have been thus introspected. In that case why do you say that they are recalled in memory ? As the last word is the cause par excellence of the knowledge of its meaning so it will also be the cause par excellence of such cognition as reveals itself as a determinant of a meaning. Such a hypothesis is contrary to reason since as a word is cognised, it is an object of cognition. One and the same thing cannot be both an object and cause par excellence of the same act. We have elaborately discussed this point in our definition of perception. We have also refuted the hypothesis that an object, qualified by its denotative word, is perceived. An elaborate refutation of this point is superfluous.

The Hypothesis that A Sentence Conveys its Own Meaning is Somehow Established.

Some other interpreters put forward an alternative suggestion. At first the first word is cognised. Then the relation of denotation holding between it and its meaning is recalled in mind. It is followed by the knowledge of its meaning. The knowledge of the meaning acts as a destructive agent of the cognition of the first word. [A law is honoured in the Vaiśeṣika system that a distinctive attribute of an all-pervasive substance is destroyed by its immediately succeeding attribute]. The auditory sense-organ, receiving the help of the cognition in question which is about to pass away, produces the cognition of the second word which is qualified by its immediately antecedent word. Thus the cognition of the second word comes into being. It is again followed by the recollection of the relation of denotation holding between the second word and its meaning. Then the knowledge of the meaning of the second word follows in its wake. It goes to destroy the cognition of the second word. The auditory sense-organ, co-operating with the cognition of the second word which is on the verge of destruction, produces the cognition of the third word as qualified by the second word in the capacity of its immediate predecessor. In this way the cognition of all the remaining words of a sentence appears. This process continues to work unless and until the last word is not cognised. When the cognition of the last word takes place the recollection of antecedent words is not more required as an accessory condition in accordance with the process of ideal construction mentioned above. The reason behind this statement is this that the remembrance of antecedent words yields such a result as is automatically established by the cognition of a word which is on the eve of destruction. The contribution of the said cognition towards the form of its immediate successor is this that an antecedent word is presented to our consciousness as qualifying its immediately succeeding word. Let us now see the result of the act of remembrance. When the last word is cognised all the antecedent words are also presented to our consciousness. The cognition of an antecedent word which is on the verge of destruction produces another cognition which refers to a relational whole in which the antecedent word qualifies its immediate successor-word. Thus, the arrangement of words in a definite order is worked out by the above cognition itself. What is the need of remembering all past-words? As an additional act of recollection is not required, there is no occasion for the simultaneity of the two acts of cognition. We have already mentioned how the cognition of the last word comes into being and presents its content to our consciousness. The cognition of the last word working out its effect in the way mentioned above, brings about the knowledge of the meaning of a sentence. Thus, the hypothesis that the meanings of the constituent words of a sentence imply the meaning of a sentence does not stand to reasons. Therefore, a sentence will convey its own meaning and the meanings of words will not point to the meaning of a sentence.

A Refutation of the Alternative Hypothesis

Some other interpreters subject the above hypothesis to severe criticism. They point out that the said hypothesis is not immune from defects. The second word is never cognised as being qualified by the first word. The cognition of the first word comes into being at first. It is followed by the recollection of the relation of denotation. This act of remembrance acts as a destructive agent to the cognition of the first word. The said cognition is now on the verge of destruction. When the meaning of the first word is conveyed to us the cognition of the first word has passed away. We are generally informed of a maxim that a piece of consciousness which has passed away renders no service favourable or unfavourable to any other event of consciousness.

Now, the upholders of the hypothesis may contend thus :— An act of consciousness which conditions another act of consciousness is opposed to the latter, as the former is destroyed by the latter. But we should also bear in mind that one act of consciousness is not necessarily opposed to another such act because the relation of the destroyer and the destroyed obtains between them. Such a statement is not sound because in some cases the relation of the destroyer and the destroyed does not hold between an act of consciousness and another act of consciousness. Though we admit the truth of the above critical remark yet we say "Let the relation of the destroyer and the destroyed be fixed between the cause-consciousness and the effect-consciousness." Though such a relation obtains between the said acts of consciousness yet the consciousness of a word is held to be the condition of the recollection of the relation of denotation just as an impression conditions the remembrance of the said relation. Because the said relation of denotation will not come into being if it is not conditioned by the cognition of a word just as it does not appear if an impression does not revive it. If it is held that the revival of an impression is the function of the said cognition then the cognition in question is surely the condition of the act of recollection since the former produces the latter through the intermediate process viz., the revival of impression. Thus, the three acts of consciousness viz., the cognition of a word, the remembrance of the relation of denotation, and the knowledge of the meaning of a word, are simultaneously present. Thus, they commit a serious blunder.

Moreover, the cognition of a word is not that of a partless whole. But it is an ideal construction of a series of consecutive letters since the hypothesis that a word consists of no parts has been refuted. We should also remember in this connection that two or three, or three or four, or five or six letters constitute a word, these letters are consecutively presented to our consciousness, and the consciousness of each letter comes into being and passes away in a consecutive order. All the letters which constitute a word are never simultaneously presented to our consciousness. The cognition of the last word turns up in this way. The cognition in question does not endure long. The antecedent ones among letters which constitute the last word will also pass away. Hence how does a judgment present its content in which the last word is a subject and its antecedent word is a predicate qualifying it ? They build castles in the air.

A sentence conveys its sense even if its constituent words are uttered at interval of time. The master of a house who is busy with various calls of duty directs the attention of his servant, uttering his name "Kaṇḍālaka" and then attends to some other business. Having finished it he says "On my horse". Another call of business interferes with his order. He pays his attention to it. Having completed it, he says again "Put harness". Having done something else he says again "And bring him." But his servant follows the sense of such a sentence viz., "Oh Kaṇḍālaka put harness on my horse and bring him". It is impossible from your point of view to make out the meaning of the sentence in question since an antecedent word does not qualify its succeeding word and all words of a sentence are not called up.

Moreover, as the followers of the master logician (Pravara) hold these logicians also subscribe to the thesis that a judgment which is relational in character does not refer to its subject and predicate. But it refers only to the subject. The distinction of the awareness of a mere successive word from that of a successive word following an antecedent word is explained by the diversity of their conditions.

Though the antecedent word qualifies its succeeding word yet it is not presented to our consciousness. Hence, the second word is only grasped by our consciousness. If this is so what is the good of admitting that an antecedent word qualifies its succeeding one ?

The suggestion that an antecedent word does not qualify its succeeding word does not hold water since the relation of denotation which obtains between the second word and its exclusive meaning has been only recalled in mind. The word has been employed, in some cases, to convey its own meaning. But it is, now, qualified by another word. But the meaning of the second word as qualified has been never grasped. Hence such a qualified meaning cannot be communicated. Let this discussion be stopped. This speaks of the unprecedented scholarship of Śaṅkara Svāmin.

Jayanta's own theory regarding the communication of the meaning of a sentence by itself is established

An objector comes up and points out "If all suggestions,

put forward by the expert logicians, are defective then you should frame a better and defectless hypothesis and place it before us." Jayanta says in reply to the above remarks, "We cannot suggest a novel theory which is highly original. Short-sighted as I am, I cannot discover even a blade of grass which my predecessors, logicians of keen insight, have failed to take notice off."

Now, you may put a question to me viz., "Why do you entertain an ardent desire for composing a logical treatise—a sphere of rational thinking of the great scholars ? My humble reply to this charge is that the ardent desire, referred to, does not invite criticism and an advice, given by others to relinquish it, will take no effect on me.

The king of Kashmere has confined me in a solitary cave—a prison cell. I have been passing my days in pleasure of composing the book in question.

Though it is a recreation to me yet, I should explain how the constituent letters communicate the meaning of a sentence, constituted by them.

Our humble suggestion on this point is as follows. The recent or remote destruction of objects which are recalled in mind does not condition our memory. It is an impression which is only responsible for memory. The objects which are remembered may have passed away recently or long ago. But their passing away does not affect the impression in question in the least. In conformity to the law of memory all antecedent words which had passed away long before and had been uttered at a long interval left an impression on our mind. This impression will revive memory. Now, if we admit that earlier words are called up and the last word is directly apprehended then we are to face the charge of the simultaneity of the two acts of consciousness. In order to avoid this problem we should rather admit that the remembrance of the last word takes place immediately before the communication of the meaning of a sentence. All the words of a sentence, being recollected, will convey the meaning of a sentence. To this effect we make the following suggestions. At the outset we cognise the first word which is a combination of some consecutive letters. It is followed by the recollection of the relation of denotation together with the impression, left on our mind, by the cognition of the first word. We suggest that the said recollection and the said impression simultaneously appear in our mind. The hypothesis of the simultaneity of the two acts of cognition has been disapproved by the recondite logical treatise but compresence of two mental phenomena, such as an event of cognition and an impression, has not been disfavoured. The knowledge of the meaning of a word follows in their wake. It also leaves an impression on our mind. Then we again combine a series of consecutive letters and construct the second word. We cognise it. Then we remember the relation of denotation which holds between it and its meaning. At the same time the cognition of the second word receiving the co-operation of its antecedent impression produces a stronger impression. Again, just as the earlier two series of consecutive letters have been combined to form the first two words so the third series of consecutive letters are combined to form the third letter. The third word is now presented to consciousness. The relation of denotation obtaining between it and its meaning is also called up. Receiving the help of its antecedent impression a stronger impression of this word and that of the knowlege of its meaning came into being. In this way the cognition of a word produces a deeper impression and the knowledge of the meaning of a word, also, produces a similar impression. All these impressions survive in our mind. Our subconscious mind is a store-house of all such impressions. In this mental background the last word of a sentence is presented to our consciousness. This consciousness is followed by the remembrance of all words as the impressions of all words survive in our mind. The impressions of the meanings of words revive their memory. As the impressions of words precede those of their meanings so these two sets are successively recalled in accordance with the order of their succession. The collection of words which are recollected constitutes a sentence. The other assemblage of meanings which are recalled constitutes the meaning of a sentence.

Now, a fresh objection arises. As recollective knowledge per se is erroneous so the knowledge of the meaning of a sentence, being representative in character, is not true. Such an objection does not hold good since the representative knowledge of a meaning in question perfectly accords with the direct acquaintance of the relation of denotation of a word. If we know that this word denotes this particular object but remember that it denotes something else then our remembrance is faulty. Just as if we know that smoke is the right probans of fire i.e., the relation of universal concomitance holds between smoke and fire but infer fire, seeing mist then our knowledge is wrong. But in the present case the consecutive letters have been recalled in that very order of succession in which they have been presented to our consciousness at the time when the relation of denotation holding between the word, constituted by these letters, and its meaning has been taught. So, the hypothesis suggested by us, suffers from no defects. Representative knowledge which immediately follows a presentative one bears a close resemblance to the latter.

There is no need of entertaining the suggestion of judgments of memory. When the meaning of the last word is known to us a judgment of introspection will arise. It will refer to all words and their meanings. It will resemble the referential knowledge of the number 'a hundred' etc. Words which are introspected constitute a sentence. Their meanings which are introspected constitute the meaning of a sentence. Such an introspection cannot be disapproved since every body bears witness to it.

Now, a fresh question arises in our mind. Why do you hold that the recollection or the introspection of all antecedent words and their meanings follows the knowledge of the meanings of the last word ? What is the motive of framing such a suggestion? If the meaning of the last word is known to us then all our task has been completed. What remains to be done ? Say what will be referred to by a judgment of memory or by that of introspection. Such an argument does not carry conviction since no body can dare deny that the meaning of a sentence which is experienced by every body is presented as an integrate whole. If its parts are neither recalled nor introspected then such a whole cannot be constructed. Thus we see that recollection or introspection renders some service. In this way, words, being recalled and referred to by a synthetic judgment, constitute a sentence. And the meanings of words, being thus recalled and referred to by such a judgment, constitute the meaning of a sentence.

An introduction to the hypothesis of mutual relations

Let not a sphoṭa which stands for a word or a sphoṭa which stands for a sentence convey a sense. Let not a sentence or the meaning of a sentence be partless. Let the hypothesis of words or sentences as suggested by you be approved. But say how are the meanings of words mutually related.

The meanings of words such as a cow, a horse, a man and an elephant remaining unrelated do not constitute the meaning of a sentence. A judgment of memory or of introspection which closely follows the knowledge of the meaning of the last word only refers to the meanings of words as cognised before. Now, we should discuss how the knowledge of their mutual relation comes up.

Rival hypothesis on this Topic

We admit that teachers differ in opinion so far as this point is concerned. Some hold that words convey their meanings as mutually related. If we do not subscribe to it, words cannot constitute a sentence. Others hold that words denote their meanings as mutually unrelated. They, being thus denoted, point to their mutual relation when they are judged from the stand-points of reciprocal reference, material non-contradiction and proximity.

This point is to be debated. Instruction plays the very important part to reveal the meaning of a word or of a sentence since a word or a sentence remains ever unintelligible if the meaning of a word or of a sentence is not taught. Are we initiated into the meaning of a sentence or into that of a word ? Are we taught that this sentence conveys this meaning or that this word conveys this meaning ? If we hold that we are initiated into the meaning of a sentence then we advocate the doctrine of Anvita-abhidhāna. If we hold that we are initiated into the meaning of a word then we subscribe to the doctrine of Abhihita-anvaya.

The doctrine of abhihita-anvaya

Now, a question arises viz., "which one (of the above two-hypotheses) is to be accepted ?" Our simple answer is that the hypothesis of Abhihita-anvaya should be approved since the ascertainment of the meaning of a sentence presupposes the determination of the meanings of its constituent words. If one is not acquainted with the meanings of words, he cannot make out the meaning of a sentence. The meanings of words are classed under different heads. We say "This word denotes a universal, this word means a substance, this word stands for an attribute and this word conveys an action. This statement becomes relevant if words express the above meanings which remain at first unrelated. But if the meaning of a word is qualified by the meanings of other words then there is no hard and fast rule that a particular meaning is determined only by another particular meaning since all meanings are simultaneously presented to our consciousness." In other words, the propounders of the hypothesis of abhihita-anvaya substantiate their hypothesis by a negative argument. They hold that if the hypothesis of anvita-abhidhāna had been true then the meaning of each word would have been presented to our consciousness as qualified by the meanings of all other words since it is impossible to draw a line of distinction. Now, the upholders of the hypothesis of anvita-abhidhāna may contend that by the joint method of agreement and difference the meaning of one word is distinguished from that of another word.

Such a contention does not hold water since there is no occasion for the application of the joint method of agreement and difference to individualise the meaning of a word. The presentation of all meanings as being mutually related does not come to a stop. We do never hold that a sentence is constructed with words the meanings of which are mutually related. But if words are isolated from a sentence, they express such meanings as are in themselves, i.e., as stand unrelated. If all words which are the source of meanings assemble together then all the meanings of words are also presented to our consciousness in their mutual relation. In that case, it is very difficult to single out the meaning of a word. Now, if a sentence is independant of the meanings of words then the sentence "Bring a cow" may be taken as the mandate "Tie down a horse." Thus we see that real meanings of words are required for the understanding of a sentence. If they are so required then they should be grasped in their well-defined character. Hence, one is compelled to admit that the relation which holds between a word and its meaning is natural. When one learns the meaning of a sentence from the usage of the experienced persons he does so deciphering the meaning of each constituent word. If one does not subscribe to this view then he will have to learn the meaning of each sentence. As sentences are infinite in number so it is impossible to obtain mastery over language. The net result of this hypothesis is this that all verbal transactions will be defunct. It is also noticed that a person who is conversant with word-meanings makes out the sense even of a new poem, composed by a poet. This is possible because of the knowledge of words and their meanings. If one subscribes to the hypothesis that a sentence is the indivisible unit of a language and the meaning of a sentence is to be learnt then none will understand the meaning of a new poem. Therefore, the hypothesis of anvita-abhidhāna is not sound.

Reasons which invalidate the rival hypothesis of anvita-abhidhāna are as follows. If the hypothesis under discussion is accepted then only one word in a sentence should be competent enough to express the meaning of the sentence and all words should be rudundant. As we know the meaning of a word, we also know the meanings of other words which qualify it. The dictum of anvita-abhidhāna-vādins is that a word conveys its own meaning as qualified by the meanings of other words. Thus we see that a single word conveys a word of objects to be denoted by other words. Now, let all our verbal transaction be executed with a single word. But, as a matter of fact, we cannot transact all our business with a single word. If we say "A cow" then all predicable attributes and actions flash in our mind. But we cannot select the acceptable meaning. To know all things at a time is in a sense to remain ignorant since a listener can take no action upon a word. To a man of taste an ocean, full of water, does not appear to be distinct from a desert since saline water does not serve the purpose of pure water. But we see no reason why the word 'cow' will convey its own meaning as qualified by the exact attribute or action which will suit the purpose of the listener.

Now, the upholder of the hypothesis of anvita-abhidhāna may contend that the word in question is accompanied by other words and these accompanying words will fix up the exact meaning of it. Does the said association of words help to convey the above meaning? Or, does the word itself communicate its own meaning? If you insist on the truth of your suggestion then we say in reply that the association of other words is not as significant as that of some words in a mantra which is muttered. It makes no difference whether these words are present or absent since a word serves no useful purpose if we do not know that it denotes such-and-such meaning. Now, if you hold that other words help to determine the meaning of the said word by conveying their own meanings then you subscribe to the hypothesis of abhihita-anvaya. Therefore, we arrive at the conclusion that the hypothesis of abhihita-anvaya is better. The meanings which are conveyed by words become related to one another from the stand-points of mutual requirement, reciprocal proximity, and absence of contradiction.

The meaning of a word which is required by that of another word is related to that. The objects denoted by words which are adjacent to one another are mutually related. If the object denoted by a word is not incompatible with another such object then they are mutually related. In other words, an object which is related should be fit to be related. If these conditions of being related are not fulfilled then a relation between two objects does not take place. For this reason, the sentence, "A hundred herds of elephants stand on the finger-end" has the meanings of its words mutually unrelated since these meanings are unfit to be related. In other words, there is material contradiction. Thus, the above sentence conveys no meaning. But if we subscribe to the hypothesis of anvita-abhidhāna then the said sentence should convey a sense since according to the above hypothesis a sentence does never express a meaning which is unrelated. But, in reality, the said sentence communicates no meaning. Hence, it is reasonable to hold that the meanings of words which are conveyed enter into relationship. Some scholars have also said to this effect that words, having conveyed their own meanings, complete their task and afterwards these meanings, being grasped, point to the meaning of a sentence.

The refutation of the hypothesis of abhihita-anvaya

Now, the upholders of the hypothesis of anvita-abhidhāna take their stand and review the remarks of the propounders of the hypothesis of abhihita-anvaya. They point out that a word does not illuminate an object just like a lamp since a listener must be initiated into the meaning of a word in order to understand it. One learns the meaning of a word, noticing the usage of experienced persons. The experienced employ sentences in order to communicate their ideas. The sentences are never replaced by words. The reason is that mere words are never used to express one's ideas.

When a matter is discussed some other matter flashes in our mind. A word is employed to communicate this new idea. This word should be considered as a sentence. A speaker employs a sentence in order to communicate a system of ideas in which all ideas are mutually connected. The listener also understands in that way. A third person who stands by them also learns the meaning of a sentence in that manner.

This is what is called the communication of the meaning of a sentence. Do you say what is a sentence ? Words which conjointly express a unity of meanings are called a sentence. Linguists hold that a collection of words, expressing a unity of meanings, is a sentence. If we subscribe to this view then a collection of words conveys a unity of meanings. If only a single word had expressed such a unity of meanings then words could not conjointly convey a complex whole of meaning. As external conditions such as faggots etc. conjointly maintain the act of cooking, all bearers conjointly carry a palanquin and three pieces of stone keep a pot boiling so all words without an exception point to the meaning of a sentence. This is what is called anvita-abhidhāna (an expression of mutually related meanings). If a word could express a self-complete meaning which is in no way connected with the meanings of other words then all words would have no usefulness to convey the meaning of a sentence.

Now, the adverse party invites the attention of the upholders of the hypothesis in question to the open question, viz., if a single word is capable of conveying the same meaning as all words conjointly do then the utterance of all other words is superfluous since a single word completes the whole task. The said objection is not tenable. It is impossible for a word to express a complete idea without receiving the assistance of other words. Now, you admit that a single word cannot convey a complete meaning. Such an admission is contrary to the corollary of your own hypothesis. The reason is as follows. Each word falls within those the operation of which yields a complete result. If such a single word is present then an operation which brings about a complete result takes place. Again, such an operation does not take place if such a single word is not present. Thus we say that a single word produces a complete result.

Now, if the above objection goes to such a length then we say "Let the collection of words convey the requisite meaning." We also feel no necessity of holding that individual words which constitute the said collection convey the meaning in question. The hypothesis, thus revised, amounts to this that a sentence and its meaning admit of no parts. Such a logical conclusion is not sound since as the working of an assemblage is noticed so the working of an individual is also observed. What is the working of a collection ? And what is the working of an individual ? The communication of the meaning of a sentence is what a collection does—whereas the exact expression of the meaning of a word is the work of an individual word. Let us cite an example. The assemblage of all conditions produces an act. viz., the act of cooking whereas individual conditions perform separate acts, e.g., faggots burn and a pot holds articles to be cooked.

If a word has a distinct operation of expressing its own meaning then it should be admitted that the meaning of a word keeps itself aloof from those of other words. Now, the upholders of the hypothesis under discussion join issue with their opponents and emphatically assert that the meaning of a word does not stand unrelated. The reason is this that a word is employed to serve the purpose of a collection of words. Though a word is included in a collection of words yet it is not a fact that the specific operation of a word is not grasped. Hence, we do not share the view that a sentence is partless since the specific contribution of each word comprised within an assemblage of words is known to us. It is also observed that words which fall within a collection of words conjointly perform the work of the collection. The said collection is not noticed to maintain itself as distinct from the constituent words themselves. Though words in a body perform a team work yet the individual activity of each work is detected by us. Let us cite an example to elucidate our point. A carriage consists of several parts. We do not single out each part and say that this part, being made up of this stuff and that part, being made up of that stuff, separately perform the action of a carriage. Similarly, a single word is never employed. Even if it is employed, it does not point to the meaning of a sentence. But a word, being combined with other words, engages itself to convey the meaning of a sentence. So, it is reasonable to think that the above word throws light on the hypothesis of a complex whole of meanings. Hence, we have stated that words conjointly convey their meaning. Words which convey their meanings in this way constitute a sentence. In other words, a collection of words which expresses a complex whole of meanings is a sentence. For this reason as we know the contribution of each part so we agree with the grammarians in not denying etymological meanings to words. Again, as we definitely know that each word goes on with its operation unless and until the final goal is reached so we agree to differ from other Mīmāṁsakas in the point that a word denotes its meaning as qualified by those of other words.

An answer to the charges levelled Against the Hypothesis of Anvita-Abhidhāna

Our objectors have pointed out that if one subscribes to the hypothesis of anvita-abhidhāna then he should admit that the meaning of each sentence is to be learnt, otherwise, a person who knows only the meanings of words cannot make out the meaning of a verse composed by a modern poet. Such an objection has been raised by one who is ignorant of the science of meanings. The word 'a cow' does not convey its meaning, viz., a white cow since an exception is noticed. It also refers to a black cow as its meaning. One cannot also hold that the word 'a cow' denotes cows having all sorts of attributes since objects, thus denoted, are infinite in number and difficult to comprehend. But the meaning of a word is fixed up by means of requirement, fitness of relation, and proximity. A sentence is only competent to suggest the meaning of a word. The ascertainment of the right meaning is arrived at by means of the joint method of agreement and difference. The application of this method is also confined only within the four walls of a sentence. Though the knowledge of the meaning of a sentence extends up to that of a word yet the starting point of the knowledge of a meaning is that of a sentence. From this we understand that there is no reference to a meaning which remains unrelated. This reason behind the above conclusion is this that an experienced man who orders and an experienced man who is ordered do never employ a mere word. This point has been stated before. Though we subscribe to the hypothesis of anvita-abhidhāna yet it is not a truism that the exact meaning of a word is not determined. With the illustration of the different functions of various parts of a carriage we have shown the different workings of various words in a sentence by means of the joint method of agreement and difference. Thus we see that the meaning of a sentence does not necessarily constitute an indivisible unit. With the help of accessory conditions such as requirement, fitness of relation and proximity we have sometimes determined the meaning of a sentence together with those of words. These meanings of words are also exactly determined. This knowledge of the meanings of words furnishes us with a clue to understand the meaning of other sentences which consist of these words since the denotation of a word, properly deciphered, does not change. Hence, we shall be able to understand the meaning of a new poem, composed by a modern poet. We have also stated before that if words denote merely isolated meanings then we shall have never an access to the meaning of a sentence since such meanings are not the means of the determination of the meaning of a sentence.

Another objection to this hypothesis has been recorded to this effect that the utterance of other words is superfluous. An answer to it has also been given. The reason behind our answer has been stated thus—"when other words come in close proximity all words play their part full well. You may ask, 'If other words come in close proximity, what does a word do?' Our answer is that the same charge may also be levelled against all conditions. But you admit that all conditions conjointly bring about an action. i.e., produce a result. Similarly, if all words co-operate to convey the meaning of a sentence, expressing their own meanings then the hypothesis of abhihitānvaya (unrelated meanings) does not stand to reason since one is never initiated into the unrelated meaning of a word. Again, if we do not admit that the meanings of words are presented to our consciousness in their relational character then we cannot establish that they are related to one another afterwards since an unrelated meaning finds no ways and means of being related.

Now, the objector may contend that unrelated meanings may relate themselves to one another with the help of accessory conditions such as requirement, fitness and proximity. This point has been already discussed. Our reply to this contention is this that the said contention is not tenable. This requirement belongs to whom? Does it belong to a word, or to its meaning, or to a knower? As a word and its meaning are unconscious so they have no requirement since requirement presupposes consciousness. Hence, we simply display empty words when we say that a word requires another word and a meaning requires another meaning. But a knower who definitely understands the meaning of a sentence enjoys the freedom of thought. But this requirement is not a source of valid knowledge since one cannot acquire the true knowledge of things by an act of will. At the outset words reveal things as they are the source of valid knowledge. Then, a desire for relating these things springs up in the mind of a person. It follows the direction of words. It is, thus, the source of the knowledge of mutual relation among things. If words are held to be responsible for the knowledge of things then we are to admit that words have long-lasting operation like arrows since, if words pass away, then the mere desire of a person cannot manufacture the mutual relation of things, denoted by words.

Thus, we see that the knowledge of the meaning of a sentence is not derived from the verbal source without an impediment. If we are in a position to demonstrate that words directly convey the meaning of a sentence then it is unwise on our part to hold that words indirectly convey the meaning of a sentence.

The concluding portion of the hypothesis of Anvita-Abhidhāna

In fine, we arrive at the conclusion that words convey relational meanings since it is the only way of communicating relation.

As we know for certain mutually related meanings so it is understood that related meanings have assembled. There is no other source of the knowledge of relation. If one says 'Bring a white cow,' he does not necessarily refer to a relation. In some cases of usage the experienced persons make mention of words denoting relation. Though an ignorant person uses a sentence involving a word which points to relation yet the relation does not function as a bond of union. Let us cite an example. If such a person says 'There are ten pomegranates' the meaning of the word 'ten' is not related to that of the word 'pomegranates'. Thus we see that the hypothesis of anvita-abhidhāna (related meanings) is reasonable.

Now, the upholder tries to find out an answer to the problem 'How do you explain the sentence that there are a hundred herds of elephants on the tip of a finger from the stand-point of anvita-abhidhāna ?'

The defender puts the same question to his objector and says O upholder of the hypothesis of abhihita-anvaya ! how do you solve this very problem ? As you hold that meanings, being expressed, enter into mutual relation so you just explain how the meanings of words contained in the sentence are related to one another after their expression.'

Now, the upholder of the hypothesis of abhihita-anvaya says in replies to the question, 'As the meanings of words of the sentence are not fit to be related, they are not mutually related. What we intend to say is this that expressed meanings are mutually related only when the conditions of mutual relation, viz., requirement, fitness and proximity are satisfied.'

The upholder of the hypothesis of anvita-abhidhāna (expression of related meanings) says, "I have also held that words convey mutually related meanings provided that they satisfy the conditions of requirement, fitness and proximity. As the said conditions are not fulfilled, words contained in the above sentence, do not express a related meaning."

The propounder of the hypothesis of abhihita-anvaya presses his point with the following words, 'As you preach the doctrine of anvita-abhidhāna so you hold that the above sentence will convey no sense since it is absurd for the meanings of words to be mutually related. In other words, if the meanings of words cannot unite themselves with one another then a sentence which contains words having unrelated meanings clearly fails to communicate its meaning. But I advocate the doctrine of abhihita-anvaya. Hence I hold that though the meanings of words in the above sentence stand unrelated yet the sentence conveys its meaning. Saying this I am not open to the charge of inconsistency.'

The upholder of the hypothesis of anvita-abhidhāna retorts thus :—'Though you are a judge, having keen insight yet you have not followed the process adopted by a word to convey its meaning. It is natural function of a word to convey its meaning. But the speaker may have merits or demerits. When they are taken into consideration it is determined whether these words of the speaker have been rightly or wrongly used. Words convey an additional sense. It is this that they point to the relation which holds between a case and a verb. But owing to the perversion of the intellect of a speaker the knowledge of relation which holds between a case and a verb becomes false.'

Some thinkers have said on this point that knowledge, derived from other proofs, contradicts the truth of the said verbal knowledge.

Now, the upholder of the doctrine of anvita-abhidhāna says, 'The intrinsic validity of verbal knowledge is, therefore, supreme. This or that sentence produces verbal knowledge without being disturbed as long as it does not face an opposition. Let us discuss whether the sentence that there are a hundred herds of elephants communicates a meaning or not. There is nothing wrong with the syntactical arrangement relating to words since the sentence consists of words which indicate the locative case, the subject standing upon the locus and the verb along with this meaning is clearly communicated to us. If the said meanings were not communicated, the said sentence would not have been constructed. But, in reality, both of us hold the same view that it is an impossible feat for the meanings of words to be mutually related since they are not fit to be so related.

If it is held that there is no syntactical arrangement of words in the above sentence then the so-called sentence should be a mere enumeration of several letters like a mention of letters such as ka, ca, ṭa, ta, pa, etc., but should not be a real sentence. If we take into consideration the mere syntactical arrangement of words in this case as we do in the case of the sentence 'There are ten pomegranates' then the hypothesis of anvita-abhidhāna does not violate the rules of reasoning.

The sentence is formally correct but materially incorrect. The opposition which it faces comes from another quarter but not from the quarter of words. This point has been clarified already. Words have an intrinsic power by dint of which they operate smoothly. Under these circumstances we can boldly assert that the Vedas will carry their intrinsic validity, facing no opposition. As the Vedas do not owe their existence to an author so they do their work i.e., correctly convey their meaning without any hindrance. The knowledge which is derived from the Vedas bears the stamp of intrinsic validity. It is above all defects. A lengthy discussion on this point is unnecessary.

Thus we see that if we subscribe to the hypothesis of anvita-abhidhāna, we can explain how a sentence communicates its meaning. May we also suggest that the learned scholars should discard the hypothesis of abhihita-anvaya since it has no educative value.

The Refutation of The Doctrine of Anvita-Abhidhāna.

The critics do not endorse the above solution. Your statement that one learns the meaning from the usage of the experienced persons is true. It is also a truism that all verbal transactions are executed by means of sentences. It is a fact that all words, like the bearers of a palanquin, assemble together to convey the meaning of a sentence by their joint effort. Let us now discuss how one acquaints himself with a meaning. Does he acquaint himself only with a composite meaning which is worked out by the totality of all words ? Or, is he taught only the meaning of each word. Now, if one is to learn an indivisible whole of meaning then it is unavoidable for him to gather the meaning of each discrete sentence. In that case, as we have pointed out, learning will be impossible since sentences are infinite in number. If the truth of the second suggestion is admitted, the exact meaning of each word should be ascertained. The propounders of the hypothesis of anvita-abhidhāna have cited an example, viz., the different parts of a carriage have distinct functions. The narration of it suggests that the distinct function of each word is to be admitted. If the truth of the above suggestion is denied then the necessity of the knowledge of the etymological meaning of a word will not be required for the understanding of the meaning of a sentence. In that case, a speaker who intends to communicate the meaning of the sentence "Bring a cow" may also use the word "a horse" instead of the word 'a cow'. Unlike the grammarians you hold that the knowledge of the meaning of a word is necessarily required for the understanding of the meaning of a sentence. By the joint method of agreement and difference one picks up the extent of the meaning of the word 'a cow'. The same extent of this meaning becomes active to constitute the meaning of a sentence in which the word 'a cow' finds a place.

The Refutation of the Hypothesis of Anvita-Abhidhāna.

O Mimāṁsakas ! You have held that the word 'cow' in

question conveys its meaning qualified by such other meanings as are required, involve no material contradiction in order to be related and are in close proximity. You do not commit this mistake because the word 'cow' is always noticed as engaged in the service of a collection of words. The word 'cow' conveys as much meaning as its force of conveying primary meaning permits it to do. We shall have to make out what is the exact primary meaning of a word, i.e., how much a word denotes and how much it does not do. Though the primary meaning of the word 'cow' is invariably associated with other meanings which are reciprocally required, are mutually related without involving material contradiction, and are in close proximity yet it cannot be left out. What cannot be brushed aside constitutes its meaning. The meaning may be only the mere universal of cowness or the concrete universal. Thus the primary meaning of the word 'cow' maintains its identity in the midst of its relation with other meanings. This meaning cannot be ignored. It is detected by the joint method of agreement and difference.

Moreover, a single word is never used. In order to use a word, a sentence shall be constructed. The series of a collection of words are essentially required for this purpose. Nobody has noticed the skill of a single word in constructing a sentence without having the aid of a collection of words. An individual word, being included in the collection of words, plays its part to convey the meaning of a sentence. Its power of conveying the primary meaning does not help it much. But its power of conveying the intended meaning helps it to communicate the meaning of a sentence. The Mimāṁsakas, having failed to recognise this distinct power of conveying the intended meaning, admit the truth of the hypothesis of anvita-abhidhāna. But such an admission is not logically sound. The power of conveying the primary meaning has no special aptitude for the expression of one and all meanings. If one is not acquainted with distinct laws which govern the communication of the meaning of a word and that of sentence then he cannot escape the charge of using superfluous words in a sentence. In other words, if a word, contained in a sentence, expresses the meaning of a sentence then other words, used in it, become superfluous.

The hypothesis of anvita-abhidhāna cannot get rid of such defects. The word 'cow' has been used in a sentence. Its meaning is related to those of other words in it. Now, the word 'cow' should denote the related meaning by its power of conveying the primary meaning. If it does not do it, the knowledge of the related meaning does not arise in our mind. How does the hypothesis of anvita-abhidhāna stand this criticism ? The hypothesis of anvita-abhidhāna leads to another absurd conclusion. The word 'cow' denotes a meaning which is related to another object. If the second object is not denoted by the word 'cow' then the related meaning cannot be communicated by it. Thus the hypothesis amounts to this that an object which relates to a cow is not apprehended but a cow as related to it is presented to our consciousness. Such a conclusion (faces) a glaring contradiction in the above hypothesis. Now, if the upholders of the said hypothesis admit that the word 'cow' also denotes the relation of a cow then they should admit that each word denotes all objects. So, we hold that the power of expressing the primary meaning cannot logically communicate all shades of meanings which the words are competent to convey. Therefore, the hypothesis of anvita-abhidhāna is not tenable.

The upholders of the hypothesis of anvita-abhidhāna should also explain the problem, viz., 'How does the syntactical relation take place in the sentence that there are a hundred elephants on the tip of a finger ?' The sense of the objection lies in this. As the meaning of the sentence involves material contradiction, how can a related meaning be denoted by a word ? Now, they may contend that in the above case the syntactical relation is merely verbal and there is no actual relation between the meanings of words. Such a contention does not hold good. If the meaning of a sentence involves material contradiction then words are not related to the real meanings to be conveyed by them. In other words, there is no syntactical relation among words. Now, the upholders of the hypothesis may further contend that the function of a word is to reveal its meaning only but a word does not judge whether a meaning is consistent or not. The critics review this contention and hold that there is an element of truth in it that a word does not judge the consistency or otherwise of its meaning. But they should also know that a word does not denote a related meaning. We cannot also frame a general proposition that all words cannot but denote related meanings. We notice instances which contradict the truth of the above general proposition. The sentences, viz., 'There are ten pomegranates' etc., are an exception to it. Now, if the upholders of the hypothesis hold that the so-called sentences are no sentences then the critics will also point out that the sentence that there are a hundred elephants on the tip of a finger is no sentence. But the knowledge of the locus, the located, the verb and their relation is merely illusory. Therefore, the hypothesis that words denote related meanings does not stand to reason.

Do words denote such meanings as stand mutually unrelated like iron-pikes ? A hypothesis which points a view like this is not also sound since usage does not justify it. If words denote unrelated meanings then it is next to impossible to find out their mutual relation since words, having completed their task, are never noticed to resume their work. In other words, a word does never accomplish its work by fits and starts. When it works it completely exhausts its capacity to bring about the result. Thus, the hypothesis of abhihita-anvaya does not get the sanction of our experience. Therefore, the above two hypotheses, i.e., the hypothesis of anvita-abhidhāna and that of abhihita-anvaya, do not come off well.

Some critics have said to this effect. The above two hypotheses do not hit our fancy. The hypothesis of anvita-abhidhāna does not take its stand upon reasoning. Similarly, the hypothesis of abhihita-anvaya does not stand to reason.

Another Hypothesis and Its Refutation.

Some other logicians use quibbles and hold that words denote meanings which, being related point to the relation of such meanings as are being expressed. This hypothesis is not to our taste.

These two distinct acts are not experienced by us. These two acts have been mentioned thus :—One is the act of expressing the meanings and the other is the act of relating them.

Do these acts occur successively or simultaneously ? If they take place successively and if the act of relating precedes then the new hypothesis is nothing but that of anvita-abhidhāna. It is not the hypothesis of anvīyamāna-abhidhāna (the expression of meanings being related). Again, if words convey their meanings at first then it is the hypothesis of abhihita-anvaya but not that of abhidhīyamāna-anvaya (the relation of meanings being expressed). In other words, they mean to say that as soon as meanings are expressed, they are cognised as being related and that meanings are related as soon as they are being expressed. These two acts are not simultaneously experienced. The act of expressing refers to words. The act of relating refers to meanings. When words are employed the act of relating which refers to meanings is not experienced.

The competent judges have arrived at the conclusion after close examination that the act of expressing is absolutely distinct from that of relating since if meanings are not expressed, they cannot be related. The judgement that this is a white cow points to the co-ordination of the two properties of an individual cow. These two properties are the universal of cowness and the colour 'white'. If there are no terms to indicate their co-ordination then how can we grasp their mutual relation ?

Thus we see that the propounders of the two hypotheses, viz., the hypothesis of anvīyamāna-abhidhāna and that of abhidhīyamāna-anvaya simply play upon words. They have coined new words only. They express no new objects which are experienced by us. All defects which cling to the above two hypotheses do not fail to infect it.

The Knowledge of meanings in Relation by means of Tātparya-Śakti

Some logicians hold that the hypothesis of anvita-abhidhāna represents the rough draft of the real thesis but that of abhihita-anvaya stands for the minute draft of it. Let us illustrate this point. If the word 'a cow' communicates its meaning as being related to abstract universals of attributes and actions but not as being related to specific attributes and actions then the hypothesis is called as anvita-abhidhāna. If the relation of a cow to a specific attribute such as the colour 'white' etc.. is communicated by other words and a minute information is thus given then the hypothesis is known as abhihita-anvaya. This new exposition makes no improvement upon the old one.

The defects which have been pointed out in the hypothesis of anvita-abhidhāna visit the new exposition of the said hypothesis viz., words express their meanings in relation to abstract universals. The same defects as have been shown to vitiate the hypothesis of abhihita-anvaya infect its new explanation, viz., the relation of the meaning of a word to a specific attribute etc., is conveyed by other words.

The hypothesis in question points to nothing new. It is in no way distinct from the hypothesis of abhihita-anvaya. When the specific meaning of a sentence is stated the hypothesis of abhihita-anvaya is adhered to. Thus it is evident that the ancient path is welcome to convey the meaning of a sentence. How do you explain everything by adopting the routine method that words point to the meaning of a sentence only by their power of expressing primary meanings ? But we find that this path is also beset with various troubles as all the previous hypothesis are infected with many defects.

The defenders of the hypothesis under discussion say in reply that the path of conveying the meaning of a sentence is immune from all defects since it has been said before that words conjointly express the meaning of a sentence. The meaning of a sentence which all words conjointly communicate is nothing but the meaning of a principal word as related to the meanings of other subordinate words. In other words, the meaning of a sentence is nothing but the organization of the meanings of words in which one plays the important part and others play the secondary ones. Where is the room for defects ?

Now, a question arises in our mind. Do you intend to revive the old hypothesis of anvita-abhidhāna ? They say in reply 'No sir ! the hypothesis in question is not that of anvita-abhidhāna'. The critics ask, 'If this is not the hypothesis of anvita-abhidhāna, how is it that words conjointly express the meaning of a sentence ?' The defenders give the following answer 'Though these words conjointly express the meaning of a sentence yet this is not the hypothesis of anvita-abhidhāna. Words conjointly bring about the related meaning but do not convey the related meaning'. The objectors again ask 'what do you say ? Do words conjointly produce the meanings of a sentence as lumps of earth and other factors in mutual co-operation produce a jar ? The defenders answer, "This is not so since words simply indicate the above meaning but do not produce it'. The objectors again put this question to them. 'Do you not indulge in quibble if you hold that words conjointly work but do not convey the related meaning ?' The answer to the above question is as follows:—

We mean to say that words indicate the mutually related meaning but do not convey such a related meaning. The power of conveying the primary meaning does not point to the related meaning. But the joint method of agreement and difference reveals the exact meaning of each word.' But these words have another power which is called Tātparya-śakti. The function of this power is to reveal the meanings of words contained in a sentence, as being in relation with one another since this power is the common effect of powers belonging to all words. This new power lasts so long as these words do not produce an independent judgment which represents a self-contained unity of ideas.

Let this suggestion be fully explained.

Perceptual or indirect non-verbal knowledge reveals its object in different manner. It incompletely or completely reveals its object which is in front of us.

But verbal knowledge is a class in itself. Its working is absolutely different. Words go on functioning unless and until a self-contained judgment is not produced.

For this reason, in this world, a single word is never employed. Because a single word cannot produce as much knowledge as serves the purpose of a listener.

Now, we put a question to you. It is this—Do words possess some other power beside the power of expressing their primary meanings ? Is it conducive to a complete result ? (A complete result stands for a self-contained judgment). An answer to this question is in the affirmative. Those who subscribe to the thesis of relation cannot refute the existence of such a power.

The relation of meanings is not conveyed by the power of conveying the primary meaning. But a sentence conveys the correlation of meanings.

Now, some logicians suggest that if the related meaning is denoted by a word then the relation of meanings is presented to our consciousness and if this condition is not fulfilled then the relation of meanings is not cognised. This suggestion is not tenable. The meanings of words are bound up together by means of a relation since words denoting these meanings work conjointly since if causes produce jointly their effects then these effects are never seen to remain isolated. A stem and a suffix, attached to it, imply each other and convey their meanings jointly. But a stem does not denote the meanings of a suffix since an injunction, the meaning of a liṅ suffix, is not denoted by the basic root, yaj, and the liṅ suffix does not denote the meaning of a basic root, such as yaj. A sacrifice is denoted by the basic root 'yaj'. It cannot be denoted by the liṅ suffix. They do not independently bring about their effects. Similarly, words conjointly produce their own effects but one word does not denote the meaning of another word. Sentences also convey their meanings with reference to their context but point to no independent meanings. This view has been expressed by some other thinkers.

As a stem and its suffix imply each other so a word implies another and a sentence implies another.

This hypothesis is better. According to it words conjointly produce their effects but the meanings conveyed by words, maintain their individuality but do not interpenetrate.

If one denies that words imply one another then words look like so many detached iron-pikes. But if the hypothesis of anvita-abhidhāna is adhered to then the use of words other than one in a sentence becomes superfluous.

But if we stick to the hypothesis that words conjointly communicate their meanings then it becomes free from all defects. This path should be followed since it is not beset with thorns.

We agree to the point that words have power to denote their own primary meanings. They have an additional power which is called 'Tātparyā-śakti'. This power continues to work unless and until the meanings of words are presented to our consciousness as being in relation with one another.

Hence, we do not subscribe to the hypothesis of anvita-abhidhāna. But of course we surely hold that a sentence conveys a unity of meanings in which they are mutually related.

We utter words with this object in view that they will conjointly produce their main effect but not that they will merely communicate their own primary meanings. In other words, we utter words with the intention of communicating the meaning of a sentence. The author of Śloka-vārttika has said to this effect.

Words which constitute a sentence engage themselves in communicating the meaning of a sentence. In order to do it they have an intervening process as its invariable associate viz., the expression of their primary meanings. Similarly, sticks of wood burn in order to accomplish their main task, viz., the act of cooking.

It is this great creeper of understanding. Knowledge is its main root. The arrangement of words is its bright sprout. The impressions due to the experience of all antecedent letters are its broad leaves. The meanings of words which have been expressed are its full blown blossoms. The excellent meaning of a sentence is its palatable fruit. One should not put it in mouth. It is to be put in heart. When it enters our heart the listeners long for no other objects.

Kumārila has said in his Tantra-Vārttika to this effect. The knowledge which is derived from words by a listener blooms in the shape of the meanings of words and lastly bears fruits in the shape of the meaning of a sentence.

The knowledge which follows from this method is sound. We have said before that the meanings of words, being mutually related, constitute the meaning of a sentence.

An objection to the ascertainment of the Meaning of the Vedas

The path to ascertain the meaning of a sentence has been shown before. All worldly transactions are conducted by means of it. The same path will help to determine the meaning of the Vedas since the words which are used in the classical Sanskrit language have also been used in the Vedic Sanskrit in the same sense.

Some critics raise an objection to this effect. Sentences which are used in the classical Sanskrit language convey such meanings as are grasped by other sources of knowledge. Hence, we are in a position to apply other ways and means to find out the meanings of words. The objects which are denoted by the Vedic sentences are supersensuous. We who are ordinary people have our mind polluted by impurities such as love, hatred etc. We possess no power of seeing transcendental objects. One who is not endowed with the mystic power of intuiting supersensuous objects is not initiated into the meaning of the Vedas, observing the usage of the experienced persons. Suppose I desire today to learn the meaning of the Vedas and may approach an expert teacher for this purpose. But he also cannot intuit supersensuous objects. So, his knowledge of the Vedas is not up to the mark. As his knowledge is limited so he will have to approach another teacher in order to receive proper instructions. The teacher whom he will approach will also sit at the feet of another teacher like me because of his imperfect knowledge. He will also wait upon another. Thus we see that the entire tradition rests upon the consecutive series of blind teachers. As Pāṇini teaches the meaning of the conventional term 'vṛddhi' in his sūtra 'Vṛddhir ādaic', as Piṅgala explains the technical term 'ma' in his work on Prosody as three consecutive long syllables, as the author of Abhidhāna-mālā, a lexicographer, mentions the synonyms of the word 'hasta' as kara and pāṇi so the Vedas themselves do not teach in the same strain viz. the words which are contained in the Vedas denote such and such meanings. Hence, the true meaning of the Vedas is incomprehensible.

Some other critics also have expressed the same view. If a person who has fondness for worldly objects does not himself understand the meaning of the Vedas then he will not learn it from others. The Vedas themselves do not explain their own meaning. Hence how is it possible for a man to gather the sense of the Vedas ?

Now, if one may argue that a learner is initiated into the meaning of the Vedas with the help of their accessories such as Nigama, Nirukta, and Vyākaraṇa. Such an argument is not sound. The reason is as follows. The authors of these works agree to differ. Words which have been taught admit of various meanings. Words, prepositions which are prefixed to verbs, and indeclinable words have no fixed meaning. Other plausible meanings of the Vedas may also be imagined.

Some critics have suggested the different meanings of one and the same Vedic text. One who is desirous of Heaven should perform the sacrifice of Agnihotra. This is the traditional meaning of the Vedic sentence 'Agnihotraṁ juhuyāt svarga-kāmaḥ'. Who knows that the same sentence does not point to the sense 'One should take the flesh of a dog ?' Is there any crucial proof to decide the truth of any one of either meanings ?

A rejoinder to the above charges is as follows. Now we understand that all our previous discussions about the Vedas are like the recital of the Rāmāyaṇa before a deaf person. These critics have heard everything with regard to the ways and means of finding out the meaning of the Vedas. But they still search for the means of explaining the Vedas. All problems, raised by the critics, stand refuted since the ways and means of interpreting the Vedas have been revealed. We have said that there is no new Vedic word. The arrangement of these words is only different. But words which have been arranged are not different from those used in the classical Sanskrit language. From the very dawn of creation the tradition of the Vedic scholars has been working. I had learnt the meaning of the Vedas long, long ago in my previous birth. If I today go to learn the meaning of the Vedas, I shall learn the same meaning.

Where are gone Grammar and Mimāṁsā Śāstra, the means of interpreting the Vedas ? These sciences still exist. But you cannot determine the meaning of the Vedas. O fool ! one word more to add. A man who is under the sway of love and hatred may not set out for the realisation of transcendental objects. But it is not a fact that such a person who is desirous of Heaven will not be able to understand that the Vedic sentence 'Agnihotraṁ juhuyāt svarga-kāmaḥ' points to the meaning 'Agni hotra sacrifice is a means to the attainment of heaven.' Now, a question may be raised, viz., 'How do we receive regular training in the supersensuous matter ?' We have said before what we have got to say with regard to this problem. The tradition of the Vedic scholars throws unflinching light on the meaning of the Vedic texts since it has been flowing from time immemorial. The Vedas, their meanings, their knowledge, their accessories and the performance of the Vedic rites are not events of our modern age. Some thinkers hold that the Vedic tradition knows no beginning. But we, the Naiyāyikas, hold that the said tradition has commenced its work from the very first day of the creation of the world. Is there any occasion to-day for heaping contumely on them ? Some wicked critics have disgraced the Vedas with the damaging interpretation of the Vedic sentence, viz., 'One should eat the flesh of a dog.' The only object which they will accomplish is that they will be ornamental flowers of hell. No novel criticism has been offered by them.

Some other thinkers take an exception to this criticism. They say 'why do you take them to task ? Have they offended against the law ? Have they made any inconsistent remark ?' One cannot learn the meaning of the Vedas from an ordinary person. You may now ask 'who is an ordinary man ? Is he an uneducated person or an educated grammarian ? Of these two types cabmen are innocent of the use of chaste and correct words. They are in the habit of using vulgar words in a loud tone. These words are 'gavi' etc. How will they be acquainted with the Vedic words ?

Though the rustic people employ a few sanskrit words, e.g., in Kasmir they use eṣi, emi etc., in Darvabhisāra 'gaccha' etc., and in Madra 'karomi', etc, yet their words are very small in number. The usage of such words is very limited since these persons are ignorant of the Vedic Literature.

Now, the defenders of the Vedic tradition may agree in the following line. The science of Sanskrit Grammar is ancillary to the Vedas. One distinguishes with its help the correct words from the incorrect ones. His mind is restrained by the following injunction-cum-prohibition that a learned man should use correct words in speaking but should not use incorrect ones. Thus, learned men always attend to their work, using correct words only. It has been thus suggested that learned men may acquire proficiency in the Vedic Literature with little effort.

This suggestion is not sound because it involves circular reasoning. If the validity of the Vedas is established then its ancillary science, Grammar, may be carefully studied. With the help of grammar one will draw a distinction between correct and incorrect words. Mature consideration given to correct and incorrect words and acquaintance with the usages of the learned scholars help us to acquire mastery over the Vedic words. When one is initiated into them his acquaintance with the Vedic vocabulary helps him to understand the Vedic work. Thus, the charge against the Vedas that they are unintelligible is answered. Then and then only the Vedas are considered to be the source of true knowledge. In other words, the movers of this proposal reason in a circle. The Vedas depend upon the grammar and the grammar depends upon the Vedas.

Now, the defenders of the Vedic tradition may take up a different line of argument. They may contend thus—If one discards with contempt the traditional view that Grammar is ancillary to the Vedas but reads grammar at his sweet will and learns to distinguish the correct words from the incorrect ones then the above hypothesis is not open to the fallacy of circular reasoning. If this is their contention, let it be thoroughly examined. Should one study grammar as he takes interest in the study of Indian dialects (Prākṛta) in order to acquire proficiency in classical Sanskrit literary works such as dramas, social dramas etc.? If the said defender admits the truth of this new suggestion then the science of grammar will be no more treated to be affiliated to the Vedas as their ancillary science like a work on Indian dialects. In that case it should be admitted that the usages of Indian dialects help to understand the meanings of the Vedic words. Thus, they jump out of the frying pan into the fire.

Another point in criticism deserves mention. One may acquire sound knowledge of grammar. He may receive instruction from a truthful person that he should always use correct words in speaking. He may form the habit of performing Vedic rites. He may develop his conscience, strictly obey Vedic injunctions and carefully avoid prohibitions. He may be a sound Vedic scholar. He may entertain respect for the Śāstras. Such a person is very seldom noticed by us. The number of such persons is not many. He uses correct words in transacting all his business which relates to a sacrifice. He moves in society, paying his sole attention to such actions as are necessary to his main duty, i.e, the performance of sacrifices. If he is not observed by his disciples in the time of his moving about in response to the call of duty then how will you utilise this great savant who is skilful in using correct language as a teacher ? Hence the suggestion that one is initiated into the meaning of Vedas, noticing the practice of a sound Vedic scholar does not stand to reason.

The Hypothesis that one learns the Vedas with the Help of Grammar is not Tenable

If one thinks that the science of grammar will constitute the means of access to the Vedic lore then he should reflect on it and solve the problem viz., 'How is it possible for grammar to open the door ?' Pāṇini does not interpret the Vedic texts as elaborately as the author of Vivaraṇa has explained the sūtras of Pāṇini. Even though we assume that Pāṇini has interpreted the Vedic texts yet short-sighted and tainted by hatred, etc., as we are, how shall we, the students of Vedic Literature, pin our faith in the truth of his interpretation ? A doubt, viz., whether his interpretation is right or wrong may arise in our mind. One may now argue that the science of grammar is a means of access to the Vedic lore because it distinguishes correct words from incorrect ones. If this is his contention then he should admit that the science of grammar bears a new relation to such rites as are enjoined by the Vedic injunctions since grammar does not enjoy the status of an independent science like the Vedas and is affiliated to the Vedas as their auxiliary science.

Now, the above speculator may contend that the Vedas are to require grammar because of the injunction 'One should use correct words in speaking' and of the prohibition 'One should not use incorrect words in speaking'. This contention is met thus. Let us examine the character of the injunction and the prohibition in question. Do they find place in a certain section of the Vedas ? Or, are they known to a well circulated topic ? Or, does it deserve discussion ?

The Distinction Between Chaste and Vulgar Words is not Tenable

Let this discussion be stopped since it is a very long one. There are no such words as bear the lable 'chaste' and similarly the label 'vulgar' is not attached to some other words. Let us now put a premium on discussion regarding the jurisdiction of an injunction and that of a prohibition. Let us take an illustration of injunction viz., 'One should sacrifice with Vrīhis' and an example of Prohibition viz., 'One should not take kalañja'. In the above two examples one knows of the characteristic features of Vrīhis and Kalañjas from the people at large. Therefore, an injunction concerning Vrīhis or a prohibition with regard to kalañjas is not impossible to understand. But as one knows what is Vrīhi and what is Kalañja from the common people so he does not know the distinction between chaste and vulgar words from the same source. (Hence, an injunction prescribing the use of chaste words and a prohibition restricting the use of vulgar words remain ever obscure). Though our ears feel tired with the hearing of words yet they depend upon simply the undiscerning knowledge of words. But the chastity or otherwise of words is never directly apprehended. As one senses the universal of soundness belonging to all sounds or the qualities of sound viz., different accents so he does not perceive with his ears the chastity or otherwise-ness of a word. As we do not perceive the chastity or otherwiseness of a word so we cannot infer it since an inference is invariably based upon perception which lies at the root of generalisation.

There are two types of words viz. (1) words coined by human beings and words used in the Vedic Literature. Of these two types of words, what has been coined by human beings denotes an object which is either perceived or inferred. As the chastity or otherwiseness of a word is neither perceived nor inferred so chaste or vulgar words do not owe their origin to human agency. Vedic words are now to be discussed. If the chastity of these words is established then they may come within the province of injunction and if their non-chastity is proved then they may fall within the jurisdiction of prohibition. In that case we cannot admit the truth of following statement viz. 'As the distinction between chaste and nonchaste words is well-established so injunction or prohibition concerns only with the proper words.' If we admit the truth of the above statement then it will be inevitably open to the fallacy of a vicious circle. If injunction and prohibition are established then the existence of chaste and non-chaste words is proved. Again, if the existence of these words is established then the existence of injunction and of prohibition is proved beyond dispute.

What is the exact meaning of the term 'chastity'? Does it mean that a chaste word is such as has denotation? If we say in the affirmative then words such as gavi etc. are full well denotative. Why are not they to be treated as chaste words? If the communication of meaning decides the chastity of a word then words like gavi etc. more quickly carry their sense than words such as 'go' etc., Hence, the so-called chaste words such as 'go' etc., firstly become non-chaste. Some hold that non-chaste words cannot directly convey their sense. They convey their meaning through the medium of their basic chaste words which are inferred. Hence, they indirectly communicate their meaning.

The above suggestion does not hold good. It simply points to another way of communicating the sense of a word. But the way which is contrary to the suggested one is well-known in this world. The rustic people who are innocent of Sanskrit Grammar are well contented with words like gavi etc. since when they hear these words their meaning is immediately conveyed to them but is not an inference. In other words, a common man having heard a vulgar word does not try to find out its basic chaste word. Recollecting the meaning of the original word and observing the invariable relation of the vulgar word with the chaste one he does not indirectly grasp the meaning of the vulgar word. As trees and fruits which grow on the northern side of the Mount of Gold are not seen before, they are beyond our reach, similarly, the chaste words of Sanskrit Literature are inaccessible to the common folk. The common man has not grasped the invariable relation of a vulgar word with a chaste one. Hence how will it be possible for him to infer the meaning of a vulgar word from that of a chaste one?

The learned scholars who are helmsmen in the ocean of

grammatical literature and are in constant touch with nice expressions do not indirectly grasp the meanings of vulgar words when they use them. In other words, they do not think in terms of Sanskrit words and gather the sense of other words through the medium of Sanskrit words. Every body has direct experience of the truth of the above statement. The power of communicating a meaning constitutes the chastity of a word. As such power belongs to chaste words such as 'go' etc. so it belongs to non-chaste words viz., 'gavi' etc. So, these non-chaste words may be considered as chaste ones. If the nonchastity of a word stands for the non-communication of meaning then it exclusively belongs to the cawing of a crow etc. But non-chastity does not belong to articulate sounds consisting of letters. Hence, the vulgar words are not non-chaste.

Now, an objector may argue the chastity of a word is not merely the pointing to an object since such a definition is too wide. It also applies to smoke and such other objects which indicate some other objects. But the power of denotation is that which tends to bring about some specific acts. Such power belongs to words like 'go' etc., but does not belong to words e.g. 'gavi' etc. Hence, words like 'gavi' etc., are not chaste.

The above criticism has been offered by a person who lacks far sight. A denotative word is that which conveys a primary meaning. We have thoroughly discussed the point that denotation means the communication of a meaning by means of the primary power. This power of denotation is equally shared by words like 'go' etc., and also by words such as 'gavi' etc. Therefore, all these words are chaste.

Now, the critics may argue that words which obey the rules of Sanskrit Etymology are chaste and those which do not obey such rules are nonchaste. This argument is logically tenable since the procedure adopted by the science of Etymology is purely conventional. It is an expression of his arbitrary will. So its findings are not absolute. Our mature intellect fails to invent any new definition of chaste and nonchaste words. Hence, we reaffirm the conclusion that a denotative word is chaste and a nondenotative word is nonchaste. Hence, an injunction concerning chaste words and a prohibition with regard to non-chaste words should be futile. The reason behind the above remark is as follows :—

'One shall speak chaste words' is a well-known maxim. Why shall we issue an injunction to this effect ? "One shall not speak non-sense" is also well known. Why does a prohibition come in ? As speaking is not possible so the prohibition of speaking non-sense is meaningless.

As the injunction, 'One should drink water', is absurd so the prohibition 'One should not eat fire', is equally absurd. A man naturally seeks to drink water. So any injunction regarding it is superfluous. What is enjoined by the Śāstras is beyond the reach of normal activities of a person. As under no circumstances it is possible for one to eat fire so any prohibition with regard to it is unnecessary. The general rule which governs prohibition is this that what is possible is prohibited. Even a camel, being afflicted by the heat of summer, will not try to eat fire in order to quench his thirst. Now, the critics may argue in the following manner. Though words like 'go' etc. and words like 'gavi' etc. are equally denotative yet an injunction and a prohibition are fruitful since their function is to impose restriction upon the indiscriminate use of words. The use of non-chaste words injoined by the Śāstras entails merit. The non-use of unchaste words prohibited by the Śāstras helps one to avoid commission of sin. Hence an injunction and a prohibition, recorded in the Śāstras, are fruitful. It has been said by Kumārila that though words, chaste and nonchaste, are denotative alike yet a restriction, imposed upon their use, is significant since it regulates merit and demerit.

Such a restriction is an impossible feat to materialise. When a restriction is to be imposed upon the use of words the use of which is to be enjoined should be individually mentioned and words the use of which is to be prohibited should be distinctly stated. The said injunction should be like this that one should utter these words. And the said prohibition should be like that one should not utter these words. If this suggestion is accepted then the above words are to be mentioned individually and their number is also to be recorded. What will be the net result if they are individually mentioned and their number is counted. This task is impossible even for Brahmā, the personal creator of this world whose span of life extends over a hundred kalpas. It is also beyond the range of imagination even of the god Ananta who has a thousand mouths wide open. It is also too difficult for the Lord of speech to perform. It is also too heavy a load for the goddess of learning to carry. As these words are infinite in number so it is absurd to have a record of them.

Now, the objectors may contend that some common properties will be discovered and words will be classed under two different heads. In other words there will be a group of sâdhu words and another group of asādhu words. But this grouping is possible if so exclusive common properties of these two groups are discovered. The critics remark that one may try to find out such common properties but it is not possible for him to find them out.

The universal of soundness which belongs to chaste and non-chaste words is an indivisible entity. Words are not divided into two classes viz. (1) a class of chaste words and (2) a class of vulgar words (words used in spoken languages and dialects). There are no two distinct species under the common genus of soundness. But a hypothesis (which suggests their existence) is unknown to the logical world. Nobody experiences that the species of chastity belongs to all chaste words and the species of vulgarity belongs to all non-chaste words.

As two distinct species are not cognised so it is not at all possible to classify words in two groups. As the basis of classification is not possible so we do not understand this: Why shall the use of words be regulated by an injunction ? Though in the Śâstras restrictive injunctions have a necessity yet one has got to explain what is the object of such injunctions. What is the purport of the injunction in question ?

Does it mean that one should utter chaste words only but not non-chaste ones ? Or, does it mean that he should only speak, uttering chaste words ? Both meanings of the said injunction are infected with defects. Some critics have made the following observation. If one is enjoined to speak chaste words only then it is not possible for him to utter non-chaste words. Hence, the prohibition that one should not speak nonchaste words is ruled out. Again, if one is enjoined to speak only then he will commit a sin when he will remain silent.

It has been said before that a word which denotes a meaning is chaste and no other definition of chastity is possible. Hence, it is impossible to accept that what has no power to denote a meaning is to be taken as a word. Therefore, there are no such words as may be called unchaste or non-chaste. The drift of this argument is that the said prohibition is meaningless.

Now, the contenders may argue that the above regulation is significant since it prohibits the use of such words as are wrongly pronounced through inadvertance or inability. Prohibition is directed towards these wrongly pronounced words.

The critics review this new suggestion and point out that if words which are wrongly pronounced through inadvertance or inability do not convey meanings then there is no possibility of applying the said prohibition to them since it follows from the text that significant words will only be taken into consideration. What is the need of taking unnecessary pains of prohibiting them ?

Again, if vulgar words denote meanings as chaste words, correctly pronounced, does then prohibition not apply to their use as it does not apply to the use of chaste words?

Now, the defenders may contend thus: Nobody can deny that there are words of Indian dialects which are exclusively used in transactions of secular business. In order to exclude their use the said prohibition that one should not speak non-chaste words has been given. Why is not the above restrictive injunction significant ? The critics join issue with the advocates and point out that as many examples of conveying one's ideas through the contraction of one's ideas through the contraction of one's eye-balls, gestures of hands, and such other expressions are noticed so regulations should also be issued prohibiting their practice.

In continuation of their criticism the critics remark that a restrictive injunction has a positive content. It enjoins something positive. Let us take an example, viz., one should lie with his wife during a fixed period after her menstruation. The person enjoined is ordered to do something positive. But a parisaṁkhyā injunction has a negative import. Let us take an example, viz., 'Five species of animals having five fingers with nails are edible.' The above injunction implies that one should not take the flesh of animals having such and such characteristic features excepting animals belonging to the well-defined five species. Now, the defenders may contend that the said restrictive injunction has also a negative import, i. e, it intends to prohibit the use of vulgar words. If this is their contention then they simply contradict themselves since they say in the same breath that the said injunction is both positive and negative (niyama and parisaṁkhyā).

Now, the defenders may contend that the said injunction has only a negative import and is a parisaṁkhyā vidhi, such a contention does not hold good since chaste and vulgar words do not simultaneously come within the jurisdiction of this injunction. In case of the above parisaṁkhyā injunction one may take the flesh of all animals having five fingers with nails. There is a possibility of taking flesh since a man is actuated by his natural propensity. Where there is a possibility there negation is significant. Thus, the taking of the flesh of certain animals has been prohibited. As there is no possibility of simultaneously using chaste and vulgar words so the injunction in question does not fall within the Parisaṁkhyā class.

The critics add a new point to their criticism. The defenders hold that the use of a chaste word brings about merit and the use of a vulgar word results in demerit. This hypothesis is not sound. It is unreasonable to assume that both produce transcendental results, viz., invisible merit and demerit since the tangible result, viz., the communication of a meaning, which stands to reason has been discarded. It has been said that a chaste word, properly used, produces the desired result in Heaven. This statement is not literally true. It falls within Arthavāda. Its object is to praise a chaste word. A word which has been improperly used is a thunderbolt and kills the institutor of a sacrifice who improperly uses a word. This statement, also, comes under Arthavāda. Its object is to condemn an improperly pronounced word. It has been clearly proved that these statements are subordinate to a sacrifice. They render assistance to a sacrifice. As they are merely laudatory or condemnatory Arthavādas so chaste and vulgar words have no connection with transcendental results, i. e., merit and demerit. A rule, laid down in the Mīmāṁsā sūtra, clearly expresses the following decision that a material substance used in a sacrifice, viz., a special kind of ladle etc., any qualitative change of a sacrificer, and accessory sacrifices are means to an end but produce no transcendental result. The injunction that one should use chaste words in conversation and the prohibition that one should not use nonchaste words in conversation are well-circulated but not based upon the authority of the Śāstras. On the basis of this hearsay evidence the science of grammar is considered to be authoritative. But we shall hope against hope if we think that it (the science of grammar) is ancillary to the Vedas on the strength of the said weak evidence. If an injunction and a prohibition are read in a particular section then they exercise their influence only upon it since their service has been meant for the said section. The universal application of the said injunction and the prohibition is not permissible. Thus, considering the problem from every possible aspect we arrive at the conclusion that the injunction and the prohibition, mentioned above, cannot constitute the basis of the authenticity of the science of grammar.

Inefficacy of the Study of Grammar

Some hold that the injunction 'One should study the Vedas along with their six ancillary sciences for their own sake' implies the obligatory character of the study of grammar since it is as ancillary as the other branches of Learning, viz., Phonetics, Ritual, Etymology, Prosody, and Astronomy are. This view does not stand to reason. It is reasonable to hold that the five branches of Learning (Phonetics to Astronomy) are really ancillary to the Vedas since each of them renders some unique services to the Vedas and many Vedic injunctions involve necessary references to them. Though grammar tries to attract attention by a show of runs and jumps yet it may be ancillary to the Vedas only because of the possible reason that it is a normative science which regulates the use of chaste words but not because of any other reason. The said function of grammar viz., the regulation of the use of chaste words is difficult to establish. This point has been brought home before. Therefore, grammar cannot compete with other ancillary sciences of the Vedas in substantiating its claim. In the above injunction concerning the study of the Vedas for their own sake the word 'niṣkāraṇa' has been used It indicates as much its non-utility but not so much its fruitfulness. The Vedas have six accessories. These accessories are not the six branches of learning. They are six ways of establishing the connection of mantras with the Vedic rites. They are called Śruti, Liṅga etc. This point will be discussed later on. Therefore, some other passages which are often quoted to prove that grammar is an accessory of the Vedas do not serve the purpose. The passages are as follows : 'A Brahmin should not use vulgar expressions since a vulgar expression is barbarism'. If a chaste word is properly used, it fulfils the desire of its employer in heaven'. 'The institutor of Agnihotra sacrifice having used vulgar expressions should observe an expiatory rite in honour of the Goddess of Learning'; and 'A speech which is strictly classical is worthy of its name'. Now, one may suggest that grammar should be based upon the usages of savants just as the science of medicine is based upon the experimental method of agreement and difference. The drift of this argument is that the science of grammar has a sound footing to stand upon. The critics review the suggestion and put the following questions. Who are these savants. Are they savants who employ classical words such as 'go' etc? Or, are they savants who use vulgar words, e. g., 'gavi' etc., in speaking and writing ? Or, are they savants who use both classical and vulgar words in speaking and writing ?

If the defenders answer the first alternative in the affirmative then they involve an unanswerable vicious circle since the science of grammar is based upon the usages of savants and savants are those who are proficient in the science of grammar. It is a fact that those who are not well up in Sanskrit Grammar are not adept in using chaste classical Sanskrit words (words which are grammatically correct). If they answer the second alternative in the affirmative then coachmen and such other persons who use vulgar words such as 'gavi' etc. should become savants and the science of grammar is nothing but a record of refinements upon those vulgar expressions. Such a conclusion appears to be absolutely irrelevant. If they answer the third alternative in the affirmative then the promiscuous use of the chaste and the vulgar words, e.g., 'go', 'gavi' etc., should go on uninterruptedly. In that case the study of grammar will be superfluous. But it is reasonable to hold that the medical science owes its origin to the reliable teachers who have composed it with the help of the experimental method of agreement and difference. Even if the science of grammar is judged from this point of view, it serves no useful purpose. Moreover, it has no utility since the author of aphorisms of grammar has made no mention of it. As Jaimini, the author of Mīmāṁsā aphorisms, has clearly stated the usefulness of Mīmāṁsā Sūtras in his Sūtra, 'athāto dharmajijñāsā', as Gautama has expressed the utility of his Nyāya-sūtras in his first Sūtra 'Pramāṇādi-jñānāt niḥśreyasādhigamaḥ' and as Kaṇāda has vindicated the efficacy of the study of his Vaiśeṣika-Sūtras in his initial sūtra 'Sādharmyādi-jñānaṁ niḥśreyasādhigamaḥ' so Pāṇini, the author of grammatical aphorisms has given no indication of the usefulness of the study of grammar. Now, the defenders may contend that Pāṇini has made no mention of its utility because it may be easily guessed. We, the critics, say, 'What do you say'? We fail to discover it up to this time even after a thorough search for it. The point in question is the subject of dispute among all parties.

There are four different ends of human life, viz., (1) Celestial happiness, (2) Wealth, (3) Realisation of secular ends and (4) Final emancipation from bondage. Now, the defenders may look forward to any one of these ends as the goal of grammatical study. Of these four ends Dharma (means to celestial happiness) does not constitute the goal of grammatical study since Dharma consists in being a sacrifice, gift, and libation etc. Or, Dharma is Apūrva, i.e., the transcendental result of the various Vedic rites. It is revealed only by the Vedas. Those who are well-acquainted with Dharma hold that the Vedas are the only source of the knowledge of Dharma. Or, we take no exception to the view if one holds that Smṛti of Manu which is based upon the Vedas, good conduct of the pious men and tradition is also authority on Dharma. But grammar-in-itself is not competent to impart instructions on Dharma. It is not reasonable to think that Dharma is the end of grammar because it is ancillary to the Vedas. Dharma is the goal of that science which gives directions to the performance of duties since such a goal is bound up with the necessary directions of duties. Dharma is not the goal of the study of grammar since it gives no such directions. Therefore, the hypothesis that Dharma is the goal of grammar has been refuted.

It is well-known that wealth is the goal of vocational subjects and Political Science. But wealth is not attained through the study of grammar since many scholars of grammar are generally noticed to be very poor. Therefore, wealth is not the goal of grammar. Fulfilment of desire is the object of the Sexual science, composed by Vātsyāyana. Grammar has got the least connection with this science. Such pleasure is beyond its reach. Mokṣa or Final Liberation is attained through the realisation of one's own self and the cessation of five kinds of kleśas (five sources of bondage—an initial error, mis-identification, love, hatred and fear of death). This is the verdict of the spiritual experts. It is not very reasonable to hold that the proper knowledge of cerebral ṣa and ṇa is a means to Final Liberation. Thus we arrive at the conclusion that none of the four ends is attained through the study of grammar.

Now, the defenders of the utility of the study of grammar may contend that no distinct end of the study of grammar has been mentioned since it is affiliated ancillary to the Vedic lore, an embodiment of all instructions conducive to all these four ends. They also add that ends which are attainable through the study of the Vedas are also attainable through the study of grammar. This contention has been already refuted.

The basic assumption that grammar is accessory to the Vedas on the strength of its instructions on chaste words has been refuted. It renders no other service to the Vedic study. Such a grammar has no utility. Moreover, a branch of learning which is not helpful to the Vedic study cannot be its ancillary.

The Vedas do not obey the injunctions issued by their subordinate science since the Mīmāṁsakas hold that they are the sole authority on the matter of injunctions. The purport of this point is that one should not logically hold that the science of grammar is an ancillary of the Vedas on the basis of non-vedic injunctions.

The celebrated Bhāṣya-kāra of Pāṇini has mentioned a few utilities of the study of grammar, viz., the preservation of the Vedas etc. As these purposes are served also by other methods so we should not absolutely depend upon grammar for the attainment of the said objects. The continuous circle of students preserve the purity of the Vedas. If one student slightly deviates from the proper pronunciation of an accent or a letter then the other students give the following warning to him. They say 'Do not mar the Vedas. This is the correct pronunciation of the Vedic sentence. Pronounce it thus.' They instruct him. Thus the Vedas are preserved. The second utility is ūha i.e., the necessary modification of a Vedic word etc., according to requirement. This modification takes place with regard to mantras, tunes, and preparatory acts for purifying substances. The modification of tunes is learnt either from the Mīmāṁsā-sūtras or from the usages of the sacrificial experts. The modification of words in a mantra is also learnt from the same source. Any modification with regard to a preparatory act of purifying something is beyond the scope of grammar. What shall grammar do in this matter ? The Vedas themselves do not constitute the object of the study of grammar. This suggestion has been already examined and criticised. Moreover, the Vedas reveal ends of human life but they are not ends in themselves. It has been said that the study of grammar provides one with an easy access to literature. Does it do so ? What do you say? One cannot master it even if he has been reading it from his childhood and continues his study for many years. If it is an easy way we do not know that will be a difficult one. Grammar can solve no doubt about the meaning of a Vedic sentence. It is Mīmāṁsā Śāstra which solves a good number of doubts eclipsing the meaning of each Vedic sentence. The science of grammar is never noticed to do this function. The mention of five-fold utilities of the study of grammar viz., the preservation of the purity of the Vedas, necessary modifications of the Vedas, the easier method of learning language and the removal of doubts has not been rightly made.

The said commentator has made mention of other minor utilities of the study of grammar. Let us illustrate one of them. The demons who were innocent of grammar wrongly pronounced 'helayaḥ helayaḥ' etc. and were crushed. The correct pronunciation of this mantra should be 'he arayaḥ, he arayaḥ' etc. These utilities have only minor significance. These are too insignificant to record. Moreover, these are indirect utilities. Kumārila in his Tantra-Vārttika has said to this effect:—

The grammarians hope against hope if they try to establish minor utilities of the grammatical study when its major utilities are not established. They behave just like a drowning man who catches at a straw, leaving aside big trees.

The Untenability of the Hypothesis that Grammar makes an Improvement upon Words.

Now, the defenders may contend thus :—There is no need of making an investigation for other utilities of the study of grammar. The only object of grammar is to make an improvement upon words. The critics say in reply to this contention that they should explain their point, viz., the saṁskāra of a word. What is this saṁskāra ? What result do we derive from it ? As sprinkling purifies Vrīhis, as looking at ghee purifies it, as the establishing of sacred fires consecrates fire so grammar does not make an improvement upon words. The Naiyāyikas hold that letters are very short-lived. They pass away as soon as they are uttered. What is the saṁskāra that a sound has ? As acceleration is the saṁskāra of the flying arrow, as impression is the saṁskāra of the soul as the branch of a tree has elasticity as its saṁskāra so what is the saṁskāra of a sound ? Again, if we subscribe to the hypothesis that letters are eternal then we are also compelled to admit that their manifestation is transient. In that case what is this saṁskāra that affects them? Does a saṁskāra work upon a letter, or upon a word, or upon a sentence ? No solution can be given to any of these three alternatives. The grammarians hold that a sentence is a partless whole. Hence, a saṁskāra which is directed towards a letter or a word has no ground to stand upon. Now, the grammarians may contend that the stems and suffixes will be elicited from sentences and the remaining words will be brought under saṁskāra. Such a contention does not hold good. Such words are non-existent. Hence, no saṁskāra can be worked upon them.

Some have criticised the above attempt thus :—Do not intelligent persons who intend to introduce saṁskāra into words after having distinguished them from a sentence by means of imagination, wreath a garland of sky-flowers, having given up flowers which emit fragrance and become ornaments of different directions.

Nobody comes across a Vedic injunction (either universal or sectional) which enjoins to formulate grammatical laws for the better analysis of words or for the synthesis of parts of words. There is no injunction on the authority of which we shall take up the better study of words. A sacrificer is enjoined to put a horn, brought to scratch the body of an antelope, into a sacrificial hole. This act exerts a purifying influence upon the rite which has been observed. A similar act in some cases precedes a rite which will be performed.

One should sprinkle Vrīhis. Sprinkling in accordance with this injunction will make the future Darśa and Pūrṇamāsa rites more perfect. In these ways it is not possible for us to make an improvement upon words. There is an injunction, viz., one should study the Vedas. It concerns only with a young boy of the twice-born class. It introduces some qualitative changes to him as he is taken to a Vedic teacher for the learning of the Vedas. Upanayana ceremony is a symbol of the beginning of the Vedic study. Or, the said injunction exerts an influence upon the Vedas thus acquired. Let us stop this discussion since it is a very long one. The drift of our discussion is this that the study of grammar is not competent enough to bring in such an improvement. It is also doubtful to hold that grammar makes an improvement upon words by formulating laws which govern inflexions, such formal changes of words as do not affect a stem and its inflexion, the elision of letters, formal changes which affect a stem and its inflexion and such other things. Let us stop this discussion. Grammar cannot work out a change which is a very hard task either in organs of speech, or in the internal air which is instrumental to the being of sound or in the organ of hearing which is instrumental to its perception, or in the soul of a speaker, or in the internal organ or in the intellect. For this reason it is certain that grammar cannot create such situation as helps the use of verbal expressions. Some may contend that the services of grammar cannot be dispensed with since it explains a few difficult compound words such as sthūlapṛṣatī etc. Such a contention is not tenable since Kalpa-sūtra, a work on rituals, and such other treatises will render the same service.

Some body has said in defence of grammar that grammar is the only means of the clear understanding of words. Kumārila, the author of Tantra-Vārttika, smiles at his claims and remarks that without the organ of hearing words are not otherwise distinctly perceived.

Moreover, though grammar has chastened words yet many ancient writers of acknowledged authority have used many irregular words which violate the rules of grammar. Pāṇini, the author of grammatical sūtras, has used irregular words in his sūtras "Janikartuḥ prakṛtiḥ" and tat-prayojako hetuśca". The compound words "Janikartuḥ" and "Tat-prayojakaḥ" are illustrations of Tat-puruṣa compound. The sixth case-ending has been dropped. But the rule "Tṛjakābhyāṁ kartari" opposes the formation of Tat-puruṣa compound in these two cases. Again, the term 'jani' denotes a root. But in the above ṣūtra the word denotes a different meaning. Kātyāyana, the author of Vārttika on Pāṇini's sūtras, has indulged in irregular usages. Let us illustrate them. In his sūtra "Dambher halgrahaṇasya jātivācakatvāt" the compound word 'jāti-vācaktvāt' is irregular since Ṣaṣṭhī-tat-puruṣa is not permissible. Let us take another example. In the sūtra "Anyabhāvyaṁ tu kāla-śabda-vyavāyāt" the word 'anyabhāvyam' is irregular. The nominal suffix 'ṣyañ' has been attached to the compound word 'anyabhāva'. The provision for the said suffix has been made in the sūtra "Guṇa-vacana-Brāhmanādibhyaḥ". The word 'anyabhāva' is not an abstract noun since it has been said that an abstract noun ceases to be so if it enters into a compound. In other words no compound word should be treated as an abstract noun. The said suffix is also attached to such words as fall within the group of words having the word 'Brāhmaṇa' at their head. The said word is not included in the list. The author of bhāṣya on Pāṇini's sūtras, has not dropped the case-ending, intending to use a compound word of the Tat-puruṣa class, containing another compound word of the Dvandva-type in the analogy of the word 'aviravika'. He has violated the rule of Pāṇini, viz. "Supodhātu-prātipadikayoḥ". He has also violated the rule of Pāṇini "Anyathaivaṁ katham itthaṁ susiddhaḥ prayogaścet" since his sentence "Anyathā kṛtvā codyam anyathā kṛtvā parihāraḥ" illustrates his irregularity. He should have attached the suffix "Ṇamul" but not "Ktvā" to the root 'kṛ' preceded by the word 'anyathā'. The above three sages are the propounders of the system of Grammar. It is a matter of grave regret that these great personages have deviated from the path of duty i.e., the use of correct expressions. Whom shall we chastise ?

In Manu's treatise and such other works a large number of words which are irregularly formed is counted. He writes "Jñātāram antimetyuktva". The euphonic combination resulting in 'antimeti' is not permissible. Āśvalāyana has also used "Akṣiṇi ajyati." The resulting form 'ajyati' is grammatically incorrect. The author of Gṛhyasūtra has used "Mūrdhni abhijighrāṇām." The suffix 'śānac' has been attached to the root 'ghrā.' It should not have been attached to the root in question. Vālmīki has written "Tubhyaṁ ca Rāghavasya". The word 'Rāghavasya' is incorrect. Vedavyāsa has made a mistake when he writes "Janme janme yadabhyastam." The word 'janma' is not chaste. It should be janman. Hence he should have written "Janmani janmani' etc. "Kumārila in his Tantravārttika says that in the works on History and Purāṇa there is no end of unchaste words.

Definition of a Chaste Word is Puzzling

There is no need of censuring the ancient personages. Our concluding remark in a nut-shell is this that grammar renders service neither to classical language nor to Vedic language. Let us point out the initial failure of grammar not to speak of other such failures. Patañjali commences his work with the title 'Atha sabdānuśāsanam' (Instruction in words). He raises a question, viz., "which words are to be discussed ?" He solves the problem by proposing to give instruction in classical and Vedic words. But he fails to enumerate the number of classical and Vedic words. We are going to discuss the matter in question. Shall we treat each word individually and give our instruction ? Or, shall we take up many words at a time and bring them under a general rule ? It is an impossible feat to treat each word individually. The ancient teachers have expressed their opinion regarding the subject-matter under discussion. They say "Bṛhaspati (the lord of speech) himself has been uniting Indra into words, one by one, for a thousand divine years but has been unable to complete his task since the number of words is inexhaustible. It is not also possible to determine all chaste words by means of general rules. The reason has been given before. In a nut-shell it is this that no common property which constitutes a mark of distinction from all vulgar words belongs to all chaste words like the species of cowness. How is an instruction in words to be imparted? He raises the problem and solves it thus : a word is to be analysed into two parts, viz., (1) its basic element and (2) inflexion attached to it and a general rule, determined by a qualification, is to be formulated. Let us take an example to illustrate the above procedure. The sūtra karmaṇyaṇ is a qualified general rule. The verbal suffix 'aṇ' is attached to a verb. This is the general rule. It is qualified by the word 'karmaṇi' karma is such as denotes an objective case and is penultimate. Thus, the meaning of the qualified general rule is this that 'aṇ' suffix is attached to a root provided it is qualified by a penultimate objective case. The defenders of the utility of grammar hold that words such as kumbhakāra, nagarakāra etc., are easily explained by means of the qualified general rule and many other words such as goda, kambalada etc., are also explained by general rules without any difficulty. We have already elaborately criticised the supposition that a word consists of two imaginary parts viz. (1) a basic element and (2) a suffix and expressed our opinion about it. Now, we shall examine the new hypothesis viz., the supposition of a qualified general rule. Such a rule is not without its defects since the determination of the two elements of a word is not exact.

Let us clearly state the ground of our objection. The general rule is that a suffix is attached to a root. In order to make it intelligible they should define a root. Now, the grammarians may say by way of repartee that a root has been defined in the sūtra 'Bhūvādayo dhātavaḥ" and its characteristic feature has been indicated. Some words have been read as synonyms in an order of succession and several such groups have been included in the list of roots. These words have been defined as roots. The inflexion 'tiṅ' and several suffixes are attached to them. The critics make the following remark :—'Very well, you have said this. But your definition does not point to the true characteristic feature of a root. If you ask 'why' ? then the reason of our critical note is as follows. Let us take an example, say 'gaṇḍate.' The noun 'gaṇḍa' should be treated as a root. Thus, the definition of a root suffers from the defect of being too wide since according to your rule inflexion 'tiṅ' is attached to a root. There is a root 'ghaṭa' which denotes activity. There is also a noun 'ghaṭa'. There is a verb 'ama' which means to be sick. When its non-essential termination 'a' becomes detached the essential form of the root is 'am'. The second case-ending in the singular number is also 'am'. There is a root 'bhū' and a noun 'bhū' also exists. There is a root 'yati' denoting 'to act well'. It has an accidental termination 'I'. When it drops off the root assumes the real form 'yat'. There is also a pronoun 'yat' which is well-known, being included in the list of pronouns. As there is no difference between the roots and the words mentioned above, so why should not inflexions 'tiṅ' etc., be attached to ghaṭa, bhū and yat (which are not roots) ? Now, the grammarians may contend that a verb is such as denotes activity. If this is their contention then the roots 'to be' (bhū) and 'to stand' (sthā) cease to be roots. They should not be included in the list of roots.'

"Now, the grammarians may revise their definition of a root and hold that there are two definitions of a root. These definitions as are follows :—(1) That which is included in the list of roots is a root and (2) That which denotes activity is a root.' Thus, 'bhū' and 'sthā' will be treated as roots since they find a place in the list of verbs. The critics put a question to them whether these two definitions will apply severally or jointly. If they say that they will apply severally then the roots 'bhū' and 'sthā' will not be treated as roots since the second definition of a root does not apply to them. If the definitions of a root do not apply to all roots then the charcteristic feature of a root remains indeterminate. In that case how will it be possible to attach inflexion 'tiṅ' and suffixes to a root ? They are attached only to roots. As roots cannot be defined where will they be attached to ? If the grammarians hold that the above two definitions of a root are to be supplied jointly then they make no improvement upon the situation i.e., the defect mentioned remains unremedied.

Some 'tin' inflexions are time-adjectives but are not denotative of tenses. If they do not denote the different times of actions then it is impossible to frame rules which speak of the connection of the various tenses with different inflexions. The sūtras e.g. 'Varttamāne laṭ', 'Bhaviṣyati lṛṭ', 'Bhūte laṅ' etc., try to do something impracticable since mentioning times they try to establish the relation of various inflections with them (times). Now, the grammarians may hold that these inflections will denote tenses i.e., times. If they change front, they contradict their own Bhāṣya-kāra who is an authority on grammar. He has said that the root in question denotes the past tense. If the findings of the Bhāṣya-kāra are accepted then the said rules are absurd since the meaning of a root cannot regulate itself. The inflexions such as liṅ etc. point to such things as are incomprehensible. Hence, they are prescribed to denote order etc. Such meanings of inflexions can be determined neither by themselves nor by their adjuncts.

Similarly, rules which govern cases are also defective. An ablative case expresses a noun or its equivalent which remains motionless when an act of separation takes place. Devadatta has fallen from a tree. A tree is said to be the ablative case. A tree is motionless. But it has not the slightest relation to the act of falling. Hence it does not fulfil the condition of being a case. A case is that which is related to a verb. A tree does not relate itself with the verb in question. A traveller has fallen behind a caravan. A person has fallen from a moving chariot. A caravan and a chariot are not motionless like a tree since an action is noticed in them. It is a truism that they have their own action. Any verb does not determine a case in a sentence. But a case is determined only with reference to a verb which finds a place in a sentence. In the above illustrations the two verbs viz., to fall behind and to fall from have been used. As a tree has no relation with the said verb so a caravan and a chariot are in no way connected with these two verbs. Each of them may be related to a particular verb and be a case. But this connection with a particular verb does not mean that a case maintains its status quo ante in relation to all verbs without an exception. If this be so then the definition of a case will be too wide. Thus we see that the definition of the ablative case has a serious flaw.

The Definition of a Chaste-word is Puzzling

A dative case is that which is intended by means of a karma. The word 'karma' requires an explanation. Does it mean an action ? Or, does it mean a case which is the most desired one ? If the first meaning is accepted then as all cases are desired for the sake of an action, i.e., for its coming into being, so each of them should be taken as a dative case. In the sentence "A student gives honorarium to his teacher" the teacher should not be a case at all since he has got no action. He has been selected only as a recipient of a gift. He has got nothing to do with the root 'to give'. He receives the gift. Therefore, he has an action to perform. But the act of receiving is distinct form of giving. An object is the destination of an action. It is the goal towards which an action proceeds. Now, the defenders may hold that the word 'karma' stands for an objective case. Such an interpretation does not stand to reason since a noun or its equivalent does not become a case because of its relation to a case. The universally accepted view is this that a noun or its equivalent which is related to an action is a case. The etymological meaning of the word 'kāraka' is that what brings about an action is a kāraka (a case).

The best instrument by which an action is produced is 'karaṇa' (an instrumental case). As the meaning of the nominal suffix 'tamap' (i.e., the suffix indicative of the superlative degree) is hard to comprehend so the word 'sādhakatama', contained in the definition of an instrumental case, is inappropriate. An affect comes into being when all conditions without an exception assemble. But it does not come into being if anyone of them is absent. Such being the state of things which particular case shall we select as the best one in order to sprinkle waters from an auspicious pitcher ?

Now, the contenders may defend that the excellence of an instrumental case lies in its having intensive operation directed towards the production of the principle effect. Such an operation is shared by all cases. But it does not exclusively belong to fuels an instance of instrumental case. In the example 'He is cooking with fuels' how do you say that fuels are the instance of an instrumental case? The purport of the objection is that fuels should not be taken as the instance of an instrumental case since they have no distinctive feature to indicate the above case-character.

A locative case is that which points to a locus. With regard to this definition something should be said by way of criticism. A locus in order to be so must contain something. What is this 'something'? Is it a root or a case? In other words, does it contain a root or a case? If you define it precisely and hold that the container of a root (an action) is a locative case then all cases should be included in the class of locative case since all cases are syntactically connected with a root. Now, the defender of the said definition may clarify the above definition thus. Let us take an example of the locative case, viz., 'He cooks rice on a pot'. A pot is a locative case since it contains rice which is being cooked. The act of cooking produces its effect on rice. Rice is the container of the resulting part of the act of cooking. A pot contains rice which is the receptacle of the act of cooking in some form. Therefore, a pot is taken as a locative case. In other words, a locative case points to the indirect locus of a root. The above contention is not tenable. The illustration that he cooks on an even spot cannot be justified if the above meaning of the definition of a locative case is accepted. One should rather say that he cooks in water. The point in objection is this that water directly contains rice which is being cooked but not a spot. Again, the illustration that he takes his food on a mat becomes grammatically incorrect since a mat is the container of a person who takes his food but not of the act of eating. Now, the defender may revise the above definition of locative case and hold that a locative case is such as contains a root through the medium of both nominative and objective cases. In that case the above two illustrations of locative case, viz., 'He cooks rice on a pot'. 'He takes food on a mat' should be incorrect since a pot and a mat are not locii of both nominative and objective cases. Now, the defender may say that the locative case is the locus of anyone of the above cases. In that case, the locus of an objective case involves a reference to the locus of a nominative case and vice versa the locus of a nominative case involves a reference to the locus of an objective case. Thus, the new revised definition of a locative case is in no way different from its immediate antecedent one. The last two definitions are identical in their sense and content. Now, if the defender holds that a locative case is the container of all cases then the illustration that he cooks rice on a pot should not be grammatically correct since a pot is not the locus of all cases. Moreover, a locative case should cease to be a case since a locative case does not find its own locus in itself. Let a few examples of locative case be examined. They are as follows :—'One takes his bath at noon', 'One eats at night', 'One rambles in the east' etc. In these cases time, space etc., having no operation to perform should be devoid of the essence of a case. Thus, they cease to be cases. Thus, the illustrations in question should be considered as grammatically incorrect.

An accusative case is that which refers to the most favourite desideratum of a subject. As the term 'sādhaka-tama', contained in the definition of an instrumental case, conveys no meaning so the word 'īpsita-tama' involved in the definition of an objective case, communicates no sense. Nobody can determine the most favourite one since an action to be accomplished being desired all cases are equally required for its completion by a subject, hence all of them are the most favourite ones. Now, the contender may say that the goal of an action is the desideratum of a subject. The objector points out that the word to which the case-ending 'am' is attached stands for some thing which is other than an accusative case. The above goal of an action cannot be an accusative case. A case stands for the cause of an action but an object is the result of an action but is not its cause. It involves contradiction to hold that what is the cause of an action is also the most favourite desideratum to be achieved by the same action.

Now, the defender may contend his case thus. An object of

an action is mentioned as a case because it is capable of producing an action. If this is your contention then the causality of an action is very strange. The causality of an instrumental case takes a unique form, that of a locative case takes another peculiar form and that of a dative case takes a third distinct form. In the case of an accusative case though boiled rice is accomplished by an action yet the former is the invariable cause of the latter since the said action is not performed if its object is not its goal. In other words, an object is the final cause of an action. The said hypothesis of the grammarians is not convincing. What is the final result cannot be said to be a means since pleasure and such other phenomena which are the mere goal of an action should also be called the means of it. One should bear in mind that the designation 'case' does not depend upon the arbitrary will of the founder of a branch of study. In other words, such a nomenclature is not due to the convention set up by a great teacher. A noun or its substitute becomes a case when it enters into relation to an action. The exact nature of the relation is this that what is the means to an action is a case. If a contrary relation takes place between them, how will a noun enjoy the status of a case ? Now, the grammarian raises an objection to the above criticism. They point out that if the above criticism is accepted then one should say that a man cooks rice but he should not say that a man cooks boiled rice since boiled rice is the result of the act of cooking. The objectors review the said critical remark and hold that they have already stated what they have got to say with regard to the definition of the accusative case. In the body of the said definition the word 'īpsitatama' (most desired) has been given. It is an objective which qualifies the accusative case. This adjective carries sense. If it applies to rice in the sentence "A man cooks rice" then it loses its significance since it has no distinctive capacity for bringing about a result.

That which is independent is the subjective case. What is independence ? You may say 'One who moves out of his own will is independent'. In that case how do you explain the sentence 'The bank of a river breaks down ?' The subject of the verb 'breaks down' is 'bank'. The bank is an inanimate object. It has no will. Hence, it cannot be the subjective case of the said verb. 'Now, the grammarians may revise their definition and hold that the case the operation of which controls those of other cases is said to be the subjective case. The objectors examine it and find defects in it. They hold that an action is to be produced by all cases. As such one fails to understand the point that the operation of which case governs that of which one since all the cases constitute an interdependent system. Now, the grammarians may hold that the case which induces other cases to do an action but itself is not induced by other cases to do it is the subject. In that case all inanimate objects cannot be the subjective case. Thus, the charge which has been already brought against the grammarians remains unsolved.

Now, the grammarians may revise their definition and hold that the subjective case is that the operation of which is expressed by a verb. The critics join issue with them and point out that they fail to grasp the import of this definition. A verb does not express the operation of a particular case. But it conveys all operations of all cases. If one does not subscribe to this assumption then all cases cannot co-operate to do the same action. Now, if a verb expresses the operations of all cases then all cases should be taken as the subject of a verb.

Now, the grammarians may revise their thesis and hold that the subjective case is that the operation of which is mainly expressed by a verb. This revised thesis is not tenable. The reason is as follows. When a sentence is communicated a verb is uttered only once. If it is uttered once then how can it express the operation of a particular case subordinately and that of another case principally ? In the Sanskrit Grammar two types of the subjective case have been mentioned. The first and the second types are represented by the independent and the causative subjects. How does a verb convey the said additional meaning ?

As the definitions of cases are not consistent so rules which govern case-endings following the above definitions, are not approved by us, the critics. The rules of the Sanskrit Grammar run like this:—'The Ablative case takes the fifth case-ending and the locative case takes the seventh case-ending. These rules cannot take effect if the ablative and the locative cases are not properly determined by their exact definitions.

Another point may be added to our critical note. In the Sanskrit grammar there are rules which govern the combining of two or more correlative words into a single compound word or the combining of a word and a nominal suffix, correlative, into a single word. Are they correlative ab initio ? Or, they have become correlative on the strength of the conventional sūtra of Pāṇini viz. 'Samarthaḥ pada-vidhiḥ' ? In any case the term 'correlation' has got to be clearly explained. The grammarians may say that if two terms relate to one and the same meaning, they are correlative. In other words, correlation consists in the relation to one and the same meaning. How do the grammarians come by this meaning of the term 'sāmarthya' (correlation) ? They may say that the said meaning is revealed through the use of compound words and nominal suffixes and the knowledge of such uses. It is also evident that correlation is cognised if there are examples of compound words and nominal suffixes and they are cognised and that if correlation exists then the examples of compound words and their knowledge becomes possible. Thus, the above hypothesis illustrates a glaring instance of vicious circle.

Another point may be added to this critical note. There are examples of compound words when the said correlation is conspicuous by its absence. They are as follows (1) aśrāddhabhoji (the negative particle is syntactically related to the root 'bhuj' but not to śrāddha. It signifies a Brāhmaṇa who does not participate in a feast due to funeral ceremony), (2) dadhighaṭaḥ (dadhi is not directly related to ghaṭa. The word 'pūrṇa' has been dropped. It means a pot full of sour milk), and gorathaḥ (the word 'go' is not directly related to rathaḥ. The intervening word 'vāhita' is missing. It stands for a cart which is carried by bullocks). Similarly, many instances of nominal suffixes are noticed in the absence of correlation. The word 'aṅgulika' is used. It means one who digs with a finger. The word 'vārkṣamūlika' has been used. It denotes one who has come from the root of a tree. These usages presuppose the instrumental and the ablative cases. These cases have not been properly defined. Hence, these usages are not correct. If a person speaks a sentence then he is a speaker. Suppose there is a place where nobody speaks. How do we say that there are no speakers on the spot ? Hence, these rules of grammar are not logically justifiable.

The definition of a nominal stem (prātipadika) as given by Pāṇini in the sūtra "Arthavadadhāturapratyayaḥ prātipadikam" is too wide since it is applicable to a sentence as well.

Now, the grammarians may contend that Pāṇini has written a complementary sūtra to mend his defects. It runs thus—'Kṛttaddhitasamāsāśca'. It has been mentioned as a special injunction since the word 'samāsa' finds a place in it. As it is a special injunction so it excludes all sentences excepting compound words from the province of nominal stems. Thus, a sentence will be excluded from a nominal stem. In other words, the definition of a nominal stem as given by Pāṇini is exact. If this is the contention of the followers of Pāṇini then the critics may as well point out that the above definition of nominal stem should not contain two adjectives, viz. (1) adhātuḥ (other than a verb) and (2) apratyayaḥ (other than an inflexion) since a verb and an inflexion will be excluded from the field of nominal stems on the strength of the special injunction.

Now, the followers of Pāṇini may contend that as a compound word and its corresponding expounding sentence convey the same meaning so they are one in different forms having similar functions and the mention of the compound word in the special injunction can exclude only a sentence but neither a verb nor an inflexion. They simply hope against a hope. The words which constitute an expounding sentence and those which constitute a compound word have no similar function. Hence, there is no necessity of holding that a compound word and its expounding sentence have similar function. Moreover, it has been established that a sentence is significant. Hence, the definition of a nominal stem suffers from the defect of being too wide.

As a nominal stem has not been exactly defined so case-endings such as 'sup' etc., cannot be added to a nominal stem in accordance with the sūtra "ṅyāp prātipadikāt" etc. There is no need of discussing this matter. So, the science of grammar is full of serious defects. Its rules exercise little influence upon verbal transactions.

The following reasons exhibit serious defects in the science of grammar. (1) The celebrated commentator of Pāṇini has taken pains to subject to a minute examination all which have been clearly expressed, which have not been stated and which have been subtly hinted at. (2) In some cases, straight definitions have been refuted under the pretext that they contain redundant long vowels or that they involve greater quantity of syllables. (3) In some cases, the interpreters hold that this plausible rule does not apply to this particular case because the commentator has not explicitly approved of its application. (4) The field of application of a sūtra has been sometimes indefinitely stated. A few illustrations have been mentioned and a big gap has been left open. Such a measure leaves room for indecision. The mention of ākṛti-gaṇa illustrates the above point. (5) In some sūtras the word 'bahula' occurs. This shows that rules involving the word 'bahula' are vague. In many cases, these rules hold good. This shows that the field of these rules has not been exactly described.

Some other critics remark that the following usages are found in the grammar. They are as follows, (1) Śobhā; (2) cīrṇam (this word cannot be analysed); (3) kandiśīka; (4) bhrājiṣṇu, (5) gaṇeya; & (6) vareṇya. These usages find no place in the authoritative collection of correct words. Definitions of memory, doubt and illusion are conspicuous by their absence in the grammar of Pāṇini. The said grammar has swerved from its duty. These critics find fault with Pāṇini's grammar and have heaped contumely on it. The defects of a grammar are as palpable as the disease of ascites. As we like to avoid the unnecessary swelling of the bulk of our work so we close our examination here.

Now, the grammarians may contend thus :- "Let us take for granted that Pāṇini, the framer of grammatical rules, has no sharp intellect and the celebrated commentators have no deep insight. But a grammarian who has very keen intellect was born. Many other commentators who had penetrative insight saw the light of the day. From such persons we have learnt the correct rules of grammar. In other words, Pāṇini's failure has not blocked the future of the Sanskrit grammar".

Such a contention does not hold good since critics, having superior intellectual attainments, have exposed the hollowness of the established conclusions, but the abler critics of the said defenders may join issue with them and find fault with their decision and the others may also subject their view to severe criticism. Hence, a regressus ad infinitum will be the inevitable conclusion. Therefore, there is no work on grammar which is free from all reproaches. The net result is that the great vow of the study of grammar simply entails a great hardship on its reader. Bṛhaspati has also given his voice to the above note. He says that it is impracticable to get by heart the vocabulary used in the Sanskrit Language if one studies each and every word, the correct rules of Sanskrit Grammar have not as yet been established, the existing grammar is open to serious defects and the hope of correction faces the fallacy of regressus ad infinitum. The followers of the great teacher Śukra hold that the science of grammar is a fell disease.

Some other critics have also said that he who is under the influence of bad stars or is cowed down with the fear of royal punishment or has been cursed by his parents embraces the study of grammar of a classical language.

Some critics have also said to this effect :-

In order to blunt the edge of one's sharp intellect Pāṇini's grammar and its commentary known as vṛtti should be prescribed for his study and sesame, a kind of pulses, wood apples and boiled rice prepared from a particular kind of rice should be prescribed for his food since these are the best instruments of benumbing keen intellect.

Even if a learned man takes pains in the study of grammar he cannot acquire proficiency in Vedic vocabulary as he is able to understand only human dialects.

There is no acknowledged avenue of understanding Vedic words. Hence, the Vedas remain unintelligible from the very beginning. How can they be the source of valid knowledge ?

The Establishment of the Hypothesis that Chaste Words are Denotative

Let the adverse criticism, recorded in the preceding chapter, be reviewed. It has been stated that words used in ordinary dialects such as 'gavi' etc. are as denotative as chaste words used in classical Sanskrit Language such as 'go', etc., are from eternity. We shall now cast a shadow of doubt on the above rival hypothesis. The objector has put forward a rival hypothesis that words used in ordinary dialects, e. g., gavi, etc. are denotative. They have logically established it. It is a piece of illusory knowledge. A critical student of Indian Philosophy who has examined these hypotheses distinguishes the true hypothesis from the false one.

After this, knowledge which dawns in his mind is true. He comes to understand that chaste words such as 'go', etc., have only denotation but words used in common dialect have no denotation. Through the influence of this knowledge he is relieved of his suspense of judgment. A labourer who carries load becomes nervous when he comes across too heavy load. If a portion of it is reduced then he entertains a doubt whether he will be able to carry the remaining portion or not. Similarly, the student of philosophy doubts whether words used in common dialects have denotation or not. Such a doubt is interesting but not idle. Then he will adopt such lines of thinking as will solve his doubts. If he follows the indicated lines of thinking then he will obtain mental satisfaction. The path of argument leads to the determination of truth. So, we refer to it. Let us now examine the hypothesis whether one undergoes the same discipline when he learns to use words adopted in ordinary dialects as he does in the case of words used in the Sanskrit language. If the use of words employed in common dialects such as gavi, etc., is learnt in the similar manner then one should conjecture that they are eternal. Let us now examine whether we have an opportunity of subscribing to such a hypothesis or not. When a student is initiated into the Vedic lore the teacher imparts minute lessons to him. The teacher is very particular about the correct pronunciation of each Vedic word. He pronounces each word with its proper accents, nasal sound and vowels. His disciple exactly repeats it. If he has any slip in his pronunciation, the teacher gives him proper instruction. Unless and until the student is able to read the Vedas in a proper manner the teacher does not allow him to leave his residence. The student also learns the Vedes with rapt attention. A student who has received proper instruction will be a teacher. He will also instruct his student in this manner. The present teacher was also a student in his young age. He was also initiated into the Vedic lore in this way by another teacher. This teacher was also taught by another teacher. Jaimini holds that in this way the study of the Vedas has been continuing from eternal time. The Naiyāyikas hold that the study of the Vedas has been in vogue from the day of creation.

In this manner if words like gavi, etc., have been guarded against deformation like words 'go', etc., and if these words are also employed to convey their meaning on their own strength then the former word will certainly share the same dignity with the latter ones which are held to be eternal. If the above condition is fulfilled then whom shall we blame ? But we have got an alternative hypothesis to suggest. The speaker pronounces the word 'go'. But the listener does not repeat it in the same manner since his organ of speech does not act properly owing to his inadvertence, sloth, etc. He tries to pronounce but actually mispronounces it. Thus the word which is pronounced becomes deformed. We learn it from our experience. Hence a doubt arises in our mind. Words which have already assumed perverted form or will take such form are used in the dialect of carters. The old uncultured fellows cannot even properly pronounce these deformed words when they talk to boys and girls of the cowherd class. Thus the origin of many deformed words may be traced to inability to pronounce chaste words. Thus a doubt arises even in the mind of a person of keen intellect. Are words like 'go', etc., which are established from eternity significant and denotative ? And are other words deformed, being mispronounced through inadvertence ? Or, do all words enjoy the same status alike ? Now, the objectors may contend that all words have the same status. If this is their contention then we point out that even to-day some words, being mispronounced by ignorant ladies and children, assume perverted forms. Now we ask "Can they discharge the onerous function of the chaste words ?" The objectors cannot say to this effect "let them bear the burden of the chaste words." The reason is that one is directly aware of the fact that these words have assumed perverted forms. In other words, the deformation of chaste words has taken place.

According to reasons stated above, words which are now used by uncultured ladies and children are considered to be debased and owing to their deformation they cannot vie with chaste words. If deformed words of recent origin do not enjoy the status of chaste words then we argue "How can words like 'gavi' etc., which may be explained otherwise, enjoy the status of chaste words like 'go' etc."

The illustrious teacher Jaimini has also said to this effect. As it requires a good deal of effort to pronounce a word so words, being mispronounced, become defective. This defect amounts to deformation. Śabara, the commentator, has stated in his commentary that a good deal of effort is required to pronounce a word properly. A wind springing up in the region of umbilicus, goes up, increases in bulk in chest, passes through trachea, dashes against the top of palate and springing back moves in the mouth and manifests various letters. A person who intends to pronounce a word may be at fault. One desires to have a fall on the dry land but falls down on the swampy ground. One thinks that he will touch once but touches twice.

The Hypothesis that Deformed words are eternal is not tenable

Now, the defenders of the eternality of deformed words come forward and hold a brief for their hypothesis. They argue in the following manner. The critics should put forward direct proofs in order to establish the late growth of unchaste words spoken by the uncultured people. The origin of words like gavi etc. is surely traced to inadvertence and such other defects. Hence they cannot enjoy the same exalted position as the chaste words, viz., go etc. do.

The critics say in reply that they will give the proper answer in no time and their wish will be fulfilled. The great thinkers who hold that deformed words such as gavi etc. have been current in this country from eternity are asked to solve the above-mentioned rational doubt. They should ponder over it. The chaste words 'hasta', 'pāṇi' and 'kara' are synonyms. Is the word 'gavi' a synonym of the word 'go' in the same sense ? Or, is the word 'gavi' the distorted form of the word 'go' owing to some possible defects either in the reception or in the pronunciation of the latter one. It is not rational to think that many synonymous words denote a single object.

If the raison d'etre of the said statement is asked, an answer is as follows. The canon of the philosophy of grammar is this that a single word denotes a single object. What leads to formulate the canon is this that if it is accepted then the relation of denotation holding between a word and its meaning is easy to establish. Again, one is to face a lot of troubles if the relation of denotation holds between many words and a single object. If a word exclusively denotes a single object then a word and its meaning remain unaltered for ever. They will never falsify each other. This word denotes only this object. This object is denoted by this word only. Thus, this canon is justifiable. But if many words signify a single object then the object may not be denoted by a particular word since there are many other words to denote the said object though the said word does not denote the said object. Hence, if the hypothesis that many words denote a particular object is accepted then there is a chance for misrepresentation. Again, if another hypothesis that a word denotes many meanings is accepted then a word has a fair chance of misrepresenting its meaning since the said word points to meanings other than the known one. Hence, any hypothesis which embodies the breach of the above rule may be a menace to the understanding of the true meaning of a word.

All the synonyms such as 'hasta', 'kara', 'pāṇi' etc. denote a single object. A few stray cases like this do not illustrate the violation of the said rule. None of the words such as 'akṣaḥ', 'pādaḥ', 'māsaḥ' etc., comes under any rule. As they are exceptional cases so one is compelled to admit that a single word denotes different meanings. This rule is quite accidenal. But the general rule is easy and straight. It conveys that one word has got a single denotation only. In other words, a word stands for a single object. Now, if one admits that the words 'go' 'gavi' and other deformed ones are synonyms then the above rule does not hold good since every chaste word has its corresponding deformed words. Hence, it yields place to another rule. The breach of the general rule is due to some defects in the speaker such as inadvertence etc., It has been said before that the deformed words such as gavi etc. do not enjoy the same elevated position in language as the chaste words such as 'go' etc., do because of their defective origin.

Moreover, the power of denotation belonging to a word is very subtle. It is neither perceived nor inferred. It is revealed only by means of presumption. If presumption is too weak to reveal it, no other source of knowledge can illuminate it. Again, if presumption is indirectly established then words like 'go' etc., cannot gather sufficient strength from presumption to communicate their meanings. Thus we see that words such as 'go' etc., possess the power of denotation by means of which they convey their meanings such as the real cow etc. The said power of denotation does not belong to deformed words such as 'gavi' etc. Why has the age-long tradition of the expert grammarians been violated by the uncultured rustic ? In other words, why do not the uncultured persons imitate the practice of the cultured ones if chaste words are only competent enough to convey their meanings ? An answer to this question is this :— the use of chaste words has been superseded by that of vulgar words just as the communication of one's intention by means of the winking of an eye and the signal, given by hands, etc. has yielded place to the use of words of the lower caste non-Aryans. Does not the power of denotation belong to the winking of an eye or to words and sentences, spoken by the lower castes ? We stick to the view that they do not possess the power of denotation. If this is true, why do they convey their sense ? We say that they have got no innate power of conveying their sense. As they have got no stable character so the innate power of denotation does not belong to them. These hints or words convey meanings on the strength of convention arbitrarily set up by the people who use them. The power of denotation as proposed by the Naiyāyikas has a universal significance. This power of denotation has been set up by God and has been in vogue since the first day of creation. It is similar to the innate power of denotation advocated by the Mīmāṁsakas. It should not be compared with the conventional power of denotation the range of application of which is very limited. The innate power of denotation or such power as has been imparted by God belongs only to words like 'go' etc., but not to deformed words such as gavi etc. Owing to the similarity of letters belonging to words 'go' and 'gavi' when the word 'gavi' is pronounced it revives the memory of the word 'go' and thus conveys the meaning of the word 'go' recalled in our mind.

How do such persons as are ignorant of words like 'go' etc., remember them ? Which is the sure means of learning them ? A special study is the sure way of their access. Which science is to be studied ? The study of grammar is called abhiyoga, which is necessary for this purpose. One has got repeatedly to study the science of grammar and closely to observe the illustrations cited in it. The complete acquisition of the science of grammar is known as its special study. By such study one acquires innumerable chaste words which are worthy of being used by the cultured persons. Such acquisition of chaste words helps him to detect the nature of unchaste words used by the uncultured ladies and the majority of rustic people because of their dissimilarity. But our objector has said that the number of chaste words is so vast that none can get them by heart by hundreds of divine years. We do not share the view of our objector. Tradition says, "The science of grammar which has been formulated by Pāṇini and elaborated by the two other sages of great repute teaches rules well tested by them. These rules give such a faultless analysis of words that they stand above all defects such as defects of being too wide or too narrow." As the Vedas distinguish virtue from vice, as the incarnation of God draws distinction between truth and falsehood, as the codes of Ethics differentiate between good and evil, as the instructions of Manu and others discriminate between the edible and non-edible, as an oath points out the difference of purity from impurity, so grammar shows the distinction between chaste and unchaste words. Every body is acquainted with the truth of the above statement. No body can deny its truth. The truth of the said statement may be easily verified even today. It is a well-known fact that there is a gulf of difference between the speech of persons well versed in the science of grammar and that of other persons such as the uncultured rustic. Thus owing to the absence of training the employment of deformed words may owe its existence to ignorance. We shall make gratuitous assumptions if we hold that the power of denotation uniformly belongs to chaste and deformed words. If we learn by heart the science of grammar, we can easily discern the difference between chaste and unchaste words. There is a standing rule that chaste words are denotative but unchaste words are not. Hence, we are in a position to conclude that all charges, levelled against our hypothesis by our objectors, are refuted. One objection still remains unanswered. It is this that there is no source of valid knowledge which points to the chastity of a word.

The chastity of a word is not a perceptible property. There is no mark which helps to infer it. The authoritative works do not reveal it. Therefore, the hypothesis of chastity is full of defects.

The chastity of a word is fit to be perceived with the aid of the authoritative works

There is another verse which contradicts the findings of the above verse. It says : The chastity of a word is a perceptible property. There is a mark which points to the existence of chastity. The authoritative works reveal it. Therefore, the hypothesis of chastity is not defective.

As we visualise the purity of water not contaminated by a piece of floating hair etc., so the auditory perception of the chastity of a word, its proper accent, the actual order of its constituent letters and such other properties are correctly presented to our consciousness. This awareness is neither indecisive nor contradicted by another true judgment nor is produced by a defective sense-organ, viz, ears. The ascertainment of the truth of the said auditory perception is nothing but the clear and distinct auditory perception of a word which is a collection of letters. When we judge a piece of auditory perception as untrue the perception possesses a contrary character. The defects which invalidate its truth have been exactly defined. Hence, we hold that the chastity or the unchastity of word is directly cognised by our sense-organ.

The objectors come forward with a pertinent question which is as follows : If the chastity or the unchastity of a word had been directly perceived with our ordinary sense-organ then persons whose intellect has not developed under the tutelage of the teachers of grammar would have been directly acquainted with the said properties (chastity or unchastity) of a word. But it is a fact that such persons do not perceive the chastity or unchastity of a word only with their ears. Therefore, the chastity or unchastity of a word is not a perceptible property.

The upholders of the above hypothesis contend that the said objection does not hold good. The complete statement of our hypothesis is this that the said property is grasped by our auditory sense-organ if it receives the aid of instructions from a sound grammarian. In other words, though our naked ears cannot detect it yet our trained ears are competent enough to do it. This is what we admit. Similarly, we cannot deny that Brāhmaṇahood is perceptible since it is perceived with our eyes which have improved under the instructions of the Śāstras. Some logicians have advanced arguments in favour of our hypothesis. If one goes up the peak of a mountain and sees an object below from the top of the mountain, then one cannot say that the said perception has not been rightly designated. Or, if the truth of determinate perception is established, perception of objects qualified by words has been also proved to be true. Let us cite another well-known parallel case of perception. Suppose, a man sees a jack-fruit tree in front of him for the first time. An experienced man who is conversant with the name of this tree comes there and initiates him into its name. He teaches him that the name of this tree is 'Panasa' (jack-fruit tree). He remembers the word of the experienced man and sees the tree. His eyes in co-operation with the memory of the said name produce a piece of knowledge intimately associated with words in the form "This is a jack-fruit tree." Thus when one acquires the relation of denotation holding between a name and the object named, a piece of verbalised knowledge of the above description is unavoidable. The author of the Nyāya-sūtra realises that this piece of word-penetrated knowledge is of course perceptual. But this is not the only form of perception. In order to give a clear expression to his view he adds the word 'avyapadeśya' to the definition of perception which has been recorded in his sūtra. The initial perception which arises from the sense-object contact only is called 'indeterminate perception'. It is not word-penetrated. When one communicates his perceptual knowledge to others it is always word-penetrated. The memory of the word (the above name), instructed by an experienced person, and the eyes jointly produce the second perception that this is a jack-fruit-tree. This is an instance of visual perception. This is the account of the above logicians. Similarly, in the present case the auditory sense-organ, accompanied by the instruction imparted by a person well versed in grammar, grasps directly the chastity or unchastity of a word. Hence, the above properties of a word are perceptible but not otherwise. The above logicians have also cited other ways of determining Brahmanhood at the sight of a man. In a country where the moral code is well maintained by the efficient administration of an influential king the good conduct of a person reveals that he is a Brahman. A king ably governs a particular country in accordance with the code of Manu and other distinguished law-givers. Owing to the personal influence of the king there are persons who observe the duties of their caste and different stages of life. Nobody belonging to a lower caste, can pose as a member of a higher caste, putting on the garb of a member of a higher caste and adopt a higher profession in that state. During the reign of such a king if we notice the good conduct of a particular person, we at once recognise his Brahmanhood. This recognition is direct. Similarly, when we notice that some persons have applied themselves to a work, hearing a distinct word we gather the sense of the word from their activities. We also remember the rules of grammar and find out the formation of a word. We find out its root and suffix. In the case of a verb we notice such an inflexion as represents its tense and number With regard to the structure of a word we also take into consideration other points, viz., the dropping of a letter, the super-addition of a letter, the supersession of a letter or a syllable by another letter or syllable and such other points. All these things constitute the infallible sign of the chastity of a word or a sentence. If the said infallible mark is present in a word and the word conveys a meaning then we rightly infer that the word is chaste. The authoritative work, viz., Vedic and Smṛti Literature instructs us to use chaste words such as madhu (honey) etc. during the observance of a sacrificial rite so that the institutor of a sacrifice surely derives the result of the said sacrifice, viz. heavenly bliss since the use of chaste words during the performance of a sacrifice is beneficial to a sacrifice. The Śāstras instruct that if a learned person uses unchaste words during the performance of a rite then he commits a sin which hinders the completion of a rite, They also bear evidence to the existence of the language of the common people who use non-Sanskritic words (unchaste words).

Now, an objector opposes the above view and holds that if the nature of unchaste words is previously determined like kalañja (a kind of fruit or the meat of a dear, killed by a poisoned arrow) then an injunction or a prohibition has room for working upon it. But the Śāstras say nothing about the nature of unchaste words. It is not also proper to think that the nature of unchaste words is implied by an injunction. This point has been stated before. The upholders of the hypothesis in question meet this objection. They hold that there is an element of truth in the above objection. But it is also a truism that Vedic literature and Dharma Śāstras furnish us with instructions on virtuous and vicious deeds. From the above statement it is implied that one should use chaste words and avoid the use of unchaste words. But it is also a bounden duty for a dutiful man to ascertain the nature of chaste and unchaste words since the injunction or the prohibition presupposes the definite knowledge of such words. Such knowledge is also true. It cannot be disregarded since an injunction requires it. Or another solution of the above problem is possible. Pāṇini has quoted a passage from the Smṛti Śāstra as an authoritative one. On the strength of its validity a Vedic injunction which enjoins the use of chaste words as the basis of the said Smṛti passage may be assumed.

We have no access to a Vedic injunction which enjoins the sipping of water before the commencement of a religious deed. But Smṛti works furnish us with this instruction. We postulate a Vedic injunction as the basis of the instruction, given by the Smṛti works. Therefore, the validity of the hypothetical Vedic injunction should not be challenged. Therefore, the chastity of a word comes within the province of the Śāstras. A person, skilled in the use of language, uses unalloyed chaste words. Good speeches, delivered by such a person, consist of the faultless order of letters. Their style is elegant and vigorous. They command applause from the learned scholars. They are a class in themselves. But the utterances of the rustic people consist of ill-chosen letters which mar the development of feelings or sentiments. They, being very harsh, irritate the mind of the audience. Everybody has direct experience of difference between the speech of a learned man and that of a vulgar person. With the aid of a grammar only we are in a position to ascertain the purity of the faultless speech of a learned person. Therefore, the distinction between chaste and unchaste words is not baseless. The Vedic passages such as "A Brāhmaṇa should not speak the language of the uncultured people and should not also use distorted words since a deformed word is as good as a word of the rustic people", being interpreted, point to the efficacy of employing chaste words.

The objector has raised a point which runs thus : There is an injunction that one should speak chaste words. It is regulative in its character. There is also a prohibition that one should not speak unchaste words. Such a prohibition is meaningless. Therefore, the said Vedic passage carries no weight. This point is not forceful. If there is an injunction that one should drink water and if there is a prohibition that one should not drink fire then the said prohibition becomes absurd since it has no scope. But the above prohibition is not of that character. The objector may argue that the very injunction that one should use chaste words implies that one should not use unchaste words. Therefore such a prohibition is absolutely unnecessary. The reply to it is as follows. As the non-Aryans have no status in the society of the Aryans so unchaste words have no place in the classical language (i.e., Sanskrit Language). Therefore they are not worthy of being used. But our experience says that the unchaste words as well convey their sense. Therefore, the use of unchaste words has a possibility. So the above prohibition is significant. Though all worldly transactions may be conducted alike by chaste and unchaste words yet the use of chaste words is conducive to merit. This injunction stands on the same footing with another injunction that one should take his meal, facing the East. These injunctions serve no worldly interest. Their goal is merit.

As a line of distinction has not been drawn between chaste and unchaste words so one apprehends that it is an impossible feat to teach all chaste words since one has got to instruct them one by one. This objection which has been raised before has been solved. We have elaborately proved that the true nature of a chaste word is both perceived and inferred. As a chaste word is recognised so rules may be easily prescribed concerning chaste words. Thus all sophism which centres round the definition of the chastity of a word stands refuted. We have said that a word is chaste if it obeys the rules of grammar and conveys a meaning. The chastity is a universal. It belongs to all homogeneous words just like the universal of cowness. Or, it is not a universal. It is the common property of all chaste words like pācakatva– the common property of all cooks. Though the chastity of a word is a common property yet it acts as a differentia. The net result of this assumption is this that all our transactions with all chaste words are made by means of it. The chastity of a word is a common property shared by all chaste words. Hence, it connotes all homogeneous chaste words.

Or, let expressiveness be equivalent to the chastity of a word. Let us accept your suggestion. Though your suggestion is accepted yet the rule, viz., "One should speak chaste words only" may be prescribed with community. Though an unchaste word does not convey a meaning, yet one may suspect that it has a meaning since on hearing it the basic chaste word is recalled to mind. This benefit of doubt may accelerate the use of unchaste words. The above rule will be fruitful since it will check the possible use of unchaste words. As the above rule imposes restriction, it, truly speaking, amounts to a negative rule since its main function is to dissuade persons from using unchaste words. Thus a regulative rule is de facto a negative rule (parisaṁkhyā vidhi). Shall we hold that the rule in question has double functions? Our solution to this problem is this that if a rule has double character, no serious defect defaces it. Let us discuss another objection. If an injunctive statement holds out a promise of reward then it is to be treated as a recommendatory statement since it has no independent voice. If one follows a recommendatory statement, he acquires no merit. If one does not follow it, he commits no sin. Thus, the rule which governs the use of chaste words and dissuades one from the use of unchaste words deserves to be neglected. This is the sum and substance of the above objection. But it does not stand to reason.

Moreover, an objection has been raised that it is an impossible feat to instruct all chaste words, one after another, since chaste and unchaste words have not been properly defined. This objection has been met since it has been elaborately stated before that the essence of chaste and unchaste words is directly cognised or inferred. On the basis of this essential property, regulative injunctions may be easily framed. Hence all sophistical arguments centering round the definition of the chastity of a word have been silenced. The definition of a chaste word is this. A chaste word is such as obeys the rules of grammar and is expressive. Thus the chastity of a word is expressiveness coupled with obedience to the rules of grammar. This common property behaves like a universal, e.g., the universal of cowness. It belongs to all individuals coming under the same class. Or, chastity is not a universal. But it is a common property like the essence of all cooks (pācakatva). Though it is not a universal yet it serves the purpose of a differentia, since the common property of all individuals belonging to a class is a distinguishing mark. The net result is that all general statements about chaste words may be made on the strength of this common property. In other words, generalisation of all chaste words is possible.

Or, though we agree to your proposal that the chastity of a word is its expressiveness yet the rule, "One should use chaste words only" deserves application. An objection may be raised to this effect that as an unchaste word, being not expressive, has no chance to be used, what is the utility of the above rule? Though an unchaste word is not expressive yet the use of such words is not impossible. Let us take a hypothetical case. On hearing an unchaste word, a person may remember a chaste word. He may doubt whether the word conveys a sense or not. Relying on the benefit of this doubt the use of unchaste words may be in vogue. In order to do away with such possibilities, the above rule will be significant. Now, a new difficulty arises, A regulative injunction has both positive and negative imports. But in this case the import of the said injunction is truly speaking, negative. Thus it is more of the nature of a parisaṁkhyā vidhi than that of a niyama vidhi since its function is mainly negative. Hence, an injunction is saddled with the functions of two distinct types of injunctions. The objectors think that it is objectionable to hold that an injunction discharges two functions. But our contention is that such functioning on the part of an injunction is not objectionable.

Let us discuss another objection raised by our opponents. The purport of their criticism is as follows :— The Vedic sentences which speak of the reward or the punishment of an action are means to an end. They enjoy no independence. Thus, they are only recommendatory in their character. As merit or demerit has no connection with rites suggested by recommendatory sentences so one who employs either chaste or unchaste words acquires neither merit nor demerit thereby. This is the sum and substance of the above objection. But the above objection does not stand to reason. Though a recommendatory sentence is not an end in itself yet it insists upon the restricted use of chaste words. Now, if one follows it, he acquires merit. But the use of unchaste words is the violation of an injunction, i.e., of the above rule. Hence, a person who employs unchaste words commits a sin. The result is that demerit accrues to him. Now, our opponent may criticise this solution. He may point out that the recommendatory sentence "Juhu is to be made up of leaves" should have also connection with merit or demerit. In other words, if one follows the instruction, given by the recommendatory sentence, he acquires merit and if one does not follow it, he commits a sin. Our answer to this charge is this that if such a consequence happens, wherein lies a defect ? Let us clarify the standpoint of the Naiyāyikas. The Naiyāyikas do not accept the division of the recommendatory sentences into two classes, viz., fruitful and fruitless. They have also shown that the constituent words of a recommendatory sentence convey a distinct meaning and purport and differ from those who believe in the hypotheses that there are fruitless recommendatory sentences in the explanation of these words. This point has been discussed before. Let us stop here. Hence, the Naiyāyikas hold that recommendatory sentences such as "If a word is properly employed, it fulfils our desires in the next world" are fruitful. The above recommendatory sentence, cited by us, points to the study of the science of grammar, since if one does not go through grammar, he can hardly use chaste and correct words. Thus, the purport of the above sentence is that one should read grammar. It is virtually an injunction. The other recommendatory sentences should be interpreted in this light.

The opponents have also raised a question, viz., "Why has not Pāṇini, himself, the author of grammatical sūtras. mentioned the utility of the study of grammar". Such an objection does not land us in difficulty, since the people all over India from the Himalayan region up to the Cape Comorin know very well that grammar is ancillary to the Vedas. If the Vedas are useless then let them who are ignorant of the Vedas be blessed. All Vedic acts which yield tangible and transcendental result will be given up. The baser persons who fall outside the pale of four castes will win a victory over us.

Now, let us turn our attention to the other aspect of the problem. If the study of the Vedas is fruitful, the Vedas along with their ancillary sciences serve our purpose. The accessory sciences have got no distinct utility to materialise. There is no need of assuming any separate mission which they fulfil. Nobody cares to expect a distinct fruit from the Prayāja sacrifice since a Prayāja sacrifice is subordinate to the Darśa-Purṇamāsa sacrifice. As Pāṇini, the author of grammatical sūtras, is aware of the character of the science of grammar, he has made no mention of its utility.

But the commentators on the Sūtras of Pāṇini have shown the principal utility of grammar and other utilities which follow from it in order to promote the interest of their audience. Hence, nobody should be taken to task.

Now, the objectors may put questions, viz., "How has grammar become ancillary to the Vedas ? What benefit do the Vedas derive from grammar ? But these are very trifling questions. The questions like the above ones do not stand to reason since either the Vedas and their ancillary sciences are eternal or they have been composed by God. Now, we should prove how Pāṇini, Piṅgala, Parāśara, etc., are designated as authors of several sciences. They are so called because they have composed them either concisely or elaborately. But really speaking, the meaning of the Vedas and its knowledge stand on the same footing with the Vedas. They are either eternal or own their existence to God. Hence, nobody should be taken to task on this issue. The sources of knowledge which comprise the Vedas and their ancillary sciences within them are counted to be fourteen in number.

The sources of knowledge are fourteen in number. They are as follows: "The four Vedas, six ancillary sciences, Mīmāṁsā, the extensive science of logic, the Purāṇas and the codes of Law (Dharmaśāstras) constitute the sources of knowledge. Many sophistical arguments have been put forward against the refinement of words. They simply exhibit verbosity but do not stand upon the solid rock of reality. The objectors have said before, "Which words fall outside the range of chaste words ? What is the refinement of a word ?" In order to avoid all these problems we do not subscribe to the hypothesis that the science of grammar owes its existence to the usages of the authoritative persons. We have already stated that the science of grammar is co-eternal with the Vedas. Though the science of grammar is eternal yet it might have been taken up by an ignorant person in the obscure past and might have been passing through the circle of ignorant persons. Thus the science of grammar has a little significance. In order to meet this possible objection we hold that the science of grammar is based upon the usages of the cultured persons as the smṛti literature is based upon the Vedas. This literature prescribes such duties as have been enjoined by the Vedas and does never prescribe such ones as have been enjoined by books other than the Vedas. The words which have been taught by the science of grammar as chaste ones are seen to be used as such by the cultured persons; just as the teaching of the medical science that a sick person is cured of his malady taking myrobalan is corroborated by the practice of reliable persons. Pāṇini has not composed the science of grammar having learnt it from the cultured personages. Caraka has not also composed his medical treatise, having ascertained the properties of various substances by means of experimental method since the beginning of the cultured persons cannot be traced out. Thus, the fallacy of a vicious circle is met. The science of grammar does not originate from the cultured persons.

The objectors have pointed out many incorrect usages of the cultured persons. They have also referred to a list of unchaste words which have been used by the ancient sages. With regard to these illlustrations the expert linguists have shown the line of defence. In order to restrain the unnecessary enlargement of this volume we cut short all these discussions.

The objectors have found fault with the definitions of a verb and a non-inflected word and with the rules which govern case-endings etc. Many erudite scholars have reviewed the said criticisms and given a fit reply to them. Now, it may be objected that these reviews may be re-examined and so on, ad infinitum. In other words, no decision will be arrived at. The objection does not hold good, since the path which has been shown by the expert linguists is free from disturbances created by the thieves in the shape of destructive critics.

If we follow the above line of defence then the other objections raised by our critics are also met with. The said objections are as follows: the treatise of grammar is incomplete since it does not contain a few words such as śobhā, cīrṇa, vareṇya, gaṇeya, bhrājiṣṇu, kāndīśika etc. The science of grammar falls short of the definitions of memory, doubt, illusion. etc. These defects have been imagined by some critics. These objections have been throughly answered by the grammarians themselves in their own works.

The Śūtra of Bṛhaspati is no sūtra at all. It is not worth considering. He has demonstrated his vain scholarship by advancing a few sophistical arguments which have been manufactured by his pure imagination. We need not enter into the contents of his arguments since they are deliberately misleading.

In fine, the science of grammar is stainless by its very nature and is elegant. It cannot be soiled if one throws the dust of slander at it.

The Study of Grammar is Compulsory

The science of grammar should be studied by all since it is the purest of all sciences and is held in esteem by all persons. It is a means to four human ends. One who wishes to realise them should study it. Moreover, one who intends to obtain mastery over polished language should study it.

Water is purer than the earth. Verses of the Vedas are purer than water. The great sages have stated that the science of grammar occupies a similar place among the three Vedas, viz., the Sāmaveda, the Yajurveda and the Ṛgveda.

In has also been said to eulogise the science of grammar. The persons who have sanctified their mouth (tongue) by studying grammar are gods but not men. They are gods who, having assumed the forms of human beings, walk on this earth.

It is better to be born as mute whales in the miry deep water than to be born as men whose speech is not refined by the study of grammar.

Manu, also, has said in his own work that a scholar who is well-versed in the science of grammar and a scholar who is well-up in the Mīmāṁsā system purify their lineage. He says that he who can analyse a word, and he who can correctly interpret the Vedic sentences employed in sacrifices, sanctify their lineage.

Puṣpadanta has also said to this effect. I have been cursed by the goddess Durgā. As a result of it my citizenship from the city of Śiva has been cancelled. Wretched as I am I lead the life of a captive. If I am to be born in the next life on this dirty earth full of miseries then I may see the light of day in such a place where my ears are filled up with the charming utterances of grammarians, utterances which are as clean as the flow of milk-emitting sprays of sweet nectar.

Those who have closely studied the science of grammar and obtained mastery over refined language may have an easy access to the Vedic words which have diverse forms. Other persons also may thoroughly understand the meaning of the Vedas with the aid of the Vedic lexicon (Nirukta) which is intimately connected with the Vedas. How is it that the Vedas shall not be the source of valid knowledge ? In other words, is there any sense in the objection that the Vedas will remain for ever a sealed book?

The Vedic collection and the science of grammar do not mutually depend upon each other. One can independently learn the science of grammar. If he acquires proficiency in language he can clearly understand the meaning of the Vedic texts. Thus, the charge of mutual dependence is answered.

Those who have not swerved an inch from the proper line of expression and remain devoted to the Vedas have held the science of grammar in esteem. How can the eternal science of grammar which has been recognised by Patañjali, the celebrated teacher, enjoy the same status with the grammar of rustic words?

The Concluding Portion

The barbarians have an access to a few loopholes. They have proclaimed loudly the falsity of the eternal Śāstras and heaped contumely on them by means of demonic language. We have refuted all their charges. The truth of the Vedas remains unshaken.

In fine, we have discussed the four sources of valid knowledge, viz., perception, inference, comparison and verbal testimony in accordance with the traditional point of view. Let those who will act upon these sources of valid knowledge realise their ends of life.

INDEX

Abhāva (Non-perception) 102
Abhihita-anvaya-vāda 843; Criticism of 846, 857; Defence of 848
Absolute, Identity of Sphoṭa with 784
Action, Nyāya view regarding the motive of 749
Activity, Nature of 704
Anvita-abhidhāna-vāda 854; established 851
Apoha, A negative general image 631
Apohas, Universal versus 639
Authoritative statement, Justification of 328
Avyapadeśya 162-64

Bhartṛhari 170
Bhāvanā 704; Factors of 709
Bhāvanā and injunction, Relation between 721

Chala 19-20
Collection of conditions, Discussion on 25-27
Comparison for and against Upamāna, 295; 297-302
Comparison, Mīmāṁsā hypothesis 304-12
Comparison of the Mīmāṁsā School 302-03
Concepts 626; Denial of 661
Concomitance universal, Buddhist view refuted 235
Consciousness and jñāna, Relation between 158
Consciousness of the Sāṁkhyists 53

Denotative relation 499; Eternality refuted 505
Dharma, Criticism of meanings of the term and its answer 577; The meaning of—from the Nyāya standpoint 577
Dhvani and its criticism 101-02
Doubt 16
Dṛṣṭānta 16

God, Existence of—upheld 406; External attributes of—including Omniscience 420; Incorporeal 422; Objections to the existence of 401; —the absolute creator 496
Grammar, Incompetent to solve the riddle 867; Inefficiency of the study of 875; Its insignificant contribution to the improvement upon words 880; The necessity and efficacy of the study of 913

Illusion, Non-discrimination hypothesis of critical 376; Projection hypothesis of 375
Inference, Alternative Three Types of 275; Definition of 226; Explanation of 264; Validity of 258; of past, present and future objects 284
Injunction (Vidhi) 715; Discussion on the meaning of 732-46; Division of 746; Forms of 747; Mīmāṁsaka view of 748
Invariable concomitance, Buddhist view of 234

Jalpa 19-20
Jāti 19-20
Jñāna, Significance of the term 157
Judgement, conditions of—produced validity refuted 357

Kalpanā 177
Kāraka, Discussion on 35-43
Knowing process is an act 35
Knowledge, Fourteen Sources of 3-5; Intrinsic, validity of Mīmāṁsā view 334; Intrinsic validity refuted 345; Its extrinsic validity examined 351; of an unreal object, impossibility of 374; of Merit, Demerit, Heaven and Hell, Sources of 2-3; of the Buddhist, the means of the new definition 46-52

Lakṣaṇa 21
Letters, denoting meaning 788; Hypothesis of the creation of 473; Manifestation of 467; Mīmāṁsaka view that—are concrete universals 451; Nyāya hypothesis of non-eternality of 439; Opposite view of the universals of 459; Review of the denotation of 772
Logic, Six Systems of 6; Utility of the study of 6-7

Manifestation—hypothesis refuted 472

Mantras, An objection to the validity of—and its answer 592
Memory and true knowledge 46
Misapprehension, Hypothesis of—reaffirmed 380; Refutation of 366
Motif 717

Negation, classification of 132; Refutation of the Prabhākara view of 131; The reality of 122
Negative act, Denial of reality to 115
Nigrahasthāna 19-20
Nirṇaya, Importance of 17-18
Non-discrimination—a substitute for Misapprehension 366
Non-erroneous 165
Non-perception, Elevenfold division of 119; Refutation of 107
Novelty in true knowledge, Role of 44
Nyāya and Tarka 5
Nyāya-sūtra, Subject-matter of 7-12
Nyāya-vistāra 5

Objections against divine authorship refuted 527

Parikṣā 21
Perception, Affirmation of transcendental 215; Buddhist objection discussed 198; Defined and refuted 225; Defined by the Mīmāṁsakas—an examination 210; Determinate 195; Place of Parāmarśa in 141-54; Kumārila's alternative interpretation 213; Mental 219; Rājā, the author of Yuktidīpikā on 225; the definition of Perception in Nyāya-sūtra 136, View of Ācārya on 139
Power of cause, Criticism of 80-81
Pramāṇa, Definition of 22; Etymological meaning of 22; Final definition of 28; Final view on the nature of 54-56; of the Sāṃkhya School, the definition of 52-53
Pramāṇas, Buddhist view on 28-33; Criticism of the view of Mīmāṁsakas on 34-46; Division of 22, 56-57; Refutation of the Buddhist hypothesis on 61-64; Two-fold division of—the Buddhist hypothesis 57-61
Pratibhā 46
Presumption, Criticism of 79-80, 85-87; Criticism of the Prabhākara view 88; Prabhākara view on 87-88; of the Bhaṭṭa School 64-76
Probability and Rumour, Criticism of the hypothesis of 133
Propositions, A syllogism of five 17
Pūrvavat, Meaning of 267

Reason Sound, Five conditions of 251
Recognition as a piece of true knowledge 46
Regressus ad infinitum, Discussion on the nature of 44-45

Śabda (Verbal knowledge authentic) 312; Criticism of the validity of 327
Śabda and inference distinguished 318
Śabda-bhāvanā, Analysis of 720
Śakti, Criticism of 80-81
Śakti refuted 81-85
Sāmānyatodṛṣta, Meaning of 273
Samplava 64
Saṁvedana 43-44
Scriptures, Reconciliation of all 562; The common authorship of the different sects of religion 558
Sense—Object—Contact 154-57
Sentence, A Third Theory regarding the communication of the meaning of and its criticism 857; Discussion on the meaning of 689, 725, 727, 763, 767-69; Hypothesis of a partless 783; Meaning of 688; Communicating its own meaning 825; Jayanta's Theory of Communication of the Meaning of 840
Śeṣavat, Meaning of 272; and Sāmānyatodṛṣta, Distinction between 279
Siddhānta 16
Sound, an attribute 477; Mīmāṁsaka's view of 426; Nyāya-counter-arguments to refute the Mīmāṁsaka view of 450; Objection to Mīmāṁsaka view of 427; Presumption in favour of eternity of 430
Sounds, Arguments in favour of the eternality of 450
Space, Determination of 293
Sphoṭa, Discussion on 776; imperceptible 801; Refutation of 790-99
Śrutārthāpatti 76-79
Suffixes, Distinction between a causative and optative 731

Tantras, Āgamas—Veracity of 544
Tarka, Importance of 17
Tātparya,—Śakti postulated 858
Tattva, Meaning of 13
The Atharvaveda included in the Trayī 533
Time, Division of 294; Existence of—and its source of knowledge 285-91

Truth or untruth, Nature of 13

Uddeśa 21
Universals, Conclusion of the discussion on 664; Discussion on 619; Real 647
Upmāna (Comparison) 295

Vedas, Authorship of 484; Conclusive proof of the veracity of the 914; Criticism of the veracity of 563; Eternality refuted 485; Fresh objection against the veracity of 585; Intrinsic validity of 349; Meaning of the—a riddle 862; Objections against the apparent shortcomings of 566; Proof of the truth of 522; Same authorship of 497; The common subject-matter of 543; Veracity due to Divine authorship 515
Vedic Collections, The position of the Atharvaveda among 529
Vedic Sentences, A reply to the objection to the truth of the—containing names of sacrifices 602
Vedic words, The conditional knowledge of the meaning of 605
Verbal knowledge affirmed, Extrinsic validity of 400
Vibhāga 21
Vitaṇḍā 19-20

Word, Denotation of—as a concrete universal 683; Discussion on the denotation of—as a mere universal 677; Function of 684; Inadequate definition of a chaste 883; The Chastity of perceptible 902; The denotation of—as a mere individual 666; The meaning of 665
Word and sentence, Relation between the meaning of 819
Words, Limitations of the meanings of 823; Partless or Sentences refuted 810; Untenability of the eternality of unchaste 896
Words and sentences, Constitution of —by letters 829; The alternative way of constituting by letters 832